Women
and
Values

Readings
in Recent
Feminist
Philosophy

Women and Values

Readings in Recent Feminist Philosophy

Second Edition

Marilyn Pearsall
University of Puget Sound

Wadsworth Publishing Company

Belmont, California
A Division of Wadsworth, Inc.

Philosophy Editor: Kenneth King
Editorial Assistant: Gay Meixel
Production: Cecile Joyner, The Cooper Company
Design: Vargas/Williams/Design
Print Buyer: Karen Hunt
Permissions Editor: Jeanne Bosschart
Copy Editor: Louise Rixey
Cover Design: Paula Goldstein
Cover Painting: Amedeo Modigliani, *Gypsy Woman with Baby,*
Chester Dale Collection, © 1992 National Gallery of Art, Washington
Compositor: Kachina Typesetting
Printer: Arcata Graphics/Fairfield

*This book is printed on
acid-free recycled paper.*

1 2 3 4 5 6 7 8 9 10—97 96 95 94 93

Library of Congress Cataloging-in-Publication Data

Women and values : readings in recent feminist philosophy / [edited
  by] Marilyn Pearsall. —2nd ed.
      p.   cm.
    Includes bibliographical references.
    ISBN 0-534-19554-7
    1. Feminist theory.   2. Feminism—United States.   3. Social
values.   4. Feminism—Moral and ethical aspects.   I. Pearsall,
Marilyn.
HQ1190.W68   1992
305.42'01—dc20   92-13426

For my daughters,
Cornelia and Sarah,
and for my son,
Anthony

Preface

Women and Values: Readings in Recent Feminist Philosophy is an anthology that deals systematically with ethical issues from a feminist perspective. In response to the exciting proliferation of books and periodicals in this field, the revised edition of *Women and Values* is a unitary text of the essential writings of feminist philosophers.

This text will be useful in a variety of teaching circumstances. It can be used, and has been successfully used, as the single textbook for semester-length courses in feminist philosophy. Its format also makes it easily compatible with other feminist materials and sources, as selected by the instructor. Moreover, it has been utilized in courses such as ethics, political science, and women's studies.

The materials gathered in this text are making an impact in current thinking and in present debates within feminism. Drawing solely upon the rich intellectual product of women thinkers, the collection brings together many issues of central concern in the field. In designing this revised edition, I have retained essays that instructors have found valuable, while adding selections that reflect significant developments in feminist inquiry. I have sought to include articles that are readable, interesting, and of high academic merit.

The text has been arranged in such a manner that it will be a flexible teaching instrument. Chapter 1 begins with a discussion of the notion of feminist theory itself. Chapter 2 presents selections that lay the groundwork necessary for later discussions. These selections focus on theories of sex difference and the nature/culture debate. Chapters 3 through 8 then present readings in value theory organized under standard headings. Chapter 3 presents readings dealing with social philosophy, Chapter 4 with political philosophy, and Chapter 5 with philosophy of law. Chapter 6 deals with philosophy of religion, and Chapter 7 with philosophy of art.

Thus, Chapters 3 through 7 focus on standard areas of value inquiry. Chapter 8 turns to ethical theory strictly so-called. I have divided Chapter 8 into two sets of readings—one consisting of theoretical considerations, the other of articles on applied ethics.

This anthology is meant to be a flexible and useful introductory text for philosophy and women's studies courses. If used for an introductory-level philosophy course, I would suggest covering Chapters 1, 2, 3, 4, and 6 (and if time permits, the first part of Chapter 8). A course in ethical theory should cover the selections in Chapters 1, 2, and both parts of Chapter 8. A course in social/political philosophy should cover Chapters 2, 3, 4, and 5. A women's studies course might well draw on Chapters 1, 5, 6, 7, and the second part of Chapter 8.

Since this is meant to be a text that is useful for philosophy classes and women's studies classes, it does not presuppose previous philosophic training or a detailed knowledge of feminism and feminist theory. Two particular features should help the student who might not have a background in either field. First, after each of the readings there are questions for discussion that should aid the student in following the content of the selection. Second, an introductory chapter has been included in which I briefly consider a survey of feminist theory and feminist approaches to moral theory.

Women's moral theory is an expression of the collective efforts of feminist thinkers, past and present. The text itself is an acknowledgment of this fact. I would also, however, like to thank those more immediately concerned with this project. I am grateful to Ken King, my editor, for his continued interest and commitment. I would also like to thank Cecile Joyner for her careful work and Lynn Hasegawa for her assistance. Discussions with

Gary Jason, in particular, as well as Michael Carella and Patricia Huckle, colleagues at San Diego State University, were especially helpful, as were comments in manuscript reviews by Barbara Allen, Carleton College; Ann E. Cudd, Occidental College; Mary Devereaux, Bucknell University; and Robin S. Dillon, University of North Carolina at Chapel Hill. I greatly appreciate the support of Terry Cooney, Associate Dean, and my new colleagues in Philosophy and Women's Studies at the University of Puget Sound.

Contents

Introduction
Toward a Feminist Transvaluation of Value Theory

Value theory is the systematic study of values. As such, it is one of the three basic fields of philosophy along with *metaphysics* (the study of the nature of reality) and *epistemology* (the study of knowledge and belief). General value theory, or *axiology*, addresses questions concerning the nature, meaning, and scope of values and value judgments.

Traditional value theory is, of course, *male* value theory, and it has been done as (male) theory-building is characteristically done. The standard approach is to carve out areas for investigation, formulate questions and a methodology for dealing with those questions, and then allow the researchers in a given area to conduct their specialized endeavor.

Thus, traditional value theory has focused on certain domains. Social philosophers discuss which social structure is the best (meaning the best for *man*kind). Similarly, political philosophers ask which political system is the "best." Philosophers of law ask which legal system is most "just." Other philosophers question the nature of art and artistic endeavor and what is a "good" work of art. Or they examine the basic concepts of religion and inquire about their meaning and function. And ethical theorists investigate the nature of "right" or "good" in respect to human conduct.

Feminist considerations arose quite outside the academic world of traditional (male) value theory. To understand the transvaluation of value theory in feminist thought, we need to understand the revolution in feminist thinking.

Feminism has a complex history as well as a philosophy. To simplify this history somewhat, it is generally said that feminist thought occurred in two waves. The first wave of feminism appeared at the start of the nineteenth century (with anticipations in the seventeenth and eighteenth centuries) with the representative text *A Vindication of the Rights of Woman,* by Mary Wollstonecraft (1792), and

later with *The Declaration of Sentiments* of the Seneca Falls Convention (1848). The first wave gave rise to the women's suffrage movement in Europe and the United States and culminated in the United States in women's right to vote (1920). Then came a period of relative dormancy in the political and theoretical activity of women.

The second wave of feminism began shortly after World War II, with the appearance of Simone de Beauvoir's now classic text, *The Second Sex* (1949). De Beauvoir's brilliant work was a turning point in the history of feminist thought. Perhaps the key to understanding the paradigm change wrought by de Beauvoir is to see that she shifted the conceptual framework of feminism from a discussion of *equality* to a discussion of *freedom.* According to de Beauvoir, women could not be equal, could not be anything but "the second sex," until they were *free* to change themselves and their conditions. So with the publication of *The Second Sex,* feminism went beyond a demand for equality—it became a call for liberation.

In *The Second Sex,* de Beauvoir agrees with the existentialist claim that man is his freedom. But, she argues, it follows that woman is her freedom, too. Why, then, is woman always and everywhere subordinate to man? De Beauvoir's insightful answer is that woman has been constituted as the Other to man's Self; she has become object to his subject, and he has mediated the world for her.

> What peculiarly signalizes the situation of woman is that she—a free and autonomous being like all human creatures—nevertheless finds herself living in a world where men compel her to assume the status of Other.

De Beauvoir argues that man enslaves woman because he flees from himself (that is, the burden of freedom) "by means of the other, whom he oppresses to that end."

So, de Beauvoir asserts, woman is not now her freedom, which means that she must project herself into the future and must undertake projects. For existential ethics, choice is central be being fully human; to be free to choose *is* to be fully human ("Man is his freedom").

> Every subject plays his part as such specifically through exploits or projects that serve as a mode of transcendence; he achieves liberty only through a continual reaching out toward other liberties. . . . Every individual concerned to justify his existence feels that [it] involves an undefined need to transcend himself, to engage in freely chosen projects.

The corollary to de Beauvoir's exhortation to women to choose their freedom is: Women cannot look to men to grant them freedom. If that were the case, women would not themselves be choosing their freedom; they must seek their own transcendence.

This line of thought forms a dramatic shift from the point of view of first-wave feminism. Whereas earlier feminism was stated as a demand for legal equality, de Beauvoir's response is that, in effect, not only must women be free to choose *not* to be the second sex, but they must choose the act of freedom: They must choose to liberate themselves. Thus the second wave is a women's liberation movement.

Another reason for seeing de Beauvoir's text as a watershed in feminist thought is that she explicitly grapples with two major theoretical systems that had not previously been addressed in feminist thought: Marxism and Freudianism. At the outset of her existentialist text, de Beauvoir rejects both systems as explanations of women's situation. She denies the Freudian claim that "anatomy is destiny," that is, that woman's situation is the outcome of her biology. And she also denies the Marxist view that a woman's identity is determined primarily by "the means of production" (the economics) of the society in which she lives. Feminist theorists of the second wave follow de Beauvoir in paying special attention to the Marxist and Freudian perspectives, utilizing or rejecting many of their concepts.

Although there are several distinct strains of contemporary feminism, they all bear the mark of de Beauvoir's initial theory to some degree.

One school of present feminist thought is exemplified by Shulamith Firestone's text, *The Dialectic of Sex* (1970), which is both an amalgam and a critique of preceding lines of thought (existentialist, Marxist, and Freudian). Firestone is one of the first thinkers to have clearly set forth the essential features of what is now called *radical feminism*. She takes up de Beauvoir's existential question, Why have women been constituted as Other, as object? And she answers it by utilizing Marxist and Freudian elements, while creating a new feminist point of view.

In the opening statement of *The Dialectic of Sex,* "Sex class is so deep as to be invisible," Firestone tells us that her view is one of a class analysis, but a class analysis with a difference. Traditional Marxist class analysis holds that there is a class struggle between the owners of the means of production and the workers; the oppressor is the bourgoisie; the oppressed is the proletariat. But the class struggle postulated by Firestone is carried on between women as a class and men as a class: Men are the oppressors, and women are the oppressed. And since the class struggle propounded by Firestone is between sex classes, sexuality in all its aspects is central to her theory. Firestone's thesis is that the origin of women's oppression (as Other, as object) is the sexual, or procreative, function of women, because women were "at the mercy of their biology." This led, she claims, to the first division of labor and to the rise of sex classes. Thus, Firestone sees sexuality as fundamental to feminism *and* Freudianism, but she rejects the idea that there is anything immutable about the nature of sexuality. Specifically, she rejects Freud's thesis that women have masculine envy, and she argues that women envy only men's power, not their anatomy.

Firestone's analysis, therefore, of what she calls "the dialectical materialism of sex" employs and yet discards Marxist and Freudian theory. It also incorporates elements of de Beauvoir's existential view in that the dialectic of sex can be resolved only by women themselves. Firestone then adds another crucial element—one reminiscent of the first wave of feminist thought, but now revolutionary rather than reformist: the notion that there must be a collective resolution of the sex class struggle.

De Beauvoir proposes the individual solution; but the individual woman, says Firestone, cannot solve the sex class struggle: Only "sisterhood is powerful."

Of *radical feminism* we can say then that its method is "consciousness-raising," that is, it raises women's (class) consciousness of their oppression. And its aim is to liberate women from the oppression of men. In other words, the universal domination of men and subordination of women must cease.

"Sexual politics," as Kate Millett calls it, must be transformed. The fundamental maxim of radical feminism, "the personal is political," means that everything that happens in the personal lives of women happens to them as a sex class and, therefore, is political. As Alison Jaggar summarizes:

> On this view, there is no distinction between the "political" and the "personal" realms: every area of life is the sphere of "sexual politics." All relations between women and men are institutionalized relationships of power and so constitute appropriate subjects for political analysis.

So, in consciousness-raising groups, women will share their personal experiences and, together, analyze their political condition.

The second wave of feminism has brought forth a number of different "types" or "camps" of feminism having diverse views on tactics and strategies for change as well as on more fundamental concepts. One way to indicate the variety of current feminist thought is to contrast each with radical feminism.

In contrast with radical feminism (and socialist feminism), liberal feminism is reformist and evolutionary rather than revolutionary. The liberal feminist is heiress to the nineteenth-century liberal tradition of the first wave, which adopts securing the rights of individuals and recognizing the equality of all individuals as its central goals. Liberal feminism, accordingly, emphasizes securing women's rights through legislation, especially through the passage of the Equal Rights Amendment (ERA). It also promotes equal opportunity for women as individuals (affirmative action).

One way to see the difference between liberal feminism and radical feminism is to ask: What is the basis of women's subordinate position? A radical feminist would construct an answer centering on the notion of women as a class—a sex class that faces class oppression and needs to act collectively.

The sex class (radical feminist) analysis indicates a radical solution: overthrow of the oppressor class. By comparison, a liberal feminist would construct an answer based on the notion of the sex roles of males and females and our socialization to them. And since women have been much less favored in their sex roles and socialization, liberal feminists argue for the attenuation of rigid sex roles and an "androgynous" ideal. The sex-role analysis also suggests the institution of meliorative measures such as providing more adequate child care facilities for working mothers, nonsexist school programs and texts, and so on.

Socialist feminists, like radical feminists, propose that meliorative measures are not sufficient, but the socialist feminist does not focus on the notion of women as a sex class. Instead, the socialist feminist adopts and extends the traditional Marxist class analysis to include a discussion of the "means of reproduction" as well as the "means of production." In their view, it is in regard to the means of reproduction that women have been exploited and alienated. Thus socialist feminists are concerned with wages for housework, the psychodynamics of the nuclear family, and motherhood.

Although socialist feminism is concerned with the fight against patriarchy, it views that task as being inseparable from the struggle against capitalism (and racism). Since it draws on the theoretical heritage of traditional Marxism, socialist feminism has perhaps a more theoretical orientation than radical feminism, which arises more directly from women's consciousness-raising (rap) groups. In its commitment to viewing the oppression of women as arising from capitalism, patriarchy, and racism, socialist feminism is characterized by a multicausal, multisystems analysis.

These as well as other types of feminism are represented in the readings that follow, in which women thinkers of all perspectives articulate and transform the various domains of value theory. Most recently, postmodern feminism has arisen out of the encounter of continental, 1960s postmodern thought and academic feminist philosophy. Feminists share with postmodernists certain ways of thinking, especially the critique of universalizing, totalizing "grand narratives" (Lyotard) that are characteristic of traditional, male-stream metaphysics. Women, as well as others, have been marginalized or silenced in this phallogocentric (qua Lacan) discourse. Postmodern feminism calls for a multiplicity of voices and for a specificity of accounts in their historical contexts (Foucault). And postmodern feminism finds deconstruction (Derrida) a potential strategy in "its disclosures of complicities where a will to knowledge would create oppositions"* such as masculine/feminine.

The writings of French feminist thinkers such as Hélène Cixous, Luce Irigaray, and Julia Kristeva are of great interest to Anglo-American feminist philosophers. As Rosemarie Tong says:**

> Postmodern feminists take DeBeauvoir's understanding of Otherness and turn it on its head. . . . Otherness, for all its associations with oppression and inferiority, is much more than an oppressed, inferior condition. Rather, it is a way of being, thinking, speaking that allows for openness, plurality, diversity, and difference.

However, the instability of the category "woman" in postmodernist theory poses an uneasy relationship with feminist practice. The questioning, or destabilizing, of the self, of personal identity, as women are seeking a female subject and a politics of autonomy, is problematic.

The revolution in feminist thought is in the process of transforming traditional academic philosophy. In particular, over the last decade a corpus of theoretical work on values and value theory informed by women's consciousness and feminist imperatives has emerged. The selections in this book have been chosen from this growing body of writings. They speak

about women and their values. The issues discussed and the conceptual schemes employed to explore them are the work of women thinkers who are the "daughters of the second wave." This collection of their essays is offered as part of the process of liberating our thinking from masculinist modes and patriarchal ideology.

To better display the profound transvaluation of value inquiry wrought by contemporary feminists, I have selected essays bearing on each of the traditional male value-domains. In these readings, feminist theorists of many persuasions present their values and voice their own felt concerns. The only restriction I imposed in selecting the readings is that these thinkers must speak from a feminist point of view, that is, from a stance that recognizes the oppression of women in male-dominated society. There is, however, ample room in this general perspective to allow for interesting and important debates among women.

We cannot predict what feminist ethical theory will eventually look like or what forms it will take, but we know it will be the collective work of many women thinkers. We are now in the process of the feminist "reconstruction of self and society." What can be said is that feminist ethics will have certain features. First, it will be highly *personal*; it will draw on the shared experiences of women's everyday lives. Second, it will have an *emancipatory* promise, for it is founded on a liberationist philosophy with postmodernist reservations. Along with social and political philosophy, philosophy of art, and philosophy of religion and their concomitant areas of inquiry, moral theory as developed by feminists may be seen as undoing patterns of conceptual dominance that before seemed permanent (what Dale Spender calls "the intellectual double-standard").

Thus it follows that feminist ethics will be highly *critical* of traditional ethics. Moral theory as developed by male philosophers has, according to women theorists, reflected and supported masculinist ideology. The concepts of "person," "equality," "justice," "freedom," "self," "nature," "subject," and many more, as they are used in ethical theory, need to be re-evaluated and re-visioned.

---

*Gayatri Chakravorty Spivak, *In Other Worlds* (Methuen, 1987) p. 180.
**Rosemarie Tong, *Feminist Thought* (Westview, 1989) p. 219.

Certain moral issues must be of particular interest to feminist philosophers, because these issues have received little or no attention in the past. Abortion, rape, pornography, prostitution, domestic violence, sex discrimination, and so on must be discussed and debated by feminists and among feminists. These *women's issues* affect women's lives and are of central concern to feminist ethics.

Thus, feminist ethics lends new meaning to moral concepts and moral issues as they become part of the feminist critique of existing values. Can we say that women will create their own ethics? In other words, is there a distinctive women's morality? If so, what will it look like? Will it have a different methodology from that of traditional (male) ethical theory? There is evidence to suggest that this might be the case; it may be that women differ from men in the way they experience and formulate moral concepts and moral issues. According to Carol Gilligan, out of "our shared fate," women may speak "in a different voice."

In any case, what we are seeing now is of the utmost significance in that feminist philosophers are engaging in a most radical critique of existing modes of ethical thought and in a most challenging exploration of moral issues. From this circumstance, we can expect profound alteration in the ways women (and men) will consider values and value theory.

Women and Values

Readings in Recent

Feminist Philosophy

1

Feminist Theory and Practice

Feminist theory is dialectically related to feminist practice and emerges from what Simone de Beauvoir calls "women's concrete situation (as wife, mother, prostitute, lesbian, as young, as old)." The dialectical relationship between feminist theory and practice is exemplified by the central feminist methodological device, consciousness-raising, which is the direct sharing by women of their personal experience.

Feminist theory arises out of the felt abuses that women testify to in consciousness-raising groups and the perceived oppression of women. As Marilyn Frye says, "What 'feminist theory' is about, to a great extent, is identifying those forces . . . which maintain the subordination of women to men." And feminist thinkers develop their theoretical analysis in great measure from looking at issues central to the experiences and lives of women, such as housework, child care, abortion, sex discrimination, sexual harrassment in the workplace, prostitution, rape, and pornography.

The close connection between feminist theory and actual feminist practice ensures that feminism does not become monolithic and authoritarian. Feminists choose to strive to represent diversities as well as commonalities among women, especially in regard to the parameters of race and class.

Jane Flax points out that theory has been male theory, which means that men have been doing the theorizing in all fields. By contrast, women have been silenced, or at least muted, in partriarchal discourse. Thus, she says, women must be wary of identifying with past modes of thought. Flax discusses feminist theorizing in terms of shared assumptions: women's oppression as a "given"; the structural and systematic nature of male domination (patriarchy); and the need to understand and confront that oppression. She outlines an agenda of feminist imperatives around three spheres: production, reproduction, and psychodynamics, which, she asserts, mutually support patriarchy.

According to Nancy Hartsock, an agenda for feminist theory must take into account the issues of women in capitalist society as well as in patriarchy. In other words, it must deal with class differences as well as the sex/gender system. She sees a socialist feminist theory arising out of women's everyday lives that addresses the need for collective action for change. In this way, Hartsock holds, feminist theory can ground socialist theory by connecting personal experience and political generality and by showing that capitalism and patriarchy are interlocking systems that oppress women.

Finally, feminist thinkers wish to engage in a discourse that encompasses women of all social, ethnic, and national backgrounds, in order to develop strategies and tactics that speak to the needs and desires of all women. Maria Lugones and Elizabeth Spelman's dialogue represents the point of view of the woman of color as well as of the white/Anglo woman concerning feminist theory. Lugones and Spelman seek a woman's voice that will speak not only for white, middle-class women but will incorporate the ideas and issues of women of color. Since no woman should be silenced, it is a feminist imperative to find ways to articulate our diversity along with our commanlity. Women of color must represent their own experience and the meaning of that experience for themselves. Lugones and Spelman's critique of androcentric theory offers some ways for us to speak together that are respectful of all women.

Women Do Theory

Jane Flax

I begin with an overview of feminist theory and a discussion of the activity of theorizing. I then present a theoretical framework that I've developed after trying various theories and finding none of them sufficient to explain the range of things I think a feminist theorist needs to explain.

Let me say a little about how I ended up doing feminist theory. I have been interested in philosophy and political theory for a long time. I am also interested in psychoanalysis, and have practiced as a feminist therapist. So, partly, I've been trying to put together more traditional ideas of theory with those I've learned as a therapist, especially from psychoanalysis.

Very early I began to connect theory with political activity. I chose political science because I thought there I would learn about politics—which was a mistake. Some political scientists seem to consider theory to be something done 3,000 years ago by Aristotle and Plato, unrelated to the present world. And yet, one of my attractions to theory was that through it, I could learn to systematize my experience. Political science was not much help.

Over time, however, I have found traditional theory to be very helpful in recognizing other people's mental processes as they try to understand the structure of the world systematically. That is, much traditional theory is a kind of internal discourse among thinkers—like a 3,000-year conversation in which people take up each others' ideas and reapply them. I'm interested in many parts of that discourse: what can politics do; what is the ideal political system; what are just relationships; what does "equality" mean?

These issues have been dealt with in the women's movement, but not always in the context of theory. For instance, what it would mean to have a really liberated society is a

From *Quest*, Vol. V. No. 1 (Summer 1979), pp. 20–26. Reprinted by permission of Jane Flax.

question of equality and justice that has been debated since the first political theory was attempted. But feminists don't often think of our questions as part of that ongoing political discourse.

In traditional political theory, however, the relationships between men and women, and the status of women, are rarely discussed. They are certainly not generally seen as problems. Some traditional political theorists talk about the family and the role it plays for the state of course; and some have argued for the liberation of women. Plato, for instance, argued that women *could* be philosopher kings since these should be chosen on merit and no inherent proof existed that women were any less intellectually capable than men.[1] Other political theorists, however, have argued that woman cannot think abstractly and has a less developed moral sense. Thus, part of the problem feminist theorists face is taking the general "grammar" and concepts of traditional theory and applying them to women and the issues that affect us.

This brings me to the questions, "what is feminist theory?" and, more generally, "what is theory?" The most important characteristic of theory is that it is a *systematic, analytic* approach to everyday experience. This everybody does unconsciously. To theorize, then, is to bring this unconscious process to a conscious level so it can be developed and refined. All of us operate on theories, though most of them are implicit. We screen out certain things; we allow others to affect us; we make choices and we don't always understand why. Theory, in other words, makes those choices conscious, and enables us to use them more efficiently.

For example, implicit in my choices about the work I could do is an understanding of where power lies, what I'm likely to be able to do, where I'm likely to meet the most frustration, and when I'm likely to be most effective. I might not think through those things consciously, but I make choices on these bases. If you push that explanation, you'll find a series of assumptions about the way the world works, what's available (to me), and what isn't. That's implicit theory-making. The problem is to make it explicit.

Blocks to Explicit Theory

One of the problems with theory is that women aren't supposed to be able to do it; women aren't supposed to be able to think abstractly. So when you say to a woman, "Okay, now let's read theory," she's likely to panic.

In addition, theoretical writing is often so full of jargon that it seems divorced from ordinary experience. Unfortunately, many theorists have an entrepreneurial interest, a territorial mentality, and they encourage everyone else to believe that their work is impossibly complex. This discourages women— and men—from engaging in theory because it seems hostile and unintelligible. I don't think that the issues *are* inherently so difficult or so far removed from ordinary understanding. I think theorists build turfs and *make* it difficult for others to understand that turf—just like any other professional.

Feminist Theory

Feminist theory is based on a series of assumptions. First, it assumes that men and women have different experiences; that the world is not the same for men and women. Some women think the experiences of women should be identical to the experiences of men. Others would like to transform the world so that there are no such dichotomous experiences. Proponents of both views, however, assume that women's experiences differ from men's, and that one task of feminist theory is to explain that difference.

Secondly, feminist theory assumes that women's oppression is not a subset of some other social relationship. Some argue that if the class system were destroyed, then women would not be oppressed—I don't classify that as

feminist theory. Feminist theory assumes that women's oppression is a unique constellation of social problems and has to be understood in itself, and not as a subset of class or any other structure.

It also assumes that women's oppression is not merely a case of what the Chinese call "bad attitudes." I have problems with the word "sexism," because the term implies that women's oppression will disappear when men become more enlightened. On the contrary, I think feminist theory assumes that the oppression of women is part of the way the structure of the world is organized, and that one task of feminist theory is to explain how and why this structure evolved.

Feminist theory names this structure "patriarchy," and assumes that it is a historical force that has a material and psychological base. What I mean by "patriarchy" is the system in which men have more power than women, and have more access to whatever society esteems. What society esteems obviously varies from culture to culture; but it you look at the spheres of power, you'll find that all who have it are male. This is a long-term historical fact rooted in real things. It's not a question of bad attitudes; it's not a historical accident—there are real advantages to men in retaining control over women. Feminist theorists want to explain why that's so.

Patriarchy works backwards as well. It affects the way men and women feel about themselves, and is so deeply internalized that we can't imagine a world without gender. As much as we talk about androgyny, or some situation in which gender isn't so significant, I don't think any of us could imagine a world in which gender would not bring with it many special meanings. *We* may still want to attach special meanings to gender, but a feminist theory would argue that the power attached to gender should disappear; it should not determine whether a person is excluded or included in whatever is esteemed by society.

Goals of Feminist Theory

Feminist theory has several purposes. The first is to understand the power differential between men and women. How did it come into being? Why does it exist now? What maintains it? How do the power relations between men and women affect other power relations—for instance, race and class—and how does patriarchy reinforce other oppressive power structures?

Secondly, the purpose is to understand women's oppression—how it evolved, how it changes over time, how it's related to other forms of oppression, and finally, how to change our oppression.

In feminist theory, one issue that emerges consistently is the necessity to understand the family, because it is one of the central mediating structures between all other structures of oppression. The family is where we're internally formed, where we learn about gender, where we experience class and race systems in personal and intimate ways. Therefore, understanding the functions of the family should be one of the crucial goals of feminist theory; yet it remains an area that is particularly undeveloped.

A third purpose of feminist theory is to overcome oppression. Feminist theory is the foundation of action and there is no pretense that theory can be neutral. Within feminist theory is a commitment to change oppressive structures and to connect abstract ideas with concrete problems for political action. It is senseless to study the situation of women without a concomitant commitment to do something about it. The theorist has to draw out the consequences of the theory and use life experience as a part of her basis for understanding, for feeding into the development of theory.

Traditional political theory has always been attached to action. Plato wrote *The Republic* partly because he thought that Athenian democracy was degenerating and he wanted to understand why, and how. It's only contemporary social science theory that claims to be objective, neutral, value-free. I don't think any form of knowledge is neutral, but certainly feminist theory cannot claim neutrality. I think that's one of the problems of women's studies programs. They are too often developed as though they are mere intellectual exercises; some may be, but the study of women is not.

The Evolving Theoretical Framework

I assume that feminist theory must point to a clear and real base for the oppression of women—feminist theory has to be rooted in human experience. I also assume that there are three basic realms of human activity.

The first is production—we need to produce food, clothing and shelter for our survival. (Obviously, different cultures will produce in different ways. Even people who live on tropical islands have to organize the gathering and preparation of coconuts.) Marx called this the material substructure of human life, and I call it the realm of production.

People also need to reproduce. Not only must we produce the next generation biologically, but we also need to reproduce good citizens for the society. We need to inculcate the values, attitudes, and beliefs appropriate to that culture. A good American citizen will have ideas and expectations very different from a good Mesopotamian citizen living 3,000 years ago. But no matter which society, somehow the unformed person must be trained in its values. In our society, acculturation is conducted by a variety of organizations, including the family and later the school, and the state is involved in setting out certain policies which translate into procedures for acculturating individuals.

The third realm of human activity is the individual's internal life. This is what Freud called "the unconscious," and what I call "psychodynamics." The psychodynamic sphere is where our biological and our mental lives meet, and must be organized. One of the most important aspects of this sphere is sexuality. One of the questions feminists must ask is how a basically "polymorphous species"[2] ends up, in most cultures, a genitally-oriented, heterosexual and monogamous species. Though all cultures allow varying degrees and varieties of sexual pleasure, every civilization channels its citizens' eroticism into practices acceptable to the society.

When we talk about the situation of women, we must examine how all three spheres cooperate to produce our oppression. The elimination of an oppressive structure in one sphere only is inadequate because the other spheres will re-emerge as even more oppressive.

For instance, in the Soviet Union, where the class system is supposedly abolished, men *still* retain the power. The upper structure of the Communist Party is almost entirely male. And while women may move into occupations (as in the United States), those occupations lose their prestige when they do.[3]

Why didn't the oppression of women disappear? For one thing, the structure of the family was not altered—no efforts were made to change the reproductive spheres.[4] So, even though one structure of oppression may have been dealt with, the other two remain intact. Hence, we cannot expect women to be fully participating persons, nor that the full range of women's experience will be expressed in social values. This is a material view of women in that it locates oppression within our material lives. And yet it also teaches us to look at each of the three spheres of human activity, to see how each one particularly impinges upon women.

The Intersection of Spheres

One of the most important characteristics of the family is that all three spheres intersect here. In our society, the family is the structure in which we learn to repress and channel our sexuality—where homosexuality is forbidden and where heterosexuality is promoted. It's also the place in which, obviously, external authority is transmitted by and translated in our parents' teachings. It's in the family that the standards of acceptable social behavior are first taught.

Even though most production is no longer done within the family, this is still the structure in which we are taught behaviors appropriate to our class. Lillian Rubin, in *Worlds of Pain*, shows that working-class people become acculturated in the proper expectations of their class and that these expectations are perpetuated from generation to generation. So, the class system impinges upon the family, not only in the obvious ways (such as the kinds of housing or childcare you can afford), but also in more subtle ways.

Other structures influence and are perpetuated by these three spheres. The state, for example, structures and benefits from the ways reproduction and psychodynamics interact in class divisions and modes of production. It also benefits from the lingering effects of the psychodynamic sphere on political and personal action.

Reproduction is obviously segregated on the basis of sex. Women are nurturers, men are authority figures—a very important distinction in terms of the developing person. This means that both acculturation and reproduction are sex-segregated.

Thus, as feminism teaches us, the class system is not the same for men and women. It's a mistake to take traditional class analysis and impose it upon the experience of women when it is clear that women's work is sex-segregated and class-segregated (80% of women work in jobs where more than half the jobs are held by women).

And finally, the psychodynamic sphere so thoroughly remembers that we're either a *male* or a *female* person, that gender becomes part of who we are. Thus, though we succeed in developing an analysis of patriarchy and capitalism, we still find ourselves repeating old, self-defeating patterns. We can't explain how this happens. Rationally, we've got it all worked out, and yet something refuses to change. That's partly because a great deal happens unconsciously, as we act out old patterns that are accessible neither to reason nor to control since the psychodynamic sphere *is* unconscious. It's the realm of dreams and associations. It's the world of sexuality; it's your internal life. But also it's hard for us to grasp because feminists haven't done much work on it.

Conclusion

My assumptions are, then, that these three spheres of life are crucial for everybody, that they're experienced differently by men and women, and that both the experience and the oppression of women are rooted in all three. I believe we must examine each sphere to see how women's and men's experience are different, and how it contributes to that difference. If we would end the oppression of women, we must transform all three spheres; change in one sphere alone will not liberate women.

The psychodynamic sphere can be changed by completely transforming the rearing of children. Dorothy Dinnerstein's book, *The Mermaid and the Minotaur,* is a good reference on the transformation of childrearing. Dinnerstein maintains that both males and females have to be present in the child's life from infancy. It's important that children not be raised by one female person, or a group of female persons. The child also needs peers. In fact, it makes day care and childrearing not something that enables women to work, but locates both right in the center of feminist demands. A feminist revolution must deal with the way children are reared. To create liberated persons requires a transformation in childrearing.

It also means that homosexuality is not just a nicety we support to appease our lesbian sisters. We must recognize that heterosexuality is also part of the structure of the oppression of women. Sexual repression is one of the ways in which women are oppressed and one of the ways in which patriarchy is maintained. On another level, restraining sexuality is a very powerful way of controlling people—as Wilhelm Reich understood in his analysis of the Nazis. Therefore, to fight for a variety of expressions of sexuality has to be part of feminism. It shouldn't be incorporated because lesbians insist, "What about us?" It's absolutely central to feminism. These are two concrete conclusions which grow out of an analysis of the psychodynamic sphere.

Notes

1. An interesting sidelight is that the head of Plato's academy was a woman who was stoned by the Christians—one of the first of the Christians' many acts against women playing an intellectual, active role.

2. Polymorphous means that we can derive erotic pleasure from a wide variety of experiences; not only from experiences between ourselves and other persons, but also between ourselves and all sorts of physical objects.

3. Seventy-five percent of physicians in the Soviet Union are women, but a physician there is like a social worker here.

4. It's not permissible to be a homosexual or to engage in sexual relations with many different persons of either gender in the Soviet Union, China or Cuba.

Study Questions

1. How does Flax define "theory"? What are the difficulties of trying to move from implicit to explicit theory making?

2. According to Flax, what assumptions are common to all feminist theories? Would all feminists agree?

3. What goals does Flax see for feminist theory?

4. What three realms of human activity does Flax mention? Why does she feel that oppression of women must be fought in all three spheres simultaneously?

5. In what areas do these three spheres overlap?

6. What implications are there for feminist theory in regard to these spheres?

Feminist Theory and the Development of Revolutionary Strategy

Nancy Hartsock

A number of writers have detailed problems of the left in America. They have pointed out that it has remained out of touch with large numbers of people, and that it has been unable to build a unified organization, or even to promote a climate in which to debate socialist issues. The left has been criticized for having a prefabricated theory made up of nineteenth-century leftovers, a strategy built on scorn for innovation in politics or for expanding political issues. Too often leftist groups have held that the working class was incapable of working out its own future and that those who would lead the working class to freedom would be those who had memorized the sacred texts and were equipped with an all-inclusive theory that would help them organize the world.

While such a list of criticisms presents a caricature of the left as a whole, it points to a number of real problems, and overcoming them will require a reorientation. Here I can only deal with one aspect of the task: the role of feminist theory and the political practice of the women's movement as a model for the rest of the left.

I want to suggest that the women's movement can provide the basis for building a new and authentic American socialism. It can provide a model for ways to build revolutionary strategy and ways to develop revolutionary theories which articulate with the realities of advanced capitalism. Developing such a model requires a redefinition of theory in general in the light of a specific examination of the nature of feminist theory and practice, a reanalysis of such fundamental questions as the nature of class, and a working out of the implications of feminist theory for the kinds of organizations we need to build.

From Zillah R. Eisenstein, ed., *Capitalistic Patriarchy and the Case for Socialist Feminism*, pp. 56–57. Copyright © 1979 by Zillah R. Eisenstein. Reprinted by permission of Monthly Review Foundation. (Notes deleted.)

Theory and Feminist Theory

Theory is fundamental to any revolutionary movement. Our theory gives us a description of the problems we face, provides an analysis of the forces which maintain social life, defines the problems we should concentrate on, and acts as a set of criteria for evaluating the strategies we develop. Theory has an even broader role, however. As Antonio Gramsci has pointed out, "One can construct, on a specific practice, a theory which, by coinciding and identifying itself with the decisive elements of the practice itself, can accelerate the historical process that is going on, rendering practice more homogeneous, more coherent, more efficient in all its elements, and thus, in other words, developing its potential to the maximum."[1] Thus, theory itself can be a force for change.

At the same time, however, Gramsci proposes that we expand our understanding of theory in a different direction. We must understand that theorizing is not just something done by academic intellectuals but that a theory is always implicit in our activity and goes so deep as to include our very understanding of reality. Not only is theory implicit in our conception of the world, but our conception of the world is itself a political choice.[2] That is, we can either accept the categories given to us by capitalist society or we can begin to develop a critical understanding of our world. If we choose the first alternative, our theory may remain forever implicit. In contrast, to choose the second is to commit ourselves to working out a critical and explicit theory. The political action of feminists over most of the last decade provides a basis for articulating the theory implicit in our practice.[3] Making the theory explict is difficult but necessary to improve the work feminists are doing.

The Nature of Feminist Theory

Women who call themselves feminists disagree on many things. To talk in such unitary terms about a social movement so diverse in its aims and goals may seem at first to be a mistake. There is a women's movement which appears on television, has national organizations, and is easy for the media to reach and present as representative of feminist thought. But there is a second movement, one harder to find, that is made up of small groups and local organizations whose members work on specific local projects, a movement which came together around the immediate needs of women in a variety of cities, a movement whose energies have gone directly into work for change. It is these groups that form the basis for my discussion of feminist theory. These groups were concerned with practical action—rape crisis centers, women's centers, building women's communities, etc. In coming together as feminists to confront the problems which dominate their lives, women have built a movement profoundly based on practice. Indeed, one of the major tasks for the women's movement is precisely the creation of revolutionary theory out of an examination of our practice.[4]

All these groups share a world view that differs from that of most socialist movements in advanced capitalist countries, and that is at the same time surprisingly close to Marx's world view. It is this mode of analysis, with its own conception of social theory as well as the concrete theories we are developing out of it, that are the sources of feminism's power and the reason I can argue that through our practice, feminists have become the most orthodox of Marxists. As Lukacs argued, orthodoxy in Marxist theory refers exclusively to method.[5]

At bottom, feminism is a mode of analysis, a method of approaching life and politics, a way of asking questions and searching for answers, rather than a set of political conclusions about the oppression of women. Women are applying that method to their own experiences as women in order to transform the social relations which define their existence. Feminists deal directly with their own daily lives—something which accounts for the rapid spread of this movement. Others have argued that socialist feminism must be recognized as a definite tendency within Marxism generally; in contrast, I am suggesting that because feminists have reinvented Marx's method, the women's movement can provide a model for the rest of the left in developing theory and strategy.

The practice of small-group consciousness-raising—with its stress on examining and understanding experience and on connecting personal experience to the structures which define women's lives—is the clearest example of the method basic to feminism. Through this practice women have learned that it was important to build their analysis from the ground up, beginning with their own experiences. They examined their lives not only as thinkers but, as Marx would have suggested, with all their senses. Women drew connections between their personal experiences and political generalities about the oppression of women; indeed they used their personal experience to develop those generalities. We came to understand our experience, our past, in a way that transformed both our experience and ourselves.[6]

The power of the method feminists developed grows out of the fact that it enables women to connect their everyday lives with an analysis of the social institutions which shape them. The institutions of capitalism (including its imperialist aspect), patriarchy, and white supremacy cease to be abstractions; they become lived, real aspects of daily experience and activity. We see the concrete interrelations among them.

All this means that within the feminist movement, an important role for theory has been reemphasized—one in which theorists work out and make "coherent the principles and the problems raised by the masses in their practical activity."[7] Feminism as a mode of analysis, especially when consciousness-raising is understood as basic to that method, requires a redefinition of the concept of intellectual or theorizer, a recasting of this social role in terms of everyday life.

Because each of us is a potential theorist, intellectual, and activist, education comes to have a very different role in the women's movement than it does in the rest of the left today. The kind of political education feminists are doing for themselves differs fundamentally from what I would call instruction, from being taught the "correct political line." Education—as opposed to instruction—is organically connected to everyday life.[8] It both grows out of and contributes to our understanding of it.

Personal and Political Change

"If what we change does not change us/we are playing with blocks."[9]

Feminist emphasis on everyday life leads to a second area of focus: the integration of personal and political change. Since we come to know the world (to change it and be changed by it) through our everyday activity, everyday life must be the basis for our political work. Even the deepest philosophical questions grow out of our need to understand our own lives. Such a focus means that reality for us consists of "sensuous human activity, practice."[10] We recognize that we produce our existence in response to specific problems posed for us by reality. By working out the links between the personal and the political, and by working out the links between daily life and social institutions, we have begun to understand existence as a social process, the product of human activity. Moreover, the realization that we not only create our social world but can change it leads to a sense of our own power and provides energy for action.

Feminism as a method makes us recognize that human activity also changes us. A fundamental redefinition of the self is an integral part of action for political change.

If our selves are social phenomena and take their meaning from the society of which we are a part, developing an independent sense of self necessarily calls other areas of our lives into question. We must ask how our relationships with other people can foster self-definition rather than dependence and can accommodate our new strengths. That is, if our individuality is the ensemble of our social relations, "to create one's personality means to acquire consciousness of them and to modify one's own personality means to modify the *ensemble* of these relations."[11] Clearly, since we do not act to produce and reproduce our lives in a vacuum, changed consciousness and changed definitions of the self can only occur in con-

junction with a restructuring of the social (both societal and personal) relations in which each of us is involved.

Thus, feminism leads us to oppose the institutions of capitalism and white supremacy as well as patriarchy. By calling attention to the specific experiences of individuals, feminism calls attention to the totality of social relations, to the social formation as a whole. A feminist mode of analysis makes it clear that patriarchy, capitalism, white supremacy, forms of social interaction, language—all exist for us as historic givens. Our daily lives are the materialization at a personal level of the features of the social formation as a whole. The historical structures that mold our lives pose questions we must respond to and define the immediate possibilities for change.

Although we recognize that human activity *is* the structure of the social world, this structure is imposed not by individuals but by masses of people, building on the work of those who came before. Social life at any point in time depends on a complex of factors, on needs already developed as well as on embryonic needs—needs whose production, shaping, and satisfaction is a historical process. Developing new selves, then, requires that we recognize the importance of large-scale forces for change as well as that the people we are trying to become—fully developed individuals—can only be the products of history and struggle.

This history and struggle necessitates the creation of a new collectivity closely linked to the creation of new individuals, a collectivity which fundamentally opposes the capitalist concept of the individual. The creation of this new collectivity

> presupposes the attainment of a "cultural-social" unity through which a multiplicity of dispersed wills, with heterogeneous aims, are welded together with a single aim, on the basis of an equal and common conception of the world, both general and particular, operating in transitory bursts (in emotional ways) or permanently (where the intellectual base is so well rooted, assimilated, and experienced that it becomes passion).[12]

Clearly, we can only transform ourselves by struggling to transform the social relations which define us: changing selves and changed social institutions are simply two aspects of the same process. Each aspect necessitates the other. To change oneself—if individuality *is* the social relations we are involved in—is to change social institutions. Feminist practice reunites aspects of life separated by capitalism and does so in a way which assimilates the intellectual aspect to passion. As Marx said: "The coincidence of the changing of circumstances and of human activity or self changing can be conceived and rationally understood only as *revolutionary practice*."[13] This process of self-changing and growing in a changed world leads us to a sense that our lives are part of a number of large processes and that all the aspects of our lives must be connected.

The Importance of Totality

By beginning with everyday life and experience, feminism has been able to develop a politics which incorporates an understanding of process and of the importance of appropriating our past as an essential element of political action. We find that we constantly confront new situations in which we act out of our changed awareness of the world and ourselves and in consequence experience the changed reactions of others. What some socialists have seen as static, feminists grasp as structures of relations in process—a reality constantly in the process of becoming something else. Feminist reasoning "regards every historically developed social form as in fluid movement and therefore takes into account its transient nature no less than its momentary existence."[14] This mode of understanding allows us to see the many ways processes are related and provides a way to understand a world in which events take their significance from the set of relationships which come to a focus in them. Thus, we are led to see that each of the interlocking institutions of capitalism, patriarchy, and white supremacy conditions the others, but each can also be understood as a different expression of the same relations.

Since each phenomenon changes form constantly as the social relations of which it is composed take on different meanings and forms, the possibility of understanding processes as

they change depends on our grasp of their role in the social whole. For example, in order to understand the increased amount of wage work by women in the United States we need to understand the relation of their work to the needs of capitalism. But we must also look at the conditions of work and the kind of work prescribed for women by patriarchy and white supremacy as different aspects of the same social system. As feminists, we begin from a position which understands that possibilities for change in any area are tied to change occurring in other areas.

Both capitalism and socialism are more than economic systems. Capitalism does not simply reproduce the physical existence of individuals. "Rather it is a definite form of activity of these individuals, a definite form of expressing their life, a definite *mode of life* on their part . . . [and this coincides with] both *what* they produce and *how* they produce."[15] A mode of life is not divisible. It does not consist of a public part and a private part, a part at the workplace and a part in the community—each of which makes up a certain fraction, and all of which add up to 100 percent. A mode of life, and all the aspects of that mode of life, take meaning from the totality of which they form a part.

In part because of shifts in the boundaries between the economic and the political and because of the increasing interconnections between the state apparatus and the economy (through means as varied as public education and government regulation of industry), it becomes even more necessary to emphasize that one can only understand and penetrate, and transform reality as a totality, and that "only a subject which is itself a totality is capable of this penetration." Only a collective individual, a united group of people "can actively penetrate the reality of society and transform it in its entirety."[16]

Feminism and Revolution

If all that I have said about feminism as a method rooted in dealing with everyday life holds true, what is it that makes this mode of analysis a force for revolution? There are three factors of particular importance: (1) The focus on everyday life and experience makes action a necessity, not a moral choice or an option. We are not fighting other people's battles but our own. (2) The nature of our understanding of theory is altered and theory is brought into an integral and everyday relation with practice. (3) Theory leads directly to a transformation of social relations both in consciousness and in reality because of its close connection to real needs.

First, how does a feminist mode of analysis make revolution necessary? The feminist method of taking up and analyzing experience is a way of appropriating reality. Experience is incorporated in such a way that our life experiences become a part of our humanness. By appropriating our experience and incorporating it into ourselves, we transform what might have been a politics of idealism into a politics of necessity. By appropriating our collective experience, we are creating prople who recognize that we cannot be ourselves in a society based on hierarchy, domination, and private property. We are acquiring a consciousness which forces us, as Marx put it, "by an ineluctable, irremediable and imperious *distress*—by practical *necessity*—to revolt against this inhumanity."[17] Incorporating, or making part of ourselves, what we learn is essential to the method of feminism.

Second, I argued that a feminist mode of analysis leads to an integration of theory and practice. For feminists, theory is the articulation of what our practical activity has already appropriated in reality. As Marx argued, as struggle develops, theorists "no longer need to seek science in their minds; they have only to take note of what is happening before their eyes and to become its mouthpiece."[18] If we look more closely at the subject about which Marx was writing on this occasion—the British working class—we find that by the time Marx wrote these words that group had already developed theory out of its practice to a considerable degree. A variety of trends had emerged, and ideas about organization and politics had been diffused over a wide area. Isolation from experienced national leadership, and the overimportance of personalities created problems,

but the facility with which English working-class people formed associations is impressive. They used a variety of forms taken over from Methodism, friendly societies, trade unions, etc. By the time Marx wrote, it was clear that most people understood that power came from organization.

In looking at history, one is especially struck with the number of false starts, the hesitancy, the backtracking that went into making what we would today recognize as class consciousness. Forming theory out of practice does not come quickly or easily, and it is rarely clear what direction the theory will finally take.

Feminists, in making theory, take up and examine what we find within ourselves; we attempt to clarify for ourselves and others what we already, at some level, know. Theory itself, then, can be seen as a way of taking up and building on our experience. This is not to say that feminists reject all knowledge that is not firsthand, that we can learn nothing from books or from history. But rather than read a number of sacred texts we make the practical questions posed for us in everyday life the basis of our study. Feminism recognizes that political philosophy and political action do not take place in separate realms. On the contrary, the concepts with which we understand the social world emerge from and are defined by human activity.

For feminists, the unity of theory and practice refers to the use of theory to make coherent the problems and principles expressed in our practical activity. Feminists argue that the role of theory is to take seriously the idea that all of us are theorists. The role of theory, then, is to articulate for us what we know from our practical activity, to bring out and make conscious the philosophy embedded in our lives. Feminists are in fact creating social theory through political action. We need to conceptualize, to take up and specify what we have already done, in order to make the next steps clear. We can start from common sense, but we need to move on to the philosophy systematically elaborated by traditional intellectuals.

A third factor in making feminism a force for revolution is that the mode of analysis I have described leads to a transformation of social relations. This is true first in a logical sense. That is, once social relations are situated within the context of the social formation as a whole, the individual phenomena change their meanings and forms. They become something other than they were. For example, what liberal theory understands as social stratification becomes clearer when understood as class. But this is not simply a logical point. As Lukacs has pointed out, the transformation of each phenomenon through relating it to the social totality ends by conferring "reality on the day to day struggle by manifesting its relation to the whole. Thus it elevates mere existence to reality."[19] This development in mass political consciousness, the transformation of the phenomena of life, is on the one hand a profoundly political act and on the other, a "point of transition."[20] Consciousness must become deed, but the act of becoming conscious is itself a kind of deed.

If we grant that the women's movement has reinvented Marx's method and for that reason can be a force for revolution, we need to ask in what specific sense the women's movement can be a model for the rest of the left. At the beginning I outlined a number of criticisms of the left, all rooted in the fact that it has lost touch with everyday life. The contrast I want to draw is one between what Gramsci recognized as "real action," action "which modifies in an essential way both man and external reality," and "gladiatorial futility, which is self-declared action but modifies only the word, not things, the external gesture and not the [person] inside."[21]

At the beginning of this paper I suggested that education took on a new significance for the women's movement because of the role of personal, everyday experience in constructing theory and transforming reality. Feminists are aware that we face the task of building a collective will, a new common sense, and this requires that we must participate in a process of education in two senses. We must, first, never tire of repeating our own arguments and, second, work to raise the general intellectual level, the consciousness of larger numbers of people in order to produce a new and different understanding of everyday life. The women's movement is working at both these tasks—the first by insisting that every woman can reconstruct the more general feminist arguments on

her own, the second by turning to the writings of more traditional intellectuals for whatever guidance we may find there.

Marx applied his method systematically to the study of capital. Feminists have not yet really begun systematic study based on the mode of analysis we have developed. Here I can only mention some of the questions which are currently being debated in the women's movement—issues on which there is not yet a consensus but whose theoretical resolution is inseparable from practical, daily work for change.

Issues for Feminist Theory

The Nature of Class

Marxists have devoted a great deal of attention to the nature of class. Most Marxist theorists agree that there are problems with traditional definitions of class. If to be working class means to have nothing to sell but labor power, then the vast majority of the American population falls within this definition. If to be working class means to contribute directly to the production of surplus value, then far fewer of us fall into the category. A number of modifications of these traditional ideas have been presented. Some writers have argued that there is a "new" working class, that what is important now is the possibility for alliances with sectors of the "new petty bourgeoisie," that knowledge and its possession (science) have become productive forces, or that the working out of the division of mental from manual labor with its attendant ritualization of knowledge is critical to the working out of class boundaries. In this maze of theories about the nature of class under advanced capitalism, a feminist mode of analysis can provide important insights into the nature of class as it structures the concrete existence of groups and individuals.

Because feminists begin from our own experience in a specific advanced capitalist society, we recognize that the lived realities of different segments of society are varied. While it is true that most people have only their labor power to sell (for wages or not), there are real differences in power, privilege, ability to control our lives, and even chances for survival. By focusing on people's daily lives we are learning that our class is not defined by our relationship to the mode of production in the simple sense that if we sell our labor power (for a day or a lifetime) or are part of the family of someone (presumably male) who does, we are working class. Being working class is a way of living life, a mode of life not exclusively defined by the simple fact that we have only our labor power to sell.

Class distinctions in capitalist society are part of a totality, a mode of life which is structured as well by the traditions of patriarchy and white supremacy. Class distinctions in the United States affect the everyday lives of women and men, white and black and Third World people in different ways. A feminist mode of analysis leads us to ask questions which recognize that we already know a great deal about class (in fact, in our daily activity we act on what we know), but need to appropriate what we know to make it into explicit theory.

One's social class is defined by one's place "in the ensemble of social practices, i.e., by [one's] place in the social division of labor as a whole," and for that reason must include political and ideological relations. "Social class, in this sense, is a concept which denotes the effects of the structure within the social division of labor (social relations and social practices)."[22] Feminists writing about class have focused on the structures produced by the interaction of political, ideological, and more strictly economic relations, and have done so from the standpoint of everyday life and activity.

Some of the best descriptions of class and its importance in the women's movement were produced by the Furies, a lesbian/feminist separatist group in Washington, D.C. When the Furies began, many members of the collective knew very little about the nature of class. But the collective included a number of lower- and working-class women who were concerned about ways middle-class women oppressed them. As one middle-class woman wrote:

Our assumptions, for example, about how to run a meeting were different from theirs, but we assumed ours were correct because they

were easiest for us—given our college educations, our ability to use words, our ability to abstract, our inability to make quick decisions, the difficulty we had with direct confrontations. . . . I learned [that] class oppression was . . . a part of my life which I could see and change. And, having seen the manifestations of class in myself, I better understood how class operated generally to divide people and keep them down.[23]

In the context of working for change, it became clear that

refusal to deal with class behavior in a lesbian/feminist movement is sheer self-indulgence and leads to the downfall of our own struggle. Middle-class women should look first at that scale of worth that is the class system in America. They should examine where they fit on that scale, how it affected them, and what they thought of the people below and above them. . . . Start thinking politically about the class system and all the power systems in this country.[24]

What specifically did the Furies learn when they looked at the way class functioned in daily life? First, they learned the sense in which we have all, no matter what our class background, taken for granted that the "middle class way is *the right way*." Class arrogance is expressed in looking down on the "less articulate," or regarding with "scorn or pity . . . those whose emotions are not repressed or who can't rap out abstract theories in thirty seconds flat." Class supremacy, the Furies found, is also apparent in a kind of passivity often assumed by middle- and especially upper-middle-class women for whom things have come easily. People who are "pushy, dogmatic, hostile, or intolerant" are looked down on. Advocating downward mobility and putting down those who are not as "revolutionary" is another form of middle-class arrogance. What is critical about all of this is that "middle-class women set the standards of what is good (and even the proper style of downward mobility which often takes money to achieve) and act 'more revolutionary than thou' towards those who are concerned about money and the future." Middle-class women retain control over approval. The small, indirect, and dishonest ways of behaving in polite society are also ways of maintaining "the supremacy of the middle class and perpetuating the feelings of inadequacy of the working class."[25]

These accounts of barriers created by class differences within the women's movement lead us toward an understanding of several important points about the nature of class. They lead us to see first that class is a complex of relations, one in which knowledge or know-how is at a premium, and second, at a deeper level, that what is involved in the daily reality of class oppression is the concrete working out of the division between mental and manual labor. Class, especially as it affects the lives of women, is a complex of a number of factors in which political and ideological aspects as well as strictly economic factors play an important role. Theorists have focused too closely on the domination of men by production pure and simple. Looking at the role of class in women's lives highlights the importance of other factors as well, such as the role of family and patriarchal traditions. For both women and men class defines the way we see the world and our place in it, how we were educated and where, and how we act—whether with assurance or uncertainty. The process of production must be seen to include the reproduction of political and ideological relations of domination and subordination. It is these factors that lead to the feelings described as "being out of control," "feeling like you don't know what to do," and feeling that you are incompetent to judge your own performance.[26]

At bottom, people are describing the way it feels to be on the "wrong" side of the division between mental and manual labor. Indeed, the division between mental and manual labor is precisely the concentrated form of class divisions in capitalism. It is critical to recognize that mental labor is the exercise of "political relations legitimized by and articulated to, the monopolization and secrecy of knowledge, i.e., the reproduction of the ideological relations of domination and subordination."[27] Mental labor involves a series of rituals and symbols. And it is always the case that the dominated group either does not know or cannot know the things that are important.

By calling attention to life rather than theory, the women's movement has called attention to cultural domination as a whole—

has begun a political analysis that does not take place in isolation from practical activity. By noticing the real differences among women in terms of class—confidence, verbal ability, ease about money, sense of group identity—we are developing new questions about class. While we have barely begun the task of reconstructing the category of class, we are learning that it is important to pay attention to the mechanisms of domination as a whole. By looking at class as a feature of life and struggle, the women's movement has established some of the terms any revolutionary movement must use: Until we confront class as a part of everyday life, until we begin to analyze what we already know about class, we will never be able to build a united and large-scale movement for revolution. In this task, we need to recognize the decisive role of the division between mental and manual labor in all its complexity for the formation of the whole mode of life that is capitalism.

Organizations and Strategies

Feminism, while it does not prescribe an organizational form, leads to a set of questions about organizational priorities. First, a feminist mode of analysis suggests that we need organizations which include the appropriation of experience as a part of the work of the organization itself. We need to systematically analyze what we learn as we work in organizations. While the analysis of our experience in small groups was valuable, we need to develop ways to appropriate our organizational experience and to use it to transform our conception of organization itself. Some feminist organizations are beginning to do this—to raise questions about the process of meetings or about the way work is done and should be done.

Because so many of us reacted to our experience in the organizations of the rest of the left by refusing to build any organizational structures at all, we have only begun to think about the way we should work in organizations with some structure. We need to build the possibilities for change and growth into our organizations rather than rely on small groups. This means that we need to systematically teach and respect different skills and allow our organizations to change and grow in new directions. We need to use our organizations as places where we begin to redefine social relations and to create new ways of working which do not follow the patterns of domination and hierarchy set by the mode of production as a whole.

A feminist mode of analysis has implications for strategy as well. We can begin to make coalitions with other groups who share our approach to politics. We cannot work, however, with people who refuse to face questions in terms of everyday life or with people who will not use their own experience as a fundamental basis for knowledge. We cannot work with those who treat theory as a set of conclusions to be pasted onto reality and who, out of their own moral commitment, make a revolution for the benefit of their inferiors. A feminist mode of analysis suggests that we must work on issues which have real impact on daily life. These issues are varied—housing, public transportation, food prices, etc. The only condition for coalition with other groups is that those groups share our method. So long as those we work with are working for change out of necessity, because they, like us, have no alternative, there is a real basis for common action.

As we work on particular issues, we must continually ask how we can use these issues to build our collective strength. The mode of analysis developed by the women's movement suggests several criteria with which to evaluate particular strategies. First, we must ask how our work will educate ourselves and others politically, how it will help us to see the connections between social institutions. Second, we must ask how a particular strategy materially affects our daily lives. This involves asking: How does it improve our conditions of existence? How will it affect our sense of ourselves and our own power to change the world? How will a particular strategy politicize people, make people aware of problems beyond individual ones? Third, we must ask how our strategies work to build organizations—to build a collective individual which will increase our power to transform social relations as a whole. Fourth, we must ask how our strategies weaken the institutions which control our lives—patriarchy, white supremacy, and capitalism. Our strategies must work not simply to weaken each of these institutions separately but must attack them on the basis of an understanding of the totality of which they form parts.

In all this, however, we must remember that there is no "ready made, pre-established, detailed set of tactics which a central committee can teach its . . . membership as if they were army recruits."[28] In general, the tactics of a mass party cannot be invented. They are "the product of a progressive series of great creative acts in the often rudimentary experiments of the class struggle. Here too, the unconscious comes before the conscious. . . ."[29]

Most important, a feminist mode of analysis makes us recognize that the struggle itself must be seen as a process with all its internal difficulties. We must avoid, on the one hand, developing a narrow sectarian outlook, and, on the other, abandoning our goal of revolution. We must continue to base our work on the necessity for change in our own lives. Our political theorizing can only grow out of appropriating the practical political work we have done. While the answers to our questions come only slowly and with difficulty, we must remember that we are involved in a continuous process of learning what kind of world we want to create as we work for change.

Notes

1. Antonio Gramsci, *Selections from the Prison Notebooks*, trans. Quinton Hoare and Geoffrey Nowell Smith (New York: International Publishers, 1971), p. 365. Gramsci adds that "the identification of theory and practice is a critical act, through which practice is demonstrated rational and necessary and theory realistic and rational."

2. Ibid., p. 327. See also p. 244.

3. I should perhaps note here that I am speaking as a participant as well as a critical observer. The experience I use as a reference point is my own as well as that of many other women.

4. Feminists are beginning to recognize the importance for the movement of conscious theorizing—for critical analysis of what we

have been doing for most of the last decade. Among the current issues and problems being reevaluated are the significance of service projects, the importance of leadership, new possibilities for developing organizational structures, and our relationship to the rest of the left.

5. George Lukacs, *History and Class Consciousness* (Cambridge, Mass: M.I.T. Press, 1971). p. 1.

6. This is not to say there have been no problems or that beginning with personal experience always led women to think in larger terms. Some groups have remained apolitical or have never moved beyond the level of personal issues; others have become so opposed to any organizations other than personal organizations that they are immobilized. Problems about the "correct line" are also part of the current debate in the women's movement.

7. Gramsci, *Selections,* p. 330.

8. Ibid., p. 43.

9. Marge Piercy, "A Shadow Play for Guilt," in *To Be of Use* (Garden City, N.Y.: Doubleday, 1973), p. 17.

10. Karl Marx, "Theses on Feuerbach," in Karl Marx and Friedrich Engels, *The German Ideology,* ed. C. J. Arthur (New York: International Publishers, 1970), p. 121. This method also overcomes the passivity characteristic of much of American life. See, for example, Richard Sennett and Jonathan Cobb, *The Hidden Injuries of Class* (New York: Vintage, 1973), p. 165, and Stanley Aronowitz, *False Promises* (New York: McGraw-Hill, 1973), p. 112.

11. See Gramsci, *Selections,* p. 352.

12. Gramsci, *Selections,* p. 349.

13. Marx, "Theses on Feuerbach," p. 121. See also Gramsci, *Selections,* pp. 352, 360.

14. Karl Marx, *Capital,* vol. 1 (Moscow: Foreign Language Publishing House, 1954), p. 20.

15. Marx and Engels, *German Ideology,* p. 114.

16. Lukacs, *History,* p. 39.

17. Karl Marx, *Selected Writings in Sociology and Social Philosophy,* trans. T. B. Botto-more (New York: McGraw-Hill, 1956), p. 232.

18. Karl Marx, *The Poverty of Philosophy* (New York: International Publishers, 1973), p. 125.

19. Lukacs, *History,* p. 22.

20. Ibid., p. 178. See also Gramsci's contention that "for a mass of people to be led to think coherently and in the same coherent fashion about the real present world, is a 'philosophical' event far more important and 'original' than the discovery by some philosophical 'genius' of a truth which remains the property of small groups of intellectuals" (*Selections,* p. 325).

21. Ibid., pp. 225, 307.

22. Poulantzas, *Classes in Contemporary Capitalism,* p. 14.

23. Ginny Berson, "Only by Association," *The Furies* 1, no. 5 (June/July 1972): 5–7.

24. Nancy Myron, "Class Beginnings," *The Furies* 1, no. 3 (March/April 1972): 3.

25. Charlotte Bunch and Coletta Reid, "Revolution Begins at Home," *The Furies* 1, no. 4 (May 1972): 2–3. See also Dolores Bargowski and Coletta Reid, "Garbage Among the Trash," *The Furies* 1, no. 6 (August 1972): 8–9.

26. These statements come from Sennett and Cobb, *Hidden Injuries of Class,* pp. 97, 115, and 157. One of the most important effects of class is to make working-class people doubt they have a legitimate right to fight back.

27. Poulantzas, *Classes,* p. 240.

28. Rosa Luxemburg, "Organizational Questions of Russian Social Democracy," *Selected Writings of Rosa Luxemburg,* ed. Dick Howard (New York: Monthly Review Press, 1971), p. 289.

29. Ibid., p. 293.

Study Questions

1. Why is theory important to a revolutionary?
2. In what way is feminism a "method"? What

is an example of this method? How does this method help women understand their daily lives?

3. In what way does feminism relate personal and social change? What implications does that have for the analysis of social institutions?

4. In what way does feminist reasoning regard social structures as fluid, as opposed to static? In what way is feminist reasoning holistic? How does this make the feminist framework more adequate for understanding social phenomena?

5. What makes the feminist mode of analysis a force for revolution?

6. How have feminists modified the traditional Marxist concept of class? In particular, what did the Furies discover?

Have We Got a Theory for You! Feminist Theory, Cultural Imperialism and the Demand for "The Woman's Voice"

Maria C. Lugones and Elizabeth V. Spelman

Prologue

(In an Hispana voice) A veces quisiera mezclar en una voz el sonido canyengue, tristón y urbano del porteñismo que llevo adentro con la cadencia apacible, serrana y llena de corage de la hispana nuevo mejicana. Contrastar y unir

el piolín y la cuerda
el traé y el pepéname
el camión y la troca
la lluvia y el llanto

Pero este querer se me va cuando veo que he confundido la solidaridad con la falta de diferencia. La solidaridad requiere el reconocer, comprender, respetar y amar lo que nos lleva a llorar en distintas cadencias. El imperialismo cultural desea lo contrario, por eso necesitamos muchas voces. Porque una sola voz nos mata a las dos.

No quiero hablar por ti sino contigo. Pero si no aprendo tus modos y tu los mios la conversación es sólo aparente. Y la apariencia se

From *Women's Studies International Forum*, Vol. 6, No. 6 (1983), pp. 573–581. Reprinted by permission of Pergamon Press.

levanta como una barrera sin sentido entre las dos. Sin sentido y sin sentimiento. Por eso no me debes dejar que te dicte tu ser y no me dictes el mio. Porque entonces ya no dialogamos. El diálogo entre nosotras requiere dos voces y no una.

Tal vez un día jugaremos juntas y nos hablaremos no en una lengua universal sino que vos me hablarás mi voz y yo la tuya.

Preface

This paper is the result of our dialogue, of our thinking together about differences among women and how these differences are silenced. (Think, for example, of all the silences there are connected with the fact that this paper is in English—for that is a borrowed tongue for one of us.) In the process of our talking and writing together, we saw that the differences between us did not permit our speaking in one voice. For example, when we agreed we expressed the thought differently; there were some things that both of us thought were true but could not express as true of each of us; sometimes we could not say "we"; and sometimes one of us could not express the thought in the first person singular, and to express it in the third person would be to present an outsider's and not an insider's perspective. Thus the use of two voices is central both to the process of constructing this paper and to the substance of it. We are both the authors of this paper and not just sections of it but we write together without presupposing unity of expression or of experience. So when we speak in unison it means just that—there are two voices and not just one.

Introduction

(In the voice of a white/Anglo woman who has been teaching and writing about feminist theory) Feminism is, among other things, a response to the fact that women either have been left out of, or included in demeaning and disfiguring ways in what has been an almost exclusively male account of the world. And so while part of what feminists want and demand for women is the right to move and to act in accordance with our own wills and not against them, another part is the desire and insistence that we give our *own* accounts of these movements and actions. For it matters to us what is said about us, who says it, and to whom it is said: having the opportunity to talk about one's life, to give an account of it, to interpret it, is integral to leading that life rather than being led through it; hence our distrust of the male monopoly over accounts of women's lives. To put the same point slightly differently, part of human life, human living, is talking about it, and we can be sure that being silenced in one's own account of one's life is a kind of amputation that signals oppression. Another reason for not divorcing life from the telling of it or talking about it is that as humans our experiences are deeply influenced by what is said about them, by ourselves or powerful (as opposed to significant) others. Indeed, the phenomenon of internalized oppression is only possible because this is so: one experiences her life in terms of the impoverished and degrading concepts others have found it convenient to use to describe her. We can't separate lives from the accounts given of them; the articula-

tion of our experience is part of our experience.

Sometimes feminists have made even stronger claims about the importance of speaking about our own lives and the destructiveness of others presuming to speak about us or for us. First of all, the claim has been made that on the whole men's accounts of women's lives have been at best false, a function of ignorance; and at worst malicious lies, a function of a knowledgeable desire to exploit and oppress. Since it matters to us that falsehood and lies not be told about us, we demand, of those who have been responsible for those falsehoods and lies, or those who continue to transmit them, not just that we speak but that they learn to be able to hear us. It has also been claimed that talking about one's life, telling one's story, in the company of those doing the same (as in consciousness-raising sessions), is constitutive of feminist method.[1]

And so the demand that the woman's voice be heard and attended to has been made for a variety of reasons: not just so as to greatly increase the chances that true accounts of women's lives will be given, but also because the articulation of experience (in myriad ways) is among the hallmarks of a self-determining individual or community. There are not just epistemological, but moral and political reasons for demanding that the woman's voice be heard, after centuries of androcentric din.

But what more exactly is the feminist demand that the woman's voice be heard? There are several crucial notes to make about it. First of all, the demand grows out of a complaint, and in order to understand the scope and focus of the demand we have to look at the scope and focus of the complaint. The complaint does not specify *which* women have been silenced, and in one way this is appropriate to the conditions it is a complaint about: virtually no women have had a voice, whatever their race, class, ethnicity, religion, sexual alliance, whatever place and period in history they lived. And if it is as women that women have been silenced, then of course the demand must be that women as women have a voice. But in another way the complaint is very misleading, insofar as it suggests that it is women as women who have been silenced, and that whether a woman is rich or poor, Black, brown or white, etc., is irrelevant to what it means for her to be a woman. For the demand thus simply made ignores at least two related points: (1) it is only possible for a woman who does not feel highly vulnerable with respect to other parts of her identity, e.g., race, class, ethnicity, religion, sexual alliance, etc., to conceive of her voice simply or essentially as a "woman's voice"; (2) just because not all women are equally vulnerable with respect to race, class, etc., some women's voices are more likely to be heard than others by those who have heretofore been giving—or silencing—the accounts of women's lives. For all these reasons, the women's voices most likely to come forth and the women's voices most likely to be heard are, in the United States anyway, those of white, middle-class, heterosexual Christian (or anyway not self-identified non-Christian) women. Indeed, many Hispanas, Black women, Jewish women—to name a few groups—have felt it an invitation to silence rather than speech to be requested—if they are requested at all—to speak about being "women" (with the plain wrapper—as if there were one) in distinction from speaking about being Hispana, Black, Jewish, working-class, etc., women.

The demand that the "woman's voice" be heard, and the search for the "woman's voice" as central to feminist methodology, reflects nascent feminist theory. It reflects nascent empirical theory insofar as it presupposes that the silencing of women is systematic, shows up in regular, patterned ways, and that there are discoverable causes of this widespread observable phenomenon; the demand reflects nascent political theory insofar as it presupposes that the silencing of women reveals a systematic pattern of power and authority; and it reflects nascent moral theory insofar as it presupposes that the silencing is unjust and that there are particular ways of remedying this injustice. Indeed, whatever else we know feminism to include—e.g., concrete direct political action—theorizing is integral to it: theories about the nature of oppression, the causes of it, the relation of the oppression of women to other forms of oppression. And certainly the concept of the woman's voice is itself a theoretical concept, in the sense that it presupposes a theory according to which our identities as human beings are

actually compound identities, a kind of fusion or confusion of our otherwise separate identities as women or men, as Black or brown or white, etc. That is no less a theoretical stance than Plato's division of the person into soul and body or Aristotle's parcelling of the soul into various functions.

The demand that the "woman's voice" be heard also invites some further directions in the exploration of women's lives and discourages or excludes others. For reasons mentioned above, systematic, sustained reflection on being a woman—the kind of contemplation that "doing theory" requires—is most likely to be done by women who vis-à-vis other women enjoy a certain amount of political, social and economic privilege because of their skin color, class membership, ethnic identity. There is a relationship between the content of our contemplation and the fact that we have the time to engage in it at some length—otherwise we shall have to say that it is a mere accident of history that white middle-class women in the United States have in the main developed "feminist theory" (as opposed to "Black feminist theory," "Chicana feminist theory," etc.) and that so much of the theory has failed to be relevant to the lives of women who are not white or middle class. Feminist theory—of all kinds—is to be based on, or anyway touch base with, the variety of real life stories women provide about themselves. But in fact, because, among other things, of the structural political and social and economic inequalities among women, the tail has been wagging the dog: feminist theory has not for the most part arisen out of a medley of women's voices; instead, the theory has arisen out of the voices, the experiences, of a fairly small handful of women, and if other women's voices do not sing in harmony with the theory, they aren't counted as women's voices—rather, they are the voices of the woman as Hispana, Black, Jew, etc. There is another sense in which the tail is wagging the dog, too: it is presumed to be the case that those who do the theory know more about those who are theorized than vice versa; hence it ought to be the case that if it is white/Anglo women who write for and about all other women, the white/Anglo women must know more about all other women than other women know about them. But in fact just in order to survive, brown and Black women have to know a lot more about white/Anglo women—not through the sustained contemplation theory requires, but through the sharp observation stark exigency demands.

(In an Hispana voice) I think it necessary to explain why in so many cases when women of color appear in front of white/Anglo women to talk about feminism and women of color, we mainly raise a complaint: the complaint of exclusion, of silencing, of being included in a universe we have not chosen. We usually raise the complaint with a certain amount of disguised or undisguised anger. I can only attempt to explain this phenomenon from a Hispanic viewpoint and a fairly narrow one at that: the viewpoint of an Argentinian woman who has lived in the US for 16 years, who has attempted to come to terms with the devaluation of things Hispanic and Hispanic people in "America" and who is most familiar with Hispano life in the Southwest of the US. I am quite unfamiliar with daily Hispano life in the urban centers, though not with some of the themes and some of the salient experiences of urban Hispano life.

When I say "we,"[2] I am referring to Hispanas. I am accustomed to use the "we" in this way. I am also pained by the tenuousness of this "we" given that I am not a native of the United States. Through the years I have come to be recognized and I have come to recognize myself more and more firmly as part of this "we." I also have a profound yearning for this firmness since I am a displaced person and I am conscious of not being of and I am unwilling to make myself of—even if this were possible—the white/Anglo community.

When I say "you" I mean not the non-Hispanic but the white/Anglo women that I address. "We" and "you" do not capture my relation to other non-white women. The complexity of that relation is not addressed here, but it is vivid to me as I write down my thoughts on the subject at hand.

I see two related reasons for our complaint-full discourse with white/Anglo women. Both of these reasons plague our world, they contaminate it through and through. It takes some hardening of oneself, some self-acceptance of our own anger to face them, for to face them is to decide that maybe we can change our situation in self-constructive ways and we know fully well that the possibilities are minimal. We know that we cannot rest from facing these reasons, that the tenderness towards others in us undermines our possibilities, that we have to fight our own niceness because it clouds our minds and hearts. Yet we know that a thoroughgoing hardening would dehumanize us. So, we have to walk through our days in a peculiarly fragile psychic state, one that we have to struggle to maintain, one that we do not often succeed in maintaining.

We and you do not talk the same language. When we talk to you we use your language: the language of your experience and of your theories. We try to use it to communicate our world of experience. But since your language and your theories are inadequate in expressing our experiences, we only succeed in communicating our experience of exclusion. We cannot talk to you in our language because you do not understand it. So the brute facts that we understand your language and that the place where most theorizing about women is taking place is your place, both combine to require that we either use your language and distort our experience not just in the speaking about it, but in the living of it, or that we remain silent. Complaining about exclusion is a way of remaining silent.

You are ill at ease in our world. You are ill at ease in our world in a very different way than we are ill at ease in yours. You are not of our world and again, you are not of our world in a very different way than we are not of yours. In the intimacy of a personal relationship we appear to you many times to be wholly there, to have broken through or to have dissipated the barriers that separate us because you are Anglo and we are raza. When we let go of the psychic state that I referred to above in the direction of sympathy, we appear to ourselves equally whole in your presence but our intimacy is thoroughly incomplete. When we are in your world many times you remake us in your own image, although sometimes you clearly and explicitly acknowledge that we are not wholly there in our being with you. When we are in your world we ourselves feel the discomfort of having our own being Hispanas disfigured or not understood. And yet, we have had to be in your world and learn its ways. We have to participate in it, make a living in it, live in it, be mistreated in it, be ignored in it, and rarely, be appreciated in it. In learning to do these things or in learning to suffer them or in learning to enjoy what is to be enjoyed or in learning to understand your conception of us, we have had to learn your culture and thus your language and self-conceptions. But there is nothing that necessitates that you understand our world: understand, that is, not as an observer understands things, but as a participant, as someone who has a stake in them understands them. So your being ill at ease in our world lacks the features of our being ill at ease in yours precisely because you can leave and you can always tell yourselves that you will be soon out of there and because the wholeness of your selves is never touched by us, we have no tendency to remake you in our image.

But you theorize about women and we are women, so you understand yourselves to be theorizing about us, and we understand you to be theorizing about us. Yet none of the feminist theories developed so far seems to me to help Hispanas in the articulation of our experience. We have a sense that in using them we are distorting our experiences. Most Hispanas cannot even understand the language used in these theories—and only in some cases the reason is that the Hispana cannot understand English. We do not recognize ourselves in these theories. They create in us a schizophrenic split between our concern for ourselves as women and ourselves as Hispanas, one that we do not feel otherwise. Thus they seem to us to force us to assimilate to some version of Anglo culture, however revised that version may be. They seem to ask that we leave our communities or that we become alienated so completely in them that we feel hollow. When we see that you feel alienated in your own communities, this confuses us because we think that maybe every feminist has to suffer this alienation. But we see that recognition of your alienation leads many of you to be empowered into the remaking of your culture, while we are paralyzed into a state of displacement with no place to go.

So I think that we need to think carefully about the relation between the articulation of our own experience, the interpretation of our own experience, and theory making by us and other non-Hispanic women about themselves and other "women."

The only motive that makes sense to me for your joining us in this investigation is the motive of friendship, out of friendship. A non-imperialist feminism requires that you make a real space for our articulating, interpreting, theorizing and reflecting about the connections among them—a real space must be a non-coerced space—and/or that you follow us into our world out of friendship. I see the "out of friendship" as the only sensical motivation for this following because the task at hand for you is one of extraordinary difficulty. It requires that you be willing to devote a great part of your life to it and that you be willing to suffer alienation and self-disruption. Self-interest has been proposed as a possible motive for entering this task. But self-interest does not seem to me to be a realistic motive, since whatever the benefits you may accrue from such a journey, they cannot be concrete enough for you at this time and they may not be worth your while. I do not think that you have any obligation to understand us. You do have an obligation to abandon your imperialism, your universal claims, your reduction of us to your selves simply because they seriously harm us.

I think that the fact that we are so ill at ease with your theorizing in the ways indicated above does indicate that there is something wrong with these theories. But what is it that is wrong? Is it simply that the theories are flawed if meant to be universal but accurate so long as they are confined to your particular group(s)? Is it that the theories are not really flawed but need to be translated? Can they be translated? Is it something about the process of theorizing that is flawed? How do the two reasons for our complaint-full discourse affect the validity of your theories? Where do *we* begin? To what extent are our experience and its articulation affected by our being a colonized people, and thus by your culture, theories and conceptions? Should we theorize in community and thus as part of community life and outside the academy and other intellectual circles? What is the point of making theory? Is theory making a good thing for us to do at this time? When are we making theory and when are we just articulating and/or interpreting our experiences?

Some Questionable Assumptions about Feminist Theorizing

(Unproblematically in Vicky's and Maria's voice) Feminist theories aren't just about what happens to the female population in any given society or across all societies; they are about the meaning of those experiences in the lives of women. They are about beings who give their own accounts of what is happening to them or of what they are doing, who have culturally constructed ways of reflecting on their lives. But how can the theorizer get at the meaning of those experiences? What should the relation be between a woman's own account of her experiences and the theorizer's account of it?

Let us describe two different ways of arriving at an account of another woman's experience. It is one thing for both me and you to observe you and come up with our different accounts of what you are doing; it is quite another for me to observe myself and others much like me culturally and in other ways and to develop an account of myself and then use that account to give an account of you. In the first case you are the "insider" and I am the "outsider." When the outsider makes clear that she is an outsider and that this is an outsider's account of your behavior, there is a touch of honesty about what she is doing. Most of the time the "interpretation by an outsider" is left understood and most of the time the distance of outsidedness is understood to mark objectivity in the interpretation. But why is the outsider as an outsider interpreting your behavior? Is she doing it so that you can understand how she sees you? Is she doing it so that other outsiders will understand how you *are*? Is she doing it so that *you* will understand how you are? It would seem that if the outsider wants you to understand how she sees you and you have given your account of how you see yourself to her, there is a possibility of genuine dialogue between the two. It also seems that the lack of reciprocity could bar genuine dialogue. For why should you engage in such a one-sided dialogue? As soon as we ask this question, a host of other conditions for the possibility of a genuine dialogue between us arise: conditions having to do with your position relative to me in the various social, political and economic structures in which we might come across each other or in which you may run face to face with my account of you and my use of your account of yourself. Is this kind of dialogue necessary for me to get at the meaning of your experiences? That is, is this kind of dialogue necessary for feminist theorizing that is not seriously flawed?

Obviously the most dangerous of the understanding of what I—an outsider—am doing in giving an account of your experience is the one that describes what I'm doing as giving an account of who and how you are whether it be given to you or to other outsiders. Why should you or anyone else believe me; that is, why should you or anyone else believe that you are as I say you are? Could I be right? What conditions would have to obtain for my being right? That many women are put in the position of not knowing whether or not to believe outsiders' accounts of their experiences is clear. The pressures to believe these accounts are enormous even when the woman in question does not see herself in the account. She is thus led to doubt her own judgment and to doubt all interpretation of her experience. This leads her to experience her life differently. Since the consequences of outsiders' accounts can be so significant, it is crucial that we reflect on whether or not this type of account can ever be right and if so, under what conditions.

The last point leads us to the second way of arriving at an account of another woman's experience, viz., the case in which I observe myself and others like me culturally and in other ways and use that account to give an account of you. In doing this, I remake you in my own image. Feminist theorizing approaches this remaking insofar as it depends on the concept of women as women. For it has not arrived at this concept as a consequence of dialogue with many women who are culturally different, or by any other kind of investigation of cultural differences which may include different conceptions of what it is to be a woman; it has simply presupposed this concept.

Our suggestion in this paper, and at this time it is no more than a suggestion, is that only when genuine and reciprocal dialogue takes place between "outsiders" and "insiders" can we trust the outsider's account. At first sight it may appear that the insider/outsider distinction disappears in the dialogue, but it is important to notice that all that happens is that we are now both outsider and insider with respect to each other. The dialogue puts us both in position to give a better account of each other's and our own experience. Here we should again note that white/Anglo women are much less prepared for this dialogue with women of color than women of color are for dialogue with them in that women of color have had to learn white/Anglo ways, self-conceptions, and conceptions of them.

But both the possibility and the desirability of this dialogue are very much in question. We need to think about the possible motivations for engaging in this dialogue, whether doing theory jointly would be a good thing, in what ways and for whom, and whether doing theory is in itself a good thing at this time for women of color or white/Anglo women. In motivating the last question let us remember the hierarchical distinctions between theorizers and those theorized about and between theorizers and doers. These distinctions are endorsed by the same views and institutions which endorse and support hierarchical distinctions between men/women, master race/inferior race, intellectuals/manual workers. Of what use is the activity of theorizing to those of us who are women of color engaged day in and day out in the task of empowering women and men of color face to face with them? Should we be articulating and interpreting their experience for them with the aid of theories? Whose theories?

Ways of Talking or Being Talked about That Are Helpful, Illuminating, Empowering, Respectful

---

(Unproblematically in Maria's and Vicky's voice) Feminists have been quite diligent about pointing out ways in which empirical, philosophical and moral theories have been androcentric. They have thought it crucial to ask, with respect to such theories: who makes them? for whom do they make them? about what or whom are the theories? why? how are theories tested? what are the criteria for such tests and where did the criteria come from? Without posing such questions and trying to answer them, we'd never have been able to begin to mount evidence for our claims that particular theories are androcentric, sexist, biased, paternalistic, etc. Certain philosophers have become fond of—indeed, have made their careers on—pointing out that characterizing a statement as true or false is only one of many ways possible of characterizing it; it might also be, oh, rude, funny, disarming, etc.; it may be intended to soothe or to hurt; or it may have the effect, intended or not, of soothing or hurting. Similarly, theories appear to be the kinds of things that are true or false; but they also are the kinds of things that can be, e.g., useless, arrogant, disrespectful, ignorant, ethnocentric, imperialistic. The immediate point is that feminist theory is no less immune to such characterizations than, say, Plato's political theory, or Freud's theory of female psychosexual development. Of course this is not to say that if feminist theory manages to be respectful or helpful it will follow that it must be true. But if, say, an empirical theory is purported to be about "women" and in fact is only about certain women, it is certainly false, probably ethnocentric, and of dubious usefulness except to those whose position in the world it strengthens (and theories, as we know, don't have to be true in order to be used to strengthen people's positions in the world).

Many reasons can be and have been given for the production of accounts of people's lives that plainly have nothing to do with illuminating those lives for the benefit of those living them. It is likely that both the method of investigation and the content of many accounts would be different if illuminating the lives of the people the accounts are about were the aim of the studies. Though we cannot say ahead of time how feminist theory making would be different if all (or many more) of those people it is meant to be about were more intimately part of the theory-making process, we do suggest some specific ways being talked about can be helpful:

1. The theory or account can be helpful if it enables one to see how parts of one's life fit

together, for example, to see connections among parts of one's life one hasn't seen before. No account can do this if it doesn't get the parts right to begin with, and this cannot happen if the concepts used to describe a life are utterly foreign.

2. A useful theory will help one locate oneself concretely in the world, rather than add to the mystification of the world and one's location in it. New concepts may be of significance here, but they will not be useful if there is no way they can be translated into already existing concepts. Suppose a theory locates you in the home, because you are a woman, but you know full well that is not where you spend most of your time? Or suppose you can't locate yourself easily in any particular class as defined by some version of Marxist theory?

3. A theory or account not only ought to accurately locate one in the world but also enable one to think about the extent to which one is responsible or not for being in that location. Otherwise, for those whose location is as oppressed peoples, it usually occurs that the oppressed have no way to see themselves as in any way self-determining, as having any sense of being worthwhile or having grounds for pride, and paradoxically at the same time feeling at fault for the position they are in. A useful theory will help people work out just what is and is not due to themselves and their own activities as opposed to those who have power over them.

It may seem odd to make these criteria of a useful theory, if the usefulness is not to be at odds with the issue of the truth of the theory; for the focus on feeling worthwhile or having pride seems to rule out the possibility that the truth might just be that such-and-such a group of people has been under the control of others for centuries and that the only explanation of that is that they are worthless and weak people, and will never be able to change that. Feminist theorizing seems implicitly if not explicitly committed to the moral view that women *are* worthwhile beings, and the metaphysical theory that we are beings capable of bringing about a change in our situations. Does

this mean feminist theory is "biased"? Not any more than any other theory, e.g., psychoanalytic theory. What is odd here is not the feminist presupposition that women are worthwhile but rather that feminist theory (and other theory) often has the effect of empowering one group and demoralizing another.

Aspects of feminist theory are as unabashedly value-laden as other political and moral theories. It is not just an examination of women's positions, for it includes, indeed begins with, moral and political judgments about the injustice (or, where relevant, justice) of them. This means that there are implicit or explicit judgments also about what kind of changes constitute a better or worse situation for women.

4. In this connection a theory that is useful will provide criteria for change and make suggestions for modes of resistance that don't merely reflect the situation and values of the theorizer. A theory that is respectful of those about whom it is a theory will not assume that changes that are perceived as making life better for some women are changes that will make, and will be perceived as making, life better for other women. This is *not* to say that if some women do not find a situation oppressive, other women ought never to suggest to the contrary that there might be very good reasons to think that the situation nevertheless *is* oppressive. But it is to say that, e.g., the prescription that life for women will be better when we're in the workforce rather than at home, when we are completely free of religious beliefs with patriarchal origins, when we live in complete separation from men, etc., are seen as slaps in the face to women whose life would be better if they could spend more time at home, whose identity is inseparable from their religious beliefs and cultural practices (which is not to say those beliefs and practices are to remain completely uncriticized and unchanged), who have ties to men—whether erotic or not—such that to have them severed in the name of some vision of what is "better" is, at that time and for those women, absurd. Our visions of what is better are always informed

by our perception of what is bad about our present situation. Surely we've learned enough from the history of clumsy missionaries, and the white suffragists of the 19th century (who couldn't imagine why Black women "couldn't see" how crucial getting the vote for "women" was) to know that we can clobber people to destruction with our visions, our versions, of what is better. *But:* this does not mean women are not to offer supportive and tentative criticism of one another. But there is a very important difference between (a) developing ideas together, in a "pre-theoretical" stage, engaged as equals in joint enquiry, and (b) one group developing, on the basis of their own experience, a set of criteria for good change for women—and then reluctantly making revisions in the criteria at the insistence of women to whom such criteria seem ethnocentric and arrogant. The deck is stacked when one group takes it upon itself to develop the theory and then have others criticize it. Categories are quick to congeal, and the experiences of women whose lives do not fit the categories will appear as anomalous when in fact the theory should have grown out of them as much as others from the beginning. This, of course, is why any organization or conference having to do with "women"—with no qualification—that seriously does not want to be "solipsistic" will from the beginning be multi-cultural or state the appropriate qualifications. How we think and what we think about does depend in large part on who is there—not to mention who is expected or encouraged to speak. (Recall the boys in the *Symposium* sending the flute girls out.) Conversations and criticism take place in particular circumstances. Turf matters. So does the fact of who if anyone already has set up the terms of the conversations.

5. Theory cannot be useful to anyone interested in resistance and change unless there is reason to believe that knowing what a theory means and believing it to be true have some connection to resistance and change. As we make theory and offer it up to others, what do we assume is the connection between theory and consciousness? Do

we expect others to read theory, understand it, believe it, and have their consciousness and lives thereby transformed? If we really want theory to make a difference to people's lives, how ought we to present it? Do we think people come to consciousness by reading? only by reading? Speaking to people through theory (orally or in writing) is a *very* specific context-dependent activity. That is, theory makers and their methods and concepts constitute a community of people and of shared meanings. Their language can be just as opaque and foreign to those not in the community as a foreign tongue or dialect.[3] Why do we engage in *this* activity and what effect do we think it ought to have? As Helen Longino has asked: "Is 'doing theory' just a bonding ritual for academic or educationally privileged feminist women?" Again, whom does our theory making serve?

Some Suggestions about How to Do Theory That Is Not Imperialistic, Ethnocentric, Disrespectful

---

(*Problematically in the voice of a woman of color*) What are the things we need to know about others, and about ourselves, in order to speak intelligently, intelligibly, sensitively, and helpfully about their lives? We can show respect, or lack of it, in writing theoretically about others no less than in talking directly with them. This is not to say that here we have a well-worked out concept of respect, but only to suggest that together all of us consider what it would mean to theorize in a respectful way.

When we speak, write, and publish our theories, to whom do we think we are accountable? Are the concerns we have in being accountable to "the profession" at odds with the concerns we have in being accountable to those about whom we theorize? Do commitments to "the profession," method, getting something published, getting tenure, lead us to talk and act in ways at odds with what we ourselves (let alone others) would regard as ordinary, decent behavior? To what extent do we presuppose that really understanding another person or culture requires our behaving in ways that are disrespectful, even violent? That is, to what extent do we presuppose that getting and/or publishing the requisite information requires or may require disregarding the wishes of others, lying to them, wresting information from them against their wills? Why and how do we think theorizing about others provides *understanding* of them? Is there any sense in which theorizing about others is a short-cut to understanding them?

Finally, if we think doing theory is an important activity, and we think that some conditions lead to better theorizing than others, what are we going to do about creating those conditions? If we think it not just desirable but necessary for women of different racial and ethnic identities to create feminist theory jointly, how shall that be arranged for? It may be the case that at this particualr point we ought not even try to do that—that feminist theory by and for Hispanas needs to be done separately from feminist theory by and for Black women, white women, etc. But it must be recognized that white/Anglo women have more power and privilege than Hispanas, Black women, etc., and at the very least they can use such advantage to provide space and time for other women to speak (with the above caveats about implicit restrictions on what counts as "the woman's voice"). And once again it is important to remember that the power of white/Anglo women vis-à-vis Hispanas and Black women is in inverse proportion to their working knowledge of each other.

This asymmetry is a crucial fact about the background of possible relationships between white women and women of color, whether as political co-workers, professional colleagues, or friends.

If white/Anglo women and women of color are to do theory jointly, in helpful, respectful, illuminating and empowering ways, the task ahead of white/Anglo women because of this asymmetry, is a very hard task. The task is a very complex one. In part, to make an analogy, the task can be compared to learning a text without the aid of teachers. We all know the lack of contact felt when we want to discuss a particular issue that requires knowledge of a text with someone who does not know the text at all. Or the discomfort and impatience that arise in us when we are discussing an issue that presupposes a text and someone walks into the conversation who does not know the text. That person is either left out or will impose herself on us and either try to engage in the discussion or try to change the subject. Women of color are put in these situations by white/Anglo women and men constantly. Now imagine yourself simply left out but wanting to do theory with us. The first thing to recognize and accept is that you disturb our own dialogues by putting yourself in the left-out position and not leaving us in some meaningful sense to ourselves.

You must also recognize and accept that you must learn the text. But the text is an extraordinarily complex one: viz., our many different cultures. You are asking us to make ourselves more vulnerable to you than we already are before we have any reason to trust that you will not take advantage of this vulnerability. So you need to learn to become unintrusive, unimportant, patient to the point of tears, while at the same time open to learning any possible lessons. You will also have to come to terms with the sense of alienation, of not belonging, of having your world thoroughly disrupted, having it criticized and scrutinized from the point of view of those who have been harmed by it, having important concepts central to it dismissed, being viewed with mistrust, being seen as of no consequence except as an object of mistrust.

Why would any white/Anglo woman engage in this task? Out of self-interest? What in engaging in this task would be, not just in her interest, but perceived as such by her before the task is completed or well underway? Why should we want you to come into our world out of self-interest? Two points need to be made here. The task as described could be entered into with the intention of finding out as much as possible about us so as to better dominate us. The person engaged in this task would act as a spy. The motivation is not unfamiliar to us. We have heard it said that now that Third World countries are more powerful as a bloc, westerners need to learn more about them, that it is in their self-interest to do so. Obviously there is no reason why people of color should welcome white/Anglo women into their world for the carrying out of this intention. It is also obvious that white/Anglo feminists should not engage in this task under this description since the task under this description would not lead to joint theorizing of the desired sort: respectful, illuminating, helpful and empowering. It would be helpful and empowering only in a one-sided way.

Self-interest is also mentioned as a possible motive in another way. White/Anglo women sometimes say that the task of understanding women of color would entail self-growth or self-expansion. If the task is conceived as described here, then one should doubt that growth or expansion will be the result. The severe self-disruption that the task entails should place a doubt in anyone who takes the task seriously about her possibilities of coming out of the task whole, with a self that is not as fragile as the selves of those who have been the victims of racism. But also, why should women of color embrace white/Anglo women's self-betterment without reciprocity? At this time women of color cannot afford this generous affirmation of white/Anglo women.

Another possible motive for engaging in this task is the motive of duty, "out of obligation," because white/Anglos have done people of color wrong. Here again two considerations: coming into Hispano, Black, Native American worlds out of obligation puts white/Anglos in a morally self-righteous position that is inappropriate. You are active, we are passive. We become the vehicles of your own redemption. Secondly, we couldn't want you to come into our worlds "out of obligation." That is like wanting someone to make love to you out of obligation. So, whether or not you have an obligation to do this (and we would deny that you do), or whether this task could even be done out of obligation, this is an inappropriate motive.

Out of obligation you should stay out of our way, respect us and our distance, and forego the use of whatever power you have over us—for example, the power to use your language in our meetings, the power to overwhelm us with your education, the power to intrude in our communities in order to research us and to record the supposed dying of our cultures, the power to engrain in us a sense that we are members of dying cultures and are doomed to assimilate, the power to keep us in a defensive posture with respect to our own cultures.

So the motive of friendship remains as both the only appropriate and understandable motive for white/Anglo feminists engaging in the task as described above. If you enter the task out of friendship with us, then you will be moved to attain the appropriate reciprocity of care for your and our well-being as whole beings, you will have a stake in us and in our world, you will be moved to satisfy the need for reciprocity of understanding that will enable you to follow us in our experiences as we are able to follow you in yours.

We are not suggesting that if the learning of the text is to be done out of friendship, you must enter into a friendship with a whole community and for the purpose of making theory. In order to understand what it is that we are suggesting, it is important to remember that during the description of her experience of exclusion, the Hispana voice said that Hispanas experience the intimacy of friendship with white/Anglo women friends as thoroughly incomplete. It is not until this fact is acknowledged by our white/Anglo women friends and felt as a profound lack in our experience of each other that white/Anglo women can begin to see us. Seeing us in our communities will make clear and concrete to you how incomplete we really are in our relationships with you. It is this beginning that forms the proper background for the yearning to understand the text of our cultures that can lead to joint theory making.

Thus, the suggestion made here is that if white/Anglo women are to understand our voices, they must understand our communities and us in them. Again, this is not to suggest that you set out to make friends with our communities, though you may become friends with some of the members, nor is it to suggest that you should try to befriend us for the purpose of making theory with us. The latter would be a perversion of friendship. Rather, from within friendship you may be moved by friendship to undergo the very difficult task of understanding the text of our cultures by understanding our lives in our communities. This learning calls for circumspection, for questioning of yourselves and your roles in your own culture. It necessitates a striving to understand while in the comfortable position of not having an official calling card (as "scientific" observers of our communities have); it demands recognition that you do not have the authority of knowledge; it requires coming to the task without ready-made theories to frame our lives. This learning is then extremely hard because it requires openness (including openness to severe criticism of the white/Anglo world), sensitivity, concentration, self-questioning, circumspection. It should be clear that it does not consist in a passive immersion in our cultures, but in a striving to understand what it is that our voices are saying. Only then can we engage in a mutual dialogue that does not reduce each one of us to instances of the abstraction called "woman."

Notes

1. For a recent example, see MacKinnon, Catharine. 1982. Feminism, Marxism, method and the state: An agenda for theory. *Signs* 7(3): 515–544.

2. I must note that when I think this "we," I think it in Spanish—and in Spanish this "we" is gendered, "nosotras." I also use "nosotros" lovingly and with ease and in it I include all members of "La raza cosmica" (Spanish-speaking people of the Americas, la gente de colores: people of many colors). In the US, I use "we" contextually with varying degrees of discomfort: "we" in the house, "we" in the department, "we" in the classroom, "we" in the meeting. The discomfort springs from the sense of community in the "we" and the varying degrees of

lack of community in the context in which the "we" is used.

3. See Bernstein, Basil. 1972. Social class, language, and socialization. In Giglioli, Pier Paolo, ed., *Language and Social Context*, pp. 157–178. Penguin, Harmondsworth, Middlesex. Bernstein would probably, and we think wrongly, insist that theoretical terms and statements have meanings *not* "tied to a local relationship and to a local social structure," unlike the vocabulary of, e.g., working-class children.

Study Questions

1. Why does Spelman (the white/Anglo woman) feel that women should speak out? Does she think that there is *one* woman's voice? Explain your answer.

2. How does Lugones (the Hispana) explain the fact that when women of color appear in front of white women they mainly raise the complaint that they are being excluded? Does she feel that Anglo feminist theory captures her experiences as a Hispana?

3. What are two different ways of arriving at an account of another woman's experience of theorizing?

4. What are some characteristics of a truly helpful feminist theory? Try to find an example of a feminist theory (from your other readings) that would *not* be "helpful" from the point of view of Lugones and Spelman.

5. What problems does Lugones see in the suggestion that women of different backgrounds "do theory together"? What does she think Anglo women need to do before such joint theorizing can take place? What motives should the Anglo woman *not* bring to the task of constructing a theory with women of color?

2

Women's Nature and Women's Values

Moral philosophy, traditionally, distinguishes "ought" from "is"; that is, it distinguishes prescriptive questions about worth and value from descriptive questions about the nature of things or matters of fact. But "ought" and "is" are intimately related in a number of ways. For one thing, "ought" implies "can." In other words, any judgment about what a person ought to do presupposes judgments about what that person is capable of doing. Thus, questions of moral philosophy cannot be separated from questions about what constitutes human nature.

How has women's nature been traditionally viewed; that is, how has it been viewed from the male perspective? Women's nature has been held to be not only different from men's but also lesser, especially in regard to rationality. Men's nature is taken to be the standard for human nature, and women, presumably, fall short of that standard. Women have been described as emotional rather than rational, intuitive rather than logical, passive rather than active, and so on. This view, in turn, justified the confinement of women to the private/domestic sphere. And because women were held to be unfit for the public (political) sphere, where rationality is supposedly required, they were denied literacy and education and were kept from participating in political, legal, economic, and religious institutions.

Feminist thinkers now challenge the very notion of human nature, and especially women's nature, as androcentrically biased. They argue that what has been called "natural" in regard to sex/gender is, in reality, socially or culturally constructed. They are also critical of the deliberate equation of male nature and human nature, because it serves to exclude women from public life and to justify their subordination as "the second sex."

As a result, feminists are engaged in reconceiving the basic question of "woman's nature." Is it true that women have a distinct nature? If so, are the differences the outcome of social learning and cultural conditioning? Should feminists seek to eliminate these differences, and if so, what would constitute the ideal form of human nature? Or should feminists celebrate any, or all, differences and explore the notion of women's nature as the basis for a system of women's values?

In her survey of classical and contemporary (psychoanalytic) theories of women's nature, Caroline Whitbeck shows how "male-stream" theories devalue women's nature and serve as rationales for the subordination of women. She considers three basic motifs in men's philosophy of women: woman as partial man, the masculine/feminine division as better/worse, and woman as defined by man's needs. Since these motifs fit men's fantasies, she says, women must create their own images.

According to Nancy Holmstrom, theories of women's nature have been used to justify women's exclusion from the public sphere, so women are rightly suspicious of them. Feminist investigators hold that past scientific research has been sexist in its assumptions. Holmstrom calls for a feminist revision of sex-difference theory that would show how women's nature is culturally produced and maintained to serve patriarchal and capitalist ends. In this way, she says, the focus of the discussion of women's nature would be dynamic rather than static. Holmstrom asserts that new social conditions will redefine women's nature.

"Woman is to nature as man is to culture" is the equation Sherry Ortner has formulated to explain the universal devaluation of women. Following de Beauvoir, Ortner sees women as tied to the natural or biological processes (primarily childbearing and childrearing). According to Ortner, man is seen as the creator of culture, which is the distinctively human project that controls nature. Women (nature) are relegated to the private sphere, while men (culture) assume the public sphere unchallenged. The feminist project, she says, is to question and challenge this oppressive dichotomy.

In her influential essay, Hélène Cixous calls for the release of woman's imaginary (and woman's body) from the repression of phallocentric discourse, in which woman is the "dark continent." She asks that women write themselves and speak their own nature. By describing their femininity, Cixous believes that women will transform the masculinist economy.

Theories of Sex Difference

Caroline Whitbeck

A survey of the theories which identify and explain differences between women and men in Western philosophy and science reveals three general themes or motifs which recur over a period of twenty-five hundred years, and still have a lively currency. In the space of this paper I shall discuss several ancient and modern theories structured by these motifs, and offer a critique of those which are currently held. In the course of the critique of Freud's and Jung's theories I shall identify factors which may explain the vitality of these motifs. These factors may be seen to contribute to, rather than be a product of, male domination. I end with some conclusions about the implications that the recognition of these motifs have for the task we women presently face, the task of articulating our experience and recovering our own consciousness.

The first of these three motifs, and one which is particularly important in structuring scientific theories on this subject, is that of woman as partial man. In theories structured by this motif the principal difference or differences among the sexes is seen as deriving from the supposed fact that women either completely lack, or have less of, some important ingredient in men's makeup. The second major motif entails an identification of two principles in nature and/or human nature. The first of these principles embodies whatever characteristics are seen as accruing to the conscious self and is taken to be male or masculine. The second principle is defined by contrast to the first and so embodies whatever characteristics are seen accruing to the nonself or other.[1] It is taken to be female or feminine.[2] (Frequently, the content ascribed to these two principles associates the masculine with the rational and

the feminine with the nonrational or even irrational, but this varies with the view of the conscious self.) The second motif occurs most often in metaphysical and psychological theories. The third and final motif holds that the essence of womanhood is defined in terms of men's needs. This motif figures most prominently in religious and mythological literature and in works which explicitly set down norms. As such the "theories" involved are more prescriptive than descriptive and are part of a social mythology and are not theories proper. However this third motif will be briefly discussed because it is also frequently found in combination with the two previous motifs in theories which do claim to describe and explain the way things are.

(i) Aristotle: Woman as Partial Man

Although we find reference to the putative fact that women are weaker than (in the sense of generally inferior to) men in Plato[3] and the pre-Socratics, it is Aristotle who provides the first extensive enumeration and explanation of differences between the sexes by the woman-as-partial-man motif.[4] Indeed, according to Aristotle, woman is defined by both a quantitative and a qualitative deficiency, though the two are related. It will be seen that his account is in many respects isomorphic to later theories, e.g., Freud's views and at least some accounts of recent findings in endocrinology. . . .

According to Aristotle, women, and likewise the females of other species, have less intrinsic, vital, or soul heat than men, or the males of the species. Thus a woman is unable to concoct, or cook, her menstrual blood to the final stage of refinement, i.e., semen. Therefore Aristotle holds, women do not contribute semen in conception, but only menstrual blood. The latter

From *The Philosophical Forum*, Vol. V, Nos. 1–2 (Fall/ Winter 1973–74), pp. 54–80. Reprinted by permission of The Philosophical Forum. (Notes deleted.)

supplies the matter of the embryo but does not contribute to its form or distinctive character. This view I shall call "the flower pot theory of pregnancy." Woman supplies the container and the earth which nourishes the seed but the seed is solely the man's. The analogy fails only in that actual seeds have a material component[5] and Aristotle envisions semen as being pure movement, which gives form to the embryo but is not itself a body.[6]

It might be objected that since a woman supplies something which the man does not, *viz.,* the material, the analog of the earth-filled flower pot, it is a mistake to say that Aristotle conceives of a woman as a partial man. This objection might be maintained even in the face of the low regard Aristotle has for the material factor in human generation. (He assimilates menstrual fluid to other products of incomplete concoction such as diarrhea.) However he explicitly says that a female is to be viewed as an infertile male and goes on to say

> the female in fact is female on account of an inability of a sort, *viz.,* it lacks the power to concoct semen out of the final state of nourishment (this is either blood or its counterpart in bloodless animals) because of the coldness of their nature.[7]

Again later in the work he says

> we should look upon the female state as being as it were a deformity though one which occurs in the ordinary course of nature.[8]

As it turns out Aristotle views women as being a bit worse off than females of other species with regard to the possession of innate heat, notwithstanding his view that females of even bloodless species are female on account of their lack of heat. He takes one result of woman's special deficiency in this regard to be the large volume of her menstrual secretions as compared with other mammals. In the human species

> the perfecting of female embryos is inferior to that of male ones since their uterus is inferior in condition. In other animals however the perfecting of female embryos is not inferior to that of male ones.[9]

The view that there is more difference between women and men than between females and males of other species would of course undercut Plato's argument from analogy with other animals for opening all societal activities to women as well as men.

The lack of semen in women has the consequence that the mother does not impart any sentient soul to the fetus but only nutritive soul. Nutritive soul is shared by all species of life including plants. Sentient soul is peculiar to animals. What about rational soul, that which in the Aristotelian scheme differentiates humans from other animals? In the *Politics* Aristotle tells us that it is proper for free adult males to rule over slaves, children and women because in slaves the deliberative faculty is entirely lacking, in children (presumably free and male) it is immature, and in women it is defective or to use the usual translation, a woman has the faculty but it is "without authority."

As we have seen, Aristotle repeatedly expresses the view that what is essential to being female is a lack of certain attributes of the male. Aristotle was one of the first to build a detailed biological theory upon this idea although this idea, and in particular the flower pot theory of pregnancy is to be found in fragments from certain of the pre-Socratics (*viz.,* Anaxagoras and Diogenes of Apollonia[10]), and Aeschylus in the *Eumenides* has Apollo assert it explicitly and deny that the mother is a parent to the child. . . .

In spite of the fact that Aristotle's account of sex differences is the exemplar of theories structured around the woman-as-partial-man motif, nonetheless Aristotle's thinking does reflect the second principle motif. This motif is revealed in his discussion of the male and female principles of generation. The male principle is, or contributes, form or movement and the female principle is, or contributes, matter. Thus Aristotle frequently speaks as though there were two distinct and perhaps opposing factors. He even says at one point that male and female differ in respect to their *logos.* A succinct expression of the two-principle theme is found in the following sentence:

> Now of course the female, *qua* female, is passive, and the male, *qua* male is active.[11]

We have already seen that Aristotle does not weaken his claim that women are partial or defective men, notwithstanding this talk of two principles. Is there any source from which

Aristotle might have inherited this conception of male and female principles? Clearly from Pythagoras or at least the Pythagoreans.

(ii) Pythagoras: The Feminine as the Second of Two Opposing Principles

---

In the Pythagoreans' account of the Monad and the Dyad we have one of the earliest Western accounts which embodies the second motif. According to the Pythagoreans, the Monad, the Principle of Oneness or unit was the original number. They envisaged it as an indivisible point, the most elementary form which can be imposed on space. Space or the Unlimited was understood as making multiplicity possible and hence the Dyad or Principle of Twoness, was derived from the Monad and Space, jointly. Subsequently, Space or the Unlimited generally was identified with the Dyad so that the Unlimited was identified with the number two, and with the even while Limit or the Limited was associated with the number one and with the odd in general. Indeed Aristotle tells us that the Pythagoreans accounted for the perceptible world in terms of ten oppositions. The first members of each pair were grouped together and identified with the Monad, whereas the second members of each pair were identified with the Dyad.

Limit-Unlimited

Odd-Even

One-Many

Right-Left

Male-Female

Rest-Motion

Straight-Curved

Light-Darkness

Good-Bad

Square-Oblong

You will notice that the Dyad is at once, female, unlimited, bad, and plural, and associ-ated with darkness, and motion. On the face of it this association of motion with the female seems to contradict Aristotle's definition of the male as active and the female as passive. However in the case of motion associated with the Dyad the sense is of change, inconstancy, whereas the motion which Aristotle associates with the male, is goal-directed action of a pur-posive cause. The above interpretation of the Pythagorean idea is borne out by attention to the last of the opposites identified with the Dyad, oblong. Odd numbers were thought of as square because a square arrangement of any number of units may be seen as the sum of successive odd numbers 1, 3, 5, 7 . . . or dis-played in two dimensions
5 5 5
3 3 5
1 3 5 . . . whereas even numbers were thought of as oblong because successive even numbers produce an oblong array 6 6 6 6
                        4 4 4 6
                        2 2 4 6

. . . the oblong produced has a changeable char-acter in that the ratio of the length of its sides changes as successive even numbers are added. Thus the motion characteristic of the Dyad is not the motion of an efficient cause proceeding rationally to accomplish some end, but recalci-trant unpredictability which Plato, and later Aristotle came to think of as characteristic of matter. For the Pythagoreans number is con-stitutive of reality and the rational form sup-plied by number is static, whereas Aristotle has a biologist's concern for the natural course of development, and thus for a dynamic rational-ity. In both cases however the female principle embodies that which opposes rationality and order.

As it happens the Pythagoreans did deem at least some women worthy of instruction, for Iamblichus (fourth century A.D.) lists all Pythagoreans known by name, and seventeen women are included in this list of two hundred and thirty-five. This fact illustrates the point that there need not be any *simple* relationship between the political and social freedom of women within a group and the theories about sex differences explicitly propounded by that group. It also warns us that what is held to distinguish the feminine principle need not be claimed to be either true of all women or a norm for women, provided that individual variation in this regard is not seen as unnatural, unseemly, or otherwise untoward.

If and when it is claimed that women need not be especially feminine nor men especially masculine, what are we to make of the fact that the terms "masculine" and "feminine" are used? This question will be dealt with below in discussion of the masculine and feminine principles in the work of C. G. Jung. However some light is shed on this question by considering the feminine symbols of astrology. Venus and the Moon are feminine "planets." The glyph for Cancer is thought to represent the breasts, and that for Virgo, the female genitals, and the fourth house represents the home and womb. Finally, the odd signs are regarded as positive, or masculine whereas the even signs are negative or feminine. Masculine here means self-expressive whereas feminine means receptive, or "self-repressive." Thus some elements of a person's destiny and psychological makeup were considered female and symbols for these elements *all* appeared somewhere in each subject's chart. What are these forces? Love and passion, beauty and the emotions in the planet Venus; flux and change, the unconscious, and maternal influences in the moon; the home and domesticity in Cancer and the fourth house; for harmony and close relationship and communication in Libra and the seventh house. In cultures which more or less confine women to the home it is clear why female symbols would be naturally associated with maternal influences, the home and domesticity. What about passion, beauty, close relation, harmony, aesthetics and emotional life in general? These areas of life have a close association with what may be broadly termed sexual feelings and hence are naturally associated with members of the opposite sex. In view of the fact that, with the exception of royalty, horoscopes were originally cast *only for men*, the opposite sex was female. Now that it has become common practice to cast the horoscopes of women, there has been some disagreement over whether in the case of a female subject the sun's positions and aspects ought to represent her own nature, as it does in the case of a man, or whether it should be understood to represent the men in her life.

The difficulty arises from the fact that the symbol for the conscious self is a masculine symbol, so that the female is seen as essentially in contrast with that self. Since rationality is the hallmark of the conscious self, the ego, rationality is seen as masculine as opposed to feminine. I will return to this subject in section (iv) below.

(iii) Women as Defined in Terms of Man's Needs

What, finally should be said about the third motif, that of woman as defined in terms of man's needs? This theme exists in a relatively pure form only in mythic religious literature and utopian social writings rather than in philosophical and scientific theories. The "theories" which embody this third motif function prescriptively, drawing morals about how the sexes ought to behave or function rather than how they do, though this is not always explicitly done. Thus this motif is more to be found in social mythology than in theories which purport to have a truth value and identify and explain existing sex differences. However it often structures subsidiary arguments and explanations offered in theories which are primarily structured by one of the two previously discussed motifs and so influences the course of some explanations, proper. Therefore it will be briefly discussed here in some of its purer instances. It is to be found in the second account of creation, the one found in Genesis 2:4b f. We are told that the point of creating woman was to provide man with a helper and companion. Indeed this was the point of making the animals too, but they did not succeed very well. For that matter woman herself was not a great success, as we shall see. The first chapter of Genesis contains a different account of creation, according to it God created man and woman together. When the narratives were put together scholars had to account for this supposed double creation. Most of the Midrashic commentators held that the first woman, Lilith, was uppity and insisted on full equality with Adam. She found Adam intolerable, and, by pronouncing the Ineffable Name, was able to fly away from Adam. A second woman was then created for Adam. The Midrashic account is as follows:

> The woman destined to become the true companion of man was taken from Adam's body, for "only when like is joined unto like the union is indissoluble." The creation of woman from man was possible because Adam originally had two faces, which were separated at the birth of Eve.
>
> When God was on the point of making Eve, He said: "I will not make her from the head of man, lest she carry her head high in arrogant pride; not from the eye, lest she be wanton-eyed; not from the ear, lest she be an eavesdropper; not from the neck, lest she be insolent; not from the mouth, lest she be a tattler; not from the heart, lest she be inclined to envy; not from the hand, lest she be a meddler; not from the foot, lest she be a gadabout. I will form her from a chaste portion of the body," and to every limb and organ as He formed it, God said, "Be chaste! Be chaste!" Nevertheless, in spite of the great caution used, woman has all the faults God tried to obviate.[12]

Not a great success as a helper. Some of the Midrashic commentators consider the fact that as bearer of children women ought to be much more complicated than men, and thus they contradict the partial man views of woman.

The definition of woman in terms of man's needs admits of variations. In particular it varies depending on whether it is the adult male or the male child's perspective that is regarded as primary. In the first case it is the role of assistant/wife that is considered as definitive for femininity and for "fulfillment" as a woman, in the second case it is the role of mother that is definitive for femininity and womanhood. In our culture the assistant/wife role is seen in terms of such traits and abilities as the following, not necessarily in this order: attractive appearance; a responsiveness to her man which makes him feel attractive; a willingness to take over routine tasks and accomplish them to perfection; the ability to produce a home/office/children which are a credit to him; a personal style which is supportive to her man which enables her to work around and modulate his moods, quirks and neuroses, disguising them even from herself; a loyalty to her man above all else; and the ability to amuse herself when not needed. Maternal worth is seen in terms of such traits and abilities as the following: physical strength, stamina, a disposition which is placid enough to nurse with ease, but versatile enough to change with each new stage of the child's development so that, for example, she is enthralled with physical functions of the infant and can stimulate the intellectual interest of a twelve-year-old. (In short she is able to produce a highly achieving but non-neurotic son.) Furthermore she is devoted to her children above all else, and able to induce their father into taking an interest in them, never sees herself as martyr, and is able to sustain herself as her children outgrow her. I submit that characteristics for the mother role are not only different from but conflict with those of the assistant/wife role. As with all roles there is a negative as well as positive aspect implicit in each, so that a woman *qua woman* is in jeopardy of becoming a *bad* assistant/wife, epitomized in a witch who steals men's potency or even literally steals his penis and the evil mother, epitomized in the witch who kills and even eats children. Success as an assistant/wife runs the danger of making a woman a bad mother, and the perfect mother is at risk for being a bad assistant/wife. What both variants of this theme have *in common* is their emphasis upon the special competence required of a good woman—though not the competence of the conquering hero or intellectual competence which might put her in competition with her man/son. This idea of special competence is foreign to both the woman-as-partial-man motif, and the theme of the feminine or the second (often explicitly non-rational or irrational) principle.

The explanations which fit under the defined-in-terms-of-man's-needs motif appear in the works of those, like the Jungians and Freudians, whose theories about sex differences are primarily structured by one of the other motifs. For example the idea of the "anima woman" whom as we shall see, the Jungians regard as expressing instinctive femininity in her life style, structured by one of the other motifs. For example the Jungians regard what they term an "anima woman" as the type of woman who "expresses instinctive femininity." An anima woman is characterized by the tendency to invite the projection of certain unconscious elements in a man's psyche, and to actively accommodate to them in the manner characteristic of a good assistant/wife. More familiar is the way in which Freudians augment their postulation that the wish to have a baby (to symbolize the missing penis) is the characteristic feminine desire, with the supposition that normal women wish to engage in *caring for* the baby and child. The first is the wish of a partial man. The second is the wish of a natural mother.

(iv) Jung: The Feminine as Non-Ego Traits in the Human Psyche

---

Next I will consider Jungian views of the structure and content of the masculine and feminine principles. It will be seen that there are numerous difficulties and inconsistencies in the Jungian account of the way in which the feminine principle relates to a woman's psyche. I am led to conclude that many of these difficulties arise because it is only from *the point of view of a man* is it natural to consider the content of the so-called "feminine principle" as feminine, and to associate it with women.

In the Jungian scheme the feminine is conceived of as one pole of a masculine-feminine polarity, in keeping with the rather Heraclitean view, that all psychic energy or libido is organized in polarities. Jungians claim that the feminine is an important element in men's as well as women's psyches. Certain qualities of personality, ways of understanding and foci of concern are viewed as feminine. According to the Jungians the feminine or, as they also term it, the eros principle, encompasses relatedness and value reached through feeling, and is contrasted with the masculine, or logos principle, which encompasses discrimination and interest in objective truth. In this respect, Jung's view is reminiscent of the now familiar supposition, found in Hegel and others, that abstract or analytic thinking and objective judgment are masculine, and that apprehension of the related concrete whole and interest in the personal and emotional side of things are feminine.

There is an empirical basis for the characterization of the eros principle as "feminine," in that Jungian analysts have amassed a body of clinical evidence showing that there is a tendency to personify these qualities in dreams, fantasies, and artistic representations by female figures. On the basis of this evidence, Jung postulates the existence of an "inner woman" in the unconscious of each man. This "inner woman" personifies the manifestations of the eros principle in his psyche. Jung calls this structure "the anima." Since "she" embodies relatedness, the anima may function to relate the man's ego to the rest of his psyche (including the so-called collective unconscious or objective psyche with its repository of archetypal and religious images). Evidence in support of Jung's view is not limited to clinical observation. Indeed, a trip through an art museum lends a good deal of credence to it. One sees muses emerging from the artist's head, represented as linking him with his creative energies, the Virgin Mary relating the human and divine, and a host of other female figures represented as relating the artist to some other realm; of course, the artist is a man.

What about women? In order to discuss the relation of women to the feminine or eros principle, we would need an initial distinction between what is held to be true of women and what is held to be true of the feminine, but this is what the Jungians do not supply.

Jung's failure to maintain a distinction between the feminine and women is exemplified in the following passage:

> Too much soul is reserved for God, too little for man. But God himself cannot flourish if man's soul is starved. The *feminine psyche* responds to this hunger, for it is the function of *Eros* to unite what Logos has sundered. The *woman* of today is faced with a tremendous cultural task—perhaps it will be the dawn of a new era.[13] (My emphasis.)

The confusion is related too in this passage from another Jungian, Gerhard Adler.

> (Man) has been obliged to acknowledge the existence of an autonomous and independent psyche. His old established belief in the

"superiority" of "*logos*" has been decisively challenged by an equally important, but diligently overlooked power of the "*eros.*" Where this challenge is accepted and answered in a constructive sense, a new and creative relationship between *man* and *woman* as equal partners can be established.[14] (My emphasis.)

The failure on the part of Jungians to maintain the distinction between woman and the feminine may be traced to another tendency, the tendency to adopt the point of view of a man, or at least, a man's ego. Thus, in the passage quoted from Jung, we find that he sees women as performing a task of reintegration for the whole culture, a task which is entirely analogous to the one that the anima, a man's unconscious "feminine" side, performs for the individual man's psyche.

Similarly, if we look into Esther Harding's *The Way of All Women*,[15] we find that Harding's first chapter entitled, "All Things to All Men," is an extended account of what she calls "a man's woman" or an "anima-woman." Harding says of her, "She figures in myths and legends, but she is always shown from the man's point of view." In playing the anima role, such a woman is viewed as being in touch with her "instinctive femininity." In contrast, the other type of woman, not-a-man's woman, is viewed as, to some extent, identified with her animus, her masculine side. It is instructive to see how odd Harding's account would appear turned around: if men were discussed as falling into two basic types depending on whether they did or did not invite animus projection on the part of women, so that a man would be understood to be fully masculine only if he were a woman's man (a lady's man?), and all other men would be viewed as identified to some extent with their unconscious feminine side.

Reading the works of Jungians, one is liable to get the impression that the conscious ego is always masculine. For example, Erich Neumann says, "every archetypal opposition easily assumes a masculine-feminine character and the opposition of the conscious and unconscious is also experienced through this symbolism, the masculine being identified with consciousness and the feminine with the unconscious. This . . . stems from the primary fact . . . that masculine consciousness is born from

maternal unconscious *(sic).* . . ." Similarly, we find Harding suggesting that the ego of an anima-woman can be largely unconscious. Harding says:

> The world of work, however, is essentially a world of competition which forces the ego into consciousness. In the case of the anima-woman, the ego often hides almost entirely in the unconscious. . . .

We may make sense of Harding's statement by supposing her to mean not that a woman's ego is largely unconscious, but that women, or at least "feminine" women, live unreflectively and are thus largely unaware of their own personalities. However, her choice of words is symptomatic of the tendency to associate women with the unconscious in defiance of the fact that conscious ego functioning is as requisite for "women's work" as for other tasks.

Another Jungian, Ann Ulanov in the book *The Feminine*, likewise says that a woman's ego is "less consciously defined than the male's and often less firm. . . ." However, she does try to give a better account of women by emphasizing what she calls the "feminine mode consciousness." Thus, she maintains that

> In contrast to the frequent identification of the feminine with the unconscious, with non-spiritual and natural processes, the symbolic (i.e., Jungian) approach describes the feminine kind of ego consciousness and its relation to the unconscious. . . .

However, Ulanov is only partially successful in her endeavor, since it turns out that feminine ego consciousness is more primitive according to the usual criteria. She says of it:

> Historically, feminine consciousness characterizes the early eras of humanity, and in individual lives, is manifest in childhood, in moments of psychological crisis, and in the creative processes. . . .

In spite of her efforts to present a more favorable account of feminine ego functioning, which Ulanov asserts to be the predominant but not exclusive type of ego functioning available to women, she, like many other female analysts, has fallen into a standpoint which I call "displaced consciousness." She has adopted man's point of view. This displaced consciousness is reflected not only in her ascription to women of a primitive form of ego functioning, and in her general failure to distinguish what is true of women from what is true of the anima, the embodiment of eros in a man's psyche, it is reflected even in her choice of pronouns. In referring to women, Ulanov invariably speaks of "them," "they," and "their experience." However, we find her saying:

> When we talk about the feminine, we talk about our concepts of the human person and of relationships between persons. We touch the most intimate aspects of our lives—our relation to sexuality, to *our wives,* our daughters, our mothers, to feminine elements in the male personality, and to the unconscious. . . . (My emphasis.)

If there is anything to the notion that eros characteristics are in some way more directly expressed in the conscious personalities of women, and logos characteristics are in some sense largely unconscious in women, then for women it would be logos or the masculine which would touch "the most intimate aspects of our (women's) lives"—our relation to sexuality, etc. However, logos does not lend itself much to intimacy. The essence of the logos principle is discrimination, differentiation, and relation to impersonal truth. Such a principle is hardly embodied in a warm, passionate and tender love. Nonetheless, guided by his equal-but-complementary principle, Jung fashioned an account of women's psyches according to which a woman's sexuality is the province of her animus, her "inner man" who embodies the logos principle.

In spite of their expressed concern to give an account of the human psyche in which the eros, or feminine principle is given equal weight with the logos, or masculine principle, the Jungians, like the Freudians, have devoted their principal efforts to constructing a model of a man's psyche, a model which is adequate to a man's experience. They have then derived from the model of a man's psyche their model of a woman's psyche. So it is that in spite of Ulanov's statement that in her book she means to be discussing the feminine as it appears in women, we find that in her section on psychological development, sex unspecified, what she gives is in fact an account of the development of a male! This is revealed in the following passages which are quoted from it:

> The third stage, which Neumann calls patriarchal, corresponds to the prepuberty years and to the onset of puberty itself. Transition to this phase is represented in initiation rituals where the boy leaves the world of women, undergoes challenges, tests, and fulfills rules laid down by the men and then joins their ranks as one of their own. . . .
>
> The fourth stage is called integrative. In this phase, the ego reclaims the elements of the non-rational feminine as woman, as the unconscious, and as anima—characteristics that were all rejected and repressed in the patriarchal. . . .

No mention is made of a girl. It is only somewhat later in the book, following a chapter explicitly devoted to the development of a man, that we finally find a chapter on the development of a woman. In that chapter Ulanov, herself, comes close to recognizing that for *both sexes,* logos characteristics are associated with the conscious ego, while eros characteristics are associated with the attractive other, with the unconscious, and with reunification of the total psyche. She says that for both sexes, it is the masculine, the logos principle, which initiates the final phase of development . . . , and later in the book, she says that in marriage it is important that both partners develop the feminine qualities within themselves and with each other. . . .

In spite of the general inadequacy of the Jungian account of a woman's psyche, the Jungian scheme *does* provide an explanation of the way in which the feminine principle has come to have much of the content that it does in our culture. Thus Ann Ulanov gives an account of the process by which a male child may come to associate eros traits and his own unconscious with women, and also to regard the sexual polarity as central. She first quotes the following passage from Erich Neumann:

> Every archetypal opposition easily assumes a masculine-feminine character and the opposition of conscious and unconscious is also experienced through this symbolism, the mascu-

line being identified with consciousness and the feminine with unconscious. This . . . stems from the primary fact . . . that masculine consciousness is born from the maternal unconscious.

She then goes on to say that in the case of a boy

The experience of the opposing sexual elements occurs sooner than it does with girls, and it has immediate decisive effects upon him. He experiences his original identity with his mother as a relation of like to unlike, as a relation to a non-self, to an "other," an opposite, symbolized by all the obvious sexual differences. In order to be himself and to have himself to himself he must stand against his early identity with the non-self; he must free his ego and go his own way. He identifies his ego with consciousness because his self-discovery coincides with his freeing himself from his mother and from the pre-ego containment in the unconscious that she symbolizes. . . .

The Jungians have drawn attention to facts about the experiences of most male infants which make it natural to form the traditional notion of the feminine. Notice that since female infants are not regularly given primary care by an adult male the complementary identification will not naturally arise in the thinking of girls and women. Indeed the masculine-feminine polarity is not likely to be a central symbol for girls and women at all.

Because of the impact of the idea of the feminine, Jung may nonetheless be right in some of what he says about women. It may well be true that in our culture at least, women *are* more likely than men to have developed skills for relating, and for integrating unconscious materials. If this is the case, then Jung may also be right in thinking that women are in a position to restore the balance in our value system which he claims to have been skewed in the direction of logos traits.

(v) Freud: Woman as Partial Man

In Freud's theory about sex differences we find many parallels to Aristotle. Like Aristotle

Freud sees women as partial men, and in each case in the equipment "missing" in women (*vis.*, semen according to Aristotle, and a penis according to Freud) has a sexual character. Like Aristotle, Freud also equates masculine with active (aims) and feminine with passive (aims). Freud's view of the primary deficiency is somewhat different from Aristotle's. Freud's suggestion that women have less libido, psychic energy, parallels Aristotle's suggestion that women have less of that quantity, innate heat, which is the vehicle of the soul, however according to Freud this quantitative "lack" is not related to the qualitative lack, the lack of a penis, being "castrated," which is the focal point of his account.

I take it that Freud's views are rather well known in philosophical and feminist circles and so shall not take space to summarize them further but instead give detailed attention to specific passages in Freud's account of feminine psychology which reveal two significant areas of incoherence. These will, I think, shed some light on the phenomenon of the recurrence of the partial man motif.

The first area of incoherence lies in Freud's account of a little girl's fantasies about the difference between male and female genitals. The term that he uses most often is "castrated." For example in "Female Sexuality" he says

She (the female child) acknowledges the *fact of her castration*, and with it too, the superiority of the male.

In women the Oedipus complex . . . is not destroyed but *created by the influence of castration*.

The point of time when the *discovery of castration* is made varies. (My emphasis.)

Now castration implies that the little girl had a penis and it was cut off. This, Freud tells us, is precisely a little boy's fantasy about why girls and women do not possess penises. It leads the boy to fear that his penis will be cut off by his father. Who, according to Freud, does the little girl fantasize cut off her penis? No one. Even Freud's own clinical observations do not support the view that little girls fantasize that they had a penis and someone cut it off. As Freud sometimes recognized, a little girl is familiar with her own genitals.

What one would expect then is that she might *at most* regard her equipment as inferior.

This, and not a fantasy of castration, is in fact what Freud has observed among his female analysands.

He reports this in the following passages:

> It was a surprise to learn that girls hold their mother responsible for their lack of a penis and do not forgive her for their being thus put at a disadvantage.[16]
>
> At the end of this first phase of attachment to the mother, there emerges, as the girl's strongest motive for turning away from her, the reproach that her mother did not give her a proper penis.[17]

Freud also reports the (presumably rare) analysand who did fantasize she was castrated. But in this case it is the *father* who in fantasy castrated her (as punishment for masturbation). This after all is what one would expect if as Freud supposed, the father is the figure who has the power and authority in the child's eyes. On Freud's account if somebody did any castrating then it should be the father, but as we have seen it is the mother whom his analysands blame for their "inferior" equipment.

For the moment at least I am not concerned with whether all or most girls have this or that fantasy, but only with whether Freud's account of a girl's fantasies is coherent. My first conclusion is that if other facts of psychic life are as Freud claims, little girls would generally not fantasize they are castrated. What Freud has done is to employ a term, "castrated" which derives from the fantasy of boys (and therefore of men) and treat it both as *fact* and as something which *little girls fantasize*. His Freudian slip leads us to ask how much of the rest of his view is a carry-over from the fantasy of little boys.

Another instance of this projection is to be found in his description of what genitals a little girl believes others to possess. We find Freud saying

> To begin with the girl regards her castration as an individual misfortune, and only gradually extends it to other females and finally to her mother as well. Her love was directed to her *phallic* mother; with the *discovery that her mother is castrated* it becomes possible to drop her as object.
>
> As a result of the discovery of a woman's lack of a penis they are debased in value for girls just *as they are for boys and later perhaps for men*.[18] (Second and third emphasis, mine.)

At the least Freud's account assumes that generally little girls learn that (some) males have penises, before they learn that (some) other females do not. A very implausible assumption, at best. However, to get to the heart of the issue I think we must attend to the term "phallic." A phallus as distinct from a penis is, the Freudians claim, a uniquely appropriate symbol for power. Freud consistently speaks of a little boy's regard for his *penis*. Perhaps the little boy connects the idea of this penis with that of a phallus through his experience of his own erections, but the prevalent power symbol is the phallus and the image associated with this symbol is that of an erect (adult) phallus. Now where is the little girl supposed to familiarize herself with an erect phallus? The sight of an infant brother's penis, even in a state of erection, is hardly likely to convey the symbol of the phallus. Well, let us assume that after all children do like to crawl into their parents' bed in the morning, and that little girls may commonly encounter early morning erections of their fathers. But how is the rest of the fantasy to get off the ground? How is the little girl supposed to attribute a phallus to her mother? Is she supposed to be *less* familiar with her mother's than her father's body? A possible but hardly likely situation. Or are little girls supposed to have an innate tendency in this specific instance to deny what they experience of their mother's body when they begin to acquaint themselves with their father's body? Such a specific psychic mechanism, if postulated, would itself require explanation. It should be noted too that empirical studies do not support Freud's description of the so-called Oedipal stage in girls.

Of course matters may be different for a little boy who may well initially assume that all persons have penises, and, having experienced as well as observed his own erections, and having connected these with his own sexual impulses, forms at least a rudimentary notion of a phallus and hence a phallic mother.

We need not impune existence of the clinical evidence supporting Freud's interpretation. Perhaps some of his women patients, having learned the symbolic meaning of the phallus, *read this symbol back* into their recollection of disappointment in their mothers when they realized their mother's subservience or weakness or passivity. (Analysts and psychiatrists are quite accustomed to interpreting hostile and resentful reactions of little boys toward fathers whom they see as subservient, weak or passive.) Such *retrospective* fantasies about the childhood experience even if common in a "normal" woman do not give us any insight into "normal" female development.

The second area of incoherence lies in Freud's account of psychological masculinity and femininity. Although for many years Freud wrestled with the problem of finding a psychological meaning for "masculine" and "feminine" the equation of masculinity with active sexual aims and of femininity with passive sexual aims appears without further explanation in his 1931 essay "Female Sexuality." However, a year later in the lecture "Femininity" he warns his hearers of what appear to be his own errors in the following tortuous passage:

We are accustomed to employ "masculine" and "feminine" as mental qualities as well, and have in the same way transferred the notion of bisexuality to mental life. Thus we speak of a person, whether male or female, as behaving in a masculine way in one connection and in a female way in another. But you will soon perceive that this is only giving way to anatomy or to convention. You cannot give the concepts of "masculine" and "feminine" *any* new connotation. The distinction is not a psychological one; when you say "feminine" you usually mean "passive." Now it is true that a relation of the kind exists. The male sex-cell is actively mobile and searches out the female one, and the latter, the ovum, is immobile and waits passively. This behaviour of the elementary sexual organisms is indeed a model for the conduct of sexual individuals during intercourse. The male pursues the female for the purpose of sexual union, seizes hold of her and penetrates into her. But by this you have precisely reduced the characteristic of masculinity to the factor of aggressiveness so far as psychology is concerned. You may well doubt whether you have gained any real advantage from this when you reflect that in some classes of animals the females are the stronger and more aggressive and the male is active only in the single act of sexual union. This is so, for instance, with the spiders. Even the functions of rearing and caring for the young, which strike us as feminine

par excellence, are not invariably attached to the female sex in animals. In quite high species we find that the sexes share the task of caring for the young between them or even that the male alone devotes himself to it. Even in the sphere of human sexual life you soon see how inadequate it is to make masculine behavior coincide with activity and feminine with passivity. A mother is active in every sense towards her child; the act of lactation itself may equally be described as the mother suckling the baby or as her being suckled by it. . . . Women can display great activity in various directions, men are not able to live in company with their own kind unless they develop a large amount of passive adaptability. If you now tell me that these facts go to prove precisely that both men and women are bisexual in the psychological sense, I shall conclude that you have decided in your own minds to make "active" coincide with "masculine" and "passive" with "feminine." But I advise you against it. It seems to me to serve no useful purpose and adds nothing to our knowledge.

One might consider characterizing femininity psychologically as giving preference to passive aims. This is not, of course, the same thing as passivity; to achieve a passive aim may call for a large amount of activity. It is perhaps the case that in a woman, on the basis of her share in the sexual function, a preference for passive behavior and passive aims is carried over into her life to a greater or lesser extent, in proportion to the limits, restricted or far-reaching, within which her sexual life thus serves as a model. But we must beware in this of underestimating the influence of social customs, which similarly force women into passive situations. All this is still far from being cleared up.[19]

And later Freud says [of the girl in her pre-Oedipal phase]

These wishes represent active as well as passive impulses; if we relate them to the differentiation of the sexes which is to appear later—though we should avoid doing so far as possible—we may call them masculine and feminine.[20]

What remains especially unclear is what is supposed to be the remaining link between what is feminine in the usual sense (i.e., being characteristic of, although not necessarily restricted to, "normal" women and girls), and what is passive in the usual sense.

What are "passive aims" and how are they at once passive and characteristic of girls and women? Freud tells us that in her phallic phase a little girl has active sexual aims and that her mother is the object of her desire but what even these active aims are, Freud admits he is at a loss to discover. All he can say is that in the cases in which a sibling is born, "the little girl wants to believe that she has given her mother the new baby just as the boy wants to."[21] At the next phase of her development, at least according to Freud, the little girl will want a baby "from" her father. As we have seen above. Freud in his *New Introductory Lectures* comes to admit that "a mother is active in every sense towards her child" so what does it come to, to say that for the girl, wanting to have a child is a passive aim? Perhaps we are to assume that the little girl sees the baby as a gift pure and simple, like a doll, or an organ transplant. *Qua* recipient the girl is passive but in this case it is not at all clear how the father could be seen as the object, or how the *sexual* aim could be passive. The aim could be sexual in some sense if the baby symbolizes a penis, as Freud claims, but if what the girl wants is a penis then *that* is what she wants and growing it or making it would be as gratifying as receiving it. If we take the baby on face value, as a baby, sexual gratification could be expected from contact with the baby, but if the aim is for just this contact and the mother is in every sense active towards her child, it is hard to see how predominantly passive aims are served. The more likely possibility is that Freud intends us to understand the giving of a child itself to be much more than giving pure and simple. Most straightforwardly what the little girl might wish to do is make a baby with her father. If that is her sexual aim the talk of *receiving* a baby is misleading. What the little girl wants to do is to make a baby with her father, and the *making* of a baby is the sexual aim. If this is what Freud means then to call this aim "passive" seems quite peculiar. Perhaps he was too impressed by the form of his own words in describing the girl as wanting a child *from* her father. The phrase is anyhow inappropriate as a description of conception unless one holds something like a flower pot theory of pregnancy, i.e., one

which assumes the very equation of masculine with active form and feminine with passive matter whose origin we are trying to discover.

(It might be the case that the girl wishes to be the recipient of solicitous attention, if any, which the mother receives on account of having the baby or being pregnant, but in the case of this straight-forwardly passive aim, having the baby is only a means to this end and not the aim itself.)

The matter is further complicated by the fact that along with the wish to "get the mother with child" *the wish to "bear her a child"* is one which Freud attributes to little girls in their active phallic period.

One is left with the conclusion that to make a baby is not in itself an especially passive aim even in Freud's view, but perhaps some particular *way* of making a baby is. In the long passage quoted above we saw that in spite of his caveats with respect to extending the model too far. Freud does offer us the image of the male being the active partner, pursuing and penetrating. Of course this is active *behavior,* and active behavior Freud tells us may be engaged in to achieve a passive aim. However having ruled out the making (giving, getting, bearing) of a child as a relevant passive sexual aim for the girl, we must assume that Freud sees the woman's and girl's desire for coitus with a man as a passive aim. Why passive? It is hard to find any reason other than that she is thought to be passive in the act, but passivity is not *generally* true of women who desire coitus. It is hard then to make much of Freud's thesis that the sexual aims which are feminine are passive.

As far as intercourse goes, *to the male* the female is the object of desire. *Qua* object of the male's active aims, the female is passive, even though in fact the female does not act in a particularly passive way nor does she primarily fantasize herself as mere recipient.

Freud's account of female fantasy makes it concur with male fantasy. However some correlation could also be expected if male fantasy secondarily influences female fantasy. Coincident with the punitive shift from active to passive aims in "normal" feminine development is a putative change of object on the part of the little girl. Her mother is replaced by her father as her primary object. Insofar as her father reciprocates (and we may assume that the little girl will be very sensitive to any reciprocation) he will convey his own (male) fantasies about intercourse and sex differences. If you recall the above discussion of "castration" and Freud's attribution of male fantasies to a little girl, you have an indication of what fantasies about sex differences will be conveyed. Furthermore if, for example, the male does fear activity on the part of the female, say through fear of castration, this may of course induce in her conscious or unconscious guilt, or fear of rejection which might make her more passive in her behavior and subsequent fantasies.

I would like to approach this issue of secondary influence in another way. Freud tells us that the psychic representation of the mother-substitute or foster mother regularly fuses with that of the mother in the child's consciousness. When, as is becoming more common even in our society, the mother-substitute is the father, and both parents give the infant a full range of care, the infant nonetheless usually grows into a "normal" woman or man. (Indeed Margaret Mead in her book *Sex and Temperament* states that the clearest departure from "normality," i.e., inversion [homosexuality, transvestism, etc.] occurs *only* in those cultures with sex stereotypes of temperament.) This "normal" outcome of development cannot occur in the manner which Freud describes. We need not follow Horney in postulating the existence of an innate, perhaps biologically based, heterosexual attraction in order to explain this outcome. It is sufficient to suppose that the heterosexual orientation of the parent or parents determines whether it is through identification or through complementing the parents' behavior in some way that the child's libidinal attachment finds most reward. (This may sound like too behavioral a description for some, but I am as willing to describe this in terms of transmission of the parents' conscious and unconscious fantasies.) Such a heterosexual object preference would be likely, although not necessary, in biological parents. We may question whether the mechanisms, whatever their precise character, which act in the above situation do not *also* operate in the more traditional family situation. If they do, then as I have suggested

above the father's male fantasies may be expected to commonly influence the way little girls learn their sexual role.

The general conclusion to which the above examination of Freud's theories leads is that if he is right about male development, then his account of female development is more an expression of male fantasies than it is true of the way in which a girl grows into even a "normal" woman.

(vi) Conclusion

We have seen that Freud and the Jungians have supplied us with more than just further examples of two of the basic motifs in explanation of sex differences. In each case we have also been given an account of how a little boy would be expected to arrive at a fantasy or symbolization embodying the motif in question. Freudians and Jungians may have given us a fairly accurate account of the origin of these motifs in the conscious and unconscious mind of boys. If so, we have found not only the source of these motifs, and an explanation of their recurrence throughout history of male-dominated Western history, but we may have located a factor which has been a contributing cause of that male domination, *viz.*, the existence of a small number of fantasies about sex differences which are common to (most) males, and which will determine what theories they will find plausible; and the absence of a similar small number of fantasies about sex differences common to most females, which might compete with the male fantasies. Thus if a little boy's narcissistic investment in his penis is as great as it is thought to be, it may be common for males to see sex differences as primarily consisting in the fact that a penis is "missing" in females. (The case is more plausible if the little boy is more familiar with the anatomy of little girls than with that of a pregnant or lactating woman.) Similarly in situations in which the mother's care of the child far exceeds that given by the father, a circumstance which is probable where breast feeding is necessary, the male child may well hit upon the contrast between the sexes to symbolize the contrast of self with other. In the latter case it is evident that the female child will not be led to either the same or the contrary symbolization by her own experience. What content does accrue to the sexual contrast is likely to vary with the infant girl's subsequent experience with males. Variety may be the rule rather than the exception with regard to a girl's fantasies about anatomical differences too, although this case is less clear.

An awareness of the entrenched motifs which have structured theories about sex differences in Western thought should have several effects. First it should make us more sensitive to those recalcitrant facts which are obscured by the fitting of data to these motifs, and thus enable us to improve the scientific researches conducted into these matters. Second, and perhaps more importantly, if we women are able to recognize the fantasies and symbolizations that arise in the male mind we will be better able to bring to consciousness our own fantasies and to understand the symbolic meaning that our own experience has for us. These reflections then may assist in a more formal way a process which has been underway for some time in rap groups. I take it that these groups are one of the principal products of the collective genius of the women's movement, that they are admirably suited to deal with certain forms of oppression peculiar to women's experience, because they enable us to discover and recover our own various fantasies and to articulate the symbolic meaning of our own experience; to know our own minds in the deepest sense.

Notes

1. Simone de Beauvoir has discussed the idea of *Woman* (though not the feminine principle) as Other in the *Second Sex* but does not discriminate between this and other motifs which I am putting forward.

2. It is common to reserve the terms "female" and "male" to mark biological diamorphism and use the terms "feminine" and "masculine" for psychological traits. Thus some depth psychologists would speak of a "feminine" principle but not a "female" one. However this distinction was not drawn historically, and in early philosophy and science no sharp distinction is drawn between the biological and the psychological contrasts.

3. E.G., Plato, *The Republic*, 455c.

4. Prior to Aristotle we have medical theories of hysteria (in the Hippocratic writings and in ancient Egyptian papyri dating from 1900 B.C.) which view this disease as arising when the uterus wanders about the body. Commentators have been puzzled by the way this conception of the uterus as an autonomous being, or "animal" could have achieved and maintained such currency in the thinking of otherwise astute medical thinkers. (See Ilza Veith *Hysteria: The History of a Disease*, Chicago, 1965.) I maintain that the view of the uterus as a separate being is natural *if one assumes that a woman is a partial man*. Her "extra" equipment which does not fit the model is then explained away as a separate individual.

5. Aristotle recognizes that seeds and eggs have a nutritive component. *Generation of Animals*, 731 a–b 3 and 732 a 29–33.

6. Because Western biology and medicine followed Aristotle (and Anaxagoras) rather than Hippocrates, Empedocles, Democritus, Alcmaeon and even Galen, in denying the existence of gametes supplied by the female parent, "semen" came to mean sperm exclusively, so that when the existence of gametes from the female was accepted in the nineteenth century, a different word, "ova," had come into use. Similarly what had been called "testes" in the female came to be called "ovaries."

7. Aristotle, *The Generation of Animals*, translated by A. L. Peck, Cambridge: Harvard University Press, p. 103 (728 a 18). This view is expressed again at 766 b 20.

8. *Ibid.*, 775 a 15. A similar statement is also found 767 b 9.

9. *Ibid.*

10. A useful companion to Diels, *Fragmente der Vorsokratiker* which includes the views of

pre-Socratics on sex differences is Kathleen Freeman's *The Pre-Socratic Philosophers*, Oxford: Basil Blackwell, 1959.

11. *Ibid.*, 729 b 14–16, p. 113.

12. Louis Ginsberg, *Legends of the Jews*, Vol. I, Philadelphia: The Jewish Publication Society of America, 1909, p. 66.

13. Carl Jung, "Woman in Europe," *Contributions to Analytical Psychology*, trans. H. G. and Gary F. Baynes (London: Routledge & Kegan Paul, 1928), pp. 132–133.

14. Gerhard Adler, *Studies in Analytical Psychology* (New York: C. G. Jung Foundation, 1966), pp. 242–243.

15. London: Longmans, Green & Co., 1936.

16. Freud "Femininity" lecture 33 of New Introductory Lectures on Psycho-Analysis in Volume 22 of the Standard Edition, edited by James Strachey, p. 127.

17. Freud, Female Sexuality in Volume 21 Standard Edition, p. 234.

18. Freud, "Femininity," p. 126.

19. Freud, "Femininity," pp. 114–116.

20. *Ibid.*, p. 120.

21. Freud, "Female Sexuality," p. 239.

Study Questions

1. What three general motifs, or views of women, does Whitbeck discuss?

2. According to Whitbeck, what is Aristotle's view of women?

3. What is the Pythagorean view of women? What does Whitbeck think that the fact that there were women Pythagoreans illustrates?

4. What is the third motif Whitbeck delineates? Where can this motif in its present form be found? (Discuss with examples.) What is the definition of woman from the adult male perspective? The male child perspective?

5. What is the Jungian view of woman? To which of the three motifs described earlier is it closest? What contradiction lurks in the Jungian view, as evidenced in the quote from Adler? The Jungian view seems to promote equality, but does it in fact do so?

6. What is Freud's view of women? To which of the three motifs is it related? What are two areas of incoherence in Freud's view of women?

Do Women Have a Distinct Nature?

Nancy Holmstrom

Feminists have good reason to be suspicious of any talk of a distinct women's nature. The very phrase contains a sexist bias in that men are implicitly taken as the norm and women as "the other," to use de Beauvoir's term. Despite some pious talk of complementarity the different characteristics attributed to men and women have always been evaluated differently, and for thousands of years theories of a distinct

From *The Philosophical Forum*, Vol. XIV, No. 1 (Fall 1982), pp. 25–42. Reprinted by permission of The Philosophical Forum. (Notes deleted.)

women's nature have been used to justify the subordination of women to men. The theories are taken to imply that these natures cannot change and also that one ought not even try to change them. Most theories of *human* nature have served a similar function. Either women have been explicitly taken to lack the traits designated by the theories as essentially human, e.g., rationality, or else traits historically more true of men than women, such as participating in politics, have been designated as essentially human. Most of these theories have been exposed by feminists as pseudo-scientific rationalizations of cultural prejudices. Not only has a distinct women's nature not been established, feminists argue, but even if it had no normative implications would follow automatically.[1]

The question can, however, be posed in unbiased terms: are there sex-differentiated natures? In this sense if women have a distinct nature then it is equally true that men have a distinct nature. This question refuses to be disposed of—in part because of the tremendous social importance the answer is presumed to have and also because of the enormous variety and complexity of the issues involved. First of all there are conceptual, methodological and ontological issues: what exactly is a nature or essence? When are similarities between things sufficient to constitute a common nature and when do differences constitute different natures? To help elucidate a methodology, I will turn to biology, which has the most developed and precise system of classifications of things in nature. I will argue that a nature or essence should be understood as an underlying structure that generates laws and that natures in this sense often play a crucial explanatory role. There are also, of course, empirical questions to be answered regarding differences between men and women that might determine their respective social roles. Examining the research on psychological sex differences, I conclude that there probably are significant differences between the sexes. However I also conclude that the most important determinants of these differences are social. The usual inference would be that men and women do not have different natures, and in the traditional sense of "natures," this is correct. However, the traditional conception depends upon a contrast between nature and society that, I argue, is mistaken, particularly in the case of human beings. Natures can also be socially constituted. Whether men and women have different natures depends, I contend, on certain theoretical considerations. As an illustration of what I mean by this claim, I discuss Marx's theory of human nature. In conclusion I discuss what would follow if men and women do have distinct natures in this sense.

Although biology has the most precise system of classifications in nature and involves few, if any, social and political factors, never-theless, even in biology there is considerable disagreement as to the criteria for differentiating species, behind which lie different philosophies of science.[2] The essentialist, or typological approach, coming from Aristotle, holds that species are differentiated by sets of individually necessary and jointly sufficient characteristics which constitute the nature or essence of that species. Since these essences were supposed to be unchanging, this approach became less dominant after the discovery of evolution. Another contemporary school of taxonomists (called pheneticists) rejects essences and argues that the only proper scientific basis for classification is the overall similarity of things. Taxonomists who emphasize evolution correctly reply that there is no such thing as overall similarity. Every individual is similar to and different from every other individual in a variety of ways. Hence there are always many possible orderings. However, this does not make all classifications arbitrary and all generalizations accidental. What similarities and differences are most important can only be decided in terms of theoretical considerations. Classifications and generalizations backed up by a theory are neither accidental nor arbitrary. Evolutionary and gene theory do not define species in terms of similarity. There can be greater variations of certain kinds within a species, e.g., between a Chihuahua and a St. Bernard, among dogs, than between two species, e.g., dogs and wolves. This is because some differences are more important than others for biological theory. Taxonomists who emphasize evolution conceive of a species as, roughly speaking, a class of individual organisms which (either do or could) consistently interbreed with fertile offspring. The actual distribution of properties among organisms is such that, contrary to the Aristotelian view, most taxa names can only be defined disjunctively. Any of the disjuncts is sufficient and the few properties that are necessary are far from sufficient. Thus most concepts of so-called natural kinds are cluster concepts. These classes of organisms change over time to such an extent that individuals in the later generations are no longer classified as belonging to the same species as those of earlier generations.

Although it is superior to the alternatives

discussed, I would agree with those philosophers called realists who argue that the evolutionary approach is still not adequate. Suppose we ask why things that fit that sort of disjunctive definition should figure in evolutionary theory? Why should such a group have the requisite stability? Why is it that they can interbreed? Realists argue that it is necessary to posit some underlying structure common to the things so defined which generates this set of properties and causes the variations in different individuals. In the case of a species, this underlying structure would be the gene pool. The disjunctive definition is sufficient to define the species, if it is, only because it is reflective of the underlying structure. The theories, which back up some generalizations and not others, should provide some account of the mechanisms generative of the regularities. In traditional terminology, the set of properties which justifies the use of the common term is called the nominal essence; the internal constitution which generates these manifest properties in accordance with laws is called the real essence. I am arguing, then, that the notion of a nature or essence—stripped of the metaphysical assumptions found in Plato and Aristotle's use of the concept—often plays an important explanatory function. Whether it is applicable to men and women depends on the facts about the sexes and the theories which explain the facts. However, it should be clear that the concept as I have explained it carries no evaluative implications. If a group has a distinct nature, nothing follows automatically about how its members ought or ought not to behave.

Since the concept of distinct male and female natures has been used to explain and justify distinct social roles for the sexes, the sexual differences we are concerned with are those which would be explanatory of those social roles. Some of the physical differences between the sexes are true by definition—which makes tautological talk of sex-differentiated natures based on these differences. To explain sexual/social roles from distinct natures in this sense would be an empty exercise. Therefore we are only concerned with physical differences between men and women if it can be shown that they determine or dispose men and

women to their respective social roles. Now why should biological differences *per se* have such systematic social implications? The linkage is usually made through psychology. Those who emphasize the biological differences between the sexes as critical to their social roles and their natures usually maintain (or simply assume) that the biological differences cause psychological differences and these in turn determine their respective social roles.[3] So what we need to find out, first of all, is whether there are psychological differences between men and women, in terms of cognitive abilities and styles and other personality characteristics, that suit them to their respective social roles, for example, that women are more nurturant than men, and therefore are the primary caretakers of their own and other peoples' children. The second question would be the source of such differences.

As we have seen, the properties that constitute the nature of a group need not be unique or common to all its members. What we should look for as a beginning, then, are statistically significant differences between the sexes. Social scientists approach the question in this way but unfortunately they rarely go further. One problem with *only* looking for statistically significant differences is that even minute differences are statistically significant given a large enough sample.[4] Furthermore it is a measure that is very manipulable. We also need to consider the magnitude of the differences between the sexes and the degree to which they overlap. Even more crucial, as we saw, is that the differences must be of a kind that is theoretically important. We need therefore to look for a theoretical framework in which to evaluate the data. As our discussion of taxonomy revealed, it is often impossible to tell what differences are important without a theory. A new theory can even change our minds about what needs to be explained. Newtonian theory, for example, showed that certain kinds of unaccelerated motion, such as a passenger in a car continuing to move when the car stops suddenly, do not need an explanation, as had previously been supposed. This is one of the reasons that after determining what if any psychological differences there are between the sexes, we then need to determine their source.

The literature in the field of psychological sex differences is actually quite confusing because the experts disagree. However, if we examine the literature we can arrive at conclusions that are fairly reliable. One of the most recent and authoritative books in the field, often cited by feminists, is *The Psychology of Sex Differences* by Eleanor Maccoby and Carol Jacklin,[5] which attempts an exhaustive analysis of the research in the field, with an emphasis on the developmental literature. According to their results, there are fewer psychological differences between men and women than commonly believed (and fewer still that appear to be biologically based). Among the beliefs about sex differences[6] that they conclude to be unfounded are: that girls are more "social" and more "suggestible" than boys, that girls have lower self-esteem and lack achievement motivation, that girls are better at rote learning while boys are more analytic and better at tasks requiring higher cognitive processing. The areas of alleged psychological sex differences that they judge to be, at present, open questions, either because of insufficient evidence or unclear results, are the following: (1) tactile sensitivity, (2) fear, timidity, anxiety, (3) activity level, (4) competitiveness, (5) dominance, (6) compliance, (7) nurturance and "maternal" behavior.[7] The alleged sex differences that they find to be fairly well established are that girls have greater verbal ability while boys have greater visual/spatial and also mathematical ability (though this did not show up until age 12–13) and that males are more "prepared for" aggression. Except for this great "preparedness" for aggression in boys, their findings simply show that with respect to a few traits more men than women have the trait to a higher degree than most people do (or vice versa). This allows that some women have as much or more of it than any man, and even that a majority of the group may lack the trait found more frequently among their group.[8]

Feminists might feel vindicated by these results, but they should be somewhat surprised too. It would be naive and idealistic to think that the differences in opportunities, expectations, socialization, and, in general, the social environment in which boys and girls and men and women live and function would have so little effect. And in fact there seem to be very good reasons for being skeptical about Maccoby and Jacklin's conclusions. Another expert in the field, Jeanne Block, points out that their conclusions conflict with other surveys of the research in the field and raises very serious questions about their methodology and the evidential support for their conclusions.[9]

One of the most interesting problems that Block points out is that Maccoby and Jacklin concentrate on sex differences in the performance of various tasks and ignore the interrelationships between intellectual performance and personality characteristics. These interrelationships are critical in understanding motivation, and there is much evidence that the differences in how the traits are linked together in the sexes are more important than the differences in average scores on various tests.[10] Achievement motivation in girls brings out the importance of this point. Females appear to have greater needs to be close to people than males. Conflict between these needs and achievement needs cuts into achievement, and since this conflict will occur more frequently in girls, this will reduce their achievement. Girls would rather "lose the game than lose the man." However, level of achievement is not the only factor to consider, because even when, at younger ages, achievement is the same or higher in girls, "it appears that female achievement behavior . . . is motivated by a desire for love rather than mastery."[11]

Most crucial for the concerns of this paper is the criticism that Maccoby and Jacklin's results are based predominantly on pre-adolescent children. Breaking down their results into different age groups, one finds that the percentage of studies in which there are clear and significant sex differences increases significantly with older age groups, especially beginning with adolescence, and this accords with other studies that show personality differences between the sexes increasing with age. All in all, then, it seems that there probably are greater personality differences between the sexes than Maccoby and Jacklin conclude, particularly among the age groups most relevant to our examination of the social roles of men and women.

The next question to consider is the source

of the psychological differences between men and women. Hoffman's research suggests that many have their origins in differences in childrearing practices.[12] However, she and others who want to argue that the psychological differences between men and women are due to differences in their socialization and in the social contexts in which they find themselves have insufficient research to appeal to. This neglect of social context is not only an obstacle to discovering the etiology of psychological sex differences but may also lead to incorrect assessment of the facts. Studies of males and females in artificial contexts (like most of Maccoby and Jacklin's data), may yield results that are not predictive of their feelings and behavior in ordinary life, where they find themselves in very different social contexts. Studies of men and women in actual social contexts would likely show greater differences between the sexes. (One reason why there are so many inconsistent findings in this area might be the different contexts in which the studies were done.)

Actually it is not only the social approach to etiology which suffers from inadequate research. As indicated earlier, there is a prevailing hostility within academic research psychology to any theoretical explanatory framework. Research psychologists do not try to determine cause and effect; they only look for statistical relationships. Longitudinal studies, more relevant to establishing cause and effect, are also more costly and more speculative. This empiricist bias obviously makes it very difficult to determine an explanation for relationships they discover.

Given this state of the research, any position on the etiology of psychological sex differences is necessarily somewhat speculative. Although serious questions have been raised as to the likelihood that any specific and variable human behavioral traits are under genetic control, I will ignore this general question about sociobiology. With respect to psychological sex differences in particular, there are a number of findings and arguments which strongly suggest that social factors are far more important determinants than biological ones: (1) Black males and white females, different biologically but with similar social handicaps, are similar in:

patterns of achievement scores, fear of success, and conformity and perceptual judgment; (2) Protestant, Jewish and Catholic women (who do not differ biologically) nevertheless experience significant differences in menstrual discomfort. (3) The same physiological state can yield very different emotional states and behavior depending on the social situation. Adrenalin produces a physiological state very much like that present in extreme fear, yet subjects injected with it became euphoric when around another person who acted euphoric and very angry when around another person who acted very angry. Thus even if sex hormonal differences between men and women affect brain functioning, as some psychologists contend, it would not follow that there necessarily would be consistent emotional and behavioral differences between men and women. (4) Different behavioral propensities, thought by many to be biologically based, disappear given certain social conditions. In one study, both sexes were rewarded for aggressive behavior, and the sex differences disappeared.[13] (5) Studies of hermaphrodites show that the crucial variable determining their gender identity is neither chromosomal sex nor hormones administered pre- or postnatally but "the consistency of the experiences of being reared as feminine, especially in the early years."[14] (6) The studies of psychological sex differences are based overwhelmingly on white middle-class Americans living in college towns. The generalizability of these findings cannot be assumed, as evidenced by the differences between whites and blacks discussed above. Moreover, anthropology reveals significant differences in sex roles in different cultures. Although rigorous cross-cultural psychological research has not been done, it appears that the personality differences between the sexes also show some cross-cultural differences.[15] If there is any connection between sex roles and psychological traits (whatever the direction of the causation), then one would expect further research to reveal that psychological sex differences vary cross-culturally. In the absence of a biological explanation, a variation according to culture strongly suggests that there is a social explanation.

The above points seem to offer dramatic

evidence in favor of environmental factors as the *primary* determinants of psychological differences. There certainly does not seem to be any direct link between biological and psychological factors. In addition, there is a general methodological argument in favor of taking environmental factors as decisive. It can be summed up as follows: "Although future research may uncover important biological factors, the present data give more than sufficient evidence that environmental shaping of sex-differentiated behavior does exist. At this time it seems evident that the environment in which all American children mature clearly projects sex role stereotypes. These stereotypic expectations and the differential responses they elicit are sufficiently clear and unambiguous to account for the cognitive and personality differences in children that ultimately lead to the different roles that they fulfill."[16] Much the same argument, using the principle of methodological simplicity, is made by J. S. Mill in *The Subjection of Women*, where he argues that there is no basis for talking about the nature of men and women so long as they have only been in the present relations to each other. I would concur with this opinion[17] and thus conclude that the most reasonable position at present is that psychological differences between the sexes are most probably overwhelmingly social in origin.

By "social" I simply mean "not biological." Such factors could include family structure, organization of the economy, and innumerable more specific factors. It is important to note that if psychological differences between the sexes do owe much to family structure, that is, to the fact that women are the primary child rearers,[18] it does not follow that the biological (reproductive) differences between the sexes are the real cause of the psychological differences. Women's ability to bear children does not automatically determine that they are the primary rearers of children. The reproductive differences between the sexes, just because they are universal, cannot explain the social and historical variations in the personalities and roles of men and women. The *significance* of the biological differences depends on social, historical facts, and, moreover, is maintained in every society by complicated social practices.

Consider this analogous example. Suppose that the division of slaves into house and field workers was based entirely on the slaves' size and strength, bigger and stronger slaves becoming field workers, smaller and weaker ones becoming house workers. It is well known that there were differences in attitudes and, to some extent, personality between house and field slaves (so-called "house niggers" and "field niggers"). What was the cause of these differences? Most writers point to the differences in work, working conditions and social relations of house and field slaves. If different social conditions would have produced different psychological results, then it would be mistaken to point to the physical differences as the cause— even though they were the basis of their being in their respective social conditions.

It seems then that there probably are not differences in male and female natures—so long as natures are understood as biologically based and immutable. However, this inference depends on certain equations and contrasts that are usually presupposed in this discussion.[19] The natural is contrasted with the social and the former is taken to be biological in origin. What's biological/natural is taken to be inevitable and what's social in origin is taken to be alterable. These assumptions are found in both popular and academic discussions of the issue, e.g., in traditional philosophical theories of essence which exclude socially variant properties as essential.

These assumptions cannot go unquestioned. Our discussion of taxonomy shows how mistaken is the assumption that the biological is unchangeable. In rejecting static essentialism and trying to fit classifications into evolutionary theory, taxonomists have rejected the equation of the natural with the unchangeable. That things change is built into nature, although, of course, until recently the big changes have been quite slow. Not only do biological facts undergo slow change on their own, but they can be changed or their results affected by social conditions and by deliberate human action. For example: the disadvantages of people with Pku deficiency can be removed by human action. We have just discussed other examples of this. So even if the differences between men and women were based more in biology than they seem to be, it would not make those differences inevitable. They could still be outweighed by deliberate human action and by social conditions, e.g., by altering childrearing practices. Therefore whether the differences between men and women are primarily biological or social in origin need not have the momentous importance it is usually assumed to have by people on both sides of the question.

If there is not in fact such a sharp contrast between what is biologically based and what is socially based then there is less reason to maintain a sharp conceptual contrast between what is natural and what is social in origin. Nor should it be assumed that what is natural is inevitable and immutable. This is not true of biological facts, as we have just seen, and if species can be understood as evolving sorts of things, there seems no reason to assume that natures must be unchanging. More precisely, if the classes of organisms classified as a particular species can change to the point where they should be classified as belonging to another species, then why should it be understood as having a different nature? If the underlying genetic basis of the classification into species can change, why can't natures themselves change? In other words, even if natures are taken to be biological in origin there seems little basis for the assumption that natures are unchanging.

Moreover there seems no reason to assume that natures must be exclusively biological. I argued earlier that natures should be understood as underlying structures that explain a range of behavior. What kinds of structures these are depends on the behavior and the organism we are seeking to explain. While human beings are undeniably biological beings they are also social beings with a history. Their biological characteristics have evolved somewhat but their social and cultural characteristics have evolved more rapidly and to a much greater extent. If we are concerned with human beings as distinct from other biological beings, then their natures are biological. But if we are concerned with humans as social beings, then their natures, i.e., the underlying structures that explain their behavior—must be understood as socially constituted and historically evolving. Hence social changes could cause

changes in natures even if they had no biological effect. This brings out the point that there are many levels of generating structures, many levels of explanation appropriate to human beings. If one accepts the view that freedom and determinism are not necessarily incompatible, then this account does not deny human freedom; it simply makes clear the constraints within which human agency functions. To what extent people are free depends on the extent to which they can be said to be self-determining. And this depends on the kinds of explanations, the kinds of determining structures of their behavior.

A similar distinction to that just made for human beings can be made for men and women. The distinction between males and females is a biological one. Hence the nature of a woman, *qua* female, is biological. However, the categories "men" and "women" are also social categories—what is called gender. Hence men and women, *qua* social beings, might have distinct natures which would be explanatory of the sex-related differences in behavior. As we saw, natures in the biological sense cannot by themselves explain sexual/social roles. If the sex differences in personality and cognitive traits discussed earlier are primarily social in origin the natures which generate and explain them would be primarily social in origin. However, this is all hypothetical. As we saw earlier, in the absence of a theoretical framework it is impossible to determine whether the psychological differences between men and women are sufficiently important to constitute differences in natures.

To clarify how a theoretical framework could be applied to help resolve this question I will discuss the example of the Marxist theory of historical materialism, which accords fairly well with the methodology set out earlier in the paper.[20] Marx argued vehemently against theories of a fixed, transhistorical human nature, offering instead a social and historical account. There are few transhistorical features of human beings, he maintained, and those there are—basic needs and capacities—are transformed throughout history and hence are in part socially constituted. "Hunger is hunger but the hunger gratified by cooked meat eaten with a knife and fork is a different hunger from that which bolts down raw meat with the aid of hand, nail and tooth."[21] These human needs are expressed, shaped, and even created through the activity of satisfying needs, that is, through labor. Because the labor of society is institutionalized into sets of social practices and social relations, Marx says that by their labor people are thereby producing their whole life. Although biological structures make possible the forms of human labor, they do not determine a particular form as the biology of other animals does. Given that in Marx's theory labor is the key to an explanation of social life and social change—which was his concern—he emphasized the characteristic form of labor rather than the biology. The differing forms of human labor (and the resultant social practices and institutions) change the mental and physical capacities of human beings. Although there will be some transhistorical features of human beings, there will also then be certain characteristic differences in the psycho-physical structures of people who do very different sorts of labor in different modes of production. These structures would generate and explain a wide range of human behavior within that mode of production which the transhistorical features would not do. These psycho-physical structures would constitute the nature of humans *qua* social beings. Although there would be certain common features, these structures as a whole vary from one mode of production to another. Hence there is no transhistorical human nature. However there would be historically specific forms of human nature, that is, human nature specific to feudalism, to capitalism, to socialism, and so on.

This approach can be applied to particular social groups, such as women, as well as to human beings. If particular social groups do labor that is sufficiently different as to generate distinct social relations, practices, and institutions associated with that labor, then they probably have distinct natures as well. There will probably be generalizations subsumable under a theory that would explain much of the group's behavior. Women appear to fit this condition. There are several levels of generalizations (sociological psychological . . .) distinctive of women which are relevant—both as cause and

as effect—to their distinct social roles. Using a Marxist theoretical framework in which to evaluate the sexual differences, we would look to see whether they are connected to the different sorts of labor women do in society and the different social relations this puts them in. Although much more investigation needs to be done, particularly cross-cultural research, there is a lot of evidence that this is so. Despite the variations, there is and has always been a sexual division of labor in which women have primary responsibility for childcare and most of the everyday household work, whatever else they do as well. In a society with a significantly different sexual division of labor, this theory implies that other differing generalizations would be true of men and women and where there was no sexual division of labor, there would likely be few or no non-accidental generalizations true of women and not men—other than biological ones, of course, and fewer perhaps of these. The generalizations true of women and not men describe behavioral dispositions reflective of specific cognitive/affective structures found more often among women which generate the different sets of traits found under different conditions. These structures would constitute the distinctive natures of women as social beings.

Much more work is necessary before we can determine whether men and women have distinct social natures. We would need to establish the validity of a particular theoretical framework and do the research dictated by that framework. In the Marxist case we would need to establish both that the sexual differences are due to the sexual division of labor and that this theoretical framework is a valid one. The point of the excursion into Marxist theory was simply to illustrate how a theoretical framework could lead to the conclusion that there are sex-differentiated natures which are social in origin. This question should be pursued with other theories as well.

Suppose men and women do have distinct natures in this social sense—whatever the theoretical grounding. What follows? Well, first of all it is important to see that many of the implications usually thought to follow do not follow when natures are understood in the sense I have explained. This nature is not fixed and inevitable; natures can change. The crucial determinants are social, not biological. That there is a distinct women's nature in this sense would not entail that every woman has this nature. If we recall that most species' names only admit of disjunctive definitions we see that there need not be any one trait that is universally more common to women than to men. There could be a common core of psychological traits found more among women than men around the world, but women of different cultures or subcultures have different subsets of this common core of traits. This would make the concept of women's (social) nature a cluster concept, as are most "natural kinds" concepts. Although probably very few women would have none of the traits generated by the distinctive cognitive/affective structures, some might have them to only a minimal degree. Individual men could have more of this women's nature than do some women. Thus someone might be biologically female but not share the gender of other females. This is because one is a biological category, the other a social category. Even women who have this nature fully do not necessarily have more in common with other such women than with any man. This women's nature is only one aspect of her individual human nature and is not necessarily more determinant than all the other factors, individually much less collectively. Furthermore, and perhaps most important, the statement that women have a distinct nature in this sense has no evaluative implications. Nothing follows about how they ought or ought not to live or how society ought to be structured. This does not logically follow from the traditional view of natures either, but it is a more plausible conclusion to draw, given that if natures are immutable, they certainly set severe constraints on possible social arrangements. Moreover, if women live and become a different way, they will not be violating their nature; their nature will simply have changed. In fact we could predict that new social conditions would redefine women's nature. Less oppressive conditions would develop potentialities presently unrealized. It is quite likely that under some social conditions there would be no sex-differentiated natures.

Given all these disclaimers, given all the ways in which my sense of a women's nature differs from the usual meaning, a reasonable objection might be that I should not call this a nature; in fact, given the sexist associations of most such talk, it is positively dangerous to do so. I agree that the term could be misleading and even dangerous in certain contexts, but "nature" is also a technical, theory-laden term that is useful in summing up certain relationships. To summarize the conditions under which I think it would be useful to employ the term about women (and men): (1) there is a cluster of traits that women tend to have more than men which are systematically related to one another and which are important in explaining a wide range of their behavior (thus not every factor explanatory of women's behavior would be part of a women's nature); (2) it seems probable that there are certain psychic structures distinctive of the sexes which generate these traits; and (3) these sexual differences can in turn be explained within a broader theoretical framework which can also explain where women differ from one another as well as where they are similar. If these conditions are met, then talk of women's (and men's) natures is a way of bringing out the importance that a person's sex, thus far in history, has tended to have for their personality and behavior. Although the term itself is not important, this fact is important and is given its due prominence if the term is used. If "nature" is understood as a theory-laden term, then talk of women's nature carries the implications of that theory. I would argue that if the theory were adequate, the concept of a woman's nature would refer to something dynamic rather than static, primarily social/historical in origin rather than innate, and so on. If understood correctly, then, the concept does have a function and need not be misleading or dangerous.

Notes

1. Joyce Trebilcot, in "Sex Roles: The Argument from Nature," argues that even if there are natural psychological differences

between the sexes, it does not follow that there ought to be distinct social/sexual roles. Christine Pierce, "Natural Law Language and Women," is particularly good on the many different and even conflicting senses of the word "natural." Both articles are in *Sex Equality*, ed. Jane English (Englewood Cliffs, NJ: Prentice-Hall, 1977), pp. 121–29, 130–42.

2. Radical critics of science would argue that social/political factors come into biological classifications as well.

3. An academic example of this point of view is Judith Bardwick, *Psychology of Women* (New York: Harper & Row, 1971).

4. Such minute differences can prove very significant in some contexts. E.g., it has been proved that a feature that gives only a minute reproductive advantage will completely replace its alternatives in 1–2000 years (pointed out to me by Rohr). However, merely being statistically significant does not make something important or anything more than minute, as is often assumed once it is called "statistically significant."

5. Eleanor Maccoby and Carol Jacklin, *The Psychology of Sex Differences* (Stanford: Stanford University Press, 1974).

6. I am speaking here about statistically significant differences, whatever the cause.

7. Their findings indicate that there may be some sex differences in these areas but that there are not general overall differences in these areas. E.g., there may be different circumstances in which males and females are compliant but no overall difference in compliance.

8. Hence the inadequacy of statistical significance as the sole criterion.

9. Block argues that their data base, their conceptual classifications, and other aspects of their methodology can all be questioned in various ways, and they shape their conclusions against differences between the sexes. For example, the studies vary considerably in statistical power, and Block says "to the extent that sex differences are assessed with respect to scores that are undependable, differences that may exist in fact will go undetected." Studies having to do with other issues are often required to report any sex differences, although there would be no reason whatsoever to expect differences (in fact, there is good reason to expect that there would not be differences since researchers not concerned with sex differences would try to control for that). As a result, "the empirical literature is replete with null findings of inconsequential import." With respect to conceptual rubrics, Block cites several questionable examples. These include: (1) a very broad definition of parental pressures for achievement; equally reasonable narrower definitions would probably reveal greater differences between the sexes; (2) a narrow definition of "impulsivity" only having to do with cognitive qualities; a broader definition including temperament (which Maccoby used in an earlier work) would show greater differences between the sexes. Certain omissions in their bibliography also influence their conclusions in the same direction. Block argues that even using their data, sex differences on several of the traits that claim to be open questions, e.g., dominance, have as much support as others that they conclude are well established. "Issues, Problems and Pitfalls in Assessing Sex Differences: A Critical Review of *The Psychology of Sex Differences*," *Merrill-Palmer Quarterly*, 22, No. 4 (1976), 283–308.

10. *Ibid.*, p. 297.

11. Hoffman, "Early Childhood Experiences and Women's Achievement Motives," *Journal of Social Issues*, 28, No. 1 (1972), 129–55. Related to this objection is the possibility that although boys and girls differ in their propensity to aggressive behavior, they may not differ in their "preparedness for aggression" but rather in the likelihood that they will express it and not inhibit it and in the way they express it, e.g., verbally or physically.

12. She suggests this explanation for the differences in achievement motives: "Since girls as compared to boys have less

encouragement for independence, more parental protectiveness, less pressure for establishing an identity separate from the mother, and less mother-child conflict which highlights this separation, they engage in less independent exploration of their environment. As a result they develop neither adequate skills nor confidence but continue to be dependent upon others" (p. 129). Although there is not adequate evidence to definitely establish this at this time, it is consistent with findings that girls are more anxious and less confident in their abilities and their judgment. The same pattern appears to be reinforced by later socialization practices (p. 144).

13. Mischel in Maccoby, pp. 56–81. Maccoby also reports that the greater propensity for aggression in boys disappears when they are given substantial childcare responsibilities. One might argue that the propensity is simply inhibited. I think this is less plausible for various reasons, but in any case it does not affect my point. This is another instance where social conditions prove more important in determining behavior than an (allegedly) biological propensity.

14. Money and Ehrhardt, *Man and Woman, Boy and Girl,* quoted in Beverly Birns' "Emergence and Socialization of Sex Differences in the Earliest Years," *Merrill-Palmer Quarterly,* 22, No. 3 (1976), 250–51.

15. Margaret Mead in *Sex and Temperament* (New York: Morrow, 1963), reports societies where the men have personalities designated as female in our culture (emotionally dependent, spoiled, etc.) and women have "masculine" personalities (independent, dominant). Carol Hoffer, in "Mende and Sherbro Women in High Office," *Canadian Journal of African Studies* (1971), 151–64, reports cultures in which women hold high political office which is enhanced by motherhood.

16. Birns, p. 251.

17. Under two conditions: (1) that natures are taken to be primarily biological and (2) that there are no strong theoretical considerations to support the claim that there are biologically based sex natures.

18. Nancy Chodorow's *The Reproduction of Mothering* (Berkeley: University of California Press, 1978) and Dorothy Dinnerstein's *The Mermaid and the Minotaur* (New York: Harper & Row, 1977) offer similar interesting hypotheses. Both authors argue that the near-universal fact that women "mother" (in a psychological as well as the many physical ways) is the key to adult male and female personality structures. Although different from "social learning" approaches (they are both more psychoanalytic), these theories both offer a social explanation in the sense I am using "social" and could easily be combined with other social explanations.

19. E.g., "a crucial issue is whether there is any basis to the claim that there are biologically derived (and therefore inescapable) psychological or personality characteristics that universally differentiate men and women." Nancy Chodorow, "Being and Doing," in *Sisterhood is Powerful,* p. 173.

20. The following is controversial. One of the most controversial areas of Marxist scholarship is whether Marx had a theory of human nature in his later works and, if so, whether it is significantly different from his earlier views. I believe the following to be consistent with both his early and his late work whether or not there are also differences between his early and later ideas.

21. *Grundrisse⁻* (Hammondsworth, England: Penguin Books, 1973), p. 92.

Study Questions

---

1. According to Holmstrom, why do women have a right to be suspicious of talk about "women's nature"?

2. What view of "species" does Holmstrom accept?

3. Holmstrom discusses a number of issues surrounding empirical psychological research on sex differences. What are some

candidates for true sex differences (mentioned in the Maccoby/Jacklin study)?

4. What does Holmstrom think is the likely cause of any such sex differences? On what basis does she reach her conclusion about the likely cause of those differences?

5. What is the Marxist view of human nature? How does Holmstrom think it might apply to "women's nature"?

6. What are a few claims that do *not* follow from the assertion that women have a distinct nature? Discuss in detail why they don't follow.

Is Female to Male as Nature Is to Culture?

Sherry B. Ortner

Much of the creativity of anthropology derives from the tension between two sets of demands: that we explain human universals, and that we explain cultural particulars. By this canon, woman provides us with one of the more challenging problems to be dealt with. The secondary status of woman in society is one of the true universals, a pan-cultural fact. Yet within that universal fact, the specific cultural conceptions and symbolizations of woman are extraordinarily diverse and even mutually contradictory. Further, the actual treatment of women and their relative power and contribution vary enormously from culture to culture, and over different periods in the history of particular cultural traditions. Both of these points—the universal fact and the cultural variation—constitute problems to be explained.

My interest in the problem is of course more than academic: I wish to see genuine change come about, the emergence of a social and cultural order in which as much of the range of human potential is open to women as is open to men. The universality of female subordination, the fact that it exists within every type of social and economic arrangement and in societies of every degree of complexity, indicates to me

that we are up against something very profound, very stubborn, something we cannot rout out simply by rearranging a few tasks and roles in the social system, or even by reordering the whole economic structure. In this paper I try to expose the underlying logic of cultural thinking that assumes the inferiority of women; I try to show the highly persuasive nature of the logic, for if it were not so persuasive, people would not keep subscribing to it. But I also try to show the social and cultural sources of that logic, to indicate wherein lies the potential for change.

It is important to sort out the levels of the problem. The confusion can be staggering. For example, depending on which aspect of Chinese culture we look at, we might extrapolate any of several entirely different guesses concerning the status of women in China. In the ideology of Taoism, *yin,* the female principle, and *yang,* the male principle, are given equal weight; "the opposition, alternation, and interaction of these two forces give rise to all phenomena in the universe." . . . Hence we might guess that maleness and femaleness are equally valued in the general ideology of Chinese culture.[1] Looking at the social structure, however, we see the strongly emphasized patrilineal descent principle, the importance of sons, and the absolute authority of the father in the family. Thus we might conclude that China is the archetypal patriarchal society. Next, looking at the actual roles played, power and influence wielded, and

From Michelle Zimbalist Rosaldo and Louise Lamphere, eds., *Woman, Culture, and Society,* pp. 67–87. © 1974 by the Board of Trustees of the Leland Stanford Junior University. Reprinted by permission of the publishers, Stanford University Press. (Notes deleted.)

material contributions made by women in Chinese society—all of which are, upon observation, quite substantial—we would have to say that women are allotted a great deal of (unspoken) status in the system. Or again, we might focus on the fact that a goddess, Kuan Yin, is the central (most worshipped, most depicted) deity in Chinese Buddhism, and we might be tempted to say, as many have tried to say about goddess-worshipping cultures in prehistoric and early historical societies, that China is actually a sort of matriarchy. In short, we must be absolutely clear about *what* we are trying to explain before explaining it.

We may differentiate three levels of the problem:

1. The universal fact of culturally attributed second-class status of woman in every society. Two questions are important here. First, what do we mean by this; what is our evidence that this is a universal fact? And second, how are we to explain this fact, once having established it?

2. Specific ideologies, symbolizations, and sociostructural arrangements pertaining to women that vary widely from culture to culture. The problem at this level is to account for any particular cultural complex in terms of factors specific to that group—the standard level of anthropological analysis.

3. Observable on-the-ground details of women's activities, contributions, powers, influence, etc., often at variance with cultural ideology (although always constrained within the assumption that women may never be officially preeminent in the total system). This is the level of direct observation, often adopted now by feminist-oriented anthropoligists.

This paper is primarily concerned with the first of these levels, the problem of the universal devaluation of women. The analysis thus depends not upon specific cultural data but rather upon an analysis of "culture" taken generically as a special sort of process in the world. A discussion of the second level, the problem of cross-cultural variation in conceptions and relative valuations of women, will entail a great deal of cross-cultural research

and must be postponed to another time. As for the third level, it will be obvious from my approach that I would consider it a misguided endeavor to focus only upon women's actual though culturally unrecognized and unvalued powers in any given society, without first understanding the overarching ideology and deeper assumptions of the culture that render such powers trivial.

The Universality of Female Subordination

What do I mean when I say that everywhere, in every known culture, women are considered in some degree inferior to men? First of all, I must stress that I am talking about *cultural* evaluations; I am saying that each culture, in its own way and on its own terms, makes this evaluation. But what would constitute evidence that a particular culture considers women inferior?

Three types of data would suffice: (1) elements of cultural ideology and informants' statements that *explicitly* devalue women, according them, their roles, their tasks, their products, and their social milieux less prestige than are accorded men and the male correlates; (2) symbolic devices, such as the attribution of defilement, which may be interpreted as *implicity* making a statement of inferior valuation; and (3) social-structural arrangements that exclude women from participation in or contact with some realm in which the highest powers of the society are felt to reside.[2] These three types of data may all of course be interrelated in any particular system, though they need not necessarily be. Further, any one of them will usually be sufficient to make the point of female inferiority in a given culture. Certainly, female exclusion from the most sacred rite or the highest political council is sufficient evidence. Certainly, explicit cultural ideology devaluing women (and their tasks, roles, products, etc.) is sufficient evidence. Symbolic indicators such as defilement are usually sufficient, although in a few cases in which, say, men and women are equally polluting to one another, a further indicator is required—and is, as far as my investigations have ascertained, always available.

On any or all of these counts, then, I would flatly assert that we find women subordinated to men in every known society. The search for a genuinely egalitarian, let alone matriarchal, culture has proved fruitless. An example from one society that has traditionally been on the credit side of this ledger will suffice. Among the matrilineal Crow, as Lowie (1956) points out, "Women . . . had highly honorific offices in the Sun Dance; they could become directors of the Tobacco Ceremony and played, if anything, a more conspicuous part in it than the men; they sometimes played the hostess in the Cooked Meat Festival; they were not debarred from sweating or doctoring or from seeking a vision." . . . Nonetheless, "Women [during menstruation] formerly rode inferior horses and evidently this loomed as a source of contamination, for they were not allowed to approach either a wounded man or men starting on a war party. A taboo still lingers against their coming near sacred objects at these times." . . . Further, just before enumerating women's rights of participation in the various rituals noted above, Lowie mentions one particular Sun Dance Doll bundle that was not supposed to be unwrapped by a woman. . . . Pursuing this trail we find: "According to all Lodge Grass informants and most others, the doll owned by Wrinkled-face took precedence not only of other dolls but of all other Crow medicines whatsoever. . . . This particular doll was not supposed to be handled by a woman." . . .[3]

In sum, the Crow are probably a fairly typical case. Yes, women have certain powers and rights, in this case some that place them in fairly high positions. Yet ultimately the line is drawn: menstruation is a threat to warfare, one of the most valued institutions of the tribe, one that is central to their self-definition; and the most sacred object of the tribe is taboo to the direct sight and touch of women.

Similar examples could be multiplied ad infinitum, but I think the onus is no longer upon us to demonstrate that female subordination is a cultural universal; it is up to those who would argue against the point to bring forth counterexamples. I shall take the universal secondary status of women as a given, and proceed from there.

Nature and Culture

How are we to explain the universal devaluation of women? We could of course rest the case on biological determinism. There is something genetically inherent in the male of the species, so the biological determinists would argue, that makes them the naturally dominant sex; that "something" is lacking in females, and as a result women are not only naturally subordinate but in general quite satisfied with their position, since it affords them protection and the opportunity to maximize maternal pleasures, which to them are the most satisfying experiences of life. Without going into a detailed refutation of this position, I think it fair to say that it has failed to be established to the satisfaction of almost anyone in academic anthropology. This is to say, not that biological facts are irrelevant, or that men and women are not different, but that these facts and differences only take on significance of superior/inferior within the framework of culturally defined value systems.

If we are unwilling to rest the case on genetic determinism, it seems to me that we have only one way to proceed. We must attempt to interpret female subordination in light of other universals, factors built into the structure of the most generalized situation in which all human beings, in whatever culture, find themselves. For example, every human being has a physical body and a sense of nonphysical mind, is part of a society of other individuals and an inheritor of a cultural tradition, and must engage in some relationship, however mediated, with "nature," or the nonhuman realm, in order to survive. Every human being is born (to a mother) and ultimately dies, all are assumed to have an interest in personal survival, and society/culture has its own interest in (or at least momentum toward) continuity and survival, which transcends the lives and deaths of particular individuals. And so forth. It is in the realm of such universals of the human condition that we must seek an explanation for the universal fact of female devaluation.

I translate the problem, in other words, into

the following simple question. What could there be in the generalized structure and conditions of existence, common to every culture, that would lead every culture to place a lower value upon women? Specifically, my thesis is that woman is being identified with—or, if you will, seems to be a symbol of—something that every culture devalues, something that every culture defines as being of a lower order of existence than itself. Now it seems that there is only one thing that would fit that description, and that is "nature" in the most generalized sense. Every culture, or, generically, "culture," is engaged in the process of generating and sustaining systems of meaningful forms (symbols, artifacts, etc.) by means of which humanity transcends the givens of natural existence, bends them to its purposes, controls them in its interest. We may thus broadly equate culture with the notion of human consciousness, or with the products of human consciousness (i.e., systems of thought and technology), by means of which humanity attempts to assert control over nature.

Now the categories of "nature" and "culture" are of course conceptual categories—one can find no boundary out in the actual world between the two states or realms of being. And there is no question that some cultures articulate a much stronger opposition between the two categories than others—it has even been argued that primitive peoples (some or all) do not see or intuit any distinction between the human cultural state and the state of nature at all. Yet I would maintain that the universality of ritual betokens an assertion in all human cultures of the specifically human ability to act upon and regulate, rather than passively move with and be moved by, the givens of natural existence. In ritual, the purposive manipulation of given forms toward regulating and sustaining order, every culture asserts that proper relations between human existence and natural forces depend upon culture's employing its special powers to regulate the overall processes of the world and life.

One realm of cultural thought in which these points are often articulated is that of concepts of purity and pollution. Virtually every culture has some such beliefs, which seem in large part (though not, of course, entirely) to be concerned with the relationship between culture and nature. . . . A well-known aspect of purity/pollution beliefs cross-culturally is that of the natural "contagion" of pollution; left to its own devices, pollution (for these purposes grossly equated with the unregulated operation of natural energies) spreads and overpowers all that it comes in contact with. Thus a puzzle—if pollution is so strong, how can anything be purified? Why is the purifying agent not itself polluted? The answer, in keeping with the present line of argument, is that purification is effected in a ritual context; purification ritual, as a purposive activity that pits self-conscious (symbolic) action against natural energies, is more powerful than those energies.

In any case, my point is simply that every culture implicitly recognizes and asserts a distinction between the operation of nature and the operation of culture (human consciousness and its products); and further, that the distinctiveness of culture rests precisely on the fact that it can under most circumstances transcend natural conditions and turn them to its purposes. Thus culture (i.e., every culture) at some level of awareness asserts itself to be not only distinct from but superior to nature, and that sense of distinctiveness and superiority rests precisely on the ability to transform—to "socialize" and "culturalize"—nature.

Returning now to the issue of women, their pan-cultural second-class status could be accounted for, quite simply, by postulating that women are being identified or symbolically associated with nature, as opposed to men, who are identified with culture. Since it is always culture's project to subsume and transcend nature, if women were considered part of nature, then culture would find it "natural" to subordinate, not to say oppress, them. Yet although this argument can be shown to have considerable force, it seems to oversimplify the case. The formulation I would like to defend and elaborate on in the following section, then, is that women are seen "merely" as being *closer* to nature than men. That is, culture (still equated relatively unambiguously with men) recognizes that women are active participants in its special processes, but at the same time sees them as being more rooted in, or having more direct affinity with, nature.

The revision may seem minor or even trivial, but I think it is a more accurate rendering of cultural assumptions. Further, the argument cast in these terms has several analytic advantages over the simpler formulation; I shall discuss these later. It might simply be stressed here that the revised argument would still account for the pan-cultural devaluation of women, for even if women are not equated with nature, they are nonetheless seen as representing a lower order of being, as being less transcendent of nature than men are. The next task of the paper, then, is to consider why they might be viewed in that way.

Why Is Woman Seen as Closer to Nature?

It all begins of course with the body and the natural procreative functions specific to women alone. We can sort out for discussion three levels at which this absolute physiological fact has significance: (1) woman's *body and its functions,* more involved more of the time with "species life," seem to place her closer to nature, in contrast to man's physiology, which frees him more completely to take up the projects of culture; (2) woman's body and its functions place her in *social roles* that in turn are considered to be at a lower order of the cultural process than man's; and (3) woman's traditional social roles, imposed because of her body and its functions, in turn give her a different *psychic structure,* which, like her physiological nature and her social roles, is seen as being closer to nature. I shall discuss each of these points in turn, showing first how in each instance certain factors strongly tend to align woman with nature, then indicating other factors that demonstrate her full alignment with culture, the combined factors thus placing her in a problematic intermediate position. It will become clear in the course of the discussion why men seem by contrast less intermediate, more purely "cultural" than women. And I reiterate that I am dealing only at the level of cultural and human universals. These arguments are intended to apply to generalized humanity; they grow out of the human condition, as humanity has experienced and confronted it up to the present day.

1. *Woman's physiology seen as closer to nature.* This part of my argument has been anticipated, with subtlety, cogency, and a great deal of hard data, by de Beauvoir.... De Beauvoir reviews the physiological structure, development, and functions of the human female and concludes that "the female, to a greater extent than the male, is the prey of the species." ... She points out that many major areas and processes of the woman's body serve no apparent function for the health and stability of the individual; on the contrary, as they perform their specific organic functions, they are often sources of discomfort, pain, and danger. The breasts are irrelevant to personal health; they may be excised at any time of a woman's life. "Many of the ovarian secretions function for the benefit of the egg, promoting its maturation and adapting the uterus to its requirements; in respect to the organism as a whole, they make for disequilibrium rather than for regulation—the woman is adapted to the needs of the egg rather than to her own requirements." ... Menstruation is often uncomfortable, sometimes painful; it frequently has negative emotional correlates and in any case involves bothersome tasks of cleansing and waste disposal; and—a point that de Beauvoir does not mention—in many cultures it interrupts a woman's routine, putting her in a stigmatized state involving various restrictions on her activities and social contacts. In pregnancy many of the woman's vitamin and mineral resources are channeled into nourishing the fetus, depleting her own strength and energies. And finally, childbirth itself is painful and dangerous.... In sum, de Beauvoir concludes that the female "is more enslaved to the species than the male, her animality is more manifest." ...

While de Beauvoir's book is ideological, her survey of woman's physiological situation seems fair and accurate. It is simply a fact that proportionately more of woman's body space, for a greater percentage of her lifetime, and at some—sometimes great—cost to her personal health, strength, and general stability, is taken up with the natural processes surrounding the reproduction of the species.

De Beauvoir goes on to discuss the negative implications of woman's "enslavement to the species" in relation to the projects in which humans engage, projects through which culture is generated and defined. She arrives thus at the crux of her argument . . . :

Here we have the key to the whole mystery. On the biological level a species is maintained only by creating itself anew; but this creation results only in repeating the same Life in more individuals. But man assures the repetition of Life while transcending Life through Existence [e.g., goal-oriented, meaningful action]; by this transcendence he creates values that deprive pure repetition of all value. In the animal, the freedom and variety of male activities are vain because no project is involved. Except for his services to the species, what he does is immaterial. Whereas in serving the species, the human male also remodels the face of the earth, he creates new instruments, he invents, he shapes the future.

In other words, woman's body seems to doom her to mere reproduction of life; the male, in contrast, lacking natural creative functions, must (or has the opportunity to) assert his creativity externally, "artificially," through the medium of technology and symbols. In so doing, he creates relatively lasting, eternal, transcendent objects, while the woman creates only perishables— human beings.

This formulation opens up a number of important insights. It speaks, for example, to the great puzzle of why male activities involving the destruction of life (hunting and warfare) are often given more prestige than the female's ability to give birth, to create life. Within de Beauvoir's framework, we realize it is not the killing that is the relevant and valued aspect of hunting and warfare; rather, it is the transcendental (social, cultural) nature of these activities, as opposed to the naturalness of the process of birth: "For it is not in giving life but in risking life that man is raised above the animal; that is why superiority has been accorded in humanity not to the sex that brings forth but to that which kills." . . .

Thus if male is, as I am suggesting, everywhere (unconsciously) associated with cul-

ture and female seems closer to nature, the rationale for these associations is not very difficult to grasp, merely from considering the implications of the physiological contrast between male and female. At the same time, however, woman cannot be consigned fully to the category of nature, for it is perfectly obvious that she is a full-fledged human being endowed with human consciousness just as a man is; she is half of the human race, without whose cooperation the whole enterprise would collapse. She may seem more in the possession of nature than man, but having consciousness, she thinks and speaks; she generates, communicates, and manipulates symbols, categories, and values. She participates in human dialogues not only with other women but also with men. As Lévi-Strauss says, "Woman could never become just a sign and nothing more, since even in a man's world she is still a person, and since insofar as she is defined as a sign she must [still] be recognized as a generator of signs." . . .

Indeed, the fact of woman's full human consciousness, her full involvement in and commitment to culture's project of transcendence over nature, may ironically explain another of the great puzzles of "the woman problem"—woman's nearly universal unquestioning acceptance of her own devaluation. For it would seem that, as a conscious human and member of culture, she has followed out the logic of culture's arguments and has reached culture's conclusions along with the men. As de Beauvoir puts it . . . :

For she, too, is an existent, she feels the urge to surpass, and her project is not mere repetition but transcendence towards a different future—in her heart of hearts she finds confirmation of the masculine pretensions. She joins the men in the festivals that celebrate the successes and victories of the males. Her misfortune is to have been biologically destined for the repetition of Life, when even in her own view Life does not carry within itself its reasons for being, reasons that are more important than life itself.

In other words, woman's consciousness— her membership, as it were, in culture—is evidenced in part by the very fact that she accepts her own devaluation and takes culture's point of view.

I have tried here to show one part of the logic of that view, the part that grows directly from the physiological differences between men and women. Because of woman's greater bodily involvement with the natural functions surrounding reproduction, she is seen as more a part of nature than man is. Yet in part because of her consciousness and participation in human social dialogue, she is recognized as a participant in culture. Thus she appears as something intermediate between culture and nature, lower on the scale of transcendence than man.

2. *Woman's social role seen as closer to nature.* Woman's physiological functions, I have just argued, may tend in themselves to motivate[4] a view of woman as closer to nature, a view she herself, as an observer of herself and the world, would tend to agree with. Woman creates naturally from within her own being, whereas man is free to, or forced to, create artificially, that is, through cultural means, and in such a way as to sustain culture. In addition, I now wish to show how woman's physiological functions have tended universally to limit her social movement, and to confine her universally to certain social contexts which *in turn* are seen as closer to nature. That is, not only her bodily processes but the social situation in which her bodily processes locate her may carry this significance. And insofar as she is permanently associated (in the eyes of culture) with these social milieux, they add weight (perhaps the decisive part of the burden) to the view of woman as closer to nature. I refer here of course to woman's confinement to the domestic family context, a confinement motivated, no doubt, by her lactation processes.

Woman's body, like that of all female mammals, generates milk during and after pregnancy for the feeding of the newborn baby. The baby cannot survive without breast milk or some similar formula at this stage of life. Since the mother's body goes through its lactation processes in direct relation to a pregnancy with a particular child, the relationship of nursing between mother and child is seen as a natural bond, other feeding arrangements being seen in most cases as unnatural and makeshift. Mothers and their children, according to cultural reasoning, belong together. Further, children beyond infancy are not strong enough to engage in major work, yet are mobile and unruly and not capable of understanding various dangers; they thus require supervision and constant care. Mother is the obvious person for this task, as an extension of her natural nursing bond with the children, or because she has a new infant and is already involved with child-oriented activities. Her own activities are thus circumscribed by the limitations and low levels of her children's strengths and skills:[5] she is confined to the domestic family group; "woman's place is in the home."

Woman's association with the domestic circle would contribute to the view of her as closer to nature in several ways. In the first place, the sheer fact of constant association with children plays a role in the issue; one can easily see how infants and children might themselves be considered part of nature. Infants are barely human and utterly unsocialized; like animals they are unable to walk upright, they excrete without control, they do not speak. Even slightly older children are clearly not yet fully under the sway of culture. They do not yet understand social duties, responsibilities, and morals; their vocabulary and their range of learned skills are small. One finds implicit recognition of an association between children and nature in many cultural practices. For example, most cultures have initiation rites for adolescents (primarily for boys; I shall return to this point below), the point of which is to move the child ritually from a less than fully human state into full participation in society and culture; many cultures do not hold funeral rites for children who die at early ages, explicitly because they are not yet fully social beings. Thus children are likely to be categorized with nature, and woman's close association with children may compound her potential for being seen as closer to nature herself. It is ironic that the rationale for boys' initiation rites in many cultures is that the boys must be purged of the defilement accured from being around mother and other women so much of the time, when in fact much of the woman's defilement may derive from her being around children so much of the time.

The second major problematic implication of women's close association with the domestic context derives from certain structural conflicts between the family and society at large in any social system. The implications of the "domestic/public opposition" in relation to the position of women have been cogently developed by Rosaldo ..., and I simply wish to show its relevance to the present argument. The notion that the domestic unit—the biological family charged with reproducing and socializing new members of the society—is opposed to the public entity—the superimposed network of alliances and relationships that *is* the society—is also the basis of Lévi-Strauss's argument in the *Elementary Structures of Kinship*. . . . Lévi-Strauss argues not only that this opposition is present in every social system, but further that it has the significance of the opposition between nature and culture. The universal incest prohibition[6] and its ally, the rule of exogamy (marriage outside the group), ensure that "the risk of seeing a biological family become established as a closed system is definitely eliminated; the biological group can no longer stand apart, and the bond of alliance with another family ensures the dominance of the social over the biological, and of the cultural over the natural." . . . And although not every culture articulates a radical opposition between the domestic and the public as such, it is hardly contestable that the domestic is always subsumed by the public; domestic units are allied with one another through the enactment of rules that are logically at a higher level than the units themselves; this creates an emergent unit—society—that is logically at a higher level than the domestic units of which it is composed.

Now, since women are associated with, and indeed are more or less confined to, the domestic context, they are identified with this lower order of social/cultural organiza-tion. What are the implications of this for the way they are viewed? First, if the specifically biological (reproductive) function of the family is stressed, as in Lévi-Strauss's formulation, then the family (and hence woman) is identified with nature pure and simple, as opposed to culture. But this is obviously too simple; the point seems more adequately formulated as follows: the family (and hence woman) represents lower-level, socially fragmenting, particularistic sort of concerns, as opposed to interfamilial relations representing higher-level, integrative, universalistic sorts of concerns. Since men lack a "natural" basis (nursing, generalized to child care) for a familial orientation, their sphere of activity is defined at the level of interfamilial relations. And hence, so the cultural reasoning seems to go, men are the "natural" proprietors of religion, ritual, politics, and other realms of cultural thought and action in which universalistic statements of spiritual and social synthesis are made. Thus men are identified not only with culture, in the sense of all human creativity, as oppposed to nature; they are identified in particular with culture in the old-fashioned sense of the finer and higher aspects of human thought—art, religion, law, etc.

Here again, the logic of cultural reasoning aligning woman with a lower order of culture than man is clear and, on the surface, quite compelling. At the same time, woman cannot be fully consigned to nature, for there are aspects of her situation, even within the domestic context, that undeniably demonstrate her participation in the cultural process. It goes without saying, of course, that except for nursing newborn infants (and artificial nursing devices can cut even this biological tie), there is no reason why it has to be mother—as opposed to father, or anyone else—who remains identified with child care. But even assuming that other practical and emotional reasons conspire to keep woman in this sphere, it is possible to show that her activities in the domestic context could as logically put her squarely in the category of culture.

In the first place, one must point out that

woman not only feeds and cleans up after children in a simple caretaker operation; she in fact is the primary agent of their early socialization. It is she who transforms newborn infants from mere organisms into cultured humans, teaching them manners and the proper ways to behave in order to become full-fledged members of the culture. On the basis of her socializing functions alone, she could not be more a representative of culture. Yet in virtually every society there is a point at which the socialization of boys is transferred to the hands of men. The boys are considered, in one set of terms or another, not yet "really" socialized; their entrée into the realm of fully human (social, cultural) status can be accomplished only by men. We still see this in our own schools, where there is a gradual inversion in the proportion of female to male teachers up through the grades: most kindergarten teachers are female; most university professors are male.[7]

Or again, take cooking. In the overwhelming majority of societies cooking is the woman's work. No doubt this stems from practical considerations—since the woman has to stay home with the baby, it is convenient for her to perform the chores centered in the home. But if it is true, as Lévi-Strauss has argued . . . , that transforming the raw into the cooked may represent, in many systems of thought, the transition from nature to culture, then here we have woman aligned with this important culturalizing process, which could easily place her in the category of culture, triumphing over nature. Yet it is also interesting to note that when a culture (e.g., France or China) develops a tradition of *haute cuisine*—"real" cooking, as opposed to trivial ordinary domestic cooking—the high chefs are almost always men. Thus the pattern replicates that in the area of socialization—women perform lower-level conversions from nature to culture, but when the culture distinguishes a higher level of the same functions, the higher level is restricted to men.

In short, we see once again some sources of woman's appearing more intermediate than man with respect to the nature/culture dichotomy. Her "natural" association with the domestic context (motivated by her natural lactation functions) tends to compound her potential for being viewed as closer to nature, because of the animal-like nature of children, and because of the infrasocial connotation of the domestic group as against the rest of society. Yet at the same time her socializing and cooking functions within the domestic context show her to be a powerful agent of the cultural process, constantly transforming raw natural resources into cultural products. Belonging to culture, yet appearing to have stronger and more direct connections with nature, she is once again seen as situated between the two realms.

3. *Woman's psyche seen as closer to nature.* The suggestion that woman has not only a different body and a different social locus from man but also a different psychic structure is most controversial. I will argue that she probably *does* have a different psychic structure, but I will draw heavily on Chodorow's paper . . . to establish first that her psychic structure need not be assumed to be innate; it can be accounted for, as Chodorow convincingly shows, by the facts of the probably universal female socialization experience. Nonetheless, if we grant the empirical near universality of a "feminine psyche" with certain specific characteristics, these characteristics would add weight to the cultural view of woman as closer to nature.

It is important to specify what we see as the dominant and universal aspects of the feminine psyche. If we postulate emotionality or irrationality, we are confronted with those traditions in various parts of the world in which women functionally are, and are seen as, more practical, pragmatic, and thisworldly than men. One relevant dimension that does seem pan-culturally applicable is that of relative concreteness vs. relative abstractness: the feminine personality tends to be involved with concrete feelings, things, and people, rather than with abstract entities; it tends toward personalism and particularism. A second, closely related, dimension seems to be that of relative subjectivity vs. relative objectivity: Chodorow cites Carlson's study (1971), which concludes that "males represent experiences of self, others, space, and time in individualistic, objective, and distant ways, while females represent experiences in relatively interpersonal, subjective, immediate ways." . . . Although this and other studies were done in Western societies, Chodorow sees their findings on the differences between male and female personality—roughly, that men are more objective and inclined to relate in terms of relatively abstract categories, women more subjective and inclined to relate in terms of relatively concrete phenomena—as "general and nearly universal differences." . . .

But the thrust of Chodorow's elegantly argued paper is that these differences are not innate or genetically programmed; they arise from nearly universal features of family structure, namely that "women, universally, are largely responsible for early child care and for (at least) later female socialization" . . . and that "the structural situation of child rearing, reinforced by female and male role training, produces these differences, which are replicated and reproduced in the sexual sociology of adult life." . . . Chodorow argues that, because mother is the early socializer of both boys and girls, both develop "personal identification" with her, i.e., diffuse identification with her general personality, behavior traits, values, and attitudes. . . . A son, however, must ultimately shift to a masculine role identity, which involves building an identification with the father. Since father is almost always more remote than mother (he is rarely involved in child care, and perhaps works away from home much of the day), building an identification with father involves a "positional identification," i.e., identification with father's male role as a collection of abstract elements rather than a personal identification with father as a real individual. . . . Further, as the boy enters the larger social world, he finds it in fact organized around more abstract and universalistic criteria . . . , as I have indicated in the previous section; thus his earlier socialization prepares him for, and is reinforced by, the type of adult social experience he will have.

For a young girl, in contrast, the personal identification with mother, which was created in early infancy, can persist into the process of learning female role identity. Because mother is immediate and present when the daughter is learning role identity, learning to be a woman involves the continuity and development of a girl's relationship to her mother, and sustains the identification with her as an individual; it does not involve the learning of externally defined role characteristics. . . . This pattern prepares the girl for, and is fully reinforced by, her social situation in later life; she will become involved in the world of women, which is characterized by few formal role differences . . . , and which involves again, in motherhood, "personal identification" with *her* children. And so the cycle begins anew.

Chodorow demonstrates to my satisfaction at least that the feminine personality, characterized by personalism and particularism, can be explained as having been generated by social-structural arrangements rather than by innate biological factors. The point need not be belabored further. But insofar as the "feminine personality" has been a nearly universal fact, it can be argued that its characteristics may have contributed further to the view of women as being somehow less cultural than men. That is, women would tend to enter into relationships with the world that culture might see as being more "like nature"—immanent and embedded in things as given—than "like culture"—transcending and transforming things through the superimposition of abstract categories and transpersonal values. Woman's relationships tend to be, like nature, relatively unmediated, more direct, whereas man not only tends to relate in a more mediated way, but in fact ultimately often relates more consistently and strongly to the mediating categories and forms than to the persons or objects themselves.

It is thus not difficult to see how the feminine personality would lend weight to a view of women as being "closer to nature." Yet at the same time, the modes of relating characteristic of women undeniably play a powerful and important role in the cultural process. For just as relatively unmediated relating is in some sense at the lower end of the spectrum of human spiritual functions, embedded and particularizing rather than transcending and synthesizing, yet that mode of relating also stands at the upper end of that spectrum. Consider the mother-child relationship. Mothers tend to be committed to their children as individuals, regardless of sex, age, beauty, clan affiliation, or other categories in which the child might participate. Now any relationship with this quality—not just mother and child but any sort of highly personal, relatively unmediated commitment—may be seen as a challenge to culture and society "from below," insofar as it represents the fragmentary potential of individual loyalties vis-à-vis the solidarity of the group. But it may also be seen as embodying the synthesizing agent for culture and society "from above," in that it represents generalized human values above and beyond loyalties to particular social categories. Every society must have social categories that transcend personal loyalties, but every society must also generate a sense of ultimate moral unity for all its members above and beyond those social categories. Thus that psychic mode seemingly typical of women, which tends to disregard categories and to seek "communion" . . . directly and personally with others, although it may appear infracultural from one point of view, is at the same time associated with the highest levels of the cultural process.

The Implications of Intemediacy

My primary purpose in this paper has been to attempt to explain the universal secondary status of women. Intellectually and personally, I felt strongly challenged by this problem; I felt compelled to deal with it before undertaking an analysis of woman's position in any particular society. Local variables of economy, ecology, history, political and social structure, values, and world view—these could explain variations within this universal, but they could not explain the universal itself. And if we were not to accept the ideology of biological determinism, then explanation, it seemed to me, could only proceed by reference to other universals of the human cultural situation. Thus the general outlines of the approach—although not of course the particular solution offered—were determined by the problem itself, and not by any predilection on my part for global abstract structural analysis.

I argued that the universal devaluation of women could be explained by postulating that women are seen as closer to nature than men, men being seen as more unequivocally occupying the high ground of culture. The culture/nature distinction is itself a product of culture, culture being minimally defined as the transcendence, by means of systems of thought and technology, of the natural givens of existence. This of course is an analytic definition, but I argued that at some level every culture incorporates this notion in one form or other, if only through the performance of ritual as an assertion of the human ability to manipulate those givens. In any case, the core of the paper was concerned with showing why women might tend to be assumed, over and over, in the most diverse sorts of world views and in cultures of every degree of complexity, to be closer to nature than men. Woman's physiology, more involved more of the time with "species of life"; woman's association with the structurally subordinate domestic context, charged with the crucial function of transforming animal-like infants into cultured beings; "woman's psyche," appropriately molded to mothering functions by her own socialization and tending toward greater personalism and less mediated modes of relating—all these factors make woman appear to be rooted more directly and deeply in nature. At the same time, however, her "membership" and fully necessary participation in culture are recognized by culture and cannot be denied. Thus she is seen to occupy an intermediate position between culture and nature.

This intermediacy has several implications for analysis, depending upon how it is interpreted. First, of course, it answers my primary question of why woman is everywhere seen as lower than man, for even if she is not seen as nature pure and simple, she is still seen as achieving less transcendence of nature than man. Here intermediate simply means "middle status" on a hierarchy of being from culture to nature.

Second, intermediate may have the significance of "mediating," i.e., performing some sort of synthesizing or converting function between nature and culture, here seen (by culture) not as two ends of a continuum but as two radically different sorts of processes in the world. The domestic unit—and hence woman, who in virtually every case appears as its primary representative—is one of culture's crucial agencies for the conversion of nature into culture, especially with reference to the socialization of children. Any culture's continued viability depends upon properly socialized individuals who will see the world in that culture's terms and adhere more or less unquestioningly to its moral precepts. The functions of the domestic unit must be closely controlled in order to ensure this outcome; the stability of the domestic unit as an institution must be placed as far as possible beyond question. (We see some aspects of the protection of the integrity and stability of the domestic group in the powerful taboos against incest, matricide, patricide, and fratricide.[8]) Insofar as woman is universally the primary agent of early socialization and is seen as virtually the embodiment of the functions of the domestic group, she will tend to come under the heavier restrictions and circumscriptions surrounding that unit. Her (culturally defined) intermediate position between nature and culture, here having the significance of her *mediation* (i.e., performing conversion functions) between nature and culture, would thus account not only for her lower status but for the greater restrictions placed upon her activities. In virtually every culture her permissible sexual activities are more closely circumscribed than man's, she is offered a much small range of role choices, and she is afforded direct access to a far more limited range of its social institutions. Further, she is almost universally socialized to have a narrower and generally more conservative set of attitudes and views than man, and the limited social contexts of her adult life reinforce this situation. This socially engendered conservatism and traditionalism of woman's thinking is another—perhaps the worst, certainly the most insidious—mode of social restriction, and would clearly be related to her traditional function of producing well-socialized members of the group.

Finally, woman's intermediate position may have the implication of greater symbolic ambiguity. . . . Shifting our image of the culture/nature relationship once again, we may envision culture in this case as a small clearing within the forest of the larger natural system. From this point of view, that which is intermediate between culture and nature is located on the continuous periphery of culture's clearing; and though it may thus appear to stand both above and below (and beside) culture, it is simply outside and around it. We can begin to understand then how a single system of cultural thought can often assign to woman completely polarized and apparently contradictory meanings, since extremes, as we say, meet. That she often represents both life and death is only the simplest example one could mention.

For another perspective on the same point, it will be recalled that the psychic mode associated with women seems to stand at both the bottom and the top of the scale of human modes of relating. The tendency in that mode is to get involved more directly with people as individuals and not as representatives of one social category or another; this mode can be seen as either "ignoring" (and thus subverting) or "transcending" (and thus achieving a higher synthesis of) those social categories, depending upon the cultural view for any given purpose. Thus we can account easily for both the subversive symbols (witches, evil eye, menstrual pollution, castrating mothers) and the feminine symbols of transcendence (mother goddesses, merciful dispensers of salvation, female symbols of justice, and the strong presence of feminine symbolism in the realms of art, religion, ritual, and law). Feminine symbolism, far more often than masculine symbolism, manifests this propensity toward polarized ambiguity—sometimes utterly exalted, sometimes utterly debased, rarely within the normal range of human possibilities.

If woman's (culturally viewed) intermediacy between culture and nature has this implication of generalized ambiguity of meaning characteristic of marginal phenomena, then we are also in a better position to account for those cultural and historical "inversions" in which women are in some way or other symbolically aligned with culture and men with nature. A number of cases come to mind: the Sirionó of Brazil, among whom, according to Ingham . . . , "nature, the raw, and maleness" are opposed to "culture, the cooked, and femaleness,"[9] Nazi Germany, in which women were said to be the guardians of culture and morals; European courtly love, in which man considered himself the beast and woman the pristine exalted object—a pattern of thinking that persists, for example, among modern Spanish peasants. . . . And there are no doubt other cases of this sort, including some aspects of our own culture's view of women. Each such instance of an alignment of women with culture rather than nature requires detailed analysis of specific historical and ethnographic data. But in indicating how nature in general, and the feminine mode of interpersonal relations in particular, can appear from certain points of view to stand both under and over (but really simply outside of) the sphere of culture's hegemony, we have at least laid the groundwork for such analyses.

In short, the postulate that woman is viewed as closer to nature than man has several implications for further analysis, and can be interpreted in several different ways. If it is viewed simply as a *middle* position on a scale from culture down to nature, then it is still seen as lower than culture and thus accounts for the pan-cultural assumption that woman is lower than man in the order of things. If it is read as a *mediating* element in the culture-nature relationship, then it may account in part for the cultural tendency not merely to devalue woman but to circumscribe and restrict her functions, since culture must maintain control over its (pragmatic and symbolic) mechanisms for the conversion of nature into culture. And if it is read as an *ambiguous* status between culture and nature, it may help account for the fact that, in specific cultural ideologies and symbolizations, woman can occasionally be aligned with culture, and in any event is often assigned polarized and contradictory meanings within a single symbolic system. Middle status, mediating functions, ambiguous meaning—all are different readings, for different contextual purposes, of woman's being seen as intermediate between nature and culture.

Conclusions

Ultimately, it must be stressed again that the whole scheme is a construct of culture rather than a fact of nature. Woman is not "in reality" any closer to (or further from) nature than man—both have consciousness, both are mortal. But there are certainly reasons why she appears that way, which is what I have tried to show in this paper. The result is a (sadly) efficient feedback system: various aspects of woman's situation (physical, social, psychological) contribute to her being seen as closer to nature, while the view of her as closer to nature is in turn embodied in institutional forms that reproduce her situation. The implications for social change are similarly circular: a different cultural view can only grow out of a different social actuality; a different social actuality can only grow out of a different cultural view.

It is clear, then, that the situation must be attacked from both sides. Efforts directed solely at changing the social institutions—through setting quotas on hiring, for example, or through passing equal-pay-for-equal-work laws—cannot have far-reaching effects if cultural language and imagery continue to purvey a relatively devalued view of women. But at the same time efforts directed solely at changing cultural assumptions—through male and female consciousness-raising groups, for example, or through revision of educational materials and mass-media imagery—cannot be successful unless the institutional base of the society is changed to support and reinforce the changed cultural view. Ultimately, both men and women can and must be equally involved in projects of creativity and transcendence. Only then will women be seen as aligned with culture, in culture's ongoing dialectic with nature.

Notes

1. It is true of course that *yin*, the female principle, has a negative valence. Nonetheless,

there is an absolute complementarity of *yin* and *yang* in Taoism, a recognition that the world requires the equal operation and interaction of both principles for its survival.

2. Some anthropologists might consider this type of evidence (socialstructural arrangements that exclude women, explicitly or de facto, from certain groups, roles, or statuses) to be a subtype of the second type of evidence (symbolic formulations of inferiority). I would not disagree with this view, although most social anthropologists would probably separate the two types.

3. While we are on the subject of injustices of various kinds, we might note that Lowie secretly bought this doll, the most sacred object in the tribal repertoire, from its custodian, the widow of Wrinkled-face. She asked $400 for it, but this price was "far beyond [Lowie's] means," and he finally got it for $80. . . .

4. Semantic theory uses the concept of motivation of meaning, which encompasses various ways in which a meaning may be assigned to a symbol because of certain objective properties of that symbol, rather than by arbitrary association. In a sense, this entire paper is an inquiry into the motivation of the meaning of woman as a symbol, asking why woman may be unconsciously assigned the significance of being closer to nature. . . .

5. A situation that often serves to make her more childlike herself.

6. David M. Schneider (personal communication) is prepared to argue that the incest taboo is not universal, on the basis of material from Oceania. Let us say at this point, then, that it is virtually universal.

7. I remember having my first male teacher in the fifth grade, and I remember being excited about that—it was somehow more grown-up.

8. Nobody seems to care much about sororicide—a point that ought to be investigated.

9. Ingham's discussion is rather ambiguous itself, since women are also associated with animals: "The contrasts man/animal and man/woman are evidently similar . . . hunting is the means of acquiring women as well as animals." . . . A careful reading of the data suggests that both women and animals are mediators between nature and culture in this tradition.

Study Questions

1. What levels of the problem of the subordination of women does Ortner distinguish? Which does Ortner focus on?

2. What sorts of evidence does Ortner think would prove that a given culture thinks women are inferior? Does Ortner prove her claim that in every human culture, women are considered inferior?

3. How is biological determinism used to explain the universal devaluation of women? On what basis does Ortner reject that explanation?

4. What does Ortner mean by "nature" and "culture"? What leads Ortner to believe that even primitive cultures distinguish nature from culture? How is that distinction relevant to the issue of the devaluation of women?

5. Discuss in detail the reasons women are seen as closer to nature.

6. Discuss the various ways men are identified with culture.

7. Why does Ortner believe that it would be inaccurate to claim that women are considered a part of nature? What implications does women's intermediate status (between nature and culture) have?

The Laugh of the Medusa

Hélène Cixous

I shall speak about women's writing: about *what it will do*. Woman must write her self: must write about women and bring women to writing, from which they have been driven away as violently as from their bodies—for the same reasons, by the same law, with the same fatal goal. Woman must put herself into the text—as into the world and into history—by her own movement.

The future must no longer be determined by the past. I do not deny that the effects of the past are still with us. But I refuse to strengthen them by repeating them, to confer upon them an irremovability the equivalent of destiny, to confuse the biological and the cultural. Anticipation is imperative.

Since these reflections are taking shape in an area just on the point of being discovered, they necessarily bear the mark of our time—a time during which the new breaks away from the old, and, more precisely, the (feminine) new from the old *(la nouvelle de l'ancien)*. Thus, as there are no grounds for establishing a discourse, but rather an arid millennial ground to break, what I say has at least two sides and two aims: to break up, to destroy; and to foresee the unforeseeable, to project.

I write this as a woman, toward women. When I say "woman," I'm speaking of woman in her inevitable struggle against conventional man; and of a universal woman subject who must bring women to their senses and to their meaning in history. But first it must be said that in spite of the enormity of the repression that has kept them in the "dark"—that dark which people have been trying to make them accept as their attribute—there is, at this time, no general woman, no one typical woman. What they have *in common* I will say. But what strikes me is the

"The Laugh of the Medusa," *Signs*, Summer 1976, translated by Keith Cohen and Paula Cohen. This is a revised version of "Le rire de la méduse," which appeared in *L'arc* (1975), pp. 39–54. Reprinted by permission of the University of Chicago Press.

infinite richness of their individual constitutions: you can't talk about *a* female sexuality, uniform, homogeneous, classifiable into codes—any more than you can talk about one unconscious resembling another. Women's imaginary is inexhaustible, like music, painting, writing: their stream of phantasms is incredible.

I have been amazed more than once by a description a woman gave me of a world all her own which she had been secretly haunting since early childhood. A world of searching, the elaboration of a knowledge, on the basis of a systematic experimentation with the bodily functions, a passionate and precise interrogation of her erotogeneity. This practice, extraordinarily rich and inventive, in particular as concerns masturbation, is prolonged or accompanied by a production of forms, a veritable aesthetic activity, each stage of rapture inscribing a resonant vision, a composition, something beautiful. Beauty will no longer be forbidden.

I wished that that woman would write and proclaim this unique empire so that other women, other unacknowledged sovereigns, might exclaim: I, too, overflow; my desires have invented new desires, my body knows unheard-of songs. Time and again I, too, have felt so full of luminous torrents that I could burst—burst with forms much more beautiful than those which are put up in frames and sold for a stinking fortune. And I, too, said nothing, showed nothing; I didn't open my mouth, I didn't repaint my half of the world. I was ashamed. I was afraid, and I swallowed my shame and my fear. I said to myself: You are mad! What's the meaning of these waves, these floods, these outbursts? Where is the ebullient, infinite woman who, immersed as she was in her naiveté, kept in the dark about herself, led into self-disdain by the great arm of parental-conjugal phallocentrism, hasn't been ashamed of her strength? Who, surprised and horrified by the fantastic tumult of her drives (for she was made to believe that a well-adjusted normal woman has a . . . divine composure), hasn't accused herself of being a monster? Who, feeling a funny desire stirring inside her (to sing, to write, to dare to speak, in short, to bring out something new), hasn't thought she was sick? Well, her shameful sickness is that she resists death, that she makes trouble.

And why don't you write? Write! Writing is for you, you are for you; your body is yours, take it. I know why you haven't written. (And why I didn't write before the age of twenty-seven.) Because writing is at once too high, too great for you, it's reserved for the great—that is for "great men"; and it's "silly." Besides, you've written a little, but in secret. And it wasn't good, because it was in secret, and because you punished yourself for writing, because you didn't go all the way, or because you wrote, irresistibly, as when we would masturbate in secret, not to go further, but to attenuate the tension a bit, just enough to take the edge off. And then as soon as we come, we go and make ourselves feel guilty—so as to be forgiven; or to forget, to bury it until the next time.

Write, let no one hold you back, let nothing stop you: not man; not the imbecilic capitalist machinery, in which publishing houses are the crafty, obsequious relayers of imperatives handed down by an economy that works against us and off our backs; and not *yourself*. Smug-faced readers, managing editors, and big bosses don't like the true texts of women—female-sexed texts. That kind scares them.

I write woman: woman must write woman. And man, man. So only an oblique consideration will be found here of man; it's up to him to say where his masculinity and femininity are at: this will concern us once men have opened their eyes and seen themselves clearly.[1]

Now women return from afar, from always: from "without," from the heath where witches are kept alive; from below, from beyond "culture"; from their childhood which men have been trying desperately to make them forget, condemning it to "eternal rest." The little girls and their "ill-mannered" bodies immured, well-preserved, intact unto themselves, in the mirror. Frigidified. But are they ever seething underneath! What an effort it takes—there's

no end to it—for the sex cops to bar their threatening return. Such a display of forces on both sides that the struggle has for centuries been immobilized in the trembling equilibrium of a deadlock.

Here they are, returning, arriving over and again, because the unconscious is impregnable. They have wandered around in circles, confined to the narrow room in which they've been given a deadly brainwashing. You can incarcerate them, slow them down, get away with the old Apartheid routine, but for a time only. As soon as they begin to speak, at the same time as they're taught their name, they can be taught that their territory is black: because you are Africa, you are black. Your continent is dark. Dark is dangerous. You can't see anything in the dark, you're afraid. Don't move, you might fall. Most of all, don't go into the forest. And so we have internalized this horror of the dark.

Men have committed the greatest crime against women. Insidiously, violently, they have led them to hate women, to be their own enemies, to mobilize their immense strength against themselves, to be the executants of their virile needs. They have made for women an antinarcissism! A narcissism which loves itself only to be loved for what women haven't got! They have constructed the infamous logic of antilove.

We the precocious, we the repressed of culture, our lovely mouths gagged with pollen, our wind knocked out of us, we the labyrinths, the ladders, the trampled spaces, the bevies—we are black and we are beautiful.

We're stormy, and that which is our breaks loose from us without our fearing any debilitation. Our glances, our smiles, are spent; laughs exude from all our mouths; our blood flows and we extend ourselves without ever reaching an end; we never hold back our thoughts, our signs, our writing; and we're not afraid of lacking.

What happiness for us who are omitted, brushed aside at the scene of inheritances; we inspire ourselves and we expire without running out of breath, we are everywhere!

From now on, who, if we say so, can say no to us? We've come back from always.

It is time to liberate the New Woman from

the Old by coming to know her—by loving her for getting by, for getting beyond the Old without delay, by going out ahead of what the New Woman will be, as an arrow quits the bow with a movement that gathers and separates the vibrations musically, in order to be more than herself.

I say that we must, for, with a few rare exceptions, there has not yet been any writing that inscribes femininity; exceptions so rare, in fact, that, after plowing through literature across languages, cultures, and ages,[2] one can only be startled at this vain scouting mission. It is well known that the number of women writers (while having increased very slightly from the nineteenth century on) has always been ridiculously small. This is a useless and deceptive fact unless from their species of female writers we do not first deduct the immense majority whose workmanship is in no way different from male writing, and which either obscures women or reproduces the classic representations of women (as sensitive—intuitive—dreamy, etc.).[3]

Let me insert here a parenthetical remark. I mean it when I speak of male writing. I maintain unequivocally that there is such a thing as *marked* writing; that, until now, far more extensively and repressively than is ever suspected or admitted, writing has been run by a libidinal and cultural—hence political, typically masculine—economy; that this is a locus where the repression of women has been perpetuated, over and over, more or less consciously, and in a manner that's frightening since it's often hidden or adorned with the mystifying charms of fiction; that this locus has grossly exaggerated all the signs of sexual opposition (and not sexual difference), where woman has never *her* turn to speak—this being all the more serious and unpardonable in that writing is precisely *the very possibility of change*, the space that can serve as a springboard for subversive thought, the precursory movement of a transformation of social and cultural structures.

Nearly the entire history of writing is confounded with the history of reason, of which it is at once the effect, the support, and one of the privileged alibis. It has been one with the phallocentric tradition. It is indeed that same self-admiring, self-stimulating, self-congratulatory phallocentrism.

With some exceptions, for there have been failures—and if it weren't for them, I wouldn't be writing (I-woman, escapee)—in that enormous machine that has been operating and turning out its "truth" for centuries. There have been poets who would go to any lengths to slip something by at odds with tradition—men capable of loving love and hence capable of loving others and of wanting them, of imagining the woman who would hold out against oppression and constitute herself as a superb, equal, hence "impossible" subject, untenable in a real social framework. Such a woman the poet could desire only by breaking the codes that negate her. Her appearance would necessarily bring on, if not revolution—for the bastion was supposed to be immutable—at least harrowing explosions. At times it is in the fissure caused by an earthquake, through that radical mutation of things brought on by a material upheaval when every structure is for a moment thrown off balance and an ephemeral wildness sweeps order away, that the poet slips something by, for a brief span, of woman. Thus did Kleist expend himself in his yearning for the existence of sister-lovers, maternal daughters, mother-sisters, who never hung their heads in shame. Once the palace of magistrates is restored, it's time to pay: immediate bloody death to the uncontrollable elements.

But only the poets—not the novelists, allies of representationalism. Because poetry involves gaining strength through the unconscious and because the unconscious, that other limitless country, is the place where the repressed manage to survive: women, or as Hoffmann would say, fairies.

She must write her self, because this is the invention of a *new insurgent* writing which, when the moment of her liberation has come, will allow her to carry out the indispensable ruptures and transformations in her history, first at two levels that cannot be separated.

a. Individually. By writing her self, woman will return to the body which has been more than confiscated from her, which has been turned into the uncanny stranger on display—the ailing or dead figure, which so often turns out to be the nasty companion, the cause and location of inhibitions. Censor the body and you censor breath and speech at the same time.

Write your self. Your body must be heard. Only then will the immense resources of the unconscious spring forth. Our naphtha will spread, throughout the world, without dollars—black or gold—nonassessed values that will change the rules of the old game.

To write. An act which will not only "realize" the decensored relation of woman to her sexuality, to her womanly being, giving her access to her native strength; it will give her back her goods, her pleasures, her organs, her immense bodily territories which have been kept under seal; it will tear her away from the super-egoized structure in which she has always occupied the place reserved for the guilty (guilty of everything, guilty at every turn: for having desires, for not having any; for being frigid, for being "too hot"; for not being both at once; for being too motherly and not enough; for having children and for not having any; for nursing and for not nursing . . .)—tear her away by means of this research, this job of analysis and illumination, this emancipation of the marvelous text of her self that she must urgently learn to speak. A woman without a body, dumb, blind, can't possibly be a good fighter. She is reduced to being the servant of the militant male, his shadow. We must kill the false woman who is preventing the live one from breathing. Inscribe the breath of the whole woman.

b. An act that will also be marked by woman's *seizing* the occasion to *speak*, hence her shattering entry into history, which has always been based *on her suppression*. To write and thus to forge for herself the antilogos weapon. To become *at will* the taker and initiator, for her own right, in every symbolic system, in every political process.

It is time for women to start scoring their feats in written and oral language.

Every woman has known the torment of getting up to speak. Her heart racing, at times entirely lost for words, ground and language slipping away—that's how daring a feat, how great a transgression it is for a woman to speak—even just open her mouth—in public. A double distress, for even if she transgresses, her words fall almost always upon the deaf male ear, which hears in language only that which speaks in the masculine.

It is by writing, from and toward women, and by taking up the challenge of speech which has been governed by the phallus, that women will confirm women in a place other than that which is reserved in and by the symbolic, that is, in a place other than silence. Women should break out of the snare of silence. They shouldn't be conned into accepting a domain which is the margin or the harem.

Listen to a woman speak at a public gathering (if she hasn't painfully lost her wind). She doesn't "speak," she throws her trembling body forward; she lets go of herself, she flies; all of her passes into her voice, and it's with her body that she vitally supports the "logic" of her speech. Her flesh speaks true. She lays herself bare. In fact, she physically materializes what she's thinking; she signifies it with her body. In a certain way she *inscribes* what she's saying, because she doesn't deny her drives the intractable and impassioned part they have in speaking. Her speech, even when "theoretical" or political, is never simple or linear or "objectified," generalized: she draws her story into history.

There is not that scission, that division made by the common man between the logic of oral speech and the logic of the text, bound as he is by his antiquated relation—servile, calculating—to mastery. From which proceeds the niggardly lip service which engages only the tiniest part of the body, plus the mask.

In women's speech, as in their writing, that element which never stops resonating, which, once we've been permeated by it, profoundly and imperceptibly touched by it, retains the power of moving us—that element is the song: first music from the first voice of love which is alive in every woman. Why this privileged relationship with the voice? Because no woman stockpiles as many defenses for countering the drives as does a man. You don't build walls around yourself, you don't forego pleasure as "wisely" as he. Even if phallic mystification has generally contaminated good relationships, a woman is never far from "mother" (I mean outside her role functions: the "mother" as nonname and as source of goods). There is always within her at least a little of that good mother's milk. She writes in white ink.

Woman for women—There always remains in woman that force which produces/is produced by the other—in particular, the other woman. *In* her, matrix, cradler; herself giver as her mother and child; she is her own sister-daughter. You might object, "What about she who is the hysterical offspring of a bad mother?" Everything will be changed once woman gives woman to the other woman. There is hidden and always ready in woman the source; the locus for the other. The mother, too, is a metaphor. It is necessary and sufficient that the best of herself be given to woman by another woman for her to be able to love herself and return in love the body that was "born" to her. Touch me, caress me, you the living no-name, give me my self as myself. The relation to the "mother," in terms of intense pleasure and violence, is curtailed no more than the relation to childhood (the child that she was, that she is, that she makes, remakes, undoes, there at the point where, the same, she mothers herself). Text: my body—shot through with streams of song; I don't mean the overbearing, clutchy "mother" but, rather, what touches you, the equivoice that affects you, fills your breast with an urge to come to language and launches your force; the rhythm that laughs you; the intimate recipient who makes all metaphors possible and desirable; body (body? bodies?), no more describable than god, the soul, or the Other; that part of you that leaves a space between yourself and urges you to inscribe in language your woman's style. In women there is always more or less of the mother who makes everything all right, who nourishes, and who stands up against separation; a force that will not be cut off but will knock the wind out of the codes. We will rethink womankind beginning with every form and every period of her body. The Americans remind us, "We are all Lesbians"; that is, don't denigrate woman, don't make of her what men have made of you.

Because the "economy" of her drives is prodigious, she cannot fail, in seizing the occasion to speak, to transform directly and indirectly *all* systems of exchange based on masculine thrift. Her libido will produce far more radical effects of political and social change than some might like to think.

Because she arrives, vibrant, over and again, we are at the beginning of a new history, or rather of a process of becoming in which several histories intersect with one another. As subject for history, woman always occurs simultaneously in several places. Woman un-thinks[4] the unifying, regulating history that homogenizes and channels forces, herding contradictions into a single battlefield. In woman, personal history blends together with the history of all women, as well as national and world history. As a militant, she is an integral part of all liberations. She must be farsighted, not limited to a blow-by-blow interaction. She foresees that her liberation will do more than modify power relations or toss the ball over to the other camp; she will bring about a mutation in human relations, in thought, in all praxis: hers is not simply a class struggle, which she carries forward into a much vaster movement. Not that in order to be woman-in-struggle(s) you have to leave the class struggle or repudiate it; but you have to split it open, spread it out, push it forward, fill it with the fundamental struggle so as to prevent the class struggle, or any other struggle for the liberation of a class or people, from operating as a form of repression, pretext for postponing the inevitable, the staggering alteration in power relations and in the production of individualities. This alteration is already upon us—in the United States, for example, where millions of night crawlers are in the process of undermining the family and disintegrating the whole of American sociality.

The new history is coming; it's not a dream, though it does extend beyond men's imagination, and for good reason. It's going to deprive them of their conceptual orthopedics, beginning with the destruction of their enticement machine.

It is impossible to *define* a feminine practice of writing, and this is an impossibility that will remain, for this practice can never be theorized, enclosed, coded—which doesn't mean that it doesn't exist. But it will always surpass the discourse that regulates the phallocentric system; it does and will take place in areas other than those subordinated to philosophico-theoretical domination. It will be conceived of only by subjects who are breakers of automatisms, by peripheral figures that no authority can ever subjugate.

Hence the necessity to affirm the flourishes of this writing, to give form to its movement, its near and distant byways. Bear in mind to begin with (1) that sexual opposition, which has always worked for man's profit to the point of reducing writing, too, to his laws, is only a historico-cultural limit. There is, there will be more and more rapidly pervasive now, a fiction that produces irreducible effects of femininity. (2) That it is through ignorance that most readers, critics, and writers of both sexes hesitate to admit or deny outright the possibility or the pertinence of a distinction between feminine and masculine writing. It will usually be said, thus disposing of sexual difference: either that all writing, to the extent that it materializes, is feminine; or, inversely—but it comes to the same thing—that the act of writing is equivalent to masculine masturbation (and so the woman who writes cuts herself out a paper penis); or that writing is bisexual, hence neuter, which again does away with differentiation. To admit that writing is precisely working (in) the in-between, inspecting the process of the same and of the other without which nothing can live, undoing the work of death—to admit this is first to want the two, as well as both, the ensemble of the one and the other, not fixed in sequences of struggle and expulsion or some other form of death but infinitely dynamized by an incessant process of exchange from one subject to another. A process of different subjects knowing one another and beginning one another anew only from the living boundaries of the other: a multiple and inexhaustible course with millions of encounters and transformations of the same into the other and into the in-between, from which woman takes her forms (and man, in his turn; but that's his other history).

In saying "bisexual, hence neuter," I am referring to the classic conception of bisexuality, which, squashed under the emblem of castration fear and along with the fantasy of a "total" being (though composed of two halves), would do away with the difference experienced as an operation incurring loss, as the mark of dreaded sectility.

To this self-effacing, merger-type bisexuality, which would conjure away castration (the writer who puts up his sign: "bisexual written here, come and see," when the odds are good that it's neither one nor the other), I oppose the *other bisexuality* on which every subject not enclosed in the false theater of phallocentric representationalism has founded his/her erotic universe. Bisexuality: that is, each one's location in self (*répérage en soi*) of the presence—variously manifest and insistent according to each person, male or female—of both sexes, nonexclusion either of the difference or of one sex, and, from this "self-permission," multiplication of the effects of the inscription of desire, over all parts of my body and the other body.

Now it happens that at present, for historico-cultural reasons, it is women who are opening up to and benefiting from this vatic bisexuality which doesn't annul differences but stirs them up, pursues them, increases their number. In a certain way, "woman is bisexual"; man—it's a secret to no one—being poised to keep glorious phallic monosexuality in view. By virtue of affirming the primacy of the phallus and of bringing it into play, phallocratic ideology has claimed more than one victim. As a woman, I've been clouded over by the great shadow of the scepter and been told: idolize it, that which you cannot brandish. But at the same time, man has been handed that grotesque and scarcely enviable destiny (just imagine) of being reduced to a single idol with clay balls. And consumed, as Freud and his followers note, by a fear of being a woman! For, if psychoanalysis was constituted from woman, to repress femininity (and not so successful a repression at that—men have made it clear), its account of masculine sexuality is now hardly refutable; as with all the "human" sciences, it reproduces the masculine view, of which it is one of the effects.

Here we encounter the inevitable man-with-rock, standing erect in his old Freudian realm, in the way that, to take the figure back to the point where linguistics is conceptualizing it "anew," Lacan preserves it in the sanctuary of the phallos (ϕ) "sheltered" from *castration's lack!* Their "symbolic" exists, it holds power—we, the sowers of disorder, know it only too well. But we are in no way obliged to deposit our lives in their banks of lack, to consider the constitution of the subject in terms of a drama manglingly restaged, to reinstate again and again the religion of the father. Because we don't want that. We don't fawn around the supreme hole. We have no womanly reason to pledge allegiance to the negative. The feminine (as the poets suspected) affirms: ". . . And yes," says Molly, carrying *Ulysses* off beyond any book and toward the new writing; "I said yes, I will Yes."

The Dark Continent is neither dark nor unexplorable—It is still unexplored only because we've been made to believe that it was too dark to be explorable. And because they want to make us believe that what interests us is the white continent, with its monuments to Lack. And we believed. They riveted us between two horrifying myths: between the Medusa and the abyss. That would be enough to set half the world laughing, except that it's still going on. For the phallologocentric sublation[5] is with us, and it's militant, regenerating the old patterns, anchored in the dogma of castration. They haven't changed a thing: they've theorized their deisre for reality! Let the priests tremble, we're going to show them our sexts!

Too bad for them if they fall apart upon discovering that women aren't men, or that the mother doesn't have one. But isn't this fear convenient for them? Wouldn't the worst be, isn't the worst, in truth, that women aren't castrated, that they have only to stop listening to the Sirens (for the Sirens were men) for history to change its meaning? You only have to look at the Medusa straight on to see her. And she's not deadly. She's beautiful and she's laughing.

Men say that there are two unrepresentable things: death and the feminine sex. That's because they need femininity to be associated with death; it's the jitters that give them a hard-on! for themselves! They need to be afraid of us. Look at the trembling Perseuses moving backward toward us, clad in apotropes. What lovely backs! Not another minute to lose. Let's get out of here.

Let's hurry: the continent is not impenetrably dark. I've been there often. I was overjoyed one day to run into Jean Genet. It was in *Pompes funèbres*.[6] He had come there led by his Jean. There are some men (all too few) who aren't afraid of femininity.

Almost everything is yet to be written by women about femininity: about their sexuality, that is, its infinite and mobile complexity, about their eroticization, sudden turn-ons of a certain miniscule-immense area of their bodies; not about destiny, but about the adventure of such and such a drive, about trips, crossings, trudges, abrupt and gradual awakenings, discoveries of a zone at one time timorous and soon to be forthright. A woman's body, with its thousand and one thresholds of ardor—once, by smashing yokes and censors, she lets it articulate the profusion of meanings that run through it in every direction—will make the old single-grooved mother tongue reverberate with more than one language.

We've been turned away from our bodies, shamefully taught to ignore them, to strike them with that stupid sexual modesty; we've been made victims of the old fool's game: each one will love the other sex. I'll give you your body and you'll give me mine. But who are the men who give women the body that women blindly yield to them? Why so few texts? Because so few women have as yet won back their body. Women must write through their bodies, they must invent the impregnable language that will wreck partitions, classes, and rhetorics, regulations and codes, they must submerge, cut through, get beyond the ultimate reserve-discourse, including the one that laughs at the very idea of pronouncing the word "silence," the one that, aiming for the impossible, stops short before the word "impossible" and writes it as "the end."

Such is the strength of women that, sweeping away syntax, breaking that famous thread (just a tiny little thread, they say) which acts for men as a surrogate umbilical cord, assuring them—otherwise they couldn't come—that the old lady is always right behind them, watching them make phallus, women will go right up to the impossible.

When the "repressed" of their culture and their society returns, it's an explosive, *utterly* destructive, staggering return, with a force never yet unleashed and equal to the most forbidding of suppressions. For when the Phallic period comes to an end, women will have been either annihilated or borne up to the highest and most violent incandescence. Muffled throughout their history, they have lived in dreams, in bodies (though muted), in silences, in aphonic revolts.

And with such force in their fragility; a fragility, a vulnerability, equal to their incomparable intensity. Fortunately, they haven't sublimated; they've saved their skin, their energy. They haven't worked at liquidating the impasse of lives without futures. They have furiously inhabited these sumptuous bodies: admirable hysterics who made Freud succumb to many voluptuous moments impossible to confess, bombarding his Mosaic statue with their carnal and passionate body words, haunting him with their inaudible and thundering denunciations, dazzling, more than naked underneath the seven veils of modesty. Those who, with a single word of the body, have inscribed the vertiginous immensity of a history which is sprung like an arrow from the whole history of men and from biblico-capitalist society, are the women, the suppliants of yesterday, who come as forebears of the new women, after whom no intersubjective relation will ever be the same. You, Dora, you the indomitable, the poetic body, you are the true "mistress" of the Signifier. Before long your efficacity will be seen at work when your speech is no longer suppressed, its point turned in against your breast, but written out over against the other.

In body—More so than men who are coaxed toward social success, toward sublimation, women are body. More body, hence more writing. For a long time it has been in body that women have responded to persecution, to the familial-conjugal enterprise of domestication, to the repeated attempts at castrating them. Those who have turned their tongues 10,000 times seven times before not speaking are either dead from it or more familiar with their tongues and their mouths than anyone else. Now, I-woman am going to blow up the Law: an explosion henceforth possible and ineluctable; let it be done, right now, *in* language.

Let us not be trapped by an analysis still encumbered with the old automatisms. It's not to be feared that language conceals an invincible adversary, because it's the language of men and their grammar. We mustn't leave them a single place that's any more theirs alone than we are.

If woman has always functioned "within" the discourse of man, a signifier that has always referred back to the opposite signifier which annihilates its specific energy and diminishes or stifles its very different sounds, it is time for her to dislocate this "within," to explode it, turn it around, and seize it; to make it hers, containing it, taking it in her own mouth, biting that tongue with her very own teeth to invent for herself a language to get inside of. And you'll see with what ease she will spring forth from that "within"—the "within" where once she so drowsily crouched—to overflow at the lips she will cover the foam.

Nor is the point to appropriate their instruments, their concepts, their places, or to begrudge them their position of mastery. Just because there's a risk of identification doesn't mean that we'll succumb. Let's leave it to the worriers, to masculine anxiety and its obsession with how to dominate the way things work—knowing "how it works" in order to "make it work." For us the point is not to take possession in order to internalize or manipulate, but rather to dash through and to "fly."[7]

Flying is woman's gesture—flying in language and making it fly. We have all learned the art of flying and its numerous techniques; for centuries we've been able to possess anything only by flying; we've lived in flight, stealing away, finding, when desired, narrow passageways, hidden crossovers. It's no accident that *voler* has a double meaning, that it plays on each of them and thus throws off the agents of sense. It's no accident: women take after birds and robbers just as robbers take after women and birds. They *(illes)*[8] go by, fly the coop, take pleasure in jumbling the order of space, in disorienting it, in changing around the furniture, dislocating things and values, breaking them all up, emptying structures, and turning propriety upside down.

What woman hasn't flown/stolen? Who hasn't felt, dreamt, performed the gesture that jams sociality? Who hasn't crumbled, held up to ridicule, the bar of separation? Who hasn't inscribed with her body the differential, punctured the system of couples and opposition? Who, by some act of transgression, hasn't overthrown successiveness, connection, the wall of circumfusion?

A feminine text cannot fail to be more than

subversive. It is volcanic; as it is written it brings about an upheaval of the old property crust, carrier of masculine investments; there's no other way. There's no room for her if she's not a he. If she's a her-she, it's in order to smash everything, to shatter the framework of institutions, to blow up the law, to break up the "truth" with laughter.

For once she blazes *her* trail in the symbolic, she cannot fail to make of it the chaosmos of the "personal"—in her pronouns, her nouns, and her clique of referents. And for good reason. There will have been the long history of gynocide. This is known by the colonized peoples of yesterday, the workers, the nations, the species off whose backs the history of men has made its gold; those who have known the ignominy of persecution derive from it an obstinate future desire for grandeur; those who are locked up know better than their jailers the taste of free air. Thanks to their history, women today know (how to do and want) what men will be able to conceive of only much later. I say woman overturns the "personal," for if, by means of laws, lies, blackmail, and marriage, her right to herself has been extorted at the same time as her name, she has been able, through the very movement of mortal alienation, to see more closely the inanity of "propriety," the reductive stinginess of the masculine-conjugal subjective economy, which she doubly resists. On the one hand she has constituted herself necessarily as that "person" capable of losing a part of herself without losing her integrity. But secretly, silently, deep down inside, she grows and multiplies, for, on the other hand, she knows far more about living and about the relation between the economy of the drives and the management of the ego than any man. Unlike man, who holds so dearly to his title and his titles, his pouches of value, his cap, crown, and everything connected with his head, woman couldn't care less about the fear of decapitation (or castration), adventuring, without the masculine temerity, into anonymity, which she can merge with, without annihilating herself: because she's a giver.

I shall have a great deal to say about the whole deceptive problematic of the gift. Woman is obviously not that woman Nietzsche dreamed of who gives only in order to.[9]

Who could ever think of the gift as a gift-that-takes? Who else but man, precisely the one who would like to take everything?

If there is a "propriety of woman," it is paradoxically her capacity to depropriate unselfishly, body without end, without appendage, without principal "parts." If she is a whole, it's a whole composed of parts that are wholes, not simple partial objects but a moving, limitlessly changing ensemble, a cosmos tirelessly traversed by Eros, an immense astral space not organized around any one sun that's any more of a star than the others.

This doesn't mean that she's an undifferentiated magma, but that she doesn't lord it over her body or her desire. Though masculine sexuality gravitates around the penis, engendering that centralized body (in political anatomy) under the dictatorship of its parts, woman does not bring about the same regionalization which serves the couple head/genitals and which is inscribed only within boundaries. Her libido is cosmic, just as her unconscious is worldwide. Her writing can only keep going, without ever inscribing or discerning contours, daring to make these vertiginous crossings of the other(s) ephemeral and passionate sojourns in him, her, them, whom she inhabits long enough to look at from the point closest to their unconscious from the moment they awaken, to love them at the point closest to their drives; and then further, impregnated through and through with these brief, identificatory embraces, she goes and passes into infinity. She alone dares and wishes to know from within, where she, the outcast, has never ceased to hear the resonance of fore-language. She lets the other language speak—the language of 1,000 tongues which knows neither enclosure nor death. To life she refuses nothing. Her language does not contain, it carries; it does not hold back, it makes possible. When id is ambiguously uttered—the wonder of being several—she doesn't defend herself against these unknown women whom she's surprised at becoming, but derives pleasure from this gift of alterability. I am spacious, singing flesh, on which is grafted no one knows which I, more or less human, but alive because of transformation.

Write! and your self-seeking text will know

itself better than flesh and blood, rising, insurrectionary dough kneading itself, with sonorous, perfumed ingredients, a lively combination of flying colors, leaves, and rivers plunging into the sea we feed. "Ah, there's her sea," he will say as he holds out to me a basin full of water from the little phallic mother from whom he's inseparable. But look, our seas are what we make of them, full of fish or not, opaque or transparent, red or black, high or smooth, narrow or bankless; and we are ourselves sea, sand, coral, seaweed, beaches, tides, swimmers, children, waves. . . . More or less wavily sea, earth, sky—what matter would rebuff us? We know how to speak them all.

Heterogeneous, yes. For her joyous benefits she is erogenous; she is the erotogeneity of the heterogeneous: airborne swimmer, in flight, she does not cling to herself; she is dispersible, prodigious, stunning, desirous and capable of others, of the other woman that she will be, of the other woman she isn't, of him, of you.

Woman be unafraid of any other place, of any same, or any other. My eyes, my tongue, my ears, my nose, my skin, my mouth, my body-for-(the)-other—not that I long for it in order to fill up a hole, to provide against some defect of mine, or because, as fate would have it, I'm spurred on by feminine "jealousy"; not because I've been dragged into the whole chain of substitutions that brings that which is substituted back to its ultimate object. That sort of thing you would expect to come straight out of "Tom Thumb," out of the *Penisneid* whispered to us by old grandmother ogresses, servants to their father-sons. If they believe, in order to muster up some self-importance, if they really need to believe that we're dying of desire, that we are this hole fringed with desire for their penis— that's their immemorial business. Undeniably (we verify it at our own expense—but also to our amusement), it's their business to let us know they're getting a hard-on, so that we'll assure them (we the maternal mistresses of their little pocket signifier) that they still can, that it's still there—that men structure themselves only by being fitted with a feather. In the child it's not the penis that the woman desires, it's not that famous bit of skin around which every man gravitates. Pregnancy cannot be traced back, except within the historical limits of the ancients, to some form of fate, to those mechanical substitutions brought about by the unconscious of some eternal "jealous woman"; not to penis envies; and not to narcissism or to some sort of homosexuality linked to the ever-present mother! Begetting a child doesn't mean that the woman or the man must fall ineluctably into patterns or must recharge the circuit of reproduction. If there's a risk there's not an inevitable trap: may women be spared the pressure, under the guise of consciousness-raising, of a supplement of interdictions. Either you want a kid or you don't—*that's your business.* Let nobody threaten you; in satisfying your desire, let not the fear of becoming the accomplice to a sociality succeed the old-time fear of being "taken." And man, are you still going to bank on everyone's blindness and passivity, afraid lest the child make a father and, consequently, that in having a kid the woman land herself more than one bad deal by engendering all at once child—mother—father—family? No; it's up to you to break the old circuits. It will be up to man and woman to render obsolete the former relationship and all its consequences, to consider the launching of a brand-new subject, alive, with defamilialization. Let us demater-paternalize rather than deny woman, in an effort to avoid the cooptation of procreation, a thrilling era of the body. Let us defetishize. Let's get away from the dialectic which has it that the only good father is a dead one, or that the child is the death of his parents. The child is the other, but the other without violence, bypassing loss, struggle. We're fed up with the reuniting of bonds forever to be severed, with the litany of castration that's handed down and genealogized. We won't advance backward anymore; we're not going to repress something so simple as the desire for life. Oral drive, anal drive, vocal drive—all these drives are our strengths, and among them is the gestation drive—just like the desire to write: a desire to live self from within, a desire for the swollen belly, for language, for blood. We are not going to refuse, if it should happen to strike our fancy, the unsurpassed pleasures of pregnancy which have actually been always exaggerated or conjured away—or cursed—in the classic texts. For if there's one thing that's been repressed, here's just the place to find it: in the taboo of the pregnant woman. This says a lot about the power she seems invested with at the time, because it has always been suspected, that, when pregnant, the woman not only doubles her market value, but—what's more important—takes on intrinsic value as a woman in her own eyes and, undeniably, acquires body and sex.

There are thousands of ways of living one's pregnancy; to have or not to have with that still invisible other a relationship of another intensity. And if you don't have that particular yearning, it doesn't mean that you're in any way lacking. Each body distributes in its own special way, without model or norm, the nonfinite and changing totality of its desires. Decide for yourself on your position in the arena of contradictions, where pleasure and reality embrace. Bring the other to life. Women know how to live detachment; giving birth is neither losing nor increasing. It's adding to life an other. Am I dreaming? Am I misrecognizing? You, the defenders of "theory," the sacrosanct yes-men of Concept, enthroners of the phallus (but not of the penis):

Once more you'll say that all this smacks of "idealism," or what's worse, you'll splutter that I'm a "mystic."

And what about the libido? Haven't I read the "Signification of the Phallus"? And what about separation, what about that bit of self for which, to be born, you undergo an ablation—an ablation, so they say, to be forever commemorated by your desire?

Besides, isn't it evident that the penis gets around in my texts, that I give it a place and appeal? Of course I do. I want all. I want all of me with all of him. Why should I deprive myself of a part of us? I want all of us. Woman of course has a desire for a "loving desire" and not a jealous one. But not because she is gelded; not because she's deprived and needs to be filled out, like some wounded person who wants to console herself or seek vengeance. I don't want a penis to decorate my body with. But I do desire the other for the other, whole and entire, male or female; because living means wanting everything that is, everything that lives, and wanting it alive. Castration? Let others toy with it. What's a desire originating from a lack? A pretty meager desire.

The woman who still allows herself to be threatened by the big dick, who's still impressed by the commotion of the phallic stance, who still leads a loyal master to the beat of the drum: that's the woman of yesterday. They still exist, easy and numerous victims of the oldest of farces: either they're cast in the original silent versions in which, as titanesses lying under the mountains they make with their quivering, they never see erected that theoretic monument to the golden phallus looming, in the old manner, over their bodies. Or, coming today out of their *infans* period and into the second, "enlightened" version of their virtuous debasement, they see themselves suddenly assaulted by the builders of the analytic empire and, as soon as they've begun to formulate the new desire, naked, nameless, so happy at making an appearance, they're taken in their bath by the new old men, and then, whoops! Luring them with flashy signifiers, the demon of interpretation—oblique, decked out in modernity—sells them the same old handcuffs, baubles, and chains. Which castration do you prefer? Whose degrading do you like better, the father's or the mother's? Oh, what pwetty eyes, you pwetty little girl. Here, buy my glasses and you'll see the Truth-Me-Myself tell you everything you should know. Put them on your nose and take a fetishist's look (you are me, the other analyst—that's what I'm telling you) at your body and the body of the other. You see? No? Wait, you'll have everything explained to you, and you'll know at last which sort of neurosis you're related to. Hold still, we're going to do your portrait, so that you can begin looking like it right away.

Yes, the naives to the first and second degree are still legion. If the New Women, arriving now, dare to create outside the theoretical, they're called in by the cops of the signifier, fingerprinted, remonstrated, and brought into the line of order that they are supposed to know; assigned by force of trickery to a precise place in the chain that's always formed for the benefit of a privileged signifier. We are pieced back to the string which leads back, if not to the Name-of-the-Father, then, for a new twist, to the place of the phallic-mother.

Beware, my friend, of the signifier that would take you back to the authority of a signified! Beware of diagnoses that would reduce your generative powers. "Common" nouns are also proper nouns that disparage your singularity by classifying it into species. Break out of the circles; don't remain within the psychoanalytic closure. Take a look around, then cut through!

And if we are legion, it's because the war of liberation has only made as yet a tiny breakthrough. But women are thronging to it. I've seen them, those who will be neither dupe nor domestic, those who will not fear the risk of being a woman; will not fear any risk, any desire, any space still unexplored in themselves, among themselves and others or anywhere else. They do not fetishize, they do not deny, they do not hate. They observe, they approach, they try to see the other woman, the child, the lover—not to strengthen their own narcissism or verify the solidity or weakness of the master, but to make love better, to invent.

Other love—In the beginning are our differences. The new love dares for the other, wants the other, makes dizzying, precipitous flights between knowledge and invention. The woman arriving over and over, again does not stand still; she's everywhere, she exchanges, she is the desire-that-gives. (Not enclosed in the paradox of the gift that takes nor under the illusion of unitary fusion. We're past that.) She comes in, comes-in-between herself me and you, between the other me where one is always infinitely more than one and more than me, without the fear of ever reaching a limit; she thrills in our becoming. And we'll keep on becoming! She cuts through defensive loves, motherages, and devourations: beyond selfish narcissism, in the moving, open, transitional space, she runs her risks. Beyond the struggle-to-the-death that's been removed to the bed, beyond the love-battle that claims to represent exchange, she scorns at an Eros dynamic that would be fed by hatred. Hatred: a heritage, again, a reminder, a duping subservience to the phallus. To love, to watch-think-seek the other in the other, to despecularize, to unhoard. Does this seem difficult? It's not impossible, and this is what nourishes life—a love that has no commerce with the apprehensive desire that provides against the lack and stultifies the strange; a love that rejoices in the exchange that multi-

plies. Wherever history still unfolds as the history of death, she does not tread. Opposition, hierarchizing exchange, the struggle for mastery which can end only in at least one death (one master—one slave, or two nonmasters ≠ two dead)—all that comes from a period in time governed by phallocentric values. The fact that this period extends into the present doesn't prevent woman from starting the history of life somewhere else. Elsewhere, she gives. She doesn't "know" what she's giving, she doesn't measure it; she gives, though, neither a counterfeit impression nor something she hasn't got. She gives more, with no assurance that she'll get back even some unexpected profit from what she puts out. She gives that there may be life, thought, transformation. This is an "economy" that can no longer be put in economic terms. Wherever she loves, all the old concepts of management are left behind. At the end of a more or less conscious computation, she finds not her sum but her differences. I am for you what you want me to be at the moment you look at me in a way you've never seen me before: at every instant. When I write, it's everything that we don't know we can be that is written out of me, without exclusions, without stipulation, and everything we will be calls us to the unflagging, intoxicating, unappeasable search for love. In one another we will never be lacking.

—Trans. Keith Cohen and Paula Cohen

Notes

1. Men still have everything to say about their sexuality, and everything to write. For what they have said so far, for the most part, stems from the opposition activity/passivity from the power relation between a fantasized obligatory virility meant to invade, to colonize, and the consequential phantasm of woman as a "dark continent" to penetrate and to "pacify." (We know what "pacify" means in terms of scotomizing the other and misrecognizing the self.) Conquering her,

they've made haste to depart from her borders, to get out of sight, out of body. The way man has of getting out of himself and into her whom he takes not for the other but for his own, deprives him, he knows, of his own bodily territory. One can understand how man, confusing himself with his penis and rushing in for the attack, might feel resentment and fear of being "taken" by the woman, of being lost in her, absorbed or alone.

2. I am speaking here only of the place "reserved" for women by the Western world.

3. Which works, then, might be called feminine? I'll just point out some examples: one would have to give them full readings to bring out what is pervasively feminine in their significance. Which I shall do elsewhere. In France (have you noted our infinite poverty in this field?—the Anglo-Saxon countries have shown resources of distinctly greater consequence), leafing through what's come out of the twentieth century—and it's not much—the only inscriptions of femininity that I have seen were by Colette, Marguerite Duras, . . . and Jean Genet.

4. *Dé·pense,* a neologism formed on the verb *penser,* hence "unthinks," but also "spends" (from *dépenser*).—Tr.

5. Standard English term for the Hegelian *Aufhebung,* the French *la relève.*

6. Jean Genet, *Pompes funèbres* (Paris, 1948), p. 185 [privately published].

7. Also, "to steal." Both meanings of the verb *voler* are played on, as the text itself explains in the following paragraph.—Tr.

8. *Illes* is a fusion of the masculine pronoun *ils,* which refers back to birds and robbers, with the feminine pronoun *elles,* which refers to women.—Tr.

9. Reread Derrida's text, "Le style de la femme," in *Nietzsche aujourd'hui* (Union Générale d'Editions, Coll. 10/18), where the philosopher can be seen operating an *Aufhebung* of all philosophy in its systematic reducing of woman to the place of seduction: she appears as the one who is taken for; the bait in person, all veils unfurled, the one who doesn't give but who gives only in order to (take).

Study Questions

1. Why does Cixous feel that "women must write themselves"? What does she see as obstacles to their writing?

2. Why does she believe that writing will return woman to her body? Specifically, what are the implications for her view of woman?

3. "She writes in white ink." What does Cixous mean by this statement? What are some implications for feminist theory?

4. Cixous believes that men fear woman as mother. What does that entail about woman's nature?

3
Social Philosophy

Social philosophy is that area of value theory that deals with questions about the nature of society and social institutions. Social theory has characteristically inquired into the relationship between the self and society. But, according to de Beauvoir, man is constituted as self and woman as other. So, feminists ask: What of woman and society?

Self is the subject, which freely chooses projects. But man has enslaved woman and made her into other, or object. Woman, therefore, has not been subject but object; she has, literally, been sex object. Feminist theorists show how women have been sexually objectified. In every society, women are defined by their sexuality. Catharine MacKinnon writes:

> Implicit in feminist theory is (the) argument: the molding, direction, and expression of sexuality organizes society into two sexes—women and men—which division underlies the totality of social relations.

Feminists demonstrate how society assigns and maintains women's sexuality in determinate social (sex) roles such as daughter, wife, mother, prostitute, lesbian, and the like.

In this section, feminist theorists address these sex roles and the social construction of "the second sex" around them. How do social institutions serve to ensure the subordination of women and the domination of men?

Sarah Hoagland discusses the notion of "femininity," which has been central to feminist theory. She argues that it is not an empirical concept but a political one. As de Beauvoir says, "a woman is made, not born," and a woman is made into the feminine, or that which is desirable to men. Lucy Gilbert and Paula Webster call this process "a formula for surrender." Hoagland describes the means by which women learn to accept their inequality and the cultural definition of woman as inferior, submissive, and vulnerable. In her analysis, Hoagland discusses forms of "resistance" and "sabotage" that women have employed to counter "the forced march to femininity."

In *The Dialectic of Sex,* Shulamith Firestone argues that whereas in the past the procreative function (as wife/mother) was the source of women's subordination, now the pivot of women's oppression is the social institution of romantic love. As she says, "Romanticism develops in proportion to the liberation of women from their biology." Romantic love, she demonstrates, is the means by which women are indoctrinated to accept their inferior status in the sex-class system. Firestone identifies the basic components of romanticism as eroticism, sex-privatization ("the process by which women are blinded to their generality as a class"), and the beauty ideal.

Jeffner Allen investigates the radical feminist formulation that the institution of motherhood maintains women's subordination. Citing de Beauvoir and Firestone, she makes motherhood the focus of her critical analysis. Her "philosophy of evac-uation," that women as a class not be synonymous with the class of mother, calls for "women's collective removal of ourselves from all forms of motherhood." She asserts the demand for a world that is open and free of the oppressive constructs of patriarchy.

Another radical feminist critique of motherhood, to which Allen's may interest-ingly be compared, is Adrienne Rich's *Of Woman Born* (New York: W. W. Norton, 1976). Rich's thesis is that motherhood as an *institution* is to be distinguished from motherhood as *experience*. The institution of motherhood in patriarchy is oppressive. However, Rich says, motherhood as the relationship of women and children may be nonoppressive if experienced, personally and collectively, outside the control of men, in the community of women.

By contrast, a socialist feminist approach to the nature of motherhood is explored by Dorothy Dinnerstein in *The Mermaid and the Minotaur* (Harper & Row, 1976). Utilizing psychoanalytic concepts, Dinnerstein connects the fear and denigration of women to the infantile experience of what seemed an all-powerful mother. As not only the giver but the withholder of gratification, mother inevitably frustrates us. At the same time, the infant fears being "swallowed up" by the mother's totality. So, Dinnerstein says, we seek asylum in the seemingly bounded and rational world of the fathers. The outcome is the devaluation of women, since women are mothers. According to Dinnerstein, amelioration of "the human malaise created by the present sexual arrangements" is to be sought in a fundamental shift so that men as well as women are primary caretakers of infants and children.

The new reproductive technologies that Firestone predicted in *The Dialectic of Sex* are now at the center of feminist concerns around motherhood. Radical feminists pose the issue of the risks for women's interests in the patriarchal control of conceptive technologies. The essay by Anne Donchin included here presents alternative perspectives that might be adopted by feminists, and an assessment of the negative and positive aspects of these techniques for women. As Jana Sawicki says, "multiple strategies for resisting their dangerous implications" are called for. Donchin indicates the relationship of mothering practices and feminist theory.

Finally, feminist social theory sees prostitution as paradigmatic of woman as sexually objectified. According to Andrea Dworkin, men see women as objectified in the roles of wife/mother *or* prostitute. Alison Jaggar proposes a philosophical investigation into the nature of prostitution. She applies what she has called the "feminist frameworks" of radical feminism, liberal feminism, and socialist feminism to the analysis. These approaches have in common the rejection of the patriarchal ideology that makes woman synonymous with her sexuality and thus objectifies her. However, they differ in their responses to the issues around prostitution. Jaggar believes that prostitution is to be viewed as part of a wider account of social arrangements and of "what is the proper role of sexuality and work in human life."

"Femininity," Resistance, and Sabotage

Sarah Lucia Hoagland

Scientists and other male elite named wimmin "feminine," the most pervasive label infecting our lives. Yet "femininity" is not an empirical concept. It did not arise as a result of, nor is it susceptible to, empirical investigation. It is not based on fact. Instead it is akin to a metaphysical category, and those in power use it to determine perception of fact, to define the social perception of wimmin. Using the feminine stereotype, scientists[1] and conservatives who are not scientists[2] portray female behavior as submissive, and in the process legitimate male domination. I will argue that behaviors typically labeled feminine indicate not submission, but rather *resistance*, to male domination; we will see that the concept "femininity" has been used to obscure and bury female resistance, as well as female autonomy and female bonding.

I have argued elsewhere that "femininity" is not an empirical concept.[3] In the first place particular character traits alleged to fall under the feminine or masculine categories are valued differently depending on whether they apply to wimmin or men. Aggression is regarded as a flaw in wimmin and an asset in men while dependence is regarded as an asset in wimmin but not men. Such valuation indicates at the very least that use of the label "feminine" is prescriptive, not descriptive: when aggression is found among wimmin it is punished. Society attempts to control and limit aggression through social sanctions against those labeled feminine in a way not attempted among those labeled masculine.

More importantly, such traits are not only valued differently, they are *perceived* differently, an indication of the metaphysical nature of femininity. An aggressive man is seen as

From Mary Vetterling-Braggin, ed., *Femininity, Masculinity, and Androgyny* (Totowa, NJ: Littlefield, Adams, 1982). Reprinted by permission of Sarah Lucia Hoagland.

normal, and a middle-class aggressive man is seen as healthy, confident, and ambitious. An aggressive womon, on the other hand, is seen as frustrated if not neurotic, and heterosexual coercion is embedded in the stereotype because such a womon is seen as in need of a "good" (i.e., more aggressive) man.

The metaphysical nature of the feminine stereotype is apparent in the "humorous" characterization of the differences between businessmen and business wimmin who behave in identical ways:[4]

A businessman is aggressive.
A business woman is pushy.
A well-dressed businessman is fashionable.
A well-dressed business woman is a clothes horse.
He's careful about detail.
She's picky.
He loses his temper because he's involved in his job.
She's bitchy.
He gets depressed from work pressures.
She has menstrual tension.
He's a man of the world.
She's been around.
He's confident.
She's conceited.
He's enthusiastic.
She's emotional.
He isn't afraid to say what he thinks.
She's opinionated.
He's a stern task maker.
She's difficult to work for.
He follows through.
She doesn't know when to quit.
He's firm.
She's stubborn.
He's an authority.
She's a tyrant.

Yet another example is Dory Previn's song, "When a Man Wants a Woman":

When a man wants a woman
He says it's a compliment
He says he's only trying to capture her
To claim her; to tame her
When he wants ev'rything ev'rything of her
Her soul, her love, her life forever and more.
He says he's persuading her
He says he's pursuing her
But when a woman wants a man
He says she's threatening him
He says she's only trying to trap him
To train him, to chain him
When she wants anything anything of him
A look, a touch, a moment of his time
He says she's demanding
He swears she's destroying him
Why is it
When a man wants a woman
He's called a hunter
But when a woman wants a man
She's called a predator

These two examples indicate that identical behavior is perceived to be different depending on whether it is attributed to wimmin or men. In both cases when a womon steps outside the limits of the feminine stereotype she is subject to derision, attack, and denial. To suggest the behavior is qualitatively different begs the question; it presupposes that wimmin and men have different natures prior to investigating the hypothesis. More significantly, such a suggestion fails to consider the context of these perceptions—a society based on the rule of the fathers. Femininity exists to limit wimmin; in these cases we are unable to *perceive* certain behavior outside the feminine stereotype.

In other cases, the behavior is detectable as challenging femininity, but it is denied to be either normal or female. If femininity were an empirical concept then female behavior would provide endless counterexamples to the feminine labeling of wimmin's characters.[5] Empirical concepts are subject to challenge and their applications to refutation. Yet wimmin who act in ways which do not fit the feminine model are not treated by scientists as counterexamples to scientific hypotheses (prejudices, prejudgments) about wimmin and wimmin's characters. Instead, scientists and others label

wimmin whose behavior is clearly not limited by the feminine model "abnormal." Recently an even more insidious move is underfoot in science. Wimmin who will not remain confined to the feminine stereotype are denied our womonhood. For example, pursuing his hypothesis that hormones pass on specific behavioral traits in conformity with sex-role stereotypes, John Money is developing an ideology that masculine minds appear in female bodies. Such a move whitens out, obliterates the concept of a strong, autonomous womon; she is now a male trapped in a female body.[6] In this view, a strong, autonomous woman must really be a man.

In general, scientists and other men in power discredit and attempt to render invisible counterexamples to the feminine stereotype, using "femininity" as a standard of womonhood, femaleness, even though they may differ on a few of the minor particulars as to what exactly constitutes femininity. Measures or standards determine fact; no amount of research into wimmin's "true natures," no appeal to fact, will either confirm or challenge the concept, the label, "femininity." The importance of realizing the coerciveness of "femininity" lies not in the tired male question of whether we can ever "discover" wimmin's "true nature." The importance lies in realizing how "femininity" determines the social perception of wimmin, and how it is used to enforce male domination and heterosexuality.

Characterizations which ordinarily pass under the label "feminine" include: passive, emotional, irrational or even nonrational, unassuming, cooperative (with whom?), unthreatening (to whom?), behind the scenes (whose scenes?), weak, gullible (when?), childlike, infantile. These characterizations present a significant picture of male fantasy. In 1946 Viola Klein documented the fanciful and contradictory nature of the scientific collection of feminine characteristics. For example, she points to a general paradox while discussing Otto Weininger's work: How can one talk about positive male and female characteristics such that each person has a few from both categories while at the same time depicting one set of those characteristics in negative terms, as voids?[7]

More than being contradictory or simply negative, however, the feminine stereotype as applied to wimmin maintains existing lines of power and promotes heterosexual bias by defining wimmin in relation to men and characterizing as normal the woman who remains totally accessible to male authority. A "normal" woman, under the male-identification of wimmin, does not bond with wimmin and she does not remain autonomous. Caroline Whitbeck has isolated three prevailing theories composing the foundation of the feminine characteristics, all of which define wimmin in relation to men: woman as partial man, woman as opposite man, and woman as helpmate to man.[8]

Following this, one of the most pervasive effects of the male naming of wimmin feminine is the obliteration of any conceptual hint of female resistance to male domination, resistance to attempts to limit or control a woman's integrity. One searches in vain for portraits and historical depictions of female autonomy, female resistance, female bonding. Patrihistorians claim that wimmin have remained content with our lot and have accepted male domination throughout time with the exception of a few suffragists and now a few "aberrant" feminists. Yet upon examination it becomes clear that within the confines of the feminine stereotype, no behavior, no set of actions *count* as resistance. Any behavior that cannot be squeezed into the confines of the feminine, passive stereotype has been discounted as an aberration or it has been buried.[9]

If nothing one can point to or even imagine counts as proof against the claim that all (normal) wimmin are feminine and accept male domination, then the claim is not empirical, it is not based on examination of fact. And we are attempting to work with a closed, coercive conceptual system. We have been unable to recognize resistance to male domination among wimmin because under the male-identified feminine stereotype, resistance is considered abnormal, an indication of insanity, or incredibly, proof of submission.

For example, acts which the namers use to support the feminine stereotype of white middle-class wimmin, the current paradigm of all womonhood, indicate resistance. Alix Kates Shulman in *Memoirs of an Ex-Prom Queen,* portrays a "fluffyheaded" housewife who regularly burns the dinner when her husband brings his boss home unexpectedly.[10] And she periodically packs raw eggs in his lunchbox. Such acts are used as "proof" of wimmin's "lesser rational ability" by those in power, but in fact they indicate resistance—sabotage. Such acts may or may not be openly called sabotage by the saboteurs. But wimmin engage in them as an affirmation of existence in a society which denies us recognition independently of a man. When we are isolated, one from another, through heterosexual coercion, these are rational alternatives to untenable situations, to traps, within a patriarchal context.

Donna Deitch's documentary, "Woman to Woman," offers a classic example of sabotage. Four wimmin, two housewives, a daughter, and the interviewer, sit around a kitchen table. One housewife protests that she is not a housewife, that she is not married to the house. The interviewer asks her to say what she does all day. The womon relates that she starts by getting up, feeding her husband, feeding her children, driving them to the school bus, driving her husband to work, returning to do the dishes, make the beds, going out to do the shopping, returning to do a wash. She continues relating her activities for a normal Monday and half of a Tuesday before she stops, shocked, and says: "Wait a minute, I AM married to the house." She complains of difficulty in getting her husband to give her money for the household, of frustration because he nevertheless holds her responsible for running the house, and of degradation because she must go to him, apologetically, at the end of each week to ask for extra money when he could have provided her with sufficient funds at the beginning of each week. Suddenly she gets a gleam in her eye, lowers her voice and leans forward, saying: "Have you ever bought something you didn't need?" Excitement brews and they all lean closer as she states: "You have to know you're alive, you have to make sure you exist." She has separated herself from her husband's perceptions of her; she is not simply an extension of his purposes, of his will, she is reclaiming (some) agency—sabotage. Yet under the feminine stereotype, we are barred from claiming her as a sister re-sister.

Significantly, femininity is used to characterize any group men in power wish to justify dominating. [In 1971] Kate Millett pointed out that femininity characterizes traits that those in power cherish in subordinates.[11] [In 1968] Naomi Weisstein noted that feminine characteristics add up to typical minority group characteristics.[12] An investigation of the literature shows that Nazis characterized Jews as feminine and used the ideology in the justification of their massacre. Men accused at the Salem witch trials were characterized as feminine.[13] And an investigation of white British anthropological writing reveals that Black South Africans were labeled feminine. The model for oppression in Anglo-European thinking is the male conception of femininity. A feminine being is one who is by nature relatively passive and dependent. It follows that those to whom the label is applied must be seeking protection (domination) by nature and should be subjected to authority "for their own good." "Femininity" portrays those not in power as wanting and needing control. It is a matter of logic, then, that those who refuse control are abnormal.

Consider the fact that white history depicts Black slaves (though not white indentured servants) as lazy, docile, and clumsy on such grounds as that slaves frequently broke tools. Yet a rational woman under slavery, comprehending that her situation is less than human, that she functions as an extension of the will of her master, will not run to pick up tools. She acts instead to differentiate herself from the will of her master, she breaks tools, carries on subversive activities—sabotage. Her master, in turn, perceiving her as subhuman and subrational, names her clumsy, childlike, foolish, perhaps, but not a saboteur.

If officially slaves were subhuman and content with their lot and masters were only acting in slaves' best interest, then any resistance to the system would be depicted by those in power as an abnormality or an indication of madness. Indeed, in recollecting the stories of her grandmother's slave days, Annie Mae Hunt tells us that "If you run off, you was considered sick."[14] That is to say, slaves existed in a Weltanschauung where running away from slavery was perceived as an indication not of (healthy) resistance but of mental imbalance. Such was the extent of control the masters exercised through the power of naming—*nothing* one did could be perceived as resistance. In fact the behaviors of slaves out of which the masters constructed and fed the slave stereotypes provide evidence of resistance and sabotage.[15]

During the Holocaust and, more significantly, after it, in the telling of the stories, Nazis as well as liberal historians have depicted Jews under Hitler's reign of terror as cooperative and willing victims. This stereotype, as is true of the slave stereotype, is still alive today. Yet again, one must ask, what would *count* as resistance? For example, Jews at Auschwitz committing suicide by hurling themselves against an electric fence would be depicted as "willing victims," and such behavior has been used to portray Jews as failing to resist Nazi aggression. In fact, Jews in concentration camps committing suicide were not willing victims. In determining the time of their own deaths they were resisting, interfering with the plans of the masters, exercising choice, and so establishing a self, differentiating themselves from the will of the masters. Holocaust literature is full of indications of Jewish resistance, of sabotage, yet the stereotype of the willing (i.e., feminine) Jewish victim persists today.[16] Again, "femininity" is used to obscure resistance.

Consider one paradigm of femininity, the white, upper-class Victorian lady. In *The Yellow Wallpaper*, Charlotte Perkins Gilman portrayed conditions faced by such wimmin in the 1880s.[17] These conditions included a prescription of total female passivity by mind gynecologists such as S. Weir Mitchell, prescriptions arising as a result of male scientists' sudden interest in wimmin as the first wave of feminism attracted their attention, prescriptions enforced by those in control. The heroine is taken by her husband to a summer home for rest. He locks her in a nursery with bars on the windows, a bed bolted to the floor, and hideous wallpaper, shredded in spots. He rebuts her despair with the rhetoric of protection, refusing to indulge her "whims" when she protests the room's atrocity. He also stifles all other attempts at creativity, flying into a rage when he discovers her writing in her diary. In the end, she manages to crawl behind the wallpaper and escape into "madness." Charlotte Perkins Gilman shows us a womon with every avenue of creativity, of integrity, patronizingly and paternalistically cut off for "her own good," to "protect" her, and we watch her slowly construct her resistance. Not surprisingly, male scientists and doctors of the day saw nothing more in the story than a testament to "feminine" insanity.[18]

Resistance, in other words, may even take the form of insanity when one is isolated within the confines of male domination and all means of maintaining integrity have been systematically cut off. Under such conditions insanity becomes a more viable alternative than submission. Mary's long descent into oblivion on morphine in *A Long Day's Journey Into Night* is another example of resistance to domination. But the coerciveness of "femininity" dictates that such behavior be perceived as part of the "mysterious" and "intricate" nature of womon rather than recognized as resistance.

Significantly, one and the same word governs insanity and anger: madness. As Phyllis Chesler has documented, mind gynecologists call wimmin mad whose behavior they can no longer understand as functioning in relation to men.[19] On the other hand, the *Oxford English Dictionary* defines "mad" as it relates to anger as "ungovernable rage or fury." One must ask, "ungovernable" by whom? Madness in anger and madness in "insanity" indicate that men have lost control.[20] When wimmin are labeled mad, it is often because we have become useless to men or a threat to male supremacy.

Thus, to maintain the feminine stereotype men will characterize more obvious forms of resistance as insanity when wimmin engage in them. Thus insanity becomes a part of the "feminine" nature and resistance is rendered institutionally invisible. Just as slaves who ran off were perceived as insane, so are wimmin who fight back against battering husbands. Wimmin who kill long-term battering husbands are, for the most part, forced to use the plea of insanity rather than that of self-defense. The most famous case is that of

Francine Hughes who killed her husband after fourteen years of beatings and psychological abuse.[21]

However, institutionally characterizing wimmin who fight back as insane was still not enough. Perceiving the plea of insanity as a license to kill even though it means incarceration for an unspecified amount of time, media men began a campaign against battered wimmin who fight back, depicting them as getting away with murder.[22] Funds for battered wives shelters are now being withdrawn on the grounds that the shelters break up the family. And agencies working on "domestic violence" focus on preserving the family intact, burying the slave conditions of wimmin within the nuclear family by obliterating the distinction between aggressor and victim.[23] Once again, the conceptual framework that renders female resistance invisible comes full circle. The concept of femininity not only blocks any social perception of female resistance, it lays the groundwork for denying the problem of male domination when female resistance threatens to break through the stereotype and become visible.

I have stressed the fact that feminine behaviors indicate resistance to point to the phenomenal reversals those in power have perpetuated. To dominate a people one must first use force, but eventually one must find other means.[24] One effective means of maintaining power is to rob the oppressed of any positive self-concept and so prevent us from identifying with each other. Then one can portray us as accepting, indeed desiring our lot, and each individual sees herself as alone and abnormal when she resists. The feminine stereotype is the most effective tool that exists for this purpose, and scientists who "investigate" femininity under the guise of establishing social fact perpetuate and legislate patriarchal value, both male domination and compulsory heterosexuality.[25]

This is true to such an extent that scientists *condemn* female competence and autonomy as threatening to males and subversive to the patriarchal family, hence as socially undesirable. Thus Daniel P. Moynihan popularized the theory of the Black matriarch who castrates Black men, and implied that for Black men to claim their manhood, Black wimmin must step behind them and become submissive.[26]

Female bonding is so threatening that it is altogether erased. For example, one will find the term "maiden aunt" employed in sociobiology in a lesbian context, burying the idea of a female rejecting a male and promoting the idea that a female is unable to attract one. The latter feeds an unsupported theory of male dominance while the former does not.[27] Among humans, Lesbians are either depicted as men or are rendered invisible.

As a final note, I wish to merely indicate an additional consequence of the heterosexual coerciveness of "femininity." The feminine stereotype provides a basis for the ideology of special protection for wimmin, thus enforcing heterosexuality. For men to maintain the conceptual framework in which they can see themselves as protectors, they must establish and maintain an atmosphere in which wimmin are in danger; they must create our victim (feminine) status. To maintain the ideology of special protection of wimmin, men have portrayed us as helpless, defenseless, innocent—victims, and thereby, targets to be attacked. If we act in self-defense and thus step out of the feminine role, becoming on their terms active and "guilty," men step up overt physical violence against us to reaffirm our victim status. When they cannot control us through protection, the safety valve they fall back on is overt violence, predation (pornography, rape, "domestic violence" [wifebeating], "incest" [daughter rape]). In short, the ideology of special protection of wimmin emerging from femininity sets us up as targets which in turn compels us to turn to men for protection and enforces heterosexuality.[28]

The patriarchal naming of wimmin feminine goes even further. The separate valuation of aggression in men and wimmin affects what is tolerated in society in terms of violence. Male violence against wimmin is an integral part of society, it is expected that men will rape, batter, maim, torture, mutilate, and murder wimmin. Rape, wifebeating and "incest" are at best ignored. But, as noted above, wimmin who fight back face the full brutality of the system.

"Femininity," I have argued, is a label whereby one group of people are defined in relation to another in such a way that domination and submission are portrayed as part of the biological essence of those involved. Under the feminine stereotype, a portrait of naive contentment with being controlled is painted such that resistance is rendered invisible or perceived as abnormal, mad, or of no consequence. Men of minority groups such as Blacks and Jews are slowly and painfully emerging from under the domination of femininity.[29] Unfortunately they often do so by laying claim to "masculinity" which does not challenge the dualism that justifies oppression. Heterosexist ideology and the failure to examine the coercive conceptual framework of "femininity" keeps wimmin locked in an ideology of male domination. Be we Black, Jewish, WASP, Iranian, Hispanic, Native American, Asian American, or a member of any of the many other cultures in which wimmin survive, be we working class, middle class, or upper class,[30] within our various situations we remain saddled with the label "femininity." Female resistance, female autonomy and Lesbian bonding do not exist within patriarchal ontology. Instead scientists and other male elite have limited the boundaries of female behavior and set us up for attack, control, and domination.

Notes

1. See, for example, E. O. Wilson, *Sociobiology: The New Synthesis* (Cambridge, Mass.: Harvard University Press, 1975).

2. See, for example, Marabel Morgan, *The Total Woman,* and *Total Joy* (Old Tappan, N.J.: Flemming H. Revell Co., 1972 and 1976).

3. Sarah L. Hoagland, "On the Status of the Concepts of Masculinity and Femininity," *Transactions of the Nebraska Academy of Sciences* 4 (August 1977): 169–72. The argument that follows is an extension of the arguments I developed in this paper.

4. Loosely adapted from "The Executive Woman," *Family Circle,* May 1976.

5. See footnote 4.

6. See the discussion of Money's thesis in Janice G. Raymond, *The Transsexual Empire: The Making of the She-Male* (Boston: Beacon Press, 1979), Chapter II.

7. Viola Klein, *The Feminine Character* (Chicago: University of Illinois Press, 1971), p. 60.

8. Caroline Whitbeck, "Theories of Sex Difference," in Chapter 2 of this volume.

9. For example, the Amazons are repeatedly depicted as mythical creatures (with attendant male fantasies such as the alleged removing of one breast) even though there is proof of their existence both in Africa and Asia. For example, in the Fall of 1979, Soviet archeologists uncovered the remains of a tribe of Amazons that lived 1200 years ago in Balabany in the Soviet Republic of Moldavia (*Chicago Sun-Times,* September 9, 1979). I have yet to see further information on this anywhere.

10. Alix Kates Shulman, *Memoirs of an Ex-Prom Queen* (New York: Bantam, 1973).

11. Kate Millett, *Sexual Politics* (New York: Avon, 1971), p. 47.

12. Naomi Weisstein, "Psychology Constructs the Female, or: The Fantasy Life of the Male Psychologist," reprint (Boston: New England Free Press, 1968).

13. Research of Betty Carpenter, personal communication, Spring 1978, Lincoln, Nebraska.

14. Ruth Winegarten, "I Am Annie Mae: The Personal Story of a Black Texas Woman," *Chrysalis* 10 (Spring 1980): 15.

15. Since formulating the thesis, I have come across documented evidence of it. See, *Puttin' on Ole Massa,* ed. Gilbert Osofsky (New York: Harper and Row, 1969); *Great Slave Narratives,* ed. Arna Bontemps (Boston: Beacon Press, 1969); and *A Documentary History of Slavery in North America,* ed. Willie Lee Rose (New York: Oxford University Press, 1976).

16. See Simone Wallace, Ellen Ledley, Paula Tobin, letter to *Off Our Backs* (December 1979): 28.

17. Charlotte Perkins Gilman, *The Yellow Wallpaper* (New York: The Feminist Press, 1973).

18. Elaine R. Hedges, "Afterword," Charlotte Perkins Gilman, op. cit.

19. Phyllis Chesler, *Women and Madness* (Garden City, N.Y.: Doubleday and Co., 1972).

20. When reading between the lines, when claiming wimmin from the past, we must examine alternatives available and in that context understand the behavior. Thus insanity itself can be a form of resistance. In addition, other behavior is depicted as insanity. As a result, there is a fine line that fades between insanity and behavior of the resister who is able to maintain the confidence of her perceptions. If everyone around you perceives your behavior in a light other than your intention, your perceptions struggle in a very different world.

21. Ann Jones, *Women Who Kill* (New York: Holt, Rinehart & Winston, 1980), pp. 285–91.

22. Ibid., p. 291.

23. Kathleen Barry, *Female Sexual Slavery* (Englewood Cliffs, N.J.: Prentice-Hall, 1979), p. 142.

24. Pat Robinson (et al.), "A Historical and Critical Essay for Black Women in the Cities," *The Black Woman,* ed. Toni Cade (New York: New American Library, 1970), pp. 198–210.

25. See Adrienne Rich, "Compulsory Heterosexuality and Lesbian Existence," *Signs* (1980), Vol. 3, no. 4, University of Chicago.

26. See Jean Carey Bond and Pat Peery, "Is the Black Male Castrated?" *The Black Woman,* ed. Toni Cade (New York: New American Library, 1970), pp. 113–19.

27. See Sarah Lucia Hoagland, "Androcentric Rhetoric in Sociobiology," *Women's Studies International Quarterly* 3, nos. 2/3 (1980): 285–93.

28. See Sarah Lucia Hoagland, "Violence, Victimization, Violation," *Sinister Wisdom* 15.

29. This is not to say, of course, that the *experience* of Black men or Jewish men has been identical to that of white wimmin or Black wimmin or Jewish wimmin. It is not to say, for example, that Black male slaves and white wimmin who were wives of Southern plantation owners had the same experiences. Black slaves were perceived as

beasts. If wives of Southern plantation owners were perceived as animals (pets), still there were significant differences. Even poor white Southern wimmin and upper-class Southern white wimmin did not have the same experiences. My point here is simply that the concept of femininity was used in the justification of the Weltanschauung of dominance and submission in such a way that resistance, in all its various forms, becomes invisible.

30. See Kathleen Barry, *Female Sexual Slavery* (Englewood Cliffs, N.J.: Prentice-Hall, 1979), Chapter 7.

Study Questions

1. What does Hoagland mean when she says that femininity is not an "empirical" concept? What reasons does she offer for her view?

2. What are some standard characterizations of femininity? In what sense are these characterizations negative, and how do they serve to reinforce the existing power relationships?

3. According to Hoagland, in what ways might seemingly typical feminine behavior (from the male point of view) instead be "resistance" or "sabotage"?

4. In what way has the male conception of femininity formed the model for oppression in Anglo-European thought?

5. How can resistance sometimes take the form of insanity?

6. How does the concept of femininity promote violence against women? Explain your answer.

The Culture of Romance

Shulamith Firestone

So far we have not distinguished "romance" from love. For there are no two kinds of love, one healthy (dull) and one not (painful) ("My dear, what you need is a mature love relationship. Get over this romantic nonsense."), but only less-than-love or daily agony. When love takes place in a power context, everyone's "love life" must be affected. Because power and love don't make it together.

So when we talk about romantic love we mean love corrupted by its power context—the sex class system—into a diseased form of love that then in turn reinforces this sex class system. We have seen that the psychological dependence of women upon men is created by continuing real economic and social oppres-

From Shulamith Firestone, *The Dialectic of Sex*, pp. 146–155. Copyright © 1970 by Shulamith Firestone. Reprinted by permission of William Morrow & Company.

sion. However, in the modern world the economic and social bases of the oppression are no longer *alone* enough to maintain it. So the apparatus of romanticism is hauled in. (Looks like we'll have to help her out, Boys!)

Romanticism develops in proportion to the liberation of women from their biology. As civilization advances and the biological bases of sex class crumble, male supremacy must shore itself up with artificial institutions, or exaggerations of previous institutions, e.g., where previously the family had a loose, permeable form, it now tightens and rigidifies into the patriarchal nuclear family. Or, where formerly women had been held openly in contempt, now they are elevated to states of mock worship.[1] Romanticism is a cultural tool of male power to keep women from knowing their condition. It is especially needed—and therefore strongest—in Western countries with the highest rate of industrialization. Today, with technology enabling women to break out of their roles for good—it was a near miss in the early twentieth century—romanticism is at an all-time high.

How does romanticism work as a cultural tool to reinforce sex class? Let us examine its components, refined over centuries, and the modern methods of its diffusion—cultural techniques so sophisticated and penetrating that even men are damaged by them.

1. *Eroticism.* A prime component of romanticism is eroticism. All animal needs (the affection of a kitten that has never seen heat) for love and warmth are channeled into genital sex: people must never touch others of the same sex, and may touch those of the opposite sex only when preparing for a genital sexual encounter ("a pass"). Isolation from others makes people starved for physical affection; and if the only kind they can get is genital sex, that's soon all they crave. In this state of hypersensitivity the least sensual stimulus produces an exaggerated effect, enough to inspire everything from schools of master painting to rock and roll. Thus *eroticism is the concentration of sexuality—often into highly-charged objects ("Chantilly Lace")—signifying the displacement of other social/affection needs onto sex.* To be plain old needy-for-affection makes one a "drip," to need a kiss is embarrassing, unless it is an erotic kiss; only "sex" is O.K., in fact it proves one's mettle. Virility and sexual performance become confused with social worth.[2]

Constant erotic stimulation of male sexuality coupled with its forbidden release through most normal channels are designed to encourage men to look at women as only things whose resistance to entrance must be overcome. For notice that this eroticism operates in only one direction. Women are the only "love" objects in our society, so much so that women regard *themselves* as erotic.[3] This functions to preserve direct sex pleasure for the male, reinforcing female dependence: women can be fulfilled sexually only by vicarious identification with the man who enjoys them. Thus eroticism preserves the sex class system.

The only exception to this concentration of all emotional needs into erotic relationships is the (sometimes) affection within the family. But here, too, unless they are *his* children, a man can no more express affection for children than he can for women. Thus his affection for the young is also a trap to saddle him into the marriage structure, reinforcing the patriarchal system.

2. *The Sex Privatization of Women.* Eroticism is only the topmost layer of the romanticism that reinforces female inferiority. As with any lower class, group awareness must be deadened to keep them from rebelling. In this case, because the distinguishing characteristic of women's exploitation as a class is sexual, a special means must be found to make them unaware that they are considered all alike sexually ("cunts"). Perhaps when a man marries he chooses from this undistinguishable lot with care, for as we have seen, he holds a special high place in his mental reserve for "The One," by virtue of her close association with himself; but in general he can't tell the difference between chicks (Blondes, Brunettes, Redheads).[4] And he likes it that way. ("A wiggle in your walk, a giggle in your talk, THAT'S WHAT I LIKE!") When a man believes all women are alike, but wants to keep women from guessing, what does he do? He keeps his beliefs to himself, and pretends, to allay her suspicions, that what she has in common with other women is precisely what makes her different. Thus her sexuality eventually becomes synonymous with her individuality. *The sex privatization of women is the process whereby women are blinded to their generality as a class which renders them invisible as individuals to the male eye.* Is not that strange Mrs. Lady next to the President in his entourage reminiscent of the discreet black servant at White House functions?

The process is insidious: When a man exclaims, "I love Blondes!" all the secretaries in the vicinity sit up; they take it personally because they have been sex-privatized. The blonde one feels personally complimented because she has come to measure her worth through the physical attributes that differentiate her from other women. She no longer recalls that any physical attribute you could name is shared by many others, that these are accidental attributes not of her own creation, that her sexuality is shared by half of humanity. But in an authentic recognition of her individuality, her blondeness would be loved, but in a different way: She would be loved first as an irreplaceable totality, and then her blondeness would be loved as one of the characteristics of that totality.

The apparatus of sex privatization is so sophisticated that it may take years to detect—if detectable at all. It explains many puzzling traits of female psychology that take such form as:

Women who are personally complimented by compliments to their sex, i.e., "Hats off to the Little Woman!"

Women who are not insulted when addressed regularly and impersonally as Dear, Honey, Sweetie, Sugar, Kitten, Darling, Angel, Queen, Princess, Doll, Woman.

Women who are secretly flattered to have their asses pinched in Rome. (Much wiser to count the number of times other girls' asses are pinched!)

The joys of "prickteasing" (generalized male horniness taken as a sign of personal value and desirability).

The "clotheshorse" phenomenon. (Women, denied legitimate outlets for expression of their individuality, "express" themselves physically, as in "I want to see something 'different.' ")

These are only some of the reactions to the sex privatization process, the confusion of one's sexuality with one's individuality. The process is so effective that most women have come to believe seriously that the world needs their particular sexual contributions to go on. ("She thinks her pussy is made of gold.") But the love songs would still be written without them.

Women may be duped, but men are quite conscious of this as a valuable manipulative technique. That is why they go to great pains to avoid talking about women in front of them ("not in front of a lady")—it would

give their game away. To overhear a bull session is traumatic to a woman: So all this time she has been considered only "ass," "meat," "twat," or "stuff," to be gotten a "piece of," "that bitch," or "this broad" to be tricked out of money or sex or love! To understand finally that she is no better than other women but completely indistinguishable comes not just as a blow but as a total annihilation. But perhaps the time that women more often have to confront their own sex privatization is in a lover's quarrel, when the truth spills out: then a man might get careless and admit that the only thing he ever *really* liked her for was her bust ("Built like a brick shithouse") or legs anyway ("Hey, Legs!"), and he can find that somewhere else if he has to.

Thus sex privatization stereotypes women: it encourages men to see women as "dolls" differentiated only by superficial attributes—not of the same species as themselves—and it blinds women to their sexploitation as a class, keeping them from uniting against it, thus effectively segregating the two classes. A side-effect is the converse: if women are differentiated only by superficial physical attributes, men appear more individual and irreplaceable than they really are.

Women, because social recognition is granted only for a *false* individuality, are kept from developing the tough individuality that would enable breaking through such a ruse. If one's existence in its generality is the only thing acknowledged, why go to the trouble to develop real character? It is much less hassle to "light up the room with a smile"—until that day when the "chick" graduates to "old bag," to find that her smile is no longer "inimitable."

3. *The Beauty Ideal.* Every society has promoted a certain ideal of beauty over all others. What that ideal is is unimportant, for any ideal leaves the majority out; ideals, by definition, are modeled on *rare* qualities. For example, in America, the present fashion vogue of French models, or the erotic ideal Voluptuous Blonde are modeled on qualities rare indeed: few Americans are of French birth, most don't look French and

never will (and besides they eat too much); voluptuous brunettes can bleach their hair (as did Marilyn Monroe, the sex queen herself), but blondes can't develop curves at will—and most of them, being Anglo-Saxon, simply aren't built like that. If and when, by artificial methods, the majority can squeeze into the ideal, the ideal changes. If it were attainable, what good would it be?

For the exclusivity of the beauty ideal serves a clear political function. Someone—most women—will be left out. And left scrambling, because as we have seen, women have been allowed to achieve individuality only through their appearance—looks being defined as "good" not out of love for the bearer, but because of her more or less successful approximation to an external standard. This image, defined by men (and currently by homosexual men, often misogynists of the worst order), becomes the ideal. What happens? Women everywhere rush to squeeze into the glass slipper, forcing and mutilating their bodies with diets and beauty programs, clothes and makeup, anything to become the punk prince's dream girl. But they have no choice. If they don't the penalties are enormous: their social legitimacy is at stake.

Thus women become more and more look-alike. But at the same time they are expected to express their individuality through their physical appearance. Thus they are kept coming and going, at one and the same time trying to express their similarity and their uniqueness. The demands of Sex Privatization contradict the demands of the Beauty Ideal, causing the severe feminine neurosis about personal appearance.

But this conflict itself has an important political function. When women begin to look more and more alike, distinguished only by the degree to which they differ from a paper ideal, they can be more easily stereotyped as a class: They look alike, they think alike, and even worse, they are so stupid they believe they are not alike.

These are some of the major components of the cultural apparatus, romanticism, which, with the weakening of "natural" limitations on women, keep sex oppression going strong. The political uses of romanticism over the centuries became increasingly complex. Operating subtly or blatantly, on every cultural level, romanticism is now—in this time of greatest threat to the male power role—amplified by new techniques of communication so all-pervasive that men get entangled in their own line. How does this amplification work?

With the cultural portrayal of the smallest details of existence (e.g., deodorizing one's underarms), the distance between one's experience and one's perceptions of it becomes enlarged by a vast interpretive network: If our direct experience contradicts its interpretation by this ubiquitous cultural network, the experience must be denied. This process, of course, does not apply only to women. The pervasion of image has so deeply altered our very relationships to ourselves that even men have become objects—if never *erotic* objects. Images become extensions of oneself; it gets hard to distinguish the real person from his latest image, if indeed, the Person Underneath hasn't evaporated altogether. Arnie, the kid who sat in back of you in the sixth grade, picking his nose and cracking jokes, the one who had a crook in his left shoulder, is lost under successive layers of adopted images: the High School Comedian, the Campus Rebel, James Bond, the Salem Springtime Lover, and so on, each image hitting new highs of sophistication until the person himself doesn't know who he is. Moreover, he deals with others through this image-extension (Boy-Image meets Girl-Image and consummates Image-Romance). Even if a woman could get beneath this intricate image facade—and it would take months, even years, of a painful, almost therapeutic relationship—she would be met not with gratitude that she had (painfully) loved the man for his real self, but with shocked repulsion and terror that she had found him out. What he wants instead is The Pepsi-Cola Girl, to smile pleasantly to his Johnny Walker Red in front of a ski-lodge fire.

But, while this reification affects both men and women alike, in the case of women it is profoundly complicated by the forms of sexploitation I have described. Woman is not only an Image, she is the Image of Sex Appeal. The stereotyping of women expands: now there is no longer the excuse of ignorance. Every woman is constantly and explicitly informed on how to "improve" what nature gave her, where to buy the products to do it with, and how to count the calories she should never have eaten—indeed, the "ugly" woman is now so nearly extinct even she is fast becoming "exotic." The competition becomes frantic, because everyone is now plugged into the same circuit. The current beauty ideal becomes all-pervasive ("Blondes have more fun . . .").

And eroticism becomes erotomania. Stimulated to the limit, it has reached an epidemic level unequalled in history. From every magazine cover, film screen, TV tube, subway sign, jump breasts, legs, shoulders, thighs. Men walk about in a state of constant sexual excitement. Even with the best of intentions, it is difficult to focus on anything else. This bombardment of the senses, in turn, escalates sexual provocation still further: ordinary means of arousal have lost all effect. Clothing becomes more provocative: hemlines climb, bras are shed. See-through materials become ordinary. But in all this barrage of erotic stimuli, men themselves are seldom portrayed as erotic objects. Women's eroticism, as well as men's, becomes increasingly directed toward women.

One of the internal contradictions of this highly effective propaganda system is to expose to men as well as women the stereotyping process women undergo. Though the idea was to better acquaint women with their feminine role, men who turn on the TV are also treated to the latest in tummy-control, false eyelashes, and floor waxes (Does she . . . or doesn't she?). Such a crosscurrent of sexual tease and exposé would be enough to make any man hate women, if he didn't already.

Thus the extension of romanticism through modern media enormously magnified its effects. If before culture maintained male supremacy through Eroticism, Sex Privatization, and the Beauty Ideal, these cultural processes are now almost too effectively carried out: the media are guilty of "overkill." The regeneration of the women's movement at this moment in history may be due to a backfiring, an in-

ternal contradiction of our modern cultural indoctrination system. For in its amplification of sex indoctrination, the media have unconsciously exposed the degradation of "femininity."

In conclusion, I want to add a note about the special difficulties of attacking the sex class system through its means of cultural indoctrination. Sex objects *are* beautiful. An attack on them can be confused with an attack on beauty itself. Feminists need not get so pious in their efforts that they feel they must flatly deny the beauty of the face on the cover of *Vogue*. For this is not the point. The real question is: is the face beautiful in a *human* way—does it allow for growth and flux and decay, does it express negative as well as positive emotions, does it fall apart without artificial props—or does it falsely imitate the very different beauty of an *inanimate* object, like wood trying to be metal?

To attack eroticism creates similar problems. Eroticism is *exciting*. No one wants to get rid of it. Life would be a drab and routine affair without at least that spark. That's just the point. Why has all joy and excitement been concentrated, driven into one narrow, difficult-to-find alley of human experience, and all the rest laid waste? When we demand the elimination of eroticism, we mean not the elimination of sexual joy and excitement but its rediffusion over—there's plenty to go around, it increases with use—the spectrum of our lives.

Notes

1. Gallantry has been commonly defined as "excessive attention to women without serious purpose," but the purpose is very serious: through a false flattery, to keep women from awareness of their lower-class condition.

2. But as every woman has discovered, a man who seems to be pressuring for sex is often greatly relieved to be excused from the literal performance: His ego has been made dependent on his continuously proving him-

self through sexual conquest; but all he may have really wanted was the excuse to indulge in affection without the loss of manly self-respect. That men are more restrained than are women about exhibiting emotion is because, in addition to the results of the Oedipus Complex, to express tenderness to a woman is to acknowledge her equality. Unless, of course, one tempers one's tenderness—takes it back—with some evidence of domination.

3. Homosexuals are so ridiculed because in viewing the male as sex object they go doubly against the norm: even women don't read Pretty Boy magazines.

4. "As for his other sports," says a recent blurb about football hero Joe Namath, "he prefers Blondes."

Study Questions

1. What does Firestone mean by "romantic love"? What caused it to develop?

2. How does eroticism (one component of romanticism) act to reinforce the sex class system?

3. What is the "sex privatization of women" (another component of romanticism), and how does it act to reinforce the sex class system?

4. What is the Beauty Ideal, and how does it act to reinforce the sex class system?

5. How has romanticism been amplified in modern American culture?

Motherhood: The Annihilation of Women

Jeffner Allen

I would like to affirm the rejection of motherhood on the grounds that motherhood is dangerous to women. If woman, in patriarchy, is she who exists as the womb and wife of man, every woman is by definition a mother: she who produces for the sake of men. A mother is she whose body is used as a resource to reproduce men and the world of men, understood both as the biological children of patriarchy and as the ideas and material goods of patriarchal culture. Motherhood is dangerous to women because it continues the structure within which females must be women and mothers and, conversely, because it denies to females the creation of a subjectivity and world that is open and free.

An active rejection of motherhood entails the development and enactment of a *philosophy of evacuation*.[1] Identification and analysis of the multiple apsects of motherhood not only show what is wrong with motherhood, but also point

to a way out. A philosophy of evacuation proposes women's collective removal of ourselves from all forms of motherhood. Freedom is never achieved by the mere inversion of an oppressive construct, that is, by seeing motherhood in a "new" light. Freedom is achieved when an oppressive construct, motherhood, is vacated by its members and thereby rendered null and void.

A small and articulate group of radical feminist and radical lesbian feminist authors agree that motherhood is oppressive to women. Simone de Beauvoir's position in *The Second Sex,* that woman's "misfortune is to have been biologically destined for the repetition of life,"[2] is reaffirmed in her recent interviews: "I think a woman must not fall into the trap of children and marriage. Even if a woman wants to have children, she must think very hard about the conditions in which she will have to bring them up, because child-bearing, at the moment, is real slavery."[3] Shulamith Firestone, following de Beauvoir, finds that, "the heart of woman's oppression is her childbearing and childrear-

From Joyce Trebilcot, ed., *Mothering* (Totowa, NJ: Rowman & Allanheld, 1984), pp. 315–328. Reprinted by permission of Rowman & Allanheld. (Notes deleted.)

ing roles."[4] That woman's "reproductive function . . . is the critical distinction upon which all inequities toward women are grounded" is also asserted by Ti-Grace Atkinson at the beginning of the second wave of the women's liberation movement.[5] Monique Wittig writes that a female becomes a woman and a mother when she is defined first, and above all else, in terms of "the capacity to give birth (biology)."[6]

The claim that a direct connection exists between woman's oppression and her role as breeder within patriarchy also entails the recognition that men impose a type of sexuality on women through the institution of motherhood. De Beauvoir agrees that "frigidity seems . . . , in the present state of malaise created by the power relationship between men and women, a reaction at least more prudent and more reasonable [than woman's being trapped in sexuality] because it reflects this malaise and makes women less dependent on men."[7] Atkinson answers affirmatively the more specific question "Do you still feel that sexual instincts would disappear if 'sexual intercourse' no longer served the function of reproduction?"[8] Wittig holds that, "Sexuality is for us (lesbian feminists) an inevitable battleground insofar as we want to get outside of genitality and of the sexual economy imposed on us by the dominant heterosexuality."[9] Andrea Dworkin states clearly and without equivocation, "There is a continuum of phallic control. In the male system, reproductive and nonreproductive sex are both phallic sex."[10] I engage in a philosophy of evacuation as a radical lesbian feminist who questions, analyzes, and describes how motherhood is dangerous to women.

Speaking of motherhood as the annihilation of women does not disclaim either women's past or present as mothers. Women as mothers make the best of motherhood. Women are mothers because within patriarchy women have no choice except motherhood. Without the institution of motherhood women could and would live otherwise. Just as no single woman, or particular mother, is free in patriarchy, no group of token women, mothers in general, are free in patriarchy. Until patriarchy no longer exists, all females, as historical beings, must resist, rebel against, and avoid producing for the sake of men. Motherhood is not a matter of woman's psychological or moral character. As an ideology by which men mark females as women, motherhood has nothing to do with a woman's selfishness or sacrifice, nurturance or nonviolence. Motherhood has everything to do with a history in which women remain powerless by reproducing the world of men and with a present in which women are expected to do the same. The central publication of the Soviet Women's Committee, for instance, writes, "Considering motherhood to be a woman's most important social function . . ."[11]

I am endangered by motherhood. In evacuation from motherhood, I claim my life, body, world, as an end in itself.

Where Do Children Come From?

The question "Where do babies come from?" is frequently dismissed with a laugh, or cut short by recourse to scientific authority. In present-day discourse, both God's prescience and the stork are generally thought to be inadequate responses. A satisfactory and "progressive" explanation is found in a scientific account of the union of egg and sperm. The appeal to science is misleading, however, for it ignores and conceals the social intercourse which first brings men and women together either indirectly, through the use of medical technology, or directly, by means of physical copulation. The question "Where do babies come from?" might be approached more appropriately through the social and historical circumstances in which conception takes place. *Children come from patriarchal (male) sexuality's use of woman's body as a resource to reproduce men and the world of men.* Similarly, *motherhood* is men's appropriation of women's bodies as a resource to reproduce patriarchy.

The scientific explanation of where children come from avoids placing conception within the continuum of social power relationships that constitute motherhood: heterosexual intercourse, pregnancy, and childraising. Compulsion marks every aspect of the motherhood continuum: the mandatory heterosexuality imposed on women by men is thought "natural"; pregnancy is viewed as a biological fact; obligatory childraising by women is so "normal" that in the United States 39 percent of black families and 12 percent of white families are headed by women.

Seduction and pregnancy, for instance, are remarkably similar: both eroticize women's subordination by acting out and deepening women's lack of power.

> Male instinct can't help ITself; women need IT either because of their sexiness or their maternal instinct. IT, the penis, is big; IT, the child, is large. Woman's body is made for IT. Women's bodies have the right fit, or proportions. Women ask for IT, want IT. IT's a maturing experience in her becoming a woman. She takes IT. No real harm is done.

In seduction and pregnancy the power imbalance between men and women assumes the appearance of sexual difference, regardless of whether such activities are "affectionate" or "brutal."

> If women didn't want IT, IT wouldn't happen. Therefore, women must choose IT. Since many choose IT, IT must be part of their nature.[12]

I am defenseless within the motherhood continuum.

IT, "male instinct," passes through heterosexual intercourse to become the IT of motherhood. In motherhood, IT, male sexuality as a man-made social power construct, marks females with ITself. IT compels women to ITself: to male sexuality and its consequences, namely, birthing and raising men and the world of men. Children come from IT, from male-defined, male-dominated social intercourse. It names ITself as "virility": belonging to, characteristic of a man; the power of procreation, especially for sexual intercourse; the masculine member, the generative organs; force, energy, drive considered typically masculine; to pursue, to hunt.[13] Virility comes from vir, which in Latin means "man." Women's "misfortune is to have been biologically destined for the repetition of life"[14] precisely because ITs power, force, energy, drive appropriates women's biological possibility in order to produce ITself. IT pursues ITs own continuation, silencing my questions: is IT needed? Is IT desired? IT pursues ITs own evolution, constituting motherhood as a given, as compulsory for women, a danger to women.

The Representation

The question remains: "Where do children come from?" Or, more precisely, if children are produced by IT, by male sexuality as a man-made social power construct, how does male sexuality appropriate women's biological possibility in order to reproduce ITself? How do men constitute the motherhood continuum of heterosexual intercourse, pregnancy, and childraising as compulsory for women?

Analysis from a radical lesbian feminist perspective suggests that motherhood is constituted by male sexuality's use of woman's body to represent ITself to ITself. As such, motherhood is a paradigmatic instance of men's creation of representational thinking and of men's appropriation of the "world" by means of representational thought.

Representational thinking does not mean the production of a picture, copy, or imitation *of* the world. Representational thinking means, rather, to conceive and grasp the world *as* picture. In representational thinking, man manipulates, pursues, and entraps the world in order to secure it as picture. Man brings into play his unlimited power for the calculating, planning, and molding of all things; by conceiving and grasping the world as picture, he gives the measure and draws up the guidelines for everything that is. As such, he creates and determines what is real, and what is not. Not only is the man who has made the picture already in the picture, he is that which he pictures to himself. Yet, to acknowledge himself as the picture would be to destroy himself as he who conceives and grasps the world as picture. Only by maintaining a privileged stand outside the picture can he claim to be the creator, and not the object, of the activity of representation. Withdrawn from representation as the representer, however, he enters into the picture as "the incalculable," "the gigantic."

The object of representational thought, in

turn, is allowed to be only insofar as it can be overpowered—manipulated, pursued, entrapped—by representational thought. Once conceived and grasped as picture, the object is said to call forth, to provoke, the particular way in which it is pictured and the activity of picturing as such. The object can, indeed, must repeat itself exactly as it has been thought. It must even claim to establish, maintain, and justify its objectification. Its sole "activity" is reproductive: the reiteration and reinforcement of itself as picture.

Reproductive thinking thereby generates, unavoidably and of necessity, an ideology that is reproductive: motherhood. Athena is born from the head of Zeus alone; children are born from the head of man alone. Athena springs fully armed from the head of Zeus; a child springs from the head of its father, fully adorned with the markings of patriarchy. Zeus sees his world in his full-grown offspring; man pictures his world in his children who soon will be adults. Even if the child is female, man incorporates the female into his world as picture. The man with the child in his head, with the child as image in his head, represents himself to himself in the child that he has made. In contrast, Athena's mother, Metis, cannot be manipulated, pursued, trapped. She cannot be bound, secured, by man's representational thought. Athena's mother, children's mothers, are not.

In representational thought, woman is made pregnable (from *prehendere*, Latin for "to take"), understood in its literal sense as vulnerable to capture, taken. She is compelled to have man's child, to reproduce throughout her world of experience men's thoughts, words, actions. She must reproduce the life of the species, that is, man and his immortality. Captured by representational thinking, woman can never be genuinely pregnant (*pregnas*, akin to *gignere*, to produce): she cannot provide her own life and world. Woman as what-in-men's-eyes-she-seems-to-be is invisible, except insofar as her body is used by man to reproduce himself and his world. Woman as what-I-am-in-my-own-eyes is not. Motherhood passes through the mind of a man, of a man who does not see woman's body as her body. The man with the child in his head does not see the woman with

the child in her body. Throughout the motherhood continuum of heterosexual intercourse, pregnancy, and compulsory childraising, motherhood exists as a dialogue between men about an invisible woman.

Key to the specific mode of representation that defines motherhood, including the articulation of women's sexuality within the confines of motherhood, is male sexuality's setting of the bounds within which life and death are to be recognized. Man, the representer, assumes a greater-than-human power over life and death. Man, the representer, fixates on life and death as the central defining moments of one's life and as the two parts, or pieces, which comprise one's life. Within the framework of man's representation of life and death, woman's body is reduced to a lifeless instrument, even when her body is a carrier of life and death. The very manner in which man represents to himself his own life and death precludes, moreover, an experience of what is always already given: the continuity and discontinuity of an individual life, the strength and power of its ongoing action in the world, the authentic subjectivity of the woman who is *as* she is.

While man is giving birth to himself, woman dies. I, bound to the representation of woman as mother, leave that representation behind: evacuation to another way of thinking, to a productive empowering of the female who has been both woman and mother.

The Mark

The question "Where do children come from?" may be answered by a radical lesbian feminist phenomenology of consciousness, in terms of the representation. The representation is that form of consciousness by which patriarchal (male) sexuality constitutes a world in which woman's body is used as a resource to reproduce men and the world of men. "Where do children come from?" may also be answered by a similarly radical phenomenology of existence, through reference to the mark. The mark is the form of specific difference imposed on women's bodies when appropriated by men as a resource to reproduce patriarchy. An idealist interpretation of the representation and a materialist analysis of the mark converge so as to portray, when taken together, the social intercourse that is motherhood. A philosophy of evacuation from motherhood proposes, accordingly, that from which women must collectively remove ourselves: patriarchal thinking, the representation, and patriarchal existence, the mark.

One may object that even within patriarchy some types of motherhood are free of the representation and the mark, that some individual women do not occupy woman's traditional position as she who is marked. Such women, when truly exceptional, successfully assume man's traditional position as the representer of motherhood. A distinction must be made, however, between the hope that it expressed by such an objection, i.e., that women might live more freely, and the fact that is ignored by the objection, i.e., how women actually live. Such an objection involves a nonappropriation of the female body, as if motherhood could miraculously pass through woman's mind and not through her body. In fact, a female cannot escape being a mother unless she no longer produces for men, unless she is no longer compelled to reproduce the biological children, material goods, and ideas of patriarchy. Identification with the patterns traced on woman's body by the representation and the mark of motherhood is a necessity for the survival of all women. Indeed, identification with any single aspect of the motherhood continuum is an identification with every aspect of the motherhood continuum, for no single aspect exists as separable from the whole of its context. Women's identification with all women as mothers is a positive endeavor which points to what can be done, to actionary possibilities for the creation of a subjectivity that is genuinely free and open. I am no longer within patriarchy when I and all females have rendered null and void the ideology and institution of motherhood.

A radical lesbian feminist perspective suggests that the mark imposed by patriarchy on the bodies of all women compels all women to exist as mothers. The mark of motherhood inscribes the domination of men into woman's body, making motherhood appear as a natural phenomenon. Yet, motherhood is not a natural phenomenon, and mothers do not exist as a natural group. On the contrary, female biological possibilities are first "naturalized" by men as women's specific difference and then claimed as the reason for the existence of motherhood. Through this "naturalization," or marking, the female's biological possibility to give birth is made to appear as the intrinsic cause of women's place in motherhood and as the origin of women's social, economic, and political place in the world. The female's biological possibility to bear a child thereby becomes the defining characteristic of all women.

The closer a mark is to the body, the more indelibly it is associated with the body and the more the individual as a whole is pursued, hunted, trapped. In the case of woman, the mark has absolute permanence, for woman's entire body, and the body of her world, is marked: MOTHER. The permanence of the mark is the sign of the permanence of the male domination that marks all women as mothers.

Marking operates by focusing on isolated fragments of the female body. Such fragments, vagina, breasts, etc., are marked with a significance that is presumed to be intrinsic, eternal, and to characterize the whole of the female body. Forms of activity and character traits termed "natural" to women are then deduced from the marking imposed on the body fragments.

The institution of motherhood is unique among those created by marking in that there is no other institution in which so many persons can be destroyed by the mark, and yet, a sufficient supply of persons to be marked remains. In all other forms of war, attrition eventually threatens the supply of persons who can be marked and thereby usually limits the activity of marking, at least for a time. The mark of motherhood is distinctive in that one of its byproducts is the regeneration of more females to be marked as women and mothers.

The object marked, woman as mother, experiences the mark as pain. The inscription of the mark of motherhood on women's bodies is never without pain—the pain of not "owning" our bodies, the pain of physical injury, the pain of being compelled to never produce a life or world of our own. Pain (from Greek *poiné*, punishment, penalty, payment) is the punishment, the penalty we must pay, for being marked by men as woman and mother. Pain has nothing to do with what we do, that is, our success or failure at being good, well-informed, or willing mothers. Pain is a sign that we, as women, are put in danger by men who mark us. *If and when* the pain of the mark is not successfully "naturalized" by men, that is, is not or does not remain imprinted on females as belonging to our nature either physiologically or psychologically, we attempt to evade pain. Our pain breaks through the force of the mark. We do not endure the pain. We do not put up with the mark. We avoid, resist, the mark. We neither need nor desire the mark. We will get out of the mark. The immense amount of pain that marking entails is both an experience that always accompanies the mark of motherhood and an experience that can lead to the end of the mark of motherhood.

Outside the social power relationship within which marking occurs, the mark does not exist. Outside patriarchy, the mark of motherhood cannot even be imagined.

Stamped, firmly imprinted on women's bodies, is the emblem that our bodies have been opened to the world of men: the shape of the pregnant woman's stomach. From conception to abortion, acts which are biologically different and yet symbolically the same, our stomachs are marked: MOTHER.

In present-day patriarchal society, the marking impressed on woman's stomach is man's proof of his virility, that he can reproduce himself. When the mark remains on women's stomachs from conception to the birth of an infant, male virility not only can, but does, reproduce itself. In contrast, when the mark remains imprinted on our stomachs from conception to the abortion of a fetus, male virility can, but does not—yet—reproduce itself. Either the time is judged as not right—yet, or the right time has passed by—already. When abortion is permitted, either officially or unofficially, there need not be an immediate and direct link between conception and the birth of an infant. There must, however, be an indirect link between male virility which can reproduce

itself and male virility which does reproduce itself. The right time must eventually be found such that man both can and does reproduce himself, either by means of biological children or through the material goods and ideas of patriarchy. Indeed, within patriarchy the fact that abortion may sometimes be permitted does not make abortion a genuinely free choice, for women have no alternative but abortion if we are already impregnated and do not want to reproduce. Nor does the right to abortion make motherhood voluntary, for a woman in patriarchy cannot abort, or do away with, the mark of motherhood itself. The right to abortion in patriarchy cannot, in principle, recognize that women may choose abortion because we will not reproduce men and the world of men, because we will not be mothers.

The woman who does not remove the mark from her stomach, who does not have an abortion, may be killed: on the West Bank one such Arab woman a week is found "poisoned or burned to death and the murder is made to look accidental."[15] Women who survive an initial decision to not remove the mark from our stomachs, to not have an abortion, in defiance of the traditions of male virility, may be persecuted as non-virgins and unmarried mothers. Yet, the women who do remove the mark from our stomachs, who abort, may also die. Five thousand women a year are estimated to die in Spain and Portugal alone as a result of complications arising from illegal abortions. In Latin America, abortion causes 20 percent to 50 percent of all maternal deaths. Complications from illegal abortions account for 4 percent to 70 percent of maternal deaths in the hospitals of developing countries. "A woman undergoing a properly performed abortion has six times less risk of death from complications than a woman having a child."[16] In childbirth our bodies as a whole are stamped with the mark of pain, terror, and possible death.

To speak of birth without violence is to ignore the violence of childbirth. The most frequent cause of death of women is childbirth:[17]

In a number of developing countries . . .
maternal mortality rates in excess of 500 per
100,000 live births are by no means exceptions.

Rates of over 1000 per 100,000 have been reported in parts of Africa.

In the areas with the highest maternal mortality, i.e., most of Africa, West, South, and East Asia, about half a million women die from maternal causes every year.

Age-specific death rates for women rise sharply at ages 20–30 in many countries, where women often have less chance than men of surviving from 15 to 45 years of age.[18]

Already, as female children, women as a whole are marked—"undesirable." College students in the United States, for instance, favor what amounts to a decrease in female births, with the overall ratio of girls to boys desired being 100:116. Also, "from 66 to 92 percent of men have been found to want an only child to be a boy . . . , and from 62 to 80 percent prefer a first child to be a boy,"[19] a chilling thought as the United States, like Western Europe, moves toward zero growth.

As female fetuses, women as a whole are stamped "to be aborted." A recent Chinese report, for example, shows that when sex determination tests were performed on 100 fetuses with the sole purpose being the determination of the fetus's gender, there were 30 planned abortions. Of those 30 aborted fetuses, 29 were female.[20]

As female infants, women as a whole are marked "dead." Men, rather than regulate men and men's use of women, claim that because there is not enough food, resources, etc., "female fertility" must be controlled by the elimination of women. From the Athens of antiquity to the present, infanticide has been, largely and for the most part, femicide.

Women as mothers are marked: Dead. Man the marker continues with himself, his sons, his mark.

The Society of Mothers

Man remains with his representation and his mark. Women need not remain. The representation and the mark, and not existing females *per se*, are integral to motherhood. Indeed, if and when the representation and the mark of motherhood can be affixed to something other than the female body, women may not be at all.

The society of mothers, comprised of all women within motherhood, is dangerous to all its members. The society of mothers continues, by definition, the ideology and institution of motherhood as oppressive to women. The motherhood lived out by the society of mothers is also the annihilation of women. When motherhood involves men's reproduction and marking of females as women and mothers, (a) motherhood may entail our physical death and our non-existence as mothers and as female infants, and (b) motherhood always entails the death of a world in which women are free. In the contemporary ideology and institution of motherhood, women's annihilation is also involved in that (a) men's representation and marking of females as women and mothers may continue and, at the same time, (b) men may represent and mark objects (from the domain of the sciences and technology of reproduction) and persons other than females (from among those men held to be "lesser" in power and merit) to reproduce men and the world of men, such that (c) the class, women as mothers, has no further use function, and thus need no longer be reproduced. Both forms of annihilation are dangerous to women. The specifically contemporary manifestation of motherhood, however, shows clearly that women are not necessary to motherhood. Patriarchal men must represent and mark something as MOTHER, but that which is so designated need not be women.

The society of mothers exhibits, in multiple forms, the dangerous situation of woman, the womb and wife of man, and mother, she who produces for men. In modern times, the collectivity of females who are compelled to live within motherhood is composed of those who must reproduce the biological children of patriarchy and those who must reproduce the material goods and ideas of patriarchal culture. Women who reproduce the biological children of patriarchy do so in widely differing manners. All such women, however, are represented and marked by motherhood. In fact, so determinate is men's regulation of women's reproduction of children that the world population growth is projected as coming to a halt in 130 years, at which time, "nearly nine-tenths of this projected 10.5 billion people will be living in developing countries. The poorest regions of the world—Africa and South Asia—will account for more than 60 percent of the world's people . . . the industrialized world's share of the world population will see a drop of today's 24 percent to about 13 percent.[21]

Members of the society of mothers who reproduce the material goods and ideas of patriarchal culture may manifest the ideology and institution of motherhood in differing ways. Despite such differences, the women remain mothers. The limitation of the society of mothers to those who reproduce only the biological children of men is to ignore that men use women's bodies in a multitude of ways to reproduce patriarchal life. Women who do not give birth to biological children are still involved in the "regeneration" of men, in virtue of our work, unpaid and paid, to continue the products, both ideal and material, of motherhood. Even when men can produce biological children by use of the sciences and technology of reproduction, women may be kept in existence as those who perform various services for men, or women may be bred out of existence. Within a patriarchal context, even the production of females by parthenogenesis need not alter the social and historical circumstances of the society of mothers into which they are born. Men may or may not continue to impose patriarchal (male) sexuality on women. Men may or may not relate in explicitly sexual modes to women, and women may still be kept in our service function as the society of mothers.

The representation and mark of motherhood claim not just the surface, but the whole of women, such that the society of mothers not only reproduces, but often defends, the patriarchal world of men: "Confined to their cities the mothers were no longer separate, free, complete individuals and they fused into an anonymous collective consciousness."[22]

In the production of the son for the father, in the production of goods for the father, for the benefit of the son, we are not our bodies, we are not ourselves. A means to men's ends, never an end in ourselves, we are selfless, worldless, annihilated. The experience of our servitude takes seriously our danger and holds, firmly and strongly, to the conviction that together we must get out of motherhood.

Priorities and Alternatives

To show how motherhood, in its many forms, is dangerous to women is also to suggest how women may get out of motherhood. Further questions such as "Why do men impose motherhood on women by means of the representation and the mark?" and "Why do women form a society of mothers?" can lead to idle speculation, unless the questioner's focus centers on how motherhood exists in actuality and how women's actions may form a horizon of possibility in light of which all women may succeed in breaking free of the ideology and institution of motherhood.

Central to a philosophy of evacuation from motherhood is the primacy of women's daily lives and the power of our possible, and sometimes actual, collective action. In breaking free from motherhood, I no longer focus on birth and death as the two most important moments of my life. I give priority, rather, to that which is always already given, my life and my world in their actual presence to me. The moment of birth and the moment of death have, in themselves, no special value. They need not determine who I am or who I may become. I—my activities, body, sexuality—am articulated by my actions and choices, which, apart from patriarchy, may be made in the openness of freedom. Similarly, I no longer give a primacy to that which I have reproduced. I claim as primary my life and world as I create and experience them. New modes of thinking and existing emerge as the evacuation from motherhood empowers the female who has been both woman and mother. In that evacuation I, as an individual female, and we, as the community of all females, lay claim, with firmness and strength, to the presence of our own freely chosen subjectivities, to the priorities and alternatives we produce as our own.

Because the evacuation from motherhood does not simply seek to alter motherhood as it exists currently, its focus is not specifically on the development of alternative means of intercourse, pregnancy, or childraising. Women who use artificial insemination and whose children have no known father, as well as women who live as lesbian mothers, clearly challenge, but need not break with, the ideology and institution of motherhood. Each of these alternatives is significant for women's survival within patriarchy, but none is sufficient for women's effective survival, that is, for the creation of a female's self-chosen, nonpatriarchal, existence.

A precondition for women's effective survival may be established, instead, by the female's power to not have children. A decision not to have children may be made, not because a female's biological possibility causes the ideology of motherhood, but because,

1. To not have children opens a time-space for the priority of claiming my life and world as my own and for the creative development of radically new alternatives.
2. The biology from which a child is born does not determine or control the course of that child's life. Females and males, younger and older, create the shapes of our lives through our individual choices.
3. Women who wish to be with younger females or males can do so collectively, with others of similar interests, or individually, through adoption.
4. Currently, there is no question of women's absolute biological extinction.

At present, and for several thousands of years past, women have conceived, borne, and raised multitudes of children without any change in the conditions of our lives as women. In the case that all females were to decide not to have children for the next twenty years, the possibilities for developing new modes of thought and existence would be almost unimaginable.

The necessary condition of women's evacuation from motherhood is, even more significantly, the claiming of our bodies as a source. Our bodies are not resources to be used by men to reproduce men and the world of men while, at the same time, giving death to ourselves. If necessary, women must bear arms, but not children, to protect our bodies from invasion by men. For our effective survival, women's repetitive reproduction of patriarchy must be replaced by the genuine, creative, production of ourselves. In particular, the areas of food, literacy, and energy sources and supplies for women must be reexamined as crucial to the claiming of our bodies as a source.

Women's hunger is one of the specific conditions affecting the possibility for men's continuing success in representing and marking women as mothers. Within the current patriarchal economy, women do not have access to sufficient crops to feed ourselves:

> In many countries where malnutrition is prevalent, up to half the cultivated acreage is growing crops for export to those who can afford them, rather than food stuffs for those who need them. . . . The cash crops are generally cultivated by men while food crops are grown by women. Practically all the agricultural land in developing countries is owned by men. Men always eat first and most of the food: Women and children go hungry and are the vast majority of malnourished everywhere, especially in Asia and Africa.[23]

Nor do women have access to the money necessary to purchase food: in 1979, women living in poverty constituted 12 percent of the total, worldwide, female population and 75 percent of all people living in poverty.

Women's literacy is the second specific condition that enhances the possibility for men's continuing success in maintaining the ideology and institution of women as mothers. Women have insufficient access to the basics of literacy, that is, reading, writing, and simple arithmetic. In fact, from a global perspective, women are two-thirds of the illiterates of the world. In almost all countries, "girls already begin school in fewer numbers than boys; on the average, the difference even at the start of school is 10–20 percent. By the time higher education is reached, the ratio between boys and girls is at least 2:1, but in many cases more."[24] In many African countries, less than 10 percent of the women read and write. The education gap between men and women is growing all over the developing world. Yet, even in industrialized societies, women have no access to determining what constitutes an education, which areas of research are the most pressing, and what comprises the development of more liberating forms of thinking and speaking.

Energy sources and supplies for women are a third area which undermines women's endeavors to break free of motherhood. In African villages, women work about three hours per day more than men because it is the women who must gather the food, water, and fuel necessary for survival. Generally speaking, technological information on alternative means of energy is not made available to such women, any more than it is to most women in industrialized countries. In all societies, women's non-control of ener⌐ sources and supplies necessary to our ⌐ keeps us in subordination to mer⌐

Women's non⌐ ⌐tion, and energy sour⌐ ⌐'s repre-sentation an⌐ ⌐others and, as such, ⌐ ⌐nda-tions of the ide⌐ ⌐her-hood. Women's s⌐ ⌐n by men go hand in ⌐ ⌐e multiple forms of vi⌐ ly enforce women's n⌐ claim our bodies as a s⌐ reproduction of mothe⌐ ages must work together⌐ defined alternatives that ex⌐ current needs and desires fo⌐ and energy. The goal of such ⌐ neither to save the world n⌐ "healthy" mothers who reprodu⌐ children. Female-defined access ⌐ education, and energy forms a necess⌐ tion for women's collective evacuatic⌐ motherhood in that such access claim⌐ source the whole of our bodies and work⌐ females who engage in evacuation f⌐ motherhood, we shape the whole of oursel⌐ and our world in the present of our own life⌐ times.

Notes

1. I am indebted to Julien Murphy for suggesting the phrase "a philosophy of evacuation."

2. Simone de Beauvoir, *The Second Sex*, trans-lated by H. M. Parshley (New York: Vintage Books, 1974), p. 72.

3. De Beauvoir, "Talking to de Beauvoir," *Spare Rib* (March 1977): 2.

4. Shulamith Firestone, *The Dialectic of Sex* (New York: Bantam Books, 1971), p. 72.

5. Ti-Grace Atkinson, *Amazon Odyssey* (New York: Links Books, 1974), p. 1.

6. Monique Wittig and Sande Zeig, *Brouillon pour un dictionnaire des amantes* (Paris: Grasset, 1976), p. 94; and Wittig, "One Is Not Born a Woman," *Feminist Issues* 1, no. 2 (Winter 1981): 1.

7. De Beauvoir, "Talking to de Beauvoir," p. 2.

8. Atkinson, "Interview with Ti-Grace Atkinson," *Off Our Backs* 9, no. 11 (December 1973): 3.

9. Wittig, "Paradigm," in *Homosexualities and French Literature*, edited by George Stambolian and Elaine Marks (Ithaca: Cornell University Press, 1979), pp. 118–19.

10. Andrea Dworkin, *Pornography: Men Possessing Women* (New York: Perigree, 1981), p. 222.

⌐ *WIN News* 7, no. 4 (1981): 68. Citation from the "Soviet Women's Committee" ⌐oklet.

⌐a Wieder, "Accouche! " *Questions Fémi-*⌐ 5 (February 1979): 53–72.

⌐ford English Dictionary.

⌐voir, *The Second Sex*, p. 72.

⌐ vol. 7, no. 2 (1981): 52. From ⌐ricain (3 January 1981).

⌐ ⌐l. 7, no. 3 (1981): 22.

⌐ ⌐7, no. 4 (1981): 24. From ⌐ Institute, *International*

⌐ ⌐n. 7, no. 3 (1981): 16. From ⌐ ⌐alth Organization, "Sixth Report ⌐e World Health Situation."

19. Jalna Hanmer, "Sex, Predetermination, Artificial Insemination and the Maintenance of Male-Dominated Culture," in *Woman, Health and Reproduction*, edited by Helen Roberts (London: Routledge & Kegan Paul, 1981), pp. 167, 168.

20. Ibid., p. 176.
21. *WIN News,* vol. 7, no. 4 (1981): 23. From the Population Institute, *International Dateline.*
22. Wittig and Zeig, *Lesbian Peoples,* p. 76.
23. *WIN News,* vol. 7, no. 4 (1981): 23, 24.
24. *WIN News,* vol. 7, no. 1 (1981): 21. From World Bank Headquarters, "Education: A World Bank Sector Policy Paper."

Study Questions

---

1. What does Allen mean by posing a "philosophy of evacuation" regarding motherhood?

2. What does Allen mean when she asks, "Where do children come from?"

3. What is "representational thinking"? How have men used this mode of thought to create "motherhood"?

4. According to Allen, what is the "mark of motherhood"?

5. In what ways does Allen think the "mark of motherhood" is physically dangerous for women?

6. What is the "society of mothers" for her?

7. What does Allen see as central to her "philosophy of evacuation"? What does that entail about the female's power to not have children? About her other powers?

The Future of Mothering: Reproductive Technology and Feminist Theory

Anne Donchin

The nurse said I would have to show you, but you reached right for my breast. You suckled right away. I remember how you grabbed with your small pursed mouth at my breast and started drawing milk from me, how sweet it felt. How could anyone know what being a mother means who has never carried a child nine months heavy under her heart, who has never borne a baby in blood and pain, who has never suckled a child . . . What do they know of motherhood?

Connie Ramos, a mother of our time.

It was part of women's long revolution. When we were breaking all the old hierarchies. Finally there was that one thing we had to give up too, the only power we ever had, in return for no more power for anyone. The original production: the power to give birth. Cause as long as we were never biologically enchained, we'd never be equal. And males never would be humanized to be loving and tender. So we all become mothers. Every child has three. To break the nuclear bonding.

Luciente, a 'mother' from a possible future.

From *Hypatia,* Vol. 1, no. 2 (Fall 1986). Reprinted by permission of the author.

Connie's dialogue with Luciente takes place within the imaginative territory explored by Marge Piercy in *Woman on the Edge of Time* (1976, 105–106). Hers is a culturally androgynous society based on feminist values and organized about a commitment to the extinction of all systematic sex-role distinctions and the elimination of biological reproduction by females. Instead genetic material taken from human males and females is stored in 'brooders' where it is fertilized and the embryos are grown until ready for birth. The bond between genes and culture is deliberately broken. Knowledge of genetic origin is obliterated. Still the citizens of Luciente's world remain divided over the desirability of genetic intervention. They watch for birth defects, for genes linked with disease susceptibility, but they do not yet breed for selected traits. The 'shapers' among them push for selective breeding; the 'mixers' "don't think people can know objectively how people should become." They see the 'shapers' proposal as a 'power surge' (Piercy 1976, 226).

The breeding practices adopted in Piercy's utopian society bear a remarkable resemblance to the reproductive arrangements instituted in Aldous Huxley's dystopian *Brave New World* (1932), though in this imaginative future, not only eugenics, but dysgenics, as well, is practiced systematically. In their laboratories they gestate both biologically 'superior' embryos and, in far larger numbers, biologically 'inferior' embryos which are subjected to the Bokanosky Process (ninety-six identical twins from a single ovum) and treated prenatally with toxins. When decanted they are barely recognizably human, but are useful in performing unskilled work and, with appropriate conditioning, can be relied upon to docilely follow the commands of superiors. Reproduction has been brought wholly within control of the state.

Since Huxley's dystopian fantasy appeared, the feasibility of such a world has drawn increasingly nearer to us. Researchers have made substantial strides in both genetic research and reproductive technologies. Artificial insemination has become a commonplace occurrence. *In vitro* fertilization and ovum transfer, though only marginally successful, are widely practiced. Economically disadvantaged women are readily available to serve as surrogate mothers for a modest fee. When mastery of the processes of extra-uterine gestation is achieved, they will be dispensible too. Already extra-corporeal membrane oxygenation (an adaptation of the heart-lung machine) is being applied successfully to infants weighing even less than one kilogram (Bartlett 1984). Once the functions of the placenta have been successfully mimicked, perpetuation *in vitro* to viability (ectogenesis) will render the biological process of pregnancy technically obsolete. Though the mere fact of technological feasibility might suggest possible development within either a Piercean or a Huxleyan social framework, subsequent achievement of effective political control over larger, more diffuse populations than even Huxley envisaged only sharpens the vision of the more portentous future. And were extra-uterine gestation to become available, the potential for such a concentration of political power would be immeasurably enhanced. Those who control the instrumentalities of power would command the means to bring either future into being.

If women's long-term interests are to be represented in determining the future direction of reproductive technology, women will need to participate collectively in shaping public policy. Unfortunately, there has been too little discussion among women about either the fundamental values at stake or the social goals that would best promote women's well-being. Though many feminist writers have expressed concern *retrospectively* about the increased dominance of medically controlled childbirth technologies and some have pointed to the direction in which prevailing interests are pushing reproductive technology, this discussion has taken place in virtual isolation from both the general context of feminist theorizing and the background of social theory with which feminist theory is intertwined.[1] There is need now to integrate grass-root feminist concerns about medically controlled reproduction with feminist theorists' attempts to reconstruct the social framework of women's collective past and draw out connections to possible feminist futures. We need to think collectively about the sort of social policy that would best serve women's most fundamental interests: whether the capacity to give birth is of such paramount value that no social aim achievable in any technological future could supplant it; whether *all* technological innovations in reproductive practices should be opposed despite their therapeutic benefit to some women individually; or if specific technological advances might be supported step by step until their deleterious social effects become clearly manifest.

In the following pages I should like to sketch out a framework within which such a feminist dialogue might proceed. First, I shall briefly discuss the utilization of reproductive technologies within the present social context, then describe the principal ethical and social positions regarding emerging reproductive technologies, considering the social values and policy alternatives implicit in each position, attempting to ferret out the implications of these developments for the interests of women. Next I will raise some conceptual and theoretical questions about the very idea of a utopian feminist future, considering first, the arguments of feminist theorists who have taken exception to the sort of utopian analysis Shulamith Firestone offers and then those feminist commentators who share Huxley's dystopian prognosis of a future where the bond between pregnancy and procreation has been severed. Finally, I will contrast their positions with the utopian feminists in order to better understand the basis of present feminist reaction to reproductive innovation, whether it stems principally from reservation about the nature of technological intervention itself or from fears about the more probable consequences of such a technological future. I will end with some observations about the presuppositions underlying theoretical differences among feminists and suggest an interim course of action to meet the present situation.

The Present Social Context

Although Great Britain and Australia have established national commissions to investigate the ethical and social implications of the new reproductive technologies and recommend appropriate social policy, in the United States the development and utilization of reproductive innovations is left to the discretion of individuals and physicians. Though there has been some consideration at the federal level of ethical issues involving *in vitro* fertilization and embryo transfer, the Ethics Advisory Board which undertook this work was disbanded after submitting its initial report in 1979. Though federally supported research into these processes cannot proceed without the approval of the disbanded committee, both private research efforts and commercial marketing of new reproductive techniques continue to go forward with virually no ethical constraints other than those researchers themselves choose to impose.[2] Individuals seeking to benefit from the fruits of reproductive research are left free to negotiate with individual physicians subject only to the constraints of private conscience and economic resources. In instances of artificial insemination, a low-tech 'cottage' industry, medical and economic constraint virtually fall out and individual choice becomes the exclusive determinant. Recipient choice is limited,

however, by available information which lies principally within the control of 'donors' (more accurately 'sperm vendors,' since in most instances they are paid for their product). Because of possible legal liability their anonymity is usually protected. Though most recipients would prefer to receive sperm from genetically screened donors, access to such information is frequently denied them. Where women attempt to procure sperm through non-medical channels from *known* donors, they risk the possibility that the donor may later claim paternity.

Hence some controls are desirable both from the perspective of those seeking to suppress the dissemination of reproductive technologies altogether and in the interests of unmarried and infertile women who hope to benefit from reproductive innovations. The principal issues, then, center around the nature of these controls and the goals toward which they are to be directed. Would women's interests be better served by continuing along the present freewheeling course that maximizes 'reproductive freedom,' limited only by the capacity to find a cooperative physician and by the patient's ability to bear the cost of the service? Or should the available options be limited by circumscribing choices, either at the level of service delivery or in the process of further research development?

Both of these positions are defended by their supporters as options which maintain continuities with social and political traditions. One emphasizes individual freedom; the other gives centrality to traditional patterns of reproduction and parenting. However, emphasis upon individualistic values tends to push in the direction of technological innovation. Attention to the focal role of the biological family in social organization, in effect, subordinates individual interests and would suppress unfettered technological development.

Social reactions to innovative reproductive practices divide roughly into three camps: the noninterventionists, who question the advisability of any practice which tampers with either nature's way of doing things or traditional social institutions; the moderate interventionists, who give primacy to reproductive freedom while acknowledging that some weight should be attached to other values as well; and the radical interventionists who divide into two distinctive factions: those who support advances in knowledge of reproductive processes for their own sake without regard to possible technological applications and those who favor reproductive research for the sake of the technological future such research will facilitate. Advocates of the first version of the radical position are to be found principally among researchers and some philosophers who argue that we should push the frontiers of knowledge forward now and concern ourselves about undesirable applications only as the need becomes manifest.[3] Most conspicuous among supporters of the second version are Marge Piercy and her model, Shulamith Firestone whose 1970 work: *The Dialectic of Sex: The Case for Feminist Revolution,* first focused feminist attention on the political significance of reproductive biology. Ursula LeGuin's fantasy: *The Left Hand of Darkness* (1976) and Joanna Russ *The Female Male* (1975) also borrow their central themes from Firestone's proposal. All look with favor upon reproductive innovations which free women from their traditional biological role.

The Noninterventionists

Among the most eloquent and articulate of the noninterventionists is Protestant theologian Paul Ramsey, who participated in the deliberations of the now defunct Ethics Advisory Board. He objects to all forms of reproductive innovation other than medical or surgical treatment of infertility (Ramsey 1972). In support of his position he offers three arguments. (1) It is a violation of the received canons of medical ethics to expose a possible human being to any unnecessary risk. Since a merely possible human cannot grant consent, there is no ground upon which it is morally permissible to jeopardize its future well being. (2) The proper role of medicine is the correction of 'medical conditions,' such as infertility. However, if there are no remedies for the physical condition itself, then it is not appropriate to in-

tervene further. (3) Procreation and parenthood are 'courses of action' appropriate to humans as natural objects toward whom an attitude of 'natural piety' is appropriate. They cannot without violation be disassembled and put together again. Instead we should work according to the functions operating in the whole of the natural order of which we are a part. Increasing mastery over nature brings increased power over humans and even greater risk of abuse.

Each of Ramsey's arguments incorporates controversial presuppositions: (1) that the canons of medical ethics are extendable to merely *possible* humans, and (2) that medicine's proper function is the reversal of a physical condition. Many physical deficits cannot be reversed, but where the function is highly valued, ways are found to circumvent the incapacity, e.g. prosthetic limbs, or eyeglasses, etc.

Many women experience sterility as such an incapacity. Having learned from infancy to associate femininity with fertility they look upon their barrenness as a mutilation. The apparent eagerness of many women to endure considerable pain and suffering at the hands of technological experts in an often futile attempt to bring about a pregnancy cannot be understood apart from this larger social context. Others fully intend to bear children but are victims of 'family planning' technologies or environmental pollutants injurious to their reproductive capacities. The social obligation to such women cannot be dismissed merely on the ground that patient *desire* is not the proper object of medical intervention. That argument fails to speak to the morally relevant features of the situation.[4]

Ramsey's final argument is complex, incorporating presumptions about both the place of humans in nature and the tendencies of human nature. There are serious ambiguities here which merit careful examination. It is not clear why the bare fact that something is natural should give it any moral weight. Why moral force should be attributed selectively to normal procreation while human intervention, say, in the use of respirators for premature infants is unquestioningly supported calls for further explanation. For such an appeal to nature to stand it would have to rest on some other ground, possibly the fear that human power over reproduction, in particular, would invite serious abuse.[5]

Despite the fragmentary character of Ramsey's arguments they do point to several widely shared concerns about the direction in which reproductive innovation is leading technologically advanced societies. His allusion to a relationship between power over nature and power over humans, in particular, captures a concern widely shared by feminist critics of technological innovation, a theme which I shall return to later and examine in detail within the context of feminist criticism.

Leon Kass, a physician and influential writer on medical ethical issues, also frames his principal objection to reproductive innovations on traditionalist grounds, but unlike Ramsey who sees the principal threat in the violation of 'nature,' Kass emphasizes values attached to human respect. However, his notion of 'respect' bears the mark of an origin closely linked to Ramsey's conception of 'nature.' Though he claims that what is at stake is the idea of the humanness of human life and the meaning of human embodiment, these conceptions appear to borrow their meaning from their affinity with social practices assumed to be naturally given rather than socially derived.

On the basis of these assumptions Kass favors legislative intervention to regulate the dangers of *in vitro* fertilization and embryo transfer which, he argues, "erode fundamental beliefs, values, institutions and practices" (Kass 1979). He proposes that the use of embryo transfer be restricted to the married couple from whom the embryo derives in order to sustain traditional bonds among sexuality, love and procreation.

Like Ramsey, Kass proposes that further research be restricted to the treatment of infertility or other measures that support the desire to have a child of 'one's own' (by implication presupposing a distinction between legitimate and inappropriate desires). He opposes use of embryos in investigative research, donation to other couples or commercial transactions (such as surrogate mothering arrangements), claiming that such practices violate the traditional human sense of our sexual nature and the experience of relatedness to our ancestors and descendants. He, too, fears the concentration of power such technological developments would place within the control of researchers and special interests, but his fear, unlike Ramsey's, is couched within an appeal to cultural practices rather than to nature. However, since his cultural arrangements seemingly owe their authority to what is 'natural' the differences between them are not so great as would first appear. Though Kass is undoubtedly correct in observing that certain innovative practices, were they to become widespread, would threaten present conceptions of historical connectedness, it is not self-evident either that such innovations would be widely adopted or that prevailing norms are more desirable than any that might supplant them. Moreover, there are other well established traditions which tend to give primacy to individual autonomous decision-making over collective social interests, traditions frequently appealed to by advocates of innovative reproductive practices.

Moderate Interventionists

The right to procreate is firmly imbedded in the Western liberal tradition. However, the *desire* to have a child of 'one's own' is not harbored exclusively by couples as pairs, as Kass' view suggests, but may extend to individuals one by one. Noel Keane (1981),[6] an attorney involved in facilitating surrogate mothering arrangements, relates the story of a 59 year old lawyer who came to his office. He and his 61 year old wife had no children. She had been infertile throughout their marriage. He had planned to leave his estate to his nieces and nephews but then became intrigued by the renewed possibility that he might still be able to will his property to a child of his own. He asked Keane to find a couple willing to assist him. The wife would be artificially inseminated with his semen and bear his child. He would guarantee financial arrangements for the child and provide for its education. Keane pursued his request and made suitable arrangements. He has also established a surrogate mothering agency and is lobbying for legislative reform that would facilitate legal enforcement of surrogate contracts.[7] Decisions either to support such individualistic practices within the law or discourage options of this kind will have an important bearing on future social policy determinations, marking the boundary between the permissible exercise of personal desire and the sphere of collective social interests. Though the desire to pass on one's genetic endowment seems a predominantly male preoccupation, women's interests in bearing and rearing children outside the institution of marriage might also be served by a social policy that allows individuals free space to construct alternative childrearing arrangements. However, the legal advantages presently available to married couples, such as Keane represents, are not so readily extended to the unmarried who seek to fulfill comparable desires.

Recent judicial decisions have repeatedly affirmed the 'right' of individuals, at least within marriage, to control their own reproductive activity. This freedom is taken to be derived from the right to privacy, to a domain within which individuals may pursue their own life plans with a minimum of societal interference. Supporters of innovative reproductive technologies are by implication advocating application of these individualistic norms to an increasingly broader range of circumstances. Extension of the scope of reproductive freedom to gratification of a desire to parent (either biologically or socially) by technological intervention is highly problematic. Legal rulings supporting reproductive freedom have leaned principally on rights of *noninterference*, on the liberty *not* to procreate. However, at issue here, is legal support for service demanded from *other* parties. In such instances, the use of innovative technologies is likely to impinge on other persons' rights of noninterference and on other social values, some that are preconditions for the very exercise of personal autonomy and others that would command comparable weight in any just social ordering.

George Annas, in testimony to the U.S. House of Representatives Committee on Science and Technology (U.S. 1985), recently pointed out that if children resulting from such techniques as surrogate embryo transfer (to a woman other than the egg donor) and the use of frozen embryos are to be adequately protected, goverment will have to intervene into the arena of human reproduction. Failure to regulate private contractual agreements, he argues, jeopardizes the integrity of the family and threatens the interests of children. The claims of some infertile couples, he contends, are outweighed by the interest of the potential child. For the sake of protecting these interests he advocates legal action: (1) defining maternity and paternity at the moment of birth, preserving the current legal presumption that the gestation mother is the legal mother so that it will be conclusive and cannot be overriden by private contractual arrangements, and (2) protecting the human embryo from commercial exploitation by restricting the freedom to use frozen embryos to the purpose specified by the donors (Annas 1984). The Warnock Commission Report incorporates comparable recommendations.

However, some object to the modesty of such regulatory recommendations, particularly those noninterventionists who accept Ramsey's and Kass' arguments in defense of early embryos and traditional conceptions of the family. Some feminists reach the same conclusions, too, though for other reasons. They fear further erosion of women's decisionmaking powers if reproductive technologies are allowed to proliferate so freely.

Radical Interventionists

Incorporation of Marge Piercy's thought-experiment into consideration of policy options for the more immediate future should promote us to consider more carefully the grounds for hesitancy to support reproductive innovations, where what is principally at issue is the nature of the activity itself or fears about the likely consequences to follow. Luciente, Piercy's protagonist from Mattapoisett, her utopian feminist world, readily acknowledges that the institution of their new reproductive arrangements required women to relinquish the power to give birth. However, they judge the benefit well worth the sacrifice since all power relations have been abolished as well. Within such a social context the choice seems obviously sensible.

There is reason to wonder, though, whether such a social framework is plausible, or even intelligible? Apart from the obvious difficulty in understanding a set of social circumstances under which the socially and politically advantaged would agree to relinquish power, it is far from clear that we can even comprehend the meanings of the radically new roles envisaged for such a society. The astonishment of Marge Piercy's character, Connie Ramos, is shared by all her readers who wonder what the word 'mother' could mean divorced from both the facts of biological mothering and the set of social expectations imbedded in traditional mothering practices. Within a social tradition that ungrudgingly grants women little status and few gratifications apart from the mothering role, there is no solid ground upon which so radically novel a conception can get a foothold. Presented with such a set of facts about alternative social structures Connie is at a loss to understand what value to place upon them. Her plight dramatizes the reaction of many feminists to Shulamith Firestone's case for feminist revolution: *The Dialectic of Sex*. Firestone's proposals for the "abolition of all cultural categories" (1970, 182) and the transformation of procreation so that "genital distinctions between the sexes would no longer matter culturally" (1970, 11) boggle the imagination; for without the mediation of a set of cultural roles and expectations we cannot know what value to place upon our experiences.

Though Firestone's advocacy of technological reproduction aims to serve feminist interests, it rests on conceptual foundations that have much in common with the presuppositions of researchers and policymakers who would pursue goals antagonistic to her own, who would support technological intervention for the sake of the monopoly of power it would make possible. Both sorts of interests view technology as "a victory over nature." They favor not only *reproductive* technology but the technological transformation of production and the elimination of labor as well. Both see human biology as a limitation to be overcome—for Firestone, because she takes the relations of procreation to be the base of society and the source of women's oppression; for those who would support "a brave new world," because the diffusion of power among women and families threatens their own power hegemony.

Feminist Reaction

In this section I will try to isolate the issues of deepest concern to feminist thinkers who see advances in reproductive technology as further encroachments on the social status of women. Some of these concerns relate to the theoretical underpinnings of Firestone's theory and, by implication, to similar analyses of the causes of and correctives for women's cultural subordination. Others focus instead on the more probable consequences of technological transformations within a social context still dominated by male power structures. In most feminist commentaries both kinds of concerns are intertwined. However, here I will attempt to disentangle them so that detachable claims can then be examined one by one on their own merits. I will focus first on one issue that enters importantly into the expression of these concerns: the presumptive neutrality of technology to gender specific social practices. Then I will briefly allude to a second significant issue: the possibility of making meaningful distinctions between the biologically given and the culturally acquired. Finally I will offer a tentative interpretation of the importance of the mothering debate for feminist theory, ending with some remarks about conditions for the participation of feminist theorists in shaping reproductive policy.

Firestone's influence on subsequent feminists is a matter of some controversy, particularly with regard to her principal claims: that mothering is more a barrier to women's self-fulfillment than a vehicle for it and that biological motherhood lies at the heart of women's oppression. Hester Eisenstein, in her most recent work, *Contemporary Feminist Thought* (1983), credits Firestone with considerable influence over subsequent feminist theorists, particularly in the early 1970's when feminism and motherhood were widely held to be in diametrical opposition. She attributes opposition to Alice Rossi's (1977) advocacy of women's nurturing role (the position that the capacity to nurture is shaped by *biological* as well as social factors) to sympathy for Firestone's position. However, Alison Jaggar in her *Feminist Politics and Human Nature* (1983) points to a lack of enthusiasm for Firestone among grass-roots feminists, probably springing, she speculates, from a widespread suspicion of advanced technology, from the observation that technology has so often been used to reinforce male dominance. Hence these feminists do not see how women could take control of technology and use it for their own ends. This latter position is given further support by Azizah al-Hibri, who argues that:

> Technological reproductive does not equalize the natural reproductive power structure—it *inverts* it. It appropriates the reproductive power from women and places it in the hands of men who now control both the sperm and the reproductive technology that could make it indispensable . . . it 'liberates' them from their 'humiliating dependency' on women in order to propagate. (1984, 266)

Further, she argues, were cloning techniques to be perfected as well, men would finally be freed from their need to share their genes with women.

Her argument challenges both the claim that it is women's biological function that lies at the root of their oppression and the derivative implication that technological reform can eliminate oppressive social practices. It rests on a very different analysis of the basis of male domination, the presumption that *envy* of women's reproductive capacities and fear of their powers create a male need to control women, limiting the free exercise of those powers. Several features of the present situation support such an alternative analysis. If the root of women's oppression were their biological role, then enormous male resistance to the technologization of procreation might be expected; for each step toward its perfection would further threaten male power. However, the contrary is the case: male dominated social

institutions provide the principal basis of support for technological transformation of reproductive practices. Moreover, al-Hibri's analysis is compatible with conclusions reached by numerous other feminist theorists. Though some, like Mary O'Brien (1981), share a similar starting point, others such as Nancy Chodorow (1978) and Dorothy Dinnerstein (1976), reach the same conclusion by very different routes, deriving support from disciplines as disparate as psychoanalysis and anthropology.

Recent criticism of Firestone's position has not focused solely on her analysis of the *sources* of women's social subordination but extends to her remedy as well. Of course, exposure of weaknesses in the argument for the biological basis of social stratification would, itself, undermine support for Firestone's solution. But the remedy is also suspect on independent grounds. Carol McMillan (1982), for instance, has noted that Firestone's theory of social institutions presupposes that relations between individuals and society are exclusively *functional*. Firestone sees all barriers to the achievement of desired goals as *technical* problems, presuming that the ends sought can be fully known in advance and we need only figure out the most technically efficient way to get there. This presupposition stems, McMillan thinks, from the presumption that reproduction is analogous to the production and manufacture of goods, where the means to bring about a desired end have no significance of themselves apart from their instrumental value (McMillan 1982, 77). Once the expertise to accomplish the aim more efficiently is at hand, earlier more 'primitive' methods can be abandoned with no loss of value.

Close reading of Firestone supports this interpretation. She compares development of artificial reproduction to the future of cybernetics and speculates that the same reticence underlying reservations about the benefits of artificial reproduction prevades our thinking about a work world where machine thinking and problem solving have displaced human efforts. She attributes this reticence to the presently prevailing distribution of power; to envisage either possibility "in the hands of present powers is to envisage a nightmare" (Firestone 1970, 90). But within 'post-revolutionary' systems both reproductive technology and cybernetics would be left free to play a wholly different role in social life. Hence, within Firestone's conceptual framework technology plays an instrumental role twice over, first by transforming the means to achieve socially desired goals without itself affecting the character of the goal, and second, by neutrally serving the interests of whichever party happens to control the means of production or reproduction.

McMillan shares company with the vast predominance of both feminist and nonfeminist women who presently hold a markedly different assessment of values bound up with childbearing and rearing practices as human activities. Unlike Firestone and the utopian feminists who presume that the values attached to mothering can be detached, lifted off and reapplied to a radically different set of social practices, they see the values identified with mothering as *integral* to procreation and nurturing. Robyn Rowland, for instance, has remarked that:

> a groundswell of women within the movement has begun to reassess the value of biological maternity. Reacting against the feeling that the women's movement coerced them to give up having children, many feminists are striving to create the experience of maternity and family in a non-exploitive way. (Rowland 1984, 358)

She points to Adrienne Rich's contention that the problem is not motherhood itself but the partiarchal *institutionalization* of motherhood (Rich 1976, 369) and argues that the sources of women's oppression lie in the nature of the social structures within which motherhood is experienced rather than in motherhood itself—which embodies within it a network of affirmative values which women ought not to abandon. She and the many women writers she cites all see technological control of these practices as usurpation of a body of values central to the fundamental interests of women. She appropriates Leon Kass' (1979) arguments to her own cause, citing his admonition that "some men may be destined to play God, to recreate other men in their own image," in support of her own fear that the new reproduc-

tive technologies will ultimately be used for the benefit of men and to the detriment of women (Rowland 1984, 356).

Writing in the same volume Janice Raymond (1984) not only decries the technological *future* that new modes of reproduction will impose on women, but the present social context "in which women supposedly 'choose' such debilitating procedures" as *in vitro* fertilization and embryo transfer. Such technologies, she believes, only give scientific and therapeutic support to female adaptation to the patriarchal ideology that reproduction is women's prime commodity, thereby reinforcing women's oppression. She, too, echoes the fears first voiced by noninterventionists, such as Paul Ramsey and Leon Kass, that submission even to presently established modes of technological intervention dehumanizes women, imposing upon them 'choices' not of their own making and forcing them to submit to a technolgy whose developers seek ultimately to render their mothering role obsolete. The arguments of Rowland and Raymond draw together both issues: that women's historical and social capabilities incorporated within childbearing and childrearing practices possess independent value wholly apart from their patriarchal context and that technological intervention into reproduction would only remove from women occasion to develop these capabilities under the guise of serving their interests. Recognizing this, women need to voice their *own* interests in accord with the moral and social values that support their sense of the good life. Unlike noninterventionists from Ramsey's background or critics of feminism such as Carol McMillan, their 'conservatism' attempts to avoid appeal to women's natural function. Their objections to alternative forms of reproduction are not couched in allusions to their supposed 'unnaturalness' but focus on a profound sense of dis-ease, stemming from the threat of further consolidation of power structures which purport to speak *for* women while simultaneously undermining women's control of their own reproductive activities. Nonetheless, despite their deliberate effort to base their case on a direct appeal to women's own expression of their interests, their arguments appear to rely on a theoretical distinction very like

Adrienne Rich employs in her analysis of motherhood. She wrote:

> I try to distinguish between two meanings of motherhood, one superimposed on the other: the *potential relationship* of any woman to her powers of reproduction and to children; and the *institution* which aims at ensuring that that potential—and all women—shall remain under male control. (Rich 1976, 13)

If the *institution* of motherhood—the "symbolic architecture" that derives from male control—could be lifted off, the *experience* of motherhood would be revealed in its true nature, grounded, Rich believes, in women's *biology.*

> In arguing that we have by no means yet explored or understood our bilogical grounding, the miracle and paradox of the female body and its spiritual and political meanings, I am really asking whether women cannot begin, at last, to *think through their body,* to connect what has been so cruelly disorganized—our great mental capacities, hardly used; our highly developed tactile sense; our genius for close observation; our complicated, pain-enduring multi-pleasured physicality. (Rich 1976, 24)

Rich's argument, like Firestone's, presupposes that we can think intelligibly about mothering experiences detached from their social context and that they can be lifted off and opened to view apart from *any* institutional structures. She assumes, too, that we can imagine them transposed into a radically different context, within which the affirmative values imbedded in mothering would be freed from the negative associations bound up with present mothering arrangements.

The foundation for these presumptions needs closer scrutiny. Despite her penetrating criticism of "male created dualisms" her own work appears to reintroduce analogous dualisms, relying, as it does, on the distinguishability of the sources of women's experiences, on the assumption that we can trace the derivation of certain experiences to women's biology and that others owe their origin to patriarchal institutions. Though such scrutiny of the logic of her work might seem to overlook its most obvious intent: to prepare a space within which to celebrate motherhood as a source of women's most cherished experiences, I wonder whether this aim can be given secure support on such a foundation. I would like to suggest now that a common thread links Rowland, Raymond and Rich's positions together and, whether or not that thread connects them all to a nature/culture dualism, they do share certain common *psychological* assumptions that hold all of them together and apart from Firestone and her company.

Like many other contemporary feminists they see the relation between the infant and mother as essentially a positive one and look to this relationship for images of what relations between woman and woman might be once women have been freed to give expression to their own values and shape social institutions that foster their unfettered expression. Their vision stands in marked contrast to the perceptions of Firestone and her generation of feminists who looked to sources outside of the mother-child relationship for models on which to build sense of the unity and solidarity of women.

In a recent paper critical of Rich's position, Janet Sayers (1984) has argued that any attempt to ground relationships between women in images of the infant-mother bond rests upon a fantasy, that in reality this relationship is marked by *contradiction,* by both positive and negative elements. She writes:

> The merits of Melanie Klein's work as far as feminism is concerned is that it draws attention to the way we often deny contradictions in personal relationships through the defensive mechanism of splitting, and draws attention to the hatred as well as love that inheres in the early infant-mother relationship—an ambivalence that is not only overlooked in feminist writing that celebrates this relation as the basis of women's solidarity as a sex, but that is also overlooked in that writing which by contrast sees in this relation the very source of women's oppression and alienation. (Sayers 1984, 240)

By way of example she cites Luce Irigaray as illustrative of the latter view, though she could as easily have cited many other feminists, including Firestone. Though her reliance on the Kleinian perspective might be called into question, her cautionary warning ought not to go unheeded. Both attitudes toward the mother-infant relation are amply represented within feminist writing. Neither can be claimed to capture the *true* expression of feminism. Her appeal to Klein is an attempt to draw together both positions within a more inclusive framework. The development of such a framework leaves much theoretical work to be done but the need for feminist action cannot be delayed until we have worked out an adequate theory of intergenerational relationships.

For the present, lacking any feminist theory capable of providing unambiguous direction in guiding the development of reproductive technology, these options lay before us: (1) we might commit ourselves unequivocally to a Richian position, accept Rowland and Raymond's analysis of the consequences of reproductive innovation and oppose all use of reproductive technology despite its short-term benefits to some women individually;[8] (2) we could join forces with the heirs of Shulamith Firestone, though it is by no means clear what implications this might have for *present* social policy considering the extent to which powerful institutional and commercial interests currently control these technologies; or (3) we could work to integrate the plurality of feminist positions into an *interim* policy, commit ourselves to intensified dialogue and attempt to influence the present direction of reproductive innovation in much the same pragmatic ways feminists are now participating in framing economic policies. Though pursuit of the third option is likely to put the cohesiveness of the feminist community to its most severe test, adoption of either of the remaining options would already presuppose a cleavage far more irreconcilable. Over this issue either the current 'wave' of the feminist movement will lose its momentum and disintegrate or feminism will emerge a far stronger, more unitary force for social transformation than ever in its prior history.

2. In the summer of 1984 the U.S. House of Representatives Subcommittee on Investigations and Oversights heard testimony on the new reproductive technologies with the intent of eventually introducing appropriate regulative legislation (U.S. 1985).

3. See, for instance, two recent philosophical works: Glover (1984) and Singer and Wells (1984).

4. Comments of Simone Novaes have been most helpful to me in efforts to understand the complex motivations of women seeking these technologies.

5. This argument was first suggested to me in a discussion of Ramsey's position by Samuel Gorovitz (1982).

6. I do not discuss other individual 'moderate interventionists' at length here only because their arguments are not directly pertinent to the issues I emphasize. However, the regulatory bodies that I do refer to—the British Warnock Committee and the Australian and Canadian commissions—all adopt versions of a moderate interventionist position. Also, most legal commentators and scientific researchers fall into this category. Some have no principled objections to the new technologies at all; others support innovations only selectively. All of them seek regulation principally to maintain continuity with prevailing liberal values.

7. Several states have already considered legislation that would bind both parties to surrogate contracts. Both Kentucky and Michigan have ruled against it.

8. Gena Corea (1985) offers much empirical evidence in support of this position.

Notes

1. A notable exception is a recent collection edited by Joan Rothchild (1983).

Study Questions

1. What concerns does Donchin voice in regard to futurist narratives of conceptive technologies such as *Woman on the Edge of Time?*

2. Specifically, what does she think are the alternative perspectives in response to innovations in reproductive practices? Explain.

3. State the non-interventionist position. How does it rely on the concept of "natural," for example?

4. According to Donchin, why are some feminists in agreement with the moderate interventionist position?

5. The radical interventionist perspective has two versions, according to Donchin. How do they differ?

6. How does Donchin summarize the Firestone model? What does she see as the central concern of feminists around new reproductive technologies?

7. Which of the options Donchin offers for feminist theory and reproductive technology would you choose? Why?

Prostitution

Alison M. Jaggar

Prostitution has long been referred to as "the social evil."[1] "Whore" or "tart" has long been the ultimate epithet to be hurled against women. Social reformers, feminists and government agencies have long sought, in their various ways, to put an end to the sale of sexual services. But there are signs that this centuries-old taboo is about to be reversed. Prostitutes themselves have organized unions calling for the decriminalization of prostitution. A recent survey showed that 59% of Republican voters favored its legalization in the United States. And her supposedly autobiographical series detailing the life of "the happy hooker" have made Xaviera Hollander a best-selling author.

Is there any reason to oppose the decriminalization of prostitution or even the western European innovation of publicly raising capital to finance prostitution hostels? The conditions of modern society appear to have undermined many traditional arguments against prostitution. Venereal disease can be detected quickly and treated effectively. Illegitimacy can be prevented by modern contraceptive techniques; indeed, prostitutes now have a lower fertility rate than other women. And changing sexual mores mean that sexual activity outside the marriage bed is increasingly taken for granted. To decide how to respond to these developments, we need a philosophical theory of prostitution. Such a theory should state exactly what prostitution is, should tell us what, if anything, is wrong with it and should help us determine what, if anything, should be done about it. In this paper, unfortunately, I am not able to offer a full-fledged theory of prostitution. Instead, I compare the relative merits of three attempts to provide such a theory and identify the philosophical basis on which a comprehensive theory of prostitution must rest. Thus I view my paper as a prolegomenon to a theory of prostitution.

The three approaches to prostitution that I shall discuss are the liberal, the classical Marxist, and the radical feminist approaches. Obviously, these do not comprise all possible views on prostitution. I choose them in part because they are all current views and in part because I find them all, to some extent, plausible. In addition, they provide interesting contrasts not only in moral and political theory but in their accounts of just what they take prostitution to be. Each begins from the paradigm case of the prostitute as a woman selling her sexual services, but each picks out very different features as essential to that situation. Thus, a comparison of these theories of prostitution illustrates an important general point about the appropriate philosophical methodology for

From Alan G. Soble, ed., *Philosophy of Sex* (Totowa, NJ: Littlefield, Adams, 1980). © 1980 by Alison Jaggar. Reprinted by permission of Alison Jaggar. (Notes deleted.)

approaching not only the issue of prostitution but also a number of other normative social issues.

Liberalism

The standard liberal position on prostitution is that it should be decriminalized. This was the conclusion of the 1963 British *Wolfenden Report of the Committee on Homosexual Offences and Prostitution* and it is the view of the American Civil Liberties Union. The Wolfenden Committee argued that "private immorality should not be the concern of the criminal law."[2] They believed that the function of the law was not "to punish prostitution *per se*," but rather to regulate "those activities which offend against public order and decency or expose the ordinary citizen to what is offensive or injurious."[3] Hence, they argued that prostitutes might be arrested for "importuning" but neither they nor their customers should be subject to any penalties for actually engaging in prostitution.

The American Civil Liberties Union argues that laws prohibiting prostitution are unconstitutional on several grounds. For one thing, they deny equal protection of the law to women. In some states, prostitution statutes apply only to females. Indeed, according to traditional case law, a prostitute is by definition female; thus by legal definition a man cannot be a prostitute. The male customer of a female prostitute, moreover, is rarely subject to legal penalty while the female prostitute invariably is. In these and other ways, prostitution laws discriminate against women. Another argument for the unconstitutionality of prostitution laws is that they often treat the mere status of being a prostitute as an offense, thereby inflicting "cruel and unusual punishment." And the use of loitering as a criterion for prostitution is said to violate a woman's right to due process. Finally, the ACLU argues that prohibitions on prostitution are an invasion of the individual's right to control his or her body without unreasonable interference from the state. This last argument is the most important, for it entails that prohibition laws cannot simply be "tidied

up" by such reforms as writing them in gender neutral language or by insisting on strict standards of evidence before convicting someone of prostitution. Instead, it argues that there should be no law prohibiting prostitution.

> The private sexual act involved in prostitution is no less a personal right for being commercial. Therefore, the government should not be able to prohibit it unless the state can meet the very heavy burden of proof that banning it is beneficial to society.[4]

This author even goes beyond the Wolfenden Report by arguing that solicitation for prostitution should be decriminalized. She doubts that it is genuinely offensive to men and claims that "to legalize prostitution while prohibiting solicitation makes as much sense as encouraging free elections but prohibiting campaigning."[5]

Their agreement on the decriminalization of prostitution does not mean that liberals share a common view about its moral status. Liberal feminists have always seen prostitution as degrading to women and conclude that it should receive no encouragement even though it should be decriminalized. This attitude is implicit in the report of the NOW Task Force on prostitution which supports

> full prosecution of any acts of coercion to any person, public agency or group to influence women to become prostitutes.[6]

Others, however, claim to see nothing wrong with prostitution. Some prostitutes view themselves as entrepreneurs, choosing to go into business for themselves rather than to work for someone else. One prostitute remarked that the work was really not tiring, that it was often less humiliating than dating. The prostitute may see herself as the boss because she can say "No" to the deal; as someone, therefore, who is less exploited than exploiting. Thus it may be argued that decriminalization will finally allow "the oldest profession" to take its place among the other professions so that prostitutes will be respected as offering a skilled service.

These liberal reflections on the moral status of prostitution, however, are generally taken as mere side comments. The central liberal line of argument is to stress the need for decriminalization by appeal to classical liberal ideals. Thus, liberal arguments emphasize the importance of equality before the law and of individual rights. They attempt to minimize government interference in the lives of individuals and they assume that there is a "private" sphere of human existence

> comprehending all that portion of a person's life and conduct which affects only himself (sic) or if it affects others, only with their free, voluntary and undeceived consent and participation.[7]

Prostitution, they believe, falls obviously within that sphere.

The usual liberal recommendation on prostitution, then, is that it should be treated as an ordinary business transaction, the sale of a service; in this case, of a sexual service. Because the prostitute engages in it out of economic motivation, liberals view prostitution as quite different from a sexual act committed by physical force or under threat of force; they view prostitution as quite different, for instance, from rape. Instead, they see it as a contract like other contracts, entered into by each individual for her or his own benefit, each striking the best bargain that she or he is able. The state has exactly the same interest in the prostitution contract as in all other contracts and may therefore regulate certain aspects by law. For instance, the law may concern itself with such matters as hygiene, control of disease, minimum standards of service and of working conditions, misleading advertising, payment of taxes and social security, etc. It should also ensure equal opportunity by redrawing the legal definition of prostitution so that an individual of either sex may be a prostitute. In these sorts of ways, the state would fulfill its traditional liberal function of ensuring fair trading practices. It should assure consumers of "a clean lay at a fair price."[8]

At first sight, the liberal approach to prostitution seems refreshingly straightforward and uncomplicated. As so often happens, however, this appearance is deceptive. One problem concerns the normative assumption that prostitution is a contract whose legitimacy is equal to that of other business contracts. Although liberals view the paradigmatic social relation as contractual, they do not believe that all contracts are legitimate. Mill, for instance, denied the legitimacy of contracts by which individuals permanently abdicated or alienated their freedom to decide on future courses of action, and on this ground he argued that the state should not enforce either lifelong marriage contracts or contracts where an individual sold her- or himself into slavery. Similarly, Joel Feinberg offers a number of different arguments which suggest why voluntary slavery contracts may be illegitimate. For instance, he suggests that it is inherently immoral to own another person and that such immorality ought to be forbidden by law; and he also suggests, on what he calls Kantian grounds, that we may not dispose of our "humanity" and that attempts to do so should not be recognized by law.[9] Without examining all the liberal arguments in detail, it is clear that the early liberal conviction that the primary purpose of the state was to uphold the sanctity of contracts has been weakened in contemporary times and liberals now also expect the state

> to provide against those contracts being made which, from the helplessness of one of the parties to them, instead of being a security for freedom, become an instrument of disguised oppression.[10]

These restrictions on legitimate contracts might be strong enough to exclude prostitution. It may well be that prostitution constitutes the sort of selling of oneself that a liberal would refuse to countenance. And it is surely not implausible to consider many prostitution contracts as instruments of not very well disguised oppression. Those liberals, therefore, are being too hasty who simply assume the legitimacy of prostitution contracts. In order to establish that prostitution is simply an ordinary business contract, they need a clear theory of what kinds of contracts are legitimate. (Robert Nozick, for instance, believes that the law should recognize and enforce people's right to sell themselves even into slavery.)[11] And they need a clear analysis of prostitution together with a normative theory of sexuality.

Liberal writers have not devoted much attention to the latter question at least. Since they ordinarily assume that sexual relations fall within the "private" realm and hence are outside the sphere of legal regulation, the development of a normative theory of sexuality has not seemed important for their political philosophy. Their main contribution to the analysis of prostitution has been to insist that a prostitute may be either male or female. Thus, liberals would rewrite laws regarding prostitution in gender-neutral language and would also, presumably, wish to revise the first part of the definition of "prostitution" in *Webster's New Twentieth Century Dictionary* which currently reads:

> *prostitute, n.* 1, a woman who engages in promiscuous sexual intercourse for pay; whore; harlot.

Here, liberals would presumably substitute "person" for "woman" and would construe "sexual intercourse" broadly enough to cover sexual encounters between individuals of either sex. Such an interpretation would also allow so-called massage parlors within the definition of "prostitution." This liberal revision of the concept of prostitution may seem at first sight to be in line with common usage, with common sense and with common justice. As we shall see, however, there are other accounts of prostitution which draw the boundaries quite differently.

A final problem with the liberal position on prostitution concerns its assumption that the prostitute enters into the transaction voluntarily. It has often been pointed out in other contexts that the liberal concept of coercion is very weak. It may well turn out that the sorts of economic considerations that impel some persons into prostitution do indeed constitute a sort of coercion and that the prostitution contract may therefore be invalidated on those grounds. This is one of the objections made by the Marxist theory of prostitution, to which I now turn.

Marxism

The Marxist approach to prostitution is considerably wider-ranging than the liberal approach, both because it attempts to understand prostitution in its social context and because it construes prostitution much more broadly. For instance, Marxists view prostitution as including not only the sale of an individual's sexual services; they see it also as the exchange of all those tangible and intangible services that a married woman provides to her husband in return for economic support. Sometimes they believe that prostitution may cover even the exchange of the services that a man provides when he marries a rich woman.

Whether or not marriage is a form of prostitution is determined, for the Marxist, by the economic class of the marriage partners. It is only where property is involved that marriage degenerates into prostitution; where no property is involved, for instance among the proletariat, marriage is based solely on mutual inclination. Thus Engels writes that, within the bourgeoisie,

> the marriage is conditioned by the class position of the parties and is to that extent always a marriage of convenience. . . . this marriage of convenience turns often enough into the crassest prostitution—sometimes of both partners, but far more commonly of the woman, who only differs from the ordinary courtesan in that she does not let out her body on piecework as a wageworker, but sells it once and for all into slavery. And of all marriages of convenience Fourier's words hold true: "As in grammar two negatives make an affirmative, so in matrimonial morality two prostitutions pass for a virtue."[12]

In describing bourgeois marriage as a form of prostitution, Marx and Engels assume not only that men as well as women may prostitute themselves; they assume also that what is sold may not be restricted to sexual services. From this, it is but a short step to describing the sale of a number of other services as types of prostitution. Indeed, in the *Economic and Philosophical Manuscripts,* Marx asserts that all wage labor is a form of prostitution. He writes, "Prostitution (in the ordinary sense) is only a *specific* expression of the *general* prostitution of the *labourer*."[13]

Someone might object that this usage of Marx's is merely metaphorical, that he is simply utilizing the pejorative connotations of "prostitution" in order to condemn wage labor. But the following entry in *Webster's New Twentieth Century Dictionary* supports the claim that Marx's broader usage is not metaphorical:

> *prostitute, n.* 2. a person, as a writer, artist, etc., who sells his services for low or unworthy purposes.

If *Webster's* too is mistaken, and if there is indeed a philosophically significant distinction to be made between the woman who sells sexual services and the individual who sells services of any kind, then that distinction must be given a philosophical rationale.

Does the Marxist corpus contain such a rationale or does it, on the other hand, provide a reason for assimilating wage labor to prostitution? I think that it contains traces of both but that the tendency to assimilate prostitution to wage labor is probably stronger. Some of Engel's objections to prostitution in the narrower sense seem to depend on two specific normative beliefs about sexuality, that sex should be linked with love and that "sexual love is by its nature exclusive."[14] It is because of the latter belief that he worries, since he views both monogamy and prostitution as results of the same state of affairs (namely, male ownership of the means of production), whether "prostitution [can] disappear without dragging monogamy with it into the abyss?"[15] He is anxious to make monogamy, or at any rate sexual fidelity, "a reality—also for men."[16] Similarly, he wants to make the "paper"[17] description of bourgeois marriage into a reality by turning an economic transaction into a free agreement based on mutual sex-love. He writes:

> Full freedom of marriage can therefore only be generally established when the abolition of capitalist production and of the property relations created by it has removed all the accompanying economic considerations which still exert such a powerful influence on the choice of a marriage partner. For then there is no other motive left except mutual inclination.[18]

Unfortunately, the theory of sexuality on which these objections to prostitution are based is left undeveloped. We are given no reason to believe that Engels's notion of "modern individual sex-love," which he describes as "the greatest moral advance we owe to [monogamy],"[19] is in fact anything more than a romantic Victorian prejudice.

Even if our intuitions about sexual relations do not agree with Engels's, however, I do not think that we are necessarily thrown back to the liberal view about prostitution. Instead I believe that it is possible to draw from the Marxist corpus another, more searching, more plausible, and more specifically Marxist critique of prostitution. This critique, however, is very similar to the critique of wage labor and thus leads us in the direction of assimilating female prostitution to the wage labor of either sex.

There are a number of different ways of explaining Marx's critique of the system of wage labor. In his earlier works, Marx stresses the concept of alienation, the estrangement of wage laborers from the process and the product of their work, from their co-workers and from their humanity itself. In his later works, Marx drops the terminology of alienation; there is considerable controversy over whether he retained the central ideas or whether there is an "epistemological break" between his earlier and his later work. Certainly in his later work Marx seems concerned to detail in a more concrete way the devastating consequences to the worker of the capitalist system. He shows how the bodies of wage laborers are distorted by industrial diseases and how their minds are damaged by the boredom of repetitive tasks. Under capitalism, he argues, workers become mere appendages to their machines, no longer human beings but merely factors in the capitalist production process. Their human capacity to work becomes reduced to the commodity of labor power and the value of this is measured not in terms of its ability to provide useful products but merely in terms of its price on the labor market. In both his earlier and his later work, Marx stresses the lack of genuine freedom that exists under capitalism. In particular, he argues that so-called free wage labor is free only in the sense that it is no longer limited by the medieval laws restricting entry into the labor market. But although individuals are free to decide for which capitalist enterprise they want to work, they are not free to refuse wage labor entirely. In order to survive, they are forced to become wage laborers. The Marxist analysis of the position of women under capitalism is notoriously sketchy; in fact, the classic analysis was left to Engels after Marx's death. Engels's explanation of the special oppression faced by women under capitalism appeals to women's exclusion from wage labor and argues that women's liberation requires that they should be drawn into "public production." Nevertheless, in spite of the importance that they place on the distinction between those who are engaged in capitalist production and those who are not, there are a number of places where Marx and Engels seem to draw parallels between the situation of women under capitalism and the situation of wage-laborers. For instance, in *The Communist Manifesto* Marx and Engels claim that the bourgeois fear that the communists will introduce "community of women" stems from the fact that

> the bourgeois sees in his wife a mere instrument of production. He hears that the instruments of production are to be exploited in common, and, naturally, can come to no other conclusions than that the lot of being common to all will likewise fall to women.[20]

Both the bourgeois wife and the wage laborer, therefore, can be seen as "instruments of production," the latter of commodities, the former of babies. Prostitutes in the narrower, more conventional sense cannot be viewed in this way, of course. They perform a service rather than create a product. Nevertheless, Marx presents prostitution as a paradigm case of the sort of alienated relationships that are created by capitalism, where money substitutes for concrete human characteristics. He writes that, under capitalism,

> What I am and can do is, therefore, not at all determined by my individuality. I am ugly, but I can buy the most beautiful woman for myself. Consequently, I am not ugly, for the effect of ugliness, its power to repel, is annulled by money.[21]

Just as the capacity to labor becomes a commodity under capitalism, so does sexuality, especially the sexuality of women. Thus prostitutes, like wage laborers, have an essential human capacity alienated. Like wage laborers, they become dehumanized and their value as

persons is measured by their market price. And like wage laborers, they are compelled to work by economic pressure; prostitution, if not marriage, may well be the best option available to them.

On the Marxist view, prostitution and wage labor (in so far as they are still separable) degrade not only the prostitute and the wage laborer. They dehumanize also the prostitute's client and the laborer's employer. Marx writes:

> in the approach to *woman* as the spoil and handmaid of communal lust is expressed the infinite degradation in which man exists for himself.[22]

Engels goes further. He writes that prostitution

> demoralizes men far more than women. Among women, prostitution degrades only the unfortunate ones who become its victims, and even these by means to the extent commonly believed. But it degrades the whole male world.[23]

(The last sentence provides an interesting comment on the extent of prostitution in Victorian England.) Marx describes the capitalist in a similar way:

> Prostitution is only a *specific* expression of the *general* prostitution of the *labourer,* and since it is a relationship in which falls not the prostitute alone, but also the one who prostitutes— and the latter's abomination is still greater—the capitalist, etc., also comes under this head.[24]

Given this critique, it is hardly surprising to find in *The Communist Manifesto* the explicit statement that it is necessary to abolish "prostitution both public and private."[25] But Marx and Engels certainly do not suggest that this end may be achieved by legal prohibition. Since all forms of prostitution result from inequality of wealth, such inequality must be eliminated. And in our time this means that capitalism must be abolished. For it is capitalism that gives men control over the means of production, thus forcing women to sell their bodies and allowing men to maintain a sexual double standard in marriage. And of course it is capitalism, by definition, that maintains the wage system and so forces the majority of the population to prostitute themselves by selling whatever capacities to labor that they may possess. Thus Marxists believe that the elimination of prostitution demands a full communist revolution. Until then, in one way or another, "capital screws us all."

The Marxist discussion of prostitution is illuminating in many respects. It brings out the real economic coercion underlying the apparently free market contract and the parallels between prostitution and wage labor must still raise questions for some people, as no doubt they did for a Victorian audience, about the moral status of the system of wage labor. (It is perhaps a measure of how far contemporary populations have internalized bourgeois values that it is possible for liberals nowadays to use the comparison not to discredit wage labor but rather to rehabilitate prostitution.) Certainly, the philosophical assimilation of prostitution to wage labor is supported by the two entries in *Webster's Dictionary*. But this assimilation may not only be illuminating. It may also obscure certain important differences between prostitution and wage labor. It may not be a matter of indifference whether the prostitute is male or female or whether it is an individual's sexuality that is sold rather than her or his capacity to labor. Radical feminism argues that an adequate account of prostitution requires an emphasis on the feminine gender of the prostitute and the sexual nature of her service.

Radical Feminism

For contemporary radical feminists, prostitution is the archetypal relationship of women to men. Karen Lindsey sums it up this way:

> We have long held that all women sell themselves: that the only available roles of a woman—wife, secretary, girlfriend—all demand the selling of herself to one or more men.[26]

Even a century ago, some feminists saw marriage as a form of prostitution and as long ago as 1909 Cicely Hamilton wrote that, although a woman cannot predict before marriage which of an infinite variety of possible tasks her husband may expect her to perform,

the only thing she can be fairly certain of is that he will require her to fulfill his idea of personal attractiveness. As a matter of business, then, and not purely from vanity, she specialises in personal attractiveness.[27]

Contemporary radical feminists have extended this insight and now perceive most social interaction between women and men as some form of prostitution. Thus, they believe that almost every man/woman encounter has sexual overtones and typically is designed to reinforce the sexual dominance of men. Correspondingly, men reward this sexual service in a variety of ways: the payment may range from a very tangible dinner to the intangible but nonetheless essential provision of male approval and patronage. Paradoxically, radical feminists argue, some women are even forced to prostitute themselves by selling their celibacy. They may retain their alimony or their social security payments only by remaining "chaste."[28]

This radical feminist view contrasts both with liberalism and with Marxism in its insistence that prostitutes must be defined as women. It differs from liberalism in its broad construal of what constitutes sexual services and from Marxism in its refusal to assimilate prostitution to other types of wage labor. It sees the social function of prostitution primarily as a means neither for sexual enjoyment nor for profit. Instead, radical feminists see prostitution as an institution to assert the dominance and power of men over women.

With respect to prostitution in the narrow conventional sense, radical feminists admit that it may indeed satisfy the physical desires of men, but they see this as being only a subsidiary function. Primarily, they believe,

> Prostitution exists to meet the desire of men to degrade women. Studies made by men reveal that very few even pretend they frequent prostitutes primarily for sexual gratification. Young boys admit they go to achieve a sense of male camaraderie and freedom. They usually go in groups and gossip about it at length afterward in a way that is good for their egos. Other men have expressed the prime motive as the desire to reaffirm the basic "filth" of all women; or to clearly separate "good" from "bad" women in their minds, or for the opportunity to treat an-

other person completely according to personal whim.[29]

In addition, conventional prostitution is seen as a way of controlling other women who are not culturally defined as prostitutes.

> The existence of a category of women defined by this function of sex object, plus the fact that every woman must guard against "slipping" into this category or being assigned to it (and the absence of a comparable group of men), is sufficient to understanding prostitution as oppressive to all women. By the ubiquitous "threat" of being treated like a "common prostitute" we are kept in our places and our freedom is further contracted.[30]

Thus,

> The [prostitution] laws are fundamental to the male protection racket—to maintaining most women as private rather than public property.[31]

From this account of prostitution, it is clear that the radical feminist does not regard it as a morally neutral institution, either in the narrow or in the broad form. The radical feminist denies the liberal contention that conventional prostitution is a victimless crime. The victims are all women, but particularly the prostitutes themselves, outcast, degraded and exploited by all the men who, directly or indirectly, enjoy the benefits of prostitution. Prostitution in its broad form is, of course, no more acceptable to the radical feminist. But,

> Unlike religious reforms of the past, feminists do not base opposition to prostitution on anti-sex values. Just as with marriage, our opposition is to the economics of the situation. Sex is a fine thing when it is the free choice of the individuals involved—free of economic coercion. No one should be dependent on selling herself for support; all love should be free love.[32]

So it is the economic coercion underlying prostitution, which requires that a woman's sexuality can be expressed only in a manner pleasing to men, that provides the basic feminist objection to prostitution. This economic coercion means that ultimately the moral status of prostitution is identical with that of rape. Like rape, prostitution perpetuates the oppression of women by encouraging the view that women are mere sexual objects, hence reinforcing male dominance and female inferiority.

Needless to say, radical feminists want to eliminate prostitution in all its forms. For this, they see two preconditions. One is that the male demand for prostitutes should be eliminated. This requires a total transformation of men's attitudes toward women and it also requires the abandonment of such conventional myths about male sexuality as that men have a much stronger biological appetite for sex than women. When masculinity is no longer so inseparably tied to heterosexual performance, feminists hypothesize that men will no longer demand prostitutes.

Recognition that the demand for prostitutes is not a biological inevitability is a comparatively recent insight in our culture. But feminists have always recognized that the *supply* of prostitutes is a function of women's inferior social status. Over fifty years ago Emma Goldman remarked:

> Nowhere is woman treated according to the merit of her work but rather as a sex. It is therefore almost inevitable that she should pay for her right to exist, to keep a position in whatever line, with sex favors. Thus it is merely a question of degree whether she sells herself to one man, in or out of marriage, or to many men. Whether our reformers admit it or not, the economic and social inferiority of woman is responsible for prostitution.[33]

Radical feminists believe, therefore, that the eradication of prostitution requires the abolition of the male monopoly of economic power together with an abandonment of the view that women are primarily sexual objects. So long as these two interdependent conditions exist, almost any significant transaction between a woman and a man must be a form of prostitution. Susan Brownmiller sums it up:

> Prostitution will not end in this country until men see women as equals. And men will never see women as equals until there's an end to prostitution. So it seems that we will have to work for the full equality of women and the end to prostitution side by side.[34]

These two tasks are indistinguishable. And, until they are achieved, radical feminists believe that, contrary to what conventional morality may indicate, women are confronted by a choice which is morally indistinguishable: it is the choice between "sucking cock and kissing ass."[35]

To many people and especially to many men, the radical feminist account of prostitution seems startling and offensive. A number of objections to it spring immediately to mind. In order to try to make the radical feminist account more plausible, I shall outline some of these objections and probable radical feminist answers to them.

One common objection to the radical feminist view of prostitution argues that it is preposterous to suppose that, when a man brings gifts to a woman he loves or takes her out to dinner, he is treating her as a prostitute. Such gestures are intended and should be received simply as tokens of affection. The radical feminist answer to this objection is that individuals' intentions do not necessarily indicate the true nature of what is going on. Both man and woman might be outraged at the description of their candlelit dinner as prostitution, but the radical feminist argues this outrage is due simply to the participants' failure or refusal to perceive the social context in which their dinner date occurs. This context is deeply sexist: the chances are that the man has more economic power than the woman; and it is certain that much of woman's social status depends on her attractiveness as defined by men. For women in our society are defined culturally as sexual objects so that "every day in a woman's life is a walking Miss America contest."[36] In these circumstances, it is almost inevitable that the man is buying "his idea of personal attractiveness."

But "almost inevitable" is not inevitable. It may be true that many more dinner dates are forms of prostitution than would appear at first sight. But surely it is not logically necessary that a man is prostituting a woman when he takes her out to dinner. What about the occasions when she pays for herself? Or even when she pays for him? Surely it is logically possible for a woman to treat a man as a prostitute? Some men even define themselves as prostitutes.

Here again the radical feminists point to the social context. They point out that the customers of so-called male prostitutes are invariably men and they argue that much of the indignity of being a so-called prostitute, for a man, is that

he is being forced to assume what is paradigmatically a woman's role, that he is being feminized. Radical feminists argue that there is an asymmetry in social attitudes towards men's and women's sexuality. The portly, grey-haired man with the young blonde woman on his arm is viewed with nudges, envy and even admiration. But the portly, grey-haired woman, if she were ever able to induce a young blonde man to lend her his arm, would be viewed with scorn, ridicule or pity. She is viewed as being "used" by her young gigolo in a way that even a "golddigging" young woman is not able to use her older lover. For, given the different social status of women and men in our society, it is always true that, in sexual encounters between women and men, a man "has" and a woman "is had." And when a man "has" another man, he is depriving him of his masculine status. Young dependent males in prison are even referred to as "women."

In arguing that prostitution is paradigmatically a relation of women to men, radical feminists are remembering the sexism that has structured our history and that continues to pervade every aspect of contemporary life. They are remembering that women appear to have been defined always as "sexual objects" and that the "traffic in women" appears to have been the earliest form of exchange.[37] They are remembering that people's personal identity is grounded on their gender-identity so firmly that, while they may "pass" for black or white or be upwardly or downwardly mobile from their class, any attempt to change their gender is met inevitably with extreme anxiety, confusion and even hostility. They are remembering that a defining feature of gender is the way in which sexuality is expressed so that homosexuals, for instance, are commonly viewed as failing to be appropriately masculine or feminine. And finally, radical feminists are remembering that not only is gender in general tied up inextricably with sexuality but also that femininity in particular is defined in large part by the ability to be attractive sexually to men. Most women have internalized the need to be "attractive" in this way and even those who have not done so usually cannot afford to be indifferent to men's opinions. Whether housewife or wage-earner, therefore, and whether or not she allows genital contact, a woman must sell her sexuality.

And since, unlike a man, she is defined largely in sexual terms, when she sells her sexuality she sells herself.

Toward a Philosophical Theory of Prostitution

Although these arguments may not establish conclusively the correctness of the radical feminist approach to prostitution, they do make it much more plausible. And the questions raised by radical feminism help to determine what is required for a philosophical account of prostitution that is adequate.

First of all, an adequate account of prostitution requires a philosophical theory of sexuality. Such a theory must be in part conceptual, in part normative. It must help us to draw the conceptual boundaries of sexual activity, enabling us to answer both how nongenital activity can still be sexual and even how genital activity may not be sexual. Given our ordinary ways of thinking, this latter suggestion may sound paradoxical but it is becoming a commonplace for feminists to define rape as a form of physical assault rather than as a form of sexual expression. Similarly, some feminists are now insisting that prostitution raises no issues of *sexual* privacy: "Prostitution is a professional or economic option, unrelated to sexual/emotional needs."[38] And we have seen other feminists deny that the main purpose of prostitution is sexual, even for men. Not only must the needed philosophical theory of sexuality help us to identify just what sexual activity is; it must also help us to make the conceptual connections and distinctions between forms of sexual expression on the one hand and gender and personal identity on the other hand. It must clarify the relationship, if any, between sexual expression and love. And it must compare the human capacity for sexual activity to the human capacity to labor. Thus it must tell us, for instance, whether there is anything especially degrading about the sale of sexual services.

An adequate account of prostitution also rests, obviously, on a philosophical account of coercion. In particular, we need to know whether economic inducements are coercive and if so, in what circumstances. Only from this philosophical basis can we work out the conceptual relationships between prostitution, rape and "free enterprise."

In addition to these conceptual and normative presuppositions, a useful account of prostitution also requires an investigation of the way in which the institution functions in contemporary society. We need to know why women engage in prostitution and why men do so. We need to understand the relationship between "the traffic in women" and other forms of exchange in our society; in other words, we need to understand the political economy of prostitution. Without such knowledge, our account of prostitution will remain at a very high level of abstraction; we will not be able to understand the specific phenomenon of prostitution in contemporary society, we shall not be able to determine what, if anything, is wrong with it and what, if anything, ought to be done about it.

But how can we ever arrive at these decisions when the various theorists, liberal, Marxist and radical feminist, all hold such widely different concepts of prostitution? Not only do the theorists disagree on what is wrong with prostitution and on what ought to be done about it; they even disagree on what it is. They each accept the paradigm case of a woman selling sexual services, but each presents a very different analysis of that paradigm case. For example, the radical feminist argues that the gender of the seller is essential to determining whether a situation is a case of prostitution, the liberal insists that it is the sale of a sexual service that is the central feature, while the Marxist focuses on the sale of an important human capacity by an individual of either sex.

How is this disagreement to be resolved? Is there a single correct analysis of prostitution on which we must agree before we can construct a normative moral and political theory about it? And is such a correct analysis to be found by looking up dictionary definitions or paying closer attention to ordinary usage?

I do not think so. I think that the issue of prostitution presents a clear example of the futility of that conventional wisdom which recommends that we begin by defining our terms. For the divergence in the competing definitions of prostitution does not result from failing to consult the dictionary or from paying insufficient attention to ordinary usage. It results from normative disagreements on what constitutes freedom, on the moral status of certain activities and, ultimately, on a certain view of what it means to be human. Thus, the disagreement on what constitutes prostitution is merely a surface manifestation of a disagreement over the fundamental categories to be used in describing social activities and over what are the important features of social life which need to be picked out. The inability of moral theorists to agree on what constitutes prostitution is an instance of the interdependence of principles and intuitions, of theory and data, even of fact and value.

The only conclusion that I draw from all this is perhaps the obvious one that prostitution is far from being a self-contained moral or political issue. What prostitution is, what is wrong with it and what should be done about it can be determined only within the context of a comprehensive social philosophy. This philosophy must explain what it is to be human, what it is to be a man or a woman, what kind of relationships should exist between individuals of the same and different sexes, what kind of social relationships will permit the institution of such relationships and what is the proper role of sexuality and work in human life. Reflections on the issues raised by prostitution shows the need for such a philosophy, but prostitution will be only one of the areas where it helps us determine what is to be done.

Notes

1. Leo Kanowitz, *Woman and the Law: The Unfinished Revolution* (Albuquerque: University of New Mexico Press, 1969), p. 15.

2. *The Wolfenden Report: Report of the Committee on Homosexual Offences and Prostitution,* Authorized American edition (New York: Stein & Day, 1963), p. 132. Another argument commonly given for the decriminalization of prostitution is that it would lessen the opportunities for blackmail, police pay-offs and protection rackets and hence break the current connection between prostitution and such crimes as blackmail, theft, rape, assault, drunkenness, drug abuse and bribery. Some prostitutes are in favor of this in the hope that it will legitimize their work.

3. *Ibid.,* p. 163.

4. Marilyn G. Haft, "Hustling for Rights," *The Civil Liberties Review* 1, Issue 2 (Winter/Spring 1974), p. 16.

5. *Ibid.,* p. 20.

6. NOW Resolution 141, passed at the sixth national conference of the National Organization for Women in Washington, D.C., in February, 1973.

7. John Stuart Mill, *On Liberty,* reprinted in *The Utilitarians* (New York: Anchor Books, 1973), p. 486.

8. Susan Brownmiller, "Speaking Out on Prostitution," in Anne Koedt and Shulamith Firestone, eds., *Notes From the Third Year* (New York: Notes From the Second Year, Inc., 1971), p. 38.

9. Joel Feinberg, "Legal Paternalism," *Canadian Journal of Philosophy,* No. 1 (1971), pp. 105–124.

10. T. H. Green, *Liberal Legislation and Freedom of Contract* III, p. 388, quoted in D. J. Manning, *Liberalism* (New York: St. Martin's Press, 1976), p. 20.

11. Robert Nozick, *Anarchy, State and Utopia* (New York: Basic Books, 1974), p. 331.

12. Frederick Engels, *The Origin of the Family, Private Property and the State* (New York: International Publishers, 1942), p. 63.

13. Karl Marx, *The Economic and Philosophical Manuscripts of 1844,* edited with an introduction by Dirk J. Struik (New York: International Publishers, 1964), p. 133, footnote.

14. Engels, *op. cit.,* p. 42. I do not know how far Marx shared this belief, but it is certainly echoed in Lenin's rejection of "the glass-of-water" theory of sex in communist society. "To be sure, thirst has to be quenched. But would a normal person normally lie down in the gutter and drink from a puddle? Or even from a glass whose edge has been greased by many lips?" V. I. Lenin, *The*

Emancipation of Women (New York: International Publishers, 1934), p. 106.

15. Engels, *op. cit.*, p. 67.

16. *Ibid.*

17. *Ibid.*, p. 72.

18. *Ibid.*

19. *Ibid.*, p. 61.

20. Karl Marx and Frederick Engels, "Manifesto of the Communist Party," reprinted in *Selected Works of Marx and Engels* (Moscow and New York: New World Paperbacks, 1968), p. 50.

21. Marx, *op. cit.*, p. 167.

22. *Ibid.*, p. 134.

23. Engels, *op. cit.*, p. 66.

24. Marx, *op. cit.*, p. 133, footnote.

25. Marx and Engels, *op. cit.*, p. 51.

26. Karen Lindsey, "Prostitution and the Law," *The Second Wave* 1, No. 4 (1972), p. 6.

27. Cicely Hamilton, *Marriage as a Trade* (London: Chapman & Hall, Ltd., 1909); selections reprinted in Nancy Reeves, *Womankind* (Chicago: Aldine-Atherton, 1971), p. 209. Some authors go so far as to charge that, contrary to public belief, marriage is less of an "honorable estate" than prostitution. "The wife who married for money, compared with the prostitute," says Havelock Ellis, "is the true scab. She is paid less, gives much more in return in labor and care, and is absolutely bound to her master. The prostitute never signs away the right over her own person, she retains her freedom and personal rights, nor is she always compelled to submit to man's embrace." Quoted by Emma Goldman, *The Traffic in Women* (New York: Times Change Press, 1970), p. 26. Contemporary radical feminists voice a similar point of view. "Wifehood is slavery with a measure of status and security; prostitution is a bit of freedom coupled with the stigma of outcast." Barbara Mehrhof and Pamela Kearon, "Prostitution," *Notes from the Third Year, op. cit.*, p. 72.

28. Mary Lathan, "Selling Celibacy," *Women: A Journal of Liberation* 3, No. 1 (1972), pp. 24–25.

29. Mehrhof and Kearon, *op. cit.*, p. 72. A similar claim is made by one of the prostitutes interviewed by Kate Millett: "There's a special indignity in prostitution, as if sex were dirty and men can only enjoy it with someone low. It involves a type of contempt, a kind of disdain, and a kind of triumph over another human being." Kate Millett, *op cit.*, p. 54.

30. Mehrhof and Kearon, *op. cit.*, p. 74.

31. Jackie MacMillan, "Prostitution as Sexual Politics," *Quest: A Feminist Quarterly* IV, No. 1 (Summer, 1977), p. 43.

32. Linda Thurston, "Prostitution and the Law," *op. cit.*, p. 8.

33. Emma Goldman, *op. cit.*, p. 20.

34. Susan Brownmiller, *op. cit.*, p. 39.

35. Cathy Nossa, "Prostitution: Who's Hustling Whom?" *Women: A Journal of Liberation* 3, No. 1 (1972), p. 29.

36. Carol Hanisch, "A Critique of the Miss American Protest" in Shulamith Firestone and Anne Koedt, eds., *Notes from the Second Year: Women's Liberation* (New York: Radical Feminism, 1970), p. 88.

37. Gayle Rubin, "The Traffic in Women," in Rayna Reiter, ed., *Towards an Anthropology of Women* (New York: Monthly Review Press, 1975), pp. 157–210.

38. Jackie MacMillan, *op cit.*, p. 47.

Study Questions

1. What is the liberal position regarding prostitution?

2. What is the radical feminist position regarding prostitution?

3. What is the Marxist position regarding prostitution, according to Jaggar?

4. Why does Jaggar deny that the difference between these views is primarily "semantical"? In what sense does she think the issue of prostitution is answerable?

4
Political Philosophy

Traditionally, political philosophy has focused on the concepts of power and authority and their relation to the state. Political philosophy has asked: What governmental system is the best, what rights do individuals possess, what limitations to state power should exist, and so on. From the feminist point of view, traditional political theory has dealt exclusively with the public realm, from which women have been systematically excluded, and has ignored the private realm, to which women have universally been consigned. Feminists have accordingly sought to reshape political theory.

The feminist imperative is to move women, personally and collectively, from powerlessness to power and in so doing to redefine the nature and function of power. Catharine MacKinnon holds that "Feminism has no theory of the state. It has a theory of power: . . . The man/woman difference and the dominance/submission dynamic define each other." In the past, women were empowered by such means as enfranchisement; the present feminist project is for women to empower themselves by a range of possible practices. The following essays present some of these.

Ti-Grace Atkinson delineates the radical feminist position, which she calls a *causal class analysis* of the oppressor class (men) and the oppressed class (women). Women, as the oppressed, she holds, were the first political class and were defined as such by their sexual/procreative function. Atkinson shows how the sexual politics of dominance and submission have been generated and maintained by men out of their own needs for potency. She calls for a programmatic analysis to ground women's tactics and strategies for feminist revolution.

Charlotte Bunch outlines the case for lesbian-feminism as a political philosophy. The basic tenet of lesbian-feminist theory is that the institution of heterosexuality is the cornerstone of male supremacy. The political ideology of heterosexism assumes that women wish to be "bonded to men—that each woman exists for a man." According to Bunch, "lesbianism is a threat to the ideological and political basis of male supremacy," because it challenges male domination in behalf of all women and, as she says, "is not for lesbians only." She calls on lesbians, however, to form their own political movement.

Separatism has been a significant political strategy for feminists. Exploring the feminist notion of female separatism as a counter to male supremacy, Marilyn Frye describes its basic modes. She discusses the notion of separatism as a conscious and systematic strategy for women, personally and politically. Frye analyzes separatism as women's denial of (men's) access to themselves. She holds that separatist practices may be instrumental in defining and empowering women.

Utilizing a postmodern account of modern disciplinary technology, Sandra Bartky shows how the project of femininity produces women as "docile bodies." She calls for the deconstruction of normative femininity and for the deployment of oppositional discourses and practices as feminist resistance.

Bell Hooks focuses on the special vantage point of women of color. She critiques the notion of a *common* oppression of women, indicating the primacy of race and class as well as gender. Hooks calls for black women to assert the perspective of their own lived experience in forming feminist discourse. As Barbara Omolade writes: "To enable black women to pursue a dialogue with white feminists, a feminist theory needs to be developed and expanded to include our priorities and experiences."

136

Radical Feminism: Declaration of War

Ti-Grace Atkinson

Almanina Barbour, a black militant woman in Philadelphia, once pointed out to me: "The Women's Movement is the first in history with a war on and no enemy." I winced. It was an obvious criticism. I fumbled about in my mind for an answer. Surely the enemy must have been defined at some time. Otherwise, what had we been shooting at for the last couple of years? into the air?

Only two responses came to me, although in looking for those two I realized that it was a question carefully avoided. The first and by far the most frequent answer was "society." The second, infrequently and always furtively, was "men."

If "society" is the enemy, what could that mean? If women are being oppressed, there's only one group left over to be doing the oppressing: men. Then why call them "society"? Could "society" mean the "institutions" that oppress women? But institutions must be maintained, and the same question arises: by whom? The answer to "who is the enemy?" is so obvious that the interesting issue quickly becomes "why has it been avoided?"

The master might tolerate many reforms in slavery but none that would threaten his essential role as master. Women have known this, and since "men" and "society" are in effect synonymous, they have feared confronting him. Without this confrontation and a detailed understanding of what *his* battle strategy has been that has kept us so successfully pinned down, the "Women's Movement" is worse than useless. It invites backlash from men, and no progress for women.

There has never been a feminist analysis. While discontent among women and the

From Ti-Grace Atkinson, *Amazon Odyssey* (1974), pp. 46–55. Reprinted by permission of Hyperion Press. (Notes deleted.)

attempt to resolve this discontent have often implied that women form a class, no political or *causal* class analysis has followed. To rephrase my last point, the persecution of women has never been taken as the starting point for a political analysis of society.

Considering that the last massing of discontent among women continued some 70 years (1850–1920) and spread the world and the recent accumulation of grievances began some three years ago here in America, the lack of a structural understanding of the problem is at first sight incomprehensible. It is the understanding of the *reasons* for this devastating omission and of the *implications* of the problem that forces one to "radical feminism."

Women who have tried to solve their problems as a class have proposed not solutions but dilemmas. The traditional feminists want equal rights for women with men. But on what grounds? If women serve a different *function* from men in society, wouldn't this necessarily affect women's "rights"? For example, do *all* women have the "right" not to bear children? Traditional feminism is caught in the dilemma of demanding equal treatment for unequal functions, because it is unwilling to challenge political (functional) classification by sex.

Radical women, on the other hand, grasp that women as a group somehow fit into a political analysis of society, but err in refusing to explore the significance of the fact that women form a class, the uniqueness of this class, and the implications of this description to the system of political classes. Both traditional feminists and radical women have evaded questioning any part of their *raison d'être:* women are a class, and the terms that make up this initial assumption must be examined.

The feminist dilemma is that it is as women—or "females"—that women are persecuted, just as it was as slaves—or "blacks" —that slaves were persecuted in America. In order to improve their condition, those individuals who are today defined as women must eradicate their own definition. Women must, in a sense, commit suicide, and the journey from womanhood to a society of individuals is hazardous. The feminist dilemma is that we have the most to do, and the least to do it with. We must create, as no other group in history has been forced to do, from the very beginning.

The "battle of the sexes" is a commonplace, both over time and distance. But it is an inaccurate description of what has been happening. A "battle" implies some balance of powers, whereas when one side suffers all the losses, such as in some kinds of raids (often referred to as the "rape" of an area), that is called a *massacre*. Women have been massacred as human beings over history, and this destiny is entailed by their definition. As women begin massing together, they take the first step from *being* massacred to *engaging in* battle (resistance). Hopefully, this will eventually lead to negotiations—in the *very* far future—and peace.

When any person or group of persons is being mistreated or, to continue our metaphor, is being attacked, there is a succession of responses or investigations:

1. Depending on the severity of the attack (short of an attack on life), the victim determines how much damage was done and what it was done with.

2. Where is the attack coming from? from whom? located where?

3. How can you win the immediate battle? defensive measures? holding actions?

4. Why did he attack you?

5. How can you win (end) the war? offensive measures? moving within his boundaries?

These first five questions are necessary but should be considered diplomatic maneuvers. They have never been answered by the so-called "Women's Movement," and for this reason I think one cannot properly call that Movement "political." It could not have had any direction relevant to women as a class.

If diplomacy fails, that is, if your enemy refuses to stop attacking you, you must force him to stop. This requires a strategy, and this strategy requires a map of the relevant landscape, including such basic information as

1. Who is the enemy?

2. Where is he located?

3. Is he getting outside support? material? manpower? from whom?

4. Where are his forces massed?

5. What's the best ammunition to knock them out?

6. What weapons is he using?

7. How can you counteract them?

8. What is your plan of attack on him to force diplomatic negotiations? Program of action (including priorities)? Techniques?

I am using some military terminology, and this may seem incongruous. But why should it? We accept the phrase "battle of the sexes." It is the proposal that *women* fight *back* that seems incongruous. It has been necessary to program women's psychic structure to nonresistance on their own behalf—for obvious reasons—they make up over half the population of the world.

Without a programmatic analysis, the "Women's Movement" has been as if running blindly in the general direction of where they *guess* the last missile that just hit them was based. For the first two years of the last organizing, I was very active in this running-blind approach. It's true that we were attacking evils, but why *those* particular evils? Were they the central issues in the persecution of women? There was no map so I couldn't be sure, but I could see no reason to believe that we knew what the key issues were, much less that we were hitting them.

It became increasingly clear to me that we were incorporating many of our external problems (e.g., power hierarchies) into our own movement, and in understanding this and beginning to ask myself some of the obvious questions I've listed above, I came to the conclusion that at this time the most radical *action* that any woman or group of women could take was a feminist analysis. The implications of such an analysis is a greater threat to the opposition to human rights for women than all the actions and threatened actions put together up until this time by women.

With this introduction to the significance of a feminist analysis, I will outline what we have so far.

As I mentioned before, the *raison d'être* of all groups formed around the problem of women is that women are a class. What is meant by that? What is meant by "women" and what is meant by "class"?

Does "women" include all women? Some groups have been driven back from the position of *all* women to some proposed "special" class such as "poor" women and eventually concentrated more on economic class than sexual class. But if we're interested in women and how women *qua* women are oppressed, this class must include *all* women.

What separates out a particular individual from other individuals as a "woman"? We recognize it's a sexual separation and that this separation has two aspects, "sociological" and "biological." The term for the sociological function is "woman" (wifman); the term for the biological function is "female" (to suckle). Both terms are descriptive of functions in the interests of someone other than the possessor.

And what is meant by "class"? We've already briefly covered the meaning as the characteristic by which certain individuals are grouped together. In the "Women's Movement" or "feminism," individuals group together to *act* on behalf of women as a class in opposition to the *class* enemies of women. It is the interaction between classes that defines political action. For this reason I call the feminist analysis a *causal class analysis.*

We have established that women are a political class characterized by a sexual function. It is clear that women, at the present time at any rate, have the *capacity* to bear children. But the question arises: "how did this biological classification become a political classification?" How or why did this elaborate superstructure of coercion develop on top of a capacity (which normally implies choice)?

It is generally agreed that women were the first political class. (Children do not properly constitute a political class since the relevant characteristic of its members [namely, age] is unstable for any given member by definition.) "Political" classes are usually defined as classes treated by other classes in some special manner distinct from the way other classes are treated. What is frequently omitted is that "political" classes are *artificial;* they define persons with certain capacities *by* those capacities, changing the contingent to the necessary, thereby appropriating the *capacities* of an individual as a *function* of society. (Definition of "political class" = individuals grouped together by other individuals as a function of the grouping individuals, depriving the grouped individuals of their human status.) A "function" of society cannot be a free individual: exercising the minimal human rights of physical integrity and freedom of movement.

If women were the first political class, and political classes must be defined by individuals outside that class, who defined them, and why, and how? It is reasonable to assume that at some period in history the population was politically undifferentiated; let's call that mass "Mankind" (generic).

The first dichotomous division of this mass is said to have been on the grounds of sex: male and female. But the genitals *per se* would be no more grounds for the human race to be divided in two than skin color or height or hair color. The genitals, in connection with a particular activity, have the *capacity* for the initiation of the reproductive process. But, I submit, it was because one half the human race bears the *burden* of the reproductive *process* and because man, the "rational" animal, had the wit to take advantage of that that the childbearers, or the "beasts of burden," were corralled into a political class. The biologically contingent burden of childbearing was equivocated into a political (or necessary) penalty, thereby modifying those individuals' definition thereby defined from the human to the functional—or animal.

There is no justification for using any individual as a function of others. Didn't *all* members of society have the right to decide if they even *wanted* to reproduce? Because one half of humanity was and still is forced to bear the burden of reproduction at the will of the other half, the first political class is defined not by its sex—sexuality was only relevant originally as a means to reproduction—but by the function of being the *container* of the reproductive process.

Because women have been taught to believe that men have protective feelings toward women (men have protective feelings toward their functions [property], not other human beings!), we women are shocked by these discoveries and ask ourselves *why* men took and continue to take advantage of us.

Some people say that men are naturally, or biologically, aggressive. But this leaves us at an impasse. If the values of society are power-oriented, there is no chance that men would agree to be medicated into a humane state.

The other alternative that has been suggested is to eliminate men as biologically incapable of humane relationships and therefore a menace to society. I can sympathize with the frustration and rage that leads to this suggestion.

But the proposal to eliminate men, as I understand it, assumes that men constitute a kind of social disease, and that by "men" is meant those individuals with certain typical genital characteristics. These genital characteristics are held to determine the organism in every biochemical respect thus determining the psychic structure as well. It may be that as in other mental derangements, and I do believe that men behave in a mentally deranged manner toward women, there is a biochemical correspondence, but this would be ultimately behaviorally determined, not genetically.

I believe that the sex roles—both male and female—must be destroyed, not the individuals who happen to possess either a penis or a vagina, or both, or neither. But many men I have spoken with see little to choose from between the two positions and feel that without the role they'd just as soon die.

Certainly it is the master who resists the abolition of slavery, especially when he is offered no recompense in power. I think that the *need* men have for the role of Oppressor is the source and foundation of all human oppression. Men suffer from a disease peculiar to Mankind which I call "metaphysical cannibalism." Men must, at the very least, cooperate in curing themselves.

Study Questions

1. What sort of feminist analysis does Atkinson propose? Why is it necessary?

2. What does Atkinson mean by "women as a class"? As "the first political class"?

3. How were women made into the first political class?

4. How does Atkinson feel men can be dealt with?

Lesbians in Revolt

Charlotte Bunch

The development of Lesbian-Feminist politics as the basis for the liberation of women is our top priority: this article outlines our present

From *Lesbianism and the Women's Movement* (Diana Press, 1975). Copyright © 1975 by Charlotte Bunch. *Editor's note:* This essay should be read in the context of the Women's Movement of the early 1970s and of the kind of anger out of which these ideas arose. Lesbian feminist theory was being formulated at that time.

ideas. In our society, which defines all people and institutions for the benefit of the rich, white male, the Lesbian is in revolt. In revolt because she defines herself in terms of women and rejects the male definitions of how she should feel, act, look, and live. To be a Lesbian is to love oneself, woman, in a culture that denigrates and despises women. The Lesbian rejects male sexual/political domination; she defies his world, his social organization, his ideology, and his definition of her as inferior. Lesbianism puts women first while the society declares the male supreme. Lesbianism threatens male supremacy at its core. When politically conscious and organized, it is central to destroying our sexist, racist, capitalist, imperialist system.

Male society defines Lesbianism as a sexual act, which reflects men's limited view of women: they think of us only in terms of sex. They also say Lesbians are not real women, so a real woman is one who gets fucked by men. We say that a Lesbian is a woman whose sense of self and energies, including sexual energies, center around women—she is woman identified. The woman-identified-woman commits herself to other women for political, emotional, physical, and economic support. Women are important to her. She is important to herself. Our society demands that commitment from women be reserved for men.

The Lesbian, woman-identified-woman, commits herself to women not only as an alternative to oppressive male/female relationships but primarily because she *loves* women. Whether consciously or not, by her actions, the Lesbian has recognized that giving support and love to men over women perpetuates the system that oppresses her. If women do not make a commitment to each other, which includes sexual love, we deny ourselves the love and value traditionally given to men. We accept our second-class status. When women do give primary energies to other women, then it is possible to concentrate fully on building a movement for our liberation.

Woman-identified Lesbianism is, then, more than a sexual preference, it is a political choice. It is political because relationships between men and women are essentially political, they involve power and dominance. Since the Lesbian actively rejects that relationship and chooses women, she defies the established political system.

Of course, not all Lesbians are consciously woman-identified, nor are all committed to finding common solutions to the oppression they suffer as women and Lesbians. Being a Lesbian is part of challenging male supremacy, but not the end. For the Lesbian or heterosexual woman, there is no individual solution to oppression.

The Lesbian may think that she is free since she escapes the personal oppression of the individual male/female relationship. But to the society she is still a woman, or worse, a visible Lesbian. On the street, at the job, in the schools, she is treated as an inferior and is at the mercy of men's power and whims. (I've never heard of a rapist who stopped because his victim was a Lesbian.) This society hates women who love women, and so, the Lesbian, who escapes male dominance in her private home, receives it doubly at the hands of male society; she is harassed, outcast, and shuttled to the bottom. Lesbians must become feminists and fight against woman oppression, just as feminists must become Lesbians if they hope to end male supremacy.

U.S. society encourages individual solutions, apolitical attitudes, and reformism to keep us from political revolt and out of power. Men who rule, and male leftists who seek to rule, try to depoliticize sex and the relations between men and women in order to prevent us from acting to end our oppression and challenging their power. As the question of homosexuality has become public, reformists define it as a private question of who you sleep with in order to sidetrack our understanding of the politics of sex. For the Lesbian-Feminist, it is not private; it is a political matter of oppression, domination, and power. Reformists offer solutions which make no basic changes in the system that oppresses us, solutions which keep power in the hands of the oppressor. The only way oppressed people end their oppression is by seizing power: People whose rule depends on the subordination of others do not voluntarily stop oppressing others. Our subordination is the basis of male power.

Sexism Is the Root of All Oppression

The first division of labor, in pre-history, was based on sex: men hunted, women built the villages, took care of children, and farmed. Women collectively controlled the land, language, culture, and the communities. Men were able to conquer women with the weapons that they developed for hunting when it became clear that women were leading a more stable, peaceful, and desirable existence. We do not know exactly how this conquest took place, but it is clear that the original imperialism was male over female: the male claiming the female body and her service as his territory (or property).

Having secured the domination of women, men continued this pattern of suppressing people, now on the basis of tribe, race, and class. Although there have been numerous battles over class, race, and nation during the past 3000 years, none has brought the liberation of women. While these other forms of oppression must be ended, there is no reason to believe that our liberation will come with the smashing of capitalism, racism, or imperialism today. Women will be free only when we concentrate on fighting male supremacy.

Our war against male supremacy does, however, involve attacking the latter-day dominations based on class, race, and nation. As Lesbians who are outcasts from every group, it would be suicidal to perpetuate these man-made divisions among ourselves. We have no heterosexual privileges, and when we publicly assert our Lesbianism, those of us who had them lose many of our class and race privileges. Most of our privileges as women are granted to us by our relationships to men (fathers, husbands, boyfriends) whom we now reject. This does not mean that there is no racism or class chauvinism within us, but we must destroy these divisive remnants of privileged behavior among ourselves as the first step toward their destruction in the society. Race, class, and national oppressions come from men, serve ruling class white men's interests, and have no place in a woman-identified revolution.

Lesbianism Is the Basic Threat to Male Supremacy

Lesbianism is a threat to the ideological, political, and economic basis of male supremacy. The Lesbian threatens the ideology of male supremacy by destroying the lie about female inferiority, weakness, passivity, and by denying women's "innate" need for men. Lesbians literally do not need men (even for procreation if the science of cloning is developed).

The Lesbian's independence and refusal to support one man undermines the personal power that men exercise over women. Our rejection of heterosexual sex challenges male domination in its most individual and common form. We offer all women something better than submission to personal oppression. We offer the beginning of the end of collective and individual male supremacy. Since men of all races and classes depend on female support and submission for practical tasks and feeling superior, our refusal to submit will force some to examine their sexist behavior, to break down their own destructive privileges over other humans, and to fight against those privileges in other men. They will have to build new selves that do not depend on oppressing women and learn to live in social structures that do not give them power over anyone.

Heterosexuality separates women from each other; it makes women define themselves through men; it forces women to compete against each other for men and the privilege which comes through men and their social standing. Heterosexual society offers women a few privileges as compensation if they give up their freedom: for example, mothers are respected and "honored," wives or lovers are socially accepted and given some economic and emotional security, a woman gets physical protection on the street when she stays with her man, etc. The privileges give heterosexual women a personal and political stake in maintaining the status quo.

The Lesbian receives none of these heterosexual privileges or compensations since she does not accept the male demands on her. She has little vested interest in maintaining the present political system since all of its institutions—church, state, media, health, schools—work to keep her down. If she understands her oppression, she has nothing to gain by supporting white rich male America and much to gain from fighting to change it. She is less prone to accept reformist solutions to women's oppression.

Economics is a crucial part of woman oppression, but our analysis of the relationship between capitalism and sexism is not complete. We know that Marxist economic theory does not sufficiently consider the role of women or Lesbians, and we are presently working on this area.

However, as a beginning, some of the ways that Lesbians threaten the economic system are clear: In this country, women work for men in order to survive, on the job and in the home. The Lesbian rejects this division of labor at its roots; she refuses to be a man's property, to submit to the unpaid labor system of housework and childcare. She rejects the nuclear family as the basic unit of production and consumption in capitalist society.

The Lesbian is also a threat on the job because she is not the passive/part-time woman worker that capitalism counts on to do boring work and be part of a surplus labor pool. Her identity and economic support do not come through men, so her job is crucial and she cares about job conditions, wages, promotion, and status. Capitalism cannot absorb large numbers of women demanding stable employment, decent salaries, and refusing to accept their traditional job exploitation. We do not understand yet the total effect that this increased job dissatisfaction will have. It is, however, clear that as women become more intent upon taking control of their lives, they will seek more control over their jobs, thus increasing the strains on capitalism and enhancing the power of women to change the economic system.

Lesbians Must Form Our Own Movement to Fight Male Supremacy

Feminist-Lesbianism, as the most basic threat to male supremacy, picks up part of the Women's Liberation analysis of sexism and gives it force and direction. Women's Liberation lacks direction now because it has failed to understand the importance of heterosexuality in maintaining male supremacy and because it has failed to face class and race as real differences in women's behavior and political needs. As long

as straight women see Lesbianism as a bedroom issue, they hold back the development of politics and strategies which would put an end to male supremacy and they give men an excuse for not dealing with their sexism.

Being a Lesbian means ending identification with, allegiance to, dependence on, and support of heterosexuality. It means ending your personal stake in the male world so that you join women, individually and collectively, in the struggle to end your oppression. Lesbianism is the key to liberation and only women who cut their ties to male privilege can be trusted to remain serious in the struggle against male dominance. Those who remain tied to men, individually or in political theory, cannot always put women first. It is not that heterosexual women are evil or do not care about women. It is because the very essence, definition, and nature of heterosexuality is men first. Every woman has experienced that desolation when her sister puts her man first in the final crunch: heterosexuality demands that she do so. As long as women still benefit from heterosexuality, receive its privileges and security, they will at some point have to betray their sisters, especially Lesbian sisters who do not receive those benefits.

Women in women's liberation have understood the importance of having meetings and other events for women only. It has been clear that dealing with men divides us and saps our energies and that it is not the job of the oppressed to explain our oppression to the oppressor. Women also have seen that collectively, men will not deal with their sexism until they are forced to do so. Yet, many of these same women continue to have primary relationships with men individually and do not understand why Lesbians find this oppressive. Lesbians cannot grow politically or personally in a situation which denies the basis of our politics: that Lesbianism is political, that heterosexuality is crucial to maintaining male supremacy.

Lesbians must form our own political movement in order to grow. Changes which will have more than token effects on our lives will be led by woman-identified Lesbians who understand the nature of our oppression and are therefore in a position to end it.

Study Questions

---

1. What does Bunch set out to show in her paper?
2. What is lesbian feminism, and how has it evolved over the last decade?
3. In what way is "woman-identified-woman" a common identification around which lesbians and feminists should unite?
4. What is the ideology of heterosexism, and how does it help to oppress women?
5. In what ways does lesbianism threaten patriarchal society?
6. Why does Bunch hold that lesbians should form their own political movement?

Some Reflections on Separatism and Power

Marilyn Frye

I have been trying to write something about separatism almost since my first dawning of feminist consciousness, but it has always been for me somehow a mercurial topic which, when I tried to grasp it, would softly shatter into many other topics like sexuality, man-hating, so-called reverse discrimination, apocalyptic utopianism, and so on. What I have to share with you today is my latest attempt to get to the heart of the matter.

In my life, and within feminism as I understand it, separatism is not a theory or a doctrine, nor a demand for certain specific behaviors on the part of feminists, though it is undeniably connected with lesbianism. Feminism seems to me to be kaleidoscopic—something whose shapes, structures and patterns alter with every turn of feminist creativity; and one element which is present through all the changes is an element of separation. This element has different roles and relations in different turns of the glass—it assumes different meanings, is variously conspicuous, variously determined or determining, depending on how the pieces fall and who is the beholder.

From *The Politics of Reality: Essays in Feminist Theory* (Trumansburg, New York: The Crossing Press, 1983). Reprinted by permission of the publisher. (Notes deleted.)

The theme of separation, in its multitude variations, is there in everything from divorce to exclusive lesbian separatist communities, from shelters for battered women to witch covens, from women's studies programs to women's bars, from expansion of daycare to abortion on demand. The presence of this theme is vigorously obscured, trivialized, mystified and outright denied by many feminist apologists, who seem to find it embarrassing, while it is embraced, explored, expanded and ramified by most of the more inspiring theorists and activists. The theme of separation is noticeably absent or heavily qualified in most of the things I take to be personal solutions and band-aid projects, like legalization of prostitution, liberal marriage contracts, improvement of the treatment of rape victims and affirmative action. It is clear to me, in my own case at least, that the contrariety of assimilation and separation is one of the main things that guides or determines assessments of various theories, actions and practices as reformist or radical, as going to the root of the thing or being relatively superficial. So my topical question comes to this: What is it about separation, in any or all of its many forms and degrees, that makes it so basic and so sinister, so exciting and so repellent?

Feminist separation is, of course, separation of various sorts or modes from men and from institutions, relationships, roles and activities which are male-defined, male-dominated and operating for the benefit of males and the maintenance of male privilege—this separation being initiated or maintained, at will, *by women*. (Masculist separatism is the partial segregation of women from men and male domains *at the will of men*. This difference is crucial.) The feminist separation can take many forms. Breaking up or avoiding close relationships or working relationships; forbidding someone to enter your house; excluding someone from your company, or from your meeting; withdrawal from participation in some activity or institution, or avoidance of participation; avoidance of communications and influence from certain quarters (not listening to music with sexist lyrics, not watching tv); withholding commitment or support; rejection of or rudeness toward obnoxious individuals.[1] Some separations are subtle realignments of identification, priorities and commitments, or working with agendas which only incidentally coincide with the agendas of the institution one works in. Ceasing to be loyal to something or someone is a separation; and ceasing to love. The feminist's separations are rarely if ever sought or maintained directly as ultimate personal or political ends. The closest we come to that, I think, is the separation which is the instinctive and self-preserving recoil from the systematic misogyny that surrounds us.[2] Generally, the separations are brought about and maintained for the sake of something else like independence, liberty, growth, invention, sisterhood, safety, health, or the practice of novel or heretical customs.[3] Often the separations in question evolve, unpremeditated, as one goes one's way and finds various persons, institutions or relationships useless, obstructive or noisome and leaves them aside or behind. Sometimes the separations are consciously planned and cultivated as necessary prerequisites or conditions for getting on with one's business. Sometimes the separations are accomplished or maintained easily, or with a sense of relief, or even joy; sometimes they are accomplished or maintained with difficulty, by dint of constant vigilance, or with anxiety, pain or grief.

Most feminists, probably all, practice some separation from males and male-dominated institutions. A separatist practices separation consciously, systematically, and probably more generally than the others, and advocates thorough and "broad-spectrum" separation as part of the conscious strategy of liberation. And, contrary to the image of the separatist as a cowardly escapist, hers is the life and program which inspires the greatest hostility, disparagement, insult and confrontation and generally she is the one against whom economic sanctions operate most conclusively. The penalty for refusing to work with or for men is usually starvation (or, at the very least, doing without medical insurance); and if one's policy of noncooperation is more subtle, one's livelihood is still constantly on the line, since one is not a loyal partisan, a proper member of the team, or what have you. The penalties for being a lesbian are ostracism, harassment and job insecurity or joblessness. The penalty for rejecting men's sexual advances is often rape and, perhaps even more often, forfeit of such things as professional or job opportunities. And the separatist lives with the added burden of being assumed by many to be a morally depraved man-hating bigot. But there is a clue here: if you are doing something that is so strictly forbidden by the patriarchs, you must be doing something right.

There is an idea floating around in both feminist and antifeminist literature to the effect that females and males generally live in a relation of parasitism,[4] a parasitism of the male on the female . . . that it is, generally speaking, the strength, energy, inspiration and nurturance of women that keeps men going, and not the strength, aggression, spirituality and hunting of men that keeps women going.

It is sometimes said that the parasitism goes the other way around, that the female is the parasite. But one can conjure the appearance of the female as parasite only if one takes a very narrow view of human living—historically parochial, narrow with respect to class and race, and limited in conception of what are the necessary goods. Generally, the female's contribution to her material support is and always has been substantial; in many times and places it has been independently sufficient. One can and should distinguish between a partial and contingent material dependence created by a certain sort of money economy and class structure, and the nearly ubiquitous spiritual, emotional and material dependence of males on females. Males presently provide, off and on, a portion of the material support of women, within circumstances apparently designed to make it difficult for women to provide them for themselves. But females provide and generally have provided for males the energy and spirit for living; the males are nurtured by the females. And this the males apparently cannot do for themselves, even partially.

The parasitism of males on females is, as I see it, demonstrated by the panic, rage and hysteria generated in so many of them by the thought of being abandoned by women. But it is demonstrated in a way that is perhaps more generally persuasive by both literary and sociological evidence. Evidence cited in Jesse Bernard's work in *The Future of Marriage* and in George Gilder's *Sexual Suicide* and *Men Alone* convincingly shows that males tend in shockingly significant numbers and in alarming degree to fall into mental illness, petty crime, alcoholism, physical infirmity, chronic unemployment, drug addiction and neurosis when deprived of the care and companionship of a female mate, or keeper. (While on the other hand, women without male mates are significantly healthier and happier than women with male mates.) And masculist literature is abundant with indications of male cannibalism, of males deriving essential sustenance from females. Cannibalistic imagery, visual and verbal, is common in pornography: images likening women to food, and sex to eating. And, as documented in Millett's *Sexual Politics* and many other feminist analyses of masculist literature, the theme of men getting high off beating, raping or killing women (or merely bullying them) is common. These interactions with women, or rather, these actions upon women, make men feel good, walk tall, feel refreshed, in*vigor*ated. Men are drained and depleted by their living by themselves and with and among other men, and are revived and refreshed, re-created, by going home and being served dinner, changing to clean clothes, having sex with

the wife; or by dropping by the apartment of a woman friend to be served coffee or a drink and stroked in one way or another; or by picking up a prostitute for a quicky or for a dip in favorite sexual escape fantasies; or by raping refugees from their wars (foreign and domestic). The ministrations of women, be they willing or unwilling, free or paid for, are what restore in men the strength, will and confidence to go on with what they call living.

If it is true that a fundamental aspect of the relations between the sexes is male parasitism, it might help to explain why certain issues are particularly exciting to patriarchal loyalists. For instance, in view of the obvious advantages of easy abortion to population control, to control of welfare rolls, and to ensuring sexual availability of women to men, it is a little surprising that the loyalists are so adamant and riled up in their objection to it. But look . . .

The fetus lives parasitically. It is a distinct animal surviving off the life (the blood) of another animal creature. It is incapable of surviving on its own resources, of independent nutrition; incapable even of symbiosis. If it is true that males live parasitically upon females, it seems reasonable to suppose that many of them and those loyal to them are in some way sensitive to the parallelism between their situation and that of the fetus. They could easily identify with the fetus. The woman who is free to see the fetus as a parasite[5] might be free to see the man as a parasite. The woman's willingness to cut off the life line to one parasite suggests a willingness to cut off the life line to another parasite. The woman who is capable (legally, psychologically, physically) of decisively, self-interestedly, independently rejecting the one parasite, is capable of rejecting, with the same decisiveness and independence, the like burden of the other parasite. In the eyes of the other parasite, the image of the wholly self-determined abortion, involving not even a ritual submission to male veto power, is the mirror image of death.

Another clue here is that one line of argument against free and easy abortion is the slippery slope argument that if fetuses are to be freely dispensed with, old people will be next. Old people? Why are old people next? And why the great concern for them? Most old people are women, indeed, and patriarchal loyalists are not generally so solicitous of the welfare of any women. Why old people? Because, I think, in the modern patriarchal divisions of labor, old people too are parasites on women. The antiabortionist folks seem not to worry about wife beating and wife murder—there is no broad or emotional popular support for stopping these violences. They do not worry about murder and involuntary sterilization in prisons, nor murder in war, nor murder by pollution and industrial accidents. Either these are not real to them or they cannot identify with the victims; but anyway, killing in general is not what they oppose. They worry about the rejection *by women, at women's discretion,* of something which lives parasitically on women. I suspect that they fret not because old people are next, but because men are next.

There are other reasons, of course, why patriarchal loyalists should be disturbed about abortion on demand; a major one being that it would be a significant form of female control of reproduction, and at least from certain angles it looks like the progress of patriarchy *is* the progress toward male control of reproduction, starting with possession of wives and continuing through the invention of obstetrics and the technology of extrauterine gestation. Giving up that control would be giving up patriarchy. But such an objection to abortion is too abstract, and requires too historical a vision, to generate the hysteria there is now in the reaction against abortion. The hysteria is, I think, to be accounted for more in terms of a much more immediate and personal presentiment of ejection by the woman-womb.

I discuss abortion here because it seems to me to be the most publicly emotional and most physically dramatic ground on which the theme of separation and male parasitism is presently being played out. But there are other locales for this play. For instance, women with newly raised consciousnesses tend to leave marriages and families, either completely through divorce, or partially, through unavailability of their cooking, housekeeping and sexual services. And women academics tend to become alienated from their colleagues and male mentors and no longer serve as sounding board, ego booster, editor, mistress or proofreader.

Many awakening women become celibate or lesbian, and the others become a very great deal more choosy about when, where and in what relationships they will have sex with men. And the men affected by these separations generally react with defensive hostility, anxiety and guilt-tripping, not to mention descents into illogical argument which match and exceed their own most fanciful images of female irrationality. My claim is that they are very afraid because they depend very heavily upon the goods they receive from women, and these separations cut them off from those goods.

Male parasitism means that males *must have access* to women; it is the Patriarchal Imperative. But feminist no-saying is more than a substantial removal (redirection, reallocation) of goods and services because Access is one of the faces of Power. Female denial of male access to females substantially cuts off a flow of benefits, but it has also the form and full portent of assumption of power.

Differences of power are always manifested in asymmetrical access. The President of the United States has access to almost everybody for almost anything he might want of them, and almost nobody has access to him. The super-rich have access to almost everybody; almost nobody has access to them. The resources of the employee are available to the boss as the resources of the boss are not to the employee. The parent has unconditional access to the child's room; the child does not have similar access to the parent's room. Students adjust to professors' office hours; professors do not adjust to students' conference hours. The child is required not to lie; the parent is free to close out the child with lies at her discretion. The slave is unconditionally accessible to the master. Total power is unconditional access; total powerlessness is being unconditionally accessible. The creation and manipulation of power is constituted of the manipulation and control of access.

All-woman groups, meetings, projects seem to be great things for causing controversy and confrontation. Many women are offended by them; many are afraid to be the one to announce the exclusion of men; it is seen as a device whose use needs much elaborate justification. I think this is because conscious and deliberate exclusion of men by women, from anything, is blatant insubordination, and generates in women fear of punishment and reprisal (fear which is often well justified). Our own timidity and desire to avoid confrontations generally keep us from doing very much in the way of all-woman groups and meetings. But when we do, we invariably run into the male champion who challenges our right to do it. Only a small minority of men go crazy when an event is advertised to be for women only—just one man tried to crash our women-only Rape Speak-Out, and only a few hid under the auditorium seats to try to spy on a women-only meeting at a NOW convention in Philadelphia. But these few are onto something their less rabid compatriots are missing. The woman-only meeting is a fundamental challenge to the structure of power. It is always the privilege of the master to enter the slave's hut. The slave who decides to exclude the master from her hut is declaring herself not a slave. The exclusion of men from the meeting not only deprives them of certain benefits (which they might survive without); it is a controlling of access, hence an assumption of power. It is not only mean, it is arrogant.

It becomes clearer now why there is always an off-putting aura of negativity about separatism—one which offends the feminine pollyanna in us and smacks of the purely defensive to the political theorist in us. It is this: First: When those who control access have made you totally accessible, your first act of taking control must be denying access, or must have denial of access as one of its aspects. This is not because you are charged up with (unfeminine or politically incorrect) negativity; it is because of the logic of the situation. When we start from a position of total accessibility there *must* be an aspect of no-saying (which is the beginning of control) in *every effective* act and strategy, the effective ones being precisely those which *shift power*, i.e., ones which involve manipulation and control of access. Second: Whether or not one says "no," or withholds or closes out or rejects, on this occasion or that, the capacity and ability to say "no" (with effect) is logically necessary to control. When we are in control of access to ourselves there will be some no-saying, and when we are more accustomed to it, when it

is more common, an ordinary part of living, it will not seem so prominent, obvious, or strained . . . we will not strike ourselves or others as being particularly negative. In this aspect of ourselves and our lives, we will strike ourselves pleasingly as active beings with momentum of our own, with sufficient shape and structure—with sufficient integrity—to generate friction. Our experience of our no-saying will be an aspect of our experience of our definition.

When our feminist acts or practices have an aspect of separation, we are assuming power by controlling access and simultaneously by undertaking definition. The slave who excludes the master from her hut thereby declares herself *not a slave*. And *definition* is another face of power.

The powerful normally determine what is said and sayable. When the powerful label something or dub it or baptize it, the thing becomes what they call it. When the Secretary of Defense calls something a peace negotiation, for instance, then whatever it is that he called a peace negotiation is an instance of negotiating peace. If the activity in question is the working out of terms of a trade-off of nuclear reactors and territorial redistributions, complete with arrangements for the resulting refugees, that is peacemaking. People laud it, and the negotiators get Noble Piece Prizes for it. On the other hand, when I call a certain speech act a rape, my "calling" it does not make it so. At best, I have to explain and justify and make clear exactly what it is about this speech act which is assaultive in just what way, and then the others acquiesce in saying the act was *like* rape or could figuratively be called a rape. My counterassault will not be counted a simple case of self-defense. And what I called rejection of parasitism, they call the loss of the womanly virtues of compassion and "caring." And generally, when renegade women call something one thing and patriarchal loyalists call it another, the loyalists get their way.*

---

*This paragraph and the succeeding one are the passage which has provoked the most substantial questions from women who read the paper. One thing that causes trouble here is that I am talking from a stance or position
(continued)

Women generally are not the people who do the defining, and we cannot from our isolation and powerlessness simply commence saying different things than others say and make it stick. There is a humpty-dumpty problem in that. But we are able to arrogate definition to ourselves when we repattern access. Assuming control of access, we draw new boundaries and create new roles and relationships. This, though it causes some strain, puzzlement and hostility, is to a fair extent within the scope of individuals and small gangs, as outright verbal redefinition is not, at least in the first instance.

One may see access as coming in two sorts, "natural" and humanly arranged. A grizzly bear has what you might call natural access to the picnic basket of the unarmed human. The access of the boss to the personal services of the secretary is humanly arranged access; the boss exercises institutional power. It looks to me,

---

(*continued*)

that is ambiguous—it is located in two different and noncommunicating systems of thought-action. *Re* the patriarchy and the English language, there is general usage over which I/we do not have the control that elite males have (with the cooperation of all the ordinary patriarchal loyalists). *Re* the new being and meaning which are being created now by lesbian-feminists, we *do* have semantic authority, and, collectively, can and do define with effect. I think it is only by maintaining our boundaries through controlling concrete access to us that we can enforce on those who are not-us our definitions of ourselves, hence force on them *the fact of our existence* and thence open up the *possibility* of our having semantic authority with them. (I wrote some stuff that's relevant to this in the last section of my paper "Male Chauvinism—A Conceptual Analysis.")[6] Our unintelligibility to patriarchal loyalists is a source of pride and delight, in some contexts; but if we don't have an effect on their usage while we continue, willy nilly, to be subject to theirs, being totally unintelligible to them could be fatal. (A friend of mine had a dream where the women were meeting in a cabin at the edge of town, and they had a sort of inspiration through the vision of one of them that they should put a sign on the door which would connect with the patriarchs' meaning-system, for otherwise the men would be too curious/frightened about them and would break the door down to get in. They put a picture of a fish on the door.) Of course, you might say that *being* intelligible to them might be fatal. Well, perhaps it's best to be in a position to make tactical decisions about when and how to be intelligible and unintelligible.

looking from a certain angle, like institutions are humanly designed patterns of access—access to persons and their services. But institutions are artifacts of definition. In the case of intentionally and formally designed institutions, this is very clear, for the relevant definitions are explicitly set forth in by-laws and constitutions, regulations and rules. When one defines the term "president," one defines presidents in terms of what they can do and what is owed them by other offices, and "what they can do" is a matter of their access to the services of others. Similarly, definitions of *dean, student, judge,* and *cop* set forth patterns of access, and definitions of *writer, child, owner,* and of course, *husband, wife,* and *man* and *girl.* When one changes the pattern of access, one forces new uses of words on those affected. The term "man" has to shift in meaning when rape is no longer possible. When we take control of sexual access to us, of access to our nurturance and to our reproductive function, access to mothering and sistering, we redefine the word "woman." The shift of usage is pressed on others by a change in social reality; it does not await their recognition of our definitional authority.

When women separate (withdraw, break out, regroup, transcend, shove aside, step outside, migrate, say *no*), we are simultaneously controlling access and defining. We are doubly insubordinate, since neither of these is permitted. And access and definition are fundamental ingredients in the alchemy of power, so we are doubly, and radically, insubordinate.

If these, then, are some of the ways in which separation is at the heart of our struggle, it helps to explain why separation is such a hot topic. If there is one thing women are queasy about it is *actually taking power.* As long as one stops just short of that, the patriarchs will for the most part take an indulgent attitude. We are afraid of what will happen to us when we really frighten them. This is not an irrational fear. It is our experience in the movement generally that the defensiveness, nastiness, violence, hostility and irrationality of the reaction to feminism tends to correlate with the blatancy of the element of separation in the strategy or project which triggers the reaction. The separations involved in women leaving homes, marriages and boyfriends, separations from fetuses, and the separation of lesbianism are all pretty dramatic. That is, they are dramatic and blatant when perceived from within the framework provided by the patriarchal world view and male parasitism. Matters pertaining to marriage and divorce, lesbianism and abortion touch individual men (and their sympathizers) because they can feel the relevance of these to themselves—they can feel the threat that they might be the next. Hence, heterosexuality, marriage and motherhood, which are the institutions which most obviously and individually maintain female accessibility to males, form the core triad of antifeminist ideology; and all-woman spaces, all-woman organizations, all-woman meetings, all-woman classes, are outlawed, suppressed, harassed, ridiculed and punished—in the name of that other fine and enduring patriarchal institution, Sex Equality.

To some of us these issues can seem almost foreign . . . strange ones to be occupying center stage. We are busily engaged in what seem to *us* our blatant insubordinations: living our own lives, taking care of ourselves and one another, doing our work, and in particular, telling it as we see it. Still, the original sin is the separation which these presuppose, and it is that, not our art or philosophy, not our speechmaking, nor our "sexual acts" (or abstinences), for which we will be persecuted, when worse comes to worst.

emphasize that it has to be separation at *our* behest—we've had enough of their imposed separation for our "protection." (There's no denying that in my real-life life, protection and maintenance of places for healing are major motives for separation.)

3. See "Separatism and Sexual Relationships," in *Philosophy and Women,* eds. S. Hill and M. Weinzweig (Wadsworth, Belmont, California, 1978).

4. I first noticed this when reading *Beyond God the Father,* by Mary Daly (Beacon Press, Boston, 1973). See also *Women's Evolution,* by Evelyn Reed (Pathfinder Press, New York, 1975) for rich hints about male cannibalism and male dependence.

5. Caroline Whitbeck: "Cross-cultural evidence suggests it's not the fetus that gets rejected in cultures where abortion is common, it is the role of motherhood, the burden, in particular, of 'illegitimacy'; where the institution of illegitimacy does not exist, abortion rates are pretty low." This suggests to me that the woman's rejection of the fetus is even more directly a rejection of the male and his world than I had thought.

6. In (improbably enough) *Philosophy and Sex,* edited by Robert Baker and Frederick Elliston (Prometheus Books, Buffalo, New York, 1976).

Notes

1. Adrienne Rich: ". . . makes me question the whole idea of 'courtesy' or 'rudeness'— surely *their* constructs, since women become 'rude' when we ignore or reject male obnoxiousness, while male 'rudeness' is usually punctuated with the 'Haven't you a sense of humor' tactic." Yes; me too. I embrace rudeness; our compulsive/compulsory politeness so often is what coerces us into their "fellowship."

2. Ti-Grace Atkinson: "Should give more attention here to our vulnerability to assault and degradation, and to separation as *protection.*" Okay, but then we have to re-

Study Questions

1. What does the systematic separatist experience? What can she conclude from what she experiences?

2. What leads Frye to think that men parasitize women, and not vice versa? How does she think that male parasitism helps explain opposition to abortion?

3. In what way does female separatism upset the power relationship between men and women?

4. How is definition another aspect of the power relations between men and women?

Foucault, Femininity and the Modernization of Patriarchal Power

Sandra Bartky

I

In a striking critique of modern society, Michel Foucault has argued that the rise of parliamentary institutions and of new conceptions of political liberty was accompanied by a darker countermovement, by the emergence of a new and unprecedented discipline directed against the body. More is required of the body now than mere political allegiance or the appropriation of the products of its labor: the new discipline invades the body and seeks to regulate its very forces and operations, the economy and efficiency of its movements.

The disciplinary practices Foucault describes are tied to peculiarly modern forms of the army, the school, the hospital, the prison, and the manufactory; the aim of these disciplines is to increase the utility of the body, to augment its forces:

> What was then being formed was a policy of coercions that act upon the body, a calculated manipulation of its elements, its gestures, its behaviour. The human body was entering a machinery of power that explores it, breaks it down and rearranges it. A "political anatomy," which was also a "mechanics of power," was being born; it defined how one may have a hold over others' bodies, not only so that they may do what one wishes, but so that they may operate as one wishes, with the techniques, the speed and the efficiency that one determines. Thus, discipline produces subjected and practiced bodies, "docile" bodies.[1]

From *Feminism and Foucault: Reflections on Resistance,* edited by Irene Diamond and Lee Quinby, Copyright © 1988 by Irene Diamond and Lee Quinby. Reprinted with the permission of Northeastern University Press, Boston.

The production of "docile bodies" requires that an uninterrupted coercion be directed to the very processes of bodily activity, not just their result; this "micro-physics of power" fragments and partitions the body's time, its space, and its movements.

The student, then, is enclosed within a classroom and assigned to a desk he cannot leave; his ranking in the class can be read off the position of his desk in the serially ordered and segmented space of the classroom itself. Foucault tells us that "Jean-Baptiste de la Salle dreamt of a classroom in which the spatial distribution might provide a whole series of distinctions at once, according to the pupil's progress, worth, character, application, cleanliness and parents' fortune." The student must sit upright, feet upon the floor, head erect; he may not slouch or fidget; his animate body is brought into a fixed correlation with the inanimate desk.

The minute breakdown of gestures and movements required of soldiers at drill is far more relentless:

> Bring the weapon forward. In three stages. Raise the rifle with the right hand, bringing it close to the body so as to hold it perpendicular with the right knee, the end of the barrel at eye level, grasping it by striking it with the right hand, the arm held close to the body at waist height. At the second stage, bring the rifle in front of you with the left hand, the barrel in the middle between the two eyes, vertical, the right hand grasping it at the small of the butt, the arm outstretched, the triggerguard resting on the first finger, the left hand at the height of the notch, the thumb lying along the barrel against the moulding. At the third stage. . . .[2]

These "body-object articulations" of the soldier and his weapon, the student and his desk effect

151

a "coercive link with the apparatus of production." We are far indeed from older forms of control that "demanded of the body only signs or products, forms of expression or the result of labour."

The body's time, in these regimes of power, is as rigidly controlled as its space: the factory whistle and the school bell mark a division of time into discrete and segmented units that regulate the various activities of the day. The following timetable, similar in spirit to the ordering of my grammar school classroom, is suggested for French "écoles mutuelles" of the early nineteenth century:

> 8:45 entrance of the monitor, 8:52 the monitor's summons, 8:56 entrance of the children and prayer, 9:00 the children go to their benches, 9:04 first slate, 9:08 end of dictation, 9:12 second slate, etc.

Control this rigid and precise cannot be maintained without a minute and relentless surveillance.

Jeremy Bentham's design for the Panopticon, a model prison, captures for Foucault the essence of the disciplinary society. At the periphery of the Panopticon, a circular structure; at the center, a tower with wide windows that opens onto the inner side of the ring. The structure on the periphery is divided into cells, each with two windows, one facing the windows of the tower, the other facing the outside, allowing an effect of backlighting to make any figure visible within the cell. "All that is needed, then, is to place a supervisor in a central tower and to shut up in each cell a madman, a patient, a condemned man, a worker or a schoolboy." Each inmate is alone, shut off from effective communication with his fellows, but constantly visible from the tower. The effect of this is "to induce in the inmate a state of conscious and permanent visibility that assures the automatic functioning of power"; each becomes to himself his own jailer. This "state of conscious and permanent visibility" is a sign that the tight, disciplinary control of the body has gotten a hold on the mind as well. In the perpetual self-surveillance of the inmate lies the genesis of the celebrated "individualism" and heightened self-consciousness that are hallmarks of modern times. For Foucault, the structure and

effects of the Panopticon resonate throughout society: Is it surprising that "prisons resemble factories, schools, barracks, hospitals, which all resemble prisons"?

Foucault's account in *Discipline and Punish* of the disciplinary practices that produce the "docile bodies" of modernity is a genuine *tour de force,* incorporating a rich theoretical account of the ways in which instrumental reason takes hold of the body with a mass of historical detail. But Foucault treats the body throughout as if it were one, as if the bodily experiences of men and women did not differ and as if men and women bore the same relationship to the characteristic institutions of modern life. Where is the account of the disciplinary practices that engender the "docile bodies" of women, bodies more docile than the bodies of men? Women, like men, are subject to many of the same disciplinary practices Foucault describes. But he is blind to those disciplines that produce a modality of embodiment that is peculiarly feminine. To overlook the forms of subjection that engender the feminine body is to perpetuate the silence and powerlessness of those upon whom these disciplines have been imposed. Hence, even though a liberatory note is sounded in Foucault's critique of power, his analysis as a whole reproduces that sexism which is endemic throughout Western political theory.

We are born male or female, but not masculine or feminine. Femininity is an artifice, an achievement, "a mode of enacting and reenacting received gender norms which surface as so many styles of the flesh." In what follows, I shall examine those disciplinary practices that produce a body which in gesture and appearance is recognizably feminine. I consider three categories of such practices: those that aim to produce a body of a certain size and general configuration; those that bring forth from this body a specific repertoire of gestures, postures, and movements; and those that are directed toward the display of this body as an ornamented surface. I shall examine the nature of these disciplines, how they are imposed and by whom. I shall probe the effects of the imposition of such discipline on female identity and subjectivity. In the final section I shall argue that these disciplinary practices must be understood in the light of the modernization of patriarchal domination, a modernization that unfolds historically according to the general pattern described by Foucault.

II

Styles of the female figure vary over time and across cultures: they reflect cultural obsessions and preoccupations in ways that are still poorly understood. Today, massiveness, power, or abundance in a woman's body is met with distaste. The current body of fashion is taut, small-breasted, narrow-hipped, and of a slimness bordering on emaciation; it is a silhouette that seems more appropriate to an adolescent boy or a newly pubescent girl than to an adult woman. Since ordinary women have normally quite different dimensions, they must of course diet.

Mass-circulation women's magazines run articles on dieting in virtually every issue. The *Ladies' Home Journal* of February 1986 carries a "Fat Burning Exercise Guide," while *Mademoiselle* offers to "Help Stamp Out Cellulite" with "Six Sleek-Down Strategies." After the diet-busting Christmas holidays and, later, before summer bikini season, the titles of these features become shriller and more arresting. The reader is now addressed in the imperative mode: Jump into shape for summer! Shed ugly winter fat with the all-new Grapefruit Diet! More women than men visit diet doctors, while women greatly outnumber men in such self-help groups as Weight Watchers and Overeaters Anonymous—in the case of the latter, by well over 90 percent.

Dieting disciplines the body's hungers: appetite must be monitored at all times and governed by an iron will. Since the innocent need of the organism for food will not be denied, the body becomes one's enemy, an alien being bent on thwarting the disciplinary project. Anorexia nervosa, which has now assumed epidemic proportions, is to women of the late twentieth century what hysteria was to women of an earlier day: the crystallization in a pathological mode of a widespread cultural obses-

sion. A survey taken recently at UCLA is astounding: of 260 students interviewed, 27.3 percent of women but only 5.8 percent of men said they were "terrified" of getting fat; 28.7 percent of women but only 7.5 percent of men said they were obsessed or "totally preoccupied" with food. The body images of women and men are strikingly different as well: 35 percent of women but only 12.5 percent of men said they felt fat though other people told them they were thin. Women in the survey wanted to weigh ten pounds less than their average weight; men felt they were within a pound of their ideal weight. A total of 5.9 percent of women and no men met the psychiatric criteria for anorexia or bulimia.

Dieting is one discipline imposed upon a body subject to the "tyranny of slenderness"; exercise is another. Since men as well as women exercise, it is not always easy in the case of women to distinguish what is done for the sake of physical fitness from what is done in obedience to the requirements of femininity. Men as well as women lift weights and do yoga, calisthenics, and aerobics, though "jazzercise" is a largely female pursuit. Men and women alike engage themselves with a variety of machines, each designed to call forth from the body a different exertion: there are Nautilus machines, rowing machines, ordinary and motorized exercycles, portable hip and leg cycles, belt massagers, trampolines, treadmills, and arm and leg pulleys. However, given the widespread female obsession with weight, one suspects that many women are working out with these apparatuses in the health club or at the gym and with an aim in mind and in a spirit quite different from men's.

But there are classes of exercises meant for women alone, these designed not to firm or to reduce the body's size overall, but to resculpture its various parts on the current model. M. J. Saffon, "international beauty expert," assures us that his twelve basic facial exercises can erase frown lines, smooth the forehead, raise hollow cheeks, banish crow's feet, and tighten the muscles under the chin. There are exercises to build the breasts and exercises to banish "cellulite," said by "figure consultants" to be a special type of female fat. There is "spot-reducing," an umbrella term that covers dozens of punishing exercises designed to reduce "problem areas" like thick ankles or "saddlebag" thighs. The very idea of "spot-reducing" is both scientifically unsound and cruel, for it raises expectations in women that can never be realized—the pattern in which fat is deposited or removed is known to be genetically determined.

It is not only her natural appetite or unreconstructed contours that pose a danger to woman: the very expressions of her face can subvert the disciplinary project of bodily perfection. An expressive face lines and creases more readily than an inexpressive one. Hence, if women are unable to suppress strong emotions, they can at least learn to inhibit the tendency of the face to register them. Sophia Loren recommends a unique solution to this problem: a piece of tape applied to the forehead or between the brows will tug at the skin when one frowns and act as a reminder to relax the face. The tape is to be worn whenever a woman is home alone.

III

There are significant gender differences in gesture, posture, movement, and general bodily comportment: women are far more restricted than men in their manner of movement and in their spatiality. In her classic paper on the subject, Iris Young observes that a space seems to surround women in imagination that they are hesitant to move beyond: this manifests itself both in a reluctance to reach, stretch, and extend the body to meet resistances of matter in motion—as in sport or in the performance of physical tasks—and in a typically constricted posture and general style of movement. Woman's space is not a field in which her bodily intentionality can be freely realized but an enclosure in which she feels herself positioned and by which she is confined. The "loose woman" violates these norms: her looseness is manifest not only in her morals, but in her manner of speech and quite literally in the free and easy way she moves.

In an extraordinary series of over two thousand photographs, many candid shots taken in the street, the German photographer

Marianne Wex has documented differences in typical masculine and feminine body posture. Women sit waiting for trains with arms close to the body, hands folded together in their laps, toes pointing straight ahead or turned inward, and legs pressed together. The women in these photographs make themselves small and narrow, harmless; they seem tense; they take up little space. Men, on the other hand, expand into the available space; they sit with legs far apart and arms flung out at some distance from the body. Most common in these sitting male figures is what Wex calls the "proffering position": the men sit with legs thrown wide apart, crotch visible, feet pointing outward, often with an arm and a casually dangling hand resting comfortably on an open, spread thigh.

In proportion to total body size, a man's stride is longer than a woman's. The man has more spring and rhythm to his step; he walks with toes pointed outward, holds his arms at a greater distance from his body and swings them farther; he tends to point the whole hand in the direction he is moving. The woman holds her arms closer to her body, palms against her sides; her walk is circumspect. If she has subjected herself to the additional constraint of high-heeled shoes, her body is thrown forward and off balance: the struggle to walk under these conditions shortens her stride still more.

But women's movement is subjected to a still finer discipline. Feminine faces, as well as bodies, are trained to the expression of deference. Under male scrutiny, women will avert their eyes or cast them downward; the female gaze is trained to abandon its claim to the sovereign status of seer. The "nice" girl learns to avoid the bold and unfettered staring of the "loose" woman who looks at whatever and whomever she pleases. Women are trained to smile more than men, too. In the economy of smiles, as elsewhere, there is evidence that women are exploited, for they give more than they receive in return; in a smile elicitation study, one researcher found that the rate of smile return by women was 93 percent, by men only 67 percent. In many typical women's jobs, graciousness, deference, and the readiness to serve are part of the work; this requires the worker to fix a smile on her face for a good part of the working day, whatever her inner state. The economy of touching is out of balance, too: men touch women more often and on more parts of the body than women touch men: female secretaries, factory workers, and waitresses report that such liberties are taken routinely with their bodies.

Feminine movement, gesture, and posture must exhibit not only constriction, but grace and a certain eroticism restrained by modesty: all three. Here is field for the operation for a whole new training: a woman must stand with stomach pulled in, shoulders thrown slightly back and chest out, this to display her bosom to maximum advantage. While she must walk in the confined fashion appropriate to women, her movements must, at the same time, be combined with a subtle but provocative hiproll. But too much display is taboo: women in short, low-cut dresses are told to avoid bending over at all, but if they must, great care must be taken to avoid an unseemly display of breast or rump. From time to time, fashion magazines offer quite precise instructions on the proper way of getting in and out of cars. These instructions combine all three imperatives of women's movement: a woman must not allow her arms and legs to flail about in all directions: she must try to manage her movements with the appearance of grace—no small accomplishment when one is climbing out of the back seat of a Fiat—and she is well-advised to use the opportunity for a certain display of leg.

All the movements we have described so far are self-movements; they arise from within the woman's own body. But in a way that normally goes unnoticed, males in couples may literally steer a woman everywhere she goes: down the street, around corners, into elevators, through doorways, into her chair at the dinner table, around the dance floor. The man's movement "is not necessarily heavy and pushy or physical in an ugly way; it is light and gentle but firm in the way of the most confident equestrians with the best trained horses."

IV

We have examined some of the disciplinary practices a woman must master in pursuit of a body of the right size and shape that also displays the proper styles of feminine motility. But woman's body is an ornamented surface too, and there is much discipline involved in this production as well. Here, especially in the application of makeup and the selection of clothes, art and discipline converge, though, as I shall argue, there is less art involved than one might suppose.

A woman's skin must be soft, supple, hairless, and smooth; ideally, it should betray no sign of wear, experience, age, or deep thought. Hair must be removed not only from the face but from large surfaces of the body as well, from legs and thighs, an operation accomplished by shaving, buffing with fine sandpaper, or applying foul-smelling depilatories. With the new high-leg bathing suits and leotards, a substantial amount of pubic hair must be removed too. The removal of facial hair can be more specialized. Eyebrows are plucked out by the roots with a tweezer. Hot wax is sometimes poured onto the mustache and cheeks and then ripped away when it cools. The woman who wants a more permanent result may try electrolysis: this involves the killing of a hair root by the passage of an electric current down a needle that has been inserted into its base. The procedure is painful and expensive.

The development of what one "beauty expert" calls "good skincare habits" requires not only attention to health, the avoidance of strong facial expressions, and the performance of facial exercises, but the regular use of skincare preparations, many to be applied more often than once a day; cleansing lotions (ordinary soap and water "upsets the skin's acid and alkaline balance"), wash-off cleansers (milder than cleansing lotions), astringents, toners, makeup removers, night creams, nourishing creams, eye creams, moisturizers, skin balancers, body lotions, hand creams, lip pomades, suntan lotions, sunscreens, and facial masks. Provision of the proper facial mask is complex: there are sulfur masks for pimples; oil or hot masks for dry areas; if these fail, then tightening masks; conditioning masks; peeling masks; cleansing masks made of herbs, cornmeal, or almonds; and mudpacks. Black women may wish to use "fade creams" to "even skin tone." Skincare preparations are never just sloshed onto the skin, but applied according to precise rules; eye cream is dabbed on gently in movements toward, never away from, the nose; cleansing cream is applied in outward directions only, straight across the forehead, the upper lip, and the chin, never up but straight down the nose and up and out on the cheeks.

The normalizing discourse of modern medicine is enlisted by the cosmetics industry to gain credibility for its claims. Dr. Christiaan Barnard lends his enormous prestige to the Glycel line of "cellular treatment activators"; these contain "glycosphingolipids" that can "make older skin behave and look like younger skin." The Clinque computer at any Clinique counter will select a combination of preparations just right for you. Ultima II contains "procollagen" in its anti-aging eye cream that "provides hydration" to "demoralizing lines." "Biotherm" eye cream dramatically improves the "biomechanical properties of the skin." The Park Avenue clinic of Dr. Zizmor, "chief of dermatology at one of New York's leading hospitals," offers not only such medical treatment as derma-brasion and chemical peeling, but "total deep skin cleansing" as well.

Really good skincare habits require the use of a variety of aids and devices: facial steamers, faucet filters to collect impurities in the water, borax to soften it, a humidifier for the bedroom, electric massagers, backbrushes, complexion brushes, loofahs, pumice stones, and blackhead removers. I will not detail the implements or techniques involved in the manicure or pedicure.

The ordinary circumstances of life as well as a wide variety of activities cause a crisis in skincare and require a stepping-up of the regimen as well as an additional laying-on of preparations. Skincare discipline requires a specialized knowledge: a woman must know what to do if she has been skiing, taking medication, doing vigorous exercise, boating, or swimming in chlorinated pools; or if she has been exposed to pollution, heated rooms, cold, sun, harsh weather, the pressurized cabins on airplanes, saunas or steam rooms, fatigue, or stress. Like the schoolchild or prisoner, the woman mastering good skincare habits is put on a timetable: Georgette Klinger requires that a shorter or longer period of attention be paid to the complexion at least four times a day. Haircare, like skincare, requires a similar investment of time,

the use of a wide variety of preparations, the mastery of a set of techniques, and, again, the acquisition of a specialized knowledge.

The crown and pinnacle of good haircare and skincare is, of course, the arrangement of the hair and the application of cosmetics. Here the regimen of haircare, skincare, manicure, and pedicure is recapitulated in another mode. A woman must learn the proper manipulation of a large number of devices—the blow dryer, styling brush, curling iron, hot curlers, wire curlers, eye-liner, lipliner, lipstick brush, eyelash curler, and mascara brush. And she must learn to apply a wide variety of products— foundation, toner, covering stick, mascara, eyeshadow, eyegloss, blusher, lipstick, rouge, lip gloss, hair dye, hair rinse, hair lightener, hair "relaxer," and so on.

In the language of fashion magazines and cosmetic ads, making-up is typically portrayed as an aesthetic activity in which a woman can express her individuality. In reality, while cosmetic styles change every decade or so, and while some variation in makeup is permitted depending on the occasion, making-up the face is, in fact, a highly stylized activity that gives little rein to self-expression. Painting the face is not like painting a picture; at best, it might be described as painting the same picture over and over again with minor variations. Little latitude is permitted in what is considered appropriate makeup for the office and for most social occasions; indeed, the woman who uses cosmetics in a genuinely novel and imaginative way is liable to be seen not as an artist but as an eccentric. Furthermore, since a properly made-up face is, if not a card of entree, at least a badge of acceptability in most social and professional contexts, the woman who chooses not to wear cosmetics at all faces sanctions of a sort that will never be applied to someone who chooses not to paint a watercolor.

V

Are we dealing in all this merely with sexual *difference?* Scarcely, The disciplinary practices I have described are part of the process by which the ideal body of femininity—and hence the feminine body-subject—is constructed; in doing this, they produce a "practiced and subjected" body, that is, a body on which an inferior status has been inscribed. A woman's face must be made-up, that is to say, made-over, and so must her body: she is ten pounds overweight; her lips must be made more kissable, her complexion dewier, her eyes more mysterious. The "art" of makeup is the art of disguise, but this presupposes that a woman's face, unpainted, is defective. Soap and water, a shave, and routine attention to hygiene may be enough for *him;* for *her* they are not. The strategy of much beauty-related advertising is to suggest to women that their bodies are deficient; but even without such more or less explicit teaching, the media images of perfect female beauty that bombard us daily leave no doubt in the minds of most women that they fail to measure up. The technologies of femininity are taken up and practiced by women against the background of a pervasive sense of bodily deficiency: this accounts for what is often their compulsive or even ritualistic character.

The disciplinary project of femininity is a "setup": it requires such radical and extensive measures of bodily transformation that virtually every woman who gives herself to it is destined in some degree to fail. Thus, a measure of shame is added to a woman's sense that the body she inhabits is deficient: she ought to take better care of herself; she might after all have jogged that last mile. Many women are without the time or resources to provide themselves with even the minimum of what such a regimen requires, for example, a decent diet. Here is an additional source of shame for poor women, who must bear what our society regards as the more general shame of poverty. The burdens poor women bear in this regard are not merely psychological, since conformity to the prevailing standards of bodily acceptability is a known factor in economic mobility.

The larger disciplines that construct a "feminine" body out of a female one are by no means race- or class-specific. There is little evidence that women of color or working-class women are in general less committed to the incarnation of an ideal femininity than their more privileged sisters: this is not to deny the many ways

in which factors of race, class, locality, ethnicity, or personal taste can be expressed within the kinds of practices I have described. The rising young corporate executive may buy her cosmetics at Bergdorf-Goodman, while the counter-server at McDonald's gets hers at the K-Mart; the one may join an expensive "upscale" health club, while the other may have to make do with the $9.49 GFX Body-Flex II Home-Gym advertised in the *National Enquirer:* both are aiming at the same general result.

In the regime of institutionalized heterosexuality, woman must make herself "object and prey" for the man: it is for him that these eyes are limpid pools, this cheek baby-smooth. In contemporary patriarchal culture, a panoptical male connoisseur resides within the consciousness of most women: they stand perpetually before his gaze and under his judgment. Woman lives her body as seen by another, by an anonymous patriarchal Other. We are often told that "women dress for other women." There is some truth in this: who but someone engaged in a project similar to my own can appreciate the panache with which I bring it off? But women know for whom this game is played: they know that a pretty young woman is likelier to become a flight attendant than a plain one, and that a well-preserved older woman has a better chance of holding onto her husband than one who has "let herself go."

Here it might be objected that performance for another in no way signals the inferiority of the performer to the one for whom the performance is intended: the actor, for example, depends on his audience but is in no way inferior to it; he is not demeaned by his dependency. While femininity is surely something enacted, the analogy to theater breaks down in a number of ways. First, as I argued earlier, the self-determination we think of as requisite to an artistic career is lacking here: femininity as spectacle is something in which virtually every woman is required to participate. Second, the precise nature of the criteria by which women are judged, not only the inescapability of judgment itself, reflects gross imbalances in the social power of the sexes that do not mark the relationship of artists and their audiences. An aesthetic of femininity, for example, that mandates fragility and a lack of muscular strength produces female bodies that can offer little resistance to physical abuse, and the physical abuse of women by men, as we know, is widespread. It is true that the current fitness movement has permitted women to develop more muscular strength and endurance than was heretofore allowed; indeed, images of women have begun to appear in the mass media that seem to eroticize this new muscularity. But a woman may by no means develop more muscular strength than her partner; the bride who would tenderly carry her groom across the threshold is a figure of comedy, not romance.

Under the current "tyranny of slenderness" women are forbidden to become large or massive; they must take up as little space as possible. The very contours a woman's body takes on as she matures—the fuller breasts and rounded hips—have become distasteful. The body by which a woman feels herself judged and which by rigorous discipline she must try to assume is the body of early adolescence, slight and unformed, a body lacking flesh or substance, a body in whose very contours the image of immaturity has been inscribed. The requirement that a woman maintain a smooth and hairless skin carries further the theme of inexperience, for an infantilized face must accompany her infantilized body, a face that never ages or furrows its brow in thought. The face of the ideally feminine woman must never display the marks of character, wisdom, and experience that we so admire in men.

To succeed in the provision of a beautiful or sexy body gains a woman attention and some admiration but little real respect and rarely any social power. A woman's effort to master feminine body discipline will lack importance just because she does it: her activity partakes of the general depreciation of everything female. In spite of unrelenting pressure to "make the most of what she has," women are ridiculed and dismissed for their interest in such "trivial" things as clothes and makeup. Further, the narrow identification of woman with sexuality and the body in a society that has for centuries displayed profound suspicion toward both does little to raise her status. Even the most adored female bodies complain routinely of their situation in ways that reveal an implicit understand-

ing that there is something demeaning in the kind of attention they receive. Marilyn Monroe, Elizabeth Taylor, and Farrah Fawcett have all wanted passionately to become actresses-artists—and not just "sex objects."

But it is perhaps in their more restricted motility and comportment that the inferiorization of women's bodies is most evident: women's typical body-language, a language of relative tension and constriction, is understood to be a language of subordination when it is enacted by men in male status hierarchies. In groups of men, those with higher status typically assume looser and more relaxed postures: the boss lounges comfortably behind the desk, while the applicant sits tense and rigid on the edge of his seat. Higher-status individuals may touch their subordinates more than they themselves get touched; they initiate more eye contact and are smiled at by their inferiors more than they are observed to smile in return. What is announced in the comportment of superiors is confidence and ease, especially ease of access to the Other. Female constraint in posture and movement is no doubt overdetermined: the fact that women tend to sit and stand with legs, feet, and knees close or touching may well be a coded declaration of sexual circumspection in a society that still maintains a double standard, or an effort, albeit unconscious, to guard the genital area. In the latter case, a woman's tight and constricted posture must be seen as the expression of her need to ward off real or symbolic sexual attack. Whatever proportions must be assigned in the final display to fear or deference, one thing is clear: woman's body language speaks eloquently, though silently, of her subordinate status in a hierarchy of gender.

VI

If what we have described is a genuine discipline—a system of "micropower" that is "essentially non-egalitarian and asymmetrical"—who then are the disciplinarians? Who is the top sergeant in the disciplinary regime of femininity? Historically, the law has had some responsibility for enforcement: in times gone by, for example, individuals who appeared in public in the clothes of the other sex could be arrested. While cross-dressers are still liable to some harassment, the kind of discipline we are considering is not the business of the police or the courts. Parents and teachers, of course, have extensive influence, admonishing girls to be demure and ladylike, to "smile pretty," to sit with their legs together. The influence of the media is pervasive, too, constructing as it does an image of the female body as spectacle, nor can we ignore the role played by "beauty experts" or by emblematic public personages such as Jane Fonda and Lynn Redgrave.

But none of these individuals—the skincare consultant, the parent, the policeman—does in fact wield the kind of authority that is typically invested in those who manage more straightforward disciplinary institutions. The disciplinary power that inscribes femininity in the female body is everywhere and it is nowhere; the disciplinarian is everyone and yet no one in particular. Women regarded as overweight, for example, report that they are regularly admonished to diet, sometimes by people they scarcely know. These intrusions are often softened by reference to the natural prettiness just waiting to emerge: "People have always said that I had a beautiful face and 'if you'd only lose weight you'd be really beautiful.'" Here, "people"—friends and casual acquaintances alike—act to enforce prevailing standards of body size.

Foucault tends to identify the imposition of discipline upon the body with the operation of specific institutions, for example, the school, the factory, the prison. To do this, however, is to overlook the extent to which discipline can be institutionally *unbound* as well as institutionally bound. The anonymity of disciplinary power and its wide dispersion have consequences that are crucial to a proper understanding of the subordination of women. The absence of a formal institutional structure and of authorities invested with the power to carry out institutional directives creates the impression that the production of femininity is either entirely voluntary or natural. The several senses of "discipline" are instructive here. On the one hand, discipline is something imposed on subjects of an "essentially non-egalitarian

and asymmetrical" system of authority. Schoolchildren, convicts, and draftees are subject to discipline in this sense. But discipline can be sought voluntarily as well—for example, when an individual seeks initiation into the spiritual discipline of Zen Buddhism. Discipline can, of course, be both at once: the volunteer may seek the physical and occupational training offered by the army without the army's ceasing in any way to be the instrument by which he and other members of his class are kept in disciplined subjection. Feminine bodily discipline has this dual character: on the one hand, no one is marched off for electrolysis at gunpoint, nor can we fail to appreciate the initiative and ingenuity displayed by countless women in an attempt to master the rituals of beauty. Nevertheless, insofar as the disciplinary practices of femininity produce a "subjected and practiced," an inferiorized, body, they must be understood as aspects of a far larger discipline, an oppressive and inegalitarian system of sexual subordination. This system aims at turning women into the docile and compliant companions of men just as surely as the army aims to turn its raw recruits into soldiers.

Now the transformation of oneself into a properly feminine body may be any or all of the following: a rite of passage into adulthood, the adoption and celebration of a particular aesthetic, a way of announcing one's economic level and social status, a way to triumph over other women in the competition for men or jobs, or an opportunity for massive narcissistic indulgence. The social construction of the feminine body is all these things, but at its base it is discipline, too, and discipline of the inegalitarian sort. The absence of formally identifiable disciplinarians and of a public schedule of sanctions only disguises the extent to which the imperative to be "feminine" serves the interest of domination. This is a lie in which all concur: making-up is merely artful play; one's first pair of high-heeled shoes is an innocent part of growing up, not the modern equivalent of foot-binding.

Why aren't all women feminists? In modern industrial societies, women are not kept in line by fear of retaliatory male violence; their victimization is not that of the South African black. Nor will it suffice to say that a false consciousness engendered in women by patriarchal ideology is at the basis of female subordination. This is not to deny that women are often subject to gross male violence or that women and men alike are ideologically mystified by the dominant gender arrangements. What I wish to suggest instead is that an adequate understanding of women's oppression will require an appreciation of the extent to which not only women's lives but their very subjectivities are structured within an ensemble of systematically duplicitous practices. The feminine discipline of the body is a case in point: the practices that construct this body have an overt aim and character far removed, indeed, radically distinct, from their covert function. In this regard, the system of gender subordination, like the wage-bargain under capitalism, illustrates in its own way the ancient tension between what-is and what-appears: the phenomenal forms in which it is manifested are often quite different from the real relations that form its deeper structure.

VII

The lack of formal public sanctions does not mean that a woman who is unable or unwilling to submit herself to the appropriate body discipline will face no sanctions at all. On the contrary, she faces a very severe sanction indeed in a world dominated by men; the refusal of male patronage. For the heterosexual woman, this may mean the loss of a badly needed intimacy; for both heterosexual women and lesbians, it may well mean the refusal of a decent livelihood.

As noted earlier, women punish themselves too for the failure to conform. The growing literature on women's body size is filled with wrenching confessions of shame from the overweight:

I felt clumsy and huge. I felt that I would knock over furniture, bump into things, tip over chairs, not fit into VW's, especially when people were trying to crowd into the back seat.

I felt like I was taking over the whole room. . . . I felt disgusting and like a slob. In the summer I felt hot and sweaty and I knew people saw my sweat as evidence that I was too fat.

I feel so terrible about the way I look that I cut off connection with my body. I operate from the neck up. I do not look in mirrors. I do not want to spend time buying clothes. I do not want to spend time with make-up because it's painful for me to look at myself.[3]

I can no longer bear to look at myself. . . . Whenever I have to stand in front of a mirror to comb my hair I tie a large towel around my neck. Even at night I slip my nightgown on before I take off my blouse and pants. But all this has only made it worse and worse. It's been so long since I've really looked at my body.[4]

The depth of these women's shame is a measure of the extent to which all women have internalized patriarchal standards of bodily acceptability. A fuller examination of what is meant here by "internalization" may shed light on a question posed earlier: Why isn't every woman a feminist?

Something is "internalized" when it gets incorporated into the structure of the self. By "structure of the self" I refer to those modes of perception and of self-perception that allow a self to distinguish itself both from other selves and from things that are not selves. I have described elsewhere how a generalized male witness comes to structure woman's consciousness of herself as a bodily being. This, then, is one meaning of "internalization." The sense of oneself as a distinct and valuable individual is tied not only to the sense of how one is perceived, but also to what one knows, especially to what one knows how to do; this is a second sense of "internalization." Whatever its ultimate effect, discipline can provide the individual upon whom it is imposed with a sense of mastery as well as a secure sense of identity. There is a certain contradiction here: while its imposition may promote a larger disempowerment, discipline may bring with it a certain development of a person's powers. Women, then, like other skilled individuals, have a stake in the perpetuation of their skills, whatever it may have cost to acquire them and quite apart from the question whether, as a gender, they would have been better off had they never had to acquire them in the first place. Hence, feminism, especially a genuinely radical feminism that questions the patriarchal construction of the female body, threatens women with a certain de-skilling, something people normally resist: beyond this, it calls into question that aspect of personal identity that is tied to the development of a sense of competence.

Resistance from this source may be joined by a reluctance to part with the rewards of compliance; further, many women will resist the abandonment of an aesthetic that defines what they take to be beautiful. But there is still another source of resistance, one more subtle, perhaps, but tied once again to questions of identity and internalization. To have a body felt to be "feminine"—a body socially constructed through the appropriate practices—is in most cases crucial to a woman's sense of herself as female and, since persons currently can *be* only as male or female, to her sense of herself as an existing individual. To possess such a body may also be essential to her sense of herself as a sexually desiring and desirable subject. Hence, any political project that aims to dismantle the machinery that turns a female body into a feminine one may well be apprehended by a woman as something that threatens her with de-sexualization, if not outright annihilation.

The categories of masculinity and femininity do more than assist in the construction of personal identities; they are critical elements in our informal social ontology. This may account to some degree for the otherwise puzzling phenomenon of homophobia and for the revulsion felt by many at the sight of female body-builders; neither the homosexual nor the muscular woman can be assimilated easily into the categories that structure everyday life. The radical feminist critique of femininity, then, may pose a threat not only to a woman's sense of her own identity and desirability but to the very structure of her social universe.

Of course, many women *are* feminists, favoring a program of political and economic reform in the struggle to gain equality with men. But many "reform," or liberal, feminists (indeed, many orthodox Marxists) are committed to the idea that the preservation of a woman's femininity is quite compatible with her struggle for liberation. These thinkers have rejected a normative femininity based upon the notion of "separate spheres" and the traditional sexual division of labor, while accepting at the same time conventional standards of feminine body display. If my analysis is correct, such a feminism is incoherent. Foucault has argued that modern bourgeois democracy is deeply flawed in that it seeks political rights for individuals constituted as unfree by a variety of disciplinary micropowers that lie beyond the realm of what is ordinarily defined as the "political." "The man described for us whom we are invited to free," he says, "is already in himself the effect of a subjection much more profound than himself." If, as I have argued, female subjectivity is constituted in any significant measure in and through the disciplinary practices that construct the feminine body, what Foucault says here of "man" is perhaps even truer of "woman." Marxists have maintained from the first the inadequacy of a purely liberal feminism: we have reached the same conclusion through a different route, casting doubt at the same time on the adequacy of traditional Marxist prescriptions for women's liberation as well. Liberals call for equal rights for women, traditional Marxists for the entry of women into production on an equal footing with men, the socialization of housework, and proletarian revolution; neither calls for the deconstruction of the categories of masculinity and femininity. Femininity as a certain "style of the flesh" will have to be surpassed in the direction of something quite different—not masculinity, which is in many ways only its mirror opposite, but a radical and as yet unimagined transformation of the female body.

VIII

Foucault has argued that the transition from traditional to modern societies has been characterized by a profound transformation in the exercise of power, by what he calls "a reversal of the political axis of individualization." In older authoritarian systems, power was embodied in the person of the monarch and exercised upon a largely anonymous body of subjects; violation of the law was seen as an insult to the royal individual. While the methods employed to enforce compliance in the past were often quite brutal, involving gross assaults against the body, power in such a system operated in a haphazard and discontinuous fashion; much in the social totality lay beyond its reach.

By contrast, modern society has seen the emergence of increasingly invasive apparatuses of power: these exercise a far more restrictive social and psychological control than was heretofore possible. In modern societies, effects of power "circulate through progressively finer channels, gaining access to individuals themselves, to their bodies, their gestures and all their daily actions." Power now seeks to transform the minds of those individuals who might be tempted to resist it, not merely to punish or imprison their bodies. This requires two things: a finer control of the body's time and of its movements—a control that cannot be achieved without ceaseless surveillance and a better understanding of the specific person, of the genesis and nature of his "case." The power these new apparatuses seek to exercise requires a new knowledge of the individual: modern psychology and sociology are born. Whether the new modes of control have charge of correction, production, education, or the provision of welfare, they resemble one another; they exercise power in a bureaucratic mode—faceless, centralized, and pervasive. A reversal has occurred: power has now become anonymous, while the project of control has brought into being a new individuality. In fact, Foucault believes that the operation of power constitutes the very subjectivity of the subject. Here, the image of the Panopticon returns: knowing that he may be observed from the tower at any time, the inmate takes over the job of policing himself. The gaze that is inscribed in the very structure of the disciplinary institution is internalized by the inmate: modern technologies of behavior are thus oriented toward the production of isolated and self-policing subjects.

Women have their own experience of the modernization of power, one that begins later but follows in many respects the course outlined by Foucault. In important ways, a woman's behavior is less regulated now than it was in the past. She has more mobility and is less confined to domestic space. She enjoys what to previous generations would have been an unimaginable sexual liberty. Divorce, access to paid work outside the home, and the increasing secularization of modern life have loosened the hold over her of the traditional family and, in spite of the current fundamentalist revival, of the church. Power in these institutions was wielded by individuals known to her. Husbands and fathers enforced patriarchal authority in the family. As in the ancien régime, a woman's body was subject to sanctions if she disobeyed. Not Foucault's royal individual but the Divine Individual decreed that her desire be always "unto her husband," while the person of the priest made known to her God's more specific intentions concerning her place and duties. In the days when civil and ecclesiastical authority were still conjoined, individuals formally invested with power were charged with the correction of recalcitrant women whom the family had somehow failed to constrain.

By contrast, the disciplinary power that is increasingly charged with the production of a properly embodied femininity is dispersed and anonymous; there are no individuals formally empowered to wield it; it is, as we have seen, invested in everyone and in no one in particular. This disciplinary power is peculiarly modern: it does not rely upon violent or public sanctions, nor does it seek to restrain the freedom of the female body to move from place to place. For all that, its invasion of the body is well-nigh total: the female body enters "a machinery of power that explores it, breaks it down and rearranges it." The disciplinary techniques through which the "docile bodies" of women are constructed aim at a regulation that is perpetual and exhaustive—a regulation of the body's size and contours, its appetite, posture, gestures and general comportment in space, and the appearance of each of its visible parts.

As modern industrial societies change and as women themselves offer resistance to patriarchy, older forms of domination are eroded. But new forms arise, spread, and become consolidated. Women are no longer required to be chaste or modest, to restrict their sphere of activity to the home, or even to realize their properly feminine destiny in maternity: normative femininity is coming more and more to be centered on woman's body—not its duties and obligations or even its capacity to bear children, but its sexuality, more precisely, its presumed heterosexuality and its appearance. There is, of course, nothing new in women's preoccupation with youth and beauty. What is new is the growing power of the image in a society increasingly oriented toward the visual media. Images of normative femininity, it might be ventured, have replaced the religiously oriented tracts of the past. New too is the spread of this discipline to all classes of women and its deployment throughout the life cycle. What was formerly the speciality of the aristocrat or courtesan is now the routine obligation of every woman, be she a grandmother or a barely pubescent girl.

To subject oneself to the new disciplinary power is to be up-to-date, to be "with-it"; as I have argued, it is presented to us in ways that are regularly disguised. It is fully compatible with the current need for women's wage labor, the cult of youth and fitness, and the need of advanced capitalism to maintain high levels of consumption. Further, it represents a saving in the economy of enforcement: since it is women themselves who practice this discipline on and against their own bodies, men get off scot-free.

The woman who checks her makeup half a dozen times a day to see if her foundation has caked or her mascara has run, who worries that the wind or the rain may spoil her hairdo, who looks frequently to see if her stockings have bagged at the ankle or who, feeling fat, monitors everything she eats, has become, just as surely as the inmate of the Panopticon, a self-policing subject, a self committed to a relentless self-surveillance. This self-surveillance is a form of obedience to patriarchy. It is also the reflection in woman's consciousness of the fact that *she* is under surveillance in ways that *he* is

not, that whatever else she may become, she is importantly a body designed to please or to excite. There has been induced in many women, then, in Foucault's words, "a state of conscious and permanent visibility that assures the automatic functioning of power." Since the standards of female bodily acceptability are impossible fully to realize, requiring as they do a virtual transcendence of nature, a woman may live much of her life with a pervasive feeling of bodily deficiency. Hence a tighter control of the body has gained a new kind of hold over the mind.

Foucault often writes as if power constitutes the very individuals upon whom it operates:

> The individual is not to be conceived as a sort of elementary nucleus, a primitive atom, a multiple and inert material on which power comes to fasten or against which it happens to strike. . . . In fact, it is already one of the prime effects of power that certain bodies, certain gestures, certain discourses, certain desires, come to be identified and constituted as individuals.[5]

Nevertheless, if individuals were wholly constituted by the power-knowledge regime Foucault describes, it would make no sense to speak of resistance to discipline at all. Foucault seems sometimes on the verge of depriving us of a vocabulary in which to conceptualize the nature and meaning of those periodic refusals of control that, just as much as the imposition of control, mark the course of human history.

Peter Dews accuses Foucault of lacking a theory of the "libidinal body," that is, the body upon which discipline is imposed and whose bedrock impulse toward spontaneity and pleasure might perhaps become the locus of resistance. Do women's "libidinal" bodies, then, not rebel against the pain, constriction, tedium, semistarvation, and constant self-surveillance to which they are currently condemned? Certainly they do, but the rebellion is put down every time a woman picks up her eyebrow tweezers or embarks upon a new diet. The harshness of a regimen alone does not guarantee its rejection, for hardships can be endured if they are thought to be necessary or inevitable.

While "nature," in the form of a "libidinal" body, may not be the origin of a revolt against "culture," domination (and the discipline it requires) are never imposed without some cost. Historically, the forms and occasions of resistance are manifold. Sometimes, instances of resistance appear to spring from the introduction of new and conflicting factors into the lives of the dominated: the juxtaposition of old and new and the resulting incoherence or "contradiction" may make submission to the old ways seem increasingly unnecessary. In the present instance, what may be a major factor in the relentless and escalating objectification of women's bodies—namely, women's growing independence—produces in many women a sense of incoherence that calls into question the meaning and necessity of the current discipline. As women (albeit a small minority of women) begin to realize an unprecedented political, economic, and sexual self-determination, they fall ever more completely under the dominating gaze of patriarchy. It is this paradox, not the "libidinal body," that produces, here and there, pockets of resistance.

In the current political climate, there is no reason to anticipate either widespread resistance to currently fashionable modes of feminine embodiment or joyous experimentation with new "styles of the flesh"; moreover, such novelties would face profound opposition from material and psychological sources identified earlier in this essay (see section VII). In spite of this, a number of oppositional discourses and practices have appeared in recent years. An increasing number of women are "pumping iron," a few with little concern for the limits of body development imposed by current canons of femininity. Women in radical lesbian communities have also rejected hegemonic images of femininity and are struggling to develop a new female aesthetic. A striking feature of such communities is the extent to which they have overcome the oppressive identification of female beauty and desirability with youth: here, the physical features of aging— "character" lines and graying hair—not only do not diminish a woman's attractiveness, they may even enhance it. A popular literature of resistance is growing, some of it analytical and reflective, like Kim Chernin's *The Obsession,* some oriented toward practical self-help, like

Marcia Hutchinson's recent *Transforming Body Image, Learning to Love the Body You Have.* This literature reflects a mood akin in some ways to that other and earlier mood of quiet desperation to which Betty Friedan gave voice in *The Feminine Mystique.* Nor should we forget that a mass-based women's movement is in place in this country that has begun a critical questioning of the meaning of femininity, if not yet in the corporeal presentation of self, then in other domains of life. We women cannot begin the re-vision of our own bodies until we learn to read the cultural messages we inscribe upon them daily and until we come to see that even when the mastery of the disciplines of femininity produces a triumphant result, we are still only women.

Notes

1. Michel Foucault, *Discipline and Punish: The Birth of the Prison,* trans. Alan Sheridan (New York: Vintage Books, 1979), p. 138.

2. Ibid., p. 28.

3. Millman, *Such a Pretty Face,* pp. 80, 195.

4. Chernin, *The Obsession,* p. 53.

5. Foucault, *Power/Knowledge,* p. 98. In fact, Foucault is not entirely consistent on this point. For an excellent discussion of contending Foucault interpretations and for the difficulty of deriving a consistent set of claims from Foucault's work generally, see Nancy Fraser, "Michel Foucault: A 'Young Conservative'?" *Ethics* 96 (October 1985): 165–84.

Study Questions

1. According to Bartky, what is the strength of the account of disciplinary practices? What does she see as the "blind spot" in the account?

2. What three categories does Bartky examine, and how does she relate them to the production of "docile bodies"?

3. Put in a single sentence the meaning of "the tyranny of slenderness." Give some examples.

4. Why does Bartky say that women's body language is a language of subordination?

5. Why does she say that the disciplinary proj-ect of femininity is a "set up"? Discuss with examples.

6. How is the project of femininity related to sexual subordination? What does Bartky mean by institutionally "unbound" as well as bound?

7. According to Bartky, in what sense is women's resistance to the regime of power possible?

Black Women: Shaping Feminist Theory

Bell Hooks

Feminism in the United States has never emerged from the women who are most victim-ized by sexist oppression; women who are daily beaten down, mentally, physically, and spirit-ually—women who are powerless to change their condition in life. They are a silent major-ity. A mark of their victimization is that they accept their lot in life without visible question, without organized protest, without collective anger or rage. Betty Friedan's *The Feminine Mystique* is still heralded as having paved the way for contemporary feminist movement—it was written as if these women did not exist. Friedan's famous phrase, "the problem that has no name," often quoted to describe the condi-tion of women in this society, actually referred to the plight of a select group of college-educated, middle and upper class, married white women—housewives bored with leisure,

with the home, with children, with buying products, who wanted more out of life. Friedan concludes her first chapter by stating: "We can no longer ignore that voice within women that says: 'I want something more than my husband and my children and my house.'" That "more" she defined as careers. She did not discuss who would be called in to take care of the children and maintain the home if more women like herself were freed from their house labor and given equal access with white men to the pro-fessions. She did not speak of the needs of women without men, without children, without homes. She ignored the existence of all non-white women and poor white women. She did not tell readers whether it was more fulfilling to be a maid, a babysitter, a factory worker, a clerk, or a prostitute, than to be a leisure class housewife.[1]

She made her plight and the plight of white women like herself synonymous with a condi-tion affecting all American women. In so do-ing, she deflected attention away from her classism, her racism, her sexist attitudes

From Bell Hooks, *Feminist Theory: From Margin to Center,* (South End Press, 1984). © Bell Hooks. Reprinted by permission of the publisher.

towards the masses of American women. In the context of her book, Friedan makes clear that the women she saw as victimized by sexism were college-educated, white women who were compelled by sexist conditioning to remain in the home. She contends:

> It is urgent to understand how the very condition of being a housewife can create a sense of emptiness, non-existence, nothingness in women. There are aspects of the housewife role that make it almost impossible for a woman of adult intelligence to retain a sense of human identity, the firm core of self or "I" without which a human being, a man or woman, is not truly alive. For women of ability, in America today, I am convinced that there is something about the housewife state itself that is dangerous.[2]

Specific problems and dilemmas of leisure class white housewives were real concerns that merited consideration and change but they were not the pressing political concerns of masses of women. Masses of women were concerned about economic survival, ethnic and racial discrimination, etc. When Friedan wrote *The Feminine Mystique,* more than one third of all women were in the work force. Although many women longed to be housewives, only women with leisure time and money could actually shape their identities on the model of the feminine mystique. They were women who, in Friedan's words, were "told by the most advanced thinkers of our time to go back and live their lives as if they were Noras, restricted to the doll's house by Victorian prejudices."[3]

From her early writing, it appears that Friedan never wondered whether or not the plight of college-educated, white housewives was an adequate reference point by which to gauge the impact of sexism or sexist oppression on the lives of women in American society. Nor did she move beyond her own life experience to acquire an expanded perspective on the lives of women in the United States. I say this not to discredit her work. It remains a useful discussion of the impact of sexist discrimination on a select group of women. Examined from a different perspective, it can also be seen as a case study of narcissism, insensitivity, sentimentality, and self-indulgence which reaches its peak when Friedan, in a chapter titled "Progressive Dehumanization," makes a comparison between the psychological effects of isolation on white housewives and the impact of confinement on the self-concept of prisoners in Nazi concentration camps.[4]

Friedan was a principal shaper of contemporary feminist thought. Significantly, the one-dimensional perspective on women's reality presented in her book became a marked feature of the contemporary feminist movement. Like Friedan before them, white women who dominate feminist discourse today rarely question whether or not their perspective on women's reality is true to the lived experiences of women as a collective group. Nor are they aware of the extent to which their perspectives reflect race and class biases, although there has been a greater awareness of biases in recent years. Racism abounds in the writings of white feminists, reinforcing white supremacy and negating the possibility that women will bond politically across ethnic and racial boundaries. Past feminist refusal to draw attention to and attack racial hierarchies suppressed the link between race and class. Yet class structure in American society has been shaped by the racial politic of white supremacy; it is only by analyzing racism and its function in capitalist society that a thorough understanding of class relationships can emerge. Class struggle is inextricably bound to the struggle to end racism. Urging women to explore the full implication of class in an early essay, "The Last Straw," Rita Mae Brown explained:

> Class is much more than Marx's definition of relationship to the means of production. Class involves your behavior, your basic assumptions about life. Your experience (determined by your class) validates those assumptions, how you are taught to behave, what you expect from yourself and from others, your concept of a future, how you understand problems and solve them, how you think, feel, act. It is these behavioral patterns that middle class women resist recognizing although they may be perfectly willing to accept class in Marxist terms, a neat trick that helps them avoid really dealing with class behavior and changing that behavior in themselves. It is these behavioral patterns which must be recognized, understood, and changed.[5]

White women who dominate feminist discourse, who for the most part make and articulate feminist theory, have little or no understanding of white supremacy as a racial politic, of the psychological impact of class, of their political status within a racist, sexist, capitalist state.

It is this lack of awareness that, for example, leads Leah Fritz to write in *Dreamers and Dealers*, a discussion of the current women's movement published in 1979:

> Women's suffering under sexist tyranny is a common bond among all women, transcending the particulars of the different forms that tyranny takes. *Suffering cannot be measured and compared quantitatively.* Is the enforced idleness and vacuity of a "rich" woman, which leads her to madness and/or suicide, greater or less than the suffering of a poor woman who barely survives on welfare but retains somehow her spirit? There is no way to measure such difference, but should these two women survey each other without the screen of patriarchal class, they may find a commonality in the fact that they are both oppressed, both miserable.[6]

Fritz's statement is another example of wishful thinking, as well as the conscious mystification of social divisions between women, that has characterized much feminist expression. While it is evident that many women suffer from sexist tyranny, there is little indication that this forges "a common bond among all women." There is much evidence substantiating the reality that race and class identity creates differences in quality of life, social status, and lifestyle that take precedence over the common experience women share—differences which are rarely transcended. The motives of materially privileged, educated, white women with a variety of career and lifestyle options available to them must be questioned when they insist that "suffering cannot be measured." Fritz is by no means the first white feminist to make this statement. It is a statement that I have never heard a poor woman of any race make. Although there is much I would take issue with in Benjamin Barber's critique of the women's movement, *Liberating Feminism*, I agree with his assertion:

Suffering is not necessarily a fixed and universal experience that can be measured by a single rod: it is related to situations, needs, and aspirations. But there must be some historical and political parameters for the use of the term so that political priorities can be established and different forms and degrees of suffering can be given the most attention.[7]

A central tenet of modern feminist thought has been the assertion that "all women are oppressed." This assertion implies that women share a common lot, that factors like class, race, religion, sexual preference, etc. do not create a diversity of experience that determines the extent to which sexism will be an oppressive force in the lives of individual women. Sexism as a system of domination is institutionalized but it has never determined in an absolute way the fate of all women in this society. Being oppressed means the *absence of choices*. It is the primary point of contact between the oppressed and the oppressor. Many women in this society do have choices, (as inadequate as they are) therefore exploitation and discrimination are words that more accurately describe the lot of women collectively in the United States. Many women do not join organized resistance against sexism precisely because sexism has not meant an absolute lack of choices. They may know they are discriminated against on the basis of sex, but they do not equate this with oppression. Under capitalism, patriarchy is structured so that sexism restricts women's behavior in some realms even as freedom from limitations is allowed in other spheres. The absence of extreme restrictions leads many women to ignore the areas in which they are exploited or discriminated against; it may even lead them to imagine that no women are oppressed.

There are oppressed women in the United States, and it is both appropriate and necessary that we speak against such oppression. French feminist Christine Delphy makes the point in her essay, "For a Materialist Feminism," that the use of the term oppression is important because it places feminist struggle in a radical political framework:

> The rebirth of feminism coincided with the use of the term "oppression." The ruling ideology,

i.e. common sense, daily speech, does not speak about oppression but about a "feminine condition." It refers back to a naturalist explanation: to a constraint of nature, exterior reality out of reach and not modifiable by human action. The term "oppression," on the contrary, refers back to a choice, an explanation, a situation that is political. "Oppression" and "social oppression" are therefore synonyms or rather social oppression is a redundance: the notion of a political origin, i.e. social, is an integral part of the concept of oppression.[8]

However, feminist emphasis on "common oppression" in the United States was less a strategy for politicization than an appropriation by conservative and liberal women of a radical political vocabulary that masked the extent to which they shaped the movement so that it addressed and promoted their class interests.

Although the impulse towards unity and empathy that informed the notion of common oppression was directed at building solidarity, slogans like "organize around your own oppression" provided the excuse many privileged women needed to ignore the differences between their social status and the status of masses of women. It was a mark of race and class privilege, as well as the expression of freedom from the many constraints sexism places on working class women, that middle class white women were able to make their interests the primary focus of feminist movement and employ a rhetoric of commonality that made their condition synonymous with "oppression." Who was there to demand a change in vocabulary? What other group of women in the United States had the same access to universities, publishing houses, mass media, money? Had middle class black women begun a movement in which they had labeled themselves "oppressed," no one would have taken them seriously. Had they established public forums and given speeches about their "oppression," they would have been criticized and attacked from all sides. This was not the case with white bourgeois feminists for they could appeal to a large audience of women, like themselves, who were eager to change their lot in life. Their isolation from women of other class and race groups provided no immediate comparative base by which to test their assumptions of common oppression.

Initially, radical participants in women's movement demanded that women penetrate that isolation and create a space for contact. Anthologies like *Liberation Now, Women's Liberation: Blueprint for the Future, Class and Feminism, Radical Feminism,* and *Sisterhood Is Powerful,* all published in the early 1970s, contain articles that attempted to address a wide audience of women, an audience that was not exclusively white, middle class, college-educated, and adult (many have articles on teenagers). Sookie Stambler articulated this radical spirit in her introduction to *Women's Liberation: Blueprint for the Future:*

> Movement women have always been turned off by the media's necessity to create celebrities and superstars. This goes against our basic philosophy. We cannot relate to women in our ranks towering over us with prestige and fame. We are not struggling for the benefit of the one woman or for one group of women. We are dealing with issues that concern all women.[9]

These sentiments, shared by many feminists early in the movement, were not sustained. As more and more women acquired prestige, fame, or money from feminist writings or from gains from feminist movement for equality in the workforce, individual opportunism undermined appeals for collective struggle. Women who were not opposed to patriarchy, capitalism, classism, or racism labeled themselves "feminist." Their expectations were varied. Privileged women wanted social equality with men of their class; some women wanted equal pay for equal work; others wanted an alternative lifestyle. Many of these legitimate concerns were easily co-opted by the ruling capitalist patriarchy. French feminist Antoinette Fouque states:

> The actions proposed by the feminist groups are spectacular, provoking. But provocation only brings to light a certain number of social contradictions. It does not reveal radical contradictions within society. The feminists claim that they do not seek equality with men, but their practice proves the contrary to be true. Feminists are a bourgeois avant-garde that maintains, in an inverted form, the dominant values. Inversion does not facilitate the passage to another kind of structure. Reformism suits everyone! Bourgeois order, capitalism,

phallocentrism are ready to integrate as many feminists as will be necessary. Since these women are becoming men, in the end it will only mean a few more men. The difference between the sexes is not whether one does or doesn't have a penis, it is whether or not one is an integral part of a phallic masculine economy.[10]

Feminists in the United States are aware of the contradictions. Carol Ehrlich makes the point in her essay, "The Unhappy Marriage of Marxism and Feminism: Can It Be Saved?," that "feminism seems more and more to have taken on a blind, safe, nonrevolutionary outlook" as "feminist radicalism loses ground to bourgeois feminism," stressing that "we cannot let this continue":

Women need to know (and are increasingly prevented from finding out) that feminism is *not* about dressing for success, or becoming a corporate executive, or gaining elective office; it is *not* being able to share a two career marriage and take skiing vacations and spend huge amounts of time with your husband and two lovely children because you have a domestic worker who makes all this possible for you, but who hasn't the time or money to do it for herself; it is *not* opening a Women's Bank, or spending a weekend in an expensive workshop that guarantees to teach you how to become assertive (but not aggressive); it is most emphatically *not* about becoming a police detective or CIA agent or marine corps general.

But if these distorted images of feminism have more reality than ours do, it is partly our own fault. We have not worked as hard as we should have at providing clear and meaningful alternative analyses which relate to people's lives, and at providing active, accessible groups in which to work.[11]

It is no accident that feminist struggle has been so easily co-opted to serve the interests of conservative and liberal feminists since feminism in the United States has so far been a bourgeois ideology. Zillah Eisenstein discusses the liberal roots of North American feminism in *The Radical Future of Liberal Feminism,* explaining in the introduction:

One of the major contributions to be found in this study is the role of the ideology of liberal individualism in the construction of feminist theory. Today's feminists either do not discuss a theory of individuality or they unselfconsciously adopt the competitive, atomistic ideology of liberal individualism. There is much confusion on this issue in the feminist theory we discuss here. Until a conscious differentiation is made between a theory of individuality that recognizes the importance of the individual within the social collectivity and the ideology of individualism that assumes a competitive view of the individual, there will not be a full accounting of what a feminist theory of liberation must look like in our Western society.[12]

The ideology of "competitive, atomistic liberal individualism" has permeated feminist thought to such an extent that it undermines the potential radicalism of feminist struggle. The usurpation of feminism by bourgeois women to support their class interests has been to a very grave extent justified by feminist theory as it has so far been conceived. (For example, the ideology of "common oppression.") Any movement to resist the co-optation of feminist struggle must begin by introducing a different feminist perspective—a new theory—one that is not informed by the ideology of liberal individualism.

The exclusionary practices of women who dominate feminist discourse have made it practically impossible for new and varied theories to emerge. Feminism has its party line and women who feel a need for a different strategy, a different foundation, often find themselves ostracized and silenced. Criticisms of or alternatives to established feminist ideas are not encouraged, e.g. recent controversies about expanding feminist discussions of sexuality. Yet groups of women who feel excluded from feminist discourse and praxis can make a place for themselves only if they first create, via critiques, an awareness of the factors that alienate them. Many individual white women found in the women's movement a liberatory solution to personal dilemmas. Having directly benefited from the movement, they are less inclined to criticize it or to engage in rigorous examination of its structure than those who feel it has not had a revolutionary impact on their lives or the lives of masses of women in our society. Nonwhite women who feel affirmed within the current structure of feminist movement (even though they may form autonomous groups) seem to also feel that their definitions of the party line, whether on the issue of black feminism or on other issues, is the only legitimate discourse. Rather than encourage a diversity of voices, critical dialogue, and controversy, they, like some white women, seek to stifle dissent. As activists and writers whose work is widely known, they act as if they are best able to judge whether other women's voices should be heard. Susan Griffin warns against this overall tendency towards dogmatism in her essay, "The Way of All Ideology":

> . . . when a theory is transformed into an ideology, it begins to destroy the self and self-knowledge. Originally born of feeling, it pretends to float above and around feeling. Above sensation. It organizes experience according to itself, without touching experience. By virtue of being itself, it is supposed to know. To invoke the name of this ideology is to confer truthfulness. No one can tell it anything new. Experience ceases to surprise it, inform it, transform it. It is annoyed by any detail which does not fit into its world view. Begun as a cry against the denial of truth, now it denies any truth which does not fit into its scheme. Begun as a way to restore one's sense of reality, now it attempts to discipline real people, to remake natural beings after its own image. All that it fails to explain it records as its enemy. Begun as a theory of liberation, it is threatened by new theories of liberation; it builds a prison for the mind.[13]

We resist hegemonic dominance of feminist thought by insisting that it is a theory in the making, that we must necessarily criticize, question, re-examine, and explore new possibilities. My persistent critique has been informed by my status as a member of an oppressed group, experience of sexist exploitation and discrimination, and the sense that prevailing feminist analysis has not been the force shaping my feminist consciousness. This is true for many women. There are white women who had never considered resisting male dominance until the feminist movement created an awareness that they could and should. My awareness of feminist struggle was stimulated by social circumstance. Growing up in a Southern, black, father-dominated, working class household, I experienced (as did my mother, my sisters, and

my brother) varying degrees of patriarchal tyranny and it made me angry—it made us all angry. Anger led me to question the politics of male dominance and enabled me to resist sexist socialization. Frequently, white feminists act as if black women did not know sexist oppression existed until they voiced feminist sentiment. They believe they are providing black women with "the" analysis and "the" program for liberation. They do not understand, cannot even imagine, that black women, as well as other groups of women who live daily in oppressive situations, often acquire an awareness of patriarchal politics from their lived experience, just as they develop strategies of resistance (even though they may not resist on a sustained or organized basis).

These black women observed white feminist focus on male tyranny and women's oppression as if it were a "new" revelation and felt such a focus had little impact on their lives. To them it was just another indication of the privileged living conditions of middle and upper class white women that they would need a theory to inform them that they were "oppressed." The implication being that people who are truly oppressed know it even though they may not be engaged in organized resistance or are unable to articulate in written form the nature of their oppression. These black women saw nothing liberatory in party line analyses of women's oppression. Neither the fact that black women have not organized collectively in huge numbers around the issues of "feminism" (many of us do not know or use the term) nor the fact that we have not had access to the machinery of power that would allow us to share our analyses or theories about gender with the American public negate its presence in our lives or place us in a position of dependency in relationship to those white and non-white feminists who address a larger audience.

The understanding I had by age thirteen of patriarchal politics created in me expectations of the feminist movement that were quite different from those of young, middle class, white women. When I entered my first women's studies class at Stanford University in the early 1970s, white women were revelling in the joy of being together—to them it was an important, momentous occasion. I had not known a life where women had not been together, where women had not helped, protected, and loved one another deeply. I had not known white women who were ignorant of the impact of race and class on their social status and consciousness (Southern white women often have a more realistic perspective on racism and classism than white women in other areas of the United States.) I did not feel sympathetic to white peers who maintained that I could not expect them to have knowledge of or understand the life experiences of black women. Despite my background (living in racially segregated communities) I knew about the lives of white women, and certainly no white women lived in our neighborhood, attended our schools, or worked in our homes.

When I participated in feminist groups, I found that white women adopted a condescending attitude towards me and other non-white participants. The condescension they directed at black women was one of the means they employed to remind us that the women's movement was "theirs"—that we were able to participate because they allowed it, even encouraged it; after all, we were needed to legitimate the process. They did not see us as equals. They did not treat us as equals. And though they expected us to provide first hand accounts of black experience, they felt it was their role to decide if these experiences were authentic. Frequently, college-educated black women (even those from poor and working class backgrounds) were dismissed as mere imitators. Our presence in movement activities did not count, as white women were convinced that "real" blackness meant speaking the patois of poor black people, being uneducated, streetwise, and a variety of other stereotypes. If we dared to criticize the movement or to assume responsibility for reshaping feminist ideas and introducing new ideas, our voices were tuned out, dismissed, silenced. We could be heard only if our statements echoed the sentiments of the dominant discourse.

Attempts by white feminists to silence black women are rarely written about. All too often they have taken place in conference rooms, classrooms, or the privacy of cozy living room settings, where one lone black woman faces the racist hostility of a group of white women.

From the time the women's liberation movement began, individual black women went to groups. Many never returned after a first meeting. Anita Cornwall is correct in "Three for the Price of One: Notes from a Gay Black Feminist," when she states, ". . . sadly enough, fear of encountering racism seems to be one of the main reasons that so many black women refuse to join the women's movement."[14] Recent focus on the issue of racism has generated discourse but has had little impact on the behavior of white feminists towards black women. Often the white women who are busy publishing papers and books on "unlearning racism" remain patronizing and condescending when they relate to black women. This is not surprising given that frequently their discourse is aimed solely in the direction of a white audience and the focus solely on changing attitudes rather than addressing racism in a historical and political context. They make us the "objects" of their privileged discourse on race. As "objects," we remain unequals, inferiors. Even though they may be sincerely concerned about racism, their methodology suggests they are not yet free of the type of paternalism endemic to white supremacist ideology. Some of these women place themselves in the position of "authorities" who must mediate communication between racist white women (naturally they see themselves as having come to terms with their racism) and angry black women whom they believe are incapable of rational discourse. Of course, the system of racism, classism, and educational elitism remain intact if they are to maintain their authoritative positions.

In 1981, I enrolled in a graduate class on feminist theory where we were given a course reading list that had writings by white women and men, one black man, but no material by or about black, Native American Indian, Hispanic, or Asian women. When I criticized this oversight, white women directed an anger and hostility at me that was so intense I found it difficult to attend the class. When I suggested that the purpose of this collective anger was to create an atmosphere in which it would be psychologically unbearable for me to speak in class discussions or even attend class, I was told that they were not angry. *I* was the one who was angry. Weeks after class ended, I received an open letter from one white female student acknowledging her anger and expressing regret for her attacks. She wrote:

> I didn't know you. You were black. In class after a while I noticed myself, that I would always be the one to respond to whatever you said. And usually it was to contradict. Not that the argument was always about racism by any means. But I think the hidden logic was that if I could prove you wrong about one thing, then you might not be right about anything at all.

And in another paragraph:

> I said in class one day that there were some people less entrapped than others by Plato's picture of the world. I said I thought we, after fifteen years of education, courtesy of the ruling class, might be more entrapped than others who had not received a start in life so close to the heart of the monster. My classmate, once a close friend, sister, colleague, has not spoken to me since then. I think the possibility that we were not the best spokespeople for all women made her fear for her self-worth and for her Ph.D.

Often in situations where white feminists aggressively attacked individual black women, they saw themselves as the ones who were under attack, who were the victims. During a heated discussion with another white female student in a racially mixed women's group I had organized, I was told that she had heard how I had "wiped out" people in the feminist theory class, that she was afraid of being "wiped out" too. I reminded her that I was one person speaking to a large group of angry, aggressive people; I was hardly dominating the situation. It was I who left the class in tears, not any of the people I had supposedly "wiped out."

Racist stereotypes of the strong, superhuman black woman are operative myths in the minds of many white women, allowing them to ignore the extent to which black women are likely to be victimized in this society and the role white women may play in the maintenance and perpetuation of that victimization. In Lillian Hellman's autobiographical work *Pentimento,* she writes, "All my life, beginning at birth, I have taken orders from black women, wanting them and resenting them, being superstitious

the few times I disobeyed." The black women Hellman describes worked in her household as family servants and their status was never that of an equal. Even as a child, she was always in the dominant position as they questioned, advised, or guided her; they were free to exercise these rights because she or another white authority figure allowed it. Hellman places power in the hands of these black women rather than acknowledge her own power over them; hence she mystifies the true nature of their relationship. By projecting onto black women a mythical power and strength, white women both promote a false image of themselves as powerless, passive victims and deflect attention away from their aggressiveness, their power, (however limited in a white supremacist, male-dominated state) their willingness to dominate and control others. These unacknowledged aspects of the social status of many white women prevent them from transcending racism and limit the scope of their understanding of women's overall social status in the United States.

Privileged feminists have largely been unable to speak to, with, and for diverse groups of women because they either do not understand fully the inter-relatedness of sex, race, and class oppression or refuse to take this inter-relatedness seriously. Feminist analyses of woman's lot tend to focus exclusively on gender and do not provide a solid foundation on which to construct feminist theory. They reflect the dominant tendency in Western patriarchal minds to mystify woman's reality by insisting that gender is the sole determinant of woman's fate. Certainly it has been easier for women who do not experience race or class oppression to focus exclusively on gender. Although socialist feminists focus on class and gender, they tend to dismiss race or they make a point of acknowledging that race is important and then proceed to offer an analysis in which race is not considered.

As a group, black women are in an unusual position in this society, for not only are we collectively at the bottom of the occupational ladder, but our overall social status is lower than that of any other group. Occupying such a position, we bear the brunt of sexist, racist, and classist oppression. At the same time, we are the group that has not been socialized to assume the role of exploiter/oppressor in that we are allowed no institutionalized "other" that we can exploit or oppress. (Children do not represent an institutionalized other even though they may be oppressed by parents.) White women and black men have it both ways. They can act as oppressor or be oppressed. Black men may be victimized by racism, but sexism allows them to act as exploiters and oppressors of women. White women may be victimized by sexism, but racism enables them to act as exploiters and oppressors of black people. Both groups have led liberation movements that favor their interests and support the continued oppression of other groups. Black male sexism has undermined struggles to eradicate racism just as white female racism undermines feminist struggle. As long as these two groups or any group defines liberation as gaining social equality with ruling class white men, they have a vested interest in the continued exploitation and oppression of others.

Black women with no institutionalized "other" that we may discriminate against, exploit, or oppress often have a lived experience that directly challenges the prevailing classist, sexist, racist social structure and its concomitant ideology. This lived experience may shape our consciousness in such a way that our world view differs from those who have a degree of privilege (however relative within the existing system). It is essential for continued feminist struggle that black women recognize the special vantage point our marginality gives us and make use of this perspective to criticize the dominant racist, classist, sexist hegemony as well as to envision and create a counter-hegemony. I am suggesting that we have a central role to play in the making of feminist theory and a contribution to offer that is unique and valuable. The formation of a liberatory feminist theory and praxis is a collective responsibility, one that must be shared. Though I criticize aspects of feminist movement as we have known it so far, a critique which is sometimes harsh and unrelenting, I do so not in an attempt to diminish feminist struggle but to enrich, to share in the work of making a liberatory ideology and a liberatory movement.

Notes

1. Although *The Feminine Mystique* has been criticized and even attacked from various fronts I call attention to it again because certain biased premises about the nature of woman's social status put forth initially in this text continue to shape the tenor and direction of feminist movement.

2. Betty Friedan, *The Feminine Mystique*, p. 15.

3. Friedan, p. 32.

4. Friedan, "Progressive Dehumanization," p. 305.

5. Rita Mae Brown, "The Last Straw," in *Class and Feminism*, p. 15.

6. Leah Fritz, *Dreamers and Dealers*, p. 51.

7. Benjamin Barber, *Liberating Feminism*, p. 30.

8. Christine Delphy, "For a Materialist Feminism," p. 211. A fuller discussion of Christine Delphy's perspective may be found in the collected essays of her work *Close to Home*.

9. Sookie Stambler, *Women's Liberation: Blueprint for the Future*, p. 9.

10. Antoinette Fouque, "Warnings," in *New French Feminists*, pp. 117–118.

11. Carol Ehrlich, "The Unhappy Marriage of Marxism and Feminism: Can It Be Saved?," p. 130.

12. Zillah Eisenstein, *The Radical Future of Liberal Feminism*, p. 5.

13. Susan Griffin, "The Way of All Ideology," *Signs*, Spring 1982, p. 648.

14. Anita Cornwell, "Three for the Price of One: Notes from a Gay Black Feminist," in *Lavender Culture*, p. 471.

Study Questions

1. Why does Hooks say that white feminists have a one-dimensional perspective? Cite an example.

2. According to Hooks, how do race and class biases dominate feminist discourse?

3. Specifically, how does she criticize the central tenet "all women are oppressed"? How does she think it reflects class interests?

4. Hooks wants to resist the hegemony of feminist discourse. What is her critique?

5. How does Hooks describe her own feminist struggle? What has been her experience in the women's movement?

6. What role should black women have in shaping feminist thought?

5
Philosophy of Law

Laws—and the sanctions by which they are enforced—represent the authority of political institutions. Accordingly, philosophers have devoted considerable attention to substantive issues surrounding legal systems: What is a just law? Should an unjust law be obeyed? What is the relationship between law and morality?

Feminist philosophers have seen the centrality of legal issues for women. And women have looked to laws and the courts for redress for the inequities and crimes that impinge upon women privately and publicly. How well do legal institutions serve women? Is there gender-balance in the courts?

In response to such questions, feminists have explored areas of law that are of special concern to women: rape, sexual slavery, pornography, incest, sexual harassment in the workplace, sex discrimination, and the like. As Rosemarie Tong writes, feminists hope "to probe the nature and limits of the law—insofar as women and their sexuality are concerned."

According to feminists, sexual harassment is sex discrimination because it endangers a woman's job and threatens her economic livelihood. Rosemarie Tong wants to show the connection between women's social inequality and the sexual harassment of women in the marketplace. As Catharine MacKinnon writes, "Sexual harassment at work connects the jobs most women do—in which a major part of their work is to be there for men—with the structure of sexual relations—in which their role is also to be there for men." Tong holds that the legal system has not fully recognized this configuration. To demonstrate the claim that sexual harassment is sex discrimination, Tong shows its connection to women's social inequality.

Many, though by no means all, feminists have viewed pornography, in the words of Robin Morgan, as "the theory of which rape is the practice." Consequently, they have organized to campaign for antipornography laws. Helen Longino argues for the antipornography position on the grounds that pornography, unlike erotica, is women-degrading. That is, it portrays women as sexually objectified, and it depicts disrespect for women as sexual beings. Thus, Longino defends the use of censorship. She contends that pornography itself is a form of violence against women since it supports the devaluation of women as a sex class.

Susan Griffin's analysis connects the criminal act of rape with the expression of culturally held norms about women's sexuality and availability in regard to men. Rape, she argues, is not an isolated or aberrant phenomenon but is, as Andrea Dworkin says, "in fact an exaggerated expression of accepted sexual relations between men and women." Griffin contends that rape is a threat to all women in that it reinforces men's dominance.

In her essay, Catharine MacKinnon examines what rape means to women and how rape acts to keep women subordinated. Is rape primarily a violent act, a sexual act, or both? Finding out calls for a re-examination of what women have considered "normal" in heterosexual intercourse. MacKinnon believes that existing legislation on rape reflects the problem of consent for women in conditions of gender inequality.

In these and other issues, feminist principles are put into practice, challenging a perceived gender bias in the legal system; that is, the manner in which sexual inequalities are enforced by the laws themselves.

Sexual Harassment

Rosemarie Tong

A March 1980 article in *Newsweek* begins:

> It may be as subtle as a leer and a series of
> off-color jokes, or as direct as grabbing a
> woman's breast. It can be found in typing pools
> and factories, Army barracks and legislature
> suites, city rooms and college lecture halls. It is
> fundamentally a man's problem, an exercise of
> power almost analogous to rape, for which
> women pay with their jobs, and sometimes
> their health. It's as traditional as underpaying
> women—and now appears to be just as illegal.
> Sexual harassment, the boss's dirty little fringe
> benefit, has been dragged out of the closet.[1]

Indeed, sexual harassment has been brought out into the open and, unlike pornography and prostitution, which have been perceived as feminist issues, sexual harassment has been labeled a woman's issue: an issue that can directly affect any women in this country. It is surely odd to distinguish between feminist and women's issues, as if the two were mutually exclusive.

But this is the way the public tends to think. Nonetheless, had it not been for feminists, the problem of sexual harassment would never have been named, let alone confronted.

Before the 1970s women largely accepted as an unpleasant fact of life what some of them called the "little rapes." With the emergence of consciousness-raising groups, many women (especially working women and students) began to feel that they need not and should not have to submit to these nagging violations of their persons. Speaking to women, Andrea Medea and Kathleen Thompson observed:

> If you are subjected . . . to this kind of
> violation every day, a gradual erosion
> begins—an erosion of your self-respect and
> privacy. You lose a little when you are shaken

From Rosemarie Tong, *Women, Sex and the Law* (Totowa, NJ: Rowman and Littlefield, 1983). By permission of the author. (Notes deleted.)

out of your daydreams by the whistles and comments of the construction workers you have to pass. You lose a little when a junior executive looks down your blouse or gives you a familiar pat at work. You lose a little to the obnoxious drunk at the next table, to that man on the subway, to the guys in the drive-in.[2]

As a result of people realizing that such abuses are common, the problem of sexual harassment was named in 1975. No sooner was the problem named than its seriousness as well as pervasiveness became apparent. For example, a 1976 issue of *Redbook* (by no means a feminist publication) reported that out of a sample of 9,000 readers, 88 percent had experienced some form of sexual harassment, and 92 percent considered the problem of sexual harassment serious.[3] Most women find that their job or academic performance degenerates as they are forced to take time and energy away from work or school to deal with sexual harassers. Indeed, fending off offensive sexual advances, especially if they are sustained over several weeks, months, or years, causes women tension, anxiety, frustration, and above all anger. Unfortunately, many women turn this anger not against their harassers, but against themselves. Gradually, they transform their initial feelings of righteous indignation into feelings of shame or guilt. Shame is experienced when a woman feels that she has not lived up to a self-imposed ideal image of herself as a person who can control men's reactions to her body. In contrast, guilt is experienced when a woman feels that she has not lived up to society's standards for female behavior, one of which instructs women to meet men's sexual wants and needs with grace, generosity, and good humor. Plagued by intense feelings of shame (failure) or guilt (transgression), an increasing number of women workers and students suffer from what has been termed "sexual harassment syndrome." Victims of this syndrome can experience psychological depression, if not also physical ailments, such as "stomachaches, headaches, nausea, involuntary muscular spasms, insomnia, hypertension, and other medical illnesses."[4]

Unfortunately, victims of sexual harassment syndrome are sometimes scoffed at. When five women students and a male assistant professor filed a class-action suit at Yale, contending that male faculty members had engaged in sexually offensive behavior, resulting in a multitude of harms, university officials responded in a defensive manner. As one spokesman for Yale said, "It's not a new thing, but it is also not a major problem." Another university official added, "There is a stronger argument that if women students aren't smart enough to outwit some obnoxious professor, they shouldn't be here in the first place. Like every other institution, Yale has its share of twisted souls."[5]

Given such varied reactions to sexual harassment and its deleterious consequences, it poses problems of definition analogous to those posed by pornography and prostitution. This article will discuss recent attempts to define sexual harassment and to distinguish it clearly from sexual attraction. Standard as well as preferred feminist legal responses to sexual harassment will be evaluated, noting that the former tend to invoke versions of both the offense principle and the harm principle, whereas the latter tend to invoke only the harm principle. Finally, the discussion will focus on when the appropriate response to an incident of sexual harassment is a legal remedy and when it is an extralegal remedy, arguing that the law is best invoked when the price one must pay for her sexual integrity is an education or occupational opportunity/position.

The Ubiquitous Phenomenon

Although definitions of sexual harassment are by no means uniform, many feminist anti-harassers agree that sexual harassment involves four conditions: (1) an annoying or unwelcome sexual advance or imposition; (2) a negative response to this sexual advance/imposition; (3) the presence of intimidation or coercion when the sexual harasser holds more power than the person sexually harassed and, frequently, (4) the suggestion that institutionally inappropriate rewards or penalties will result from compliance or refusal to comply.

This preliminary definition, critics point out, leaves much to be desired. First, it fails to illuminate the connection between the sexual advance/imposition, the negative response, and the institutional consequences. For instance, how forceful must the response be? How serious must the consequences be? Second, the definition fails to make clear who this society's power-holders are. Must one be an employer or a professor in order to have power over a woman employee or a woman student? Or does the mere fact that a person is male give him an automatic power over a female's fate? Third, it fails to distinguish between the kind of coercion that consists of a threatened penalty and the kind that consists of a promised reward. Properly speaking, is not the latter form of coercion more aptly described as a pressure tactic or an incentive technique? Fourth, and most important, the definition fails to indicate which of the four conditions are necessary for sexual harassment and which are sufficient.

In response to these criticisms, but especially the last one, feminists have refined their definition of sexual harassment. As they see it, there are two types of sexual harassment: coercive and noncoercive. Coercive sexual harassment includes (1) sexual misconduct that offers a benefit or reward to the person to whom it is directed, as well as (2) sexual misconduct that threatens some harm to the person to whom it is directed. An example of the first instance would be offering someone a promotion only if she provides a sexual favor. An example of the second instance would be stating that one will assign a student a failing grade unless she performs a sexual favor. In contrast, noncoercive sexual harassment denotes sexual misconduct that merely annoys or offends the person to whom it is directed. Examples of noncoercive sexual misconduct are repeatedly using a lewd nickname ("Boobs") to refer to an attractive co-worker, or prowling around the women's dormitory after midnight. What coercive and noncoercive modes of sexual harassment have in common, of course, is that they are un-solicited, unwelcome, and generally unwanted by the women to whom they are directed.[6]

Coercive Sexual Harassment

According to feminists, a coercive act is "one where the person coerced is made to feel com-pelled to do something he or she would not normally do."[7] This compulsion is accom-plished by the coercer's "adversely changing the options available for the victim's choos-ing."[8] The paradigm case of coercion is, of course, the use of physical or psychological re-straint, but *threats* of physical or psychological restraint/reprisal are also coercive to a lesser degree. Although it is difficult to determine whether a sexual harasser has in fact narrowed for the worse the options available for a woman's choosing, John Hughes and Larry May provide two tests to facilitate such de-terminations: would the woman have "freely chosen" to change her situation before the alleged threat was made for her situation after the broaching of the alleged threat; and, would the woman be made "worse off" than she other-wise would be by not complying with the offer?[9]

Relying on Hughes and May's twofold test, feminists maintain that sexual advances/ impositions that threaten some harm to the person to whom they are directed are clearly coercive. "If you don't go to bed with me, Suzy, I'll fail you in this course." Assuming that Suzy has not been secretly longing to sleep with her professor or to flunk her course, she would not freely choose to change her situation to one in which the only way she can attain a passing grade is by sleeping with him. Therefore, be-cause Suzy's professor has adversely altered her options, he has coerced her into a very tight corner; and since a coercive sexual advance is by definition an instance of sexual harass-ment, Suzy's professor is guilty of sexual ha-rassment.

In contrast to sexual advances backed by threats, feminists admit that sexual advances backed by offers do not constitute clear cases of sexual harassment. Nonetheless, like sexual threats, sexual offers are coercive. It is just that the bitter pill of coercion is coated with a sugary promise: "If you go to bed with me, Suzy, I'll give you an 'A' in this course." According to critics, however, feminists confuse seduction with sexual harassment when they conflate sex-ual offers with sexual threats—when they insist that every time a man pressures a woman for a sexual favor by promising her a reward he coerces her into saying an unwilling yes to his request. In this connection, Michael Bayles asks feminists to ponder the following hypothetical case:

> Assume there is a mediocre woman graduate student who would not receive an assistantship. Suppose the department chairman offers her one if she goes to bed with him, and she does so. In what sense has the graduate student acted against her will? She apparently pre-ferred having the assistantship and sleeping with the chairman to not sleeping with the chairman and not having the assistantship . . . the fact that choice has undesirable con-sequences does not make it against one's will. One may prefer having clean teeth without having to brush them; nonetheless, one is not acting against one's will when one brushes them.[10]

As Bayles sees it, the department chairman has not coerced the graduate student to sleep with him. Rather he has seduced her to sleep with him. Consequently, whatever the chair-man is guilty of, it is not sexual harassment. Bayles's reasons for insisting that the graduate student has not been coerced are two. First, she would have freely chosen to move from the preoffer stage (no chance of an assistantship) to the postoffer stage (a chance of an assistant-ship). Second, her options after the sexual offer are not worse than before. If she refuses the sexual offer, she will not lose a chance for an assistantship because she was never in the run-ning; and if she accepts the sexual offer, she will have not only a chance for an assistantship, but an assistantship. Despite the superficial plausibility of Bayles's analysis, feminists (once again following Hughes and May) insist that a deeper reading of the graduate student's di-lemma indicates that she has in fact been coerced by her department chairman. In the first place, assuming the graduate student has not been dying to go to bed with her chairman, and that she is not a calculating mercenary who has been hoping for a sexual offer to bail her out of a dead-end career trajectory, it is not clear that she would have freely chosen to move from the preoffer stage to the postoffer stage. The best reason for her not wishing to move to the postoffer stage is that it places her in a "damned if you do, damned if you don't" predicament.

On the one hand, if the graduate student refuses to sleep with her chairman, she will of course *not* receive an undeserved assistantship. In addition, she will place herself at considerable risk. Perhaps the chairman is talking sweetly today only because he thinks the graduate student will be in his bed tomorrow. Should she disappoint him, he may turn against her. This is a real possibility, given the unpredictable character of sexual feelings and the history of reprisals against women who turn down sexual offers. On the other hand, if the graduate student agrees to sleep with the chairman—either because she wants an assistantship or because she fears angering him (a possibility that Bayles overlooks)—she increases her vulnerability to other professors as well as to the chairman. Other professors might imitate their chairman's behavior—after all, he got away with it—adding a degree of instability and potential for arbitrary treatment not only to this particular student's future, but to all female graduate students' futures. Once such considerations are factored in, feminists observe that the chairman has in fact boxed his graduate student into a corner from which she cannot emerge unscathed. Consequently, whatever else the chairman is guilty of (such as depriving a worthy candidate of an assistantship), he is also guilty of sexual harassment.

Noncoercive Sexual Harassment

Clear cases of coercive sexual harassment affect a woman's options so adversely that she gives in to her harasser's threats or offers simply because her other options seem so much worse. Unlike the sexual seducer who showers a woman with gifts so that she will at long last *willingly* leap into his arms, the coercive sexual harasser waves his stick or carrot in front of a woman, not caring how *unwilling* she is when she jumps into his bed. Significantly, what distinguishes the noncoercive sexual harasser from both the sexual seducer and the coercive

sexual harasser is that his primary aim is not to get a woman to perform sexually for him, but simply to annoy or offend her.

Although it is possible to argue that the ogler's, pincher's, or squeezer's sexual misconduct is coercive, it is difficult. Many women fear calling attention not only to the sexual misconduct of their employers and professors, who can cost them their jobs or academic standing, but also to the sexual misconduct of strangers—strangers who have no long-term economic or intellectual power over them, but who nonetheless have the short-term power of physical strength over them. For example, in a recent *New York Times* article, Victoria Balfour reported that although women are frequently sexually harassed at movie theaters, they very rarely complain to theater managers. One highly educated woman who had been afraid to report an incident of sexual harassment to the theater manager commented: "He might think that somehow I had done something that made the man want to bother me, that I had provoked him. To me, harassment has its implications, like rape."[11] Two other women silently endured a harasser for the duration of another film. Although their harasser's behavior was extremely offensive, they did not report the incident: "He was staring heavily, breathing heavily and making strange noises. We didn't move because we were afraid if we got somebody to deal with him, he'd be waiting outside afterward with a knife."[12] All three of these women kept silent because they feared provoking their harassers to some heinous deed.

To claim that these theatergoers were *coerced* into silence is, according to feminists, to accomplish some good at the risk of effecting considerable harm. On the one hand, the public ought to realize that, for women, being bothered at the movies, in the subways, and on the streets by youthful girl-watchers, middle-aged creeps, and dirty old men is a routine occurrence. On the other hand, women ought not to think of themselves as helpless victims who dare not confront their harassers for fear of retaliatory violence. Therefore, on balance, feminists are of the opinion that it is best to reserve the term *coercive* for cases of sexual harassment that involve specific threats or offers, especially if these threats or offers are made in the context of the workplace or academy. This is not to suggest, however, that feminists think that cases of noncoercive sexual harassment are always less serious than cases of coercive sexual harassment. No woman wants to be coerced into a man's bed; but neither does a woman want to be hounded by a man who takes delight in insulting, belittling, or demeaning her, and who may even find satisfaction in driving her to distraction. This being the case, feminists insist that the law attend to cases of unwanted *noncoercive* as well as unwanted coercive sexual harassment. But this is no light request to make of a law that, like some Freudians, is still wondering what women really want.

Standard Legal Responses

Although the law is better suited to deal with cases of coercive sexual harassment than with cases of noncoercive sexual harassment, it has attempted to provide remedies for both types of misconduct. Traditionally, the two major legal avenues open to victims of sexual harassment have been criminal proceedings and civil suits, which invoke tort law. The rationale behind the criminal-proceedings approach depends straightforwardly on the harm principle, whereas the rationale behind civil suits relies on a mixture of the harm and offense principles. The fact that these two rationales differ is not without consequence. The civil law (=tort law) tends to take sexual harassment even less seriously than the criminal law does.

Criminal Proceedings: Invoking the Harm Principle

Criminal proceedings are now, as in the past, less frequently employed than civil suits. This is not surprising given that the criminal sanction is appropriate only if the sexually harassed woman is a victim of rape, indecent assault, common assault, assault causing bodily harm, threats, intimidation, or solicitation. That is, unless a woman is *seriously* harmed by her harasser, a prosecutor is not likely to press

criminal charges, and if she is seriously harmed, the prosecutor is not likely to charge her harasser with sexual harassment but with rape, indecent assault, and so on.

The prosecutor's course of action is prima facie rational. If a woman's "harasser" is in no way connected with her place of education or employment, it is confusing and trivializing to describe his rape of her as an extreme incident of sexual harassment. But if a woman is coerced to submit to sexual intercourse as a condition of successful employment or education, then her rape is technically best described as aggravated sexual harassment. If the prosecutor wishes to be precise about the whole affair, then he should work toward an aggravated sexual harassment conviction rather than a rape conviction. But be this as it may, a victim of sexual harassment who seeks the aegis of the criminal law is not likely to get very far. Should an adult working woman or an adult student complain of indecent assault, the police are not likely either to lay charges for her or to pursue her case absent of witnesses, other than herself, to the episode. Says one police officer:

> If a girl came to us and told us her boss had called her into the office, put his arm around her, and grabbed her breast, we would first investigate to see if there was some additional evidence. No judge would convict without further evidence. Our practice is that we will not deal with complaints of this kind without some corroborating evidence. It's just too easy for her employer, an upstanding man in the community, to testify that she had asked him for a raise, that he had turned her down, and that this false cry of assault was her ploy to get even.[13]

If a victim of sexual harassment encounters such a police officer, she may, in absence of his support, lay criminal charges herself. Should she pursue this cource of action, however, the district attorney would probably not argue her case. She would be forced to hire a private prosecutor to do her arguing and "it is common knowledge that the judges who hear private prosecutors treat them with much less concern than they do police-laid charges."[14] Realizing this, victims of sexual harassment have tended to bypass the criminal sanction unless they are able to find other women who have been similarly harassed by the particular man involved. The sole victim of *even* extreme forms of sexual harassment is unlikely to be taken seriously. Oftentimes police officers and prosecutors are unable to recognize the special coercion, the extra harm, inherent in extreme forms of sexual harassment that occur in the workplace or the academy. They are apt to think that such cases are episodes of mutually agreeable sexual relations gone awry: "A guy and a gal are together—she's prepared to go along for a few months—after that she wants to cut it off and he doesn't."[15] In short, male members of the criminal justice system are quite reluctant to invoke the harm principle against sexual harassers because they remain unconvinced, on some level, that sexual harassment can indeed constitute a serious harm to a woman's physical or psychological integrity.

Civil Torts: Invoking the Harm and Offense Principles

Given the criminal law's limitations, victims of sexual harassment have turned instead to the civil law, which seems better suited to succor the individual woman who has been sexually harassed. Whereas criminal liability exists to exact a penalty from a wrongdoer in order to protect society as a whole, tort liability exists primarily to compensate the injured person by requiring the wrongdoer to pay for the damage he or she had done. Like criminal law, tort law designates that liability is progressively greater as the defendant's actions range from mere inadvertence, to negligence of likely consequences, to intentional invasion of another's rights under the mistaken notion that no harm is being committed, to instances where the motive is a "malevolent desire to do harm."[16] Because tort law is oriented to victim compensation in a way that the criminal law is not, and because guilty tort-feasors are punished less severely than guilty criminal offenders, in many more instances than the criminal law, tort law will take a strict liability approach, often requiring even the person who merely acted inadvertently or negligently to compensate the individual(s) harmed by his or her thoughtless or careless action(s). Likewise, tort law will, in many more instances than the criminal law,

address what I have termed "offenses" (behavior that embarrasses, shames, disgusts, or annoys someone), sometimes requiring the merely offensive person to compensate his or her victim.

1. *Types of Torts:* While new torts are emerging all the time, there are several existing torts that may be particularly applicable to cases of sexual harassment: battery, assault, and the intentional infliction of mental or emotional disturbance.

a. *The Battery Tort:* Battery is defined as "an intentional and unpermitted contact, other than that permitted by social usage."[17] While contact must be intentional, intent to cause all the damages that resulted from the contact is not necessary to establish liability. In other words, a harasser may be guilty of battery simply because he intended to touch a woman without her consent, even though he meant her no harm or offense. So, for example, battery includes instances in which a compliment is intended. Absent her consent, it is tortious, for example, to kiss an "unappreciative woman" under the mistletoe. Because the battery tort considers contact with the body or anything already in contact with the body (such as clothing), it is a useful tort for victims to use against harassers who go beyond verbal abuse. Usually physical contact is not tortious unless it represents socially unacceptable behavior ("breast squeezing" or "fanny-pinching"). Nonetheless, in some cases, socially acceptable behavior ("cheek kissing" or "hand pressing") may be tortious if it is known by the harassers that the receiver of such contacts objects to and does not permit them. In either event, the victim of battery may win her suit, especially since she need not prove—as the victim of rape has had to prove until recently—her lack of consent through some show of resistance.

b. *The Assault Tort:* Where physical contact has not occurred, the tort of assault may be actionable. Assault is "an intentional act, short of contact, which produces *apprehension* of a battery."[18] As Catharine MacKinnon notes, the tort of assault applies to the person placed in fear of an immediately harmful and minimally offensive "touching of the mind, if not the body." Since the invasion is mental, the defendant must have intended at least to arouse psychic apprehension in his victim. Although the fear-producing event must consist of "more than words alone," without words the intentions of the harasser may remain equivocal.[19]

Because the lines between psychic and physical battery are easily crossed, battery and assault doctrines are frequently combined in practice. Catharine MacKinnon provides several examples of successful torts brought under this combined doctrine in the early 1900s. In an age of heightened sexual sensibilities, it was not unusual for cases to be brought forward such as the one in which "a railroad was found responsible for the embarrassment and humiliation of a woman passenger caused when a drunken man, of whose boisterous conduct and inebriated condition the railroad was aware, fell down on top of her and kissed her on the cheek."[20] In another case, "a woman recovered damages for assault and battery against a man who squeezed her breast and laid his hand on her face."[21]

The Intentional Infliction of Mental or Emotional Disturbance Tort

Contemporary sexual mores make it difficult to take altogether seriously the cases MacKinnon describes in today's courts. Unlike her early twentieth-century counterpart, today's woman does not take umbrage at every peck on the cheek or laying on of hands. This does not mean, however, that today's woman either *does* or *should* take in stride every obnoxious ogle, every offensive touch, and every suggestive gesture. As in the past, unwanted or annoying sexual advances/impositions can affect a woman adversely. For this reason, the tort of intentional infliction, in words or acts, of mental or emotional disturbance is gaining currency. Although this tort may be the most difficult to use against sexual harassers, because it includes only those offenses that cause "purely emotional disturbance,"[22] it is also the most promising in that it probably covers those

forms of sexual harassment calculated to wear down a woman's resistance.

Consider, for example, the specific tort of intentional infliction of nervous shock. In order for this tort to apply, the sexual harasser must have either purposely, knowingly, or recklessly desired to cause alarm or fright in his victim. Moreover, his conduct must have been serious enough to cause nervous shock in a normal person (unless he was aware of his victim's peculiar susceptibility to emotional shock), and the victim's nervous shock must have physical or psychopathological consequences. Given that sexual harassers often badger their victims systematically over a long period of time, some women do suffer from nervous shock, or sexual harassment syndrome. An example may clarify matters. Over an eight-month period, David Eccles had "persistently telephoned" Marcia Samms at all hours of the night or day, begging her to have sexual intercourse with him. Although Mrs. Samms repeatedly told Eccles to stop bothering her, he kept on soliciting her. Eventually, Mrs. Samms became so emotionally distressed that she brought suit against Eccles for three thousand dollars in damages. The Supreme Court of Utah in *Samms* v. *Eccles* (1961) found that Mrs. Samms had grounds for suit (cause of action).[23] The court decision reads:

> We quite agree with the idea that under usual circumstances, the solicitation to sexual intercourse would not be actionable even though it may be offensive to the offeree. It seems to be a custom of longstanding and one which in all likelihood will continue. The assumption is usually indulged that most solicitations occur under such conditions as to fall within the well known phrase of Chief Judge Magruder that "there is no harm in asking." The Supreme Court of Kentucky has observed that an action will not lie in favor of a woman against a man who, without trespass or assault, makes such a request; and that the reverse is also true: that a man would have no right of action against a woman for such a solicitation. But the situation just described, where tolerance for the conduct referred to is indulged, is clearly distinguishable from the aggravated circumstances the plaintiff claims existed here.[24]

1. *Problems with the Tort Approach:* This case is important in that it offers recourse to

women who are subjected to both aggravated and severely disturbing sexual harassment. Nonetheless, for at least three reasons
the tort approach is problematic not only in
this form, but in its battery and assault
forms.

a. *The Issue of Consent:* At least in battery cases,
the harasser may claim that the woman consented to his sexual advances. This objection
is significant because the harasser is not liable for his actions if the woman agreed to
submit to them. Unfortunately, it is no easy
matter to determine if a woman consented
to a sexual advance. For this reason, in cases
of sexual harassment, as in cases of rape and
woman-battering, the law has straddled between two approaches: One focuses on
whether the sexual misconduct was clearly
consented to; the other focuses on the consequences of the sexual misconduct without
emphasizing issues of consent. Where the
law has favored the consent strategy, it has
adopted methods similar to those it uses in
rape cases. That is, it has sought to establish
consent (a mental state) by looking to the
victim's resistance or lack thereof (a behavioral manifestation).

In some sense the victim who fails to resist
the man who paws her does consent to his
pawing. But given that women are still
socialized to be "nice" to men, it will take a
strong woman to say a loud "No, thank you"
to a man who has more arms than an octo-
pus has tentacles. Andrea Medea and Kathleen Thompson report that one woman
went so far as to follow her eventual rapist
into a dark alley because she feared "offend-
ing" him by implying that he might rape her.
Rather than berating the woman for her
naivete, Medea and Thompson ask their
female readers to recall all those times and
places in which they paid attention to a man
for fear of hurting his feelings.

Realizing that many women are currently
unable to express forecefully their nonconsent to an unwanted sexual advance/
imposition, the law has recently experi-
mented with the so-called consequences
approach. This approach assumes that it is
easier to measure the effect that unwanted
sexual propositions have on female victims
than it is to determine whether a female

victim's lack of overt resistance to them is a
sign of her tacit consent to them. If Jane
experiences depression, anxiety, frustration, and even nausea or vomiting as a result
of being repeatedly manhandled by Dick,
she has been sexually harassed whether or
not she was able to communicate her nonconsent to Dick by telling him to "shove off"
or by splashing a glass of ice water on his
face.

The consequences approach is an *effective*
way to handle sexual harrassment cases. But
critics wonder whether it is a *fair* way to
handle such cases, since Dick, for example,
may have sincerely believed that Jane was
enjoying his pawings and pattings. Under
such circumstances, it does not seem unambiguously just to penalize Dick, since
much of Anglo-American law teaches that
unless a man knowingly or recklessly harms
someone, he is not to be sanctioned for the
harm he effects, unless, of course, a standard of negligence is employed. This being
the case, even when the consequences
approach is employed and the harassed
woman does not have to prove her lack of
consent, her case is strengthened where she
has made her dissent quite clear through
words and actions.

b. *The Issue of Hypersensitivity:* Where consent is
not an issue, the harasser may claim that he
had no reason to believe that the woman he
touched or threatened to touch would be
offended or frightened. That is, he had no
reason to believe that his target was a
hypersensitive individual. In such cases, the
harasser will be liable only if his conduct
would have been offensive to a person of
ordinary sensibilities. So, for example, Dick
is liable for the battery of Jane, whom he
patted on the posterior, if, but only if, a
person of ordinary sensibilities would have
been offended by such physical contact. But
since this person of ordinary sensibilities is
generally termed "the ordinary *man*," problems could arise for the female victim of
sexual harassment. As Catharine MacKinnon notes:

Ordinary women probably find offensive sexual contact and proposals that ordinary men
find trivial or sexually stimulating coming from

women. Sex is peculiarly an area where a presumption of gender sameness, or judgments by men of women, are not illuminating as standards for equal treatment, since to remind a man of his sexuality is to build his sense of potency, while for a man to remind a woman of hers is often experienced as intrusive, denigrating, and depotentiating.[25]

To summarize, although a typical man in this culture may like it when a strange woman squeezes muscles, a typical woman will probably not like it when a strange man squeezes her breasts or buttocks. And there will be times when a man will not be able to understand, say, why a woman does not always (or usually) appreciate wolf whistles. Of course, these differences of perspective could be remedied by a supplemental ordinary *woman* test, but this would require the law to confront squarely its male-biases—a major review for which it may not be ready.

2. *The Issue of Harm:* Where neither consent nor hypersensitivity is an issue, the harasser may argue that his victim did not suffer the harm she claims to have suffered. Such a defense is likely to set off a battle between *his* medical experts and *her* medical experts, the former arguing that Jane is of sound body and mind, the latter insisting that Jane is the shell of her former self. Unless such battles can be avoided, it may not be worth the victim's time, energy, and reputation to sue her harasser.

Feminist Legal Responses: Antidiscrimination Law

Even if it can be shown that a woman has not consented to her harasser's sexual advances, that she is not a hypersensitive individual, and that she has indeed suffered harm as a result of her harasser's sexual misconduct, it is not clear that the tort approach best serves sexually harassed women's interests. Catharine MacKinnon notes that the "aura of the pedestal," more properly viewed as a "cage," distorts cases such as the one in which a judge preached, "every woman has the right to assume that a passenger car is not a brothel and that when she travels in it, she will meet nothing, see nothing,

hear nothing, to wound her delicacy or insult her womanhood."[26] But to construe resistance to sexual harassment as a return to prudery is, according to feminists, to miss the point: Sexual harassment is not so much an issue of offensive behavior as an issue of abusive power.

But if sexual harassment is more an issue of power than an issue of offense, the tort approach, which emphasizes unseemly sexual conduct, must, in the estimation of feminists, be supplemented by a legal approach stressing that women often submit to unwanted sexual advances simply because their position in society is inferior relative to men. Not only are most men physically more powerful than most women, but it is men and not women who hold the balance of power in the political, economic, and social institutions that govern us all. Because antidiscrimination law is sensitive to these power dynamics, it can accomplish more for sexually harassed women than tort law. Whereas tort law views sexual harassment as an outrage to an individual woman's sensibilities and to a society's purported values, antidiscrimination law casts the same act either as one of *economic* coercion, in which the material survival of women in general is threatened, or as one of *intellectual* coercion, in which the spiritual survival of women in general is similarly jeopardized. If a woman wishes to argue that she has been sexually harassed not because she is vulnerable Sally Jones, but because she is a woman, a member of a gender that suffers from institutionalized inferiority and relative powerlessness, then the antidiscrimination approach obviously suits her purposes best.

Discriminatory Sexual Harassment: A Historical Survey

Despite the cogency of this line of reasoning, feminists were *initially* unable to convince the courts that sexual harassment could in fact constitute sex-based discrimination in the workplace and in the academy. The workplace decisions, resting on Title VII, which prohibits sex-based discrimination in employment, represent an upward struggle from the first case brought under it, *Corne v. Bausch and Lomb, Inc.*,[27] through several subsequent cases (*Miller v. Bank of America*[28] and *Tomkins v. Public Service*

Electric and Gas Co.,[29] to the landmark case *Barnes* v. *Costle).*[30] To a greater or lesser extent all these cases reveal two attitudes the courts had to overcome on the way to recognizing discriminatory sexual harassment: (1) sexual attraction between a man and a woman is a personal matter in which the courts should not intervene; and (2) the practice of sexual harassment is so prevalent that if courts became involved they would be flooded with complaints, many of which might be false or trivial.

In *Corne* v. *Bausch and Lomb, Inc.,* two female clerical workers sued for a violation of their civil rights based on sex discrimination. As a result of the offensive and unwelcome sexual liberties their male supervisor had taken with them, these two women were forced to resign their positions. In dismissing their complaint, the court gave several reasons, the chief of which was that sexual harassment is a "personal proclivity, peculiarity, or mannerism," which employers cannot be expected to extirpate in their employees.[31] Said the court, "The only sure way an employer could avoid such charges would be to have employees who were asexual."[32] Incidentally, the trial judge found unimaginable precisely what Margaret Mead has encouraged; namely, that society establish a sexual taboo in the workplace (and by parity of reasoning, in the academy). Flatly stated, Mead's incest taboo asserts that "You don't make passes at or sleep with the people you work with."[33]

Although many feminists think Mead's asexual approach is too drastic, it gains strength in view of *Miller* v. *Bank of America.* In this case the court dismissed the complaint of a female bank worker who was fired when she refused to be "sexually cooperative" with her male supervisor. The court concluded that "The attraction of males to females and females to males is a natural sex phenomenon and it is probable that this attraction plays at least a subtle part in most personnel decisions. Such being the case, it would seem wise for the courts to refrain from delving into these matters."[34] This decision is particularly distressing not only because it conflates sexual attraction (a desirable social phenomenon) with sexual harassment (an undesirable social phenomenon), but because it suggests that unwanted manhandling is something that

"big girls" must accept unless the company that employs their harassers *explicitly* endorses such hanky panky as a matter of policy (or some sort of fringe benefit for male employees).

That the courts have had trouble taking sexual harassment seriously as well as distinguishing between sexual attraction and sexual harassment is even more apparent in a case that followed *Miller.* In *Tomkins* v. *Public Service Electric and Gas Co.,* the court dismissed Tomkins's complaint, commenting that a sexually motivated assault that takes place in a "corporate corridor" is no more the concern of Title VII than a sexually motivated assault that takes place in a "back alley."[35] Title VII does not address the labyrinthine issue of sexual desires, and were the courts to encourage women to sue male co-workers and employees whose sexual attentions they had tired of, "an invitation to dinner could become an invitation to a federal lawsuit, if some harmonious relationship turned sour at a later time."[36] This court decision supposes that vindictive women would sue their male subordinates on trumped-up charges; similarly, hysterical or hypersensitive women would sue their male superordinates for the most trivial of reasons.

Fortunately, not all courts are as benighted as those that ruled in *Corne, Miller,* and *Tomkins.* In *Barnes* v. *Train (Costle),* the Washington, D.C., District Court originally found against the plaintiff, a woman who was first denied promotion and then fired for having refused the sexual advances of her supervisor. Ironically, the woman's supervisor was none other than the director of the Environmental Protection Agency's Equal Employment Opportunities Division. The suit was initially rejected on the grounds that sexual harassment does not constitute sex discrimination. The court contended that the woman plaintiff had been denied promotion not because of her sex, but because of her refusal to accede to the director's sexual demands. Conceding that the supervisor's behavior may have been inexcusable, the court nonetheless insisted that the behavior did not constitute an "arbitrary barrier to continued employment based on plaintiff's sex."[37] On appeal, the D.C. circuit court reversed, declaring that discrimination *was* involved, since the declined invitation had been issued only because the plaintiff was a woman. Said Judge Robinson for the court:

> But for her womanhood, from aught that appears, her participation in sexual activity would never have been solicited. To say, then, that she was victimized in her employment simply because she declined the invitation is to ignore the asserted fact that she was invited only because she was a woman subordinate to the inviter in the hierarchy of agency personnel. Put another way, she became the target of her superior's sexual desires because she was a woman, and was asked to bow to his demands as the price for holding her job.[38]

As a result of this decision, the courts now seem prepared to find sex-based discrimination in the workplace.

In the same way that Title VII is an available remedy for sexually harassed working women, Title IX (1972 Education Amendments) is an available remedy for sexually harassed students. With the exception of the still-pending *Alexander* v. *Yale* case, in which five women students and a male assistant professor filed a class-action suit, contending that male faculty members had engaged in sexually offensive conversations and behavior resulting in a multitude of harms, the courts have not, as yet, handled Title IX cases.[39] However, should such cases be generated and processed, they will probably follow Title VII precedents. Such litigations explicitly promise to reveal the limits of antidiscrimination law as it has developed so far. In handling the grievances of working women and also of female students (who are sexually harassed more frequently by their fellow students than by their male professors), the courts will have to confront squarely the problem of peer-on-peer sexual harassment, a type of harassment that they have already encountered in *Continental Can Co.* v. *Minnesota*.[40] In this case, the Minnesota Supreme Court extended employer liability beyond the actions of supervisory personnel to those of co-workers. To the degree that *Continental Can Co.* sets a precedent for other jurisdictions, it requires the courts to rethink the three major conditions for discriminatory sexual harassment outlined in *Barnes*. There the court ruled that sex-based discrimination may be found only (1) when the

victims of sexual harassment are of only one sex; (2) when the harasser is in a position to affect the terms or conditions of the victim's employment; and (3) when the harassment has a verifiably adverse impact on the victim (that is, it is not trivial).

Discriminatory Sexual Harassment: A Doctrinal Analysis

The first major condition for discriminatory sexual harassment is that it does not exist unless *only women* or *only men* are being harassed by a particular supervisor or professor. Arguably, neither Title VII nor Title IX prohibits a bisexual male supervisor/professor from sexually harassing his employees/students—provided that he harasses men as well as women.

1. *The Disparate Treatment Approach:* Regarding Title VII, sexual harassment is discriminatory when a male supervisor, for example, sexually pursues a woman simply because she is a woman, pawing and patting her when there is nothing except her sexuality to separate her from similarly situated male employees. Likewise, it is discriminatory when a female supervisor sexually pursues a man simply because he is a man, coming on to him when there is nothing except his sexuality to separate him from similarly situated female employees. Much the same could be said about male homosexual or lesbian supervisors with the necessary adjustments.

   The problem with the "disparate-treatment" approach is that only a fraction of women/men present in an employment situation is likely to be victimized by any particular incident of sexual harassment. As a result, there will be a tendency to detach the incident from the group referent necessary to establish a case under Title VII. This is precisely what happened in the cases preceding *Barnes* v. *Costle*. In these cases the courts suggested that the female employees had been singled out for sexual attention not so much because they were members of the gender group women, but either because of their unique personal characteristics, such as red hair, or because of their sex-specific characteristics, such as large breasts. (A sex-specific characteristic is one that is not shared by both genders and which is possessed by only a subset of the gender class in question.) Since there is no sex discrimination unless a plaintiff can show that her personal injury contains a sufficient gender referent, a red-headed, large-breasted, sexually harassed woman employee must be able to explain why her employer has not harassed similarly situated blond, flat-chested women, if all he was interested in was *a woman* and not a specific kind of woman with red hair and large breasts. Supposedly, if she cannot explain this, she does not have cause to invoke Title VII, although she may have grounds for an assault or battery tort action.

But all this seems rather ludicrous. The sexually harassed red-haired or large-breasted woman does have an explanation for her employer's conduct: He would not be sexually harassing her were she a man or were she her employer's boss. In other words, when a woman invokes Title VII rather than slapping her harasser with an assault or battery suit, she wants to stress that had she not been a female employee in a subordinate position she would not have been sexually harassed.

Implicit in this argument is the suggestion that harassment is not an expression of sexual lust, but a show of power. Contrary to the *Tomkins* court, there is a difference, at least of degree, between an incident of sexual harassment that occurs in a "corporate corridor" and one that occurs in a "back alley." An employer has control over one's life in a way that a stranger does not. And when a company tolerates the sexual harassment of one female employee, it makes an implicit statement to all female employees, telling them that their merits are to be measured not in terms of their skills or job performance, but in terms of their sexual attractiveness and compliance. In short, when a heterosexual male employer harasses only one female employee, he not only treats her disparately but also affects her reference group disparately.

2. *The Disparate-Impact Approach:* According to the "disparate-impact" approach to discriminatory sexual harassment, the motivating impetus for harassment is indeed sexuality (whether male or female), which results in discrimination "only when conjoined with social traditions of male heterosexual predominance in academic and employment hierarchies."[41] Therefore, this approach suggests that when an individual male employee is sexually harassed by a female employer, the discrimination he experiences is of the disparate-treatment rather than the disparate-impact variety. Given the way society is still structured, men are less likely than women to become fearful as a group when one of their number is sexually harassed by an employer of the opposite sex.

3. *Comparing the Disparate-Treatment and Disparate-Impact Approaches:* Regarding women, the disparate-impact approach to discriminatory sexual harassment seems more serviceable and promising than the disparate-treatment approach. Because the disparate-impact approach focuses on structural considerations (women's general position in society), it reminds the courts that women have yet to achieve parity with men either in the workplace or in the academy. In the past, the courts were either not served this reminder or they chose to ignore it. More recently, the courts have taken off their blinders. Increasingly, they are realizing that sexual harassment is a serious problem for many working and learning women. For example, the female worker may find herself at the mercy of her male supervisor, who, in an attempt to avoid liability and follow the letter of his company's official antiharassment policy, may not discharge or demote her, but may instead make working conditions so intolerable for her that she will "voluntarily" resign. Fortunately, the courts have come to see these "voluntary" resignations for what they are: "constructive discharges."

As a result of such realizations, the courts are taking a stronger line with respect to those institutions that fail to protect their employees from even the more subtle forms of adverse consequences attendant upon discriminatory sexual harassment: the assignment of undesirable work, close surveillance of performance, failure to enlist co-worker cooperation where necessary, unwillingness to provide adequate training, and failure to release recommendations for promotion. Despite a history of vacillation, the courts now seem prepared to hold employers liable for all acts of sexual harassment perpetrated by their employees, "regardless of whether the employer knew or should have known of their occurrence" except sexual harassment by co-workers.[42] In other words, if Tilly is sexually harassed by her foreman, then the foreman's employer is liable for his actions. It matters not that the employer did not know, or should not have been expected to know, what his foreman was doing. The employer is strictly liable. In contrast, if Tilly is harassed by her co-worker Joe, then the employer must have *actual* or constructive knowledge of Joe's misbehavior in order to be liable for it.

This last point is worth developing because most sexual harassment occurs between peers. There is no reason to view such sexual harassment as discriminatory, however offensive it may be, unless an employer (such as a corporation or a university) is understood to tolerate, endorse, or condone it. By failing to sanction the sexually-harassing conduct of its nonmanagerial and nonsupervisory employees, the employer lets them poison the work atmosphere. If the men on the assembly line are making passes at Rosy the Riveter and Betty the Bolter, and the employer, Cast Iron Works, does nothing to stop them, even though its managers and supervisors either know or should know what is going on, then Cast Iron Works is liable for their misbehavior where the other tests of liability under Title VII are met. Similarly, if the fraternity boys are sexually harassing members of the Feminist Alliance and the university does nothing to stop them, even though its deans and professors either know or should know what is going on, then the university is liable for their misbehavior when the other tests of liability under Title IX are met.

Extralegal Remedies

The current trend of the courts is to hold employers (corporations or universities) responsible for what goes on in the workplace or in the academy. In fact, Title IX already requires universities to adopt and publish grievance procedures providing for prompt and equitable resolution of student complaints of sexual harassment. Because sexual harassment has been kept in the closets of colleges and universities for many years, most grievance procedures are not capable of providing prompt and equitable resolution of student complaints. In the past, students have complained about members of the faculty or school who have harassed them, and some of this harassment has been explicitly sexual; however, quite a bit of it has been so-called gender harassment.

Gender harassment is related to sexual harassment as genus is to species: Sexual harassment is a form of gender harassment. Catharine MacKinnon comments "Gender *is* a power division and sexuality is one sphere of its expression. One thing wrong with sexual harassment . . . is that it eroticizes women's subordination. It acts out and deepens the powerlessness of women as a gender, *as women*."[43] Whereas gender harassment is a relatively abstract way to remind women that their gender role is one of subordination, sexual harassment is an extremely concrete way to remind women that their subordination as a gender is intimately tied to their sexuality, in particular to their reproductive capacities and in general to their bodily contours.

Examples of verbal sexual harassment include those comments (in this case, written comments) to which female coal miners were subjected at the Shoemaker Mine in the late 1970s. Because women had never worked in the mine before, they were, from the moment they appeared on the scene, scrutinized by male eyes. Although the tension between the female and male coal miners was considerable, it was bearable until a rash of graffiti appeared on the mine walls. The graffiti focused on the women's physical characteristics. For example, one women who had small breasts was called "inverted nipples," and another woman who supposedly had protruding lower vaginal lips was called the "low-lip express."[44] Subjected to such offensive social commentary on this and other occasions, the female miners found it increasingly difficult to maintain their sense of self-respect, and their personal and professional lives began to deteriorate.

In contrast to these examples of verbal sexual harassment stand more sanitized but not necessarily less devastating examples of verbal gender harassment. Unlike instances of verbal sexual harassment that focus on women's bodies, these latter comments, illustrations, and jokes call attention to women's gender traits and roles. It is interesting that a gender harasser may describe female gender traits and roles either in negative terms (women are irrational, hysterical, defective) or in seemingly positive terms (women are nurturing, self-sacrifing, closer to nature). In both cases, however, the gender harasser will add credence to the "*kinder, kirche, kuche*" theory of womanhood, according to which women's biology and psychology naturally suit them for bearing and raising children, praying in church, and cooking.

Although women are routinely subjected to gender harassment, society as a whole remains unconvinced that female students, for example, should take umbrage when their professors gender harass them. Nonetheless, given the educational mission of academic institutions, and the fact that women students may be more vulnerable to their professors' sexist remarks ("Women can't do math") than their professors' sexual inneundos ("It's a joy having your body—oops! your *person*—in this class, Miss Jones"), Title IX should, and probably does, cover cases of gender harassment.

In this connection, it is important to note that Title VII has already covered several gender-harassment cases. Recently, for example, a woman named Ms. Bay, who was employed by EFCS (Executive Financial Counselling Serivce) in Philadelphia, won a successful sex-discrimination suit against her boss, Gordon Campbell. Although Mr. Campbell never sexually harassed Ms. Bay by calling attention to or touching her body in any way, he did gender harass her. On one occasion Mr. Campbell asked Ms. Bay whether her husband would "suffer for food and clean clothes while she was away on business trips." On other occasions he contacted clients, on his own initiative, to inquire whether they objected to dealing with a woman and to see what they thought of Ms. Bay, "although such evaluations had never been requested for a male member of the EFCS staff." On still another occasion he arranged a seminar training program for a male employee while providing no such training program for Ms. Bay, despite her requests and despite Mr. Campbell's private comments to his superiors that her seminar performance was weak and in need of improvement. After listening to the recounting of these and other incidents, the judge ruled that, although Ms. Bay quit, she was really fired because "any reasonable person would have reacted to the situation at EFCS much as she did."[45]

Realizing that liability for sexual harassment and gender harassment belong to them as well as to authorities in the workplace, academic deans and other college personnel have tried to handle student harassment complaints informally. Their attempts have not always been successful. Not wanting to make mountains out of molehills, and arguing that young women freqently "imagine" things, some college officials have downplayed student reports of gender and sexual harassment. Even where they have taken such reports seriously and acted upon them, they have tended to keep them quiet in the name of discretion, preferring to let things "cool off" or "work themselves out." As a result of the students' rights movement, students have pressed their respective colleges and universities to handle such matters in a more formal and public manner. Students have also become much more concerned about student-on-student sexual harassment, which is a very pervasive fact of campus life. Understandably, deans and professors, who have by and large abandoned their *in loco parentis* roles, fear to invade their students' privacy. Realizing that students who come from diverse backgrounds will, as a matter of course, experience some difficulty in adjusting to one another's sexual mores, they fear making an issue out of what may be nothing more than normal social adjustment. And even when college officials discern a problem on campus, they resist setting up quasi-legal procedures to handle it. Predictably, deans and professors tend to argue that the way to handle sensitive problems such as sexual harassment is through educational forums rather than litigation.

Indeed, education is needed. Despite the breakdown of many sexual stereotypes, the macho ideal of the strong man lives on, as does the ideal of the vulnerable female. In large measure, this fact explains the growing incidence of "date-rape" on campuses. Crossed signals and mixed messages characterize many student sexual relations. Says one man:

> I get told "no," . . . and I keep going. I guess if someone said, "Look, sorry, I thought I wanted to, but I changed my mind, no way!" I'd listen, but if we're lying on the bed and she puts her little hands up in front of her chest and says, "Oh, please, no, I'm not sure about this," I ignore it. Nobody complains afterward.[46]

Women have to learn to say no, and men have to learn to take a *no* at face value. Moreover, women have to stop blaming themselves when men sexually harass them. This may be particularly difficult for a young woman to do. She may not have met enough different types of men to realize that it's not always something about her or her body that turns a man on, but something about his need to assert himself. Arguably, the more secure a man is about his masculinity, the less need he will have to harass women sexually or otherwise. Failing to understand this, a young woman may berate herself for her harasser's conduct. She may punish herself for being sexed by starving or neglecting her body. The epidemic of anorexia on many campuses is not unrelated to young women's fear of their own sexuality; and the unkempt appearance of some young women is often evidence of their attempt to kill the "temptress" in themselves.

Not surprisingly, educators want to help students escape these destructive prisons. But, as always, education is a long-term process. In the interim, college officials must set up and enforce internal grievance procedures to handle both faculty-on-student and student-on-student sexual harassment. Such quasi-legal remedies are not in opposition to a college's educational mission. On the contrary, they serve to remind the college community that it is susceptible to the same human foibles and power plays that characterize society in general.

Internal grievance procedures have been set up in many workplaces as well as at many academic institutions even though Title VII does not require employers to *maintain* grievance procedures. Since agreement has arisen in Title VII sexual harassment cases that there is no cause for judicial action *if* the employer takes prompt and remedial action upon acquiring knowledge of an incident, prudent employers have decided to set up mechanisms that can facilitate quick and corrective action. Unfortunately, these internal grievance procedures can be subverted. Company officials can convince all but the most determined of women that it is in her best interest to keep things quiet. One government official, who was interviewed by Constance Backhouse and Leah Cohen, opined that women should avoid both internal grievance procedures and complaints made directly to a personnel manager or management:

> The personnel director will most likely go to the sexual harasser and have a quiet little chat and a good laugh and express any number of the following statements:
> She brought it on herself.
> She can take care of herself.
> She was obviously willing.
> She is vindictive, as a result of a love affair gone sour.
> In fact, this is an isolated incident, not a serious problem.
> She is a troublemaker.[47]

This official went on to add that, if at all possible, the sexually harassed woman should either start looking for another job—"A woman is in real jeopardy if she can't get along in government. Who will hire you in private industry, if you are fired by the government?"—or if this is not a viable option, she should start looking for a "tough feminist lawyer" who will take the case as a "personal challenge."[48]

Conclusion

Sexual harassment is a phenomenon deeply rooted in the sexist assumptions that women can turn men "on" or "off" at will, and that sexual harassment is nothing more serious than old-fashioned flirtation. As such, it clearly must be approached on social and cultural as well as legal levels. However, because of its intangible or blurry-edged nature, sexual harassment often seems to be a problem with which the law, in its insistence on clear definitions and consistent guidelines, does not seem best suited to deal. The broad concept of institutional liability, which encourages the development of internal grievance procedures and internal education programs, may thus be the ideal way of confronting and remedying cases of sexual harassment. But the ideal is not always realized, and women—especially women workers and students—find themselves without effective remedies, short of quitting their jobs or leaving school. As Catharine MacKinnon has noted, the sexual subordination of women interacts with other forms of social power that men have over women. To be precise: "Economic power is to sexual harassment as physical force is to rape."[49] And regarding Title IX, intellectual power is to gender harassment on the campus as economic power is to gender or sexual harassment in the workplace as physical force is to rape anywhere. Rape and harassment are abuses of power as well as expressions of male sexuality. The power that makes rape or harassment effective derives from the superior position that the rapist or harasser holds by virtue of his social position.

As in the past, men remain powerful today. Their power is currently derived not so much from their brawn or their brains as from the fact that the major institutions of society—law, education, medicine, government, business, and science—are still largely controlled by them. Only when these institutions, for whatever reasons, begin to evolve in ways that allow women full access to them will the balance of power between men and women equalize. Fortunately, this institutional evolution is already in process.

In particular, the law is being tailored to fit women's as well as men's needs. Avenues of legal action against sexual harassers are both a powerful educational tool and an important means for women to assert and protect their rights to personal respect and self-determination, especially in the workplace and in the academy, while they wait for those rights to be accepted into the canon of cultural assumptions.

Faced with the possibility of legal consequences, men may be forced to reconsider their assumptions about women, employers may be forced to recognize their workers as workers rather than sexually exploitable conveniences, and institutes of higher education may be forced to extend their promise of an environment supportive rather than inhibitive of intellectual growth to female students. Once this happens, the incidences of gender harassment, especially its sexual forms, are likely to decrease. Where neither men nor women have superior power as a group, there is no need to use "sexuality" as a cruel weapon, reminding the powerless just how limited their options are.

Notes

1. A. Press et al., "Abusing Sex at the Office," *Newsweek*, March 10, 1980, p. 81.

2. Andrea Medea and Kathleeen Thompson, *Against Rape* (New York: Farrar, Straus & Giroux, 1974), p. 50.

3. Constance Backhouse and Leah Cohen, *Sexual Harassment on the Job* (Englewood Cliffs, N.J.: Prentice-Hall, 1982), p. 34.

4. Ibid., pp. 38–39.

5. Ibid., pp. 39–40.

6. John C. Hughes and Larry May, "Sexual Harassment," *Social Theory and Practice* 6 (Fall 1980): 251.

7. Ibid., p. 252.

8. Ibid.

9. Ibid.

10. Ibid., p. 249; cf. Michael Bayles, "Coercive

Offers and Public Benefits," *The Personalist* 55 (Spring 1974): 142–43.

11. Victoria Balfour, "Harassment at Movies: Complaints Rare," *New York Times,* November 17, 1982, p. C24.

12. Ibid.

13. Backhouse and Cohen, *Sexual Harassment on the Job,* p. 101.

14. Ibid.

15. Ibid., p. 103.

16. Frank J. Till, *Sexual Harassment: A Report on the Sexual Harassment of Students* (Washington, D.C.: National Advisory Council on Women's Educational Programs, 1980), pt. II, p. 13.

17. Ibid.

18. Ibid.

19. Catharine MacKinnon, *Sexual Harassment of Working Women* (New Haven, Conn.: Yale University Press, 1979), pp. 165–66.

20. Ibid., p. 166.

21. Ibid.

22. Ibid., p. 167.

23. *Samms* v. *Eccles* (1961), in Wright I. Linden, *Canadian Tort Law,* 6th ed. (Toronto: Butterworths, 1975), pp. 52–54.

24. Ibid.

25. MacKinnon, *Sexual Harassment of Working Women,* p. 171.

26. Ibid., p. 172.

27. 390 F. Supp. 161 (1975), U.S. Dist. Ct., D. Arizona.

28. 418 F. Supp. 233 (1976), U.S. Dist. Ct., N.D. California.

29. 422 F. Supp. 553 (1976), U.S. Dist. Ct., New Jersey.

30. 561 F. 2nd. 983 (1977), U.S. Ct. of Appeals, D.C. Circuit.

31. Backhouse and Cohen, *Sexual Harassment on the Job,* p. 119.

32. Ibid.

33. Margaret Mead, "A Proposal: We Need Taboos on Sex at Work," *Redbook,* April 1978, p. 31.

34. *Miller* v. *Bank of America,* 418 F. Supp. 233 (1976), U.S. Dist. Ct., N.D. California.

35. Backhouse and Cohen, *Sexual Harassment on the Job,* p. 121.

36. Ibid., p. 122.

37. *Barnes* v. *Train (Costle),* 13 FEP Cases 123, 124 (D.D.C. 1974).

38. *Barnes* v. *Costle,* 561 F. 2d at 992, n. 68 (D.C. Cir. 1977).

39. *Alexander et al.* v. *Yale University,* 459 F. Supp. 1 (D. Conn. 1977).

40. *Continental Can Co.* v. *Minnesota* (Minn. S.C. 1980).

41. Ibid., pp. 260–61.

42. Till, *Sexual Harassment,* pt. II, p. 9.

43. MacKinnon, *Sexual Harassment of Working Women,* pp. 220–21.

44. Raymond M. Lane, "A Man's World: An Update on Sexual Harassment," *The Village Voice,* December 16, 1981, p. 20.

45. *Philadelphia Inquirer,* September 9, 1982, p. 1A.

46. Karen Barrett, "Sex on a Saturday Night," *Ms.,* September 1982, p. 50.

47. Backhouse and Cohen, *Sexual Harassment on the Job,* p. 72.

48. Ibid.

49. MacKinnon, *Sexual Harassment of Working Women,* pp. 217–18.

Study Questions

1. Why might one call sexual harassment a *women's* issue as opposed to a *feminist* issue? Does Tong agree with that characterization?

2. Why and how do feminists distinguish between coercive and noncoercive sexual harassment? What tests can be applied to tell whether coercion has taken place?

3. Consider the case of the "mediocre woman graduate student." How does Bayles argue that such a case is *not* sexual harassment?

How does Tong reply? Do you agree with her reply?

4. Why are criminal proceedings rarely employed in sexual harassment cases?

5. What is tort law? How does it differ from criminal law? Why is tort law possibly a more adequate avenue of attack against sexual harassment? In what way is the tort approach problematic?

6. Why do feminists think that the tort approach needs to be supplemented by an antidiscrimination approach? What obstacles did the view initially face in the courts? What case proved a turning point? Why?

Pornography, Oppression, and Freedom: A Closer Look

Helen E. Longino

A question which is often asked at the beginning of any discussion on pornography is "How do you define it?" The answer is difficult. A good clear definition of pornography has eluded everyone. Twenty years ago, the United States Supreme Court was defining pornography as material which "taken as a whole appeals to prurient interest." Ten years later, Justice Potter Stewart said, "I can't define it, but I know it when I see it." Today federal law states that the definition of pornography is to be left up to the individual communities to decide. This, of course, has totally confused the country. What seems to be acceptable in San Francisco may be appalling in a small town, and communities themselves are having trouble deciding what they think is "patently offensive" and without "serious literary, artistic, political or scientific value." Feminists have a further objection to this definition: If pornography does not offend local community standards, we say, then something is wrong because it should!

In this paper, . . . feminist philosopher Helen Longino puts forth a serious definition of pornography which we believe withstands a rigorous and critical examination and which may prove helpful to teachers, doctors, laypeople, and jurists—anyone, in fact, who is interested in a good working definition of the term. She goes on to apply this definition to the question of pornography and the First Amendment.

Introduction

The much-touted sexual revolution of the 1960's and 1970's not only freed various modes of sexual behavior from the constraints of social disapproval, but also made possible a flood of pornographic material. According to figures

From Laura Lederer, ed., *Take Back the Night* (New York: Morrow, 1980), pp. 26–39. Reprinted by permission of Helen E. Longino. (Notes deleted.)

provided by WAVPM (Women Against Violence in Pornography and Media), the number of pornographic magazines available at newsstands has grown from zero in 1953 to forty in 1977, while sales of pornographic films in Los Angeles alone have grown from $15 million in 1969 to $85 million in 1976.

Traditionally, pornography was condemned as immoral because it presented sexually explicit material in a manner designed to appeal to "prurient interests" or a "morbid" interest in nudity and sexuality, material which furthermore lacked any redeeming social value and which exceeded "customary limits of candor." While these phrases, taken from a definition of "obscenity" proposed in the 1954 American Law Institute's *Model Penal Code,* require some criteria of application to eliminate vagueness, it seems that what is objectionable is the explicit description or representation of bodily parts or sexual behavior for the purpose of inducing sexual stimulation or pleasure on the part of the reader or viewer. This kind of objection is part of a sexual ethic that subordinates sex to procreation and condemns all sexual interactions outside of legitimized marriage. It is this code which was the primary target of the sexual revolutionaries in the 1960's, and which has given way in many areas to more open standards of sexual behavior.

One of the beneficial results of the sexual revolution has been a growing acceptance of the distinction between questions of sexual mores and questions of morality. This distinction underlies the old slogan, "Make love, not war," and takes harm to others as the defining characteristic of immorality. What is immoral is behavior which causes injury to or violation of another person or people. Such injury may be physical or it may be psychological. To cause pain to another, to lie to another, to hinder another in the exercise of her or his rights, to exploit another, to degrade another, to misrepresent and slander another are instances of immoral behavior. Masturbation or engaging voluntarily in sexual intercourse with another consenting adult of the same or the other sex, as long as neither injury nor violation of either individual or another is involved, are not immoral. Some sexual behavior is morally objectionable, but not because of its sexual character. Thus, adultery is immoral not because it involves sexual intercourse with someone to whom one is not legally married, but because it involves breaking a promise (of sexual and emotional fidelity to one's spouse). Sadistic, abusive, or forced sex is immoral because it injures and violates another.

The detachment of sexual chastity from moral virtue implies that we cannot condemn forms of sexual behavior merely because they strike us as distasteful or subversive of the Protestant work ethic, or because they depart from standards of behavior we have individually

adopted. It has thus seemed to imply that no matter how offensive we might find pornography, we must tolerate it in the name of freedom from illegitimate repression. I wish to argue that this is not so, that pornography is immoral because it is harmful to people.

What Is Pornography?

I define pornography as *verbal or pictorial explicit representations of sexual behavior that,* in the words of the Commission on Obscenity and Pornography, *have as a distinguishing characteristic "the degrading and demeaning portrayal of the role and status of the human female . . . as a mere sexual object to be exploited and manipulated sexually."* In pornographic books, magazines, and films, women are represented as passive and as slavishly dependent upon men. The role of female characters is limited to the provision of sexual services to men. To the extent that women's sexual pleasure is represented at all, it is subordinated to that of men and is never an end in itself as is the sexual pleasure of men. What pleases women is the use of their bodies to satisfy male desires. While the sexual objectification of women is common to all pornography, women are the recipients of even worse treatment in violent pornography, in which women characters are killed, tortured, gang-raped, mutilated, bound, and otherwise abused, as a means of providing sexual stimulation or pleasure to the male characters. It is this development which has attracted the attention of feminists and been the stimulus to an analysis of pornography in general.

Not all sexually explicit material is pornography, nor is all material which contains representations of sexual abuse and degradation pornography.

A representation of a sexual encounter between adult persons which is characterized by mutual respect is, once we have disentangled sexuality and morality, not morally objectionable. Such a representation would be one in which the desires and experiences of each participant were regarded by the other participants as having a validity and a subjective importance equal to those of the individual's own desires and experiences. In such an encounter, each participant acknowledges the other participant's basic human dignity and personhood. Similarly, a representation of a nude human body (in whole or in part) in such a manner that the person shown maintains self-respect—e.g., is not portrayed in a degrading position— would not be morally objectionable. The educational films of the National Sex Forum, as well as a certain amount of erotic literature and art, fall into this category. While some erotic materials are beyond the standards of modesty held by some individuals, they are not for this reason immoral.

A representation of a sexual encounter which is not characterized by mutual respect, in which at least one of the parties is treated in a manner beneath her or his dignity as a human being, is no longer simple erotica. That a representation is of degrading behavior does not in itself, however, make it pornographic. Whether or not it is pornographic is a function of contextual features. Books and films may contain descriptions or representations of a rape in order to explore the consequences of such an assault upon its victim. What is being shown is abusive or degrading behavior which attempts to deny the humanity and dignity of the person assaulted, yet the context surrounding the representation, through its exploration of the consequences of the act, acknowledges and reaffirms her dignity. Such books and films, far from being pornographic, are (or can be) highly moral, and fall into the category of moral realism.

What makes a work a work of pornography, then, is not simply its representation of degrading and abusive sexual encounters, but its implicit, if not explicit, approval and recommendation of sexual behavior that is immoral, i.e., that physically or psychologically violates the personhood of one of the participants. Pornography, then, is verbal or pictorial material which represents or describes sexual behavior that is degrading or abusive to one or more of the participants *in such a way as to endorse the degradation.* The participants so treated in virtually all heterosexual pornography are women or children, so heterosexual pornography is, as a matter of fact, material which endorses sexual behavior that is degrading and/or abusive to women and children. As I use the term "sexual behavior," this includes sexual encounters between persons, behavior which produces sexual stimulation or pleasure for one of the participants, and behavior which is preparatory to or invites sexual activity. Behavior that is degrading or abusive includes physical harm or abuse, and physical or psychological coercion. In addition, behavior which ignores or devalues the real interests, desires, and experiences of one or more participants in any way is degrading. Finally, that a person has chosen or consented to be harmed, abused, or subjected to coercion does not alter the degrading character of such behavior.

Pornography communicates its endorsement of the behavior it represents by various features of the pornographic context: the degradation of the female characters it represented as providing pleasure to the participant males and, even worse, to the participant females, and there is no suggestion that this sort of treatment of others is inappropriate to their status as human beings. These two features are together sufficient to constitute endorsement of the represented behavior. The contextual features which make material pornographic are intrinsic to the material. In addition to these, extrinsic features, such as the purpose for which the material is presented— i.e., the sexual arousal/pleasure/satisfaction of its (mostly) male consumers—or an accompanying text, may reinforce or make explicit the endorsement. Representations which in and of themselves do not show or endorse degrading behavior may be put into a pornographic context by juxtaposition with others that are degrading, or by a text which invites or recommends degrading behavior toward the subject represented. In such a case the whole complex—the series of representations or representations with text—is pornographic.

The distinction I have sketched is one that applies most clearly to sequential material—a verbal or pictorial (filmed) story—which represents an action and provides a temporal context for it. In showing the before and after, a narrator or film-maker has plenty of opportunity to acknowledge the dignity of the person violated or clearly to refuse to do so. It is somewhat more difficult to apply the distinction to single still representations. The contextual features cited above, however, are clearly present in still photographs or pictures that glamorize degradation and sexual violence. Phonograph album covers and advertisements offer some prime examples of such glamorization. Their representations of women in chains (the Ohio Players), or bound by ropes and black and blue (the Rolling Stones) are considered high-quality commercial "art" and glossily prettify the violence they represent. Since the standard function of prettification and glamorization is the communication of desirability, these albums and ads are communicating the desirability of violence against women. Representations of women bound or chained, particularly those of women bound in such a way as to make their breasts, or genital or anal areas vulnerable to any passerby, endorse the scene they represent by the absence of any indication that this treatment of women is in any way inappropriate.

To summarize: Pornography is not just the explicit representation or description of sexual behavior, nor even the explicit representation or description of sexual behavior which is degrading and/or abusive to women. Rather, it is material that explicitly represents or describes degrading and abusive sexual behavior so as to endorse and/or recommend the behavior as described. The contextual features, moreover, which communicate such endorsement are intrinsic to the material; that is, they are features whose removal or alteration would change the representation or description.

This account of pornography is underlined by the etymology and original meaning of the word "pornography." *The Oxford English Dictionary* defines pornography as "Description of the life, manners, etc., of prostitutes and their patrons [from πόρνη (porne) meaning "harlot" and γράφειν (graphein) meaning "to write"]; hence the expression or suggestion of obscene or unchaste subjects in literature or art."

Let us consider the first part of the definition for a moment. In the transactions between prostitutes and their clients, prostitutes are paid, directly or indirectly, for the use of their bodies by the client for sexual pleasure.[1] Tradi-

tionally males have obtained from female prostitutes what they could not or did not wish to get from their wives or women friends, who, because of the character of their relation to the male, must be accorded some measure of human respect. While there are limits to what treatment is seen as appropriate toward women as wives or women friends, the prostitute as prostitute exists to provide sexual pleasure to males. The female characters of contemporary pornography also exist to provide pleasure to males, but in the pornographic context no pretense is made to regard them as parties to a contractual arrangement. Rather, the anonymity of these characters makes each one Everywoman, thus suggesting not only that all women are appropriate subjects for the enactment of the most bizarre and demeaning male sexual fantasies, but also that this is their primary purpose. The recent escalation of violence in pornography—the presentation of scenes of bondage, rape, and torture of women for the sexual stimulation of the male characters or male viewers—while shocking in itself, is from this point of view merely a more vicious extension of a genre whose success depends on treating women in a manner beneath their dignity as human beings.

Pornography: Lies and Violence against Women

What is wrong with pornography, then, is its degrading and dehumanizing portrayal of women (and *not* its sexual content). Pornography, by its very nature, requires that women be subordinate to men and mere instruments for the fulfillment of male fantasies. To accomplish this, pornography must lie. Pornography lies when it says that our sexual life is or ought to be subordinate to the service of men, that our pleasure consists in pleasing men and not ourselves, that we are depraved, that we are fit subjects for rape, bondage, torture, and murder. Pornography lies explicitly about women's sexuality, and through such lies fosters more lies about our humanity, our dignity, and our personhood.

Moreover, since nothing is alleged to justify the treatment of the female characters of pornography save their womanhood, pornography depicts all women as fit objects of violence by virtue of their sex alone. Because it is simply being female that, in the pornographic vision, justifies being violated, the lies of pornography are lies about all women. Each work of pornography is on its own libelous and defamatory, yet gains power through being reinforced by every other pornographic work. The sheer number of pornographic productions expands the moral issue to include not only assessing the morality or immorality of individual works, but also the meaning and force of the mass production of pornography.

The pornographic view of women is thoroughly entrenched in a booming portion of the publishing, film, and recording industries, reaching and affecting not only all who look to such sources for sexual stimulation, but also those of us who are forced into an awareness of it as we peruse magazines at newsstands and record albums in record stores, as we check the entertainment sections of city newspapers, or even as we approach a counter to pay for groceries. It is not necessary to spend a great deal of time reading or viewing pornographic material to absorb its male-centered definition of women. No longer confined within plain brown wrappers, it jumps out from billboards that proclaim "Live X-rated Girls!" or "Angels in Pain" or "Hot and Wild," and from magazine covers displaying a woman's genital area being spread open to the viewer by her own fingers.[2] Thus, even men who do not frequent pornography shops and movie houses are supported in the sexist objectification of women by their environment. Women, too, are crippled by internalizing as self-images those that are presented to us by pornographers. Isolated from one another and with no source of support for an alternative view of female sexuality, we may not always find the strength to resist a message that dominates the common cultural media.

The entrenchment of pornography in our culture also gives it a significance quite beyond its explicit sexual messages. To suggest, as pornography does, that the primary purpose of women is to provide sexual pleasure to men is to deny that women are indepedently human or have a status equal to that of men. It is,

moreover, to deny our equality at one of the most intimate levels of human experience. This denial is especially powerful in a hierarchical, class society such as ours, in which individuals feel good about themselves by feeling superior to others. Men in our society have a vested interest in maintaining their belief in the inferiority of the female sex, so that no matter how oppressed and exploited by the society in which they live and work, they can feel that they are at least superior to someone or some category of individuals—a woman or women. Pornography, by presenting women as wanton, depraved, and made for the sexual use of men, caters directly to that interest.[3] The very intimate nature of sexuality which makes pornography so corrosive also protects it from explicit public discussion. The consequent lack of any explicit social disavowal of the pornographic image of women enables this image to continue fostering sexist attitudes even as the society publicly proclaims its (as yet timid) commitment to sexual equality.

In addition to finding a connection between the pornographic view of women and the denial to us of our full human rights, women are beginning to connect the consumption of pornography and committing rape and other acts of sexual violence against women. Contrary to the findings of the Commission of Obscenity and Pornography, a growing body of research is documenting (1) a correlation between exposure to representations of violence and the committing of violent acts generally, and (2) a correlation between exposure to pornographic materials and the committing of sexually abusive or violent acts against women. While more study is needed to establish precisely what the causal relations are, clearly so-called hard-core pornography is not innocent.

From "snuff" films and miserable magazines in pornographic stores to *Hustler,* to phonograph album covers and advertisements, to *Vogue,* pornography has come to occupy its own niche in the communications and entertainment media and to acquire a quasi-institutional character (signaled by the use of diminutives such as "porn" or "porno" to refer to pornographic material, as though such familiar naming could take the hurt out). Its acceptance by the mass media, whatever the motivation, means a cultural endorsement of its message.

As much as the materials themselves, the social tolerance of these degrading and distorted images of women in such quantities is harmful to us, since it indicates a general willingness to see women in ways incompatible with our fundamental human dignity and thus to justify treating us in those ways.[4] The tolerance of pornographic representations of the rape, bondage, and torture of women helps to create and maintain a climate more tolerant of the actual physical abuse of women.[5] The tendency on the part of the legal system to view the victim of a rape as responsible for the crime against her is but one manifestation of this.

In sum, pornography is injurious to women in at least three distinct ways:

1. Pornography, especially violent pornography, is implicated in the committing of crimes of violence against women.

2. Pornography is the vehicle for the dissemination of a deep and vicious lie about women. It is defamatory and libelous.

3. The diffusion of such a distorted view of women's nature in our society as it exists today supports sexist (i.e., male-centered) attitudes, and thus reinforces the oppression and exploitation of women.

Society's tolerance of pornography, especially pornography on the contemporary massive scale, reinforces each of these modes of injury. By not disavowing the lie, it supports the male-centered myth that women are inferior and subordinate creatures. Thus, it contributes to the maintenance of a climate tolerant of both psychological and physical violence against women.

Pornography and the Law

Congress shall make no law respecting the establishment of religion, or prohibiting the free exercise thereof; or abridging the freedom of speech, or of the press; or the right of the people peaceably to assemble, and to petition the Government for a redress of grievances.

—*First Amendment, Bill of Rights of the United States Constitution*

Pornography is clearly a threat to women. Each of the modes of injury cited above offers sufficient reason at least to consider proposals for the social and legal control of pornography. The almost universal response from progressives to such proposals is that constitutional guarantees of freedom of speech and privacy preclude recourse to law. While I am concerned about the erosion of constitutional rights and also think for many reasons that great caution must be exercised before undertaking a legal campaign against pornography, I find objections to such a campaign that are based on appeals to the First Amendment or to a right to privacy ultimately unconvincing.

Much of the defense of the pornographer's right to publish seems to assume that, while pornography may be tasteless and vulgar, it is basically an entertainment that harms no one but its consumers, who may at worst suffer from the debasement of their taste; and that therefore those who argue for its control are demanding an unjustifiable abridgment of the rights to freedom of speech of those who make and distribute pornographic materials and of the rights to privacy of their customers. The account of pornography given above shows that the assumptions of this position are false. Nevertheless, even some who acknowledge its harmful character feel that it is granted immunity from social control by the First Amendment, or that the harm that would ensue from its control outweighs the harm prevented by its control.

There are three ways of arguing that control of pornography is incompatible with adherence to constitutional rights. The first argument claims that regulating pornography involves an unjustifiable interference in the private lives of individuals. The second argument takes the First Amendment as a basic principle constitutive of our form of government, and claims that the production and distribution of pornographic material, as a form of speech, is an activity protected by that amendment. The third argument claims not that the pornographer's rights are violated, but that others' rights will be if controls against pornography are instituted.

The privacy argument is the easiest to dispose of. Since the open commerce in pornographic materials is an activity carried out in the public sphere, the publication and distribution of such materials, unlike their use by individuals, is not protected by rights to privacy. The distinction between the private consumption of pornographic material and the production and distribution of, or open commerce in, it is sometimes blurred by defenders of pornography. But I may entertain, in the privacy of my mind, defamatory opinions about another person, even though I may not broadcast them. So one might create without restraint—as long as no one were harmed in the course of preparing them—pornographic materials for one's personal use, but be restrained from reproducing and distributing them. In both cases what one is doing—in the privacy of one's mind or basement—may indeed be deplorable, but immune from legal proscription. Once the activity becomes public, however—i.e., once it involves others—it is no longer protected by the same rights that protect activities in the private sphere.[6]

In considering the second argument (that control of pornography, private or public, is wrong in principle), it seems important to determine whether we consider the right to freedom of speech to be absolute and unqualified. If it is, then obviously all speech, including pornography, is entitled to protection. But the right is, in the first place, not an unqualified right: There are several kinds of speech not protected by the First Amendment, including the incitement to violence in volatile circumstances, the solicitation of crimes, perjury and misrepresentation, slander, libel, and false advertising.[7] That there are forms of proscribed speech shows that we accept limitations on the right to freedom of speech if such speech, as do the forms listed, impinges on other rights. The manufacture and distribution of material which defames and threatens all members of a class by its recommendation of abusive and degrading behavior toward some members of that class simply in virtue of their membership in it seems a clear candidate for inclusion on the list. The right is therefore not an unqualified one.

Nor is it an absolute or fundamental right, underived from any other right: If it were there would not be exceptions or limitations. The first ten amendments were added to the Constitution as a way of guaranteeing the "blessings of liberty" mentioned in its preamble, to protect citizens against the unreasonable usurpation of power by the state. The specific rights mentioned in the First Amendment—those of religion, speech, assembly, press, petition—reflect the recent experiences of the makers of the Constitution under colonial government as well as a sense of what was and is required generally to secure liberty.

It may be objected that the right to freedom of speech is fundamental in that it is part of what we mean by liberty and not a right that is derivative from a right to liberty. In order to meet this objection, it is useful to consider a distinction explained by Ronald Dworkin in his book *Taking Rights Seriously*. As Dworkin points out, the word "liberty" is used in two distinct, if related, senses: as "license," i.e., the freedom from legal constraints to do as one pleases, in some contexts; and as "independence," i.e., "the status of a person as independent and equal rather than subservient," in others. Failure to distinguish between these senses in discussions of rights and freedoms is fatal to clarity and understanding.

If the right to free speech is understood as a partial explanation of what is meant by liberty, then liberty is perceived as license: The right to do as one pleases includes a right to speak as one pleases. But license is surely not a condition the First Amendment is designed to protect. We not only tolerate but require legal constraints on liberty as license when we enact laws against rape, murder, assault, theft, etc. If everyone did exactly as she or he pleased at any given time, we would have chaos if not lives, as Hobbes put it, that are "nasty, brutish, and short." We accept government to escape, not to protect, this condition.

If, on the other hand, by liberty is meant independence, then freedom of speech is not necessarily a part of liberty; rather, it is a means to it. The right to freedom of speech is not a fundamental, absolute right, but one derivative from, possessed in virtue of, the more basic right to independence. Taking this view of liberty requires providing arguments showing that the more specific rights we claim are necessary to guarantee our status as persons "independent and equal rather than subservient."

In the context of government, we understand independence to be the freedom of each individual to participate as an equal among equals in the determination of how she or he is to be governed. Freedom of speech in this context means that an individual may not only entertain beliefs concerning government privately, but may express them publicly. We express our opinions about taxes, disarmament, wars, social-welfare programs, the function of the police, civil rights, and so on. Our right to freedom of speech includes the right to criticize the government and to protest against various forms of injustice and the abuse of power. What we wish to protect is the free expression of ideas even when they are unpopular. What we do not always remember is that speech has functions other than the expression of ideas.

Regarding the relationship between a right to freedom of speech and the publication and distribution of pornographic materials, there are two points to be made. In the first place, the latter activity is hardly an exercise of the right to the free expression of ideas as understood above. In the second place, to the degree that the tolerance of material degrading to women supports and reinforces the attitude that women are not fit to participate as equals among equals in the political life of their communities, and that the prevalence of such an attitude effectively prevents women from so participating, the absolute and fundamental right of women to liberty (political independence) is violated.

This second argument against the suppression of pornographic material, then, rests on a premise that must be rejected, namely, that the right to freedom of speech is a right to utter anything one wants. It thus fails to show that the production and distribution of such material is an activity protected by the First Amendment. Furthermore, an examination of the issues involved leads to the conclusion that tolerance of this activity violates the rights of women to political independence.

The third argument (which expresses concern that curbs on pornography are the first step toward political censorship) runs into the same ambiguity that besets the arguments based on principle. These arguments generally have as an underlying assumption that the maximization of freedom is a worthy social goal. Control of pornography diminishes freedom—directly the freedom of pornographers, indirectly that of all of us. But again, what is meant by "freedom"? It cannot be that what is to be maximized is license—as the goal of a social group whose members probably have at least some incompatible interests, such a goal would be internally inconsistent. If, on the other hand, the maximization of political independence is the goal, then that is in no way enhanced by, and may be endangered by, the tolerance of pornography. To argue that the control of pornography would create a precedent for suppressing political speech is thus to confuse license with political independence. In addition, it ignores a crucial basis for the control of pornography, i.e., its character as libelous speech. The prohibition of such speech is justified by the need for protection from the injury (psychological as well as physical or economic) that results from libel. A very different kind of argument would be required to justify curtailing the right to speak our minds about the institutions which govern us. As long as such distinctions are insisted upon, there is little danger of the government's using the control of pornography as precedent for curtailing political speech.

In summary, neither as a matter of principle nor in the interests of maximizing liberty can it be supposed that there is an intrinsic right to manufacture and distribute pornographic material.

The only other conceivable source of protection for pornography would be a general right to do what we please as long as the rights of others are respected. Since the production and distribution of pornography violates the rights of women—to respect and to freedom from defamation, among others—this protection is not available.

Conclusion

I have defined pornography in such a way as to distinguish it from erotica and from moral realism, and have argued that it is defamatory and libelous toward women, that it condones crimes against women, and that it invites tolerance of the social, economic, and cultural oppression of women. The production and distribution of pornographic material is thus a social and moral wrong. Contrasting both the current volume of pornographic production and its growing infiltration of the communications media with the status of women in this culture makes clear the necessity for its control. Since the goal of controlling pornography does not conflict with constitutional rights, a common obstacle to action is removed.

Appeals for action against pornography are sometimes brushed aside with the claim that such action is a diversion from the primary task of feminists—the elimination of sexism and of sexual inequality. This approach focuses on the enjoyment rather than the manufacture of pornography, and sees it as merely a product of sexism which will disappear when the latter has been overcome and the sexes are socially and economically equal. Pornography cannot be separated from sexism in this way: Sexism is not just a set of attitudes regarding the inferiority of women but the behaviors and social and economic rules that manifest such attitudes. Both the manufacture and distribution of pornography and the enjoyment of it are instances of sexist behavior. The enjoyment of pornography on the part of individuals will presumably decline as such individuals begin to accord women their status as fully human. A cultural climate which tolerates the degrading representation of women is not a climate which facilitates the development of respect for women. Furthermore, the demand for pornography is stimulated not just by the sexism of individuals but by the pornography industry itself. Thus, both as a social phenomenon and in its effect on individuals, pornography, far from being a mere product, nourishes sexism. The campaign against it is an essential component of women's struggle for legal, economic, and social equality, one which requires the support of all feminists.[8]

Notes

1. In talking of prostitution here, I refer to the concept of, rather than the reality of prostitution. The same is true of my remarks about relationships between women and their husbands or men friends.

2. This was a full-color magazine cover seen in a rack at the check-out counter of a corner delicatessen.

3. Pornography thus becomes another tool of capitalism. One feature of some contemporary pornography—the use of Black and Asian women in both still photographs and films—exploits the racism as well as the sexism of its white consumers. For a discussion of the interplay between racism and sexism under capitalism as it relates to violent crimes against women, see Angela Y. Davis, "Rape, Racism, and the Capitalist Setting," *The Black Scholar*, Vol. 9, No. 7, April 1978.

4. This tolerance has a linguistic parallel in the growing acceptance and use of nonhuman nouns such as "chick," "bird," "filly," "fox," "doll," "babe," "skirt," etc., to refer to women, and of verbs of harm such as "fuck," "screw," "bang," to refer to sexual intercourse. See Robert Baker and Federick Elliston, " 'Pricks' and 'Chicks': A Plea for Persons," *Philosophy and Sex* (Buffalo, N.Y.: Prometheus Books, 1975).

5. This is supported by the fact that in Denmark the number of rapes committed has increased while the number of rapes reported to the authorities has decreased over the past twelve years. See *WAVPM Newspage*, Vol. II, No. 5, June, 1978, quoting M. Harry, "Denmark Today—The Causes and Effects of Sexual Liberty" (paper presented to The Responsible Society, London, England, 1976). See also Eysenck and Nias, *Sex, Violence and the Media* (New York: St. Martin's Press, 1978), pp. 120–124.

6. Thus, the right to use such materials in the privacy of one's home, which has been upheld by the United States Supreme Court (*Stanley* v. *Georgia*, 394 U.S. 557), does not

include the right to purchase them or to have them available in the commercial market. See also *Paris Adult Theater I* v. *Slaton*, 431 U.S. 49.

7. The Supreme Court has also traditionally included obscenity in this category. As not everyone agrees it should be included, since as defined by statutes, it is a highly vague concept, and since the grounds accepted by the Court for including it miss the point, I prefer to omit it from this list.

8. Many women helped me to develop and crystalize the ideas presented in this paper. I would especially like to thank Michele Farrell, Laura Lederer, Pamela Miller, and Dianne Romain for their comments in conversation and on the first written draft. Portions of this material were presented orally to members of the Society for Women in Philosophy and to participants in the workshops on "What Is Pornography?" at the Conference on Feminist Perspectives on Pornography, San Francisco, November 17, 18, and 19, 1978. Their discussion was invaluable in helping me to see problems and to clarify the ideas presented here.

Study Questions

1. According to Longino, what is one of the benefits of the sexual revolution? What does she think constitutes immorality?

2. How does Longino define "pornography"? How does her definition differ from the earlier traditional one?

3. According to Longino, how are women and children portrayed in pornography?

4. What does Longino mean when she says that "pornography communicates its endorsement of the behavior it represents by various features of the pornographic context?"

5. How does pornography lie? How, according to the author, do these lies serve men's purposes?

6. Longino considers three arguments that attempt to show that control of pornography is incompatible with adherence to constitutional rights. What are these arguments, and how does she respond to them?

Rape: The All-American Crime

Susan Griffin

I have never been free of the fear of rape. From a very early age I, like most women, have thought of rape as part of my natural environment—something to be feared and prayed against like fire or lightning. I never asked why men raped; I simply thought it one of the many mysteries of human nature.

I was, however, curious enough about the violent side of humanity to read every crime magazine I was able to ferret away from my grandfather. Each issue featured at least one "sex crime," with pictures of a victim, usually in

From *Ramparts*, September 1971, pp. 26–35. Reprinted by permission of Susan Griffin.

a pearl necklace, and of the ditch or the orchard where her body was found. I was never certain why the victims were always women, nor what the motives of the murderer were, but I did guess that the world was not a safe place for women. I observed that my grandmother was meticulous about locks, and quick to draw the shades before anyone removed so much as a shoe. I sensed that danger lurked outside.

At the age of eight, my suspicions were confirmed. My grandmother took me to the back of the house where the men wouldn't hear, and told me that strange men wanted to do harm to little girls. I learned not to walk on dark streets, not to talk to strangers, or get into strange cars, to lock doors, and to be modest. She never explained why a man would want to harm a little girl, and I never asked.

If I thought for a while that my grandmother's fears were imaginary, the illusion was brief. That year, on the way home from school, a schoolmate a few years older than I tried to rape me. Later, in an obscure aisle of the local library (while I was reading *Freddy the Pig*) I turned to discover a man exposing himself. Then, the friendly man around the corner was arrested for child molesting.

My initiation to sexuality was typical. Every woman has similar stories to tell—the first man who attacked her may have been a neighbor, a family friend, an uncle, her doctor, or perhaps her own father. And women who grow up in New York City always have tales about the subway.

But though rape and the fear of rape are a daily part of every woman's consciousness, the subject is so rarely discussed by that unofficial staff of male intellectuals (who write the books which study seemingly every other form of male activity) that one begins to suspect a conspiracy of silence. And indeed, the obscurity of rape in print exists in marked contrast to the frequency of rape in reality, for *forcible rape is the most frequently committed violent crime in America today*. The Federal Bureau of Investigation classes three crimes as violent: murder, aggravated assault and forcible rape. In 1968, 31,600 rapes were *reported*. According to the FBI and independent criminologists, however, to approach accuracy this figure must be multiplied by at least a factor of ten to compensate for the fact that most rapes are not reported; when these compensatory mathematics are used, there are more rapes committed than aggravated assaults and homicides.

When I asked Berkeley, California's Police Inspector in charge of rape investigation if he knew why men rape women, he replied that he had not spoken with "these people and delved into what really makes them tick, because that really isn't my job. . . ." However, when I asked him how a woman might prevent being raped, he was not so reticent, "I wouldn't advise any female to go walking around alone at night . . . and she should lock her car at all times." The Inspector illustrated his warning with a grisly story about a man who lay in wait for women in the back seats of their cars, while they were shopping in a local supermarket. This man eventually murdered one of his rape victims. "Always lock your car," the Inspector repeated, and then added, without a hint of irony, "Of course, you don't have to be paranoid about this type of thing."

The Inspector wondered why I wanted to write about rape. Like most men he did not understand the urgency of the topic, for, after all, men are not raped. But like most women I had spent considerable time speculating on the true nature of the rapist. When I was very young, my image of the "sexual offender" was a nightmarish amalgamation of the bogey man and Captain Hook: he wore a black cape, and he cackled. As I matured, so did my image of the rapist. Born into the psychoanalytical age, I tried to "understand" the rapist. Rape, I came to believe, was only one of many unfortunate evils produced by sexual repression. Reasoning by tautology, I concluded that any man who would rape a woman must be out of his mind.

Yet, though the theory that rapists are insane is a popular one, this belief has no basis in fact. According to Professor Menachem Amir's study of 646 rape cases in Philadelphia, *Patterns in Forcible Rape*, men who rape are not abnormal. Amir writes, "Studies indicate that sex offenders do not constitute a unique or psychopathological type; nor are they as a group invariably more disturbed than the control groups to which they are compared." Alan Taylor, a parole officer who has worked with rapists in the prison facilities at San Luis Obispo, California, stated the question in plainer language, "Those men were the most normal men there. They had a lot of hang-ups, but they were the same hang-ups as men walking out on the street."

Another canon in the apologetics of rape is that, if it were not for learned social controls, all men would rape. Rape is held to be natural behavior, and not to rape must be learned. But in truth rape is not universal to the human species. Moreover, studies of rape in our culture reveal that, far from being impulsive behavior, most rape is planned. Professor Amir's study reveals that in cases of group rape (the "gangbang" of masculine slang) 90 percent of the rapes were planned; in pair rapes, 83 percent of the rapes were planned; and in single rapes, 58 percent were planned. These figures should significantly discredit the image of the rapist as a man who is suddenly overcome by sexual needs society does not allow him to fulfill.

Far from the social control of rape being learned, comparisons with other cultures lead one to suspect that, in our society, it is rape itself that is learned. (The fact that rape is against the law should not be considered proof that rape is not in fact encouraged as part of our culture.)

This culture's concept of rape as an illegal, but still understandable, form of behavior is not a universal one. In her study *Sex and Temperament*, Margaret Mead describes a society that does not share our views. The Arapesh do not ". . . have any conception of the male nature that might make rape understandable to them." Indeed our interpretation of rape is a product of our conception of the nature of male sexuality. A common retort to the question, why don't women rape men, is the myth that men have greater sexual needs, that their sexuality is more urgent than women's. And it is the nature of human beings to want to live up to what is expected of them.

And this same culture which expects aggression from the male expects passivity from the female. Conveniently, the companion myth about the nature of female sexuality is that all women secretly want to be raped. Lurking beneath her modest female exterior is a subconscious desire to be ravished. The following description of a stag movie, written by Brenda Starr in Los Angeles' underground paper, *Everywoman*, typifies this male fantasy. The movie "showed a woman in her underclothes reading on her bed. She is interrupted by a rapist with a knife. He immediately wins her over with his charm and they get busy sucking and fucking." An advertisement in the *Berkeley Barb* reads, "Now as all women know from their daydreams, rape has a lot of advantages. Best of all it's so simple. No preparation necessary, no planning ahead of time, no wondering if you should or shouldn't; just whang! bang!" Thanks to Masters and Johnson even the scientific canon recognizes that for the female,

"whang! bang!" can scarcely be described as pleasurable.

Still, the male psyche persists in believing that, protestations and struggles to the contrary, deep inside her mysterious feminine soul, the female victim has wished for her own fate. A young woman who was raped by the husband of a friend said that days after the incident the man returned to her home, pounded on the door and screamed to her, "Jane, Jane. You loved it. You know you loved it."

The theory that women like being raped extends itself by deduction into the proposition that most or much of rape is provoked by the victim. But this too is only myth. Though provocation, considered a mitigating factor in a court of law, may consist of only "a gesture," according to the Federal Commission on Crimes of Violence, only 4 percent of reported rapes involved any precipitative behavior by the woman.

The notion that rape is enjoyed by the victim is also convenient for the man who, though he would not commit forcible rape, enjoys the idea of its existence, as if rape confirms that enormous sexual potency which he secretly knows to be his own. It is for the pleasure of the armchair rapist that detailed accounts of violent rapes exist in the media. Indeed, many men appear to take sexual pleasure from nearly all forms of violence. Whatever the motivation, male sexuality and violence in our culture seem to be inseparable. James Bond alternately whips out his revolver and his cock, and though there is no known connection between the skills of gun-fighting and love-making, pacifism seems suspiciously effeminate.

In a recent fictional treatment of the Manson case, Frank Conroy writes of his vicarious titillation when describing the murders to his wife:

"Every single person there was killed." She didn't move.

"It sounds like there was torture," I said. As the words left my mouth I knew there was no need to say them to frighten her into believing that she needed me for protection.

The pleasure he feels as his wife's protector is inextricably mixed with pleasure in the violence itself. Conroy writes, "I was excited by the killings, as one is excited by catastrophe on a grand scale, as one is alert to pre-echoes of unknown changes, hints of unrevealed secrets, rumblings of chaos. . . ."

The attraction of the male in our culture to violence and death is a tradition Manson and his admirers are carrying on with tireless avidity (even presuming Manson's innocence, he dreams of the purification of fire and destruction). It was Malraux in his *Anti-Memoirs* who said that, for the male, facing death was *the* illuminating experience analogous to childbirth for the female. Certainly our culture does glorify war and shrouds the agonies of the gunfighter in veils of mystery.

And in the spectrum of male behavior, rape, the perfect combination of sex and violence, is the penultimate act. Erotic pleasure cannot be separated from culture, and in our culture male eroticism is wedded to power. Not only should a man be taller and stronger than a female in the perfect love-match, but he must also demonstrate his superior strength in gestures of dominance which are perceived as amorous. Though the law attempts to make a clear division between rape and sexual intercourse, in fact the courts find it difficult to distinguish between a case where the decision to copulate was mutual and one where a man forced himself upon his partner.

The scenario is even further complicated by the expectation that, not only does a woman mean "yes" when she says "no," but that a really decent woman ought to begin by saying "no," and then be led down the primrose path to acquiescence. Ovid, the author of Western Civilization's most celebrated sex-manual, makes this expectation perfectly clear:

> . . . and when I beg you to say "yes," say "no."
> Then let me lie outside your bolted door. . . .
> So love grows strong. . . .

That the basic elements of rape are involved in all heterosexual relationships may explain why men often identify with the offender in this crime. But to regard the rapist as the victim, a man driven by his inherent sexual needs to take what will not be given him, reveals a basic ignorance of sexual politics. For in our culture heterosexual love finds an erotic expression through male dominance and female submission. A man who derives pleasure from raping a woman clearly must enjoy force and dominance as much or more than the simple pleasures of the flesh. Coitus cannot be experienced in isolation. The weather, the state of the nation, the level of sugar in the blood—all will affect a man's ability to achieve orgasm. If a man can achieve sexual pleasure after terrorizing and humiliating the object of his passion, and in fact while inflicting pain upon her, one must assume he derives pleasure directly from terrorizing, humiliating and harming a woman. According to Amir's study of forcible rape, on a statistical average the man who has been convicted of rape was found to have a normal sexual personality, tending to be different from the normal, well-adjusted male only in having a greater tendency to express violence and rage.

And if the professional rapist is to be separated from the average dominant heterosexual, it may be mainly a quantitative difference. For the existence of rape as an index to masculinity is not entirely metaphorical. Though this measure of masculinity seems to be more publicly exhibited among "bad boys" or aging bikers who practice sexual initiation through group rape, in fact, "good boys" engage in the same rites to prove their manhood. In Stockton, a small town in California which epitomizes silent-majority America, a bachelor party was given last summer for a young man about to be married. A woman was hired to dance "topless" for the amusement of the guests. At the high point of the evening the bridegroom-to-be dragged the woman into a bedroom. No move was made by any of his companions to stop what was clearly going to be an attempted rape. Far from it. As the woman described, "I tried to keep him away—told him of my Herpes Genitalis, et cetera, but he couldn't face the guys if he didn't screw me." After the bridegroom had finished raping the woman and returned with her to the party, far from chastizing him, his friends heckled the woman and covered her with wine.

It was fortunate for the dancer that the bridegroom's friends did not follow him into the bedroom for, though one might suppose that in group rape, since the victim is outnumbered, less force would be inflicted on her, in fact, Amir's studies indicate, "the most excessive degrees of violence occurred in group rape." Far from discouraging violence, the presence of other men may in fact encourage sadism, and even cause the behavior. In an unpublished study of group rape by Gilbert Geis and Duncan Chappell, the authors refer to a study by W. H. Blanchard which relates, "The leader of the male group . . . apparently precipitated and maintained the activity, despite misgivings, because of a need to fulfill the role that the other two men had assigned to him. 'I was scared when it began to happen,' he says. 'I wanted to leave but I didn't want to say it to the other guys—you know—that I was scared.' "

Thus it becomes clear that not only does our culture teach men the rudiments of rape, but society, or more specifically other men, encourage the practice of it.

> Every man I meet wants to protect me. Can't figure out what from.
>
> *Mae West*

If a male society rewards aggressive, domineering sexual behavior, it contains within itself a sexual schizophrenia. For the masculine man is also expected to prove his mettle as a protector of women. To the naive eye, this dichotomy implies that men fall into one of two categories: those who rape and those who protect. In fact, life does not prove so simple. In a study euphemistically entitled "Sex Aggression by College Men," it was discovered that men who believe in a double standard of morality for men and women, who in fact believe most fervently in the ultimate value of virginity, are more liable to commit "this aggressive variety of sexual exploitation."

(At this point in our narrative it should come as no surprise that Sir Thomas Malory, creator of that classic tale of chivalry, *The Knights of the Round Table,* was himself arrested and found guilty for repeated incidents of rape.)

In the system of chivalry, men protect women against men. This is not unlike the protection relationship which the mafia established with small businesses in the early part of this century. Indeed, chivalry is an age-old protection racket which depends for its existence on rape.

According to the male mythology which defines and perpetuates rape, it is an animal instinct inherent in the male. The story goes that sometime in our pre-historical past, the male, more hirsute and burly than today's counterparts, roamed about an uncivilized landscape until he found a desirable female. (Oddly enough, this female is *not* pictured as more muscular than the modern woman.) Her mate does not bother with courtship. He simply grabs her by the hair and drags her to the closest cave. Presumably, one of the major advantages of modern civilization for the female has been the civilizing of the male. We call it chivalry.

But women do not get chivalry for free. According to the logic of sexual politics, we too have to civilize our behavior. (Enter chastity. Enter virginity. Enter monogamy.) For the female, civilized behavior means chastity before marriage and faithfulness within it. Chivalrous behavior in the male is supposed to protect that chastity from involuntary defilement. The fly in the ointment of this otherwise peaceful system is the fallen woman. She does not behave. And therefore she does not deserve protection. Or, to use another argument, a major tenet of the same value system: what has once been defiled cannot again be violated. One begins to suspect that it is the behavior of the fallen woman, and not that of the male, that civilization aims to control.

The assumption that a woman who does not respect the double standard deserves whatever she gets (or at the very least "asks for it") operates in the courts today. While in some states a man's previous rape convictions are not considered admissible evidence, the sexual reputation of the rape victim is considered a crucial element of the facts upon which the court must decide innocence or guilt.

The court's respect for the double standard manifested itself particularly clearly in the case of the People v. Jerry Plotkin. Mr. Plotkin, a 36-year-old jeweler, was tried for rape last spring in a San Francisco Superior Court. According to the woman who brought the charges, Plotkin, along with three other men, forced her at gunpoint to enter a car one night in October 1970. She was taken to Mr. Plotkin's fashionable apartment where he and the three other men first raped her and then, in the delicate language of the *S.F. Chronicle,* "subjected her to perverted sex acts." She was, she said, set free in the morning with the warning that she would be killed if she spoke to anyone about the event. She did report the incident to the police who then searched Plotkin's apartment and discovered a long list of names of women. Her name was on the list and had been crossed out.

In addition to the woman's account of her abduction and rape, the prosecution submitted four of Plotkin's address books containing the names of hundreds of women. Plotkin claimed he did not know all of the women since some of the names had been given to him by friends and he had not yet called on them. Several women, however, did testify in court that Plotkin had, to cite the *Chronicle,* "lured them up to his apartment under one pretext or another, and forced his sexual attentions on them."

Plotkin's defense rested on two premises. First, through his own testimony Plotkin established a reputation for himself as a sexual libertine who frequently picked up girls in bars and took them to his house where sexual relations often took place. He was the Playboy. He claimed that the accusation of rape, therefore, was false—this incident had simply been one of many casual sexual relationships, the victim one of many playmates. The second premise of the defense was that his accuser was also a sexual libertine. However, the picture created of the young woman (fully 13 years younger than Plotkin) was not akin to the light-hearted, gay-bachelor image projected by the defendant. On the contrary, the day after the defense cross-examined the woman, the *Chronicle* printed a story headlined, "Grueling Day for Rape Case Victim." (A leaflet passed out by women in front of the courtroom was more succinct, "rape was committed by four men in a private apartment in October; on Thursday, it was done by a judge and a lawyer in a public courtroom.")

Through skillful questioning fraught with innuendo, Plotkin's defense attorney James Martin MacInnis portrayed the young woman as a licentious opportunist and unfit mother. MacInnis began by asking the young woman (then employed as a secretary) whether or not it was true that she was "familiar with liquor" and had worked as a "cocktail waitress." The young woman replied (the *Chronicle* wrote "admitted") that she had worked once or twice as a cocktail waitress. The attorney then asked if she had worked as a secretary in the financial district but had "left that employment after it was discovered that you had sexual intercourse on a couch in the office." The woman replied, "That is a lie. I left because I didn't like working in a one-girl office. It was too lonely." Then the defense asked if, while working as an attendant at a health club, "you were accused of having a sexual affair with a man?" Again the woman denied the story, "I was never accused of that."

Plotkin's attorney then sought to establish that his client's accuser was living with a married man. She responded that the man was separated from his wife. Finally he told the court that she had "spent the night" with another man who lived in the same building.

At this point in the testimony the woman asked Plotkin's defense attorney, "Am I on trial? . . . It is embarrassing and personal to admit these things to all these people. . . . I did not commit a crime. I am a human being." The lawyer, true to the chivalry of his class, apologized and immediately resumed questioning her, turning his attention to her children. (She is divorced, and the children at the time of the trial were in a foster home.) "Isn't it true that your two children have a sex game in which one gets on top of another and they—""That is a lie!" the young woman interrupted him. She ended her testimony by explaining "They are wonderful children. They are not perverted."

The jury, divided in favor of acquittal ten to two, asked the court stenographer to read the woman's testimony back to them. After this reading, the Superior Court acquitted the defendant of both the charges of rape and kidnapping.

According to the double standard a woman who has had sexual intercourse out of wedlock cannot be raped. Rape is not only a crime of aggression against the body; it is a transgression against chastity as defined by men. When a woman is forced into a sexual relationship, she has, according to the male ethos, been violated. But she is also defiled if she does not behave according to the double standard, by maintaining her chastity, or confining her sexual activities to a monogamous relationship.

One should not assume, however, that a woman can avoid the possibility of rape simply by behaving. Though myth would have it that mainly "bad girls" are raped, this theory has no basis in fact. Available statistics would lead one to believe that a safer course is promiscuity. In a study of rape done in the District of Columbia, it was found that 82 percent of the rape victims had a "good reputation." Even the Police Inspector's advice to stay off the streets is rather useless, for almost half of reported rapes occur in the home of the victim and are committed by a man she has never before seen. Like indiscriminate terrorism, rape can happen to any woman, and few women are ever without this knowledge.

But the courts and the police, both dominated by white males, continue to suspect the rape victim, *sui generis,* of provoking or asking for her own assault. According to Amir's study, the police tend to believe that a woman without a good reputation cannot be raped. The rape victim is usually submitted to countless questions about her own sexual mores and behavior by the police investigator. This preoccupation is partially justified by the legal requirements for prosecution in a rape case. The rape victim must have been penetrated, and she must have made it clear to her assailant that she did not want penetration (unless of course she is unconscious). A refusal to accompany a man to some isolated place to allow him to touch her does not, in the eyes of the court, constitute rape. She must have said "no" at the crucial genital moment. And the rape victim, to qualify as such, must also have put up a physical struggle—unless she can prove that to do so would have been to endanger her life.

But the zealous interest the police frequently exhibit in the physical details of a rape case is only partially explained by the requirements of the court. A woman who was raped in Berkeley was asked to tell the story of her rape four different times "right out in the street," while her assailant was escaping. She was then required to submit to a pelvic examination to prove that penetration had taken place. Later, she was taken to the police station where she was asked the same questions again: "Were you forced?" "Did he penetrate?" "Are you sure your life was in danger and you had no other choice?" This woman had been pulled off the street by a man who held a 10-inch knife at her throat and forcibly raped her. She was raped at midnight and was not able to return to her home until five in the morning. Police contacted her twice again in the next week, once by telephone at two in the morning and once at four in the morning. In her words, "The rape was probably the least traumatic incident of the whole evening. If I'm ever raped again, . . . I wouldn't report it to the police because of all the degradation. . . ."

If white women are subjected to unnecessary and often hostile questioning after having been raped, third-world women are often not believed at all. According to the white male ethos (which is not only sexist but racist), third-world women are defined from birth as "impure." Thus the white male is provided with a pool of women who are fair game for sexual imperialism. Third-world women frequently do not report rape and for good reason. When blues singer Billie Holliday was 10 years old, she was taken off to a local house by a neighbor and raped. Her mother brought the police to rescue her, and she was taken to the local police station crying and bleeding:

> When we got there, instead of treating me and Mom like somebody who called the cops for help, they treated me like I'd killed somebody. . . . I guess they had me figured for having enticed this old goat into the whorehouse. . . . All I know for sure is they threw me into a cell . . . a fat white matron . . . saw I was still bleeding, she felt sorry for me and gave me a couple glasses of milk. But nobody else did anything for me except give me filthy looks and snicker to themselves.
>
> After a couple of days in a cell they dragged me into a court. Mr. Dick got sentenced to five years. They sentenced me to a Catholic institution.

Clearly the white man's chivalry is aimed only to protect the chastity of "his" women.

As a final irony, that same system of sexual values from which chivalry is derived has also provided womankind with an unwritten code of behavior, called femininity, which makes a feminine woman the perfect victim of sexual aggression. If being chaste does not ward off the possibility of assault, being feminine certainly increases the chances that it will succeed. To be submissive is to defer to masculine strength; is to lack muscular development or any interest in defending oneself; is to let doors be opened, to have one's arm held when crossing the street. To be feminine is to wear shoes which make it difficult to run; skirts which inhibit one's stride; underclothes which inhibit the circulation. Is it not an intriguing observation that those very clothes which are thought to be flattering to the female and attractive to the male are those which make it impossible for a woman to defend herself against aggression?

Each girl as she grows into womanhood is taught fear. Fear is the form in which the female internalizes both chivalry and the double standard. Since, biologically speaking, women in fact have the same if not greater potential for sexual expression as do men, the woman who is taught that she must behave differently from a man must also learn to distrust her own carnality. She must deny her own feelings and learn not to act from them. She fears herself. This is the essence of passivity, and of course, a woman's passivity is not simply sexual but functions to cripple her from self-expression in every area of her life.

Passivity itself prevents a woman from ever considering her own potential for self-defense and forces her to look to men for protection. The woman is taught fear, but this time fear of the other; and yet her only relief from this fear is to seek out the other. Moreover, the passive woman is taught to regard herself as impotent, unable to act, unable even to perceive, in no way self-sufficient, and, finally, as the object and not the subject of human behavior. It is in this sense that a woman is deprived of the status of a human being. She is not free to be.

Since Ibsen's Nora slammed the door on her patriarchical husband, woman's attempt to be free has been more or less fashionable. In this 19th-century portrait of a woman leaving her marriage, Nora tells her husband, "Our home has been nothing but a playroom. I have been your doll-wife just as at home I was papa's doll-child." And, at least on the stage, "The Doll's House" crumbled, leaving audiences with hope

for the fate of the modern woman. And today, as in the past, womankind has not lacked examples of liberated women to emulate: Emma Goldman, Greta Garbo and Isadora Duncan all denounced marriage and the double standard, and believed their right to freedom included sexual independence; but still their example has not affected the lives of millions of women who continue to marry, divorce and remarry, living out their lives dependent on the status and economic power of men. Patriarchy still holds the average woman prisoner not because she lacks the courage of an Isadora Duncan, but because the material conditions of her life prevent her from being anything but an object.

In the *Elementary Structures of Kinship*, Claude Levi-Strauss gives to marriage this universal description, "It is always a system of exchange that we find at the origin of the rules of marriage." In this system of exchange, a woman is the "most precious possession." Levi-Strauss continues that the custom of including women as booty in the marketplace is still so general that "a whole volume would not be sufficient to enumerate instances of it." Levi-Strauss makes it clear that he does not exclude Western Civilization from his definition of "universal" and cites examples from modern wedding ceremonies. (The marriage ceremony is still one in which the husband and wife become one, and "that one is the husband.")

The legal proscription against rape reflects this possessory view of women. An article in the 1952–53 *Yale Law Journal* describes the legal rationale behind laws against rape: "In our society sexual taboos, often enacted into law, buttress a system of monogamy based upon the law of 'free bargaining' of the potential spouses. Within this process the woman's power to withhold or grant sexual access is an important bargaining weapon." Presumably then, laws against rape are intended to protect the right of a woman, not for physical self-determination, but for physical "bargaining." The article goes on to explain explicitly why the preservation of the bodies of women is important to men:

> The consent standard in our society does more than protect a significant item of social currency for women; it fosters, and is in turn bolstered by, a masculine pride in the exclusive

possession of a sexual object. The consent of a woman to sexual intercourse awards the man a privilege of bodily access, a personal "prize" whose value is enhanced by sole ownership. An additional reason for the man's condemnation of rape may be found in the threat to his status from a decrease in the "value" of his sexual possession which would result from forcible violation.

The passage concludes by making clear whose interest the law is designed to protect. "The man responds to this undercutting of status as *possessor* of the girl with hostility toward the rapist; no other restitution device is available. The law of rape provides an orderly outlet for his vengeance." Presumably the female victim in any case will have been sufficiently socialized so as not to consciously feel any strong need for vengeance. If she does feel this need, society does not speak to it.

The laws against rape exist to protect rights of the male as possessor of the female body, and not the right of the female over her own body. Even without this enlightening passage from the *Yale Law Review,* the laws themselves are clear: In no state can a man be accused of raping his wife. How can any man steal what already belongs to him? It is in the sense of rape as theft of another man's property that Kate Millett writes, "Traditionally rape has been viewed as an offense one male commits against another—a matter of abusing his woman." In raping another man's woman, a man may aggrandize his own manhood and concurrently reduce that of another man. Thus a man's honor is not subject directly to rape, but only indirectly, through "his" woman.

If the basic social unit is the family, in which the woman is a possession of her husband, the superstructure of society is a male hierarchy, in which men dominate other men (or patriarchal families dominate other patriarchal families). And it is no small irony that, while the very social fabric of our male-dominated culture denies women equal access to political, economic and legal power, the literature, myth and humor of our culture depicts women not only as the power behind the throne, but the real source of the oppression of men. The religious version of this fairy tale blames Eve for both carnality and eating of the tree of knowledge, at the same time making her gullible to the obvious devices of a serpent. Adam, of course, is merely the trusting victim of love. Certainly this is a biased story. But no more biased than the one television audiences receive today from the latest slick comedians. Through a media which is owned by men, censored by a State dominated by men, all the evils of this social system which make a man's life unpleasant are blamed upon "the wife." The theory is: were it not for the female who waits and plots to "trap" the male into marriage, modern man would be able to achieve Olympian freedom. She is made the scapegoat for a system which is in fact run by men.

Nowhere is this more clear than in the white racist use of the concept of white womanhood. The white male's open rape of black women, coupled with his overweening concern for the chastity and protection of his wife and daughters, represents an extreme of sexist and racist hypocrisy. While on the one hand she was held up as the standard for purity and virtue, on the other the Southern white woman was never asked if she wanted to be on a pedestal, and in fact any deviance from the male-defined standards for white womanhood was treated severely. (It is a powerful commentary on American racism that the historical role of blacks as slaves, and thus possessions without power, has robbed black women of legal and economic protection through marriage. Thus black women in Southern society and in the ghettoes of the North have long been easy game for white rapists.) The fear that black men would rape white women was, and is, classic paranoia. Quoting from Ann Breen's unpublished study of racism and sexism in the South *"The New South: White Man's Country,"* Frederick Douglass legitimately points out that, had the black man wished to rape white women, he had ample opportunity to do so during the civil war, when white women, the wives, sisters, daughters and mothers of the rebels, were left in the care of blacks. But yet not a single act of rape was committed during this time. The Ku Klux Klan, who tarred and feathered black men and lynched them in the honor of the purity of white womanhood, also applied tar and feathers to a Southern white woman accused of bigamy, which leads one to suspect that Southern white men were not so much outraged at the violation of the woman as a person, in the few instances where rape was actually committed by black men, but at the violation of his property rights." In the situation where a black man was found to be having sexual relations with a white woman, the white woman could exercise skin-privilege, and claim that she had been raped, in which case the black man was lynched. But if she did not claim rape, she herself was subject to lynching.

In constructing the myth of white womanhood so as to justify the lynching and oppression of black men and women, the white male has created a convenient symbol of his own power which has resulted in black hostility toward the white "bitch," accompanied by an unreasonable fear on the part of many white women of the black rapist. Moreover, it is not surprising that after being told for two centuries that he wants to rape white women, occasionally a black man does actually commit that act. But it is crucial to note that the frequency of this practice is outrageously exaggerated in the white mythos. Ninety percent of reported rape is intra- not inter-racial.

In *Soul on Ice,* Eldridge Cleaver has described the mixing of a rage against white power with the internalized sexism of a black man raping a white woman. "Somehow I arrived at the conclusion that, as a matter of principle, it was of paramount importance for me to have an antagonistic, ruthless attitude toward white women. . . . Rape was an insurrectionary act. It delighted me that I was defying and trampling upon the white man's law, upon his system of values and that I was defiling his women—and this point, I believe, was the most satisfying to me because I was very resentful over the historical fact of how the white man has used the black woman." Thus a black man uses white women to take out his rage against white men. But in fact, whenever a rape of a white woman by a black man does take place, it is again the white man who benefits. First, the act itself terrorizes the white woman and makes her more dependent on the white male for protection. Then, if the woman prosecutes her attacker, the white man is afforded legal opportunity to exercise overt racism. Of course, the knowledge of the rape helps to perpetuate two myths

which are beneficial to white male rule—the bestiality of the black and the desirability of white women. Finally, the white man surely benefits because he himself is not the object of attack—he has been allowed to stay in power.

Indeed, the existence of rape in any form is beneficial to the ruling class of white males. For rape is a kind of terrorism which severely limits the freedom of women and makes women dependent on men. Moreover, in the act of rape, the rage that one man may harbor toward another higher in the male hierarchy can be deflected toward a female scapegoat. For every man there is always someone lower on the social scale on whom he can take out his aggressions. And this is any woman alive.

This oppressive attitude towards women finds its institutionalization in the traditional family. For it is assumed that a man "wears the pants" in his family—he exercises the option of rule whenever he so chooses. Not that he makes all the decisions—clearly women make most of the important day-to-day decisions in a family. But when a conflict of interest arises, it is the man's interest which will prevail. His word, in itself, is more powerful. He lords it over his wife in the same way his boss lords it over him, so that the very process of exercising his power becomes as important an act as obtaining whatever it is his power can get for him. This notion of power is key to the male ego in this culture, for the two acceptable measures of masculinity are a man's power over women and his power over other men. A man may boast to his friends that "I have 20 men working for me." It is also aggrandizement of his ego if he has the financial power to clothe his wife in furs and jewels. And, if a man lacks the wherewithal to acquire such power, he can always express his rage through equally masculine activities—rape and theft. Since male society defines the female as a possession, it is not surprising that the felony most often committed together with rape is theft. As the following classic tale of rape points out the elements of theft, violence and forced sexual relations merge into an indistinguishable whole.

The woman who told this story was acquainted with the man who tried to rape her. When the man learned that she was going to be staying alone for the weekend, he began early in the day a polite campaign to get her to go out with him. When she continued to refuse his request, his chivalrous mask dropped away:

I had locked all the doors because I was afraid, and I don't know how he got in; it was probably through the screen door. When I woke up, he was shaking my leg. His eyes were red, and I knew he had been drinking or smoking. I thought I would try to talk my way out of it. He started by saying that he wanted to sleep with me, and then he got angrier and angrier, until he started to say, "I want pussy," "I want pussy." Then, I got scared and tried to push him away. That's when he started to force himself on me. It was awful. It was the most humiliating, terrible feeling. He was forcing my legs apart and ripping my clothes off. And it was painful. I did fight him—he was slightly drunk and I was able to keep him away. I had taken judo a few years back, but I was afraid to throw a chop for fear that he'd kill me. I could see he was getting more and more violent. I was thinking wildly of some way to get out of this alive, and then I said to him, "Do you want money. I'll give you money." We had money but I was also thinking that if I got to the back room I could telephone the police—as if the police would have even helped. It was a stupid thing to think of because obviously he would follow me. And he did. When he saw me pick up the phone, he tried to tie the cord around my neck. I screamed at him that I did have the money in another room, that I was going to call the police because I was scared, but that I would never tell anybody what happened. It would be an absolute secret. He said, okay, and I went to get the money. But when he got it, all of a sudden he got this crazy look in his eye and he said to me, "Now I'm going to kill you." Then I started saying my prayers. I knew there was nothing I could do. He started to hit me— I still wasn't sure if he wanted to rape me at this point—or just to kill me. He was hurting me, but hadn't yet gotten me into a stranglehold because he was still drunk and off balance. Somehow we pushed into the kitchen where I kept looking at this big knife. But I didn't pick it up. Somehow, no matter how much I hated him at that moment, I still couldn't imagine putting the knife in his flesh, and then I was afraid he would grab it and stick it into me. Then he was hitting me again and somehow we pushed through the back door of the kitchen and onto the porch steps. We fell down the steps and that's when he started to strangle me. He was on top

of me. He just went on and on until finally I lost consciousness. I did scream, though my screams sounded like whispers to me. But what happened was that a cab driver happened by and frightened him away. The cab driver revived me—I was out only a minute at the most. And then I ran across the street and I grabbed the woman who was our neighbor and screamed at her, "Am I alive? Am I still alive?"

Rape is an act of agression in which the victim is denied her self-determination. It is an act of violence which, if not actually followed by beatings or murder, nevertheless always carries with it the threat of death. And finally, rape is a form of mass terrorism, for the victims of rape are chosen indiscriminately, but the propagandists for male supremacy broadcast that it is women who cause rape by being unchaste or in the wrong place at the wrong time—in essence, by behaving as though they were free.

The threat of rape is used to deny women employment. (In California, the Berkeley Public Library, until pushed by the Federal Employment Practices Commission, refused to hire female shelvers because of perverted men in the stacks.) The fear of rape keeps women off the streets at night. Keeps women at home. Keeps women passive and modest for fear that they be thought provocative.

It is part of human dignity to be able to defend oneself, and women are learning. Some women have learned karate; some to shoot guns. And yet we will not be free until the threat of rape and the atmosphere of violence is ended, and to end that the nature of male behavior must change.

But rape is not an isolated act that can be rooted out from patriarchy without ending patriarchy itself. The same men and power structure who victimize women are engaged in the act of raping Vietnam, raping black people and the very earth we live upon. Rape is a classic act of domination where, in the words of Kate Millett, "the emotions of hatred, contempt, and the desire to break or violate personality," takes place. This breaking of the personality characterizes modern life itself. No simple reforms can eliminate rape. As the symbolic expression of the white male hierarchy, rape is the quintessential act of our civilization, one which, Valerie

Solanis warns, is in danger of "humping itself to death."

Study Questions

1. How does Griffin think all women get initiated to sexuality?
2. Does Griffin believe that rapists are insane? Explain your answer.
3. Does Griffin believe that if it weren't for social control, all men would rape? Explain.
4. What two myths about sexuality, according to Griffin, are prevalent in our culture?
5. "In our culture male eroticism is wedded to power." What does Griffin mean by this, and how does it tie in with the existence of rape? Does it mean that the difference between a "normal" man and the rapist is merely a matter of degree?
6. Does Griffin believe that the system of chivalry is incompatible with the existence of rape? Explain your answer.
7. In what way is the rape victim often "put on trial"?
8. Griffin says "femininity" makes sexual aggression against women easier. Explain what she means by this.
9. What view of women is implicit in the institution of monogamy? How does it account for the existence of laws against rape?
10. How does rape in any form benefit males as a class? How does the threat of rape serve to oppress women, according to Griffin?

Rape: On Coercion and Consent

Catharine A. MacKinnon

If sexuality is central to women's definition and forced sex is central to sexuality, rape is indigenous, not exceptional, to women's social condition. In feminist analysis, a rape is not an isolated event or moral transgression or individual interchange gone wrong but an act of terrorism and torture within a systemic context of group subjection, like lynching. The fact that the state calls rape a crime opens an inquiry into the state's treatment of rape as an index to its stance on the status of the sexes.

Under law, rape is a sex crime that is not regarded as a crime when it looks like sex. The law, speaking generally, defines rape as intercourse with force or coercion and without consent.[1] Like sexuality under male suprema-

From Catharine A. MacKinnon, *Toward a Feminist Theory of the State* (Harvard University Press, 1989). Copyright © 1989 by Catharine MacKinnon. Reprinted by permission of the publisher.

cy, this definition assumes the sadomasochistic definition of sex: intercourse with force or coercion can be or become consensual. It assumes pornography's positive-outcome-rape scenario: dominance plus submission is force plus consent. This equals sex, not rape. Under male supremacy, this is too often the reality. In a critique of male supremacy, the elements "with force and without consent" appear redundant. Force is present because consent is absent.

Like heterosexuality, male supremacy's paradigm of sex, the crime of rape centers on penetration.[2] The law to protect women's sexuality from forcible violation and expropriation defines that protection in male genital terms. Women do resent forced penetration. But penile invasion of the vagina may be less pivotal to women's sexuality, pleasure or violation, than it is to male sexuality. This definitive element of rape centers upon a male-defined loss. It also centers upon one way men define loss of exclusive access. In this light, rape, as legally defined, appears more a crime against female monogamy (exclusive access by one man) than against women's sexual dignity or intimate integrity. Analysis of rape in terms of concepts of property, often invoked in marxian analysis to criticize this disparity, fail to encompass the realities of rape.[3] Women's sexuality is, socially, a thing to be stolen, sold, bought, bartered, or exchanged by others. But women never own or possess it, and men never treat it, in law or in life, with the solicitude with which they treat property. To be property would be an improvement. The moment women "have" it—"have sex" in the dual gender/sexuality sense—it is lost as theirs. To have it is to have it taken away. This may explain the male incomprehension that, once a woman has had sex, she loses anything when subsequently raped. To them women have nothing to lose. It is true that dignitary harms, because nonmaterial, are ephemeral to the legal mind. But women's loss through rape is not only less tangible; it is seen as unreal. It is difficult to avoid the conclusion that penetration itself is considered a violation from the male point of view, which is both why it is the centerpiece of sex and why women's sexuality, women's gender definition, is stigmatic. The question for social explanation becomes not why some women tolerate rape but how any women manage to resent it.

Rape cases finding insufficient evidence of force reveal that acceptable sex, in the legal perspective, can entail a lot of force. This is both a result of the way specific facts are perceived and interpreted within the legal system and the way the injury is defined by law. The level of acceptable force is adjudicated starting just above the level set by what is seen as normal male sexual behavior, including the normal level of force, rather than at the victim's, or women's, point of violation.[4] In this context, to seek to define rape as violent not sexual is as understandable as it is futile. Some feminists have reinterpreted rape as an act of violence, not sexuality, the threat of which intimidates all women.[5] Others see rape, including its violence, as an expression of male sexuality, the social imperatives of which define as well as threaten all women.[6] The first, epistemologically in the liberal tradition, comprehends rape as a displacement of power based on physical force onto sexuality, a preexisting natural sphere to which domination is alien. Susan Brownmiller, for example, examines rape in riots, wars, pogroms, and revolutions; rape by police, parents, prison guards; and rape motivated by racism. Rape in normal circumstances, in everyday life, in ordinary relationships, by men as men, is barely mentioned.[7] Women are raped by guns, age, white supremacy, the state—only derivatively by the penis. The view that derives most directly from victims' experiences, rather than from their denial, construes sexuality as a social sphere of male power to which forced sex is paradigmatic. Rape is not less sexual for being violent. To the extent that coercion has become integral to male sexuality, rape may even be sexual to the degree that, and because, it is violent.

The point of defining rape as "violence not sex" has been to claim an ungendered and nonsexual ground for affirming sex (heterosexuality), while rejecting violence (rape). The problem remains what it has always been: telling the difference. The convergence of sexuality with violence, long used at law to deny the reality of women's violation, is recognized by rape survivors with a difference: where the legal system has seen the intercourse in rape, victims see the rape in intercourse. The uncoerced context for sexual expression becomes as elusive as the physical acts come to feel indistinguishable. Instead of asking what is the violation of rape, their experience suggests that the more relevant question is, what is the nonviolation of intercourse? To know what is wrong with rape, know what is right about sex. If this, in turn, proves difficult, the difficulty is as instructive as the difficulty men have in telling the difference when women see one. Perhaps the wrong of rape has proved so difficult to define because the unquestionable starting point has been that rape is defined as distinct from intercourse,[8] while for women it is difficult to distinguish the two under conditions of male dominance.

In the name of the distinction between sex and violence, reform of rape statutes has sought to redefine rape as sexual assault.[9] Usually, assault is not consented to in law; either it cannot be consented to, or consensual assault remains assault.[10] Yet sexual assault consented to is intercourse, no matter how much force was used. The substantive reference point implicit in existing legal standards is the sexually normative level of force. Until this norm is confronted as such, no distinction between violence and sexuality will prohibit more instances of women's experienced violation than does the existing definition. Conviction rates have not increased under the reform statutes.[11] The question remains what is seen as force, hence as violence, in the sexual arena.[12] Most rapes, as women live them, will not be seen to violate women until sex and violence are confronted as mutually definitive rather than as mutually exclusive. It is not only men convicted of rape who believe that the only thing they did that was different from what men do all the time is get caught.

Consent is supposed to be women's form of control over intercourse, different from but equal to the custom of male initiative. Man proposes, woman disposes. Even the ideal is not mutual. Apart from the disparate consequences of refusal, this model does not envision a situation the woman controls being placed in, or choices she frames. Yet the consequences are attributed to her as if the sexes began at arm's length, on equal terrain, as in the contract fiction. Ambiguous cases of consent in law are archetypically referred to as "half won arguments in parked cars."[13] Why not half lost? Why isn't half enough? Why is it an argument? Why do men still want "it," feel entitled to "it," when women do not want them? The law of rape presents consent as free exercise of sexual choice under conditions of equality of power without exposing the underlying structure of constraint and disparity. Fundamentally, desirability to men is supposed a woman's form of power because she can both arouse it and deny its fulfillment. To woman is attributed both the cause of man's initiative and the denial of his satisfaction. This rationalizes force. Consent in this model becomes more a metaphysical quality of a woman's being than a choice she makes and communicates. Exercise of women's so-called power presupposes more fundamental social powerlessness.[14]

The law of rape divides women into spheres of consent according to indices of relationship to men. Which category of presumed consent a woman is in depends upon who she is relative to a man who wants her, not what she says or does. These categories tell men whom they can legally fuck, who is open season and who is off limits, not how to listen to women. The paradigm categories are the virginal daughter and other young girls, with whom all sex is proscribed, and the whorelike wives and prostitutes, with whom no sex is proscribed. Daughters may not consent; wives and prostitutes are assumed to, and cannot but.[15] Actual consent or nonconsent, far less actual desire, is comparatively irrelevant. If rape laws existed to enforce women's control over access to their sexuality, as the consent defense implies, no would mean no, marital rape would not be a widespread exception,[16] and it would not be effectively legal to rape a prostitute.

All women are divided into parallel provinces, their actual consent counting to the degree that they diverge from the paradigm case in their category. Virtuous women, like young girls, are unconsenting, virginal, rapable. Unvirtuous women, like wives and prostitutes, are consenting, whores, unrapable. The age line under which girls are presumed disabled from consenting to sex, whatever they say, rationalizes a condition of sexual coercion which women never outgrow. One day they cannot say yes, and the next day they cannot say no. The law takes the most aggravated case for female powerlessness based on gender and age combined and, by formally prohibiting all sex as rape, makes consent irrelevant on the basis of an assumption of powerlessness. This defines those above the age line as powerful, whether they actually have power to consent or not. The vulnerability girls share with boys— age—dissipates with time. The vulnerability girls share with women—gender—does not. As with protective labor laws for women only, dividing and protecting the most vulnerable becomes a device for not protecting everyone who needs it, and also may function to target those singled out for special protection for special abuse. Such protection has not prevented high rates of sexual abuse of children and may contribute to eroticizing young girls as forbidden.

As to adult women, to the extent an accused knows a woman and they have sex, her consent is inferred. The exemption for rape in marriage is consistent with the assumption underlying most adjudications of forcible rape: to the extent the parties relate, it was not really rape, it was personal.[17] As marital exemptions erode, preclusions for cohabitants and voluntary social companions may expand. As a matter of fact, for this purpose one can be acquainted with an accused by friendship or by meeting him for the first time at a bar or a party or by hitchhiking. In this light, the partial erosion of the marital rape exemption looks less like a change in the equation between women's experience of sexual violation and men's experience of intimacy, and more like a legal adjustment to the social fact that acceptable heterosexual sex is increasingly not limited to the legal family. So although the rape law may not now always assume that the woman consented simply because the parties are legally one, indices of closeness, of relationship ranging from nodding acquaintance to living together, still contraindicate rape. In marital rape cases, courts look for even greater atrocities than usual to undermine their assumption that if sex happened, she wanted it.[18]

This approach reflects men's experience that women they know do meaningfully consent to sex with them. *That* cannot be rape; rape must be by someone else, someone unknown. They do not rape women they know. Men and women are unequally socially situated with regard to the experience of rape. Men are a good deal more likely to rape than to be raped. This forms their experience, the material conditions of their epistemological position. Almost half of all women, by contrast, are raped or victims of attempted rape at least once in their lives. Almost 40 percent are victims of sexual abuse in childhood.[19] Women are more likely to be raped than to rape and are most often raped by men whom they know.[20]

Men often say that it is less awful for a woman to be raped by someone she is close to: "The emotional trauma suffered by a person victimized by an individual with whom sexual intimacy is shared as a normal part of an ongoing marital relationship is not nearly as severe as that suffered by a person who is victimized by one with whom that intimacy is not shared."[21] Women often feel as or more traumatized from being raped by someone known or trusted, someone with whom at least an illusion of mutuality has been shared, than by some stranger. In whose interest is it to believe that it is not so bad to be raped by someone who has fucked you before as by someone who has not? Disallowing charges of rape in marriage may, depending upon one's view of normalcy, "remove a substantial obstacle to the resumption of normal marital relationships."[22] Note that the obstacle is not the rape but the law against it. Apparently someone besides feminists finds sexual victimization and sexual intimacy not all that contradictory under current conditions. Sometimes it seems as though women and men live in different cultures.

Having defined rape in male sexual terms, the law's problem, which becomes the victim's problem, is distinguishing rape from sex in specific cases. The adjudicated line between rape and intercourse commonly centers on some assessment of the woman's "will." But how should the law or the accused know a woman's will? The answer combines aspects of force with aspects of nonconsent with elements of resistance, still effective in some states.[23] Even when nonconsent is not a legal element of the offense, juries tend to infer rape from evidence of force or resistance. In Michigan, under its reform rape law, consent was judicially held to be a defense even though it was not included in the statute.[24]

The deeper problem is that women are socialized to passive receptivity; may have or perceive no alternative to acquiescence; may prefer it to the escalated risk of injury and the humiliation of a lost fight; submit to survive. Also, force and desire are not mutually exclusive under male supremacy. So long as dominance is eroticized, they never will be. Some women eroticize dominance and submission; it beats feeling forced. Sexual intercourse may be deeply unwanted, the woman would never have initiated it, yet no force may be present. So much force may have been used that the woman never risked saying no. Force may be used, yet the woman may prefer the sex—to avoid more force or because she, too, eroticizes dominance. Women and men know this. Considering rape as violence not sex evades, at the moment it most seems to confront, the issue of who controls women's sexuality and the dominance/submission dynamic that has defined it. When sex is violent, women may have lost control over what is done to them, but absence of force does not ensure the presence of that control. Nor, under conditions of male dominance, does the presence of force make an interaction nonsexual. If sex is normally something men do to women, the issue is less whether there was force than whether consent is a meaningful concept.[25]

To explain women's gender status on a rape theory, Susan Brownmiller argues that the threat of rape benefits all men.[26] How is unspecified. Perhaps it benefits them sexually, hence as a gender: male initiatives toward women carry the fear of rape as support for persuading compliance, the resulting appearance of which has been considered seduction and termed consent. Here the victims' perspective grasps what liberalism applied to women denies: that forced sex as sexuality is not exceptional in relations between the sexes but constitutes the social meaning of gender. "Rape is a man's act, whether it is a male or a female man and whether it is a man relatively permanently or relatively temporarily; and being raped is a woman's experience, whether it is a female or a male woman and whether it is a woman relatively permanently or relatively temporarily."[27] To be rapable, a position that is social not biological, defines what a woman is.

Marital rape and battery of wives have been separated by law. A feminist analysis suggests that assault by a man's fist is not so different from assault by a penis, not because both are violent but because both are sexual. Battery is often precipitated by women's noncompliance with gender requirements.[28] Nearly all incidents occur in the home, most in the kitchen or bedroom. Most murdered women are killed by their husbands or boyfriends, usually in the bedroom. The battery cycle accords with the rhythms of heterosexual sex.[29] The rhythm of lesbian sadomasochism is the same.[30] Perhaps violent interchanges, especially between genders, make sense in sexual terms.

The larger issue raised by sexual aggression for the interpretation of the relation between sexuality and gender is: what is heterosexuality? If it is the erotization of dominance and

submission, altering the participants' gender does not eliminate the sexual, or even gendered, content of aggression. If heterosexuality is males over females, gender matters independently. Arguably, heterosexuality is a fusion of the two, with gender a social outcome, such that the acted upon is feminized, is the "girl" regardless of sex, the actor correspondingly masculinized. Whenever women are victimized, regardless of the biology of the perpetrator, this system is at work. But it is equally true that whenever powerlessness and ascribed inferiority are sexually exploited or enjoyed—based on age, race, physical stature or appearance or ability, or socially reviled or stigmatized status—the system is at work.

Battery thus appears sexual on a deeper level. Stated in boldest terms, sexuality is violent, so perhaps violence is sexual. Violence against women is sexual on both counts, doubly sexy. If this is so, wives are beaten, as well as raped, as women—as the acted upon, as gender, meaning sexual, objects. It further follows that acts by anyone which treat a woman according to her object label, woman, are in a sense sexual acts. The extent to which sexual acts are acts of objectification remains a question of one's account of women's freedom to live their own meanings as other than illusions, of individuals' ability to resist or escape, even momentarily, prescribed social meanings short of political change. Clearly, centering sexuality upon genitality distinguishes battery from rape at exactly the juncture that both existing law, and seeing rape as violence not sex, do.

Most women get the message that the law against rape is virtually unenforceable as applied to them. Women's experience is more often delegitimated by this than the law is. Women, as realists, distinguish between rape and experiences of sexual violation by concluding that they have not "really" been raped if they have ever seen or dated or slept with or been married to the man, if they were fashionably dressed or not provably virgin, if they are prostitutes, if they put up with it or tried to get it over with, if they were force-fucked for years. The implicit social standard becomes: if a woman probably could not prove it in court, it was not rape.

The distance between most intimate violations of women and the legally perfect rape measures the imposition of an alien definition. From women's point of view, rape is not prohibited; it is regulated. Even women who know they have been raped do not believe that the legal system will see it the way they do. Often they are not wrong. Rather than deterring or avenging rape, the state, in many victims' experiences, perpetuates it. Women who charge rape say they were raped twice, the second time in court. Under a male state, the boundary violation, humiliation, and indignity of being a public sexual spectacle makes this more than a figure of speech.[31]

Rape, like many other crimes, requires that the accused possess a criminal mind (*mens rea*) for his acts to be criminal. The man's mental state refers to what he actually understood at the time or to what a reasonable man should have understood under the circumstances. The problem is that the injury of rape lies in the meaning of the act to its victim, but the standard for its criminality lies in the meaning of the act to the assailant. Rape is only an injury from women's point of view. It is only a crime from the male point of view, explicitly including that of the accused.

The crime of rape is defined and adjudicated from the male standpoint, presuming that forced sex is sex and that consent to a man is freely given by a woman. Under male supremacist standards, of course, they are. Doctrinally, this means that the man's perceptions of the woman's desires determine whether she is deemed violated. This might be like other crimes of subjective intent if rape were like other crimes. With rape, because sexuality defines gender norms, the only difference between assault and what is socially defined as a noninjury is the meaning of the encounter to the woman. Interpreted this way, the legal problem has been to determine whose view of that meaning constitutes what really happened, as if what happened objectively exists to be objectively determined. This task has been assumed to be separable from the gender of the participants and the gendered nature of their exchange, when the objective norms and the assailant's perspective are identical.

As a result, although the rape law oscillates between subjective tests and objective standards invoking social reasonableness, it uniformly presumes a single underlying reality, rather than a reality split by the divergent meanings inequality produces. Many women are raped by men who know the meaning of their acts to their victims perfectly well and proceed anyway.[32] But women are also violated every day by men who have no idea of the meaning of their acts to the women. To them it is sex. Therefore, to the law it is sex. That becomes the single reality of what happened. When a rape prosecution is lost because a woman fails to prove that she did not consent, she is not considered to have been injured at all. It is as if a robbery victim, finding himself unable to prove he was not engaged in philanthropy, is told he still has his money. Hermeneutically unpacked, the law assumes that, because the rapist did not perceive that the woman did not want him, she was not violated. She had sex. Sex itself cannot be an injury. Women have sex every day. Sex makes a woman a woman. Sex is what women are for.

Men set sexual mores ideologically and behaviorally, define rape as they imagine women to be sexually violated through distinguishing that from their image of what they normally do, and sit in judgment in most accusations of sex crimes. So rape comes to mean a strange (read Black) man who does not know his victim but does know she does not want sex with him, going ahead anyway. But men are systematically conditioned not even to notice what women want. Especially if they consume pornography, they may have not a glimmer of women's indifference or revulsion, including when women say no explicitly. Rapists typically believe the woman loved it. "Probably the single most used cry of rapist to victim is 'You bitch . . . slut . . . you know you want it. You all want it' and afterward, 'there now, you really enjoyed it, didn't you?' "[33] Women, as a survival strategy, must ignore or devalue or mute desires, particularly lack of them, to convey the impression that the man will get what he wants regardless of what they want. In this context, to measure the genuineness of consent from the individual assailant's point of view is to adopt as law the point of view which creates the problem. Measuring consent from the socially reasonable, meaning objective man's, point of view reproduces the same problem under a more elevated label.[34]

Men's pervasive belief that women fabricate rape charges after consenting to sex makes sense in this light. To them, the accusations are false because, to them, the facts describe sex. To interpret such events as rapes distorts their experience. Since they seldom consider that their experience of the real is anything other than reality, they can only explain the woman's version as maliciously invented. Similarly, the male anxiety that rape is easy to charge and difficult to disprove, also widely believed in the face of overwhelming evidence to the contrary, arises because rape accusations express one thing men cannot seem to control: the meaning to women of sexual encounters.

Thus do legal doctrines, incoherent or puzzling as syllogistic logic, become coherent as ideology. For example, when an accused wrongly but sincerely believes that a woman he sexually forced consented, he may have a defense of mistaken belief in consent or fail to satisfy the mental requirement of knowingly proceeding against her will.[35] Sometimes his knowing disregard is measured by what a reasonable man would disregard. This is considered an objective test. Sometimes the disregard need not be reasonable so long as it is sincere. This is considered a subjective test. A feminist inquiry into the distinction between rape and intercourse, by contrast, would inquire into the meaning of the act from women's point of view, which is neither. What is wrong with rape in this view is that it is an act of subordination of women to men. It expresses and reinforces women's inequality to men. Rape with legal impunity makes women second-class citizens.

This analysis reveals the way the social conception of rape is shaped to interpret particular encounters and the way the legal conception of rape authoritatively shapes that social conception. When perspective is bound up with situation, and situation is unequal, whether or not a contested interaction is authoritatively considered rape comes down to whose meaning wins. If sexuality is relational, specifically if it is a power relation of gender, consent is a communication under conditions of inequality. It transpires somewhere between what the woman actually wanted, what she was able to

express about what she wanted, and what the man comprehended she wanted.

Discussing the conceptually similar issue of revocation of prior consent, on the issue of the conditions under which women are allowed to control access to their sexuality from one penetration to the next, one commentator notes: "Even where a woman revokes prior consent, such is the male ego that, seized of an exaggerated assessment of his sexual prowess, a man might genuinely believe her still to be consenting; resistance may be misinterpreted as enthusiastic cooperation; protestations of pain or disinclination, a spur to more sophisticated or more ardent love-making; a clear statement to stop, taken as referring to a particular intimacy rather than the entire performance."[36] This vividly captures common male readings of women's indications of disinclination under many circumstances[37] and the perceptions that determine whether a rape occurred. The specific defense of mistaken belief in consent merely carries this to its logical apex. From whose standpoint, and in whose interest, is a law that allows one person's conditioned unconsciousness to contraindicate another's violation? In conceiving a cognizable injury from the viewpoint of the reasonable rapist, the rape law affirmatively rewards men with acquittals for not comprehending women's point of view on sexual encounters.

Whether the law calls this coerced consent or defense of mistaken belief in consent, the more the sexual violation of women is routine, the more pornography exists in the world the more legitimately, the more beliefs equating sexuality with violation become reasonable, and the more honestly women can be defined in terms of their fuckability. It would be comparatively simple if the legal problem were limited to avoiding retroactive falsification of the accused's state of mind. Surely there are incentives to lie. The deeper problem is the rape law's assumption that a single, objective state of affairs existed, one that merely needs to be determined by evidence, when so many rapes involve honest men and violated women. When the reality is split, is the woman raped but not by a rapist? Under these conditions, the law is designed to conclude that a rape did not occur. To attempt to solve this problem by adopting reasonable belief as a standard without asking, on a substantive social basis, to whom the belief is reasonable and why—meaning, what conditions make it reasonable—is one-sided: male-sided.[38] What is it reasonable for a man to believe concerning a woman's desire for sex when heterosexuality is compulsory? What is it reasonable for a man (accused or juror) to believe concerning a woman's consent when he has been viewing positive-outcome-rape pornography?[39] The one whose subjectivity becomes the objectivity of "what happened" is a matter of social meaning, that is, a matter of sexual politics. One-sidedly erasing women's violation or dissolving presumptions into the subjectivity of either side are the alternatives dictated by the terms of the object/subject split, respectively. These alternatives will only retrace that split to women's detriment until its terms are confronted as gendered to the ground.

Notes

1. W. LaFave and A. Scott, *Substantive Criminal Law* (St. Paul: West, 1986), sec. 5.11 (pp. 688–689); R. M. Perkins and R. N. Boyce, *Criminal Law* (Mineola, N.Y.: Foundation Press, 1980), p. 210.

2. One component of Sec. 213.0 of the Model Penal Code (Philadelphia: American Law Institute, 1980) defines rape as sexual intercourse with a female not the wife of the perpetrator, "with some penetration however slight." Most states follow. New York requires penetration (sec. 130.00 [I]). Michigan's gender-neutral sexual assault statute includes penetration by objects (sec. 750.520 a[h]; 720.520[b]). The 1980 Annotation to Model Penal Code (Official Draft and Revised Comments, sec. 213.1[d]) questions and discusses the penetration requirement at 346–348. For illustrative case law, see Liptroth v. State, 335 So.2d 683 (Ala. Crim. App. 1976), *cert. denied* 429 U.S. 963 (1976); State v. Kidwell, 556 P.2d 20, 27 Ariz. App. 466 (Ariz. Ct. App. 1976); People v. O'Neal, 50 Ill. App. 3d 900, 365 N.E. 2d 1333 (Ill. App.

Ct. 1977); Commonwealth v. Usher, 371 A.2d 995 (Pa. Super. Ct. 1977); Commonwealth v. Grassmyer, 237 Pa. Super. 394, 352 A.2d 178 (Pa. Super. Ct. 1975) (statutory rape conviction reversed because defendant's claim that five-year-old child's vaginal wound was inflicted with a broomstick could not be disproved and commonwealth could therefore not prove requisite penetration; indecent assault conviction sustained). Impotence is sometimes a defense and can support laws that prevent charging underage boys with rape or attempted rape; Foster v. Commonwealth, 31 S.E. 503, 96 Va. 306 (1896) (boy under fourteen cannot be guilty of attempt to commit offense that he is legally assumed physically impotent to perpetrate).

3. In the manner of many socialist-feminist adaptations of marxian categories to women's situation, to analyze sexuality as property short-circuits analysis of rape as male sexuality and presumes rather than develops links between sex and class. Concepts of property need to be rethought in light of sexuality as a form of objectification. In some ways, for women legally to be considered property would be an improvement, although it is not recommended.

4. For contrast between the perspectives of the victims and the courts, see Rusk v. State, 43 Md. App. 476, 406 A.2d 624 (Md. Ct. Spec. App. 1979) *(en banc)*, rev'd, 289 Md. 230, 424 A.2d 720 (1981); Gonzales v. State, 516 P.2d 592 (1973).

5. Susan Brownmiller, *Against Our Will: Men, Women, and Rape* (New York: Simon and Schuster, 1975), p. 15.

6. Diana E. H. Russell, *The Politics of Rape: The Victim's Perspective* (New York: Stein & Day, 1977); Andrea Medea and Kathleen Thompson, *Against Rape* (New York: Farrar, Straus and Giroux, 1974); Lorenne M. G. Clark and Debra Lewis, *Rape: The Price of Coercive Sexuality* (Toronto: Women's Press, 1977); Susan Griffin, "Rape: The All-American Crime," in Chapter 5 of this volume. Ti-Grace Atkinson connects rape with "the institution of sexual inter-

course," *Amazon Odyssey: The First Collection of Writings by the Political Pioneer of the Women's Movement* (New York: Links Books, 1974), pp. 13–23. Kalamu ya Salaam, "Rape: A Radical Analysis from the African-American Perspective," in *Our Women Keep Our Skies from Falling* (New Orleans: Nkombo, 1980), pp. 25–40.

7. Racism is clearly everyday life. Racism in the United States, by singling out Black men for allegations of rape of white women, has helped obscure the fact that it is men who rape women, disproportionately women of color.

8. Pamela Foa, "What's Wrong with Rape?" in *Feminism and Philosophy*, ed. Mary Vetterling-Braggin, Frederick A. Elliston, and Jane English (Totowa, N.J.: Littlefield, Adams, 1977), pp. 347–359; Michael Davis, "What's So Bad about Rape?" (Paper presented at the annual meeting of the Academy of Criminal Justice Sciences, Louisville, Ky., March 1982). "Since we would not want to say that there is anything morally wrong with sexual intercourse per se, we conclude that the wrongness of rape rests with the matter of the woman's consent"; Carolyn M. Shafer and Marilyn Frye, "Rape and Respect," in Vetterling-Braggin, Elliston, and English, *Feminism and Philosophy*, p. 334. "Sexual contact is not inherently harmful, insulting or provoking. Indeed, ordinarily it is something of which we are quite fond. The difference is [that] ordinary sexual intercourse is more or less consented to while rape is not"; Davis, "What's So Bad?" p. 12.

9. Liegh Bienen, "Rape III—National Developments in Rape Reform Legislation," 6 *Women's Rights Law Reporter* 170 (1980). See also Camille LeGrande, "Rape and Rape Laws: Sexism in Society and Law," 61 *California Law Review* 919 (May 1973).

10. People v. Samuels, 58 Cal. Rptr. 439, 447 (1967).

11. Julia R. Schwendinger and Herman Schewendinger, *Rape and Inequality* (Berkeley: Sage Library of Social Research, 1983), p. 44; K. Polk, "Rape Reform and Criminal Justice Processing,"

Crime and Delinquency 31 (April 1985): 191–205. "What can be concluded about the achievement of the underlying goals of the rape reform movement? . . . If a major goal is to increase the probability of convictions, then the results are slight at best . . . or even negligible" (p. 199) (California data). See also P. Bart and P. O'Brien, *Stopping Rape: Successful Survival Strategies* (Elmsford, N.Y.: Pergamon, 1985), pp. 129–131.

12. See State v. Alston, 310 N.C. 399, 312 S.E.2d 470 (1984) and discussion in Susan Estrich, *Real Rape* (Cambridge: Harvard University Press, 1987), pp. 60–62.

13. Note, "Forcible and Statutory Rape: An Exploration of the Operation and Objectives of the Consent Standard," 62 *Yale Law Journal* 55 (1952).

14. A similar analysis of sexual harassment suggests that women have such "power" only so long as they behave according to male definitions of female desirability, that is, only so long as they accede to the definition of their sexuality (hence, themselves, as gender female) on male terms. Women have this power, in other words, only so long as they remain powerless.

15. See Comment, "Rape and Battery between Husband and Wife," 6 *Stanford Law Review* 719 (1954). On rape of prostitutes, see, e.g., People v. McClure, 42 Ill. App. 952, 356 N.E. 2d 899 (1st Dist. 3d Div. 1976) (on indictment for rape and armed robbery of prostitute where sex was admitted to have occurred, defendant acquitted of rape but "guilty of robbing her while armed with a knife"); Magnum v. State, 1 Tenn. Crim. App. 155, 432 S.W. 2d 497 (Tenn. Crim. App. 1968) (no conviction for rape; conviction for sexual violation of age of consent overturned on ground that failure to instruct jury to determine if complainant was "a bawd, lewd or kept female" was reversible error; "A bawd female is a female who keeps a house of prostitution, and conducts illicit intercourse. A lewd female is one given to unlawful indulgence of lust, either for sexual indulgence or profit . . . A kept female is one who is supported and kept by a man for his own illicit in-

tercourse"; complainant "frequented the Blue Moon Tavern; she had been there the night before . . . she kept company with . . . a married man separated from his wife . . . There is some proof of her bad reputation for truth and veracity"). Johnson v. State, 598 S.W. 2d 803 (Tenn. Crim. App. 1979) (unsuccessful defense to charge of rape that "even [if] technically a prostitute can be raped . . . the act of the rape itself was no trauma whatever to this type of unchaste woman"); People v. Gonzales, 96 Misc. 2d 639, 409 N.Y.S. 2d 497 (Crm. Crt. N.Y. City 1978) (prostitute can be raped if "it can be proven beyond a reasonable doubt that she revoked her consent prior to sexual intercourse because the defendant . . . used the coercive force of a pistol).

16. People v. Liberta, 64 N.Y. 2d 152, 474 N.E. 2d 567, 485 N.Y.S. 2d 207 (1984) (marital rape recognized, contrary precedents discussed). For a summary of the current state of the marital exemption, see Joanne Schulman, "State-by-State Information on Marital Rape Exemption Laws," in Diana E. H. Russell, *Rape in Marriage* (New York: Macmillan, 1982), pp. 375–381; Patricia Searles and Ronald Berger, "The Current Status of Rape Reform Legislation: An Examination of State Statutes," 10 *Women's Rights Law Reporter* 25 (1987).

17. On "social interaction as an element of consent" in a voluntary social companion context, see Model Penal Code, sec. 213.1. "The prior social interaction is an indicator of consent in addition to actor's and victim's behavioral interaction during the commission of the offense"; Wallace Loh, "Q: What Has Reform of Rape Legislation Wrought? A: Truth in Criminal Labeling," *Journal of Social Issues* 37, no. 4 (1981): 47.

18. E.g., People v. Burnham, 176 Cal. App. 3d 1134, 222 Cal. Rptr. 630 (Cal. App. 1986).

19. Diana E. H. Russell and Nancy Howell, "The Prevalence of Rape in the United States Revisited," *Signs: Journal of Women in Culture and Society* 8 (Summer 1983): 668–695; and D. Russell, *The Secret Trauma: Incestuous Abuse of Women and Girls* (New York: Basic Books, 1986).

20. Pauline Bart found that women were more likely to be raped—that is, less able to stop a rape in progress—when they knew their assailant, particularly when they had a prior or current sexual relationship; "A Study of Women Who Both Were Raped and Avoided Rape," *Journal of Social Issues* 37 (1981): 132. See also Linda Belden, "Why Women Do Not Report Sexual Assault" (Portland, Ore.: City of Portland Public Service Employment Program, Portland Women's Crisis Line, March 1979); Menachem Amir, *Patterns in Forcible Rape* (Chicago: University of Chicago Press, 1971), pp. 229–252.

21. Answer Brief for Plaintiff-Appellee, People v. Brown, Sup. Ct. Colo., Case No. 81SA102 (1981): 10.

22. Note, "Forcible and Statutory Rape," p. 55.

23. La. Rev. Stat. 14.42. Delaware law requires that the victim resist, but "only to the extent that it is reasonably necessary to make the victim's refusal to consent known to the defendant"; 11 Del. Code 761(g). See also Sue Bessmer, *The Laws of Rape* (New York: Praeger, 1984).

24. See People v. Thompson, 117 Mich. App. 522, 524, 324 N.W. 2d 22, 24 (Mich. App. 1982); People v. Hearn, 100 Mich. App. 749, 300 N.W. 2d 396 (Mich. App. 1980).

25. See Carol Pateman, "Women and Consent," *Political Theory* 8 (May 1980): 149–168: "Consent as ideology cannot be distinguished from habitual acquiescence, assent, silent dissent, submission, or even enforced submission. Unless refusal of consent or withdrawal of consent are real possibilities, we can no longer speak of 'consent' in any genuine sense . . . Women exemplify the individuals whom consent theorists declared are incapable of consenting. Yet, simultaneously, women have been presented as always consenting, and their explicit non-consent has been treated as irrelevant or has been reinterpreted as 'consent' " (p. 150).

26. Brownmiller, *Against Our Will,* p. 5.

27. Shafer and Frye, "Rape and Respect," p. 334.

28. See R. Emerson Dobash and Russell Dobash, *Violence against Wives: A Case against the Patriarchy* (New York: Free Press, 1979), pp. 14–21.

29. On the cycle of battering, see Lenore Walker, *The Battered Woman* (New York: Harper & Row, 1979).

30. Samois, *Coming to Power* (Palo Alto, Calif.: Alyson Publications, 1983).

31. If accounts of sexual violation are a form of sex, as argued in Chapter 11, victim testimony in rape cases is a form of live oral pornography.

32. This is apparently true of undetected as well as convicted rapists. Samuel David Smithyman's sample, composed largely of the former, contained self-selected respondents to his ad, which read: "Are you a rapist? Researchers Interviewing Anonymously by Phone to Protect Your Identity. Call . . ." Presumably those who chose to call defined their acts as rapes, at least at the time of responding; "The Undetected Rapist" (Ph.D. diss., Claremont Graduate School, 1978), pp. 54–60, 63–76, 80–90, 97–107.

33. Nancy Gager and Cathleen Schurr, *Sexual Assault: Confronting Rape in America* (New York: Grosset & Dunlap, 1976), p. 244.

34. Susan Estrich proposes this; *Real Rape*, pp. 102–103. Her lack of inquiry into social determinants of perspective (such as pornography) may explain her faith in reasonableness as a legally workable standard for raped women.

35. See Director of Public Prosecutions v. Morgan, 2 All E.R.H.L. 347 (1975) [England]; Pappajohn v. The Queen, 111 D.L.R. 3d 1 (1980) [Canada]; People v. Mayberry, 542 P.2d 1337 (Cal. 1975).

36. Richard H. S. Tur, "Rape: Reasonableness and Time," 3 *Oxford Journal of Legal Studies* 432, 441 (Winter 1981). Tur, in the context of the *Morgan* and *Pappajohn* cases, says the "law ought not to be astute to equate wickedness and wishful, albeit mistaken, thinking" (p. 437). Rape victims are typically less concerned with wickedness than with injury.

37. See Silke Vogelmann-Sine, Ellen D. Ervin, Reenie Christensen, Carolyn H. Warmsun, and Leonard P. Ullmann, "Sex Differences in Feelings Attributed to a Woman in Situations Involving Coercion and Sexual Advances," *Journal of Personality* 47 (September 1979): 429–430.

38. Estrich has this problem in *Real Rape*.

39. E. Donnerstein, "Pornography: Its Effect on Violence against Women," in *Pornography and Sexual Aggression,* ed. N. Malamuth and E. Donnerstein (Orlando, Fla.: Academic Press, 1984), pp. 65–70. Readers who worry that this could become an argument for defending accused rapists should understand that the reality to which it points already provides a basis for defending accused rapists. The solution is to attack the pornography directly, not to be silent about its exonerating effects, legal or social, potential or actual.

Study Questions

1. According to MacKinnon, how does the law define rape? What is a feminist analysis of rape?

2. Why does MacKinnon reject a definition of rape as violence? Explain in some detail.

3. What is the problem with the notion of force?

4. How does the law of rape operate in regard to consent? What does MacKinnon say are the categories of consent?

5. What message do women get about rape in the legal system?

6. Why does MacKinnon claim that the notion of consent does not serve women well?

7. What does she mean by "the woman (is) raped but not by a rapist"?

8. Why does she say that consent "under conditions of inequality" is questionable? How can this be changed?

6
Philosophy of Religion

Religious institutions profoundly affect our public lives as well as our private lives. Religion affects our public lives in that religious values permeate political, social, legal, and educational structures. Religion also affects our private lives in that religious attitudes inform our domestic and sexual relationships. Thus philosophers have been concerned with the nature and function of those religious values.

Philosophers, historically, have raised such questions as: What is the function of religion? What is the nature of religious concepts? Does God exist, and if so, what is God's nature? How can religious statements be established, and for whom are they valid?

Some feminist thinkers have a strong interest in these matters. From the woman's point of view, the most important questions about religion have not yet been addressed. So feminists are raising such issues as: Is religion by its very nature patriarchal and oppressive? Should women involve themselves with religious institutions to make them more responsive to us? What would it mean to have women-centered religion, which would express matriarchal values or feminist spirituality?

Mary Daly calls for women to reject world religions and their "processions," since they all legitimate patriarchy and are not salvageable. She proposes that women exorcise their minds of patriarchal religious myths by means of "ludic cerebration." Daly speaks of "the qualitative leap" by which women will move "beyond God the Father" and live their own transcendence, in their own time/space. She calls this process "the journey of *becoming*."

Theology may be distinguished from the philosophy of religion as that area that deals with the concept of deity. Carol Christ proposes "thealogy," or the study of the Goddess concept. In positing a male God, she believes that patriarchal religion has supported the devaluation of women. Christ argues that a Goddess symbol would empower women by affirming female strength, by reclaiming the female body, and by valuing female energy.

Gail Stenstad asks: What happens if we hold monotheistic ideology in question? She focuses on ways women might deny patriarchal theologizing the right to set rules. Stenstad calls for anarchic thinking that is characterized by fluidity and multiplicity of meaning. She cites Susan Griffin and Luce Irigaray as voices questioning the master discourse.

The Qualitative Leap Beyond Patriarchal Religion

Mary Daly

The writing of this article presents a minor dilemma. I do not wish simply to rewrite ideas which I have presented elsewhere. Yet there is a background, or frame of reference, or context, out of which the present article is written. To resolve this I am setting forth in very skeletal form, in the form of twenty-three statements, a context discussed at length in a number of articles and in two books.[1]

Prolegomena

1. There exists a planetary sexual caste system, essentially the same in Saudi Arabia and in New York, differing only in degree.

2. This system is masked by sex role segregation, by the dual identity of women, by ideologies and myths.

3. Among the primary loci of sexist conditioning is grammar.

4. The "methods" of the various "fields" are not adequate to express feminist thought. Methodolatry requires that women perform Methodicide, an act of intellectual bravery.

5. All of the major world religions function to legitimate patriarchy. This is true also of the popular cults such as the Krishna movement and the Jesus Freaks.

6. The myths and symbols of Christianity are essentially sexist. Since "God" is male, the male is God. God the Father legitimates all earthly Godfathers, including Vito Corleone, Pope Paul, President Gerald Ford, the Godfathers of medicine (e.g., the American Medical Association), of science (e.g., NASA), of the media, of psychiatry, of education, and of all the -ologies.

7. The myth of feminine evil, expressed in the story of the Fall, is reinforced by the myth of salvation/redemption by a single human being of the male sex. The idea of a unique divine incarnation in a male, the God-man of the "hypostatic union," is inherently sexist and oppressive. Christolatry is idolatry.

8. A significant and growing cognitive minority of women, radical feminists, are breaking out from under the sacred shelter of patriarchal religious myths.

9. This breaking out, facing anomy when the meaning structures of patriarchy are seen through and rejected, is a communal, political event. It is a revelatory event, a creative, political ontophany.

10. The bonding of the growing cognitive minority of women who are radical feminists, commonly called *sisterhood*, involves a process of new naming, in which words are wrenched out of their old semantic context and heard in a new semantic context. For example, the "sisterhoods" of patriarchy, such as religious congregations of women, were really mini-brotherhoods. *Sisterhood* heard with new ears is bonding for women's own liberation.

11. There is an inherent dynamic in the women's revolution in Judeo-Christian society which is Antichurch, whether or not feminists specifically concern ourselves with churches. This is so because the Judeo-Christian tradition legitimates patriarchy—the prevailing power structure and prevailing world view—which the women's revolution leaves behind.

12. The women's revolution is not only Anti-

From *Quest*, Vol. 1, No. 4 (Spring 1975), pp. 20–40. Reprinted by permission of Mary Daly.

227

church. It is a postchristian spiritual revolution.

13. The ethos of Judeo-Christian culture is dominated by The Most Unholy Trinity: Rape, Genocide, and War. It is rapism which spawns racism. It is gynocide which spawns genocide, for sexism (rapism) is fundamental socialization to objectify "the other."

14. The women's revolution is concerned with transvaluation of values, beyond the ethics dominated by The Most Unholy Trinity.

15. The women's revolution is not merely about equality within a patriarchal society (a contradiction in terms). It is about *power* and redefining power.

16. Since Christian myths are inherently sexist, and since the women's revolution is not about "equality" but about power, there is an intrinsic dynamic in the feminist movement which goes beyond efforts to reform Christian churches. Such efforts eventually come to be recognized as comparable to a Black person's trying to reform the Ku Klux Klan.

17. Within patriarchy, power is generally understood as power *over* people, the environment, things. In the rising consciousness of women, power is experienced as *power of presence* to ourselves and to each other, as we affirm our own being against and beyond the alienated identity (nonbeing) bestowed upon us within patriarchy. This is experienced as *power of absence* by those who would objectify women as "the other," as magnifying mirrors.

18. The presence of women to ourselves which is *absence* to the oppressor is the essential dynamic opening up the women's revolution to human liberation. It is an invitation to men to confront non-being and hence affirm their be-ing.

19. It is unlikely that many men will accept this invitation willingly, or even be able to hear it, since they have profound vested (though self-destructive) interest in the present social arrangements.

20. The women's movement is a new mode of relating to the self, to each other, to men, to the environment—in a word—to the cosmos. It is self-affirming, refusing objectification of the self and of the other.

21. Entrance into new feminist time/space, which is moving time/space located on the boundaries of patriarchal institutions, is active participation in ultimate reality, which is de-reified, recognized as Verb, as intransitive Verb with no object to block its dynamism.

22. Entrance into radical feminist consciousness involves recognition that all male-dominated "revolutions," which do not reject the universally oppressive reality which is patriarchy, are in reality only reforms. They are "revolutions" only in the sense that they are spinnings of the wheels of the same senescent system.

23. Entrance into radical feminist consciousness implies an awareness that the women's revolution is the "final cause" (pun intended) in the radical sense that it is the cause which can move the other causes. It is the catalyst which can bring about real change, since it is the rising up of the universally and primordially objectified "Other," discrediting the myths which legitimate rapism. Rapism is by extension the objectification and destruction of all "others" and inherently tends to the destruction of the human species and of all life on this planet.

Radical feminism, the becoming of women, is very much an Otherworld Journey. It is both discovery and creation of a world other than patriarchy. Some observation reveals that patriarchy is "everywhere." Even outer space and the future have been colonized. As a rule, even the more imaginative science fiction writers (seemingly the most foretelling futurists) cannot/will not create a space and time in which women get far beyond the role of space stewardess. Nor does this situation exist simply "outside" women's minds, securely fastened into institutions which we can physically leave behind. Rather, it is also internalized, festering inside women's heads, even feminist heads.

The journey of women *becoming*, then, involves exorcism of the internalized Godfather, in his various manifestations (His name is legion). It involves dangerous encounters with these demons. Within the Christian tradition, particularly in medieval times, evil spirits have sometimes been associated with the Seven Deadly Sins, both as personifications and as causes.[2] A "standard" and prevalent listing of the Sins is, of course, the following: pride, avarice, anger, lust, gluttony, envy, and sloth.[3] I am contending that these have all been radically misnamed, that is, inadequately and even perversely "understood" within Christianity. These concepts have been used to victimize the oppressed, particularly women. They are particularized expressions of the overall use of "evil" to victimize women. The feminist journey involves confrontations with the demonic distortions of evil.

Why has it seemed "appropriate" in this culture that a popular book and film (*The Exorcist*) center around a Jesuit who "exorcises" a girl-child who is "possessed"? Why is there no book or film about a woman who exorcises a Jesuit?[4] Within a culture possessed by the myth of feminine evil, the naming, describing, and theorizing about good and evil has constituted a web of deception, a Maya. The journey of women becoming is breaking through this web—a Fall into free space. It is reassuming the role of subject, as opposed to object, and naming good and evil on the basis of our own intuitive intellection.

Breaking through the web of the Male Maya is both exorcism and ecstasy. These are two aspects of the same journey. Since women have been prohibited from real journeying, that is, from encountering the strange, the unknown, the women's movement is movement into uncharted territory. The process involves removal of the veils which prevent confrontation with the unknown. Let it be noted that "journey" is a multidimensional word and that the various meanings and images conjured up by the word are not sharply distinguishable. One thinks of mystical journeys, quests, adventurous travel, advancement in skills, in sports, in intellectual probing, in psychological integration and transformation. So also the "veils," the insulations against the unknown imposed upon women by male mediators, are multidimensional and intertwined. The veils are woven of religious myths (for example, the myth of the "good woman," the Virgin Mother who has only a Son, not a Daughter), legal restrictions, social customs, medical and psycho-analytic ideologies and practices, academic restrictions (withholding of access to "higher" education, to certain professions), grammatical conditioning ("he" supposedly includes "she"), economic limitations. The very process of exorcism, of casting off the blinding veils, is movement outside the patriarchally imposed sense of reality and identity. This demystification process, standing/moving outside The Lie, *is* ecstasy.

The process of encountering the unknown, of overcoming the "protection" racket, also involves a continual conversion of the previously unknown into the familiar.[5] This requires the use of tools and instruments now in the possession of women's captors. Amazon expeditions into the male-controlled "fields" such as law, medicine, psychology, philosophy, theology, literature, history, sociology, biology, and physics are necessary in order to leave the Fathers' cave and live in the sun. A crucial problem has been to learn how to plunder righteously while avoiding being caught too long in the cave. In universities, and in virtually all of the professions, there are poisonous gases which are almost invisible and odorless, and which gradually stifle women's minds and spirits. Those who carry out the necessary expeditions run the risk of shrinking into the mold of the mystified Athena, the twice-born who forgets and denies her Mother and Sisters. "Reborn" from the Father, she becomes Daddy's Girl, the mutant who serves the master's purposes. The token woman, who in reality is enchained, possessed, "knows" that she is free. She is a useful tool of the patriarchs, particularly against her sister Artemis, who knows better, respects her womanself, bonds with her sisters, and refuses to sell her freedom, her original birthright, for a mess of respectability.

Exorcism, Processions, and Remythologization

What clues can we find concerning the "nature" and direction of the Other-world journey of radically feminist (i.e., conscious) women? Some important hints can be discovered in *Three Guineas*, an astonishing book published in the 1930s by a prophetic foremother. In that book Virginia Woolf links processions (e.g., academic, churchly, military, judicial) with professions and processions. She asks: What are these ceremonies and why should we take part in them? What are these professions and why should we make money out of them? Where, in short, is it leading us, the procession of the sons of educated men?[6]

Clearly, they are leading us to destruction of the human species and of the planet. The rigid, stylized, hierarchical, gynocidal and genocidal processions of male-controlled professions—of church, state, university, army—are all intimately interconnected. These processions capture and reify process. They are deadly. It is important to understand them in order to understand what feminist process/journeying is *not*.

Patriarchal processions both generate and reflect the archetypal image of "procession" from and return to God the Father. In Christian myth, this is a cyclic pattern: separation and return. Christians participate in the procession—they join the parade—through Baptism, which explicitly contains a rite of exorcism. This mythic symbolic procession toward "God," then, begins with belief in possession by evil forces ("possession" technically in a broad sense, of course), release from which requires captivity by the church. What is ultimately sought is reconciliation with the Father.

Clearly, the ultimate symbol of "procession" is the All Male Trinity itself. In various abstruse ways theologians have elaborated upon the "mystery," or as some would say, the "symbol," of the Trinity. What is of great significance here is the fact that this is a myth of Father and Son (no Mother or Daughter involved) in total unity, so total that this "love" is expressed by the Third Person, the Holy Spirit. This is the epitome of male bonding beyond the wildest dreams of Lionel Tiger. It is (almost?) erotic male homosexual mythos, the perfect All Male Marriage, the All Male Divine Family. It is asymmetric patriarchy carried to the sublime absurdity of contradiction, christened "mystery." To the timid objections sometimes voiced by Christian women, the classic answer has been: "You're included. The Holy Spirit is feminine." The conclusion of this absurd logic

arrives quickly if one asks: How then, did "he" impregnate the Virgin Mary?

Mere human males, of course, cannot fully identify with the divine Son. Perfect consubstantiality with the Father, therefore, cannot be achieved. The earthly processions of the sons of men have as their basic paradigm an attempted identification with the Father. (God the Father, the Godfather, the Oedipal Father). The junior statesman dreams of becoming The President. The academic junior scholar (disciple) dreams of becoming The Professor (Master). The acolyte dreams of becoming The Priest. And, as Woolf recognized, the death-oriented military processions reveal the real direction of the whole scenario, which is a funeral procession of the human species. God the Father requires human sacrifice.

Women becoming must indeed recognize the fact of having been possessed by the structures of evil. However, the solution is not "rebirth" or Baptism by the Father's surrogates, for it is this socialized "rebirth" which is the captivity from which we are trying to escape. Radical feminism is *not* reconciliation with the Father. It begins with saying "No" to the Father, who attempts to eradicate our Mother and to transform us into mutants by forcing "rebirth" (whether from the head of Zeus or from the rib of Adam or from baptismal "grace"). More than this: radical feminism means saying "Yes" to our original birth, the original movement-surge toward life. This is both a remembering and a rediscovering. Athena remembers and rediscovers her Mother. That which is generated between us is Sisterhood. We are then no longer confined by our identities as "Mother" or "Daughter." The Daughter is *not* obedient to the Mother "unto death." The Mother does not send her forth to be crucified for the sins of women or of men. Rather, they go forth as Sisters. Radical feminism releases the inherent dynamic in the Mother-Daughter relationship toward Sisterhood, which is thwarted within the Male-mastered system. The Mother does *not* demand self-sacrifice of the Daughter. Rather, both demand of each other affirmation of the self and of each other in an ongoing personal/political process which is mythic in its depths—which is both exorcising and remythologizing process.

The "sacrifice" that is required is not mutilation at the hands of men, but rather the discipline needed for action together, for self-defense and self-actualization on a planet dominated by the Reign of Terror which is the Reign of the Godfathers. It is important that we consider the actual conditions of this terrain through which we must make our journey.

The Land of the Fathers

As Phyllis Chesler has pointed out, the story of the Virgin Mary, impregnated by God to bring forth his only Son, is classic patriarchal rape-incest myth. The Madonna has no Divine Daughter. Moreover, as the same author perceptively says, she foregoes sexual pleasure, physical prowess, and economic and intellectual power in order to become a "mother" for her "divine" son.[7] And this is the primary role-model for women in our culture. This is the life that women are condemned to live out —an alienation which is personal, social, mythic—and which is all the deeper because unrecognized, unacknowledged.

In a society in which women are in fact *robbed* of physical prowess, of economic and intellectual power, we live in a State of Siege.[8] As Jeanne Lafferty and Evelyn Clark wrote:

Every female person knows the humiliation of being constantly harassed and solicited by males. Having her person talked at, whistled at, yelled at, grunted at, hooted and howled at, visually dismembered or stared and winked at by males everywhere—on the street, at work, at school, at home—everywhere.[9]

This is the very real condition of women in a rapist society. Moreover, the dismemberment is not always only visual. Male fetishism concerning women's bodies, the cutting into objectified parts which is the prime material of advertising and pornography, has at its logical outcome the brutal rape murders and actual physical dismemberments which take place in such a society. In a world ruled by God the Father this is not considered a serious problem. A feminist author wrote:

"Rape is too personal and too terrible a crime to be left to the punishment of indifferent male law."[10]

In a society possessed by the sexual caste system, that is, in a rapist society, there is a deep struggle on the part of those designated "victims" to cast out the deception that warps the soul. The deception inflicted upon women is a kind of mindbinding comparable to the footbinding procedure which mutilated millions of Chinese women for a thousand years.[11] Just as footbinding destroyed the capacity for physical movement—walking, running, dancing—mindbinding damages the capacity for autonomous creativity, action, thinking, imagining, willing. Stripping away the mindbindings of lies that reduce women to the status of physical, mental, and spiritual rapes is the basic loving act in such a society.

The Qualitative Leap

Creative, living, political hope for movement beyond the gynocidal reign of the Fathers will be fulfilled only if women continue to make qualitative leaps in living our transcendence. A short-circuited hope of transcendence has caused many to remain inside churches, and patriarchal religion sometimes has seemed to satisfy the hunger for transcendence. The problem has been that both the hunger and the satisfaction generated within such religions have to a great extent alienated women from our deepest aspirations. Spinning in vicious circles of false needs and false consciousness, women caught on the patriarchal wheel have not been able to experience women's own experience.

I suggest that what is required is *ludic cerebration,* the free play of intuition in our own space, giving rise to thinking that is vigorous, informed, multidimensional, independent, creative, tough. *Ludic cerebration* is thinking out of experience. I do not mean the experience of dredging out All That Was Wrong with Mother, or of instant intimacy in group encounters, or of waiting at the doctoral dispensary, or of self-lobotomization in order to publish, perish, and then be promoted. I mean the experience of being. *Being* is the verb that says the dimensions of depth in all verbs, such as intuiting, reasoning, loving, imaging, making, acting, as well as the couraging, hoping, and playing that are always there when one is really living.

It may be that some new things happen within patriarchy, but one thing essentially stays the same: women are always marginal beings. From this vantage point of the margin it is possible to look at what is between the margins with the lucidity of The Compleat Outsider. To change metaphors: the systems within the System do not appear so radically different from each other to those excluded by all. Hope for a qualitative leap lies in *us* by reason of that deviance from the "norm" which was first imposed but which can also be *chosen* on our own terms. This means that there has to be a shift from "acceptable" female deviance (characterized by triviality, diffuseness, dependence upon others for self-definition, low self-esteem, powerlessness) to deviance which may be unacceptable to others but which is acceptable to the self and *is* self-acceptance.

For women concerned with philosophical/theological questions, it seems to me, this implies the necessity of some sort of choice. One either tries to avoid "acceptable" deviance ("normal" female idiocy) by becoming accepted as a male-identified professional, or else one tries to make the qualitative leap toward self-acceptable deviance as ludic cerebrator, questioner of everything, madwoman, and witch.

I do mean witch. The heretic who rejects the idols of patriarchy is the blasphemous creatrix of her own thoughts. She is finding her life and intends not to lose it. The witch that smolders within every woman who cared and dared enough to become a philosophically/spiritually questing feminist in the first place seems to be crying out these days: "Light my fire!" The qualitative leap, the light of those flames of spiritual imagination and cerebral fantasy can be a new dawn.

On "Androgyny"

Feminists have searched for a word to express the concept/reality of psychic wholeness, of integration, which we are just beginning to glimpse intuitively, experientially, as realizable. In this search for the right word we have experienced the poverty of the language bequeathed to us, and we have recognized the manner in which it constricts and even distorts our thought. In my book *Beyond God the Father,* I frequently use the word "androgyny" to express this intuition and incipient experience of wholeness which transcends sex-role stereotyping—the societally imposed "eternal feminine" and "eternal masculine." Feminist ethicist Janice Raymond has written perceptively of an "intuition of androgyny" as identical with the intuition of being.[12] Two young theologians, graduates of Harvard Divinity School, used the term to convey a feminist understanding of wholeness in a much discussed jointly published article.[13] Feminist poet Adrienne Rich used the word in her poem *The Stranger*, which concludes with the following lines:

> I am the androgyne
> I am the living mind you fail to
>   describe
> in your dead language
> the lost noun, the verb surviving
> only in the infinitive
> the letters of my name are written
>   under the lids
> of the newborn child.[14]

All of these authors now experience some hesitancy about using the word "androgyny" to express our vision(s). This hesitancy is at least in part due to an increasing understanding of the political use and abuse of language. This increased sophistication has resulted from some distressing misinterpretations of the word.

In speaking to audiences, I have sometimes had the impression that people hearing this term vaguely envisage two distorted halves of a human being stuck together—something like John Wayne and Brigitte Bardot scotchtaped together—as if two distorted "halves" could make a whole. That is, there is a kind of reification of wholeness, instead of recognition that what is being described is continual process. This non-understanding of "androgyny," which feminists have used when attempting to describe the *process* of integration, is also reflected in the assumption on the part of some women (and men) that a woman who is successful in a career on male terms (for example, a successful business executive) and at the same time a model housewife has achieved "androgyny." In fact, this career housewife as described fails to criticize radically either the "masculine" or the "feminine" roles/worlds. She simply compartmentalizes her personality in order to function within both, instead of recognizing/rejecting/transcending the inherent oppressiveness of such institutions as big business and the nuclear family.

When one becomes conscious of the political usages of language, she recognizes also that the term "androgyny" is adaptable to such mystifying usage as the expression "human liberation" has been subjected to. That is, it can easily be used to deflect attention from the fact that women and men at this point in history cannot simply "get together and work it out," ignoring the profound differences in socialization and situation within the sexual caste system. Both "androgyny" and "human liberation" function frequently to encourage false transcendence, masking—even though unintentionally—the specific content of the oppression of women, and suggesting that wholeness depends upon identification with men. Some of us do still use the term "androgyny," of course, but less frequently, more circumspectly, and with some apprehension that we will be misunderstood.

Some feminists began to feel somewhat less comfortable with the word "androgyny" when the implications of a small terse fact surfaced to consciousness. That fact is etymological: the first part of the word obviously is derived from the Greek *aner, andros* (man), while the second part is from *gyne* (woman). This, of course, carries its own message. A first reaction was to employ the word "gynandry," which, from the perspective of women's becoming, is more appropriate. But it soon became evident that the priority problem in the etymology of the word was really symptomatic of deeper problems.

In fact, the term "androgyny" comes to us heavily fraught with traditional associations, that is, associations of male-centered tradition(s). The image conveyed by the word is that of a "feminized" male. This fact has been brought home to me in public discussions with male Christian theologians who, confronted

with the problem of the inherent oppressiveness of Christolatry, have responded earnestly that there really is no problem since "Jesus was androgynous." Whatever this may mean, it has little relevance to the problem of women's becoming *now*, and in fact it distracts from the real issues confronting us. Dressing up old symbols just will not work for women who are conscious of sexist religiosity.

"Gynandry" helps to shift images away from the traditional biases, but only to a limited degree. Placing the female part of the word first does not dissolve the inherent dependency of the word itself upon stereotypes in order that there be any meaningful content at all. To put it another way, in an "androgynous" or "gynandrous" society it would be senseless to speak of "androgyny" or "gynandry," since people would have no idea of the sex-stereotyped characteristics and/or roles referred to by the components of the terms. Use of these terms at this point in history is dysfunctional to the extent that it encourages on some level a perpetuation of stereotypes (as is the case with Jungian ideology of the "anima" and "animus"). "Gynandry" or "androgyny" *can* function in a liberating way if they are seen as "transitional" words, or, more precisely, as self-liquidating words. They should be understood as having a built-in planned obsolescence.[15]

Wanted: "God" or "The Goddess"?

Feminist consciousness is experienced by a significant number of women as ontological becoming, that is, being. This process requires existential courage, courage to be and to *see*, which is both revolutionary and revelatory, revealing our participation in ultimate reality as Verb, as intransitive Verb.

The question obviously arises of the need for anthropomorphic symbols for this reality. There is no inherent contradiction between speaking of ultimate reality as Verb and speaking of this as personal. The Verb is more personal than a mere static noun. However, if we choose to *image* the Verb in anthropomorphic symbols, we can run into a problematic phenomenon which sociologist Henri Desroche calls "crossing." "Crossing" refers to a notable tendency among oppressed groups to attempt to change or adapt the ideological tools of the oppressor, so that they can be used *against* him and *for* the oppressed. The problem here is the fact that the functioning of "crossing" does not generally move far enough outside the ideological framework it seeks to undermine. In the "Black theology" of James Cone, for example, we find a Black God and a Black Messiah, but this pigmentation operation does not significantly alter the behavior of Jahweh & Son. Cone's Black God is as revengeful and sexist as his White prototype. For feminist eyes it is clear that this God is at least as oppressive as the old (for black women as well as for white women). The message in the alteration of symbol is simply about *which* male-ruled racial group will be on top and which will be on the bottom. The basic presupposition of *hierarchy* remains unaltered: that is, the presupposition that there must be an "us" or a "them" on top, and a corresponding "them" or "us" on the bottom.

Some women religious leaders within Western culture in modern times have performed something like a "crossing" operation, notably such figures as Mary Baker Eddy and Ann Lee, in stressing the "maternal" aspect of the divinity. The result has been mixed. Eddy's "Father-Mother God" is, after all, the Christian God. Nor does Ann Lee really move completely outside the Christian framework. It is interesting that their writings lack the thirst for vengeance that characterizes Cone's all too Christian Black theology, which is certainly in their favor. But it is also necessary to note that their theologies lack explicit relevance to the concrete problems of the oppression of women. Intellection and spirituality remain cut off from creative political movement. In earlier periods also there were women within the Christian tradition who tried to "cross" the Christian all-male God and Christ to some degree. An outstanding example was Juliana of Norwich, an English recluse and mystic who lived in the last half of the fourteenth century. Juliana's "God" and "Jesus" were—if language conveys anything—hermaphroditic constructs, with the primary identity clearly male. While there are many levels on which I could analyze Juliana's words

about "our beloved Mother, Jesus, (who) feeds us with himself,"[16] suffice it to say here that this hermaphroditic image is somewhat less than attractive. The "androgynous" God and Jesus present problems analogous to and related to those problems which occur in connection with the use of the term "androgyny" to describe the direction of women's becoming. There is something like a "liberation of the woman within" the (primarily male) God and Jesus.

Indeed, it is harder to perform a transsexual operation on the Judeo-Christian divinity than a mere pigmentation operation. This is one reason, no doubt, why Cone is able to achieve a purely Black God and Black Messiah rather than a Mulatto, whereas the Christian women mentioned brought forth hermaphrodites, with emphasis upon maleness. Indeed, they did something on the symbolic level which is analogous to "liberating the woman within the man." Since they went only this far, they accomplished little or nothing, in social or mythic terms, toward the genuine liberation of women.

One fact that stands out here is that these were women whose imaginations were still partially controlled by Christian myth. My contention is that they were caught in a contradiction (which is not the case in the work of Black *male* theologians). I am saying that there is a profound contradiction between the inherent logic of radical feminism and the inherent logic of the Christian symbol system. I would not have said this ten years ago, at the time of writing the original edition of *The Church and the Second Sex*, which expressed hope for reform of Christianity in general and Roman Catholicism in particular. Nor would some women today say this—women who still perceive their identity as both Christian and feminist.

Both the reformers and those who leave Judaism and Christianity behind are contributing and will contribute in different ways to the process of the becoming of women. The point here is not to place value judgments upon individual persons and their efforts—and there are heroic efforts at all points of the feminist spectrum. Rather, it is to disclose an inherent logic in feminism. The courage which some women have in affirming this logic comes in part from having been on the feminist journey for quite awhile. Encouragement comes also from knowing increasing numbers of women who have chosen the route of the logical conclusion. Some of these women have "graduated" from Christianity or religious Judaism, and some have never even been associated closely with church or synagogue, but have discovered spiritual and mythic depths in the women's movement itself. What we share is a sense of becoming in cosmic process, which I prefer to call the Verb, Be-ing, and which some would still call "God."

For some feminists concerned with the spiritual depth of the movement, the word "God" is becoming increasingly problematic, however. This by no means indicates a movement in the direction of "atheism" or "agnosticism" or "secularism," as these terms are usually understood. Rather, the problem arises precisely because of the spiritual and mythic quality perceived in feminist process itself. Some use expressions such as "power of being." Some reluctantly still use the word "God" while earnestly trying to divest the term of its patriarchal associations, attempting to think perhaps of the "God of the philosophers" rather than the overtly masculist and oppressive "God of the theologians." But the problem becomes increasingly troublesome, the more the "God" of the various Western philosophers is subjected to feminist analysis. "He"—"Jahweh"—still often hovers behind the abstractions, stunting our own thought, giving us a sense of contrived double-think. The word "God" just may be inherently oppressive.

Indeed, the word "Goddess" has also been problematic, but for different reasons. Some have been worried about the problem of "crossing." However, that difficulty appears more and more as a pseudo-difficulty when it is recognized that "crossing" is likely to occur only when one is trying to work *within* a sexist tradition. For example, Christian women who in their "feminist liturgies" experiment with referring to "God" as "she" and to the Trinity as "The Mother, the Daughter, and the Holy Spirit," are still working within all the boundaries of the same symbolic framework and the same power structure. Significantly, their services are at the same place and time as "the usual,"

and are regarded by most of the constituency of the churches as occasional variations of "business as usual."

As women who are outside the Christian church inform ourselves of evidence supporting the existence of ancient matriarchy and of evidence indicating that the Gods of patriarchy are indeed contrived, pale derivatives and reversals of the Great Goddess of an earlier period, the fear of mere "crossing" appears less appropriate and perhaps even absurd. There is also less credibility allowable to the notion that "Goddess" would function like 'God' in reverse, that is, to legitimate an oppressive "female-dominated" society, if one is inclined to look seriously at evidence that matriarchal society was not structured like patriarchy, that it was non-hierarchical.[17]

Would "Goddess" be likely to function oppressively, like "God"? Given the present situation of women, the danger is not imminent. "Would it function that way in the future?" My inclination is to think not, but it is not my intention to attempt to "prove" this point at this time. The question has a quality of "abstraction" and remoteness from the present social realities and it is, it seems to me, diversionary. When it is raised, and it is usually raised by men, one senses an "atmosphere" about the question, an aroma of masculine hysteria, a fear of invading hordes of "matriarchs" (read, female patriarchs) taking over The Man's world.

There are, however, two points concerning the symbol "Goddess" which I think *are* relevant to the existing situation. First, it can at the very least be pointed out that whenever the pendulum has swung extremely in one direction (and it *has*—for millennia), it is psychologically/socially/ethically important to emphasize "the other side." The hermaphroditic image hardly seems satisfactory for anyone. For an increasing minority of women—and even for some men[18]—"Goddess" is becoming more functional, meaningful, and loaded with healing associations. As this minority grows, Western society will be shaken by the presence of gynarchic symbolism in a new and potent way. It should be noted that women are inclined to speak and write of "The Goddess," whereas one seldom says "The God." In our culture it has been assumed that "goddesses" are many and trivial, whereas the "real" divinity *is* "God," who does not even require the definite article. The use of the expression, "The Goddess," is a way of confronting this trivialization, of exorcising the male "God," and of affirming a different myth/reality.

A second, and related, point has to do with the fact that the "self-transcending immanence," the sence of giving birth to ourselves, the sense of power of being within, which is being affirmed by many women, does not seem to be denoted, imaged, adequately pointed to, or perhaps even associated with the term "God." With her permission, I will relate a story told to me by a theologian for whose insights I have the greatest respect. This woman told me that in the past when riding in planes (and feeling fearful about the situation) she often conjured up images remembered from childhood of "God" as "having the whole world in his hands." Later, this image/prayer? became meaningless. When she was on a plane recently, the ride suddenly became extremely "bumpy" and rough. It occurred to her to "try on" the name/image "Goddess." The result, as she described it, was immediate, electrifying, consoling. She sensed a presence and had/heard? the thought: "Just let go. Just sit on the seat and sit on the air waves and ride." The ride, though as rough as before, became a joyful experience.[19]

Clearly, it would be inappropriate and arrogant to try to "explain" or "interpret" this experience of another person. I can only comment that many women I know are finding power of being within the self, rather than in "internalized" father images. As a philosopher, my preference has been for abstractions. Indeed I have always been annoyed and rather embarrassed by "anthropomorphic" symbols, preferring terms such as "ground and power of being" (Tillich), "beyond subjectivity and objectivity" (James), "the Encompassing" (Jaspers), or the commonly used "Ultimate Reality," or "cosmic process." More recently I have used the expression "Intransitive Verb." Despite this philosophical inclination, and also because of it, I find it impossible to ignore the realm of symbols, or to fail to recognize that many women are experiencing and participating in a remythologizing process, which is a new dawn.

It is necessary to add a few remarks about the functioning of the confusing and complex "Mary" symbol within Christianity. Through it, the power of the Great Goddess symbol is enchained, captured, used, cannibalized, tokenized, domesticated, tranquillized. In spite of this, I think that many women and at least some men, when they have heard of or imaged the "Mother of God," have, by something like a selective perception process, screened out the standardized, lobotomized, dull, derivative and dwarfed Christian reflections of a more ancient symbol; they have perceived something that might more accurately be described as the Great Goddess, and which, in human terms, can be translated into "the strong woman who can relate because she can stand alone." A woman of Jewish background commented that "Mother of God" had always seemed strange and contradictory to her. Not having been programmed to "know" about the distinctions between the "divine" and the "human" nature of "Christ," or to "know" that the "Mother of God" is less than God, this woman had been able to hear the expression with the ears of an extraenvironmental listener. It sounded, she said, something like "infinite plus one."[20] When this symbolic nonsense is recognized, it is more plausible simply to *think* "infinite," and to *image* something like "Great Mother," or "Goddess."

It may appear that the suffix "-ess" presents a problem, when one considers other usages of that suffix, for example, in "poetess," or in "authoress." In these cases, there is a tone of depreciation, a suggestion that women poets and authors are in a separate and "inferior" category to be judged by different standards than their male counterparts. However, the suffix does not always function in this "diminishing" way. For example, there appear to be no "diminuitive" overtones suggested by the word "actress." So also it seems that the term "Goddess"— or "The Goddess"—*is not only non-diminuitive,* but very strong. Indeed, it calls before the mind images of a powerful and ancient tradition before, behind, and beyond Christianity. These are multidimensional images of women's present and future becoming/ be-ing.

"Priests" or *"Priestesses"*?

I would suggest that "priestess" has diminuitive connotations if it is applied within the framework of Christianity (Episcopalian priestesses?), since of course within the limitations of that framework the role "acted out" by women has to be seen as derivative. It is only when one considers the possibility that the Christian tradition is itself derivative from a far more ancient and woman-centered tradition, that one's perception of priesthood changes. For women to be priestesses then is no longer perceived simply as a derivative phenomenon, but as primary and authentic. But then neither is it a Christian phenomenon. The priesthood of women need not seek legitimation within Christian churches. Nor need it be seen as a title or office conferred upon certain officially designated women to the exclusion of others.

Moreover, there are impossible contradictions in the idea of woman-identified Christian priests. While it may be possible for a twice-born Athena to "say Mass," or to commit baptism "in the name of the Father and of the Son and of the Holy Ghost," this sort of behavior presents incredible problems, that is, problems of credibility. Moreover, as I have said, it is inconsistent simply to try to fit a "feminine" symbolism into these sclerotic vessels. The "form" would still be the message, with some alterations in "content."

Is it true, as Malcolm Boyd has recently argued, that "when the (Christian) priest is a woman, even God is no longer a male"?[21] At one time, some years ago, I might have agreed with this. However, it is important to look at Protestant churches which have been ordaining women for years. Clearly, their God (and Gods) are still male. Large patriarchal institutions are still male. Large patriarchal institutions are still quite capable of absorbing a few tokens and in fact of profiting from this, appearing "liberal" while at the same time attracting women who are doubly devoted to the task of serving male Gods. I say "doubly devoted" because, as the cliché goes, a woman has to be twice as "good" as a man to get half as much recognition.

It is instructive to read the list of 110 Catholic signers who have called for the ordination of women "to the priesthood of the universal church."[22] Having read some writings of some of them, I question (1) whether they can possibly understand what the logic of feminism is all about (i.e., leaving behind and thus leaving to die the inherently oppressive structures of patriarchal religions); (2) whether they *do* "understand" what the logic of feminism is about and see "containment" as an important tactic for holding women in bondage as long as possible.

The women's movement *is* about refusal to be merely contained as well as refusal to be mere containers. It is about saying "Yes" to ourselves, which is the deepest way of saying "Yes" to others. At some point in her history a woman may sincerely see ordination to the Christian priesthood as her way of saying this "Yes." It is my hope that such women will *continue* their journey. Ambition to "ordination" perhaps reaches a respectable altitude for the jet age, but it does not reach very far, I think, into feminist space/time. It is my hope that these sisters will raise their ambitions and their self-respect higher, immeasurably higher, that they will one day outgrow their books of common prayer and dream less common dreams.

Notes

1. *Beyond God the Father: Toward a Philosophy of Women's Liberation* (Boston: Beacon Press, 1973); *The Church and the Second Sex,* With a New Feminist Postchristian Introduction by the Author (New York: Harper Colophon, 1975).

2. An elaborate historical study of the Sins is to be found in Morton W. Bloomfield, *The Seven Deadly Sins* (Michigan State University Press, 1952, 1967).

3. Bloomfield gives a variety of "listings" of Deadly Sins in different periods and cultures, with useful contextual information.

4. See Dolores Bargowski's review of the film in *Quest: A Feminist Quarterly* I, No. 1 (Summer, 1974), pp. 53–57.

5. This idea is developed in a remarkable article. See Peggy Allegro, "The Strange and the Familiar," *Amazon Quarterly*, I, 1, pp. 29–41.

6. Virginia Woolf, *Three Guineas* (New York: Harcourt, Brace, and World, Inc., 1938, 1966), p. 63.

7. Phyllis Chesler, *Women and Madness* (New York: Doubleday, 1972), pp. 24–26.

8. This expression was used by Emily Culpepper in an unpublished paper titled "Reflections on Ethics and Self Defense: Establishing a Firm Stance."

9. "Self Defense and the Preservation of Females," in *The Female State: A Journal of Female Liberation*, Issue 4 (April 1970), p. 96.

10. Elizabeth Gould Davis, author of *The First Sex* (New York: G. P. Putnam's Sons, 1971), wrote this in an article about her own devastating rape in *Prime Time*, June, 1974, p. 3.

11. The horrors of footbinding are recounted by Andrea Dworkin, *Woman Hating* (New York: Dutton, 1974), pp. 95–117. These tiny "feet" were malodorous, mutilated humps. Women fell from one to the other. These stumps were described in fantastically deceptive euphemistic language and were the objects of sadistic male fetishism.

12. "Beyond Male Morality," in *Women and Religion*, revised edition, edited by Judith Plaskow and Joan Romero (Missoula, Montana: American Academy of Religion and The Scholars' Press, 1974), pp. 115–125.

13. Linda L. Barufaldi and Emily E. Culpepper, "Androgyny and the Myth of Masculine/Feminine," *Christianity and Crisis*, April 16, 1973, pp. 69–71.

14. Adrienne Rich, *Diving into the Wreck Poems*, 1971–72 (New York: W. W. Norton, 1973).

15. In a speech delivered at the Modern Languages Association Forum, December, 1973, Cynthia Secor noted that there is no "Androgyne Quarterly"—most probably because there are no androgynes around to publish it.

16. Juliana of Norwich, *Revelations of Divine Love*, edited by Clifton Walters (Baltimore, Maryland: 1966), Ch. 61.

17. See Robert Briffault, *The Mothers* (New York: Macmillan, 1927), Vol. I. See also J. J. Bachofen, *Myth, Religion and Mother-Right*, trans. by Ralph Manheim (Princeton: Princeton University Press, 1967).

18. Kenneth Pitchford chooses Goddess imagery, which occurs frequently in his more recent poems.

19. The story was told by Professor Nelle Morton of Drew Theological Seminary, and paraphrased by myself.

20. Comment of Linda Franklin, Boston College student.

21. *Ms.*, December, 1974.

22. Reported in *National Catholic Reporter*, November 8, 1974, p. 5.

Study Questions

---

1. What does Daly mean when she says that women must exorcise the internalized Godfather?

2. What does Daly think of "Amazon expeditions into the male-controlled" fields?

3. What does Daly think of the male-controlled professions?

4. How does Daly view the notion of the Trinity? Of the story of the Virgin Mary?

5. What does it mean to say our society is "rapist"?

6. What is "ludic cerebration," and why does Daly recommend it for women as a "qualitative leap"?

7. How does Daly view the desirability of androgyny?

8. What does Daly think of attempts to perform a "crossing" operation on the concept of the Christian God?

9 Does Daly think that Christian women should try to become ordained ministers or priests in their churches?

10. Does Daly think that feminists should substitute the concept of "Goddess" for that of "God"?

Why Women Need the Goddess: Phenomenological, Psychological, and Political Reflections

Carol P. Christ

At the close of Ntosake Shange's stupendously successful Broadway play "For Colored Girls Who Have Considered Suicide When the Rainbow Is Enuf," a tall beautiful black woman rises from despair to cry out, "I found God in myself and I loved her fiercely."[1] Her discovery is echoed by women around the country who meet spontaneously in small groups on full moons, solstices, and equinoxes to celebrate the Goddess as symbol of life and death powers and waxing and waning energies in the universe and in themselves.[2]

> It is the night of the full moon. Nine women stand in a circle, on a rocky hill above the city. The western sky is rosy with the setting sun; in the east the moon's face begins to peer above the horizon. . . . The woman pours out a cup of wine onto the earth, refills it and raises it high. "Hail, Tana, Mother of mothers!" she cries. "Awaken from your long sleep, and return to your children again!"[3]

What are the political and psychological effects of this fierce new love of the divine in themselves for women whose spiritual experience has been focused by the male God of Judaism and Christianity? Is the spiritual dimension of feminism a passing diversion, an escape from difficult but necessary political work? Or does the emergence of the symbol of Goddess among women have significant political and psychological ramifications for the feminist movement?

To answer this question, we must first understand the importance of religious symbols and rituals in human life and consider the effect of male symbolism of God on women.

From *Heresies* (Spring 1978), in C. P. Christ and J. Plaskow, eds., *WomanSpirit Rising* (New York: Harper & Row, 1979), Chapter IV. Reprinted by permission of Carol P. Christ. (Notes deleted.)

According to anthropologist Clifford Geertz, religious symbols shape a cultural ethos, defining the deepest values of a society and the persons in it. "Religion," Geertz writes, "is a system of symbols which act to produce powerful, pervasive, and long-lasting moods and motivations"[4] in the people of a given culture. A "mood" for Geertz is a psychological attitude such as awe, trust, and respect, while a "motivation" is the *social* and *political* trajectory created by a mood that transforms mythos into ethos, symbol system into social and political reality. Symbols have both psychological and political effects, because they create the inner conditions (deep-seated attitudes and feelings) that lead people to feel comfortable with or to accept social and political arrangements that correspond to the symbol system.

Because religion has such a compelling hold on the deep psyches of so many people, feminists cannot afford to leave it in the hands of the fathers. Even people who no longer "believe in God" or participate in the institutional structure of patriarchal religion still may not be free of the power of the symbolism of God the Father. A symbol's effect does not depend on rational assent, for a symbol also functions on levels of the psyche other than the rational. Religion fulfills deep psychic needs by providing symbols and rituals that enable people to cope with limit situations in human life (death, evil, suffering) and to pass through life's important transitions (birth, sexuality, death). Even people who consider themselves completely secularized will often find themselves sitting in a church or synagogue when a friend or relative gets married, or when a parent or friend has died. The symbols associated with these important rituals cannot fail to affect the deep or unconscious structures of the mind of even a person who has rejected these symbolisms on a conscious level—especially if the person is under stress. The reason for the continuing effect of religious symbols is that the mind abhors a vacuum. Symbol systems cannot simply be rejected, they must be replaced. Where there is not any replacement, the mind will revert to familiar structures at times of crisis, bafflement, or defeat.

Religions centered on the worship of a male God create "moods" and "motivations" that keep women in a state of psychological dependence on men and male authority, while at the same legitimating the *political* and *social* authority of fathers and sons in the institutions of society.

Religious symbol systems focused around exclusively male images of divinity create the impression that female power can never be fully legitimate or wholly beneficent. This message need never be explicitly stated (as, for example, it is in the story of Eve) for its effect to be felt. A woman completely ignorant of the myths of female evil in biblical religion nonetheless acknowledges the anomaly of female power when she prays exclusively to a male God. She may see herself as like God (created in the image of God) only by denying her own sexual identity and affirming God's transcendence of sexual identity. But she can never have the experience that is freely available to every man and boy in her culture, of having her full sexual identity affirmed as being in the image and likeness of God. In Geertz' terms, her "mood" is one of trust in male power as salvific and distrust of female power in herself and other women as inferior or dangerous. Such a powerful, pervasive, and longlasting "mood" cannot fail to become a "motivation" that translates into social and political reality.

In *Beyond God the Father,* feminist theologian Mary Daly detailed the psychological and political ramifications of father religion for women. "If God in 'his' heaven is a father ruling his people," she wrote, "then it is the 'nature' of things and according to divine plan and the order of the universe that society be male dominated. Within this context, a *mystification of roles* takes place: The husband dominating his wife represents God 'himself.' The images and values of a given society have been projected into the realm of dogmas and 'Articles of Faith,' and these in turn justify the social structures which have given rise to them and which sustain their plausibility."[5]

Philosopher Simone de Beauvoir was well aware of the function of patriarchal religion as legitimater of male power. As she wrote, "Man enjoys the great advantage of having a god endorse the code he writes; and since man exercises a sovereign authority over women it is especially fortunate that this authority has been vested in him by the Supreme Being. For the Jew, Mohammedans, and Christians, among others, man is Master by divine right; the fear of God will therefore repress any impulse to revolt in the downtrodden female."[6]

This brief discussion of the psychological and political effects of God religion puts us in an excellent position to begin to understand the significance of the symbol of Goddess for women. In discussing the meaning of the Goddess, my method will first be phenomenological. I will isolate a meaning of the symbol of the Goddess as it has emerged in the lives of contemporary women. I will then discuss its psychological and political significance by contrasting the "moods" and "motivations" engendered by Goddess symbols with those engendered by Christian symbolism. I will also correlate Goddess symbolism with themes that have emerged in the women's movement, in order to show how Goddess symbolism undergirds and legitimates the concerns of the women's movement, much as God symbolism in Christianity undergirded the interests of men in patriarchy. I will discuss four aspects of Goddess symbolism here: the Goddess as affirmation of female power, the female body, the female will, and women's bonds and heritage. There are, of course, many other meanings of the Goddess that I will not discuss here.

The sources for the symbol of the Goddess in contemporary spirituality are traditions of Goddess worship and modern women's experience. The ancient Mediterranean, pre-Christian European, native American, Mesoamerican, Hindu, African, and other traditions are rich sources for Goddess symbolism. But these traditions are filtered through modern women's experiences. Traditions of Goddesses, subordination to Gods, for example, are ignored. Ancient traditions are tapped selectively and eclectically, but they are not considered authoritative for modern consciousness. The Goddess symbol has emerged spontaneously in the dreams, fantasies, and thoughts of many women around the country in the past several years. Kirsten Grimstad and Susan Rennie reported that they were surprised to discover widespread interest in spirituality, including the Goddess, among feminists around the country in the summer of 1974.[7] *WomanSpirit* magazine, which published its first issue in 1974 and has contributors from across the United States, has expressed the grass roots nature of the women's spirituality movement. In 1976, a journal, *Lady Unique,* devoted to the Goddess emerged. In 1975, the first women's spirituality conference was held in Boston and attended by 1,800 women. In 1978, a University of Santa Cruz course on the Goddess drew over 500 people. Sources for this essay are these manifestations of the Goddess in modern women's experiences as reported in *WomanSpirit, Lady Unique,* and elsewhere, and as expressed in conversations I have had with women who have been thinking about the Goddess and women's spirituality.

The simplest and most basic meaning of the symbol of Goddess is the acknowledgment of the legitimacy of female power as a beneficent and independent power. A woman who echoes Ntosake Shange's dramatic statement, "I found God in myself and I loved her fiercely," is saying "Female power is strong and creative." She is saying that the divine principle, the saving and sustaining power, is in herself, that she will no longer look to men or male figures as saviors. The strength and independence of female power can be intuited by contemplating ancient and modern images of the Goddess. This meaning of the symbol of Goddess is simple and obvious, and yet it is difficult for many to comprehend. It stands in sharp contrast to the paradigms of female dependence on males that have been predominant in Western religion and culture. The internationally acclaimed novelist Monique Wittig captured the novelty and flavor of the affirmation of female power when she wrote, in her mythic work *Les Guerilleres,*

There was a time when you were not a slave, remember that. You walked alone, full of laughter, you bathed bare-bellied. You say you have lost all recollection of it, remember . . .

you say there are no words to describe it, you say it does not exist. But remember. Make an effort to remember. Or, failing that, invent.[8]

While Wittig does not speak directly of the Goddess here, she captures the "mood" of joyous celebration of female freedom and independence that is created in women who define their identities through the symbol of Goddess. Artist Mary Beth Edelson expressed the political "motivations" inspired by the Goddess when she wrote,

The ascending archetypal symbols of the feminine unfold today in the psyche of modern Every woman. They encompass the multiple forms of the Great Goddess. Reaching across the centuries we take the hands of our Ancient Sisters. The Great Goddess alive and well is rising to announce to the patriarchs that their 5,000 years are up—Hallelujah! Here we come.[9]

The affirmation of female power contained in the Goddess symbol has both psychological and political consequences. Psychologically, it means the defeat of the view engendered by patriarchy that women's power is inferior and dangerous. This new "mood" of affirmation of female power also leads to new "motivations"; it supports and undergirds women's trust in their own power and the power of other women in family and society.

If the simplest meaning of the Goddess symbol is an affirmation of the legitimacy and beneficence of female power, then a question immediately arises, "Is the Goddess simply female power writ large, and if so, why bother with the symbol of Goddess at all? Or does the symbol refer to a Goddess 'out there' who is not reducible to a human potential?" The many women who have rediscovered the power of Goddess would give three answers to this question: (1) The Goddess is divine female, a personification who can be invoked in prayer and ritual; (2) the Goddess is symbol of the life, death, and rebirth energy in nature and culture, in personal and communal life; and (3) the Goddess is symbol of the affirmation of the legitimacy and beauty of female power (made possible by the new becoming of women in the women's liberation movement). If one were to ask these women which answer is the "correct" one, different responses would be given. Some would assert that the Goddess definitely is *not* "out there," that the symbol of a divinity "out there" is part of the legacy of patriarchal oppression, which brings with it the authoritarianism, hierarchicalism, and dogmatic rigidity associated with biblical monotheistic religions. They might assert that the Goddess symbol reflects the sacred power within women and nature, suggesting the connectedness between women's cycles of menstruation, birth, and menopause, and the life and death cycles of the universe. Others seem quite comfortable with the notion of Goddess as a divine female protector and creator and would find their experience of Goddess limited by the assertion that she is not *also* out there as well as within themselves and in all natural processes. When asked what the symbol of Goddess means, feminist priestess Starhawk replied, "It all depends on how I feel. When I feel weak, she is someone who can help and protect me. When I feel strong, she is the symbol of my own power. At other times I feel her as the natural energy in my body and the world." How are we to evaluate such a statement? Theologians might call these the words of a sloppy thinker. But my deepest intuition tells me they contain a wisdom that Western theological thought has lost.

To theologians, these differing views of the "meaning" of the symbol of Goddess might seem to threaten a replay of the trinitarian controversies. Is there, perhaps, a way of doing theology, which would not lead immediately into dogmatic controversy, which would not require the theologians to say definitively that one understanding is true and the others are false? Could people's relation to a common symbol be made primary and varying interpretations be acknowledged? The diversity of explications of the meaning of the Goddess symbol suggests that symbols have a richer significance than any explications of their meaning can express, a point literary critics have long insisted on. This phenomenological fact suggests that theologians may need to give more than lip service to a theory of symbol in which the symbol is viewed as the primary fact and the meanings are viewed as secondary. It also suggests that a *thea*logy of the Goddess would be very different from the *theo*logy we have known in the West. But to spell out this notion of the primacy of *symbol* in thealogy in contrast to the primacy of the *explanation* in theology would be the topic of another paper. Let me simply state that women, who have been deprived of a female religious symbol system for centuries, are therefore in an excellent position to recognize the power and primacy of symbols. I believe women must develop a theory of symbol and thealogy congruent with their experience at the same time as they "remember and invent" new symbol systems.

A second important implication of the Goddess symbol for women is the affirmation of the female body and the life cycle expressed in it. Because of women's unique position as menstruants, birthgivers, and those who have traditionally cared for the young and the dying, women's connection to the body, nature, and this world has been obvious. Women were denigrated because they seemed more carnal, fleshy, and earthy than the culture-creating males. The misogynist anti*body* tradition in Western thought is symbolized in the myth of Eve who is traditionally viewed as a sexual temptress, the epitome of women's carnal nature. This tradition reaches its nadir in the *Malleus Maleficarum (The Hammer of Evil-Doing Women),* which states, "All witchcraft stems from carnal lust, which in women is insatiable."[10] The Virgin Mary, the positive female image in Christianity does not contradict Christian denigration of the female body and its powers. The Virgin Mary is revered because she, in her perpetual virginity, transcends the carnal sexuality attributed to most women.

The denigration of the female body is expressed in cultural and religious taboos surrounding menstruation, childbirth, and menopause in women. While menstruation taboos may have originated in a perception of the awesome powers of the female body, they degenerated into a simple perception that there is something "wrong" with female bodily functions. Menstruating women were forbidden to enter the sanctuary in ancient Hebrew and premodern Christian communities. Although only Orthodox Jews still enforce religious taboos against menstruant women, few women in our culture grow up affirming their menstruation as a connection to sacred power.

Most women learn that menstruation is a curse and grow up believing that the bloody facts of menstruation are best hidden away. Feminists challenge this attitude to the female body. Judy Chicago's art piece "Menstruation Bathroom" broke these menstrual taboos. In a sterile white bathroom, she exhibited boxes of Tampax and Kotex on an open shelf, and the wastepaper basket was overflowing with bloody tampons and sanitary napkins.[11] Many women who viewed the piece felt relieved to have their "dirty secret" out in the open.

The denigration of the female body and its powers is further expressed in Western culture's attitudes toward childbirth. Religious iconography does not celebrate the birthgiver, and there is no theology or ritual that enables a woman to celebrate the process of birth as a spiritual experience. Indeed, Jewish and Christian traditions also had blood taboos concerning the woman who had recently given birth. While these religious taboos are rarely enforced today (again, only by Orthodox Jews), they have secular equivalents. Giving birth is treated as a disease requiring hospitalization, and the woman is viewed as a passive object, anesthetized to ensure her acquiescence to the will of the doctor. The women's liberation movement has challenged these cultural attitudes, and many feminists have joined with advocates of natural childbirth and home birth in emphasizing the need for women to control and take pride in their bodies, including the birth process.

Western culture also gives little dignity to the postmenopausal or aging woman. It is no secret that our culture is based on a denial of aging and death, and that women suffer more severely from this denial than men. Women are placed on a pedestal and considered powerful when they are young and beautiful, but they are said to lose this power as they age. As feminists have pointed out, the "power" of the young woman is illusory, since beauty standards are defined by men, and since few women are considered (or consider themselves) beautiful for more than a few years of their lives. Some men are viewed as wise and authoritative in age, but old women are pitied and shunned. Religious iconography supports this cultural attitude toward aging women. The

purity and virginity of Mary and the female saints is often expressed in the iconographic convention of perpetual youth. Moreover, religious mythology associates aging women with evil in the symbol of the wicked old witch. Feminists have challenged cultural myths of aging women and have urged women to reject patriarchal beauty standards and to celebrate the distinctive beauty of women of all ages.

The symbol of Goddess aids the process of naming and reclaiming the female body and its cycles and processes. In the ancient world and among modern women, the Goddess symbol represents the birth, death and rebirth processes of the natural and human worlds. The female body is viewed as the direct incarnation of waxing and waning, life and death, cycles in the universe. This is sometimes expressed through the symbolic connection between the twenty-eight-day cycles of menstruation and the twenty-eight-day cycles of the moon. Moreover, the Goddess is celebrated in the triple aspect of youth, maturity, and age, or maiden, mother, and crone. The potentiality of the young girl is celebrated in the nymph or maiden aspect of the Goddess. The Goddess as mother is sometimes depicted giving birth, and giving birth is viewed as a symbol for all the creative, life-giving powers of the universe. The life-giving powers of the Goddess in her creative aspect are not limited to physical birth, for the Goddess is also seen as the creator of all the arts of civilization, including healing, writing, and the giving of just law. Women in the middle of life who are not physical mothers may give birth to poems, songs, and books, or nurture other women, men, and children. They too are incarnations of the Goddess in her creative, life-giving aspect. At the end of life, women incarnate the crone aspect of the Goddess. The wise old woman, the woman who knows from experience what life is about, the woman whose closeness to her own death gives her a distance and perspective on the problems of life, is celebrated as the third aspect of the Goddess. Thus, women learn to value youth, creativity, and wisdom in themselves and other women.

The possibilities of reclaiming the female body and its cycles have been expressed in a number of Goddess-centered rituals. Hallie

Mountainwing and Barbry MyOwn created a summer solstice ritual to celebrate menstruation and birth. The women simulated a birth canal and birthed each other into their circle. They raised power by placing their hands on each other's bellies and chanting together. Finally they marked each other's faces with rich, dark menstrual blood saying, "This is the blood that promises renewal. This is the blood that promises sustenance. This is the blood that promises life."[12] From hidden dirty secret to symbol of the life power of the Goddess, women's blood has come full circle. Other women have created rituals that celebrate the crone aspect of the Goddess. Z. Budapest believes that the crone aspect of the Goddess is predominant in the fall, especially at Halloween, an ancient holiday. On this day, the wisdom of the old woman is celebrated, and it is also recognized that the old must die so that the new can be born.

The "mood" created by the symbol of the Goddess in triple aspect is one of positive, joyful affirmation of the female body and its cycles and acceptance of aging and death as well as life. The "motivations" are to overcome menstrual taboos, to return the birth process to the hands of women, and to change cultural attitudes about age and death. Changing cultural attitudes toward the female body could go a long way toward overcoming the spirit-flesh, mind-body dualisms of Western culture, since, as Ruether has pointed out, the denigration of the female body is at the heart of these dualisms. The Goddess as symbol of the revaluation of the body and nature thus also undergirds the human potential and ecology movements. The "mood" is one of affirmation, awe, and respect for the body and nature, and the "motivation" is to respect the teachings of the body and the rights of all living beings.

A third important implication of the Goddess symbol for women is the positive valuation of will in a Goddess-centered ritual, especially in Goddess-centered ritual magic and spellcasting in womanspirit and feminist witchcraft circles. The basic notion behind ritual magic and spellcasting is energy as power. Here the Goddess is a center or focus of power and energy; she is the personification of the energy that flows between beings in the natural and human

worlds. In Goddess circles, energy is raised by chanting or dancing. According to Starhawk, "Witches conceive of psychic energy as having form and substance that can be perceived and directed by those with a trained awareness. The power generated within the circle is built into a cone form, and at its peak is released—to the Goddess, to reenergize the members of the coven, or to do a specific work such as healing."[13] In ritual magic, the energy raised is directed by willpower. Women who celebrate in Goddess circles believe they can achieve their wills in the world.

The emphasis on the will is important for women, because women traditionally have been taught to devalue their wills, to believe that they cannot achieve their will through their own power, and even to suspect that the assertion of will is evil. Faith Wildung's poem "Waiting," from which I will quote only a short segment, sums up women's sense that their lives are defined not by their own will, but by waiting for others to take the initiative.

Waiting for my breasts to develop
Waiting to wear a bra
Waiting to menstruate
. . .
Waiting for life to begin, Waiting—
Waiting to be somebody
. . .
Waiting to get married
Waiting for my wedding day
Waiting for my wedding night
. . .
Waiting for the end of the day
Waiting for sleep. Waiting . . .[14]

Patriarchal religion has enforced the view that female initiative and will are evil through the juxtaposition of Eve and Mary. Eve caused the fall by asserting her will against the command of God, while Mary began the new age with her response to God's initiative, "Let it be done to me according to thy word" (Luke 1:38) . Even for men, patriarchal religion values the passive will subordinate to divine initiative. The classical doctrines of sin and grace view sin as the prideful assertion of will and grace as the obedient subordination of the human will to the divine initiative or order. While this view of will might be questioned from a human perspective, Valerie Saiving has argued that it has particularly deleterious consequences for women in Western culture. According to Saiving, Western culture encourages males in the assertion of will, and thus it may make some sense to view the male form of sin as an excess of will. But since culture discourages females in the assertion of will, the traditional doctrines of sin and grace encourage women to remain in their form of sin, which is self-negation or insufficient assertion of will.[15] One possible reason the will is denigrated in a patriarchal religious framework is that both human and divine will are often pictured as arbitrary, self-initiated, and exercised without regard for other wills.

In a Goddess-centered context, in contrast, the will is valued. *A woman is encouraged to know her will, to believe that her will is valid, and to believe that her will can be achieved in the world*, three powers traditionally denied to her in patriarchy. In a Goddess-centered framework, a woman's will is not subordinated to the Lord God as king and ruler, nor to men as his representatives. Thus a woman is not reduced to waiting and acquiescing in the wills of others as she is in patriarchy. But neither does she adopt the egocentric form of will that pursues self-interest without regard for the interests of others.

The Goddess-centered context provides a different understanding of the will than that available in the traditional patriarchal religious framework. In the Goddess framework, will can be achieved only when it is exercised in harmony with the energies and wills of other beings. Wise women, for example, raise a cone of healing energy at the full moon or solstice when the lunar or solar energies are at their high points with respect to the earth. This discipline encourages them to recognize that not all times are propitious for the achieving of every will. Similarly, they know that spring is a time for new beginnings in work and love, summer a time for producing external manifestations of inner potentialities, and fall or winter times for stripping down to the inner core and extending roots. Such awareness of waxing and waning processes in the universe discourages arbitrary ego-centered assertion of will, while at the same time encouraging the assertion of individual will in cooperation with natural energies and

the energies created by the wills of others. Wise women also have a tradition that whatever is sent out will be returned and this reminds them to assert their wills in cooperative and healing rather than egocentric and destructive ways. This view of will allows women to begin to recognize, claim, and assert their wills without adopting the worst characteristics of the patriarchal understanding and use of will. In the Goddess-centered framework, the "mood" is one of positive affirmation of personal will in the context of the energies of other wills or beings. The "motivation" is for women to know and assert their wills in cooperation with other wills and energies. This of course does not mean that women always assert their wills in positive and life-affirming ways. Women's capacity for evil is, of course, as great as men's. My purpose is simply to contrast the differing attitudes toward the exercise of will *per se*, and the female will in particular, in Goddess-centered religion and in the Christian God-centered religion.

The fourth and final aspect of Goddess symbolism that I will discuss here is the significance of the Goddess for a revaluation of women's bonds and heritage. As Virginia Woolf has said, "Chloe liked Olivia," a statement about a woman's relation to another woman, is a sentence that rarely occurs in fiction. Men have written the stories, and they have written about women almost exclusively in their relations to men.[16] The celebrations of women's bonds to each other, as mothers and daughters, as colleagues and coworkers, as sisters, friends, and lovers, is beginning to occur in the new literature and culture created by women in the women's movement. While I believe that the revaluing of each of these bonds is important, I will focus on the mother-daughter bond, in part because I believe it may be the key to the others.

Adrienne Rich has pointed out that the mother-daughter bond, perhaps the most important of woman's bonds, "resonant with charges . . . the flow of energy between two biologically alike bodies, one of which has lain in amniotic bliss inside the other, one of which has labored to give birth to the other,"[17] is rarely celebrated in patriarchal religion and culture. Christianity celebrates the father's relation to the son and the mother's relation to the son, but the story of mother and daughter is missing. So, too, in patriarchal literature and psychology the mothers and the daughters rarely exist. Volumes have been written about the oedipal complex, but little has been written about the girl's relation to her mother. Moreover, as de Beauvoir has noted, the mother-daughter relation is distorted in patriarchy because the mother must give her daughter over to men in a male-defined culture in which women are viewed as inferior. The mother must socialize her daughter to become subordinate to men, and if her daughter challenges patriarchal norms, the mother is likely to defend the patriarchal structures against her own daughter.[18]

These patterns are changing in the new culture created by women in which the bonds of women to women are beginning to be celebrated. Holly Near has written several songs that celebrate women's bonds and women's heritage. In one of her finest songs she writes of an "old-time woman" who is "waiting to die." A young woman feels for the life that has passed the old woman by and begins to cry, but the old woman looks her in the eye and says, "If I had not suffered, you wouldn't be wearing those jeans/Being an old-time woman ain't as bad as it seems."[19] This song, which Near has said was inspired by her grandmother, expresses and celebrates a bond and a heritage passed down from one woman to another. In another of Near's songs, she sings of "a hiking-boot mother who's seeing the world/For the first time with her own little girl." In this song, the mother tells the drifter who has been traveling with her to pack up and travel alone if he thinks "traveling three is a drag" because "I've got a little one who loves me as much as you need me/And darling, that's loving enough."[20] This song is significant because the mother places her relationship to her daughter above her relationship to a man, something women rarely do in patriarchy.

Almost the only story of mothers and daughters that has been transmitted in Western culture is the myth of Demeter and Persephone that was the basis of religious rites celebrated by women only, the Thesmophoria, and later formed the basis of the Eleusian mysteries, which were open to all who spoke Greek. In this story, the daughter, Persephone, is raped away from her mother, Demeter, by the God of the underworld. Unwilling to accept this state of affairs, Demeter rages and withholds fertility from the earth until her daughter is returned to her. What is important for women in this story is that a mother fights for her daughter and for her relation to her daughter. This is completely different from the mother's relation to her daughter in patriarchy. The "mood" created by the story of Demeter and Persephone is one of celebration of the mother-daughter bond, and the "motivation" is for mothers and daughters to affirm the heritage passed on from mother to daughter and to reject the patriarchal pattern where the primary loyalties of mother and daughter must be to men.

The symbol of Goddess has much to offer women who are struggling to be rid of the "powerful, pervasive, and long-lasting moods and motivations" of devaluation of female power, denigration of the female body, distrust of female will, and denial of the women's bonds and heritage that have been engendered by patriarchal religion. As women struggle to create a new culture in which women's power, bodies, will, and bonds are celebrated, it seems natural that the Goddess would reemerge as symbol of the newfound beauty, strength, and power of women.

Notes

1. From the original cast album, Buddah Records, 1976.

2. See Susan Rennie and Kristen Grimstad, "Spiritual Explorations Cross-Country," *Quest*, 1975, *I*(4), 1975, 49–51; and *WomanSpirit* magazine.

3. See Starhawk, "Witchcraft and Women's Culture," *WomanSpirit Rising* (New York: Harper & Row, 1979).

4. "Religion as a Cultural System," in William L. Lessa and Evon V. Vogt, eds., *Reader in*

Comparative Religion, 2nd ed. (New York: Harper & Row, 1972), p. 206.

5. Boston: Beacon Press, 1974, p. 13; italics added.

6. *The Second Sex,* trans. H. M. Parshley (New York: Alfred A. Knopf, 1953).

7. See Grimstad and Rennie.

8. *Les Guerilleres,* trans. David LeVay (New York: Avon Books, 1971), p. 89. Also quoted in Morgan MacFarland, "Witch-craft: The Art of Remembering," *Quest,* 1975, *I*(4), 41.

9. "Speaking for Myself," *Lady Unique,* 1976, *I*, 56.

10. Heinrich Kramer and Jacob Sprenger (New York: Dover, 1971), p. 47.

11. Judy Chicago, *Through the Flower* (New York: Doubleday & Company, 1975), plate 4, pp. 106–107.

12. Barbry MyOwn, "Ursa Maior: Menstrual Moon Celebration," in Anne Kent Rush, ed., *Moon, Moon* (Berkeley, Calif., and New York: Moon Books and Random House, 1976), pp. 374–387.

13. Starhawk.

14. In Judy Chicago, pp. 213–217.

15. "The Human Situation: A Feminine View," in *Journal of Religion,* 1960, *40*, 100–112.

16. *A Room of One's Own* (New York: Harcourt Brace Jovanovich, 1928), p. 86.

17. Rich, p. 226.

18. De Beauvoir, pp. 448–449.

19. "Old Time Woman," lyrics by Jeffrey Langley and Holly Near, from *Holly Near: A Live Album,* Redwood Records, 1974.

20. "Started Out Fine," by Holly Near from *Holly Near: A Live Album.*

Study Questions

1. Why does religion have such a compelling hold on people?

2. What "mood" does the traditional religious symbol system create in women, and why?

3. What is the basic meaning of the Goddess symbol? Why is that meaning so difficult for some to comprehend?

4. What controversy surrounds the question "Does the Goddess really exist?" Need a thealogy (as opposed to a theology) take such a question as all-important?

5. What implications does the Goddess symbol have for women's view of their bodies? How does this contrast with male-created theology? How does the Goddess symbol help "reclaim" the female body?

6. How does the Goddess symbol aid the positive valuation of the will? Why is that important for women?

7. How does the Goddess symbol aid the positive valuation of the bonds between women?

Anarchic Thinking: Breaking the Hold of Monotheistic Ideology on Feminist Philosophy

Gail Stenstad

Historically, the institutions of domination have established themselves by destroying community. . . . We must be intimately concerned with preserving and creating community (Starhawk, 97).

The constant calls for unity and homogenization in the Western world derive from our long-standing ideology of monotheism . . . monotheism is a political and psychological ideology as well as a religious one (Adler, 24).

And, I would add, monotheism is also a philosophical ideology. I want to begin by taking the words of two pagans seriously and to suggest that they have important implications for feminist philosophy. What happens if we hold monotheistic ideology in question not only in regard to religion, but in regard to our doing of philosophy in other areas as well?

We have become well aware of the ways in which patriarchal institutions and practices have isolated women and kept them divided from one another. Feminists are not likely to fall into the trap of viewing other women as competitors for men. We are trying to bridge the barriers of race and class. The notion of community among women *as women* has become thinkable. But we may have fallen into another trap: that of confusing unity and homogenization with community.

Feminist philosophy has, over the years, been primarily concerned with theory-building. The practice of theory-building presupposes some philosophical notions that serve to validate the contents of theories: truth, reality and objectivity. A theory seeks to give an objectively true account of the domain of real-

Source: Part of the material in this chapter first appeared in *Hypatia* 3, 2 (Summer 1988): 87–100. Copyright © 1988 by Gail Stenstad. Reprinted with permission of the author.

ity with which it is concerned. The best theory is that which most closely approximates the true and the real. The root assumption is that there really *is* one truth, one reality, and that it is the business of philosophy to give an account of it. The rider is that it is our responsibility to conform our lives to it. The true. Goodness as conformity to the true. Conformity: sameness. God the father. God the son and his priests. All the same. Women: those who are defined in terms of privation (lack of a penis). Difference as lack. Lacking: truth, reality, goodness. Now, we do not feel our difference from men as a lack. But what about our differences from each other? I would suggest that if we persist in theory-building, we risk doing to each other what the patriarchs have tried to do to us.

It has been pointed out by feminists who are women of color that the prominent feminist theories (whether liberal, radical, or socialist) speak primarily from and to the experience of white, middle-class women. If, in our quite understandable desire for a viable political strategy, we fall for the assumption that such strategy requires *a* theoretical base, we silence the voices of and trivialize the experiences of the majority of our sisters. Also, with the exception of some of the radical theorists (such as Mary Daly), theorists tend to either ignore the women's spirituality movement, or castigate it as an escapist diversion from (political) realities. And what about cleaning women, waitresses, and farm laborers: where do they find a voice within any of our theories? Adherence to theory results in the creation of in-groups and out-groups (those who "see the truth" and those who do not). Then the divisions and lack of community become issues in themselves, and we think, "if only we could devise the ultimate feminist theory, the one on which we could all agree." Which amounts to saying, "if only we were all the same." I would suggest that the root of the problem is our adherence to the assumptions that underlie theory-building. Feminists in the 1980s have begun to question such assumptions. For example, feminists working in science and the philosophy of science have begun to call the assumption of pure objectivity in research into question. I would suggest that we need to question these assumptions even more radically.

We need to do much more than confront patriarchal thinking in its own terms and by its own rules. We also need to think in ways that deliberately break the rules, ways that deny to patriarchy the right to set a standard for feminist thinking. Why should we, in our resistance to patriarchy and our attempt to create something different from it, continue to echo some of its most fundamental presuppositions (that there is *a* truth, *a* reality, *the* good, etc.)? One of the most subversive things feminists can do is to think anarchically and then to speak and act from this thinking. Anarchic, unruled, thinking is atheoretical thinking; that is, it is thinking that does not work from, posit, or yield objective distance, supra-historical truth, hierarchical orderings, or a unitary reality. It is thinking that has "renounced the claim to a binding doctrine," accepting no one ultimate referent on which such a doctrine could be based (Heidegger 1971, 185). Thus it is open to a multiplicity of meanings, interpretations, styles and possibilities.

In some ways the difference between theoretical thinking and anarchic thinking is analogous to the difference between monotheism and polytheism. Theoretical thinking and monotheism both tend toward "the one." Monotheism, obviously, is oriented toward one god; historically, many monotheistic religions have also been very concerned with one-ness in doctrine, with arriving at doctrine that can be taken to be the only true or correct one. "One lord, one faith, one baptism." This sort of focus creates an in-group and an out-group: the saved and the damned. While none but the most rigid theorists would go so far in demarcating an in-group and an out-group, accusations of "incorrectness" have been used to silence disagreement. Further, in its very structure, any claim to possess *the* truth, or *the*

correct account of reality or the good, creates an out-group, whether we like it or not. The out-group is all those whose truth or reality or values are different from those posited in the theory. As Margot Adler has pointed out, polytheism has room to include a monotheistic perspective (though the reverse is not the case). A belief in many gods, or in many possibilities of sacred manifestation, can allow for an individual's preference for any one (or more) of those manifestations (Adler, viii). Likewise, anarchic thinking does not abandon or exclude or negate the insights achieved by theoretical thinking, but rather demotes "the theory" to a situational analysis, useful and accurate within limits clearly demarcated in each case. Other, very different analyses, based on other women's situations and experiences, are not ruled out.

How can we think anarchically? What sets anarchic thinking in motion, and what keeps it moving? What are some of the important elements of the actual practice of anarchic thinking? These are the questions I need to address next.

What sets anarchic thinking in motion? There are no limiting rules for what is worthy of thought. The traditional distinction between passion and reason, with only the latter assigned to the realm of "real thinking," is not operative here.

> Let's never give ourselves orders, commands, or prohibitions. Let our imperatives be only appeals to move, to be moved, together (Irigaray 1985b, 217).

Anything that deeply concerns us, touches us in mind and heart, sparks thinking. It might be something as particular as one sentence heard or read, or as general as wonder in the face of life. It might be the bruises on the face of a battered woman, or the nearly incomprehensible prospect of nuclear annihilation. It could be some oppressive situation calling for action, or the success of an act of resistance to oppression. It might be the touch of a hand or the sound of a voice.

Then what? Once we get underway in anarchic thinking, what moves it along? One of the main things that keeps thinking moving is the play of unresolved tension. The important elements or moments of anarchic thinking all seem to act to maintain such tension, and thus to keep anarchic thinking fluid, always in motion, always on the way. Such fluidity serves as well to maintain openness to possibilities that would otherwise remain closed. Persistence in questioning, working and playing with ambiguities, being alert for the presence of the strange within the familiar, and allowing for concealment or unclarity in the midst of disclosure are four elements of anarchic thinking that stand out as particularly significant in this respect.

Persistence in questioning keeps anarchic thinking moving. As feminists, we are questioning the authority of patriarchal structures, institutions and practices. The tidiest and most comprehensive theories, the most self-evident presuppositions, solid truths, and hard facts become questionable. Hairline cracks open up into which we can insert our questions. These questions and our thoughtful responses engender further questions. That is, there is a great deal of caution about letting any of our own "answers" stand unquestioned. Since we are not looking for a theoretical resolution of this question-and-response tension, thinking remains in motion.

We might ask ourselves: how do we view the language we think about and with?

> Words are not terms, and thus are not like buckets and kegs from which we can scoop a content that is there. Words are wellsprings that are found and dug up in the telling (Heidegger 1968, 130).

Anarchic thinking welcomes the ambiguities, the multiplicity of meanings, of the words we encounter and use. Anarchic thinking embraces multiple interpretations of texts. The tensions that arise from such ambiguity and multiplicity serve to keep thinking moving.

Another of the tensions that keeps anarchic thinking moving and opens up new possibilities is the tension between the familiar and the strange or uncanny. Theory-building seeks, in a sense, to make the strange familiar, to tame it and place it in its proper slot in the totality. Anarchic thinking, on the other hand, takes note of the previously unnoticed or unheeded

strangeness in what is familiar. Feminists are already acquainted with this making-strange in the works of, for example, Mary Daly, Luce Irigaray, and Susan Griffin. Daly has made some of the most familiar, taken-for-granted presuppositions and activities of patriarchy appear to us as something strange or even bizarre. I will discuss Griffin and Irigaray in more detail below.

The effect of this making-strange is to decenter the familiar, the taken-for-granted, the true, the real, etc. The boundaries set for our thinking by familiarity are transgressed. The previously unthinkable becomes thinkable. Anarchic thinking is boundary thinking, pushing at the very boundaries of the thinkable, stretching them, rearranging them, breaking them. The practice of thinking at the boundary transforms our thinking; it transforms *us*. When a boundary or limit is seen for what it is, it is loosened; its power to limit is subverted. The transformative experience of anarchic thinking is perhaps one of its most subversive effects. It is a powerful way to clear out lingering internalizations of patriarchal presuppositions. This clears the way, as well, for us to think creatively.

Susan Griffin's *Woman and Nature* serves as a powerful example of this transformative boundary-thinking. *Woman and Nature* is not a theoretical work. Some of the key movements in the text, the movement from dis-membering to re-membering and the closely intertwined movement from silence to speech, serve as a powerful demonstration of the practice of anarchic thinking and the transformative experience which accompanies it.

The book begins by quoting or paraphrasing the voices of the philosophers, the theologians, the scientists, the engineers, the technicians. These voices (the voices of patriarchy, echoing and re-echoing each other) are all very, very familiar. Plato, Aristotle, Aquinas, Bacon, Descartes, Kant, and Schopenhauer. Copernicus, Kepler, Newton, Boyle, and Bohr. The *Malleus Malleficarum*. Pavlov and Freud. The foresters, dairymen, and doctors. All speaking from an ever-increasing objective distance, analyzing, ordering, establishing hierarchies (in which we again and again find ourselves at the bottom), proclaiming the truth, defining reality, dividing the real into useful layers and manageable bits. Listen to Griffin:

> Separation. The clean from the unclean . . .
> The changing from the sacred Death from the
> city. Wilderness from the city. The cemetery.
> The Garden. The Zoological Garden. The
> ghetto. The ghetto of Jews. The ghetto of
> moors. The quarter of prostitutes. The ghetto
> of blacks. The neighborhood of lesbians. The
> prison. The witchhouse. The underworld.
> The underground. The sewer. Space divided.
> The inch. The foot. The mile. The boundary.
> The skin of the sea otter . . . from the sea otter
> . . . the tusk of the elephant . . . from the
> elephant . . . the pelt of the fox . . . from the
> fox . . . the weed from the flower, the metal
> from the mountains, uranium from the metal,
> plutonium from uranium, the electron from
> the atom . . . energy splitting, the chromosome
> split, spirit burned from flesh, desire devastated from the earth (95–8).

As we experience the violence of the tradition with which we are familiar, as we experience the numbing into fearful silence of women's voices down through time, the familiar becomes very, very strange.

> We open our mouths. We try to speak. We try
> to remember (44).

We question and question and question. We notice ambiguities. We ponder alternate interpretations of the familiar words. We begin to speak with each other.

> . . . what is buried emerges . . . What is unearthed is stunning, the one we were seeking
> . . . is ourselves (160).
> We are flesh, we breathe. . . . We speak (46).
> The time of our silence is over . . . we do not
> deny our voices (174–5).

The transformative experience of reading and thinking along with Susan Griffin does not yield some one thought or way of thinking or voice but rather, as she said, *voices*, many voices, all of our voices, however similar or different they may be. Since this thinking is atheoretical, it will not fall into the trap of replacing patriarchal truth and reality with some unitary truth or reality of our own. Anarchic thinking, on the contrary, empowers a multiplicity of strong feminist voices. The speaking (or writing) that

is empowered by anarchic thinking gives voice to the movement of the thinking and not the new possibilities that arise along the way. Our own transformative experience in reading (or hearing) and thinking along with such a voice provokes us to continue the movement of thinking *in our own ways* and to give voice to the new possibilities we encounter and create.

Thus far I have characterized the practice of anarchic thinking as calling for persistence in questioning, openness to ambiguity and multiple interpretations, and attentiveness to the strange-within-the-familiar. As exemplified in Griffin's work, such thinking decenters the familiar, the taken-for-granted, the "true" and the "real." It stretches, rearranges and breaks the boundaries of the thinkable—the thinkable as delimited by the kinds of thinking to which patriarchal institutions give their seal of approval. In so doing, it clears the way for the possibility of creative thinking, of thinking something genuinely different. Those who attempt to think differently, creatively, and to communicate this thinking to others, however, encounter another boundary or barrier: our expectations of language itself. We expect language to disclose something clearly. When we encounter language (whether our own or another's) that seems unclear, that seems to conceal as much as it discloses, we tend to resist or even reject it. It may be helpful here to consider that such expectations of language are linked to traditional, rule-bound thinking. Analysis wants to divide, define, clarify, and master its material. Instrumental rationality takes this further, using such analysis for the purpose of control, of power-over.

In creative feminist thinking, this traditional, rule-bound thinking may run up against something that is opaque to it, something resistant to its penetration, something incalculable and elusive. For example, the possibility of "speaking as (a) woman," as it is explored by Irigaray, is *deliberately* presented as something opaque to traditional modes of thinking. If we are bound to such modes of thinking, we would see Irigaray's "woman's voice" as something irrational, to be rejected out of hand, or as an obstacle to be overcome, to be forcibly penetrated and made clear and mastered. I would suggest that anarchic thinking instead allows for opacity and for language that conceals as it reveals. One thing that the self-concealing quality of such language creates is a shelter from patriarchal and/or instrumental and/or analytic violation. But this somewhat defensive move is only one (and perhaps a lesser) thing that occurs. The other is the way in which its elusiveness actually makes a place for, and *makes way* for the opening up of creative possibilities.

To see how anarchic thinking can help us think these creative possibilities, let us take a closer (though necessarily very brief) look at what Irigaray is trying to accomplish.

> [Whatever we attempt to say], in order to be interpreted, [has] to pass through the master discourse: the one that prescribes . . . [i.e.,] the discourse on discourses, philosophical discourse. . . . But this philosophical mastery . . . cannot simply be approached head-on, nor simply within the realm of the philosophical. Thus it was necessary to deploy other languages . . . so that something of the feminine as the limit of the philosophical might be heard (Irigaray 1985b, 149–150).

We cannot simply use the logical and analytical tools of philosophy to break the limits of philosophical discourse, the master discourse. So Irigaray has deployed two other strategies. The first, which places us *at* the limit, is transformative mimesis, a repetition of the master discourse that evokes the oppressiveness of what is said (and has been said, over and over and over); the familiar discourse becomes strange, alienating, and perhaps optional. We have already encountered a similar transformative move in Griffin. To attempt to go *beyond* the limit, Irigaray explores the possibility of "speaking as (a) woman."

The first question that arises in this attempt is: what is this (word) "woman"? We know what "woman" has been in the master discourse and we know as well how far it is from what we might say of ourselves. But what shall we say of ourselves? To say "woman is __" (fill in the blank) is to acquiesce to the syntax and presuppositions of the master discourse. This syntax allows us to fill in the blank with: a being, entity, subject, object, proper name, concept, formal identity, or intelligible ideality, i.e., something formulated, formed, fixed, finished, complete. In the master discourse, if

"woman" is none of these things, then "she" is simply . . . a blank, a nothing. We know we are not simply nothing. Yet we cannot, according to Irigaray, "fill in the blank" in the master discourse.

> One woman + one woman + one woman will never add up to some generic entity: woman (1985a, 230).

Neither blank, nor definite and finished, "woman" is multiple, ambiguous, indefinite, unfinished, something not fixable within the master grid (1985b, 156; 1985a, 229–230).

When we then go on to explore the creative possibility of "*speaking* as (a) woman," we are thus already speaking from a place of multiplicity and indefiniteness. Therefore, says Irigaray,

> . . . there is simply no way I can give an account of "speaking (as) woman"; it is spoken, but not in metalanguage (1985b, 134).

No metalanguage, no rules of syntax: no *proper* meanings, *proper* names, *proper* attribution, etc. Yet, it is spoken. We have all heard it, if only seldom, in the words of some of our poets (Piercy, Rich, Shange and others). Most philosophers would ask, here, can a speaking for which there is no metalanguage be thinkable? The hidden agenda in this question is that (1) "thinkable" means philosophically thinkable, in the traditional manner, and that (2) something that is not "thinkable" in this sense should not be used in doing philosophy. I would reject the notion that thinking is restricted to what the tradition has allowed it to be, and suggest that *to hear*, in this context, is *to think*. It is, as Mary Daly put it, to "hear forth new words" (Daly, 414).

> [These words are] inaudible for whoever listens to them with ready-made grids, with a fully elaborated code in hand. . . . One would have to listen with another ear, as if hearing another meaning always in the process of weaving itself, of embracing itself with words, but also getting rid of words in order not to become fixed, congealed in them. For if "she" says something, it is not, it is already no longer identical with what she means. What she says is no longer identical with anything, moreover; rather, it is contiguous. It touches (upon) (Irigaray 1985b, 29).

As the words are woven together, arising to disclose something, they are also, at once, withdrawing. There is no self-identity, no pure disclosure. The demand for a pure disclosure is a demand of the master discourse.

Anarchic thinking allows us to hear/think words that are not identical with but are, rather, contiguous with their meaning, words that touch (upon) their meaning, fluidly. In this context, "I hear" is not "I see" but "I am touched." I hear words that draw near and slip away, intimately, yielding only intimations. These intimations spark my desire to draw nearer, to listen . . . to listen not only to the reticence of what is held back, but also for what might arise. I listen for the words of she who attempts to "speak as (a) woman," whoever she may be. . . .

Breaking the hold of monotheistic ideology on feminist philosophy, anarchic thinking shapes a sheltering place for attentiveness and response to the elusiveness of voices other than those allowed for within the master discourse. It makes the master discourse's demand for a pure and conceptually analyzable disclosure optional. Anarchic thinking opens up a space for an *other* thinking, and an *other* speaking, where what has not been sayable can be said . . . and thought, without violation.

References

Adler, Margot. 1986. *Drawing Down the Moon.* Boston: Beacon Press.

Daly, Mary. 1978. *Gyn/Ecology.* Boston: Beacon Press.

Griffin, Susan. 1978. *Woman and Nature: The Roaring Inside Her.* New York: Harper & Row.

Heidegger, Martin. 1971. *Poetry, Language, Thought.* Translated by Albert Hofstadter. New York: Harper Colophon Books.

———. 1968. *What Is Called Thinking?* Translated by J. Glenn Gray. New York: Harper Colophon Books.

Irigaray, Luce. 1985a. *Speculum of the Other Woman.* Translated by Gillian C. Gill. Ithaca: Cornell University Press.

———. 1985b. *This Sex Which Is Not One.* Translated by Catherine Porter. Ithaca: Cornell University Press.

McWhorter, LaDelle. 1987. "Thinking Through the Metaphysics of the Real." Unpublished paper.

Starhawk. 1982. *Dreaming the Dark.* Boston: Beacon Press.

Study Questions

1. How does Stenstad criticize theory-building among women? What does she say about community?

2. What practices does Stenstad explore that she claims will promote anarchic thinking among women?

3. In what does *defamiliarizing* consist? What is its effect?

4. According to Stenstad, what strategy does Irigaray deploy to transform women's thinking?

5. What does she think might be the outcome for feminists of breaking the hold of the ideology of monotheism?

7
Philosophy of Art

Art, like religion, is an aspect of human activity found in all cultures. The field of philosophy that deals with the nature and function of art and the relation of art and society is *aesthetics*. Like ethics, aesthetics is concerned with value judgments and their validity. (In the case of aesthetics, the judgments are about the worth of works of art.)

Feminist theorists are changing the focus of philosophy of art. Feminist philosophers in this field address such questions as: Is there a women's art? How does women's art relate to women's culture and experience? What criteria should feminists apply to assess film, literature, visual arts, music, architecture, and the like?

E. Ann Kaplan's essay offers a critical analysis of art in the patriarchal setting. Specifically, she examines the way in which women are sexually objectified in art, and in turn, how women learn to accept this objectification. In film, this takes the form of "the gaze," which is the cinematic expression of men's objectification of women's bodies and the internalization of this process by women themselves. Kaplan seeks new approaches to film art and aesthetics.

In her essay, Mary Russo focuses on carnival in order to see how the notion of the carnivalesque woman might constitute liberatory practice. She considers the deployment of the grotesque and of masquerade in a feminist aesthetic. Specifically referring to Hélène Cixous and Luce Irigaray, Russo shows how making a spectacle might be recuperative of femininity and the female subject.

Sue-Ellen Case takes up the question of placing woman in the subject position and changing her conditioning as object (of the male gaze) in cultural practices. Case considers camp and masquerade as performance with feminist intent. Specifically, she details how a lesbian configuration might be operative.

"What is the relation of the woman of color to the woman artist?" is the question addressed by Trinh Minh-ha. She focuses on the problems of freedom and commitment for an ethnic consciousness within a feminist aesthetic.

256

Is the Gaze Male?

E. Ann Kaplan

Since the beginning of the recent women's liberation movement, American feminists have been exploring the representation of female sexuality in the arts—literature, painting, film, and television.[1] The first wave of feminist critics adopted a broadly sociological approach, looking at sex roles women were seen to occupy in all kinds of imaginative works, from high art to mass entertainment. Roles were assessed as "positive" or "negative" according to some externally constructed criteria for the fully autonomous, independent woman.

Feminist film critics were the first to object to this prevailing critical approach, largely because of the general developments taking place in film theory at the beginning of the 1970s.[2] They noted the lack of awareness about the way images are constructed through the mechanism of whatever artistic practice is involved; representations, they pointed out, are mediations, embedded through the art form in the dominant ideology. Influenced by the work of Claude Lévi-Strauss, Roland Barthes, Jacques Lacan, Christian Metz, Julia Kristeva, and others, women began to apply the tools of psychoanalysis, semiology, and structuralism in analyzing the representation of women in film.[3] I will not duplicate the history of these theoretical developments here; let it suffice to note, by way of introduction, that increasing attention has been given first, to cinema as a signifying practice, to *how meaning is produced* in film rather than to something that used to be called its "content"; and second, to the links between the processes of psychoanalysis and those of cinema.[4] Feminists have been particularly concerned with how sexual difference is constructed psychoanalytically through

From Ann Snitow, Christine Stansell, and Sharon Thompson, eds., *Powers of Desire* (New York: Monthly Review Press, 1983), pp. 309–327. Reprinted by permission of E. Ann Kaplan. (Notes deleted.)

the Oedipal process, especially as this is read by Lacan.[5] For Lacan, woman cannot enter the world of the symbolic, of language, because at the very moment of the acquisition of language, she learns that she lacks the phallus, the symbol that sets language going through a recognition of difference; her relation to language is a negative one, a lack. In patriarchal structures, thus, woman is located as other (enigma, mystery), and is thereby viewed as outside of (male) language.

The implications of this for cinema are severe: dominant (Hollywood) cinema is seen as constructed according to the unconscious of patriarchy, which means that film narratives are constituted through a phallocentric language and discourse that parallels the language of the unconscious. Women in film, thus, do not function as signifiers for a signified (a real woman) as sociological critics have assumed, but signifier and signified have been elided into a sign that represents something in the male unconscious.[6]

Two basic Freudian concepts—voyeurism and fetishism—have been used to explain what exactly woman represents and the mechanisms that come into play for the male spectator watching a female screen image. (Or, to put it rather differently, voyeurism and fetishism are mechanisms the dominant cinema uses to *construct* the male spectator in accordance with the needs of his unconscious.) The first, voyeurism, is linked to the scopophilic instinct (i.e., the male pleasure in his own sexual organ transferred to pleasure in watching other people having sex). Critics argue that the cinema relies on this instinct, making the spectator essentially a voyeur. The drive that causes little boys to peek through keyholes of parental bedrooms to learn about their sexual activities (or to get sexual gratification by thinking about these activities) comes into play when the male adult watches films, sitting in a dark room. The original eye of the camera, controlling and limiting what can be seen, is reproduced by the projector aperture that lights up one frame at a time; and both processes (camera and projector) duplicate the eye at the keyhole, whose gaze is confined by the keyhole "frame." The spectator is obviously in the voyeur position when there are sex scenes on the screen, but screen images of women are sexualized no matter what the women are doing literally, or what kind of plot may be involved.

According to Laura Mulvey (the British filmmaker and critic whose theories are central to new developments), this eroticization of women on the screen comes about through the way the cinema is structured around three explicitly male looks or gazes: there is the look of the camera in the situation where events are being filmed (called the profilmic event)—while technically neutral, this look, as we have seen, is inherently voyeuristic and usually "male" in the sense of a man doing the filming; there is the look of the men within the narrative, which is structured so as to make women objects of their gaze; and finally there is the look of the male spectator that imitates (or is necessarily in the same position as) the first two looks.[7]

But if women were simply eroticized and objectified, things might not be too bad, since objectification may be an inherent component of both male and female eroticism. (As I will show later on, however, things in this area are not symmetrical.) But two further elements enter in: to begin with, men do not simply look; their gaze carries with it the power of action and of possession that is lacking in the female gaze. Women receive and return a gaze, but cannot act on it. Second, the sexualization and objectification of women is not simply for the purposes of eroticism; from a psychoanalytic point of view, it is designed to annihilate the threat that woman (as castrated, and possessing a sinister genital organ) poses. In her 1932 article "The Dread of Woman," Karen Horney goes to literature to show that "men have never tired of fashioning expressions for the violent force by which man feels himself drawn to the woman, and side by side with his longing, the dread that through her he might die and be undone."[8] Later on, Horney conjectures that even man's glorification of women "has its source not only in his cravings for love, but also in his desire to conceal his dread. A similar relief, however, is also sought and found in the disparagement of women that men often display ostentatiously in their "attitudes."[9] Horney goes on to explore the basis of the dread of women not only in castration (more related to the father), but in fear of the vagina.

But psychoanalysts agree that, for whatever reason—the fear of castration (Freud), or the attempt to deny the existence of the sinister female genital (Horney)—men endeavor to find the penis in women.[10] Feminist film critics have seen this phenomenon (clinically known as fetishism) operating in the cinema; the camera (unconsciously) fetishizes the female form, rendering it phallus-like so as to mitigate woman's threat. Men, that is, turn "the represented figure itself into a fetish so that it becomes reassuring rather than dangerous" (hence overvaluation, the cult of the female star).[11]

The apparently contradictory attitudes of glorification and disparagement pointed out by Horney thus turn out to be a reflection of the same ultimate need to annihilate the dread that woman inspires. In the cinema, the twin mechanisms of fetishism and voyeurism represent two different ways of handling this dread. As Mulvey points out, fetishism "builds up the physical beauty of the object, turning it into something satisfying in itself," while voyeurism, linked to disparagement, has a sadistic side, and is involved with pleasure through control or domination, and with punishing the woman (guilty for being castrated).[12] For Claire Johnston, both mechanisms result in woman's not being presented qua *woman* at all. Extending the *Cahiers du Cinéma* analysis of *Morocco,* Johnston argues that Sternberg represses "the idea of woman as a social and sexual being," thus replacing the opposition man/woman with male/nonmale.[13]

With this brief look at feminist film theories as background, we can turn to the question of the gaze: as it stands, current work using psychoanalysis and semiology has demonstrated that the dominant cinematic apparatus is constructed by men for a male spectator. Women as women are absent from the screen *and* from the audience. Several questions now arise: first, is the gaze *necessarily* male (i.e., for reasons inherent in the structure of language, the unconscious, all symbolic systems, and thereby all social structures)? Or would it be possible to structure things so that women own the gaze? Second, would women want to own the gaze, if it were possible? Third, in either case, what does it mean to be a female spectator? Women are in fact present in audiences: what is happening to them as they watch a cinematic apparatus that constructs a male viewer? Does a woman spectator of female images have any choice other than either identifying as female object of desire, or if subject of desire, then appropriating the male position? Can there be such a thing as the female subject of desire? Finally, if a female subject is watching images of lesbians, what can this mean to her? How do such images inform women's actual, physical relations with other women?

It is extremely important for feminist film critics to begin to address these questions. First, behind these questions, posed largely in structural terms, lie the larger questions concerning female desire and female subjectivity: Is it possible for there to be a female voice, a female discourse? What can a feminine specificity mean? Second, those of us working within the psychoanalytic system need to find a way out of an apparently overwhelming theoretical problem that has dramatic consequences for the way we are constituted, and constitute ourselves, not just in representation but also in our daily lives. Is there any escape from the overdetermined, phallocentric sign? The whole focus on the materialization of the signifier has again brought daily experience and art close together. Now critics read daily life as structured according to signifying practices (like art, "constructed," not naively experienced), rather than the earlier oversimplification of seeing art as a mere reflection/imitation of lived experience (mirroring it, or, better, presenting it as through a transparent pane of glass).

Finally, the growing interest in psychoanalytic and semiological approaches has begun to polarize the feminist film community, and I want to begin by addressing some objections to current theoretical work, since they will lead us back to the larger questions of the female gaze and female desire. In a roundtable discussion in 1979, some women voiced their displeasure with theories that were themselves originally devised by men, and with women's preoccupation with how we have been seen/placed/positioned by the dominant male order. Julia LeSage, for instance, argues that the use of Lacanian criticism has been destructive in reifying women "in a childlike position that patriarchy has wanted to see them in"; for LeSage, the Lacanian framework establishes "a discourse which is totally male."[14] And Ruby Rich objects to theories that rest with the apparent elimination of women from both screen and audience. She asks how we can move beyond our placing, rather than just analyzing it.

As if in response to Rich's request, some feminist film critics have begun to take up the challenge of moving beyond the preoccupation with how women have been constructed in patriarchal cinema. In a recent paper on *Gentlemen Prefer Blondes,* Lucie Arbuthnot and Gail Seneca attempt to appropriate for themselves some of the images hitherto defined as repressive. They begin by expressing their dissatisfaction not only with current feminist film theory as outlined above, but also with the new theoretical feminist films, which, they say, "focus more on denying men their cathexis with women as erotic objects than in connecting women with each other." In addition, these films, by "destroying the narrative and the possibility for viewer identification with the characters, destroy both the male viewer's pleasure and our pleasure."[15] Asserting their need for identification with strong female screen images, they argue that Hollywood films offer many examples of pleasurable identification; in a clever analysis, the relationship between Marilyn Monroe and Jane Russell in *Gentlemen Prefer Blondes* is offered as an example of strong women, who care for one another, providing a model we need.

However, looking at the construction of the film as a whole, rather than simply isolating certain shots, it is clear that Monroe and Russell are positioned, and position themselves, as objects for a specifically male gaze. The men's weakness does not mitigate their diegetic power, leaving to the women merely the limited control they can wield through their sexuality. The film constructs them as "to-be-looked-at," and their manipulations end up merely comic, since "capturing" the men involves their "being captured." The images of Monroe show her fetishized placement, aimed at reducing her sexual threat, while Russell's stance is a parody of the male position.[16] The result is that the two women repeat, in exaggerated form, dominant gender stereotypes.

Yet Arbuthnot and Seneca begin from important points: first, the need for films that construct *women* as the spectator and yet do not offer *repressive* identifications (as, for example, Hollywood women's films do); and second, the need for feminist films that satisfy our craving for *pleasure*. In introducing the notion of pleasure, Arbuthnot and Seneca pinpoint a central and little-discussed issue. Mulvey was aware of the way feminist films as counter-cinema would deny pleasure, but she argued that this denial was a necessary prerequisite for freedom, and did not go into the problems involved. Arbuthnot and Seneca locate the paradox in which feminist film critics have been caught without realizing it: namely, that we have been analyzing Hollywood (rather than, say, avant-garde) films, largely because they bring us pleasure; but we have (rightly) been wary of admitting the degree to which the pleasure comes from identifying with our own objectification. Our positioning as "to-be-looked-at," as object of the gaze, has, through our positioning, come to be sexually pleasurable.

However, it will not do to simply enjoy our oppression unproblematically; to appropriate Hollywood images to ourselves, taking them out of the context of the total structure in which they appear, will not get us very far. In order to fully understand *how it is* that women take pleasure in the objectification of women, one has to have recourse to psychoanalysis. Since criticisms like those voiced by LeSage, Rich, and Arbuthnot and Seneca are important, and reflect the deepening rift in the feminist film

community, it is worth dwelling for a moment on why psychoanalysis is necessary as a feminist tool at this point in our history.

As Christian Metz, Stephen Heath, and others have shown, the processes of cinema mimic in many ways those of the unconscious. The mechanisms Freud distinguishes in relation to dream and the unconscious have been likened to the mechanisms of film.[17] In this analysis, film narratives, like dreams, symbolize a latent, repressed content, only now the "content" refers not to an individual unconscious but to that of patriarchy in general. If psychoanalysis is a tool that will unlock the meaning of dreams, it should also unlock that of films.

But of course the question still remains as to the ideology of psychoanalysis: is it true, as Talking Lips argues at the start of the film *Sigmund Freud's Dora*, that psychoanalysis is a discourse shot through with bourgeois ideology, functioning "almost as an Ideological State Apparatus," with its focus the individual, "outside of real history and real struggle?"[18] Or is psychoanalysis, although developed at a time when bourgeois capitalism was the dominant form, a theory that applies *across* history rather than being *embedded in* history?

Of these two possibilities, the first seems to me to be true. Psychoanalysis and cinema are inextricably linked both to each other and to capitalism, because both are products of a particular stage of capitalist society. The psychic patterns created by capitalist social and interpersonal structures (especially the nuclear family) required at once a machine for their unconscious release and an analytic tool for understanding and adjusting disturbances caused by the structures confining people. To this extent, both mechanisms support the status quo; but they are not eternal and unchanging, being rather inserted in history and linked to the particular social formation that produced them.

For this very reason, we have to begin by using psychoanalysis if we want to understand how we have been constituted, and the kind of linguistic and cultural universe we live in. Psychoanalysis may indeed have been used to oppress women, in the sense of forcing us to accept a positioning that is inherently antithetical to subjectivity and autonomy; but if that is the case, we need to know exactly *how* this has functioned to repress what we could potentially become. Given our positioning as women raised in a historical period dominated by Oedipal structuring and discourse, we must start by examining the psychoanalytic processes as they have worked to position us as other (enigma, mystery), and as eternal and unchanging, however paradoxical this may appear. For it is only in this way that we can begin to find the gaps and fissures through which we can reinsert woman in history, and begin to change ourselves as a first step toward changing society.

Let us now return to the question of women's pleasure in being objectified and see what we can learn about it through psychoanalysis. We saw earlier that the entry of the father as the third term disrupts the mother/child dyad, causing the child to understand the mother's castration and possession by the father. In the symbolic world the girl now enters she learns not only subject/object position but the sexed pronouns "he" and "she." Assigned the place of object (since she lacks the phallus, the symbol of the signifier), she is the recipient of male desire, the passive recipient of his gaze. If she is to have sexual pleasure, it can only be constructed around her objectification; it cannot be a pleasure that comes from desire for the other (a subject position)—that is, her desire is to be desired.

Given the male structuring around sadism that I have already discussed, the girl may adopt a corresponding masochism. In practice, this masochism is rarely reflected in more than a tendency for women to be passive in sexual relations; but in the realm of fantasy, masochism is often quite prominent. In an interesting paper, "The 'Woman's Film': Possession and Address," Mary Ann Doane has shown that in the one film genre that constructs a female spectator, that spectator is made to participate in what is essentially a masochistic fantasy. Doane notes that in the major classical genres, the female body *is* sexuality, providing the erotic object for the male spectator. In the woman's film, the gaze must be de-eroticized (since the spectator is now assumed to be female), but in doing this the films effectively disembody their spectator. The repeated masochistic scenarios are designed to immobilize the female viewer, refuse her the imaginary identification that, in uniting body and identity, gives back to the male spectator his idealized (mirror) self, together with a sense of mastery and control.

Later on in her paper, Doane shows that Freud's "A Child Is Being Beaten" is important in distinguishing the way a common masochistic fantasy works out for boys and for girls. In the male fantasy, "sexuality remains on the surface" and the man "retains his own role and his own gratification in the context of the scenario. The 'I' of identity remains." But the female fantasy is, first, desexualized, and, second, "necessitates the woman's assumption of the position of spectator, outside of the event." In this way, the girl manages, as Freud says, "to escape from the demands of the erotic side of her life altogether."[19]

Perhaps we can phrase this a little differently and say that in locating herself in fantasy in the erotic, the woman places herself as either passive recipient of male desire, or, at one remove, positions herself as *watching* a woman who is passive recipient of male desires and sexual actions. Although the evidence we have to go on is slim, it does seem that women's sexual fantasies would confirm the predominance of these positionings. Nancy Friday's volumes, for instance, provide discourses on the level of dream, and, however questionable as scientific evidence, show narratives in which the woman speaker largely arranges the scenario for her sexual pleasure so that things are done to her, or in which she is the object of men's lascivious gaze.[20] Often, there is pleasure in anonymity, or in a strange man approaching her when she is with her husband. Rarely does the dreamer initiate the sexual activity, and the man's large, erect penis usually is central in the fantasy. Nearly all the fantasies have the dominance-submission pattern, with the woman in the latter place.

It is significant that in the lesbian fantasies that Friday has collected women occupy *both* positions, the dreamer excited either by dominating another woman, forcing her to have sex, or enjoying being so dominated.

These fantasies suggest either that the female positioning is not as monolithic as critics often imply, or that women occupy the "male" position when they become dominant. Whichever the case may be, the prevalence of the dominance-submission pattern as a sexual turn-on is clear. At a discussion about pornography organized by Julia LeSage at the Northwestern Conference on Feminist Film Criticism, gay and straight women admitted their pleasure (in both fantasy and actuality) in being "forced" or "forcing" someone else. Some women claimed that this was a result of growing up in Victorian-style households where all sexuality was repressed, but others denied that it had anything to do with patriarchy. Women wanted, rightly, to accept themselves sexually, whatever the turn-on mechanism.[21] But to simply celebrate whatever gives us sexual pleasure seems to me both problematic and too easy: we need to analyze how it is that certain things turn us on, how sexuality has been constructed in patriarchy to produce pleasure in the dominance-submission forms, before we advocate these modes.

It was predictable that many of the male fantasies in Friday's book *Men in Love* would show the speaker constructing events so that he is in control: again, the "I" of identity remains central, as it was not in the female narrations.[22] Many male fantasies focus on the man's excitement arranging for his woman to expose herself (or even give herself) to other men, while he watches. The difference between this male voyeurism and the previous female form is striking: the women do not own the desire, even when they watch; their watching is to place responsibility for sexuality at yet one more remove, to distance themselves from sex; the man, on the other hand, owns the desire and the woman, and gets pleasure from exchanging the woman, as in Lévi-Strauss' kinship system.

Yet some of the fantasies in Friday's book show men's wish to be taken over by an aggressive woman who would force them to become helpless, like the little boy in his mother's hands. The Women Against Pornography guided trip around Times Square corroborated this; after a slide show that focused totally on male sadism and violent sexual exploitation of women, we were taken on a tour that showed literature and film loops expressing as many fantasies of male as of female submission. The situations were the predictable ones, showing young boys (but sometimes men) seduced by women in a form of authority—governesses, nursemaids, nurses, schoolteachers, stepmothers. (Of course, it is significant that the corresponding dominance-submission female fantasies have men in authority positions that carry much more status—professors, doctors, policemen, executives: these men seduce the innocent girls, or young wives, who cross their paths.)

Two interesting things emerge from all this: one is that dominance-submission patterns are apparently a crucial part of both male and female sexuality as constructed in western capitalism. The other is that men have a far wider range of positions available: more readily both dominant and submissive, they vacillate between supreme control and supreme abandonment. Women, meanwhile, are more consistently submissive, but not excessively abandoned. In their own fantasies, women do not position themselves as exchanging men, although a man might find being exchanged an exciting fantasy.

But the important question remains: when women are in the dominant position, are they in the *masculine* position? Can we envisage a female dominant position that would differ qualitatively from the male form of dominance? Or is there merely the possibility for both sex genders to occupy the positions we now know as masculine and feminine?

The experience of recent films of the 1970s and 1980s would support the latter possibility, and explain why many feminists have not been excited by the so-called liberated woman on the screen, or by the fact that some male stars have recently been made to seem the object of the female gaze. Traditionally male stars did not necessarily (or even primarily) derive their glamour from their looks or their sexuality, but from the power they were able to wield within the filmic world in which they functioned (i.e., John Wayne); these men, as Laura Mulvey has shown, became ego ideals for the men in the audience, corresponding to the image in the mirror, who was more in control of motor coordination than the young child looking in. "The male figure," Mulvey notes, "is free to command the stage . . . of spatial illusion in which he articulates the look and creates the action."[23]

Recent films have begun to change this pattern: a star like John Travolta (*Saturday Night Fever, Urban Cowboy, Moment by Moment*) has been rendered the object of women's gaze and in some of the films (i.e., *Moment by Moment*) placed explicitly as a sexual object to a woman who controlled the film's action. Robert Redford likewise has begun to be used as the object of female desire (i.e., in *Electric Horseman*). But it is significant that in all these films, when the man steps out of his traditional role as the one who controls the whole action, and when he is set up as a sex object, the woman then takes on the masculine role as bearer of the gaze and initiator of the action. She nearly always loses her traditionally feminine characteristics in so doing—not those of attractiveness, but rather of kindness, humaneness, motherliness. She is now often cold, driving, ambitious, manipulating, just like the men whose position she has usurped.

Even in a supposedly feminist film like *My Brilliant Career* the same processes are at work. The film is interesting because it places in the foreground the independent-minded heroine's dilemma in a clearly patriarchal culture: in love with a wealthy neighbor, the heroine makes him the object of her gaze, but the problem is that, as female, her desire has no power. Men's desire naturally carries power with it, so when the hero finally concedes his love for her, he comes to get her. However, being able to conceive of "love" only as "submission," an end to autonomy and to her life as a creative writer, the heroine now refuses. The film thus plays with established positions, but is unable to work through them to something else.

What we can conclude from the discussion so far is that our culture is deeply committed to clearly demarcated sex differences, called masculine and feminine, that revolve on, first, a complex gaze-apparatus; and, second, dominance-submission patterns. This positioning of the two sex genders clearly privileges the male through the mechanisms of voyeurism and fetishism, which are male operations, and because his desire carries power/action, where woman's usually does not. But as a result of the recent women's movement, women have been permitted in representation to assume (step into) the position defined as masculine, as long as the man then steps into *her* position, so as to keep the whole structure intact.

It is significant, of course, that while this substitution is made to happen relatively easily in the cinema, in real life any such "swapping" is fraught with the immense psychological difficulties that only psychoanalysis can unravel. In any case, such "exchanges" do not do much for either sex, since nothing has essentially changed: the roles remain locked into their static boundaries. Showing images of mere reversal may in fact provide a safety valve for the social tensions that the women's movement has created by demanding a more dominant role for women.

We have thus arrived at the point where we must question the necessity for the dominance-submission structure. The gaze is not necessarily male (literally), but to own and activate the gaze, given our language and the structure of the unconscious, is to be in the masculine position. It is for this reason that Julia Kristeva and others have said that it is impossible to know what the feminine might be; while we must reserve the category "women" for social demands and publicity. Kristeva says that by "woman" she means "that which is not represented, that which is unspoken, that which is left out of meanings and ideologies."[24] For similar reasons, Sandy Flitterman and Judith Barry have argued that feminist artists must avoid claiming a specific female power residing in the body of women that represents "an inherent feminine artistic essence which could find expression if allowed to be explored freely." The impulse toward this kind of art is understandable in a culture that denies satisfaction in being a woman, but it results in motherhood's being redefined as the seat of female creativity, while women, "are proposed as the bearers of culture, albeit an alternative one."[25]

Barry and Flitterman argue that this form of feminist art, along with some others that they outline, is dangerous in not taking into account "the social contradictions involved in 'femininity.'" They suggest that "a radical feminist art would include an understanding of how women are constituted through social practices in culture," and argue for "an aesthetics designed to subvert the production of 'woman' as commodity," much as Claire Johnston and Laura Mulvey had earlier stated that to be feminist, a cinema had to be a counter-cinema.[26]

The problem with all these arguments is that they leave women trapped in the position of negativity—subverting rather than positing. Although the feminists asserting this point of view are clearly right in placing in the foreground women's repression in representation and culture (and in seeing this work as a necessary first step), it is hard to see how women can move forward from these awarenesses. If certain feminist groups (i.e., Women Against Pornography) err on the side of eliding reality with fantasy (i.e., in treating an image's violating of women on the same level as a literal act of violation on the street), feminist critics err on the side of seeing a world constructed only of signifiers, of losing contact with the "referred" world of the social formation.

The first error was in positing an unproblematic relationship between art and life in the sense that (1) art was seen as able simply to imitate life, as if through a transparent pane of glass; and (2) that representation was thought to affect social behavior directly; but the second error is to see art and life as both equally "constructed" by the signifying practices that define and limit each sphere. The signifier is here made material, in the sense that it is all there is to know. Discussing semiology in relation to Marxism, Terry Eagleton points out the dangers of this way of seeing for a Marxist view of history. History evaporates in the new scheme, since the signified can never be grasped, we cannot talk about our reality as human subjects. But, as he goes on to show, more than the signified (which in Saussure's scheme obediently followed the signifier, despite its being arbitrary) is at stake: "It is also," he says "a question of the referent, which we all long ago bracketed out of being. In rematerializing the sign, we are in imminent danger of de-materializing its referent; a linguistic materialism gradually reverts itself into a linguistic idealism."[27]

Eagleton no doubt overstates the case when he talks about "sliding away from the referent,"

since neither Saussure nor Althusser denied that there *was* a referent. But it is true that while semiologists talk about the eruption of "the real" (i.e., accidents, death, revolution), on a daily basis they tend to be preoccupied with life as dominated by the prevailing signifying practices of a culture. It may be true that all lived experience is mediated through signifying practices, but we should not therefore pay exclusive attention to this level of things. In attempting to get rid of an unwelcome dualism, inherent in western thought at least since Plato, and rearticulated by Kant on the brink of the modern period, some semiologists run the danger of collapsing levels of things that need to remain distinct if we are to work effectively in the political arena to bring about change.

Thus while it is essential for feminist film critics to examine signifying processes carefully in order to fully understand the way women have been constructed in language and the nonverbal arts, it is equally important not to lose sight of the need to find strategies for changing discourse, since these changes would, in turn, affect the structuring of the social formation.

Some feminist film critics have begun to face this challenge. The directors of *Sigmund Freud's Dora,* for example, suggest that raising questions is the first step toward establishing a female discourse, or, perhaps, that asking questions is the only discourse available to women as a resistance to patriarchal domination. Since questions lead to more questions, a kind of movement is in fact taking place, although it is in a nontraditional mode. Sally Potter structured her film *Thriller* around this very notion, and allowed her heroine's investigation of herself as heroine to lead to some (tentative) conclusions. And Laura Mulvey has suggested that even if one accepts the psychoanalytic positioning of women, all is not lost, since the Oedipus complex is not completed in women; she notes that "there's some way in which women aren't colonized," having been "so specifically excluded from culture and language."[28]

From this position, psychoanalytic theory allows us to see that there is more possibility for women to change themselves (and perhaps to bring about social change) just because they have not been processed, as have little boys, through a clearly defined, and ultimately simple, set of psychic stages. The girl's relationship to her mother remains forever unresolved, incomplete; in heterosexuality, she is forced to turn away from her primary love object, destined never to return to it, while the boy, through marrying someone like his mother, can regain his original plenitude in another form. The girl must transfer her need for love to the father, who, as Nancy Chodorow has shown, never completely satisfies.[29]

Mulvey thus suggests that patriarchal culture is not monolithic, not cleanly sealed. There are gaps, fissures through which women can begin to ask questions and introduce change. The directors of *Sigmund Freud's Dora* end their film with a series of letters from a daughter (who is sometimes called Dora) read out by her mother, some of which deal with the place of the mother in psychoanalysis. The daughter's comments illuminate the fact that Freud dismisses Dora's mother (in his famous account of the case history), instead of talking about her "as the site of the intersection of many representations" (of which the historical mother is just one). She suggests that Freud's omission was not merely an oversight, but, given his system, a necessity.

Mulvey and Wollen's earlier film, *Riddles of the Sphinx,* confronted the repression of mothering in patriarchal culture directly; the film argued that women "live in a society ruled by the father, in which the place of the mother is repressed. Motherhood, and how to live it or not to live it, lies at the root of the dilemma."[30] In an interview, Mulvey noted the influence of psychoanalysis on her conception of the mother-child exchange ("the identification between the two, and the implications that has for narcissism and recognition of the self in the 'other' "), but she went on to say that this is an area rarely read from the mother's point of view.[31]

Motherhood thus becomes one place from which to begin to reformulate our position as women, just because men have not dealt with it theoretically or in the social realm (i.e., by providing free childcare, free abortions, maternal leave, after-school child programs, etc.). Motherhood has been repressed on all levels except that of hypostatization, romanticization,

and idealization. Yet women have been struggling with lives as mothers—silently, quietly, often in agony, often in bliss, but always on the periphery of a society that tries to make us all, men and women, forget our mothers.

But motherhood, and the fact that we were all mothered, will not be repressed; or, if the attempt is made, there will be effects signaling "the return of the repressed." The entire construction of woman in patriarchy as a lack could be viewed as emerging from the need to repress mothering and the painful memory traces it has left in the man. The phallus as signified can be set in motion only given the other with a lack, and this has resulted in the male focus on castration. But is it possible that this focus was designed to mask an even greater threat that mothering poses? And if we look from the position of women, need this lack in reality have the dire implications men would have us believe? The focus on women as (simply) sex object, or (more complexly) as fetishized (narcissistic male desire) that we have been tracing through Hollywood films, may be part of the apparatus that represses mothering. The insistence on rigidly defined sex roles, and the dominance-submission, voyeurism-fetishism mechanisms may be constructed to this end.

In placing the problem of mothering in the foreground in this way, one is not necessarily falling into the trap of essentialism. First, I am not denying that motherhood has been constructed in patriarchy by its very place as repressed; nor, second, am I saying that women are inherently mothers; nor, third, that the only ideal relationship that can express female specificity is mothering. I am saying, rather, that motherhood is one of the areas that has been left vague, allowing us to reformulate the position as given, rather than discovering a specificity outside the system we are in. It is a place to start rethinking sex-difference, not an end.

Let me review briefly some of the main ways in which motherhood can be thought of within psychoanalysis. First, and most conservatively, motherhood has been analyzed as an essentially narcissistic relationship, and as involved with the problem of castration. In this way, it parallels male fetishism; just as men fetishize women in order to reduce their threat (finding themselves thus in the other), so women fetishize the child, looking in the child for the phallus to "make up" for castration; second, motherhood can be seen as narcissistic, not in the sense of finding the phallus in the child, but of finding *the self* in the child (this parallels male fetishizing of women in another way); women here do not relate to the child as other, but as an extension of their own egos; third, and most radically (but this is also the position that can lead to essentialism), one could argue that since the law represses mothering, a gap is left through which it may be possible to subvert patriarchy.

The problem with this latter (and most hopeful) position, however, is that of how to express motherhood after the period of the imaginary. One could argue that women are faced with an impossible dilemma: to remain in blissful unity with the child in the imaginary (or to try to hold onto this realm as long as possible), or to enter the symbolic in which mothering is repressed, cannot be "spoken," cannot represent a position of power. Here the only resistance is silence.

But is this not one of those places where a rigid adherence to the theoretical formulation of imaginary and symbolic betrays the inadequacy of the theory? Is not mothering, in fact, now being "spoken," even through patriarchal discourse? Both Dorothy Dinnerstein and Nancy Chodorow "speak" a discourse about mothering that, while remaining within psychoanalysis, breaks new ground.[32] And the feminist films about mothering now appearing begin to investigate and move beyond patriarchal representations.[33]

On the social/historical level, in addition, we are living in a period in which mothers are increasingly living alone with their children, offering the possibility for new psychic patterns to emerge; fathers are increasingly becoming involved with childrearing, and also living alone with their children. Freud's own kind of science (which involved studying the people brought up in strict Victorian, bourgeois households) applied rigorously to people today results in very different conclusions. Single mothers are forced to make themselves subject in relation to their children; they are forced to invent new symbolic roles, which combine positions previously assigned to fathers with traditional female ones. The child cannot position the mother as object to the father's law, since in single-parent households *her* desire sets things in motion.

A methodology is often not per se either revolutionary or reactionary, but open to appropriation for a variety of usages. At this point, feminists may have to use psychoanalysis, but in a manner opposite to the traditional one. Other kinds of psychic processes obviously can exist and may stand as models for when we have worked our way through the morass that confronts us as people having grown up in western capitalist culture. Julia Kristeva, for example, suggests that desire functions in a very different manner in China, and urges us to explore Chinese culture, from a very careful psychoanalytic point of view, to see what is possible.[34]

Many of the mechanisms we have found in Hollywood films which echo deeply embedded myths in western capitalist culture are thus not inviolable, eternal, unchanging, or inherently necessary. They rather reflect the unconscious of patriarchy, including a fear of the pre-Oedipal plenitude with the mother. The domination of women by the male gaze is part of men's strategy to contain the threat that the mother embodies, and to control the positive and negative impulses that memory traces of being mothered have left in the male unconscious. Women, in turn, have learned to associate their sexuality with domination by the male gaze, a position involving a degree of masochism in finding their objectification erotic. We have participated in and perpetuated our domination by following the pleasure principle, which leaves us no options, given our positioning.

Everything, thus, revolves around the issue of pleasure, and it is here that patriarchal repression has been most negative. For things have been structured to make us forget the mutual, pleasurable bonding that we all, male and female, enjoyed with our mothers. Some recent experimental (as against psychoanalytic) studies have shown that the gaze is first set in motion in the mother-child relationship. But this is a *mutual* gazing, rather than the subject-object kind that reduces one of the parties to the place of submission. Patriarchy has worked hard to prevent the eruption of a (mythically) feared return of the matriarchy that might take place were the close mother-child bonding returned to dominance, or allowed to stand in place of the law of the father.

This is by no means to argue that a return to matriarchy would be either possible or desirable. What rather has to happen is that we move beyond long-held cultural and linguistic patterns of oppositions: male/female (as these terms currently signify); dominant/submissive; active/passive; nature/civilization; order/chaos; matriarchal/patriarchal. If rigidly defined sex differences have been constructed around fear of the other, we need to think about ways of transcending a polarity that has only brought us all pain.

Notes

1. See works by Kate Millett, Linda Nochlin, Molly Haskell, articles in the few issues of *Women in Film* (1972–1975), and articles in *Screen* and *Screen Education* throughout the 1970s.

2. See especially work by Christian Metz, Jean-Louis Comolli, Raymond Bellour, Roland Barthes, and essays in *Cahiers du Cinema* in France; in England, the work by Stephen Heath, Colin McCabe, Paul Willémen, and others in *Screen* and elsewhere.

3. See especially the work of Claire Johnston, Pam Cook, and Laura Mulvey from England, and subsequent work by the *Camera Obscura* group.

4. Christine Gledhill, "Recent Developments in Feminist Film Criticism," *Quarterly Review of Film Studies* 3, no. 4 (1978): 458–93; E. Ann Kaplan, "Aspects of British Feminist Film Criticism," *Jump Cut*, nos. 12–13 (December 1976): 52–56; and Kaplan, "Integrating Marxist and Psychoanalytic Concepts in Feminist Film Criticism," *Millenium Film Journal* (April 1980): 8–17.

5. Jacques Lacan, "The Mirror Phase as Formative of the Function of the 'I'" (1949), in *New Left Review* 51 (September/October 1968): 71–77. See also essays on Lacan in Anthony Wilden, *System and Structure: Essays in Communication and Exchange* (London: Tavistock Publications, 1972).

6. For a background to semiological concepts, see work by Roland Barthes, Julia Kristeva, and Umberto Eco among others. Terence Hawkes, *Structuralism and Semiology* (London: Methuen, 1977), and Rosalind Coward and John Ellis, *Language and Materialism* (London: Routledge and Kegan Paul, 1977) provide useful summaries of relevant material.

7. Laura Mulvey, "Visual Pleasure and Narrative Cinema," *Screen* 16, no. 3 (Autumn 1975): 6–18.

8. Karen Horney, "The Dread of Woman" (1932), in *Feminine Psychology* (New York: W. W. Norton, 1967), p. 134.

9. Ibid., p. 136.

10. For a useful discussion of fetishism, see Otto Fenichel, *The Psychoanalytic Theory of Neurosis* (New York: W. W. Norton, 1945), pp. 341–345.

11. Mulvey, "Visual Pleasure," p. 14.

12. Ibid.

13. Claire Johnston, "Woman's Cinema as Counter-Cinema," in *Notes on Women's Cinema,* ed. Claire Johnston (London: Screen Pamphlet, 1973), p. 26.

14. "Women and Film: A Discussion of Feminist Aesthetics," *New German Critique* 13 (Winter 1978): 93.

15. Lucy Arbuthnot and Gail Seneca, "Pre-Text and Text in *Gentlemen Prefer Blondes*," paper delivered at the Conference on Feminist Film Criticism, Northwestern University, November 1980.

16. See Maureen Turim, "Gentlemen Consume Blondes," in *Wideangle* 1, no. 1 (1979): 52–59. Carol Rowe also (if somewhat mockingly) shows Monroe's phallicism in her film *Grand Delusion.*

17. See the essays in *Edinburgh Magazine* 1 (1977) by Coward, Metz, Heath, and Johnston. Also the issue of *Screen* 16, no. 2 (Summer 1975), on "Psychoanalysis and Cinema," especially the piece by Metz.

18. See E. Ann Kaplan, "Feminist Approaches to History, Psychoanalysis, and Cinema in *Sigmund Freud's Dora*," *Millenium Film Journal* 7/8/9 (Fall/Winter 1979): 173–85.

19. Mary Ann Doane, "The Woman's Film: Possession and Address," paper delivered at the Conference on Cinema History, Asilomar, Monterey, May 1981, pp. 3–8.

20. Nancy Friday, *My Secret Garden: Women's Sexual Fantasies* (New York: Pocket Books, 1981).

21. Unpublished transcript of a discussion, organized by Julia LeSage, at the Conference on Feminist Criticism, Northwestern University, November 1980. See also for discussion of dominance-submission patterns, Pat Califia, "Feminism and Sadomasochism," *Heresies* 12, pp. 32ff.

22. Nancy Friday, *Men in Love* (New York: Dell, 1980).

23. Mulvey, "Visual Pleasure," pp. 12–13.

24. Julia Kristeva, "La femme ce n'est jamais ça," trans. Marilyn A. August, in *New French Feminisms,* ed. E. Marks and I. de Courtivron (Amherst: University of Massachusetts Press, 1980), p. 37.

25. Sandy Flitterman and Judith Barry, "Textual Strategies: The Politics of Art-Making," *Screen* 2, no. 3 (Summer 1980): 37.

26. Ibid., p. 36.

27. Terry Eagleton, "Aesthetics and Politics," *New Left Review* (1978).

28. "Women and Representation: A Discussion with Laura Mulvey" (collective project by Jane Clarke, Sue Clayton, Joanna Clelland, Rosie Elliott, and Mandy Merck), *Wedge* (London) 2 (Spring 1979): 49.

29. Nancy Chodorow, "Psychodynamics of the Family," in *The Reproduction of Mothering* (Berkeley: University of California Press, 1978), pp. 191–209.

30. "*Riddles of the Sphinx:* A Film by Laura Mulvey and Peter Wollen; Script," *Screen* 18, no. 2 (Summer 1977): 62.

31. Jacquelyn Suter and Sandy Flitterman, "Textual Riddles: Woman as Enigma or Site of Social Meanings? An Interview with Laura Mulvey," *Discourse* 1, no. 1 (Fall 1979): 107.

32. Dinnerstein, *The Mermaid and the Minotaur* (New York: Harper and Row, 1976) and Chodorow, *The Reproduction of Mothering.*

33. See, for example, films by Laura Mulvey and Peter Wollen, Michelle Citron, Marjorie Keller, and Helke Sander.

34. Kristeva, "Les Chinoises à 'contre-courant,' " *New French Feminisms,* p. 240.

Study Questions

1. How has feminist film criticism changed as a consequence of the work by Lacan and others?

2. How has the Freudian concept of voyeurism been used to explain what women (in film) represent? In Laura Mulvey's view, how does the voyeurism manifest itself in the types of looks or gazes involved in cinema?

3. In what way has the phenomenon of fetishism operated in the cinema?

4. In what ways have the growing use of psychoanalytic and semiological approaches to cinema polarized feminist film criticism?

5. In what two ways might a feminist critic view *Gentlemen Prefer Blondes*?

6. Kaplan indicates that pleasure (in film viewing) is an important issue, one often overlooked by feminists. Why does she say this? How does she think psychoanalysis can help us understand women's pleasure in being objectified?

7. Why does Kaplan believe that dominance-submission patterns are apparently a crucial part of sexuality in a capitalist system?

8. What does Kaplan think that the films of the present time showing "women as liberated" really tell us about dominance and masculinity? How does "the gaze" figure in respect to those films?

9. In Kaplan's view, how has much feminist art criticism failed in the attempt to create a true female discourse? How have some feminist film critics begun to face the challenge?

10. From the point of view of psychoanalytic theory, why is there more possibility for women than men to change themselves? In what ways might women invent new symbolic roles?

Female Grotesques: Carnival and Theory

Mary Russo

Pretext

There is a phrase that still resonates from childhood. Who says it? The mother's voice—not my own mother's, perhaps, but the voice of an aunt, an older sister, or the mother of a friend. It is a harsh, matronizing phrase, and it is directed toward the behavior of other women:

> "She" [the other woman] is making a spectacle out of herself.

Making a spectacle out of oneself seemed a specifically feminine danger. The danger was of an exposure. Men, I learned somewhat later in life, "exposed themselves," but that operation was quite deliberate and circumscribed. For a woman, making a spectacle out of herself had more to do with a kind of inadvertency and loss of boundaries: the possessors of large, aging, and dimpled thighs displayed at the public beach, of overly rouged cheeks, of a voice shrill in laughter, or of a sliding bra strap—a loose, dingy bra strap especially—were at once caught out by fate and blameworthy. It was my impression that these women had done something wrong, had stepped, as it were, into the limelight out of turn—too young or too old, too early or too late—and yet anyone, any *woman*, could make a spectacle out of herself if she was

From Teresa de Lauretis, ed., *Feminist Studies/Critical Studies* (Bloomington, IN: Indiana University Press, 1986). Reprinted by permission of the author.

not careful. It is a feature of my own history and education that in contemplating these dangers, I grew to admire both the extreme strategies of the cool, silent, and cloistered St. Clare (enclosed, with a room of her own) and the lewd, exuberantly parodistic Mae West.

Although the models, of course, change, there is a way in which radical negation, silence, withdrawal, and invisibility, and the bold affirmations of feminine performance, imposture, and masquerade (purity and danger) have suggested cultural politics for women.

Theory of Carnival and the Carnival of Theory

These extremes are not mutually exclusive, and in various and interesting ways they have figured round each other. Feminist theory and cultural production more generally have most recently brought together these strategies in approaching the questions of difference and the reconstruction or counterproduction of knowledge. In particular, the impressive amount of work across the discourse of carnival, or, more properly, the carnivalesque—much of it in relation to the work of the Russian scholar Mikhail Bakhtin[1]—has translocated the issues of bodily exposure and containment, disguise and gender masquerade, abjection and marginality, parody and excess, to the field of the social constituted as a symbolic system. Seen as a productive category, affirmative and celebratory (a Nietzschean gay science), the discourse of carnival moves away from modes of critique that would begin from some Archimedean point of authority without, to models of transformation and counterproduction situated within the social system and symbolically at its margins.[2]

The reintroduction of the body and categories of the body (in the case of carnival, the "grotesque body") into the realm of what is called the political has been a central concern of feminism. What would seem to be of great interest at this critical conjuncture in relation to this material would be an assessment of how the materials on carnival as historical performance may be configured with the materials on carnival as semiotic performance; in other words, how the relation between the symbolic and cultural constructs of femininity and Womanness and the experience of *women* (as variously identified and subject to multiple determinations) might be brought together toward a dynamic model of a new social subjectivity. The early work of Julia Kristeva on semiotics, subjectivity, and textual revolution and the more recent contributions of Teresa de Lauretis in mapping the terrain of a genuinely sociological and feminist semiotics are crucial to this undertaking.[3] This project is the grand one. More modestly, an examination of the materials on carnival can also recall limitations, defeats, and indifferences generated by carnival's complicitous place in dominant culture. There are especial dangers for women and other excluded or marginalized groups within carnival, though even the double jeopardy that I will describe may suggest an ambivalent redeployment of taboos around the female body as grotesque (the pregnant body, the aging body, the irregular body) and as unruly when set loose in the public sphere.

Female Grotesques

I would begin by citing briefly some of the important work on carnival in various fields (I could not pretend to be exhaustive, since the volume of recent work on Bakhtin alone is staggering). Here, I can only indicate some major lines of interest and weakness in the theory of carnival and cite some similar instances in what might be called the carnival of theory, that is, in the rhetorical masking, gesturing, and mise-en-scène of contemporary writing.

Not at all surprising, much of the early work on carnival in anthropology and social history dates from the late sixties, when enactments of popular protest, counterculture, experimental theater, and multimedia art were all together suggestive of the energies and possibilities of unlimited cultural and social transformation. In many ways this essay is generated from the cultural surplus of that era. The work of Mary Douglas and Victor Turner, which was as influential in social history as, more recently, the work of Clifford Geertz, saw in the human body the prototype of society, the nation-state, and the city, and in the social dramas of transition and "rituals of status reversal" evidence of the reinforcement of social structure, hierarchy, and order through inversion. In liminal states, thus, temporary loss of boundaries tends to redefine social frames, and such topsy-turvy or time-out is inevitably set right and on course.[4] This structural view of carnival as essentially conservative is both strengthened and enlarged by historical analysis, which tends, of course, to be the political history of domination. The extreme difficulty of producing lasting social change does not diminish the usefulness of these symbolic models of transgression, and the histories of subaltern and counterproductive cultural activity are never as neatly closed as structural models might suggest.

Natalie Davis, in what remains the most interesting piece on carnival and gender, "Women on Top," argues dialectically that in early modern Europe, carnival and the image of the carnivalesque woman "undermined as well as reinforced" the renewal of existing social structure:

> The image of the disorderly woman did not always function to keep women in their place. On the contrary, it was a multivalent image that could operate, first, to widen behavioral options for women within and even outside marriage, and second, to sanction riot and political disobedience for both men and women in

a society that allowed the lower orders few formal means of protest. Play with an unruly woman is partly a chance for temporary release from the traditional and stable hierarchy; but it is also part of the conflict over efforts to change the basic distribution of power within society.[5]

Among Davis's very interesting examples of the second possibility—that is, that the image of the unruly or carnivalesque woman actually worked to incite and embody popular uprisings—is the Wiltshire enclosure riots of 1641, where rioting men were led by male cross-dressers who called themselves "Lady Skimmington" (a skimmington was a ride through the streets mocking a henpecked husband, the name probably referring to the big skimming ladle that could be used for husband beatings).[6] The projection of the image of the fierce virago onto popular movements, especially a movement such as this one, involving the transgression of boundaries, is suggestive from the point of view of social transformation. What may it tell us about the construction of the female subject in history within this political symbology? Merely to sketch out the obvious problems in working toward an answer to this question, one might begin with the assumption that the history of the enclosure riots and the image of the unruly woman are not direct reflections of one another; both contain ambiguities and gender asymmetries that require historical and textual readings.

These readings are difficult in both areas. First, the history of popular movements has been largely the history of men; a stronger history of women in mixed and autonomous uprisings is needed to assess the place of women as historical subjects in relation to such uprisings. Second, as a form of representation, masquerade of the feminine (what psychoanalytic theory will insist is femininity par excellence) has its distinct problems. The carnivalized woman such as Lady Skimmington, whose comic female masquerade of those "feminine" qualities of strident wifely aggression, behind whose skirts men are protected and provoked to actions, is an image that, however counterproduced, perpetuates the dominant (and in this case misogynistic) representation of women by men. In the popular

tradition of this particular example, Lady Skimmington is mocked alongside her henpecked husband, for she embodies the most despised aspects of "strong" femininity, and her subordinate position in society is in part underlined in this enactment of power reversal.

Furthermore, although the origins of this image in male-dominated culture may be displaced, there remain questions of enactment and gender-layering. Are women who have taken on this role (as opposed to men cross-dressing) as effective as male cross-dressers? Or is it, like the contemporary "straight" drag of college boys in the amateur theatricals of elite universities, a clear case of sanctioned play for men, while it is something always risking self-contempt for women to put on "the feminine"? In addition, one must ask of any representation other questions—questions of style, genre, and contextuality which may cut across the issue of gender. Is the parodistic and hyperbolic style of Lady Skimmington as a leader of men a sign of insurgency and lower-class solidarity for women and men? Does this comic female style work to free women from a more confining aesthetic? Or are women again so identified with style itself that they are as estranged from its liberatory and transgressive effects as they are from their own bodies as signs in culture generally? In what sense can women really produce or make spectacles out of themselves?

Historical inquiry may yield instances of performance (symbolic and political) that may bypass the pessimism of psychoanalytically oriented answers to this last question, but only if that history begins to understand the complexity of treating signifying systems and "events" together. In this regard, even the work on female political iconography and social movements by very distinguished historians, such as Maurice Agulhon and Eric Hobsbawm, remains problematic.[7] This methodological difficulty does not prevent historians from becoming increasingly aware of gender differences in relation to the carnivalesque. Other social historians have documented the insight of the anthropologist Victor Turner that the marginal position of women and others in the "indicative" world makes their presence in the "subjunctive" or possible world of the topsy-turvy carnival "quintessentially" dangerous; in fact, as Emmanuel Le Roy Ladurie shows in *Carnival at Romans*, Jews were stoned, and there is evidence that women were raped, during carnival festivities.[8] In other words, in the everyday indicative world, women and their bodies, certain bodies, in certain public framings, in certain public spaces, are always already transgressive—dangerous, and in danger.

With these complexities no doubt in mind, Davis concluded her brilliant article with the hope that "the woman on top might even facilitate innovation in historical theory and political behavior" (p. 131). Since the writing of her article, the conjuncture of a powerful women's movement and feminist scholarship has facilitated further interrogation of the relationship between symbology and social change. The figure of the female transgressor as public spectacle is still powerfully resonant, and the possibilities of redeploying this representation as a demystifying or utopian model have not been exhausted.

The Carnivalesque Body

Investigation of linguistic and cultural contexts in relation to categories of carnival and the body have been recently inspired by a new reception in English-speaking countries of the work of the Russian scholar and linguist Mikhail Bakhtin. Like the work of Davis and Le Roy Ladurie, Bakhtin's work on carnival is at one level a historical description of carnival in early modern Europe. It offers, as well, a proscriptive model of a socialist collectivity.

In his introduction to his study of Rabelais, Bakhtin enumerates three forms of carnival folk culture: ritual spectacles (which include feasts, pageants, and marketplace festivals of all kinds); comic verbal compositions, parodies both oral and written; and various genres of billingsgate (curses, oaths, profanations, marketplace speech). The laughter of carnival associated with these spectacles and unconstrained speech in the Middle Ages was for Bakhtin entirely positive. The Romantic period, in contrast, saw laughter "cut down to cold

humour, irony, sarcasm" (*RW*, pp. 37–38). The privatism and individualism of this later humor make it unregenerative and lacking in communal hilarity. Without pretense to historical neutrality, Bakhtin's focus on carnival in early modern Europe contains a critique of modernity and its stylistic effects as a radical diminishment of the possibilities of human freedom and cultural production. He considers the culture of modernity to be as austere and bitterly isolating as the official religious culture of the Middle Ages, which he contrasts with the joy and heterogeneity of carnival and the carnivalesque style and spirit. Bakhtin's view of Rabelais and carnival is in some ways nostalgic for a socially diffuse oppositional context which has been lost, but which is perhaps more importantly suggestive of a future social horizon that may release new possibilities of speech and social performance.

The categories of carnivalesque speech and spectacle are heterogeneous, in that they contain the protocols and styles of high culture in and from a position of debasement. The masks and voices of carnival resist, exaggerate, and destabilize the distinctions and boundaries that mark and maintain high culture and organized society. It is as if the carnivalesque body politic had ingested the entire corpus of high culture and, in its bloated and irrepressible state, released it in fits and starts in all manner of recombination, inversion, mockery, and degradation. The political implications of this heterogeneity are obvious: it sets carnival apart from the merely oppositional and reactive; carnival and the carnivalesque suggest a redeployment or counterproduction of culture, knowledge, and pleasure. In its multivalent oppositional play, carnival refuses to surrender the critical and cultural tools of the dominant class, and in this sense, carnival can be seen above all as a site of insurgency, and not merely withdrawal.

The central category under which Bakhtin organizes his reading of Rabelais as a carnivalesque text is "grotesque realism," with particular emphasis on the grotesque body. The grotesque body is the open, protruding, extended, secreting body, the body of becoming, process, and change. The grotesque body is opposed to the classical body, which is monumental, static, closed, and sleek, corresponding to the aspirations of bourgeois individualism; the grotesque body is connected to the rest of the world. Significantly, Bakhtin finds his concept of the grotesque embodied in the Kerch terracotta figurines of senile, pregnant hags. Here is Bakhtin describing the figurines:

> This is typical and very strongly expressed grotesque. It is ambivalent. It is pregnant death, a death that gives birth. There is nothing completed, nothing calm and stable in the bodies of these old hags. They combine senile, decaying, and deformed flesh with the flesh of new life, conceived but as yet unformed. (*RW*, pp. 25–26) "Moreover," he writes, "the old hags are laughing" (*RW*, p. 25).

Homologously, the grotesque body is the figure of the socialist state to come, a state unfinished, which, as it "outgrows itself, transgresses its own limits" (*RW*, p. 26). For Bakhtin, this body is, as well, a model for carnival language; a culturally productive linguistic body in constant semiosis. But for the feminist reader, this image of the pregnant hag is more than ambivalent. It is loaded with all of the connotations of fear and loathing associated with the biological processes of reproduction and of aging. Bakhtin, like many other social theorists of the nineteenth and twentieth centuries, fails to acknowledge or incorporate the social relations of gender in his semiotic model of the body politic, and thus his notion of the Female Grotesque remains, in all directions, repressed and undeveloped.

Yet, Bakhtin's description of these ancient crones is at least exuberant. Almost to prove his point about the impossibility of collective mirth over such images in the period of late capitalism, here is a version of the same female grotesque in the voice of Paul Céline:

> Women you know, they wane by candlelight, they spoil, melt, twist, ooze! [. . . The end of tapers is a horrrible sight, the end of ladies too. . . .][9]

Quoted and glossed by Julia Kristeva as a portrait of "a muse in the true tradition of the lowly genres—apocalyptic, Menippean, and carnivalesque," this passage suggests the dark festival of transgression that she charts in *Powers of Horror*. This book, which contrasts in tone with Kristeva's indispensable application of Bakhtin in, for instance, "Word, Dialogue, and the Novel" and *Polylogue*, draws on Mary Douglas's categories of purity and defilement to arrive, through the analytical processes of transference, at the brink of abjection.

Through the convolutions of Céline's relentlessly misogynist and anti-Semitic writing, Kristeva as author and problematized subject has projected herself toward the grotesque, which she sees as the "undoer of narcissism and of all imaginary identity as well" (p. 208). Her study is richly intertextual. As Kristeva focusses on Céline, her own text increasingly takes on his rhetoric of abjection, which interestingly comes to rest in the category of the maternal. Kristeva writes: "Abject . . . the jettisoned object, is radically excluded and draws me toward the place where meaning collapses . . . on the edge of non-existence and hallucination" (p. 2). And elsewhere: "Something maternal . . . bears upon the uncertainty of what I call abjection" (p. 208). The fascination with the maternal body in childbirth, the fear of and repulsion from it throughout the chosen texts of Céline, constitutes it here again as a privileged sight of liminality and defilement. Kristeva writes:

> When Céline locates the ultimate of abjection—and thus the supreme and sole interest of literature—in the birth-giving scene, he makes amply clear which fantasy is involved: something horrible to see at the impossible doors of the invisible—the mother's body. The scene of scenes is here not the so-called primal scene but the one of giving birth, incest turned inside out, flayed identity. Giving birth: the height of bloodshed and life, scorching moment of hesitation (between inside and outside, ego and other, life and death), horror and beauty, sexuality and the blunt negation of the sexual. . . . At the doors of the feminine, at the doors of abjection, as I defined the term earlier, we are also, with Céline, given the most daring X-ray of the "drive foundations" of fascism.[10]

While there are many general reasons for questioning the use of the maternal in recent French criticism, here, I think, the point may be that the accumulated horror and contempt that these descriptions of the maternal body suggest generate a subliminal defense of the maternal, which then reemerges in Kristeva as an idealized category far from the realities of motherhood, either as a construction or as a lived experience.[11] Jews, unlike mothers, would seem to merely drop out of the field of abjection, as the anti-Semitism of Céline becomes for Kristeva a problem of maintaining the categorical imperatives of identity and the political.[12]

The book ends on a note of mystical subjectivity: near "the quiet shore of contemplation" (p. 210), far from the polis. On the verge, at the limit of this avant-garde frontier, there remains, for Kristeva, only writing.[13] Peter Stallybrass and Allon White, in their book on the politics and poetics of transgression, have called the exclusion of the already marginalized in moves such as these "displaced abjection."[14] As I have argued, both in the history of carnival and in its theory, the category of the female body as grotesque (in, for instance, pregnancy or aging) brings to light just such displacements. How this category might be used affirmatively to destabilize the idealizations of female beauty or to realign the mechanisms of desire, would be the subject of another study.

Carnival of Theory

There has been, as well, a carnival of theory at the discursive level, in the poetics of postmodernist criticism and feminist writing. It has included all manner of textual travesty, "mimetic rivalry," semiotic delinquency, parody, teasing, posing, flirting, masquerade, seduction, counterseduction, tight-rope walking, and verbal aerialisms of all kinds. Performances of displacement, double displacements, and more have permeated much feminist writing in our attempts to survive or muscle in on the discourses of Lacanian psychoanalysis, deconstruction, avant-garde writing, and postmodernist visual art. It could even be said, with reservation, that in relation to academic institutions, what has come to be called "theory" has constituted a kind of carnival space. The practice of criticism informed by this theory has

taken great license stylistically, and in its posing posed a threat of sorts.

It is interesting to consider the discourse of carnival and poststructuralism together. In 1980, Michèle Richman, in her essay entitled "Sex and Signs: Language of French Feminist Criticism," saw in the proliferation of literature on festival in France a reaction primarily to structuralism and to the structuralist economy of exchange within which, as Lévi-Strauss described it, women circulate as signs but are not theorized as sign producers.[15] The festival or carnival discourse drew upon the work of Marcel Mauss (and, as importantly, on the writings of Georges Bataille) on the gift or *dépense* as that which exceeds this linguistically modeled economy. As Richman indicates, the discussion of *dépense* was relocated within a more general libidinal economy of desire. The generosity of femininity and feminine writing (*écriture féminine*) is privileged over male *dépense*, which is understood as being simultaneously a demand. The female body is the site of this desirous excess.

In terms strikingly similar to Bakhtin's formulation of the grotesque body as continuous process, Hélène Cixous calls this body "the body without beginning and without end."[16] Female sexuality and especially the mother's body, as it figures simultaneously demarcation and dissolution of identity, serve this cultural project of disrupting the political economy of the sign as it is produced in dominant discourse. This *écriture féminine*, which has been admirably discussed elsewhere by many American feminists, can be and has been done by men (in fact, modernist writers such as Joyce are often mentioned as models); how the male-authored or travestied "feminine" is different, and how the inscription of the female body in the texts produced by women may be usefully contextualized elsewhere are still important and unanswered questions, although the critiques of this feminization of writing as essentialist must be taken into account in reconsiderations of these topics.[17]

Beyond essentialism, there are, as I have indicated earlier, other historical and anthropological warnings to heed. Even within France there have been critiques of the feminine textual festival. Annie Leclerc has chided the "delirious adultors of the festival," and Catherine Clément in *La jeune née* parallels the carnivalesque with hysterical crisis. In terms similar to earlier critiques of carnival, she sees the cultural category of hysteria as

> the only form of contestation possible in certain types of social organization, within the context of the village community; it is also a safety valve. This language not yet at the point of verbal expression, restrained within the bond of the body . . . remains convulsive. Men look but they do not hear.[18]

Historically, Clément is right: hysterics and madwomen generally have ended up in the attic or in the asylum, their gestures of pain and defiance having served only to put them out of circulation. As a figure of representation, however, hysteria may be less recuperable. The famous photographs commissioned by Charcot, which chart the various stages of hysteria in the patients of Salpêtrière, fix in attitude and gesture, in grimaces and leaps, a model of performance not unlike the fashionable histrionics of the great Romantic actresses and circus artists of the late nineteenth century. These paid performers were, like women hysterics, "seen but not heard," in one sense, since the scene of their livelihood, their context, it can be argued, was arranged by and for the male viewer. Nonetheless, they used their bodies in public, in extravagant ways that could have only provoked wonder and ambivalence in the female viewer, as such latitude of movement and attitude was not permitted most women without negative consequences.

This hyperbolic style, this "overacting," like the staged photographs of Salpêtrière (whatever Charcot's claims were to scientific documentation), can be read as double representations: as mimicries of the somatizations of the women patients whose historical performances were lost to themselves and recuperated into the medical science and medical discourse which maintain their oppressive hold on women. The photographs of Salpêtrière especially strike us as uncanny because of the repetitiveness of the hysterical performance. It is not only the content of hysterical behavior that strikes us as grotesque but its representation: if hysteria is a dis-play, these photographs display the display.

If hysteria is understood as feminine in its image, accoutrements, and stage business (rather than in its physiology), then it may be used to rig us up (for lack of the phallic term) into discourse. The possibility, indeed the necessity, of using the female body in this sense allows for the distance necessary for articulation. Luce Irigaray describes this provisional strategy as follows:

> To play with mimesis is thus, for a woman, to try to recover the place of her exploitation by discourse, without allowing herself simply to be reduced to it. It means to resubmit herself—inasmuch as she is on the side of "perceptible," of "matter"—to "ideas," in particular to ideas about herself, that are elaborated in/by masculine logic, but so as to make "visible," by an effect of playful repetition, what was supposed to remain invisible: the cover-up of a possible operation of the feminine in language. It also means to "unveil" the fact that, if women are such good mimics, it is because they are not simply reabsorbed into this function.[19]

What is called mimesis here is elsewhere, with various modifications, called masquerade. (Irigaray herself reserves the latter term to refer negatively to the false position of women experiencing desire only as male desire for them.) Female sexuality as masquerade is a well-noted psychoanalytic category. Jacques Lacan, a great *poseur* himself, has written of female sexuality as masking a lack, pretending to hide what is in fact not there:

> Paradoxical as this formulation might seem, I would say that it is in order to be the phallus, that is to say, the signifier of the desire of the Other, that the woman will reject an essential part of her femininity, notably all its attributes through masquerade. It is for what she is not that she expects to be desired as well as loved.[20]

The mask here is seen as feminine (for men and women) rather than something that hides a stable feminine identity. Femininity is a mask which masks nonidentity. According to Lacan, that produces an unexpected side effect for the man anxious to appear manly:

> The fact that femininity takes refuge in this mask, because of the *Verdrangung* inherent to the phallic mark of desire, has the strange con-

sequence that, in the human being, virile display itself appears as feminine.[21]

In film theory, Mary Ann Doane has problematicized the female spectator, using the essay of Joan Riviere on "Womanliness and Masquerade."[22] Her argument is that masquerade can "manufacture a distance from the image, to generate a problematic within which the image is manipulable, producible, and readable by the women."[23] It is, in other words, a way around the theorization of the spectator only in terms of the male gaze and male categories of voyeurism and fetishistic pleasure. More generally, her discussion of Riviere is extremely useful in explaining the asymmetries of transvestism, which for a woman has always been necessary in some sense in order for her to take part in a man's world. For a woman to dress, act, or position herself in discourse as a man is easily understandable and culturally compelling. To "act like a woman" beyond narcissism and masochism is, for psychoanalytic theory, trickier. That is the critical and hopeful power of the masquerade. Deliberately assumed and foregrounded, femininity as mask, for a man, is a take-it-or-leave-it proposition; for a woman, a similar flaunting of the feminine is a take-it-*and*-leave-it *possibility*. To put on femininity with a vengeance suggests the power of taking it off.

These considerations account for some of the interest in masquerade for those contemporary artists and critics whose work on imposture and dissimulation tends to stress the constructed, the invented, and (to use Gayatri Spivak's wonderful phrase) the "scrupulously fake."[24] Spivak reads Nietzsche's characterization of female sexual pleasure as masquerade ("they 'give themselves,' even when they—give themselves. The female is so artistic") as an originary displacement, occluding "an unacknowledged envy: a man cannot fake an orgasm."[25] Reading Derrida, she sees the figure of woman displaced twice over. "Double displacement," she suggests, might be undone in carefully fabricated "useful and scrupulous fake readings in place of the passively active fake orgasm." Such readings may suggest new ways of making new spectacles of oneself.

Other work on masquerade has a more ex-plicitly sociopolitical dimension, which greatly enriches psychoanalytic and deconstructive approaches to the material (I am thinking, for instance, of Dick Hebdige's work on subculture and Homi Bhabha's recent work on mimicry and the colonial subject).[26] For feminist theory, particularly, a more specifically historical and social use of masquerade may be needed, perhaps in the context of larger discussions of social groups and categories of the feminine mask in colonized and subcultural contexts, or in relation to other guises of the carnivalesque body. Nonetheless, the hyperboles of masquerade and carnival suggest, at least, some preliminary "acting out" of the dilemmas of femininity.

General Laughter and the Laughter of Carnival

Feminist theory itself has been travestied, hidden, and unacknowledged in many discussions of subjectivity and gender. It is part of what Elaine Showalter has called "critical cross-dressing."[27] The fathers of French theory alluded to here are in fact all masters of *mise-en-scène*. Even Derrida, whose persona has been more diffidently drawn in his writings, has been recently showcased as a carnival master.

The interview with Derrida published in *Critical Exchange*, in which he speaks of women and feminism, is quite as interesting for what he says about feminists as for the *mise-en-scène*.[28] Derrida restates his reservations about feminism as a form of phallogocentrism (fair enough). Later, he says that feminism is tantamount to phallogocentrism (not so fair).[29] James Creech, who edited and translated the interview, states that he attempted "to reproduce its conversational tone, with interruptions, ellipses, suspensions and laughter that marked a very cordial and freeform discussion. Essentially nothing has been edited out, and the reader can follow the sub-text of associations which lead from one moment of discussion to another" (p. 30). The transcription is punctuated by parenthetical laughter and occasionally, in bold face, "General Laughter." For instance:

Certain feminists, certain women struggling in the name of feminism—may see in deconstruction only what will not allow itself to be feminist. That's why they try to constitute a sort of target, a silhouette, a shooting gallery almost, where they spot phallocentrism and beat up on it [*tappent dessus*]. Just as Said and others constitute an enemy in the image [LAUGHTER] of that against which they have ready arms, in the same way, I think certain feminists as they begin to read certain texts, focus on particular themes out of haste and say, "Well, there you have it. . . ." (I don't know exactly who one could think of in this regard, but I know it goes on.) In France I recall a very violent reaction from a feminist who upon reading *Spurs* and seeing the multiplication of phallic images—spurs, umbrellas, etc.—said, "So, it's a phallocentric text," and started kicking up a violent fuss, charging about like a bull perhaps. . . . [GENERAL LAUGHTER] (p. 30)

This is a startling scene—the feminist as raging bull ("I don't know exactly who one can think of in this regard, but I know it goes on"). The bull in the shooting gallery, spotting and targeting, "kicking up a violent fuss, charging about." Is this textual spotting and targeting a reverse image? Is phallogocentrism really tantamount to feminism here? Is this a male dressed as a female dressing as a male? What kind of drag is this? Who is waving the red flag? And, who must join this "general laughter"? The laughter of carnival is communal and spontaneous, but general laughter in this context is coercive, participated in, like much comedy, by the marginalized only in an effort to pass. But it can be heard from another position.

A counter scene is offered in the films of Yvonne Rainer, whose past as a performance artist puts her in a particularly good position to stage theory and intellectual comedy. In her film *The Man Who Envied Women* (1985) ("I don't know exactly who one can think of in this regard, but I know it goes on"), the man stands behind a female student, his hands gripping her shoulders as she asks the difference between the subject-in-process and the everyday individual with choices and identifications to make. He replies (paraphrasing Foucault): in the very enactment of the power relations that are being almost simultaneously affirmed and denied.

In another film, *Journeys from Berlin/1971* (1980), the joke is Jean-Paul Sartre's in another interview. Reference is made to Sartre's trip to West Germany to visit the imprisoned terrorists awaiting trial. When asked why he visited only the cell of Andreas Baader and not that of his accomplice Ulrike Meinhof, he replies, "The gang is called Baader-Meinhof not Meinhof-Baader, isn't it?" In the voice-over, two people laugh, the man because he is pleased with the old intellectual's intellectual prowess, the woman because she hears the joke as on Sartre himself in decadence.

What Rainer stages is a dialogical laughter, the laughter of intertext and multiple identifications. It is the conflictual laughter of social subjects in a classist, racist, ageist, sexist society. It is the laughter we have now: other laughter for other times. Carnival and carnival laughter remain on the horizon with a new social subjectivity.

For now, right now, as I acknowledge the work of feminists in reconstituting knowledge, I imagine us going forward, growing old (I hope), or being grotesque in other ways. I see us viewed by ourselves and others, in our bodies and in our work, in ways that are continuously shifting the terms of viewing, so that looking at us, there will be a new question, the question that never occurred to Bakhtin in front of the Kerch terracotta figurines—

Why are these old hags laughing?

Notes

1. Mikhail Bakhtin, *Rabelais and His World*, trans. Helene Iswolsky (Bloomington: Indiana University Press, 1984). An earlier edition of this translation was published in 1968 by MIT Press. References to *Rabelais and His World* will be identified as *RW* and included in the text.

2. I am indebted to Peter Stallybrass, whose forthcoming book with Allon White, *The Politics and Poetics of Transgression*, contains a rigorous historical and critical introduction to carnival as political discourse.

3. See Julia Kristeva, *La Révolution du langage*

poétique: l'avant-garde à la fin du 19e siècle: Lautréamont et Mallarmé (Paris: Seuil, 1977) and *Polylogue* (Paris: Seuil, 1977); and Teresa de Lauretis, *Alice Doesn't: Feminism, Semiotics, Cinema* (Bloomington: Indiana University Press, 1984).

4. Mary Douglas, *Purity and Danger; An Analysis of Concepts of Pollution and Taboo* (London: Routledge and Kegan Paul, 1966); Victor Turner, *From Ritual to Theater; The Human Seriousness of Play* (New York: Performing Arts Journal Publications, 1982) and *The Ritual Process: Structure and Antistructure* (Chicago: University of Chicago Press, 1968). Clifford Geertz, *The Interpretation of Cultures* (New York: Basic Books, 1973).

5. Natalie Zemon Davis, "Women on Top," in her *Society and Culture in Early Modern France* (Stanford: Stanford University Press, 1965), pp. 124–52. I am quoting from p. 131.

6. Ibid., p. 148. As Davis points out, this image of the "strong woman" is problematic: "The unruly woman not only directed some of the male festive organizations; she was sometimes their butt. The village scold or the domineering wife might be ducked in the pond or pulled through the streets muzzled or branked or in creel" (p. 140).

7. Maurice Agulhon, *Marianne into Battle: Republican Imagery and Symbolism in France, 1789–1880* (Cambridge: Cambridge University Press, 1981); Eric Hobsbawm, "Man and Woman in Socialist Iconography," *History Workshop: A Journal of Socialist Historians,* no. 6 (Autumn 1978), pp. 107–121.

8. Victor Turner, "Frame, Flow, and Reflection: Ritual and Drama as Public Liminality," in *Performance in Postmodern Culture,* ed. Michel Benamou and Charles Caramello, Center for Twentieth Century Studies, Theories of Contemporary Culture, vol. 1 (Madison: Coda Press, 1977), pp. 35–55.

9. Paul Céline, quoted in Julia Kristeva, *Powers of Horror: An Essay on Abjection,* trans. Leon S. Roudiez (New York: Columbia University Press, 1982), p. 169.

10. Kristeva, *Powers of Horror,* pp. 155–56. See also chapter 8, "Those Females Who Can Wreck the Infinite" (pp. 157–73).

11. I am grateful to Ann Rosalind Jones for this insight. For an excellent critique of Kristeva's most recent work, see her "Julia Kristeva on Femininity: The Limits of a Semiotic Politics," *Feminist Review,* no. 18 (Winter 1984), pp. 56–73.

12. "His fascination with Jews, which was full of hatred and which he maintained to the end of his life, the simple-minded anti-Semitism that besots the tumultuous pages of the pamphlets, are no accident; they thwart the disintegration of identity that is coextensive with a scription that affects the most archaic distinctions, that bridges the gaps insuring life and meaning. Céline's anti-Semitism, like political commitment, for others—like, as a matter of fact, any political commitment, to the extent that it settles the subject within a socially justified illusion—is a security blanket" (Kristeva, *Powers of Horror,* pp. 136–37).

13. Writing, or "literature," is a "vision of the apocalypse that seems to me rooted no matter what its socio-historical condition might be, on the fragile border (borderline cases) where identities (subject/object, etc.) do not exist or only barely so—doubly, fuzzy, heterogeneous, animal, metamorphosed, altered, abject" (ibid., p. 207).

14. Stallybrass and White, *Politics and Poetics,* p. 21.

15. Michèle Richman, "Sex and Signs: The Language of French Feminist Criticism," *Language and Style* 13 (Fall 1980): 62–80.

16. Hélène Cixous, quoted in ibid., p. 74. The work of Luce Irigaray and Michèle Montrelay is especially important to this discussion.

17. The dangers of essentialism in posing the female body, whether in relation to representations or in relation to "women's history," have been well stated, so well stated, in fact, that "antiessentialism" may well be the greatest inhibition to work in cultural theory and politics at the moment, and must be displaced. For an account of re-

cent debates around the female body and film, see Constance Penley, "Feminism, Film, and Theory and the Bachelor Machine," *M/F,* no. 10 (1985), pp. 39–61.

18. Catherine Clément, quoted in Richman, "Sex and Signs," p. 69.

19. Luce Irigaray, *The Sex Which Is Not One,* trans. Catherine Porter (Ithaca, N.Y.: Cornell University Press, 1985), p. 76.

20. Jacques Lacan, *Feminine Sexuality: Jacques Lacan and the "Ecole Freudienne,"* ed., Juliet Mitchell and Jacqueline Rose, trans. Jacqueline Rose (New York: W. W. Norton, 1982), p. 84.

21. Ibid., p. 85.

22. Mary Ann Doane, "Film and Masquerade: Theorizing the Female Spectator," *Screen* 23, nos. 3/4 (Sept./Oct. 1982): 74–87, and "Woman's Stake: Filming the Female Body," *October* 17 (Summer 1981): 23–36. See also Kaja Silverman, "*Histoire d'O:* The Construction of a Female Subject," in *Pleasure and Danger: Exploring Female Sexuality,* ed. Carole S. Vance (Boston: Routledge and Kegan Paul, 1984), pp. 320–49, and "Changing the Fantasmatic Scene," *Framework* 20 (1983): 27–36. For a discussion of masquerade in relation to postmodernism, see Craig Owens, "Posing," in *Difference: On Representation and Sexuality Catalog* (New York: New Museum of Contemporary Art, 1985).

23. Doane, "Film and Masquerade," p. 87.

24. Gayatri Spivak, "Displacement and the Discourse of Woman," in *Displacement: Derrida and After,* ed. Mark Krupnick, Center for Twentieth Century Studies, Theories of Contemporary Culture, vol. 4 (Bloomington: Indiana University Press, 1983), p. 186.

25. Spivak, p. 170. As Spivak quotes Derrida, "She is twice model, in a contradictory fashion, at once lauded and condemned. . . . (First), like writing. . . . But, insofar as she does not believe, herself, in truth . . . she is again the model, this time the good model, or rather the bad model as good model: she plays dissimulation, ornament, lying, art, the artistic philosophy . . ." (p. 171).

26. Dick Hebdige, *Subculture: The Meaning of Style* (London: Methuen, 1979); Homi Bhabha, "Of Mimicry and Man: The Ambivalence of Colonial Discourse," *October* 28 (Spring 1984): 125–33. Conversely, both Hebdige and Bhabha have largely ignored gender difference.

27. Elaine Showalter, "Critical Cross-Dressing: Male Feminists and the Woman of the Year," *Raritan* 3 no. 2 (Fall 1983): 130–49.

28. James Creech, Peggy Kamuf, and Jane Todd, "Deconstruction in America: An Interview with Jacques Derrida," *Critical Exchange* 17 (Winter 1985): 30.

29. Derrida says, "So let's just say that the most insistent and the most organized motif in my texts is neither feminist nor phallocentric. And that at a certain point I try to show that the two are tanamount to the same thing" (ibid., p. 31).

Study Questions

1. What does Russo mean by "making a spectacle"? Why is it a female danger?

2. In what ways might a feminist relate carnival to a new model of women's subjectivity?

3. Why does Russo believe that carnival could be transgressive? How might it be applied to women?

4. Russo indicates that the body is central to Bakhtin's theory of carnival. Why does she say this? What is an example of the grotesque body?

5. What does Kristeva say about the maternal body? Why does Russo think that female masquerade myths upset the male gaze?

6. What is the place of carnival laughter in the carnival of (feminist) theory?

Toward a Butch-Femme
Aesthetic

Sue-Ellen Case

In the 1980s, feminist criticism has focused increasingly on the subject position: both in the explorations for the creation of a female subject position and the deconstruction of the inherited subject position that is marked with masculinist functions and history. Within this focus, the problematics of women inhabiting the traditional subject position have been sketched out, the possibilities of a new heterogeneous, heteronomous position have been explored, and a desire for a collective subject has been articulated. While this project is primarily a critical one, concerned with language and symbolic structures, philosophic assumptions, and psychoanalytic narratives, it also implicates the social issues of class, race, and sexuality. Teresa de Lauretis's article "The Technology of Gender" (in *Technologies of Gender,* 1987) reviews the recent excavations of the subject position in terms of ideology, noting that much of the work on the subject, derived from Foucault and Althusser, denies both agency and gender to the subject. In fact, many critics leveled a similar criticism against Foucault in a recent conference on postmodernism, noting that while his studies seem to unravel the web of ideology, they suggest no subject position outside the ideology, nor do they construct a subject who has the agency to change ideology ("Postmodernism," 1987). In other words, note de Lauretis and others, most of the work on the subject position has only revealed the way in which the subject is trapped within ideology and thus provides no programs for change.

For feminists, changing this condition must be a priority. The common appellation of this bound subject has been the "female subject," signifying a biological, sexual difference, inscribed by dominant cultural practices. De

From Lynda Hart, ed., *Making a Spectacle* (Ann Arbor, MI: University of Michigan, 1989). Reprinted by permission.

Lauretis names her subject (one capable of change and of changing conditions) the feminist subject, one who is "at the same time inside and outside the ideology of gender, and conscious of being so, conscious of that pull, that division, that doubled vision" (1987, 10). De Lauretis ascribes a sense of self-determination at the micropolitical level to the feminist subject. This feminist subject, unlike the female one, can be outside of ideology, can find self-determination, can change. This is an urgent goal for the feminist activist/theorist. Near the conclusion of her article (true to the newer rules of composition), de Lauretis begins to develop her thesis: that the previous work on the female subject, assumes, but leaves unwritten, a heterosexual context for the subject and this is the cause for her continuing entrapment. Because she is still perceived in terms of men and not within the context of other women, the subject in heterosexuality cannot become capable of ideological change (1987, 17–18).

De Lauretis's conclusion is my starting place. Focusing on the feminist subject, endowed with the agency for political change, located among women, outside the ideology of sexual difference, and thus the social institution of heterosexuality, it would appear that the lesbian roles of butch and femme, as a dynamic duo, offer precisely the strong subject position the movement requires. Now, in order for the butch-femme roles to clearly emerge within this sociotheoretical project, several tasks must be accomplished: the lesbian subject of feminist theory would have to come out of the closet, the basic discourse or style of camp for the lesbian butch-femme positions would have to be clarified, and an understanding of the function of roles in the homosexual lifestyle would need to be developed, particularly in relation to the historical class and racial relations embedded in such a project. Finally, once these tasks have been completed, the performance practice, both on and off the stage, may be studied as that of a feminist subject, both inside and outside ideology, with the power to self-determine her role and her conditions on the micropolitical level. Within this schema, the butch-femme couple inhabit the subject position together— "you can't have one without the other," as the song says. The two roles never appear as . . . discrete. The combo butch-femme as subject is reminiscent of Monique Wittig's "j/e" or coupled self in her novel *The Lesbian Body*. These are not split subjects, suffering the torments of dominant ideology. They are coupled ones that do not impale themselves on the poles of sexual difference or metaphysical values, but constantly seduce the sign system, through flirtation and inconstancy into the light fondle of artifice, replacing the Lacanian slash with a lesbian bar.

However, before all of this *jouissance* can be enjoyed, it is first necessary to bring the lesbian subject out of the closet of feminist history. The initial step in that process is to trace historically how the lesbian has been assigned to the role of the skeleton in the closet of feminism; in this case, specifically the lesbian who relates to her cultural roots by identifying with traditional butch-femme role-playing. First, regard the feminist genuflection of the 1980s—the catechism of "working-class-women-of-color" feminist theorists feel impelled to invoke at the outset of their research. What's wrong with this picture? It does not include the lesbian position. In fact, the isolation of the social dynamics of race and class successfully relegates sexual preference to an attendant position, so that even if the lesbian were to appear, she would be as a bridesmaid and never the bride. Several factors are responsible for this ghosting of the lesbian subject: the first is the growth of moralistic projects restricting the production of sexual fiction or fantasy through the antipornography crusade. This crusade has produced an alliance between those working on social feminist issues and right-wing homophobic, born-again men and women who also support censorship. This alliance in the electorate, which aids in producing enough votes for an ordinance, requires the closeting of lesbians for the so-called greater cause. Both Jill

Dolan and Alice Echols develop this position in their respective articles.

Although the antipornography issue is an earmark of the moralistic 1980s, the homophobia it signals is merely an outgrowth of the typical interaction between feminism and lesbianism since the rise of the feminist movement in the early 1970s. Del Martin and Phyllis Lyon describe the rise of the initial so-called lesbian liberatory organization, the Daughters of Bilitis (DOB), in their influential early book, *Lesbian/Woman* (1972). They record the way in which the aims of such organizations were intertwined with those of the early feminist, or more precisely, women's movement. They proudly exhibit the way in which the DOB moved away from the earlier bar culture and its symbolic systems to a more dominant identification and one that would appease the feminist movement. DOB's goal was to erase butch-femme behavior, its dress codes, and lifestyle from the lesbian community and to change lesbians into lesbian feminists.

Here is the story of one poor victim who came to the DOB for help. Note how similar this narrative style is to the redemptive, corrective language of missionary projects: "Toni joined Daughters of Bilitis . . . at our insistence, and as a result of the group's example, its unspoken pressure, she toned down her dress. She was still very butch, but she wore women's slacks and blouses . . . one of DOB's goals was to teach the lesbian a mode of behavior and dress acceptable to society. . . . We knew too many lesbians whose activities were restricted because they wouldn't wear skirts. But Toni did not agree. 'You'll never get me in a dress,' she growled, banging her fist on the table." The description of Toni's behavior, her animal growling noise, portrays her as uncivilized, recalling earlier, colonial missionary projects. Toni is portrayed as similar to the inappropriately dressed savage whom the missionary clothes and saves. The authors continue: "But she became fast friends with a gay man, and over the months he helped her to feel comfortable with herself as a woman" (*Lesbian/ Woman* 1972, 77). Here, in a lesbian narrative, the missionary position is finally given over to a man (even if gay) who helps the butch to feel like a woman. The contemporary lesbian-identified reader can only marvel at the conflation of gender identification in the terms of dominant, heterosexual culture with the adopted gender role-playing within the lesbian subculture.

If the butches are savages in this book, the femmes are lost heterosexuals who damage birthright lesbians by forcing them to play the butch roles. The authors assert that most femmes are divorced heterosexual women who know how to relate only to men and thus force their butches to play the man's role, which is conflated with that of a butch (*Lesbian/Woman* 1972, 79). Finally, the authors unveil the salvationary role of feminism in this process and its power to sever the newly constructed identity of the lesbian feminist from its traditional lesbian roots: "The minority of lesbians who still cling to the traditional male-female or husband-wife pattern in their partnerships are more than likely old-timers, gay bar habituées or working class women." This sentence successfully compounds ageism with a (homo)phobia of lesbian bar culture and a rejection of a working-class identification. The middle-class upward mobility of the lesbian feminist identification shifts the sense of community from one of working-class, often women-of-color lesbians in bars, to that of white upper-middle-class heterosexual women who predominated in the early women's movement. The book continues: "the old order changeth however" (here they even begin to adopt verb endings from the King James Bible) "as the women's liberation movement gains strength against this pattern of heterosexual marriages, the number of lesbians involved in butch-femme roles diminishes" (*Lesbian/Woman* 1972, 80).

However, this compulsory adaptation of lesbian feminist identification must be understood as a defensive posture, created by the homophobia that operated in the internal dynamics of the early movement, particularly within the so-called consciousness-raising groups. In her article with Cherríe Moraga on butch-femme relations, Amber Hollibaugh, a femme, described the feminist reception of lesbians this way: "the first discussion I ever heard of lesbianism among feminists was: 'We've been sex objects to men and where did it get us? And

here when we're just learning how to be friends with other women, you got to go and sexualize it' ... they made men out of every sexual dyke" (1983, 402). These kinds of experiences led Hollibaugh and Moraga to conclude: "In our involvement in a movement largely controlled by white middle-class women, we feel that the values of their culture . . . have been pushed down our throats . . . ," and even more specifically, in the 1980s, to pose these questions: "why is it that it is largely white middle-class women who form the visible leadership in the anti-porn movement? Why are women of color not particularly visible in this sex-related single issue movement?" (1983, 405).

When one surveys these beginnings of the alliance between the heterosexual feminist movement and lesbians, one is not surprised at the consequences for lesbians who adopted the missionary position under a movement that would lead to an antipornography crusade and its alliance with the Right. Perhaps too late, certain members of the lesbian community who survived the early years of feminism and continued to work in the grass-roots lesbian movement, such as Joan Nestle, began to perceive this problem. As Nestle, founder of the Lesbian Herstory Archives in New York, wrote: "We lesbians of the 1950s made a mistake in the 1970s: we allowed ourselves to be trivialized and reinterpreted by feminists who did not share our culture" (1981, 23). Nestle also notes the class prejudice in the rejection of butch-femme roles: "I wonder why there is such a consuming interest in the butch-fem lives of upper-class women, usually more literary figures, while real-life, working butch-fem women are seen as imitative and culturally backward . . . the reality of passing women, usually a working-class lesbian's method of survival, has provoked very little academic lesbian-feminist interest. Grassroots lesbian history research is changing this" (1981, 23).

So the lesbian butch-femme tradition went into the feminist closet. Yet the closet, or the bars, with their hothouse atmosphere have produced what, in combination with the butch-femme couple, may provide the liberation of the feminist subject—the discourse of camp. Proust described this accomplishment in his novel *The Captive:*

The lie, the perfect lie, about people we know, about the relations we have had with them, about our motive for some action, formulated in totally different terms, the lie as to what we are, whom we love, what we feel in regard to those people who love us . . .—that lie is one of the few things in the world that can open windows for us on to what is new and unknown, that can awaken in us sleeping senses for the contemplation of the universes that otherwise we should never have known. (Proust, 213; in Sedgwick 1987)

The closet has given us camp—the style, the discourse, the *mise en scène* of butch-femme roles. In his history of the development of gay camp, Michael Bronski describes the liberative work of late-nineteenth-century authors such as Oscar Wilde in creating the homosexual camp liberation from the rule of naturalism, or realism. Within his argument, Bronski describes naturalism and realism as strategies that tried to save fiction from the accusation of daydream, imagination, or masturbation and to affix a utilitarian goal to literary production—that of teaching morals. In contrast, Bronski quotes the newspaper *Fag Rag* on the functioning of camp: "We've broken down the rules that are used for validating the difference between real/true and unreal/false. The controlling agents of the status quo may know the power of lies; dissident subcultures, however, are closer to knowing their value" (1984, 41). Camp both articulates the lives of homosexuals through the obtuse tone of irony and inscribes their oppression with the same device. Likewise, it eradicates the ruling powers of heterosexist realist modes.

Susan Sontag, in an avant-garde assimilation of camp, described it as a "certain mode of aestheticism . . . one way of seeing the world as an aesthetic phenomenon . . . not in terms of beauty, but in terms of the degree of artifice" (1966, 275). This artifice, as artifice, works to defeat the reign of realism as well as to situate the camp discourse within the category of what can be said (or seen). However, the fixed quality of Sontag's characteristic use of camp within the straight context of aestheticization has produced a homosexual strategy for avoiding such assimilation: what Esther Newton has described as its constantly changing, mobile quali-

ty, designed to alter the gay camp sensibility before it becomes a fad (1972, 105). Moreover, camp also protects homosexuals through a "first-strike wit" as *Fag Rag* asserts: "Wit and irony provide the only reasonable modus operandi in the American Literalist Terror of Straight Reality" (1984, 46).

Oscar Wilde brought this artifice, wit, irony, and the distancing of straight reality and its conventions to the stage. Later, Genet staged the malleable, multiple artifice of camp in *The Screens,* which elevates such displacement to an ontology. In his play, *The Blacks,* he used such wit, irony and artifice to deconstruct the notion of "black" and to stage the dynamics of racism. *The Blacks* displaced the camp critique from homophobia to racism, in which "black" stands in for "queer" and the campy queen of the bars is transformed into an "african queen." This displacement is part of the larger use of the closet and gay camp discourse to articulate other social realities. Even Sedgwick attests to this displacement when she writes: "I want to argue that a lot of energy of attention and demarcation that has swirled around issues of homosexuality since the end of the nineteenth century . . . has been impelled by the distinctly indicative relation of homosexuality to wider mappings of secrecy and disclosure, and of the private and the public, that were and are critically problematical for the gender, sexual, and economic structures of the heterosexist culture at large. . . . 'The closet' and 'coming out' are now verging on all-purpose phrases for the potent crossing and recrossing of almost any politically-charged lines of representation. . . . The apparent floating-free from its gay origins of that phrase 'coming out of the closet' in recent usage might suggest that the trope of the closet is so close to the heart of some modern preoccupations that it could be . . . evacuated of its historical gay specificity. But I hypothesize that exactly the opposite is true." Thus, the camp success in ironizing and distancing the regime of realist terror mounted by heterosexist forces has become useful as a discourse and style for other marginal factions.

Camp style, gay-identified dressing and the articulation of the social realities of homosexuality have also become part of the straight, postmodern canon, as Herbert Blau articulated it in a special issue of *Salmagundi*: "becoming homosexual is part of the paraphilia of the postmodern, not only a new sexual politics but the reification of all politics, supersubtilized beyond the unnegotiable demands of the sixties, from which it is derived, into a more persuasive rhetoric of unsublimated desire" (1983, 233). Within this critical community, the perception of recognizable homosexuals can also inspire broader visions of the operation of social codes. Blau states: "there soon came pullulating toward me at high prancing amphetamined pitch something like the end of Empire or like the screaming remains of the return of the repressed—pearl-white, vinyl, in polo pants and scarf–an englistered and giggling outburst of resplendent queer . . . what was there to consent to and who could possibly legitimate that galloping specter I had seen, pure ideolect, whose plunging and lungless soundings were a full-throttled forecast of much weirder things to come?" (1983, 221–22). Initially, these borrowings seem benign and even inviting to the homosexual theorist. Contemporary theory seems to open the closet door to invite the queer to come out, transformed as a new, postmodern subject, or even to invite straights to come into the closet, out of the roar of dominant discourse. The danger incurred in moving gay politics into such heterosexual contexts is in only slowly discovering that the strategies and perspectives of homosexual realities and discourse may be locked inside a homophobic "concentration camp." Certain of these authors, such as Blau, even introduce homosexual characters and their subversions into arguments that conclude with explicit homophobia. Note Blau's remembrance of things past: "thinking I would enjoy it, I walked up Christopher Street last summer at the fag end of the depleted carnival of Gay Pride Day, with a disgust unexpected and almost uncontained by principle. . . . I'll usually fight for the right of each of us to have his own perversions, I may not, under the pressure of theory and despite the itchiness of my art, to try on yours and, what's worse, rather wish you wouldn't. Nor am I convinced that what you are doing isn't perverse in the most pejorative sense" (1983, 249). At least Blau, as in all of his writing, honestly and openly records his personal prejudice. The indirect or subtextual homophobia in this new assimilative discourse is more alluring and ultimately more powerful in erasing the social reality and the discursive inscriptions of gay, and more specifically, lesbian discourse.

Here, the sirens of sublation may be found in the critical maneuvers of heterosexual feminist critics who metaphorize butch-femme roles, transvestites and campy dressers into a "subject who masquerades," as they put it, or is "carnivalesque" or even, as some are so bold to say, who "cross-dresses." Even when these borrowings are nested in more benign contexts than Blau's, they evacuate the historical, butch-femme couples' sense of masquerade and cross-dressing the way a cigar-store Indian evacuates the historical dress and behavior of the Native American. As is often the case, illustrated by the cigar-store Indian, these symbols may only proliferate when the social reality has been successfully obliterated and the identity has become the private property of the dominant class. Such metaphors operate simply to display the breadth of the art collection, or style collection, of the straight author. Just as the French term *film noir* became the name for B-rate American films of the forties, these notions of masquerade and cross-dressing, standing in for the roles of working-class lesbians, have come back to us through French theory on the one hand and studies of the lives of upper-class lesbians who lived in Paris between the wars on the other. In this case, the referent of the term Left Bank is not a river, but a storehouse of critical capital.

Nevertheless, this confluence of an unresolved social, historical problem in the feminist movement and these recent theoretical strategies, re-assimilated by the lesbian critic, provide a ground that could resolve the project of constructing the feminist subject position. The butch-femme subject could inhabit that discursive position, empowering it for the production of future compositions. Having already grounded this argument within the historical situation of butch-femme couples, perhaps now it would be tolerable to describe the theoretical maneuver that could become the butch-femme subject position. Unfortunately, these strategies must emerge in the bodiless world of "spectatorial positions" or "subject positions," where transvestites wear no clothes and subjects tread only "itineraries of desire." In this terrain of discourse, or among theorized spectators in darkened movie houses with their gazes fixed on the dominant cinema screen, "the thrill is gone" as Nestle described it. In the Greenwich Village bars, she could "spot a butch 50 feet away and still feel the thrill of her power" as she saw "the erotic signal of her hair at the nape of her neck, touching the shirt collar; how she held a cigarette; the symbolic pinky ring flashing as she waved her hand" (1981, 21–22). Within this theory, the erotics are gone, but certain maneuvers maintain what is generally referred to as "presence."

The origins of this theory may be found in a Freudian therapist's office, where an intellectual heterosexual woman, who had become frigid, had given way to rages, and, puzzled by her own coquettish behavior, told her story to Joan Riviere sometime around 1929. This case caused Riviere to publish her thoughts in her ground-breaking article entitled "Womanliness as a Masquerade" that later influenced several feminist critics such as Mary Russo and Mary Ann Doane and the French philosopher Jean Baudrillard. Riviere began to "read" this woman's behavior as the "wish for masculinity" which causes the woman to don "the mask of womanliness to avert anxiety and the retribution feared from men" (1929, 303). As Riviere saw it, for a woman to read an academic paper before a professional association was to exhibit in public her "possession of her father's penis, having castrated him" (1929, 305–6). In order to do recompense for this castration, which resided in her intellectual proficiency, she donned the mask of womanliness. Riviere notes: "The reader may now ask how I define womanliness or where I draw the line between genuine womanliness and the 'masquerade' . . . they are the same thing" (1929, 306). Thus began the theory that all womanliness is a masquerade worn by women to disguise the fact that they have taken their father's penis in their intellectual stride, so to speak. Rather than remaining the well-adjusted castrated woman, these intellectuals have taken the penis for their own and protect it with the mask of the castrated, or woman-

hood. However, Riviere notes a difference here between heterosexual women and lesbian ones—the heterosexual women don't claim possession openly, but through reaction-formations; whereas the homosexual women openly display their possession of the penis and count on the males' recognition of defeat (1929, 312). This is not to suggest that the lesbian's situation is not also fraught with anxiety and reaction-formations, but this difference in degree is an important one.

I suggest that this kind of masquerade is consciously played out in butch-femme roles, particularly as they were constituted in the 1940s and 1950s. If one reads them from within Riviere's theory, the butch is the lesbian woman who proudly displays the possession of the penis, while the femme takes on the compensatory masquerade of womanliness. The femme, however, foregrounds her masquerade by playing to a butch, another woman in a role; likewise, the butch exhibits her penis to a woman who is playing the role of compensatory castration. This raises the question of "penis, penis, who's got the penis," because there is no referent in sight; rather, the fictions of penis and castration become ironized and "camped up." Unlike Riviere's patient, these women play on the phallic economy rather than to it. Both women alter this masquerading subject's function by positioning it between women and thus foregrounding the myths of penis and castration in the Freudian economy. In the bar culture, these roles were always acknowledged as such. The bars were often abuzz with the discussion of who was or was not a butch or femme, and how good they were at the role (see Davis and Kennedy 1986). In other words, these penis-related posturings were always acknowledged as roles, not biological birthrights, nor any other essentialist poses. The lesbian roles are underscored as two optional functions for women in the phallocracy, while the heterosexual woman's role collapses them into one compensatory charade. From a theatrical point of view, the butch-femme roles take on the quality of something more like a character construction and have a more active quality than what Riviere calls a reaction-formation. Thus, these roles qua roles lend agency and self-determination to the historically passive subject, providing her with at least two options for gender identification and with the aid of camp, an irony that allows her perception to be constructed from outside ideology, with a gender role that makes her appear as if she is inside of it.

Meanwhile, other feminist critics have received this masquerade theory into a heterosexual context, retaining its passive imprint. In Mary Ann Doane's influential article entitled "Film and the Masquerade: Theorising the Female Spectator," Doane, unfortunately, resorts to a rather biologistic position in constructing the female spectator and theorizing out from the female body. From the standpoint of something more active in terms of representation such as de Lauretis's feminist subject or the notion of butch-femme, this location of critical strategies in biological realities seems revisionist. That point aside, Doane does devise a way for women to "appropriate the gaze for their own pleasure" (1982, 77) through the notion of the transvestite and the masquerade. As the former, the female subject would position herself as if she were a male viewer, assimilating all of the power and payoffs that spectatorial position offers. As the latter, she would, as Riviere earlier suggested, masquerade as a woman. She would "flaunt her femininity, produce herself as an excess of femininity— foreground the masquerade," and reveal "femininity itself . . . as a mask" (1982, 81). Thus, the masquerade would hold femininity at a distance, manufacturing "a lack in the form of a certain distance between oneself and one's image" (1982, 82). This strategy offers the female viewer a way to be the spectator of female roles while not remaining close to them, nor identifying with them, attaining the distance from them required to enter the psychoanalytic viewing space. The masquerade that Doane describes is exactly that practiced by the femme—she foregrounds cultural femininity. The difference is that Doane places this role in the spectator position, probably as an outgrowth of the passive object position required of women in the heterosexist social structures. Doane's vision of the active woman is as the active spectator. Within the butch-femme economy, the femme actively performs her masquerade as the subject of representation. She

delivers a performance of the feminine masquerade rather than, as Doane suggests, continues in Riviere's reactive formation of masquerading compensatorily before the male-gaze-inscribed-dominant-cinema-screen. *Flaunting* has long been a camp verb and here Doane borrows it, along with the notion of "excess of femininity," so familiar to classical femmes and drag queens. Yet, by reinscribing it within a passive, spectatorial role, she gags and binds the traditional homosexual role players, whose gender play has nothing essential beneath it, replacing them with the passive spectatorial position that is, essentially, female.

Another feminist theorist, Mary Russo, has worked out a kind of female masquerade through the sense of the carnivalesque body derived from the work of Mikhail Bakhtin. In contrast to Doane, Russo moves on to a more active role for the masquerader, one of "making a spectacle of oneself." Russo is aware of the dangers of the essentialist body in discourse, while still maintaining some relationship between theory and real women. This seems a more hopeful critical terrain to the lesbian critic. In fact, Russo even includes a reference to historical instances of political resistance by men in drag (1985, 3). Yet in spite of her cautions, like Doane, Russo's category is once again the female subject, along with its biologically determined social resonances. Perhaps it is her reliance on the male author Bakhtin and the socialist resonances in his text (never too revealing about gender) that cause Russo to omit lesbian or gay strategies or experiences with the grotesque body. Instead, she is drawn to depictions of the pregnant body and finally Kristeva's sense of the maternal, even though she does note its limitations and problematic status within feminist thought (1985, 6). Finally, this swollen monument to reproduction, with all of its heterosexual privilege, once more stands alone in this performance area of the grotesque and carnivalesque. Though she does note the exlusion, in this practice, of the "already marginalized" (6), once again, they do not appear. Moreover, Russo even cites Showalter's notion that feminist theory itself is a kind of "critical cross-dressing," while still suppressing the lesbian presence in the feminist community that made such a concept available to the straight theorists (1985, 8). Still true to the male, hetero-sexual models from which her argument de-rives, she identifies the master of *mise en scène* as Derrida. Even when damning his characteriza-tion of the feminist as raging bull and asking "what kind of drag is this," her referent is the feminist and not the bull . . . dyke (1985, 9). This argument marks an ironic point in his-tory: once the feminist movement had obscured the original cross-dressed butch through the interdiction of "politically in-correct," it donned for itself the strategies and characteristics of the role-playing, safely theo-rized out of material reality and used to sup-press the referent that produced it.

In spite of their heterosexist shortcomings, what, in these theories, can be employed to understand the construction of the butch-femme subject on the stage? First, how might they be constructed as characters? Perhaps the best example of some workings of this potential is in Split Britches' production of *Beauty and the Beast.*[1] The title itself connotes the butch-femme couple: Shaw as the butch becomes the Beast who actively pursues the femme, while Weaver as the excessive femme becomes Beauty. Within the dominant system of repre-sentation, Shaw, as butch Beast, portrays as bestial women who actively love other women. The portrayal is faithful to the historical situa-tion of the butch role, as Nestle describes it: "None of the butch women I was with, and this included a passing woman, ever presented themselves to me as men; they did announce themselves as tabooed women who were willing to identify their passion for other women by wearing clothes that symbolized the taking of responsibility. Part of this responsibility was sexual expertise . . . this courage to feel com-fortable with arousing another woman became a political act" (1981, 21). In other words, the butch, who represents by her clothing the de-sire for other women, becomes the beast—the marked taboo against lesbianism dressed up in the clothes of that desire. Beauty is the desired one and the one who aims her desirability at the butch.

This symbolism becomes explicit when Shaw and Weaver interrupt the Beauty/Beast nar-rative to deliver a duologue about the history of their own personal butch-femme roles. Weaver

uses the trope of having wished she was Kathar-ine Hepburn and casting another woman as Spencer Tracy, while Shaw relates that she thought she was James Dean. The identifica-tion with movie idols is part of the camp assimilation of dominant culture. It serves mul-tiple purposes: (1) they do not identify these butch-femme roles with "real" people, or literal images of gender, but with fictionalized ones, thus underscoring the masquerade; (2) the his-tory of their desire, or their search for a sexual partner becomes a series of masks, or identities that stand for sexual attraction in the culture, thus distancing them from the "play" of seduc-tion as it is outlined by social mores; (3) the association with movies makes narrative fiction part of the strategy as well as characters. This final fiction as fiction allows Weaver and Shaw to slip easily from one narrative to another, to yet another, unbound by through-lines, plot structure, or a stable sense of character because they are fictional at their core in the camp style and through the butch-femme roles. The in-stability and alienation of character and plot is compounded with their own personal butch-femme play on the street, as a recognizable couple in the lower East Side scene, as well as within fugitive narratives onstage, erasing the difference between theatre and real life, or actor and character, obliterating any kind of essentialist ontology behind the play. This al-lows them to create a play with scenes that move easily from the narrative of beauty and the beast, to the duologue on their butch-femme history, to a recitation from *Macbeth,* to a solo lip-synced to Perry Como. The butch-femme roles at the center of their ongoing personali-ties move masquerade to the base of perfor-mance and no narrative net can catch them or hold them, as they wriggle into a variety of characters and plots.

This exciting multiplicity of roles and nar-ratives signals the potency of their agency. Somehow the actor overcomes any text, yet the actor herself is a fiction and her social self is one as well. Shaw makes a joke out of suturing to any particular role or narrative form when she dies, as the beast. Immediately after dying, she gets up to tell the audience not to believe in such cheap tricks. Dies. Tells the audience that Ronald Reagan pulled the same trick when he was shot—tells them that was not worth the suturing either. Dies. Asks for a Republican doctor. Dies. Then rises to seemingly close the production by kissing Weaver. Yet even this final butch-femme tableau is followed by a song to the audience that undercuts the performance itself.

Weaver's and Shaw's production of butch-femme role-playing in and out of a fairy tale positions the representation of the lesbian couple in a childhood narrative: the preadolescent proscription of perversity. Though they used *Beauty and the Beast* to stage butch-femme as outsiders, the quintessential childhood narrative that proscribes cross-dressing is *Little Red Riding Hood,* in which the real terror of the wolf is produced by his image in grandmother's clothing. The bed, the eating metaphor, and the cross-dressing by the wolf, provide a gridlock closure of any early thoughts of transgressing gender roles. Djuna Barnes wrote a version of this perspective in *Nightwood.* When Nora sees the transvestite doctor in his bed, wearing women's nightclothes, she remarks: "God, children know something they can't tell; they like Red Riding Hood and the wolf in bed!" Barnes goes on to explicate that sight of the cross-dressed one: "Is not the gown the natural raiment of extremity? . . . He dresses to lie beside himself, who is so constructed that love, for him, can only be something special. . . ." (1961, 78–80). *Beauty and the Beast* also returns to a childhood tale of taboo and liberates the sexual preference and role-playing it is designed to repress, in this case, specifically the butch-femme promise. As some lesbians prescribed in the early movement: identify with the monsters!

What, then, is the action played between these two roles? It is what Jean Baudrillard terms *séduction* and it yields many of its social fruits. Baudrillard begins his argument in *De la séduction,* by asserting that seduction is never of the natural order, but always operates as a sign, or artifice (1979, 10). By extension, this suggests that butch-femme seduction is always located in semiosis. The kiss, as Shaw and Weaver demonstrate in their swooping image of it, positioned at its most clichéd niche at the end of the narrative, is always the high camp kiss. Again, Baudrillard: seduction doesn't "re-

cuperate the autonomy of the body . . . truth . . . the sovereignty of this seduction is transsexual, not bisexual, destroying all sexual organization. . . ." (1979, 18). The point is not to conflict reality with another reality, but to abandon the notion of reality through roles and their seductive atmosphere and lightly manipulate appearances. Surely, this is the atmosphere of camp, permeating the *mise en scène* with "pure" artifice. In other words, a strategy of appearances replaces a claim to truth. Thus, butch-femme roles evade the notion of "the female body" as it predominates in feminist theory, dragging along its Freudian baggage and scopophilic transubstantiation. These roles are played in signs themselves and not in ontologies. Seduction, as a dramatic action, transforms all of these seeming realities into semiotic play. To use Baudrillard with Riviere, butch-femme roles offer a hypersimulation of woman as she is defined by the Freudian system and the phallocracy that institutes its social rule.[2]

Therefore, the female body, the male gaze, and the structures of realism are only sex toys for the butch-femme couple. From the perspective of camp, the claim these have to realism destroys seduction by repressing the resonances of vision and sound into its medium. This is an idea worked out by Baudrillard in his chapter on pornography, but I find it apt here. That is, that realism, with its visual organization of three dimensions, actually degrades the scene; it impoverishes the suggestiveness of the scene by its excess of means (1979, 49). This implies that as realism makes the spectator see things its way, it represses her own ability to free-associate within a situation and reduces the resonances of events to its own limited, technical dimensions. Thus, the seduction of the scene is repressed by the authoritarian claim to realistic representation. This difference is marked in the work of Weaver and Shaw in the ironized, imaginative theatrical space of their butch-femme role-playing. Contrast their freely moving, resonant narrative space to the realism of Marsha Norman, Beth Henley, Irene Fornes's *Mud,* or Sam Shepard's *A Lie of the Mind.* The violence released in the continual zooming-in on the family unit, and the heterosexist ideology linked with its stage partner, realism, is directed against women and their hint of seduction. In *A Lie of the Mind,* this becomes literally woman-battering. Beth's only associative space and access to transformative discourse is the result of nearly fatal blows to her head. One can see similar violent results in Norman's concerted moving of the heroine toward suicide in *'night, Mother* or Henley's obsession with suicide in *Crimes of the Heart* or the conclusive murder in Fornes's *Mud.* The closure of these realistic narratives chokes the women to death and strangles the play of symbols, or the possibility of seduction. In fact, for each of them, sexual play only assists their entrapment. One can see the butch Peggy Shaw rising to her feet after these realistic narrative deaths and telling us not to believe it. Cast the realism aside—its consequences for women are deadly.

In recuperating the space of seduction, the butch-femme couple can, through their own agency, move through a field of symbols, like tiptoeing through the two lips (as Irigaray would have us believe), playfully inhabiting the camp space of irony and wit, free from biological determinism, elitist essentialism, and the heterosexist cleavage of sexual difference. Surely, here is a couple the feminist subject might perceive as useful to join.

Notes

1. There is no published version of this play. In fact, there is no satisfactory way to separate the spoken text from the action. For further discussions of this group's work see Kate Davy, "Constructing the Spectator: Reception, Context, and Address in Lesbian Performance," *Performing Arts Journal* 10, no. 2 (1986): 43–52; Jill Dolan, "The Dynamics of Desire: Sexuality and Gender in Pornography and Performance," *Theatre Journal* 39, no. 2 (1987): 156–74.

2. The term *hypersimulation* is borrowed from Baudrillard's notion of the simulacrum rather than his one of seduction. It is useful here to raise the ante on terms like artifice and to suggest, as Baudrillard does, its relation to the order of reproduction and late capitalism.

References

Barnes, Djuna, 1961. *Nightwood.* New York: New Directions.

Baudrillard, Jean. 1979. *De la seduction.* Paris: Editions Galilee.

Blau, Herbert. 1983. "Disseminating Sodom." *Salmagundi* 58–59: 221–51.

Bronski, Michael. 1984. *Culture Clash: The Making of Gay Sensibility.* Boston: South End Press.

Davis, Madeline, and Kennedy, Elizabeth Lapovsky. 1986. "Oral History and the Study of Sexuality in the Lesbian Community: Buffalo, New York, 1940–1960." *Feminist Studies* 12, no. I:7–26.

de Lauretis, Teresa. 1987. *Technologies of Gender.* Bloomington, Ind.: Indiana University Press.

Doane, Mary Ann. 1982. "Film and the Masquerade: Theorising the Female Spectator." *Screen* 23:74–87.

Dolan, Jill. 1987. "The Dynamics of Desire: Sexuality and Gender in Pornography and Performance." *Theatre Journal* 39, no. 2:156–74.

Echols, Alice. 1983. "The New Feminism of Yin and Yang." In *Powers of Desire: The Politics of Sexuality,* ed. Ann Snitow, Christine Stansell, and Sharon Thompson, 440–59. New York: Monthly Review Press.

Hollibaugh, Amber, and Moraga, Cherrié. 1983. "What We're Rollin' Around in Bed With: Sexual Silences in Feminism." In *Powers of Desire: The Politics of Sexuality,* ed. Ann Snitow, Christine Stansell, and Sharon Thompson, 395–405. New York: Monthly Review Press.

Martin, Del, and Lyon, Phyllis. 1972. *Lesbian/ Woman.* New York: Bantam.

Nestle, Joan. 1981. "Butch-Fem Relationships: Sexual Courage in the 1950s." *Heresies* 12:21–24. All pagination here is from that publication.

Newton, Esther. 1972. *Mother Camp: Female Impersonators in America*. Englewood Cliffs, N.J.: Prentice-Hall.

"Postmodernism: Text, Politics, Instruction." 1987. International Association for Philosophy and Literature. Lawrence, Kansas, April 30–May 2.

Riviere, Joan. 1929. "Womanliness as a Masquerade." *International Journal of Psycho-Analysis* 10:303–13.

Russo, Mary. 1985. "Female Grotesques: Carnival and Theory." See Chapter 7 of this volume.

Sedgwick, Eve. 1990. "The Epistemology of the Closet." Berkeley: University of California Press.

Sontag, Susan. 1966. *Against Interpretation*. New York: Farrar, Strauss & Giroux.

Wittig, Monique. 1975. *The Lesbian Body*. Trans. David LeVay. New York: William Morrow.

Study Questions

1. According to Case, changing the notion of the female subject is an imperative. How does she support this claim?

2. How does she portray the lesbian subject in feminist history?

3. What is the discourse of camp? In what sense does it relate to the feminist subject?

4. Why does Case say that the butch-femme configuration might be a feminist subject?

5. How does masquerade theory relate to the lesbian subject position?

6. Why does Case criticize Russo's formulation as heterosexist?

7. In what kind of performance does Case think the female subject might be recuperated? Why is *Beauty and the Beast* a good example?

Commitment from the Mirror-Writing Box

Trinh T. Minh-ha

The Triple Bind

Neither black/red/yellow nor woman but poet or writer. For many of us, the question of priorities remains a crucial issue. Being merely "a writer" without doubt ensures one a status of far greater weight than being "a woman of color who writes" ever does. Imputing race or sex to the creative act has long been a means by which the literary establishment cheapens

From Trinh T. Minh-ha, *Woman, Native, Other* (Bloomington, IN: Indiana University Press, 1989). Reprinted by permission.

and discredits the achievements of non-mainstream women writers. She who "happens to be" a (non-white) Third World member, a woman, and a writer is bound to go through the ordeal of exposing her work to the abuse of praises and criticisms that either ignore, dispense with, or overemphasize her racial and sexual attributes. Yet the time has passed when she can confidently identify herself with a profession or artistic vocation without questioning and relating it to her color-woman condition. Today, the growing ethnic-feminist consciousness has made it increasingly difficult for her to turn a blind eye not only to the specification of the writer as historical subject (who writes? and in what context?), but also to writing itself as a practice located at the intersection of subject and history—a literary practice that involves the possible knowledge (linguistical and ideological) of itself as such. On the one hand, no matter what position she decides to take, she will sooner or later find herself driven into situations where she is made to feel she must choose from among three conflicitng identities. Writer of color? Woman writer? Or woman of color? Which comes first? Where does she place her loyalties? On the other hand, she often finds herself at odds with language, which partakes in the white-male-is-norm ideology and is used predominantly as a vehicle to circulate established power relations. This is further intensified by her finding herself also at odds with her relation to writing, which when carried out uncritically often proves to be one of domination: as holder of speech, she usually writes from a position of power, creating as an "author," situating herself *above* her work and existing *before* it, rarely simultaneously *with* it. Thus, it has become almost impossible for her to take up her pen without at the same time questioning her relation to the material that defines her and her creative work. As focal point of cultural consciousness and social change, writing weaves into language the complex relations of a subject caught between the problems of race and gender and the practice of literature as the very place where social alienation is thwarted differently according to each specific context.

Silence in Time

Writing, reading, thinking, imagining, speculating. These are luxury activities, so I am reminded, permitted to a privileged few, whose idle hours of the day can be viewed otherwise than as a bowl of rice or a loaf of bread less to share with the family. "If we wish to increase the supply of rare and remarkable women like the Brontës," wrote our reputed foresister Virginia Woolf, "we should give the Joneses and the Smiths rooms of their own and five hundred [pounds] a year. One cannot grow fine flowers in a thin soil."[1] Substantial creative achievement demands not necessarily genius, but acumen, bent, persistence, time. And time, in the framework of industrial development, means a wage that admits of leisure and living conditions that do not require that writing be incessantly interrupted, deferred, denied, at any rate subordinated to family responsibilities. "When the claims of creation cannot be primary," Tillie Olsen observes, "the results are atrophy; unfinished work; minor effort and accomplishment; silences." The message Olsen conveys in *Silences* leaves no doubt as to the circumstances under which most women writers function. It is a constant reminder of those who never come to writing: "the invisible, the as-innately-capable: the born to the wrong circumstances—diminished, excluded, foundered."[2] To say this, however, is not to say that writing should be held in veneration in all milieus or that every woman who fails to write is a disabled being. (What Denise Paulme learned in this regard during her first period of fieldwork in Africa is revealing. Comparing her life one day with those of the women in an area of the French Sudan, she was congratulating herself on not having to do a chore like theirs—pounding millet for the meals day in and day out—when she overheard herself commented upon by one of the women nearby: "That girl makes me tired with her everlasting paper and pencil: what sort of a life is that?" The lesson, Paulme concluded, "was a salutary one, and I have never forgotten it.")[3] To point out that, in general, the situation of women does not favor literary productivity is to imply that it is almost impossible for them (and especially for those bound up with the Third World) to engage in writing as an occupation without their letting themselves be consumed by a deep and pervasive sense of guilt. Guilt over the selfishness implied in such activity, over themselves as housewives and "women," over their families, their friends and all other "less fortunate" women. The circle in which they turn proves to be vicious, and writing in such a context is always practiced at the cost of other women's labor. Doubts, lack of confidence, frustrations, despair: these are sentiments born with the habits of distraction, distortion, discontinuity and silence. After having toiled for a number of years on her book, hattie gossett exclaims to herself:

Who do you think you are [to be writing a book]? and who cares what you think about anything enough to pay money for it . . . a major portion of your audience not only cant read but seems to think readin is a waste of time? plus books like this arent sold in the ghetto bookshops or even in airports?[4]

The same doubt is to be heard through Gloria Anzaldúa's voice:

Who gave us permission to perform the act of writing? Why does writing seem so unnatural for me? . . . The voice recurs in me: *Who am I, a poor Chicanita from the sticks, to think I could write?* How dared I even consider becoming a writer as I stooped over the tomato fields bending, bending under the hot sun . . .

How hard it is for us to *think* we can choose to become writers, much less *feel* and *believe* that we can.[5]

Rites of Passage

S/he who writes, writes. In uncertainty, in necessity. And does not ask whether s/he is given the permission to do so or not. Yet, in the context of today's market-dependent societies, "to be a writer" can no longer mean purely to perform the act of writing. For a laywo/man to enter the priesthood—the sacred world of writers—s/he must fulfill a number of unwritten conditions. S/he must undergo a series of rituals, be baptized and ordained. S/he must *submit* her writings to the law laid down by the corporation of literary/literacy victims and be prepared to *accept* their verdict. Every woman who writes and wishes to become established as a writer has known the tast of *rejection*. Sylvia Plath's experience is often cited. Her years of darkness, despair and disillusion, her agony of slow rebirth, her moments of fearsome excitement at the start of the writing of *The Bell Jar,* her unsuccessful attempts at re-submitting her first book of poems under ever-changing titles and the distress with which she upbraided herself are parts of the realities that affect many women writers:

Nothing stinks like a pile of unpublished writing, which remark I guess shows I still don't

have a pure motive (O it's-such-fun-I-just-can't-stop-who-cares-if-it's-published-or-read) about writing . . . I still want to see it finally ritualized in print.[6]

Accumulated unpublished writings do stink. They heap up before your eyes like despicable confessions that no one cares to hear; they sap your self-confidence by incessantly reminding you of your failure to incorporate. For publication means the breaking of a first seal, the end of a "no-admitted" status, the end of a soliloquy confined to the private sphere and the start of a possible sharing with the unknown other—the reader, whose collaboration with the writer alone allows the work to come into full being. Without such a rite of passage, the woman-writer-to-be/woman-to-be-writer is condemned to wander about, begging for permission to join in and be a member. If it is difficult for any woman to find acceptance for her writing, it is all the more so for those who do not match the stereotype of the "real woman"—the colored, the minority, the physically or mentally handicapped. Emma Santos, who spent her days running to and fro between two worlds—that of hospitals and that of the "normal" system—equally rejected by Psychiatry and by Literature, is another writer whose first book has been repeatedly dismissed (by twenty-two publishing houses). Driven to obsession by a well-known publisher who promised to send her an agreement but never did, she followed him, spied on him, called him twenty times a day on the phone, and ended up feeling like "a pile of shit making after great men of letters." Writing, she remarks, is "a shameful, venereal disease," and Literature, nothing more than "a long beseeching." Having no acquaintance, no friend to introduce her when she sought admission for her work among the publishers, she describes her experience as follows:

I receive encouraging letters but I am goitrous. Publishers, summons, these are worse than psychiatrists, interrogatories. The publishers perceive a sick and oblivious girl. They would have liked the text, the same one, without changing a single word, had it been presented by a young man from the [Ecole] Normale Superieure, *agrégé* of philosophy, worthy of the Goncourt prize.[7]

The Guilt

To capture a publisher's attention, to convince, to negotiate: these constitute one step forward into the world of writers, one distress, one guilt. One guilt among the many yet to come, all of which bide their time to loom up out of their hiding places, for the path is long and there is an ambush at every turn. Writing: not letting it merely haunt you and die over and over again in you until you no longer know how to speak. Getting published: not loathing yourself, not burning it, not giving up. Now I (the all-knowning subject) feel almost secure with such definite "not-to-do's." Yet I/i (the plural, non-unitary subject) cannot set my mind at rest with them without at the same time recognizing their precariousness. i (the personal race- and gender-specific subject) have, in fact turned a deaf ear to a number of primary questions: Why write? For whom? What necessity? What writing? What impels you and me and hattie gossett to continue to write when we know for a fact that our books are not going to be "sold in the ghetto bookshops or even in airports?" And why do we care for their destinations at all? "A writer," proclaims Toni Cade Bambara, "like any other cultural worker, like any other member of the community, ought to try to put her/his skills in the service of the community." It is apparently on account of such a conviction that Bambara "began a career as the neighborhood scribe," helping people write letters to faraway relatives as well as letters of complaint, petitions contracts and the like.[8] For those of us who call ourselves "writers" in the context of a community whose major portion "not only cant read but seems to think readin is a waste of time" (gossett), being "the neighborhood scribe" is no doubt one of the most gratifying and unpretentious ways of dedicating oneself to one's people. Writing as a social function—as differentiated from the ideal of art for art's sake—is the aim that Third World writers, in defining their roles, highly esteem and claim. *Literacy* and *literature* intertwine so tightly, indeed, that the latter has never ceased to imply both the ability to read and the condition of being well read—and thereby to convey the sense of *polite learning* through the arts of *grammar* and *rhetoric*. The illiterate, the ignorant versus the wo/man of "letters" (of wide reading), the highly educated. With such discrimination and opposition, it is hardly surprising that the writer should be viewed as a social parasite. Whether s/he makes common cause with the upper classes or chooses to disengage her/himself by adopting the myth of the bohemian artist, the writer is a kept wo/man who for her/his living largely relies on the generosity of that portion of society called the literate. A room of one's own and a pension of five hundred pounds per year solely for making ink marks on paper: this, symbolically speaking, is what many people refer to when they say the writer's activity is "gratuitous" and "useless." No matter how devoted to the vocation s/he may be, the writer cannot subsist on words and mere fresh air, nor can s/he really "live by the pen," since her/his work—arbitrarily estimated as it is—has no definite market value. Reading in this context may actually prove to be "a waste of time," and writing, as Woolf puts it, "a reputable and harmless occupation." Reflecting on her profession as a writer (in a 1979 interview), Toni Cade Bambara noted that she probably did not begin "getting really serious about writing until maybe five years ago. Prior to that, in spite of all good sense, I always thought writing was rather frivolous, that it was something you did because you didn't feel like doing any work." The concept of "writing" here seems to be incompatible with the concept of "work." As the years went by and Toni Cade Bambara got more involved in writing, however, she changed her attitude and has "come to appreciate that it is a perfectly legitimate way to participate in struggle."[9]

Commitment as an ideal is particularly dear to Third World writers. It helps to alleviate the Guilt: that of being privileged (Inequality), of "going over the hill" to join the clan of literates (Assimilation), and of indulging in a "useless" activity while most community members "stoop over the tomato fields, bending under the hot sun" (a perpetuation of the same privilege). In a sense, committed writers are the ones who write both to awaken to the consciousness of their guilt and to give their readers a guilty conscience. Bound to one another by an awareness of their guilt, writer and reader may thus assess their positions, engaging themselves wholly in their situations and carrying their weight into the weight of their communities, the weight of the world. Such a definition naturally places the committed writers on the side of Power. For every discourse that breeds fault and guilt is a discourse of authority and arrogance. To say this, however, is not to say that all power discourses produce equal oppression or that those established are necessary. Discussing African literature and the various degrees of propaganda prompted by commitment, Ezekiel Mphahlele observes that although "propaganda is always going to be with us"—for "there will always be the passionate outcry against injustice, war, fascism, poverty"—the manner in which a writer protests reflects to a large extent her/his regard for the reader and "decides the literary worth of a work." "Commitment," Mphahlele adds, "need not give rise to propaganda: the writer can make [her/]his stand known without advocating it . . . in two-dimensional terms, i.e., in terms of one response to one stimulus."[10] Thus, in the whirlwind of prescriptive general formulas such as: Black art must "respond *positively* to the reality of revolution" or Black art must "expose the enemy, *praise* the people, and *support* the revolution" (Ron Karenga, my italics), one also hears distinct, unyielding voices whose autonomy asserts itself as follows:

> Black pride need not blind us to our own weaknesses: in fact it should help us to perceive our weaknesses . . .
>
> I do not care for black pride that drugs us into a condition of stupor and inertia. I do not care for it if leaders use it to dupe the masses.[11]

> To us, the man who adores the Negro is as sick as the man who abominates him.[12]

Freedom and the Masses

The notion of *art engagé* as defined by Jean-Paul Sartre, an influential apologist for socially effective literature, continues to grow and to circulate among contemporary engaged writers. It is easy to find parallels (and it is often directly quoted) in Third World literary discourses. "A free man addressing free men," the Sartrian writer "has only one subject—freedom." He writes to "appeal to the reader's freedom to collaborate in the production of his work" and paints the world "only so that free men may feel their freedom as they face it."[13] The function of literary art, in other words, must be to remind us of that freedom and to defend it. Made to serve a political purpose, literature thus places itself within the context of the proletarian fight, while the writer frees himself from his dependence on elites—or in a wider sense, from any privilege—and creates, so to speak, an art for an unrestricted public known as "art for the masses." From the chain of notions dear to Sartre—choice, responsibility, contingency, situation, motive, reason, being, doing, having—two notions are set forth here as being most relevant to Third World engaged literary theories: freedom and the masses. What is freedom in writing? And what can writing-for-the-masses be? Reflecting on being a writer, "female, black, and free," Margaret Walker, for example, defines freedom as "a philosophical state of mind and existence." She proudly affirms:

> My entire career in writing . . . is determined by these immutable facts of my human condition . . .
>
> Writing is my life, but it is an avocation nobody can buy. In this respect I believe I am a free agent, stupid perhaps, but *me* and still free . . .
>
> The writer is still in the avant-garde for Truth and Justice, for Freedom, Peace, and Human Dignity . . . Her place, let us be reminded, is anywhere she chooses to be, doing what she has to do, creating, healing, and always being herself.[14]

These lines agree perfectly with Sartre's ideal of liberty. They may be said to echo his concepts of choice and responsibility—according to which each person, being an absolute choice of self, an absolute emergence at an absolute date, must assume her/his situation with the proud consciousness of being the author of it. (For one is nothing but this "being-in-situation" that is the total contingency of the world, of one's birth, past and environment, and of the fact of one's fellow wo/man.) By its own rationale, such a sense of responsibility (attributed to the lucid, conscientious, successful man of action) renders the relationship between freedom and commitment particularly problematic. Is it not, indeed, always in the name of freedom that My freedom hastens to stamp out those of others? Is it not also in the name of the masses that My personality bestirs itself to impersonalize those of my fellow wo/men? Do the masses become masses by themselves? Or are they the result of a theoretical and practical operation of "massification"? From where onward can one say of a "free" work of art that it is written for the infinite numbers which constitute the masses and not merely for a definite public stratum of society?

For the People, by the People and from the People

Like all stereotypical notions, the notion of the masses has both an upgrading connotation and a degrading one. One often speaks of the masses as one speaks of the people, magnifying thereby their number, their strength, their mission. One invokes them and pretends to write on their behalf when one wishes to give weight to one's undertaking or to justify it. The Guilt mentioned earlier is always lurking below the surface. Yet to oppose the masses to the elite is already to imply that those forming the masses are regarded as an aggregate of average persons condemned by their lack of personality or by their dim individualities to stay with the herd, to be docile and anonymous. Thus the notion of "art *for* the masses" supposes not only a split between the artist and her/his audience—the spectator-consumer—but also a passivity on the part of the latter. For art here is not attributed to the masses; it is ascribed to the active few, whose role is precisely to produce *for* the great numbers. This means that despite the shift of emphasis the elite-versus-masses opposition remains intact. In fact it must remain so, basically unchallenged, if it is to serve a conservative political and ideological purpose—in other words, if (what is defined as)

"art" is to exist at all. One of the functions of this "art for the masses" is, naturally, to contrast with the other, higher "art for the elite," and thereby to enforce its elitist values. The wider the distance between the two, the firmer the stand of conservative art. One can no longer let oneself be deceived by concepts that oppose the artist or the intellectual to the masses and deal with them as with two incompatible entities. Criticisms arising from or dwelling on such a *myth* are, indeed, quite commonly leveled against innovators and more often used as tools of intimidation than as reminders of social interdependency. It is perhaps with this perspective in mind that one may better understand the variants of Third World literary discourse, which claims not exactly an "art for the masses," but an "art for the people, by the people and from the people." In an article on *"Le Poète noir et son peuple"* (The Black Poet and His People), for example, Jacques Rabemananjara virulently criticized Occidental poets for spending their existence indulging in aesthetic refinement and sublties that bear no relation to their peoples' concerns and aspirations, that are merely sterile intellectual delights. The sense of dignity, Rabemananjara said, forbids black Orpheus to go in for the cult of art for art's sake. Inspirer inspired by his people, the poet has to play the difficult role of being simultaneously the torch lighting the way for his fellowmen and their loyal interpreter. "He is more than their spokesman: he is their voice." His noble mission entitles him to be "not only the messenger, but the very message of his people."[15] The concept of a popular and functional art is here poised against that of an intellectual and aesthetic one. A justified regression? A shift of emphasis again? Or an attempt at fusion of the self and the other, of art, ideology and life? Let us listen to other, perhaps less didactic voices; that of Aimé Césaire in *Return to My Native Land:*

I should come back to this land of mine and say to it: "Embrace me without fear. . . . If all I can do is speak, at least I shall speak for you."

And I should say further: "My tongue shall serve those miseries which have no tongue, my voice the liberty of those who founder in the dungeons of despair."

And I should say to myself: "And most of all beware, even in thought, of assuming the sterile attitude of the spectator, for life is not a spectacle, a sea of griefs is not a proscenium, a man who wails is not a dancing bear."[16]

that of Nikki Giovanni in *Gemini:*

> Poetry is the culture of a people. We are poets even when we don't write poems. . . . We are all preachers because we are One. . . . I don't think we younger poets are doing anything significantly different from what we as a people have always done. The new Black poetry is in fact just a manifestation of our collective historical needs.[17]

and that of Alice Walker in an essay on the importance of models in the artist's life:

> It is, in the end, the saving of lives that we writers are about. . . . We do it because we care. . . . We care because we know this: *The life we save is our own.*[18]

One may say of art for art's sake in general that it is itself a reaction against the bourgeois "functional" attitude of mind which sees in the acquisition of art the highest, purest form of consumption. By making explicit the gratuitousness of their works, artists show contempt for their wealthy customers, whose purchasing power allows them to subvert art in its subversiveness, reducing it to a mere commodity or a service. As a reaction, however, art for art's sake is bound to be "two-dimensional"—"one response to one stimulus" (Mphahlele)—and, therefore, to meet with no success among writers of the Third World. "I cannot imagine," says Wole Soyinka, "that our 'authentic black innocent' would ever have permitted himself to be manipulated into the false position of countering one pernicious Manicheism with another."[19] An art that claims to be at the same time sender and bearer of a message, to serve the people and "to come off the street" (Cade Bambara), should then be altogether "functional, collective, and committing or committed" (Karenga). The reasoning circle closes on the notion of commitment, which again emerges, fraught with questions.

Notes

1. Virginia Woolf, *Women and Writing* (New York: Harcourt Brace Jovanovich, 1979), 54.
2. Tillie Olsen, *Silences* (1978, rpt. New York: Delta/Seymour Lawrence Ed., 1980), 13, 39.
3. Denise Paulme, ed., *Women of Tropical Africa,* tr. H. M. Wright (1963, rpt. Berkeley: University of California Press, 1974), 2.
4. hattie gossett, "Who Told You Anybody Wants To Hear From You? You Ain't Nothing But a Black Woman!" *This Bridge Called My Back: Writings by Radical Women of Color,* ed. Cherrie Morraga & Gloria Anzaldúa (Watertown, MA: Persephone Press, 1981), 175.
5. Gloria Anzaldúa, "Speaking in Tongues: A Letter to 3rd World Women Writers," *This Bridge Called My Back,* 166.
6. Sylvia Plath, *The Bell Jar* (1971, rpt. New York: Bantam Books, 1981), 211. See Biographical Note by Lois Ames.
7. Emma Santos, *L'Itinéraire psychiatrique* (Paris: Des Femmes, 1977), 46–77. For previous quotes see pp. 47, 50, 125 (my translations).
8. Toni Cade Bambara, "What It Is I Think I'm Doing Anyhow," *The Writer on Her Work,* ed. J. Sternburg (New York: W. W. Norton, 1980), 167.
9. "Commitment: Toni Cade Bambara Speaks," interview with Beverly Guy-Sheftall in *Sturdy Black Bridges: Visions of Black Women in Literature,* ed. R. P. Bell, B. J. Parker, & B. Guy-Sheftall (New York: Anchor/Doubleday, 1979), 232.
10. Ezekiel Mphahlele, *Voices in the Whirlwind* (New York: Hill & Wang, 1972), 186–87.
11. Ibid., 196.
12. Franz Fanon, *Black Skin White Masks,* tr. Charles Lam Markmann (New York: Grove Press, 1967), 8.

13. Jean-Paul Sartre, *Situations, II Qu'est-ce que la littérature?* (Paris: Gallimard, 1948), 97, 112.

14. Margaret Walker, "On Being Female, Black, and Free," *The Writer on Her Work*, 95, 102, 106.

15. Jacques Rabemananjara, "Le Poète noir et son peuple," *Présence Africaine* 16 (Oct.–Nov. 1957), 10–13.

16. Aimé Césaire, *Return to My Native Land* (Paris: Présence Africaine, 1971), 60–62.

17. Nikki Giovanni, *Gemini: An Extended Autobiographical Statement on My First Twenty-Five Years of Being a Black Poet* (New York: Viking Press, 1971), 95–96.

18. Alice Walker, "Saving the Life That Is Your Own: The Importance of Models in the Artist's Life," *The Third Woman: Minority Women Writers of the United States*, ed. D. Fisher (Boston: Houghton Mifflin, 1980), 158.

19. Wole Soyinka, *Myth, Literature, and the African World* (New York: Cambridge University Press, 1976), 138.

Study Questions

1. Minh-ha indicates that the woman writer of color has a question of loyalties. Why does she say this?

2. What are some problems about or obstacles to an ethnic-feminist consciousness? How is it related to her identity?

3. Why does Minh-ha speak of writing as a rite of passage? Cite an example.

4. How does she think that "a room of one's own" might be viewed by the Third World woman writer?

5. Will the commitment of the ethnic-feminist writer/artist necessarily preclude freedom, according to Minh-ha? Explain.

6. In her view, how does the committed writer mediate the notion of "art for art's sake"?

8

Feminist Ethics

Ethics is the philosophy of morality and, with aesthetics, makes up the centrality of the area of philosophy called axiology (value theory). Ethics is concerned with questions of right and wrong conduct, the nature of moral obligation, and the notion of the good life. The core question, posed by Aristotle, is "What kind of life shall I best lead?"

Feminist ethics starts, in one sense, with the realization that Aristotle's famous question in "male-stream" philosophy does not apply—or has not applied—to women. As de Beauvoir says, women have been objects and not subjects. By that she means that women have been denied the right to be full moral agents; they have not been those who "choose a life."

Feminist ethics, therefore, now poses the question: Is it good for women? (This is a recurring question in the feminist manifestos of the second wave.) In this way, feminist theorists seek the re-visioning of moral philosophy. The feminist imperative is to challenge the hegemony of male ethical theory and to insist on "the woman's voice."

Feminist ethics, then, arises directly out of women's lives and women's issues. (These had been given only passing consideration in patriarchal value theory.) For example, we see much concern with reproductive rights, since these reflect the centrality of women's demand for control over "our bodies, ourselves."

The moral issues concerning abortion have been, accordingly, the subject of significant analysis by feminist philosophers. Paradigmatic of female sexual autonomy, abortion issues affect all women, directly or indirectly. Judith Thomson's argument for abortion was one of the first systematic analyses. Her discussion focuses on the question of what one person owes another and the kind of use one person can make of another's body. This changes the locus of concern from the personhood of the fetus to the notion of rights to one's person.

In response to Thomson's article, Mary Anne Warren contends that personhood is indeed the central issue in the question of abortion, but she returns the discussion to the personhood of the fetus. She introduces the notion of the moral community as the basis for legitimating personhood and for validating judgments of the kind involved in decisions affecting abortion.

Another feminist response to Thomson's argument is offered in the essay by Kathryn Addelson. She compares Thomson's approach to the issue with the approach of a feminist abortion clinic. Addelson believes that this comparison yields a contrast between two ways of organizing morality. The first, the dominant tradition, uses concepts and categories such as "rights," "property," and "contract," while the second, or feminist, mode asks, "What leads to a meaningful life for women?" Addelson believes that Thomson's argument is characteristic of the dominant viewpoint rather than of the viewpoint of women, who are socially subordinate. Her discussion leads to an exploration of moral concepts and their significance for a feminist re-visioning.

In the last set of writings, feminist thinking is brought to bear on the central question of feminist ethical theory: Is there a women's morality? And, if so, what are its main features? In other words, what *is* a feminist ethics? According to Hester Eisenstein, and as the selections show, it is "a woman-centered analysis which presupposes the centrality, normality, and value of women's experience and women's culture."

Women's moral development may be different from men's, according to Carol Gilligan, and traditional moral theory does not account for this difference. Gilligan believes that women's morality centers on the notions of caring and responsibility. She contrasts this ethics with the "standard" ethics of rights and rules that men have formulated. Like Addelson, Gilligan believes that women's moral development must be recognized and women's morality validated by our ethical theory.

All women, whether as mothers or daughters, are involved in maternal practices, according to Sara Ruddick. She argues for the rational configuration of what she calls "maternal thinking," which arises out of these practices. She also sees maternal thinking as expressive of ethical modes such as the notion of "attentive love," and she proposes that these modes transform morality in general.

Nel Noddings approaches the topic of female ethics by critiquing examples of male ethics. She discusses the standpoint of women as the basis of an ethics, especially the notion of caring. Noddings details the features of a morality of caring that will be non-oppressive for women.

Adrienne Rich speaks to the notion of women-bonding and to the kind of morality that will support this goal. She says that in the past women were not expected to have honor: "they lied and were lied to." Rich exhorts women to create a climate of honor among themselves, and she states that it is especially important for women to take truthfulness to each other seriously if they are to have a life together.

Joyce Trebilcot considers women's morality in terms of a re-visioning of certain central concepts such as "nurturance," "strength," and "lesbian." Trebilcot believes that women are redefining themselves, and she shows how a feminist naming of ourselves is called for in order to create ourselves as moral subjects.

In the final essay, Katie Cannon explores the moral agency of the black community. She believes that dominant ethics is not applicable to the material conditions of black women. She posits a moral wisdom, in place of an ethics of freedom, which she finds in the black women's literary tradition. Citing texts by Zora Neale Hurston and Toni Morrison, Cannon finds the meaning of the moral life in a womanist (Alice Walker) context.

A Defense of Abortion

Judith Jarvis Thomson

Most opposition to abortion relies on the premise that the fetus is a human being, a person, from the moment of conception. The premise is argued for, but, as I think, not well. Take, for example, the most common argument. We are asked to notice that the development of a human being from conception through birth into childhood is continuous; then it is said that to draw a line, to choose a point in this development and say "before this point the thing is not a person, after this point it is a person" is to make an arbitrary choice, a choice for which in the nature of things no good reason can be given. It is concluded that the fetus is, or anyway that we had better say it is, a person from the moment of conception. But this conclusion does not follow. Similar things might be said about the development of an acorn into an oak tree, and it does not follow that acorns are oak trees, or that we had better say they are. Arguments of this form are sometimes called "slippery slope arguments"—the phrase is perhaps self-explanatory—and it is dismaying that opponents of abortion rely on them so heavily and uncritically.

I am inclined to agree, however, that the prospects for "drawing a line" in the development of the fetus look dim. I am inclined to think also that we shall probably have to agree that the fetus has already become a human person well before birth. Indeed, it comes as a surprise when one first learns how early in its life it begins to acquire human characteristics. By the tenth week, for example, it already has a face, arms and legs, fingers and toes; it has internal organs, and brain activity is detectable.[1] On the other hand, I think that the

From *Philosophy of Public Affairs*, Vol. 1, No. 1 (Fall 1971), pp. 47–66. Copyright © 1971 by Princeton University Press. Reprinted by permission of Princeton University Press.

premise is false, that the fetus is not a person from the moment of conception. A newly fertilized ovum, a newly implanted clump of cells, is no more a person than an acorn is an oak tree. But I shall not discuss any of this. For it seems to me to be of great interest to ask what happens if, for the sake of argument, we allow the premise. How, precisely, are we supposed to get from there to the conclusion that abortion is morally impermissible? Opponents of abortion commonly spend most of their time establishing that the fetus is a person, and hardly any time explaining the step from there to the impermissibility of abortion. Perhaps they think the step too simple and obvious to require much comment. Or perhaps instead they are simply being economical in argument. Many of those who defend abortion rely on the premise that the fetus is not a person, but only a bit of tissue that will become a person at birth; and why pay out more arguments than you have to? Whatever the explanation, I suggest that the step they take is neither easy nor obvious, that it calls for closer examination than it is commonly given, and that when we do give it this closer examination we shall feel inclined to reject it.

I propose, then, that we grant that the fetus is a person from the moment of conception. How does the argument go from here? Something like this, I take it. Every person has a right to life. So the fetus has a right to life. No doubt the mother has a right to decide what shall happen in and to her body; everyone would grant that. But surely a person's right to life is stronger and more stringent than the mother's right to decide what happens in and to her body, and so outweighs it. So the fetus may not be killed; an abortion may not be performed.

It sounds plausible. But now let me ask you to imagine this. You wake up in the morning and find yourself back to back in bed with an unconscious violinist. A famous unconscious violinist. He has been found to have a fatal kidney ailment and the Society of Music Lovers has canvassed all the available medical records and found that you alone have the right blood type to help. They have therefore kidnapped you, and last night the violinist's circulatory system was plugged into yours, so that your kidneys can be used to extract poisons from his blood as well as your own. The director of the hospital now tells you, "Look, we're sorry the Society of Music Lovers did this to you—we would never have permitted it if we had known. But still, they did it, and the violinist now is plugged into you. To unplug you would be to kill him. But never mind, it's only for nine months. By then he will have recovered from his ailment, and can safely be unplugged from you." Is it morally incumbent on you to accede to this situation? No doubt it would be very nice of you if you did, a great kindness. But do you *have* to accede to it? What if it were not nine months, but nine years? Or longer still? What if the director of the hospital says, "Tough luck, I agree, but you've now got to stay in bed, with the violinist plugged into you, for the rest of your life. Because remember this. All persons have a right to life, and violinists are persons. Granted you have a right to decide what happens in and to your body, but a person's right to life outweighs your right to decide what happens in and to your body. So you cannot ever be unplugged from him." I imagine you would regard this as outrageous, which suggests that something really is wrong with that plausible-sounding argument I mentioned a moment ago.

In this case, of course, you were kidnapped; you didn't volunteer for the operation that plugged the violinist into your kidneys. Can those who oppose abortion on the ground I mentioned make an exception for a pregnancy due to rape? Certainly. They can say that persons have a right to life only if they didn't come into existence because of rape; or they can say that all persons have a right to life, but that some have less of a right to life than others, in particular, that those who came into existence because of rape have less. But these statements have a rather unpleasant sound. Surely the question of whether you have a right to life at all, or how much of it you have,

shouldn't turn on the question of whether or not you are the product of a rape. And in fact the people who oppose abortion on the ground I mentioned do not make this distinction, and hence do not make an exception in case of rape.

Nor do they make an exception for a case in which the mother has to spend the nine months of her pregnancy in bed. They would agree that would be a great pity, and hard on the mother; but all the same, all persons have a right to life, the fetus is a person, and so on. I suspect, in fact, that they would not make an exception for a case in which, miraculously enough, the pregnancy went on for nine years, or even the rest of the mother's life.

Some won't even make an exception for a case in which continuation of the pregnancy is likely to shorten the mother's life; they regard abortion as impermissible even to save the mother's life. Such cases are nowadays very rare, and many opponents of abortion do not accept this extreme view. All the same, it is a good place to begin: a number of points of interest come out in respect to it.

1. Let us call the view that abortion is impermissible even to save the mother's life "the extreme view." I want to suggest first that it does not issue from the argument I mentioned earlier without the addition of some fairly powerful premises. Suppose a woman has become pregnant, and now learns that she has a cardiac condition such that she will die if she carries the baby to term. What may be done for her? The fetus, being a person, has a right to life, but as the mother is a person too, so has she a right to life. Presumably they have an equal right to life. How is it supposed to come out that an abortion may not be performed? If mother and child have an equal right to life, shouldn't we perhaps flip a coin? Or should we add to the mother's right to life her right to decide what happens in and to her body, which everybody seems to be ready to grant—the sum of her rights now outweighing the fetus' right to life?

The most familiar argument here is the following. We are told that performing the abortion would be directly killing[2] the child, whereas doing nothing would not be killing the mother, but only letting her die. Moreover, in killing the child, one would be killing an innocent person, for the child has committed no crime, and is not aiming at his mother's death. And then there are a variety of ways in which this might be continued. (1) But as directly killing an innocent person is always and absolutely impermissible, an abortion may not be performed. Or, (2) as directly killing an innocent person is murder, and murder is always and absolutely impermissible, an abortion may not be performed.[3] Or, (3) as one's duty to refrain from directly killing an innocent person is more stringent than one's duty to keep a person from dying, an abortion may not be performed. Or, (4) if one's only options are directly killing an innocent person or letting a person die, one must prefer letting the person die, and thus an abortion may not be performed.[4]

Some people seem to have thought that these are not further premises which must be added if the conclusion is to be reached, but that they follow from the very fact that an innocent person has a right to life.[5] But this seems to me to be a mistake, and perhaps the simplest way to show this is to bring out that while we must certainly grant that innocent persons have a right to life, the theses in (1) through (4) are all false. Take (2), for example. If directly killing an innocent person is murder, and thus is impermissible, then the mother's directly killing the innocent person inside her is murder, and thus is impermissible. But it cannot seriously be thought to be murder if the mother performs an abortion on herself to save her life. It cannot seriously be said that she *must* refrain, that she *must* sit passively by and wait for her death. Let us look again at the case of you and the violinist. There you are, in bed with the violinist, and the director of the hospital says to you. "It's all most distressing, and I deeply sympathize, but you see this is putting an additional strain on your kidneys, and you'll be dead within the month. But you *have* to stay where you are all the same. Because unplugging you will be directly killing an innocent violinist, and that's murder, and

that's impermissible." If anything in the world is true, it is that you do not commit murder, you do not do what is impermissible, if you reach around to your back and unplug yourself from that violinist to save your life.

The main focus of attention in writings on abortion has been on what a third party may or may not do in answer to a request from a woman for an abortion. This is in a way understandable. Things being as they are, there isn't much a woman can safely do to abort herself. So the question asked is what a third party may do, and what the mother may do, if it is mentioned at all, is deduced, almost as an afterthought, from what it is concluded that third parties may do. But it seems to me that to treat the matter in this way is to refuse to grant to the mother that very status of person which is so firmly insisted on for the fetus. For we cannot simply read off what a person may do from what a third party may do. Suppose you find yourself trapped in a tiny house with a growing child. I mean a very tiny house, and a rapidly growing child—you are already up against the wall of the house and in a few minutes you'll be crushed to death. The child on the other hand won't be crushed to death; if nothing is done to stop him from growing he'll be hurt, but in the end he'll simply burst open the house and walk out a free man. Now I could well understand it if a bystander were to say, "There's nothing we can do for you. We cannot choose between your life and his, we cannot be the ones to decide who is to live, we cannot intervene." But it cannot be concluded that you too can do nothing, that you cannot attack it to save your life. However innocent the child may be, you do not have to wait passively while it crushes you to death. Perhaps a pregnant woman is vaguely felt to have the status of house, to which we don't allow the right of self-defense. But if the woman houses the child, it should be remembered that she is a person who houses it.

I should perhaps stop to say explicitly that I am not claiming that people have a right to do anything whatever to save their lives. I think, rather, that there are drastic limits to the right of self-defense. If someone threatens you with death unless you torture someone else to death, I think you have not the right, even to save your life, to do so. But the case under consideration here is very different. In our case there are only two people involved, one whose life is threatened, and one who threatens it. Both are innocent: the one who is threatened is not threatened because of any fault, the one who threatens does not threaten because of any fault. For this reason we may feel that we bystanders cannot intervene. But the person threatened can.

In sum, a woman surely can defend her life against the threat to it posed by the unborn child, even if doing so involves its death. And this shows not merely that the theses in (1) through (4) are false; it shows also that the extreme view of abortion is false, and so we need not canvass any other possible ways of arriving at it from the argument I mentioned at the outset.

2. The extreme view could of course be weakened to say that while abortion is permissible to save the mother's life, it may not be performed by a third party, but only by the mother herself. But this cannot be right either. For what we have to keep in mind is that the mother and the unborn child are not like two tenants in a small house which has, by an unfortunate mistake, been rented to both: the mother *owns* the house. The fact that she does adds to the offensiveness of deducing that the mother can do nothing from the supposition that third parties can do nothing. But it does more than this: it casts a bright light on the supposition that third parties can do nothing. Certainly it lets us see that a third party who says "I cannot choose between you" is fooling himself if he thinks this is impartiality. If Jones has found and fastened on a certain coat, which he needs to keep him from freezing, but which Smith also needs to keep him from freezing, then it is not impartiality that says "I cannot choose between you" when Smith owns the coat. Women have said again and again "This body is *my* body!" and they have

reason to feel angry, reason to feel that it has been like shouting into the wind. Smith, after all, is hardly likely to bless us if we say to him, "Of course it's your coat, anybody would grant that it is. But no one may choose between you and Jones who is to have it."

We should really ask what it is that says "no one may choose" in the face of the fact that the body that houses the child is the mother's body. It may be simply a failure to appreciate this fact. But it may be something more interesting, namely the sense that one has a right to refuse to lay hands on people, even where it would be just and fair to do so, even where justice seems to require that somebody do so. Thus justice might call for somebody to get Smith's coat back from Jones, and yet you have a right to refuse to be the one to lay hands on Jones, a right to refuse to do physical violence to him. This, I think, must be granted. But then what should be said is not "no one may choose," but only "*I* cannot choose," and indeed not even this, but "*I* will not *act*," leaving it open that somebody else can or should, and in particular that anyone in a position of authority, with the job of securing people's rights, both can and should. So this is no difficulty. I have not been arguing that any given third party must accede to the mother's request that he perform an abortion to save her life, but only that he may.

I suppose that in some views of human life the mother's body is only on loan to her, the loan not being one which gives her any prior claim to it. One who held this view might well think it impartiality to say "I cannot choose." But I shall simply ignore this possibility. My own view is that if a human being has any just, prior claim to anything at all, he has a just, prior claim to his own body. And perhaps this needn't be argued for here anyway, since, as I mentioned, the arguments against abortion we are looking at do grant that the woman has a right to decide what happens in and to her body.

But although they do grant it, I have tried to show that they do not take seriously what is done in granting it. I suggest the same thing will reappear even more clearly when we turn away from cases in which the mother's life is at stake, and attend, as I propose we now do, to the vastly more common cases in which a woman wants an abortion for some less weighty reason than preserving her own life.

3. Where the mother's life is not at stake, the argument I mentioned at the outset seems to have a much stronger pull. "Everyone has a right to life, so the unborn person has a right to life." And isn't the child's right to life weightier than anything other than the mother's own right to life, which she might put forward as ground for an abortion?

This argument treats the right to life as if it were unproblematic. It is not, and this seems to me to be precisely the source of the mistake.

For we should now, at long last, ask what it comes to, to have a right to life. In some views having a right to life includes having a right to be given at least the bare minimum one needs for continued life. But suppose that what in fact *is* the bare minimum a man needs for continued life is something he has no right at all to be given? If I am sick unto death, and the only thing that will save my life is the touch of Henry Fonda's cool hand on my fevered brow, then all the same, I have no right to be given the touch of Henry Fonda's cool hand on my fevered brow. It would be frightfully nice of him to fly in from the West Coast to provide it. It would be less nice, though no doubt well meant, if my friends flew out to the West Coast and carried Henry Fonda back with them. But I have no right at all against anybody that he should do this for me. Or again, to return to the story I told earlier, the fact that for continued life that violinist needs the continued use of your kidneys does not establish that he has a right to be given the continued use of your kidneys. He certainly has no right against you that *you* should give him continued use of your kidneys. For nobody has any right to use your kidneys unless you give him such a right; and nobody has the right against you that you shall give him this right—if you do

allow him to go on using your kidneys, this is a kindness on your part, and not something he can claim from you as his due. Nor has he any right against anybody else that *they* should give him continued use of your kidneys. Certainly he had no right against the Society of Music Lovers that they should plug him into you in the first place. And if you now start to unplug yourself, having learned that you will otherwise have to spend nine years in bed with him, there is nobody in the world who must try to prevent you, in order to see to it that he is given something he has a right to be given.

Some people are rather stricter about the right to life. In their view, it does not include the right to be given anything, but amounts to, and only to, the right not to be killed by anybody. But here a related difficulty arises. If everybody is to refrain from killing that violinist, then everybody must refrain from doing a great many different sorts of things. Everybody must refrain from slitting his throat, everybody must refrain from shooting him—and everybody must refrain from unplugging you from him. But does he have a right against everybody that they shall refrain from unplugging you from him? To refrain from doing this is to allow him to continue to use your kidneys. It could be argued that he has a right against us that *we* should allow him to continue to use your kidneys. That is, while he had no right against us that we should give him the use of your kidneys, it might be argued that he anyway has a right against us that we shall not now intervene and deprive him of the use of your kidneys. I shall come back to third-party interventions later. But certainly the violinist has no right against you that *you* shall allow him to continue to use your kidneys. As I said, if you do allow him to use them, it is a kindness on your part, and not something you owe him.

The difficulty I point to here is not peculiar to the right to life. It reappears in connection with all the other natural rights; and it is something which an adequate account of rights must deal with. For present purposes it is enough just to draw attention to it. But I would stress that I am not arguing that people do not have a right to life—quite to the contrary, it seems to me that the primary control we must place on the acceptability of an account of rights is that it should turn out in that account to be a truth that all persons have a right to life. I am arguing only that having a right to life does not guarantee having either a right to be given the use of or a right to be allowed continued use of another person's body—even if one needs it for life itself. So the right to life will not serve the opponents of abortion in the very simple and clear way in which they seem to have thought it would.

4. There is another way to bring out the difficulty. In the most ordinary sort of case, to deprive someone of what he has a right to is to treat him unjustly. Suppose a boy and his small brother are jointly given a box of chocolates for Christmas. If the older boy takes the box and refuses to give his brother any of the chocolates, he is unjust to him, for the brother has been given a right to half of them. But suppose that, having learned that otherwise it means nine years in bed with that violinist, you unplug yourself from him. You surely are not being unjust to him, for you gave him no right to use your kidneys, and no one else can have given him any such right. But we have to notice that in unplugging yourself, you are killing him; and violinists, like everybody else, have a right to life, and thus in the view we were considering just now, the right not to be killed. So here you do what he supposedly has a right you shall not do, but you do not act unjustly to him in doing it.

The emendation which may be made at this point is this: the right to life consists not in the right not to be killed, but rather in the right not to be killed unjustly. This runs a risk of circularity, but never mind: it would enable us to square the fact that the violinist has a right to life with the fact that you do not act unjustly toward him in unplugging yourself, thereby killing him. For if you do not kill him unjustly, you do not violate his right to life, and so it is no wonder you do him no injustice.

But if this emendation is accepted, the gap in the argument against abortion stares us plainly in the face: it is by no means enough to show that the fetus is a person, and to remind us that all persons have a right to life—we need to be shown also that killing the fetus violates its right to life, i.e., that abortion is unjust killing. And is it?

I suppose we may take it as a datum that in a case of pregnancy due to rape the mother has not given the unborn person a right to the use of her body for food and shelter. Indeed, in what pregnancy could it be supposed that the mother has given the unborn person such a right? It is not as if there were unborn persons drifting about the world, to whom a woman who wants a child says "I invite you in."

But it might be argued that there are other ways one can have acquired a right to the use of another person's body than by having been invited to use it by that person. Suppose a woman voluntarily indulges in intercourse, knowing of the chance it will issue in pregnancy, and then she does become pregnant; is she not in part responsible for the presence, in fact the very existence, of the unborn person inside her? No doubt she did not invite it in. But doesn't her partial responsibility for its being there itself give it a right to the use of her body?[6] If so, then her aborting it would be more like the boy's taking away the chocolates, and less like your unplugging yourself from the violinist—doing so would be depriving it of what it does have a right to, and thus would be doing it an injustice.

And then, too, it might be asked whether or not she can kill it even to save her own life: If she voluntarily called it into existence, how can she now kill it, even in self-defense?

The first thing to be said about this is that it is something new. Opponents of abortion have been so concerned to make out the independence of the fetus, in order to establish that it has a right to life, just as its mother does, that they have tended to overlook the possible support they might gain from making out that the fetus is *dependent* on the mother, in order to establish that she has a special kind of responsibility for it, a responsibility that gives it rights against her which are not possessed by any independent person—such as an ailing violinist who is a stranger to her.

On the other hand, this argument would give the unborn person a right to its mother's body only if her pregnancy resulted from a voluntary act, undertaken in full knowledge of the chance a pregnancy might result from it. It would leave out entirely the unborn person whose existence is due to rape. Pending the availability of some further argument, then, we would be left with the conclusion that unborn persons whose existence is due to rape have no right to the use of their mothers' bodies, and thus that aborting them is not depriving them of anything they have a right to and hence is not unjust killing.

And we should also notice that it is not at all plain that this argument really does go even as far as it purports to. For there are cases and cases, and the details make a difference. If the room is stuffy, and I therefore open a window to air it, and a burglar climbs in, it would be absurd to say, "Ah, now he can stay, she's given him a right to the use of her house—for she is partially responsible for his presence there, having voluntarily done what enabled him to get in, in full knowledge that there are such things as burglars, and that burglars burgle." It would be still more absurd to say this if I had had bars installed outside my windows, precisely to prevent burglars from getting in, and a burglar got in only because of a defect in the bars. It remains equally absurd if we imagine it is not a burglar who climbs in, but an innocent person who blunders or falls in. Again, suppose it were like this: people-seeds drift about in the air like pollen, and if you open your windows, one may drift in and take root in your carpets or upholstery. You don't want children, so you fix up your windows with fine mesh screens, the very best you can buy. As can happen, however, and on very, very rare occasions does happen, one of the screens is defective; and a seed drifts in and takes root. Does the person-plant who now develops have a right

to the use of your house? Surely not—despite the fact that you voluntarily opened your windows, you knowingly kept carpets and upholstered furniture, and you knew that screens were sometimes defective. Someone may argue that you are responsible for its rooting, that it does have a right to your house, because after all you *could* have lived out your life with bare floors and furniture, or with sealed windows and doors. But this won't do—for by the same token anyone can avoid a pregnancy due to rape by having a hysterectomy, or anyway by never leaving home without a (reliable!) army.

It seems to me that the argument we are looking at can establish at most that there are *some* cases in which the unborn person has a right to the use of its mother's body, and therefore *some* cases in which abortion is unjust killing. There is room for much discussion and argument as to precisely which, if any. But I think we should sidestep this issue and leave it open, for at any rate the argument certainly does not establish that all abortion is unjust killing.

5. There is room for yet another argument here, however. We surely must all grant that there may be cases in which it would be morally indecent to detach a person from your body at the cost of his life. Suppose you learn that what the violinist needs is not nine years of your life, but only one hour: all you need do to save his life is to spend one hour in that bed with him. Suppose also that letting him use your kidneys for that one hour would not affect your health in the slightest. Admittedly you were kidnapped. Admittedly you did not give anyone permission to plug him into you. Nevertheless it seems to me plain you *ought* to allow him to use your kidneys for that hour—it would be indecent to refuse.

Again, suppose pregnancy lasted only an hour, and constituted no threat to life or health. And suppose that a woman becomes pregnant as a result of rape. Admittedly she did not voluntarily do anything to bring about the existence of a child. Admittedly she did nothing at all which would give the unborn person a right to the use of her body. All the same it might well be said, as in the newly emended violinist story, that she *ought* to allow it to remain for that hour—that it would be indecent of her to refuse.

Now some people are inclined to use the term "right" in such a way that it follows from the fact that you ought to allow a person to use your body for the hour he needs, that he has a right to use your body for the hour he needs, even though he has not been given that right by any person or act. They may say that it follows also that if you refuse, you act unjustly toward him. This use of the term is perhaps so common that it cannot be called wrong; nevertheless it seems to me to be an unfortunate loosening of what we would do better to keep a tight rein on. Suppose that box of chocolates I mentioned earlier has not been given to both boys jointly, but was given only to the older boy. There he sits, stolidly eating his way through the box, his small brother watching enviously. Here we are likely to say "You ought not to be so mean. You ought to give your brother some of those chocolates." My own view is that it just does not follow from the truth of this that the brother has any right to any of the chocolates. If the boy refuses to give his brother any, he is greedy, stingy, callous—but not unjust. I suppose that the people I have in mind will say it does follow that the brother has a right to some of the chocolates, and thus that the boy does act unjustly if he refuses to give his brother any. But the effect of saying this is to obscure what we should keep distinct, namely the difference between the boy's refusal in this case and the boy's refusal in the earlier case, in which the box was given to both boys jointly, and in which the small brother thus had what was from any point of view clear title to half.

A further objection to so using the term "right" that from the fact that A ought to do a thing for B, it follows that B has a right against A that A do it for him, is that it is going to make the question of whether or not a man has a right to a thing turn on how easy it is to provide him with it; and this seems not merely unfortunate, but morally unacceptable. Take the case of Henry Fonda again. I said earlier that I had no right to the touch of his cool hand on my fevered brow, even though I needed it to save my life. I said it would be frightfully nice of him to fly in from the West Coast to provide me with it, but that I had no right against him that he should do so. But suppose he isn't on the West Coast. Suppose he has only to walk across the room, place a hand briefly on my brow—and lo, my life is saved. Then surely he ought to do it, it would be indecent to refuse. Is it to be said "Ah, well, it follows that in this case she has a right to the touch of his hand on her brow, and so it would be an injustice in him to refuse"? So that I have a right to it when it is easy for him to provide it, though no right when it's hard? It's rather a shocking idea that anyone's rights should fade away and disappear as it gets harder and harder to accord them to him.

So my own view is that even though you ought to let the violinist use your kidneys for the one hour he needs, we should not conclude that he has a right to do so—we should say that if you refuse, you are, like the boy who owns all the chocolates and will give none away, self-centered and callous, indecent in fact, but not unjust. And similarly, that even supposing a case in which a woman pregnant due to rape ought to allow the unborn person to use her body for the hour he needs, we should not conclude that he has a right to do so; we should conclude that she is self-centered, callous, indecent, but not unjust, if she refuses. The complaints are no less grave; they are just different. However, there is no need to insist on this point. If anyone does wish to deduce "he has a right" from "you ought," then all the same he must surely grant that there are cases in which it is not morally required of you that you allow that violinist to use your kidneys, and in which he does not have a right to use them, and in which you do not do him an injustice if you refuse. And so also for mother and unborn child. Except in such cases as the unborn person has a right to demand it—and we were leaving open the possibility that there may be such cases—nobody is morally *required* to make large sacrifices, of health, of all other interests and concerns, of all other duties and commitments, for nine years, or even for nine months, in order to keep another person alive.

6. We have in fact to distinguish between two kinds of Samaritan: the Good Samaritan and what we might call the Minimally Decent Samaritan. The story of the Good Samaritan, you will remember, goes like this:

> A certain man went down from Jerusalem to Jericho, and fell among thieves, which stripped him of his raiment, and wounded him, and departed, leaving him half dead.
>
> And by chance there came down a certain priest that way; and when he saw him, he passed by on the other side.
>
> And likewise a Levite, when he was at the place, came and looked on him, and passed by on the other side.
>
> But a certain Samaritan, as he journeyed, came where he was; and when he saw him he had compassion on him.
>
> And went to him, and bound up his wounds, pouring in oil and wine, and set him on his own beast, and brought him to an inn, and took care of him.
>
> And on the morrow, when he departed, he took out two pence, and gave them to the host, and said unto him, "Take care of him; and whatsoever thou spendest more, when I come again, I will repay thee."
>
> *(Luke 10:30–35)*

The Good Samaritan went out of his way, at some cost to himself, to help one in need of it. We are not told what the options were, that is, whether or not the priest and the Levite could have helped by doing less than the Good Samaritan did, but assuming they could have, then the fact they did nothing at all shows they were not even Minimally Decent Samaritans, not because they were not Samaritans, but because they were not even minimally decent.

These things are a matter of degree, of course, but there is a difference, and it comes out perhaps most clearly in the story of Kitty Genovese, who, as you will remember, was murdered while thirty-eight

people watched or listened, and did nothing at all to help her. A Good Samaritan would have rushed out to give direct assistance against the murderer. Or perhaps we had better allow that it would have been a Splendid Samaritan who did this, on the ground that it would have involved a risk of death for himself. But the thirty-eight not only did not do this, they did not even trouble to pick up a phone to call the police. Minimally Decent Samaritanism would call for doing at least that, and their not having done it was monstrous.

After telling the story of the Good Samaritan, Jesus said "Go, and do thou likewise." Perhaps he meant that we are morally required to act as the Good Samaritan did. Perhaps he was urging people to do more than is morally required of them. At all events it seems plain that it was not morally required of any of the thirty-eight that he rush out to give direct assistance at the risk of his own life, and that it is not morally required of anyone that he give long stretches of his life—nine years or nine months—to sustaining the life of a person who has no special right (we were leaving open the possibility of this) to demand it.

Indeed, with one rather striking class of exceptions, no one in any country in the world is *legally* required to do anywhere near as much as this for anyone else. The class of exceptions is obvious. My main concern here is not the state of the law in respect to abortion, but it is worth drawing attention to the fact that in no state in this country is any man compelled by law to be even a Minimally Decent Samaritan to any person; there is no law under which charges could be brought against the thirty-eight who stood by while Kitty Genovese died. By contrast, in most states in this country women are compelled by law to be not merely Minimally Decent Samaritans, but Good Samaritans to unborn persons inside them. This doesn't by itself settle anything one way or the other, because it may well be argued that there should be laws in this country—as there are in many European countries—compelling at least Minimally

Decent Samaritanism.[7] But it does show that there is a gross injustice in the existing state of the law. And it shows also that the groups currently working against liberalization of abortion laws, in fact working toward having it declared unconstitutional for a state to permit abortion, had better start working for the adoption of Good Samaritan laws generally, or earn the charge that they are acting in bad faith.

I should think, myself, that Minimally Decent Samaritan laws would be one thing, Good Samaritan laws quite another, and in fact highly improper. But we are not here concerned with the law. What we should ask is not whether anybody should be compelled by law to be a Good Samaritan, but whether we must accede to a situation in which somebody is being compelled—by nature, perhaps—to be a Good Samaritan. We have, in other words, to look now at third-party interventions. I have been arguing that no person is morally required to make large sacrifices to sustain the life of another who has no right to demand them, and this even where the sacrifices do not include life itself; we are not morally required to be Good Samaritans or anyway Very Good Samaritans to one another. But what if a man cannot extricate himself from such a situation? What if he appeals to us to extricate him? It seems to me plain that there are cases in which we can, cases in which a Good Samaritan would extricate him. There you are, you were kidnapped, and nine years in bed with that violinist lie ahead of you. You have your own life to lead. You are sorry, but you simply cannot see giving up so much of your life to the sustaining of his. You cannot extricate yourself, and ask us to do so. I should have thought that—in light of his having no right to the use of your body—it was obvious that we do not have to accede to your being forced to give up so much. We can do what you ask. There is no injustice to the violinist in our doing so.

7. Following the lead of the opponents of abortion, I have throughout been speaking of the fetus merely as a person, and what I have been asking is whether or not the argument we began with, which proceeds only from the fetus' being a person, really does establish its conclusion. I have argued that it does not.

But of course there are arguments and arguments, and it may be said that I have simply fastened on the wrong one. It may be said that what is important is not merely the fact that the fetus is a person, but that it is a person for whom the woman has a special kind of responsibility issuing from the fact that she is its mother. And it might be argued that all my analogies are therefore irrelevant—for you do not have that special kind of responsibility for that violinist, Henry Fonda does not have that special kind of responsibility for me. And our attention might be drawn to the fact that men and women both *are* compelled by law to provide support for their children.

I have in effect dealt (briefly) with this argument in section 4 above; but a (still briefer) recapitulation now may be in order. Surely we do not have any such "special responsibility" for a person unless we have assumed it, explicitly or implicitly. If a set of parents do not try to prevent pregnancy, do not obtain an abortion, and then at the time of birth of the child do not put it out for adoption, but rather take it home with them, then they have assumed responsibility for it, they have given it rights, and they cannot *now* withdraw support from it at the cost of its life because they now find it difficult to go on providing for it. But if they have taken all reasonable precautions against having a child, they do not simply by virtue of their biological relationship to the child who comes into existence have a special responsibility for it. They may wish to assume responsibility for it, or they may not wish to. And I am suggesting that if assuming responsibility for it would require large sacrifices, then they may refuse. A Good Samaritan would not refuse—or anyway, a Splendid Samaritan, if the sacrifices that had to be made were enormous. But then so would a Good Samaritan assume responsibility for that violinist; so would Henry Fonda, if he is a

Good Samaritan, fly in from the West Coast and assume responsibility for me.

8. My argument will be found unsatisfactory on two counts by many of those who want to regard abortion as morally permissible. First, while I do argue that abortion is not impermissible, I do not argue that it is always permissible. There may well be cases in which carrying the child to term requires only Minimally Decent Samaritanism of the mother, and this is a standard we must not fall below. I am inclined to think it a merit of my account precisely that it does *not* give a general yes or a general no. It allows for and supports our sense that, for example, a sick and desperately frightened fourteen-year-old schoolgirl, pregnant due to rape, may *of course* choose abortion, and that any law which rules this out is an insane law. And it also allows for and supports our sense that in other cases resort to abortion is even positively indecent. It would be indecent in the woman to request an abortion, and indecent in a doctor to perform it, if she is in her seventh month, and wants the abortion just to avoid the nuisance of postponing a trip abroad. The very fact that the arguments I have been drawing attention to treat all cases of abortion, or even all cases of abortion in which the mother's life is not at stake, as morally on a par ought to have made them suspect at the outset.

Secondly, while I am arguing for the permissibility of abortion in some cases, I am not arguing for the right to secure the death of the unborn child. It is easy to confuse these two things in that up to a certain point in the life of the fetus it is not able to survive outside the mother's body; hence removing it from her body guarantees its death. But they are importantly different. I have argued that you are not morally required to spend nine months in bed, sustaining the life of that violinist; but to say this is by no means to say that if, when you unplug yourself, there is a miracle and he survives, you then have a right to turn round and slit his throat. You may detach yourself even if this costs him his life; you have no right to be guaranteed his death, by some other means, if unplugging

yourself does not kill him. There are some people who will feel dissatisfied by this feature of my argument. A woman may be utterly devastated by the thought of a child, a bit of herself, put out for adoption and never seen or heard of again. She may therefore want not merely that the child be detached from her, but more, that it die. Some opponents of abortion are inclined to regard this as beneath contempt—thereby showing insensitivity to what is surely a powerful source of despair. All the same, I agree that the desire for the child's death is not one which anybody may gratify, should it turn out to be possible to detach the child alive.

At this place, however, it should be remembered that we have only been pretending throughout that the fetus is a human being from the moment of conception. A very early abortion is surely not the killing of a person, and so is not dealt with by anything I have said here.

Notes

1. Daniel Callahan, *Abortion: Law, Choice and Morality* (New York, 1970), p. 373. This book gives a fascinating survey of the available information on abortion. The Jewish tradition is surveyed in David M. Feldman, *Birth Control in Jewish Law* (New York, 1968), Part 5; the Catholic tradition in John T. Noonan, Jr., "An Almost Absolute Value in History," in *The Morality of Abortion*, ed. John T. Noonan, Jr. (Cambridge, Mass., 1970).

2. The term "direct" in the arguments I refer to is a technical one. Roughly, what is meant by "direct killing" is either killing as an end in itself, or killing as a means of some end, for example, the end of saving someone else's life. See footnote 5 for an example of its use.

3. Cf. *Encyclical Letter of Pope Pius XI on Christian Marriage*, St. Paul Editions (Boston, n.d.), p. 32: "however much we may pity the

mother whose health and even life is gravely imperiled in the performance of the duty allotted to her by nature, nevertheless what could ever be a sufficient reason for excusing in any way the direct murder of the innocent? This is precisely what we are dealing with here." Noonan (*The Morality of Abortion*, p. 43) reads this as follows: "What cause can ever avail to excuse in any way the direct killing of the innocent? For it is a question of that."

4. The thesis in (4) is in an interesting way weaker than those in (1), (2), and (3): they rule out abortion even in cases in which both mother *and* child will die if the abortion is not performed. By contrast, one who held the view expressed in (4) could consistently say that one needn't prefer letting two persons die to killing one.

5. Cf. the following passage from Pius XII, *Address to the Italian Catholic Society of Midwives:* "The baby in the maternal breast has the right to life immediately from God.—Hence there is no man, no human authority, no science, no medical, eugenic, social, economic or moral 'indication' which can establish or grant a valid juridical ground for a direct deliberate disposition of an innocent human life, that is a disposition which looks to its destruction either as an end or as a means to another end perhaps in itself not illicit.—The baby, still not born, is a man in the same degree and for the same reason as the mother" (quoted in Noonan, *The Morality of Abortion*, p. 45).

6. The need for a discussion of this argument was brought home to me by members of the Society for Ethical and Legal Philosophy, to whom this paper was originally presented.

7. For a discussion of the difficulties involved, and a survey of the European experience with such laws, see *The Good Samaritan and the Law*, ed. James M. Ratcliffe (New York, 1966).

Study Questions

1. What premise of the antiabortion argument does Thomson grant for the sake of argument?

2. What, specifically, is Thomson trying to show by using the example of the violinist?

3. According to Thomson, what is the extreme view on the impermissibility of abortion? What are the major arguments for this view? How does she reply?

4. How does Thomson respond to the objection that a pregnant woman who voluntarily engaged in sexual intercourse is responsible for the existence of the fetus, and thus it would be unjust for her to deprive the fetus of life?

5. In what way does Thomson think that it might be true that you ought to do something for another person, even though that person has no right to expect that you do?

6. What is Thomson trying to prove by distinguishing between a Good Samaritan and a Minimally Decent Samaritan?

7. Does Thomson think that all abortions are morally acceptable? Why or why not?

On the Moral and Legal Status of Abortion

Mary Anne Warren

We will be concerned with both the moral status of abortion, which for our purposes we may define as the act which a woman performs in voluntarily terminating, or allowing another person to terminate, her pregnancy, and the legal status which is appropriate for this act. I will argue that, while it is not possible to produce a satisfactory defense of a woman's right to obtain an abortion without showing that a fetus is not a human being, in the morally relevant sense of that term, we ought not to conclude that the difficulties involved in determining whether or not a fetus is human make it impossible to produce any satisfactory solution to the problem of the moral status of abortion. For it is possible to show that, on the basis of intuitions which we may expect even the opponents of abortion to share, a fetus is not a person, and hence not the sort of entity to which it is proper to ascribe full moral rights.

Of course, while some philosophers would deny the possibility of any such proof,[1] others will deny that there is any need for it, since the moral permissibility of abortion appears to them to be too obvious to require proof. But the inadequacy of this attitude should be evident from the fact that both the friends and the foes of abortion consider their position to be morally self-evident. Because proabortionists have never adequately come to grips with the conceptual issues surrounding abortion, most, if not all, of the arguments which they advance in opposition to laws restricting access to abortion fail to refute or even weaken the traditional antiabortion argument, i.e., that a fetus is a human being, and therefore abortion is murder.

These arguments are typically of one of two sorts. Either they point to the terrible side effects of the restrictive laws, e.g., the deaths due to illegal abortions, and the fact that it is

From *The Monist,* Vol. 57, No. 1 (1973). Reprinted by permission of *The Monist,* La Salle, Illinois 61301.

poor women who suffer the most as a result of these laws, or else they state that to deny a woman access to abortion is to deprive her of her right to control her own body. Unfortunately, however, the fact that restricting access to abortion has tragic side effects does not, in itself, show that the restrictions are unjustified, since murder is wrong regardless of the consequences of prohibiting it; and the appeal to the right to control one's body, which is generally construed as a property right, is at best a rather feeble argument for the permissibility of abortion. Mere ownership does not give me the right to kill innocent people whom I find on my property, and indeed I am apt to be held responsible if such people injure themselves while on my property. It is equally unclear that I have any moral right to expel an innocent person from my property when I know that doing so will result in his death.

Furthermore, it is probably inappropriate to describe a woman's body as her property, since it seems natural to hold that a person is something distinct from her property, but not from her body. Even those who would object to the identification of a person with his body, or with the conjunction of his body and his mind, must admit that it would be very odd to describe, say, breaking a leg, as damaging one's property, and much more appropriate to describe it as injuring one*self.* Thus it is probably a mistake to argue that the right to obtain an abortion is in any way derived from the right to own and regulate property.

But however we wish to construe the right to abortion, we cannot hope to convince those who consider abortion a form of murder of the existence of any such right unless we are able to produce a clear and convincing refutation of the traditional antiabortion argument, and this has not, to my knowledge, been done. With respect to the two most vital issues which that argument involves, i.e., the humanity of the fetus and its implication for the moral status of abortion, confusion has prevailed on both sides of the dispute.

Thus, both proabortionists and antiabortionists have tended to abstract the question of whether abortion is wrong to that of whether it is wrong to destroy a fetus, just as though the rights of another person were not necessarily involved. This mistaken abstraction has led to the almost universal assumption that if a fetus is a human being, with a right to life, then it follows immediately that abortion is wrong (except perhaps when necessary to save the woman's life), and that it ought to be prohibited. It has also been generally assumed that unless the question about the status of the fetus is answered, the moral status of abortion cannot possibly be determined.

Two recent papers, one by B. A. Brody,[2] and one by Judith Thomson,[3] have attempted to settle the question of whether abortion ought to be prohibited apart from the question of whether or not the fetus is human. Brody examines the possibility that the following two statements are compatible: (1) that abortion is the taking of innocent human life, and therefore wrong; and (2) that nevertheless it ought not to be prohibited by law, at least under the present circumstances.[4] Not surprisingly, Brody finds it impossible to reconcile these two statements, since, as he rightly argues, none of the unfortunate side effects of the prohibition of abortion is bad enough to justify legalizing the *wrongful* taking of human life. He is mistaken, however, in concluding that the incompatibility of (1) and (2), in itself, shows that "the legal problem about abortion cannot be resolved independently of the status of the fetus problem" [p. 369].

What Body fails to realize is that (1) embodies the questionable assumption that if a fetus is a human being, then of course abortion is morally wrong, and that an attack on *this* assumption is more promising, as a way of reconciling the humanity of the fetus with the claim that laws prohibiting abortion are unjustified, than is an attack on the assumption that if abortion is the wrongful killing of innocent human beings then it ought to be prohibited. He thus overlooks the possibility that a fetus may have a right to life and abortion still be morally permissible, in that the right of a woman to terminate an unwanted pregnancy might override the right of the fetus to be kept alive. The immorality of abortion is no more demonstrated by the humanity of the fetus, in itself, than the immorality of killing in self-defense is demonstrated by the fact that the assailant is a human being. Neither is it demonstrated by the *innocence* of the fetus, since there may be situations in which the killing of innocent human beings is justified.

It is perhaps not surprising that Brody fails to spot this assumption, since it has been accepted with little or no argument by nearly everyone who has written on the morality of abortion. John Noonan is correct is saying that "the fundamental question in the long history of abortion is, How do you determine the humanity of a being?"[5] He summarizes his own antiabortion argument, which is a version of the official position of the Catholic Church, as follows:

> . . . it is wrong to kill humans, however, poor, weak, defenseless, and lacking in opportunity to develop their potential they may be. It is therefore morally wrong to kill Biafrans. Similarly, it is morally wrong to kill embryos.[6]

Noonan bases his claim that fetuses are human upon what he calls the theologians' criterion of humanity: that whoever is conceived of human beings is human. But although he argues at length for the appropriateness of this criterion, he never questions the assumption that if a fetus is human then abortion is wrong for exactly the same reason that murder is wrong.

Judith Thomson is, in fact, the only writer I am aware of who has seriously questioned this assumption; she has argued that, even if we grant the antiabortionist his claim that a fetus is a human being, with the same right to life as any other human being, we can still demonstrate that, in at least some and perhaps most cases, a woman is under no moral obligation to complete an unwanted pregnancy.[7] Her argument is worth examining, since if it holds up it may enable us to establish the moral permissibility of abortion without becoming involved in problems about what entitles an entity to be considered human, and accorded full moral rights. To be able to do this would be a great gain in the power and simplicity of the proabortion position, since, although I will argue that these problems can be solved at least as decisively as can any other moral problem, we should certainly be pleased to be able to avoid having to solve them as part of the justification of abortion.

On the other hand, even if Thomson's argument does not hold up, her insight, i.e., that it requires *argument* to show that if fetuses are human then abortion is properly classified as murder, is an extremely valuable one. The assumption she attacks is particularly invidious, for it amounts to the decision that it is appropriate, in deciding the moral status of abortion, to leave the rights of the pregnant woman out of consideration entirely, except possibly when her life is threatened. Obviously, this will not do; determining what moral rights, if any, a fetus possesses is only the first step in determining the moral status of abortion. Step two, which is at least equally essential, is finding a just solution to the conflict between whatever rights the fetus may have, and the rights of the woman who is unwillingly pregnant. While the historical error has been to pay far too little attention to the second step, Ms. Thomson's suggestion is that if we look at the second step first we may find that a woman has a right to obtain an abortion *regardless* of what rights the fetus has.

Our own inquiry will also have two stages. In Section I, we will consider whether or not it is possible to establish that abortion is morally permissible even on the assumption that a fetus is an entity with a full-fledged right to life. I will argue that in fact this cannot be established, at least not with the conclusiveness which is essential to our hopes of convincing those who are skeptical about the morality of abortion, and that we therefore cannot avoid dealing with the question of whether or not a fetus really does have the same right to life as a (more fully developed) human being.

In Section II, I will propose an answer to this question, namely, that a fetus cannot be considered a member of the moral community, the set of beings with full and equal moral rights, for the simple reason that it is not a person, and that it is personhood, and not genetic humanity, i.e., humanity as defined by Noonan, which is the basis for membership in this community.

I will argue that a fetus, whatever its stage of development, satisfies none of the basic criteria of personhood, and is not even enough *like* a person to be accorded even some of the same rights on the basis of this resemblance. Nor, as we will see, is a fetus's *potential* personhood a threat to the morality of abortion, since, whatever the rights of potential people may be, they are invariably overridden in any conflict with the moral rights of actual people.

I

We turn now to Professor Thomson's case for the claim that even if a fetus has full moral rights, abortion is still morally permissible, at least sometimes, and for some reasons other than to save the woman's life. Her argument is based upon a clever, but I think faulty, analogy. She asks us to picture ourselves waking up one day, in bed with a famous violinist. Imagine that you have been kidnapped, and your bloodstream hooked up to that of the violinist, who happens to have an ailment which will certainly kill him unless he is permitted to share your kidneys for a period of nine months. No one else can save him, since you alone have the right type of blood. He will be unconscious all that time, and you will have to stay in bed with him, but after the nine months are over he may be unplugged, completely cured, that is provided that you have cooperated.

Now then, she continues, what are your obligations in this situation? The antiabortionist, if he is consistent, will have to say that you are obligated to stay in bed with the violinist: for all people have a right to life, and violinists are people, and therefore it would be murder for you to disconnect yourself from him and let him die [p. 174]. But this is outrageous, and so there must be something wrong with the same argument when it is applied to abortion. It would certainly be commendable of you to agree to save the violinist, but it is absurd to suggest that your refusal to do so would be murder. His right to life does not obligate you to do whatever is required to keep him alive; nor does it justify anyone else in forcing you to do so. A law which required you to stay in bed with the violinist would clearly be an unjust law, since it is no proper function of the law to force unwilling people to make huge sacrifices for the sake of other people toward whom they have no such prior obligation.

Thomson concludes that, if this analogy is an apt one, then we can grant the anti-abortionist his claim that a fetus is a human being, and still hold that it is at least sometimes the case that a pregnant woman has the right to refuse to be a Good Samaritan towards the fetus, i.e., to obtain an abortion. For there is a great gap between the claim that x has a right to life, and the claim that y is obligated to do whatever is necessary to keep x alive, let alone that he ought to be forced to do so. It is y's duty to keep x alive only if he has somehow contracted a *special* obligation to do so; and a woman who is unwillingly pregnant, e.g., who was raped, has done nothing which obligates her to make the enormous sacrifice which is necessary to preserve the conceptus.

This argument is initially quite plausible, and in the extreme case of pregnancy due to rape it is probably conclusive. Difficulties arise, however, when we try to specify more exactly the range of cases in which abortion is clearly justifiable even on the assumption that the fetus is human. Professor Thomson considers it a virtue of her argument that it does not enable us to conclude that abortion is *always* permissible. It would, she says, be "indecent" for a woman in her seventh month to obtain an abortion just to avoid having to postpone a trip to Europe. On the other hand, her argument enables us to see that "a sick and desperately frightened schoolgirl pregnant due to rape may *of course* choose abortion, and that any law which rules this out is an insane law" [p. 187]. So far, so good; but what are we to say about the woman who becomes pregnant not through rape but as a result of her own carelessness, or because of contraceptive failure, or who gets pregnant intentionally and then changes her mind about wanting a child? With respect to such cases, the violinist analogy is of much less use to the defender of the woman's right to obtain an abortion.

Indeed, the choice of a pregnancy due to rape, as an example of a case in which abortion

is permissible even if a fetus is considered a human being, is extremely significant; for it is only in the case of pregnancy due to rape that the woman's situation is adequately analogous to the violinist case for our intuitions about the latter to transfer convincingly. The crucial difference between a pregnancy due to rape and the *normal* case of an unwanted pregnancy is that in the normal case we cannot claim that the woman is in no way responsible for her predicament; she could have remained chaste, or taken her pills more faithfully, or abstained on dangerous days, and so on. If, on the other hand, you are kidnapped by strangers, and hooked up to a strange violinist, then you are free of any shred of responsibility for the situation, on the basis of which it could be argued that you are obligated to keep the violinist alive. Only when her pregnancy is due to rape is a woman clearly just as non-responsible.[8]

Consequently, there is room for the anti-abortionist to argue that in the normal case of unwanted pregnancy a woman has, by her own actions, assumed responsibility for the fetus. For if x behaves in a way which he could have avoided, and which he knows involves, let us say, a 1 percent chance of bringing into existence a human being, with a right to life, and does so knowing that if this should happen then that human being will perish unless x does certain things to keep him alive, then it is by no means clear that when it does happen x is free of any obligation to what he knew in advance would be required to keep that human being alive.

The plausibility of such an argument is enough to show that the Thomson analogy can provide a clear and persuasive defense of a woman's right to obtain an abortion only with respect to those cases in which the woman is in no way responsible for her pregnancy, e.g., where it is due to rape. In all other cases, we would almost certainly conclude that it was necessary to look carefully at the particular circumstances in order to determine the extent of the woman's responsibility, and hence the extent of her obligation. This is an extremely unsatisfactory outcome, from the viewpoint of the opponents of restrictive abortion laws, most of whom are convinced that a woman has a right to obtain an abortion regardless of how and why she got pregnant.

Of course a supporter of the violinist analogy might point out that it is absurd to suggest that forgetting her pill one day might be sufficient to obligate a woman to complete an unwanted pregnancy. And indeed it *is* absurd to suggest this. As we will see, the moral right to obtain an abortion is not in the least dependent upon the extent to which the woman is responsible for her pregnancy. But unfortunately, once we allow the assumption that a fetus has full moral rights, we cannot avoid taking this absurd suggestion seriously. Perhaps we can make this point more clear by altering the violinist story just enough to make it more analogous to a normal unwanted pregnancy and less to a pregnancy due to rape, and then seeing whether it is still obvious that you are not obligated to stay in bed with the fellow.

Suppose, then, that violinists are peculiarly prone to the sort of illness the only cure for which is the use of someone else's bloodstream for nine months, and that because of this there has been formed a society of music lovers who agree that whenever a violinist is stricken they will draw lots and the loser will, by some means, be made the one and only person capable of saving him. Now then, would you be obligated to cooperate in curing the violinist if you had voluntarily joined this society, knowing the possible consequences, and then your name had been drawn and you had been kidnapped? Admittedly, you did not promise ahead of time that you would, but you did deliberately place yourself in a position in which it might happen that a human life would be lost if you did not. Surely, this is at least a prima facie reason for supposing that you have an obligation to stay in bed with the violinist. Suppose that you had gotten your name drawn deliberately; surely *that* would be quite a strong reason for thinking that you had such an obligation.

It might be suggested that there is one important disanalogy between the modified violinist case and the case of an unwanted pregnancy, which makes the woman's responsibility significantly less, namely, the fact that the fetus *comes into existence* as the result of the woman's actions. This fact might give her a right to refuse to keep it alive, whereas she would not have had this right had it existed previously, independently, and then as a result of her actions become dependent upon her for its survival.

My own intuition, however, is that x has no more right to bring into existence, either deliberately or as a foreseeable result of actions he could have avoided, a being with full moral rights (y), and then refuse to do what he knew beforehand would be required to keep that being alive, than he has to enter into an agreement with an existing person, whereby he may be called upon to save that person's life, and then refuse to do so when so called upon. Thus, x's responsibility for y's existence does not seem to lessen his obligation to keep y alive, if he is also responsible for y's being in a situation in which only he can save him.

Whether or not this intuition is entirely correct, it brings us back once again to the conclusion that once we allow the assumption that a fetus has full moral rights it becomes an extremely complex and difficult question whether and when abortion is justifiable. Thus the Thomson analogy cannot help us produce a clear and persuasive proof of the moral permissibility of abortion. Nor will the opponents of the restrictive laws thank us for anything less; for their conviction (for the most part) is that abortion is obviously *not* a morally serious and extremely unfortunate, even though sometimes justified act, comparable to killing in self-defense or to letting the violinist die, but rather is closer to being a morally neutral act, like cutting one's hair.

The basis of this conviction, I believe, is the realization that a fetus is not a person, and thus does not have a full-fledged right to life. Perhaps the reason why this claim has been so inadequately defended is that it seems self-evident to those who accept it. And so it is, insofar as it follows from what I take to be perfectly obvious claims about the nature of personhood, and about the proper grounds for ascribing moral rights, claims which ought, indeed, to be obvious to both the friends and foes of abortion. Nevertheless, it is worth examining these claims, and showing how they demonstrate the moral innocuousness of abortion, since this apparently has not been adequately done before.

II

The question which we must answer in order to produce a satisfactory solution to the problem of the moral status of abortion is this: How are we to define the moral community, the set of beings with full and equal moral rights, such that we can decide whether a human fetus is a member of this community or not? What sort of entity, exactly, has the inalienable rights to life, liberty, and the pursuit of happiness? Jefferson attributed these rights to all *men,* and it may or may not be fair to suggest that he intended to attribute them *only* to men. Perhaps he ought to have attributed them to all human beings. If so, then we arrive, first, at Noonan's problem of defining what makes a being human, and second, at the equally vital question which Noonan does not consider, namely, What reason is there for identifying the moral community with the set of all human beings, in whatever way we have chosen to define that term?

1. Defining "Human"

One reason why this vital second question is so frequently overlooked in the debate over the moral status of abortion is that the term "human" has two distinct, but not often distinguished, senses. This fact results in a slide of meaning, which serves to conceal the fallaciousness of the traditional argument that since (1) it is wrong to kill innocent human beings, and (2) fetuses are innocent human beings, then (3) it is wrong to kill fetuses. For if "human" is used in the same sense in both (1) and (2) then, whichever of the two senses is meant, one of these premises is question-begging. And if it is used in two different senses then of course the conclusion doesn't follow.

Thus, (1) is a self-evident moral truth,[9] and avoids begging the question about abortion, only if "human being" is used to mean something like "a full-fledged member of the moral community." (It may or may not also be meant to refer exclusively to members of the species *Homo sapiens.*) We may call this the *moral* sense of "human." It is not to be confused with what we will call the *genetic* sense, i.e., the sense in which *any* member of the species is a human being, and no member of any other species could be. If (1) is acceptable only if the moral sense is intended, (2) is non-question-begging only if what is intended is the genetic sense.

In "Deciding Who Is Human," Noonan argues for the classification of fetuses with human beings by pointing to the presence of the full genetic code, and the potential capacity for rational thought (p. 135). It is clear that what he needs to show, for his version of the traditional argument to be valid, is that fetuses are human in the moral sense, the sense in which it is analytically true that all human beings have full moral rights. But, in the absence of any argument showing that whatever is genetically human is also morally human, and he gives none, nothing more than genetic humanity can be demonstrated by the presence of the human genetic code. And, as we will see, the *potential* capacity for rational thought can at most show that an entity has the potential for *becoming* human in the moral sense.

2. Defining the Moral Community

Can it be established that genetic humanity is sufficient for moral humanity? I think that there are very good reasons for not defining the moral community in this way. I would like to suggest an alternative way of defining the moral community, which I will argue for only to the extent of explaining why it consists of all and only *people,* rather than all and only human beings,[10] and probably the best way of demonstrating its self-evidence is by considering the concept of personhood, to see what sorts of entity are and are not persons, and what the decision that a being is or is not a person implies about its moral rights.

What characteristics entitle an entity to be considered a person? This is obviously not the place to attempt a complete analysis of the concept of personhood, but we do not need such a fully adequate analysis just to determine whether and why a fetus is or isn't a person. All we need is a rough and approximate list of the most basic criteria of personhood, and some idea of which, or how many, of these an entity must satisfy in order to properly be considered a person.

In searching for such criteria, it is useful to look beyond the set of people with whom we are acquainted, and ask how we would decide whether a totally alien being was a person or not. (For we have no right to assume that genetic humanity is necessary for personhood.) Imagine a space traveler who lands on an unknown planet and encounters a race of beings utterly unlike any he has ever seen or heard of. If he wants to be sure of behaving morally toward these beings, he has to somehow decide whether they are people, and hence have full moral rights, or whether they are the sort of thing which he need not feel guilty about treating as, for example, a source of food.

How should he go about making this decision? If he has some anthropological background, he might look for such things as religion, art, and the manufacturing of tools, weapons, or shelters, since these factors have been used to distinguish our human from our prehuman ancestors, in what seems to be closer to the moral than the genetic sense of "human." And no doubt he would be right to consider the presence of such factors as good evidence that the alien beings were people, and morally human. It would, however, be overly anthropocentric of him to take the absence of these things as adequate evidence that they were not, since we can imagine people who have progressed beyond, or evolved without ever developing, these cultural characteristics.

I suggest that the traits which are most central to the concept of personhood, or humanity in the moral sense, are, very roughly, the following:

1. Consciousness (of objects and events external and/or internal to the being), and in particular the capacity to feel pain

2. Reasoning (the *developed* capacity to solve new and relatively complex problems)

3. Self-motivated activity (activity which is relatively independent of either genetic or direct external control)

4. The capacity to communicate, by whatever means, messages of an indefinite variety of types, that is, not just with an indefinite number of possible contents, but on indefinitely many possible topics

5. The presence of self-concepts, and self-awareness, either individual or racial, or both.

Admittedly, there are apt to be a great many problems involved in formulating precise definitions of these criteria, let alone in developing universally valid behavioral criteria for deciding when they apply. But I will assume that both we and our explorer know approximately what (1)–(5) mean, and that he is also able to determine whether or not they apply. How, then, should he use his findings to decide whether or not the alien beings are people? We needn't suppose that an entity must have *all* of these attributes to be properly considered a person; (1) and (2) alone may well be sufficient for personhood, and quite probably (1)–(3) are sufficient. Neither do we need to insist that any one of these criteria is *necessary* for personhood, although once again (1) and (2) look like fairly good candidates for necessary conditions, as does (3), if "activity" is construed so as to include the activity of reasoning.

All we need to claim, to demonstrate that a fetus is not a person, is that any being which satisfies *none* of (1)–(5) is certainly not a person. I consider this claim to be so obvious that I think anyone who denied it, and claimed that a being which satisfied none of (1)–(5) was a person all the same, would thereby demonstrate that he had no notion at all of what a person is—perhaps because he had confused the concept of a person with that of genetic humanity. If the opponents of abortion were to deny the appropriateness of these five criteria, I do not know what further arguments would convince them. We would probably have to admit that our conceptual schemes were indeed irreconcilably different, and that our dispute could not be settled objectively.

I do not expect this to happen, however, since I think that the concept of a person is one which is very nearly universal (to people), and that it is common to both proabortionists and antiabortionists, even though neither group has fully realized the relevance of this concept to the resolution of their dispute. Furthermore, I think that on reflection even antiabortionists ought to agree not only that (1)–(5) are central to the concept of personhood, but also that it is a part of this concept that all and only people have full moral rights. The concept of a person is in part a moral concept; once we have admitted that *x* is a person we have recognized, even if we have not agreed to respect, *x*'s right to be treated as a member of the moral community. It is true that the claim that *x* is a *human being* is more commonly voiced as part of an appeal to treat *x* decently than is the claim that *x* is a person, but this is either because "human being" is here used in the sense which implies personhood, or because the genetic and moral senses of "human" have been confused.

Now if (1)–(5) are indeed the primary criteria of personhood, then it is clear that genetic humanity is neither necessary nor sufficient for establishing that an entity is a person. Some human beings are not people, and there may well be people who are not human beings. A man or woman whose consciousness has been permanently obliterated but who remains alive is a human being which is no longer a person; defective human beings, with no appreciable mental capacity, are not and presumably never will be people; and a fetus is a human being which is not yet a person, and which therefore cannot coherently be said to have full moral rights. Citizens of the next century should be prepared to recognize highly advanced, self-aware robots or computers, should such be developed, and intelligent inhabitants of other worlds, should such be found, as people in the fullest sense, and to respect their moral rights. But to ascribe full moral rights to an entity which is not a person is as absurd as to ascribe moral obligations and responsibilities to such an entity.

3. Fetal Development and the Right to Life

Two problems arise in the application of these suggestions for the definition of the moral community to the determination of the precise moral status of a human fetus. Given that the paradigm example of a person is a normal adult human being, then (1) How like this paradigm, in particular how far advanced since conception, does a human being need to be before it begins to have a right to life by virtue, not of being fully a person as of yet, but of being *like* a

person? and (2) To what extent, if any, does the fact that a fetus has the *potential* for becoming a person endow it with some of the same rights? Each of these questions requires some comment.

In answering the first question, we need not attempt a detailed consideration of the moral rights of organisms which are not developed enough, aware enough, intelligent enough, etc., to be considered people, but which resemble people in some respects. It does seem reasonable to suggest that the more like a person, in the relevant respects, a being is, the stronger is the case for regarding it as having a right to life, and indeed the stronger its right to life is. Thus we ought to take seriously the suggestion that, insofar as "the human individual develops biologically in a continuous fashion . . . the rights of a human person might develop in the same way."[11] But we must keep in mind that the attributes which are relevant in determining whether or not an entity is enough like a person to be regarded as having some of the same moral rights are no different from those which are relevant to determining whether or not it is fully a person—i.e., are no different from (1)–(5)—and that being genetically human or having recognizably human facial and other physical features, or detectable brain activity, or the capacity to survive outside the uterus, are simply not among these relevant attributes.

Thus it is clear that even though a seven- or eight-month fetus has features which make it apt to arouse in us almost the same powerful protective instinct as is commonly aroused by a small infant, nevertheless it is not significantly more personlike than is a very small embryo. It is *somewhat* more personlike; it can apparently feel and respond to pain, and it may even have a rudimentary form of consciousness, insofar as its brain is quite active. Nevertheless, it seems safe to say that it is not fully conscious, in the way that an infant of a few months is, and that it cannot reason, or communicate messages of indefinitely many sorts, does not engage in self-motivated activity, and has no self-awareness. Thus, in the *relevant* respects, a fetus, even a fully developed one, is considerably less personlike than is the average mature mammal, indeed the average fish. And I think that a rational person must conclude that if the right to life of a fetus is to be based upon its resemblance to a person, then it cannot be said to have any more right to life than, let us say, a newborn guppy (which also seems to be capable of feeling pain), and that a right of that magnitude could never override a woman's right to obtain an abortion, at any stage of her pregnancy.

There may, of course, be other arguments in favor of placing legal limits upon the stage of pregnancy in which an abortion may be performed. Given the relative safety of the new techniques of artificially inducing labor during the third trimester, the danger to the woman's life or health is no longer such an argument. Neither is the fact that people tend to respond to the thought of abortion in the later stages of pregnancy with emotional repulsion, since mere emotional responses cannot take the place of moral reasoning in determining what ought to be permitted. Nor, finally, is the frequently heard argument that legalizing abortion, especially late in the pregnancy, may erode the level of respect for human life, leading, perhaps, to an increase in unjustified euthanasia and other crimes. For this threat, if it is a threat, can be better met by educating people to the kinds of moral distinctions which we are making here than by limiting access to abortion (which limitation may, in its disregard for the rights of women, be just as damaging to the level of respect for human rights).

Thus, since the fact that even a fully developed fetus is not personlike enough to have any significant right to life on the basis of its personlikeness shows that no legal restrictions upon the stage of pregnancy in which an abortion may be performed can be justified on the grounds that we should protect the rights of the older fetus; and since there is no other apparent justification for such restrictions, we may conclude that they are entirely unjustified. Whether or not it would be *indecent* (whatever that means) for a woman in her seventh month to obtain an abortion just to avoid having to postpone a trip to Europe, it would not, in itself, be *immoral*, and therefore it ought to be permitted.

We have seen that a fetus does not resemble a person in any way which can support the claim that it has even some of the same rights.

But what about its *potential*, the fact that if nurtured and allowed to develop naturally it will very probably become a person? Doesn't that alone give it at least some right to life? It is hard to deny that the fact that an entity is a potential person is a strong prima facie reason for not destroying it; but we need not conclude from this that a potential person has a right to life, by virtue of that potential. It may be that our feeling that it is better, other things being equal, not to destroy a potential person is better explained by the fact that potential people are still (felt to be) an invaluable resource, not to be lightly squandered. Surely, if every speck of dust were a potential person, we would be much less apt to conclude that every potential person has a right to become actual.

Still, we do not need to insist that a potential person has no right to life whatever. There may well be something immoral, and not just imprudent, about wantonly destroying potential people, when doing so isn't necessary to protect anyone's rights. But even if a potential person does have some prima facie right to life, such a right could not possibly outweigh the right of a woman to obtain an abortion, since the rights of any actual person invariably outweigh those of any potential person, whenever the two conflict. Since this may not be immediately obvious in the case of a human fetus, let us look at another case.

Suppose that our space explorer falls into the hands of an alien culture, whose scientists decide to create a few hundred thousand or more human beings, by breaking his body into its component cells, and using these to create fully developed human beings, with, of course, his genetic code. We may imagine that each of these newly created men will have all of the original man's abilities, skills, knowledge, and so on, and also have an individual self-concept, in short that each of them will be a bona fide (though hardly unique) person. Imagine that the whole project will take only seconds, and that its chances of success are extremely high, and that our explorer knows all of this, and also knows that these people will be treated fairly. I maintain that in such a situation he would have every right to escape if he could, and thus to deprive all of these potential people of their potential lives; for his right to life outweighs all of theirs together, in spite of the fact that they are all genetically human, all innocent, and all have a very high probability of becoming people very soon, if only he refrains from acting.

Indeed, I think he would have a right to escape even if it were not his life which the alien scientists planned to take, but only a year of his freedom, or, indeed, only a day. Nor would he be obligated to stay if he had gotten captured (thus bringing all these people-potentials into existence) because of his own carelessness, or even if he had done so deliberately, knowing the consequences. Regardless of how he got captured, he is not morally obligated to remain in captivity for *any* period of time for the sake of permitting any number of potential people to come into actuality, so great is the margin by which one actual person's right to liberty outweighs whatever right to life even a hundred thousand potential people have. And it seems reasonable to conclude that the rights of a woman will outweigh by a similar margin whatever right to life a fetus may have by virtue of its potential personhood.

Thus, neither a fetus's resemblance to a person, nor its potential for becoming a person provides any basis whatever for the claim that it has any significant right to life. Consequently, a woman's right to protect her health, happiness, freedom, and even her life,[12] by terminating an unwanted pregnancy, will always override whatever right to life it may be appropriate to ascribe to a fetus, even a fully developed one. And thus, in the absence of any overwhelming social need for every possible child, the laws which restrict the right to obtain an abortion, or limit the period of pregnancy during which an abortion may be performed, are a wholly unjustified violation of a woman's most basic moral and constitutional rights.

Postscript on Infanticide

Since the publication of this article, many people have written to point out that my argument appears to justify not only abortion, but infanticide as well. For a newborn infant is not significantly more personlike than an advanced fetus, and consequently it would seem that if the destruction of the latter is permissible so too must be that of the former. Inasmuch as most people, regardless of how they feel about the morality of abortion, consider infanticide a form of murder, this might appear to represent a serious flaw in my argument.

Now, if I am right in holding that it is only people who have a full-fledged right to life, and who can be murdered, and if the criteria of personhood are as I have described them, then it obviously follows that killing a new-born infant isn't murder. It does *not* follow, however, that infanticide is permissible, for two reasons. In the first place, it would be wrong, at least in this country and in this period of history, and other things being equal, to kill a new-born infant, because even if its parents do not want it and would not suffer from its destruction, there are other people who would like to have it, and would, in all probability, be deprived of a great deal of pleasure by its destruction. Thus, infanticide is wrong for reasons analogous to those which make it wrong to wantonly destroy natural resources, or great works of art.

Secondly, most people, at least in this country, value infants and would much prefer that they be preserved, even if foster parents are not immediately available. Most of us would rather be taxed to support orphanages than allow unwanted infants to be destroyed. So long as there are people who want an infant preserved, and who are willing and able to provide the means of caring for it, under reasonably humane conditions, it is *ceteris paribus*, wrong to destroy it.

But, it might be replied, if this argument shows that infanticide is wrong, at least at this time and in this country, doesn't it also show that abortion is wrong? After all, many people value fetuses, are disturbed by their destruction, and would much prefer that they be preserved, even at some cost to themselves. Furthermore, as a potential source of pleasure to some foster family, a fetus is just as valuable as an infant. There is, however, a crucial difference between the two cases: so long as the fetus is unborn, its preservation, contrary to the wishes of the pregnant woman, violates her rights to freedom, happiness, and self-determination. Her rights override the rights of those who would like the fetus preserved, just as if someone's life or limb is threatened by a wild animal, his right to protect himself by destroying the animal overrides the rights of those who would prefer that the animal not be harmed.

The minute the infant is born, however, its preservation no longer violates any of its mother's rights, even if she wants it destroyed, because she is free to put it up for adoption. Consequently, while the moment of birth does not mark any sharp discontinuity in the degree to which an infant possesses the right to life, it does mark the end of its mother's right to determine its fate. Indeed, if abortion could be performed without killing the fetus, she would never possess the right to have the fetus destroyed, for the same reasons that she has no right to have an infant destroyed.

On the other hand, it follows from my argument that when an unwanted or defective infant is born into a society which cannot afford and/or is not willing to care for it, then its destruction is permissible. This conclusion will, no doubt, strike many people as heartless and immoral; but remember that the very existence of people who feel this way, and who are willing and able to provide care for unwanted infants, is reason enough to conclude that they should be preserved.

Notes

1. For example, Roger Wertheimer, who in "Understanding the Abortion Argument," *Philosophy and Public Affairs*, 1, no. 1 (Fall, 1971), [*supra*, pp. 43–57], argues that the problem of the moral status of abortion is insoluble, in that the dispute over the status of the fetus is not a question of fact at all, but only a question of how one responds to the facts.

2. B. A. Brody, "Abortion and the Law," *The Journal of Philosophy*, 68, no. 12 (June 17, 1971), 357–69.

3. Judith Thomson, "A Defense of Abortion," *Philosophy and Public Affairs*, 1, no. 1 (Fall, 1971) [*infra*, pp. 173–87]. Reprinted in Chapter 8 of this volume.

4. I have abbreviated these statements somewhat, but not in a way which affects the argument.

5. John Noonan, "Abortion and the Catholic Church: A Summary History," *Natural Law Forum*, 12 (1967), 125.

6. John Noonan, "Deciding Who Is Human," *Natural Law Forum*, 13 (1968), 134.

7. "A Defense of Abortion."

8. We may safely ignore the fact that she might have avoided getting raped, e.g., by carrying a gun, since by similar means you might likewise have avoided getting kidnapped, and in neither case does the victim's failure to take all possible precautions against a highly unlikely event (as opposed to reasonable precautions against a rather likely event) mean that she is morally responsible for what happens.

9. Of course, the principle that it is (always) wrong to kill innocent human beings is in need of many other modifications, e.g., that it may be permissible to do so to save a greater number of other innocent human beings, but we may safely ignore these complications here.

10. We use "human" to mean genetically human, since the moral sense seems closely connected to, and perhaps derived from, the assumption that genetic humanity is sufficient for membership in the moral community.

11. Thomas L. Hayes, "A Biological View," *Commonweal, 85* (March 17, 1967), 667–78; quoted by Daniel Callahan, in *Abortion, Law, Choice, and Morality* (London: Macmillan & Co., 1970).

12. That is, insofar as the death rate, for the woman, is higher for childbirth than for early abortion.

Study Questions

1. What two common proabortion arguments does Warren reject, and why?

2. What assumption does Warren believe most writers on abortion make without argument?

3. To what analogy offered by Thomson does Warren object? What was Thomson trying to show by that analogy, and what is Warren's objection? How does Warren modify the Thomson analogy to bring out her objection to it?

4. What criteria of personhood does Warren offer? Under these criteria, what types of human beings are not persons? Do you agree with her point?

5. Does Warren believe that a seven- or eight-month fetus is very much like a person in the morally relevant respects? Explain her reasons. Do you agree?

6. What is Warren's reply to the objection that a fetus has a right to life because it is a potential person?

7. Does Warren's defense of abortion commit her to defending infanticide? Why or why not?

Moral Revolution

Kathryn Pyne Addelson

Part I: Introduction

Has a covert bias been introduced into our world view by the near exclusion of women from the domain of intellectual pursuits?

Philosophers and scientists both have argued long and hard that it is a virtue of science that the sex, race, ethnic background, or creed of the investigator is irrelevant to scientific results, provided only that scientific method is practiced correctly. They have taken that to be one consequence of the *objectivity* of science, and some have even felt that the remedy for bias is to become *more* scientific. Although philosophers and scientists generally conclude that there is no bias, the question somehow keeps arising. One reason it cannot be laid to rest is that detecting bias is itself a philosophic or scientific enterprise, and the methods used

Revised and condensed from Julia A. Sherman and Evelyn T. Beck, eds., *The Prism of Sex* (Madison, WI: University of Wisconsin Press, 1979). Copyright © 1978 by Kathryn Pyne Parsons. Reprinted by permission of Kathryn Pyne Addelson. (Notes deleted.)

in the detection may themselves be questioned as to bias. In fact, the major question concerns how to define what bias amounts to.

Sometimes bias in intellectual work has been said to be the result of doing "bad science," or "bad philosophy." In principle, the work is biased because of the biases of the investigators using the theory. Let me give an example from Judith Jarvis Thomson's paper, "A Defense of Abortion,"[1] which I'll consider in some detail in Part II below. In this paper, she says that most philosophical discussions of abortion have taken the point of view of a third party (lawgiver, abortionist, interested onlooker) and not the point of view of the pregnant woman. She argues that the moral decision from the point of view of the pregnant woman is quite different and that we can't generalize from the third-party point of view to hers. For example, considerations of self-defense may enter for the pregnant woman when they don't enter for an outsider. This criticism Judith Thomson raises shows bias in the *application* of the philosophical theory she is working with. It doesn't correct the philosophical theory itself. Her criticism shows that other papers on abortion have been biased *in the use of the theory*. The bias would be corrected by reforming the way the theory is applied.

Some criticisms of bias in the use of a theory show that fairly basic assumptions of the theory may need to be corrected to do "good science" with it. Let's take an example from sociology. Arlene Daniels reports on a paper by Joan Acker:

> [Joan Acker] points out that stratification literature—whether written by functionalists, Marxists, or others—contains assumptions about the social position of women that are quite inadequate. The first assumption is that the family is the unit in the stratification system. From this view, a number of other assumptions are derived, such as that the social position of a family is determined by the male head of household or that the status of females living in families is determined by the males to whom they are attached. But these assumptions do not accurately reflect the actual state of relationships for large segments of the population. There are many females and female heads of households who are not attached to males. Why should such persons be ignored or placed in some residual category indicating their irrelevance to any major analysis of the stratification system? No male stratification theorists have previously questioned the usefulness of a world view that excludes the conditions of so much of the population from consideration. But it has been convenient to assume that females have no relevant role in stratification processes independent of their ties to men.[2]

In this passage, Arlene Daniels isn't suggesting that the functionalist or Marxist theories have to be thrown out because they are sexist. She is saying that they contain inadequate assumptions about the social position of women, and that those assumptions need to be corrected by reforming the theory.

There is a more radical kind of bias that may infect a theory, a kind which can't be corrected by reforming the application of the theory or a few of its assumptions. To reform this kind of bias, we need a scientific revolution in which the old theory is scrapped and a new theory introduced. Let me give another example from sociology. In *Another Voice*, Lyn Lofland reviewed urban sociology. She says:

> . . . women in that portion of the literature of urban sociology here under review are mostly and simply, just there. They are part of the locale or neighborhood or area—described like other important aspects of the setting such as income, ecology, or demography—but largely irrelevant to the analytic *action*. . . . To the degree that urban researchers have taken seriously (and of course many have not) the Blumerian injunction to "look upon human group life as chiefly a vast interpretative process in which people, singly and collectively, *guide themselves* by *defining* the objects, events and situations they encounter," they have done so primarily for the male participants in the human group life. The female participants are "just there."[3]

Lyn Lofland feels a radical change in urban sociology is necessary to correct this bias and that no mere reform will do. She says: " . . . the problems which lead to the portrayal of women as 'only there' are among the central conceptual, focal, and methodological difficulties of urban sociology itself."[4] She suggests that to remedy this bias, completely new models, concepts, and variables would have to be developed out of studies which gave proper investigation to women; the resulting theory, she feels, would very likely differ in a radical way from the one currently used by many urban sociologists. Such a radical change in theory is a *scientific revolution*.

Since the publication of Thomas Kuhn's *Structure of Scientific Revolutions* in 1962, a good deal of research has been done on scientific revolutions.[5] Charles Darwin's evolutionary theory constituted a scientific revolution of very great magnitude, since it brought with it a revolution in patterns of thinking in philosophy of science and many other sciences in addition to biology. Lavoisier's revolution, which transformed alchemy to chemistry, was important but of smaller magnitude. The Copernican revolution in astronomy and the Newtonian in physics were also far-reaching.

The bias which Lyn Lofland found in urban sociology has ancient roots. In this paper, as a philosopher, I shall be investigating a bias of the third sort in contemporary American moral philosophy. A main bias in moral philosophy for two millenia has been the bias which Lyn Lofland points out in urban sociology: the moral-social world has been taken to be the world as men know it. A meaningful life (or a "good life") has been a life seen from the perspective of males and open only to males—and in fact, only to higher-class white adult males, so that the bias is classist and racist and ageist as well as sexist. I believe a moral, social, and philosophical revolution is necessary to change it.

Part II: A Defense of Abortion

In September 1971, the first issue of *Philosophy and Public Affairs* was published. It was a very different kind of journal from the philosophy journals existing then. Its purpose was to highlight the philosophical dimension in issues of public concern and to encourage "philosophically inclined writers from various disciplines . . . [to] bring their distinctive methods to bear on problems that concern everyone." The journal had an effect on the direction of work in philosophy.

In the first issue of *Philosophy and Public Affairs,* there was a paper by Judith Jarvis Thomson titled "A Defense of Abortion." In the paper, Judith Thomson considers whether or not abortion is ever morally justifiable, concluding that it sometimes is. In the years since this paper was published, it has become one of the classic works used when the abortion problem is considered in philosophy courses and in medicine and ethics courses. It is an example of excellent work in its tradition—which I'll call the "Judith Thomson tradition," even though its roots lie in the seventeenth century, and even though some philosophers in the tradition today disagree with some of Judith Thomson's analyses.

Analyzing Arguments

There is a particular pattern of analysis, a particular method, which philosophers in Judith Thomson's tradition use, and there is a particular pattern of thinking which they take to be *moral reasoning. Moral reasoning* constitutes a technical category within this philosophic tradition, but it is really supposed to capture the kind of thinking people would do in moral matters if they were thinking properly. Let me go over the Judith Thomson paper to show the method and to indicate what moral reasoning is supposed to be.

In the introduction to an anthology in which Judith Thomson's abortion paper is reprinted, editor Joel Feinberg says: "Abortion raises subtle problems for private conscience, public policy, and constitutional law. Most of these problems are essentially philosophical, requiring a degree of clarity about basic concepts that is seldom achieved in legislative debates and letters to the newspaper."[6] As the analytic philosopher sees it, matters of private conscience have to do with a *moral agent* doing whatever *moral reasoning* is necessary to decide whether a *moral act* (or kind of moral act) is *morally justifiable.* Moral reasoning may show that an act is morally unjustifiable as well, of course. One way of showing that an act is justifiable is by finding a *moral principle* which covers it. One moral principle that Judith Thomson considers is "Every person has a right to life." Often, though, the matter is much more complicated, and the moral reasoning requires a *moral argument.*

Philosophers in this tradition spend a great deal of time analyzing arguments. It is a main part of their method. In the process of examining arguments, the philosopher clarifies and develops concepts, and often establishes the basis for a new position. Superficially, the widely used tactic of examining arguments makes this philosophy seem destructive and merely critical. But this is misleading. Razing buildings in a city would look merely destructive unless you realized that the buildings were unsafe for people to live in and that, perhaps, the neighborhood people wanted to build a park on the site.

Here is the line of argument Judith Thomson criticizes:

A. The fetus is a *person* from the moment of conception.
B. Every person has a *right to life.*
∴ C. The fetus has a *right to life.*
D. The mother has a *right* to decide what will happen in and to her body.
E. A person's *right to life* is stronger and more stringent than the mother's *right* to

decide what happens in and to her own
body and so outweighs it.

∴ F. The fetus may not be killed.

Since aborting the birth amounts (in nearly all
cases) to killing the fetus, the conclusion of
interest is

∴ G. Abortion is impermissible.

Using the word *mother* here reflects a bias—
not Judith Thomson's bias, since she is just
citing an argument which some "right-to-lifers"
give. A pregnant woman is not a mother, nor is
a woman giving birth a mother, except in the
barest of biological senses. In the context of this
argument, using *mother* constitutes an emotional and moral bias, and it begs the question. So
I'll use the term *pregnant woman*.

The method of examining arguments is an
exact science in philosophy, and there are various questions to ask in doing the examination.
For example, a foremost question to ask is
whether the argument is *valid*. That amounts to
asking whether the conclusion follows by the
laws of logic from the premises. In the argument I set out above, which Judith Thomson
will be examining, C is a conclusion from premises A and B. Conclusions may also be premises,
and C is in fact a premise in the argument
which has F as a conclusion. So a question which
Judith Thomson raises is whether the argument having A, B, C, D, and E as premises, and
F as conclusion is valid.

In fact, that argument is not valid. Like nearly all arguments given in real life, it is *en-
thymematic*—that is, it has many suppressed
premises not set out explicitly in the argument.
If our arguments in real life weren't enthyme-
matic, we would all die of boredom because the
premises which have to be made explicit include enormous numbers of trivial premises
that everyone would agree to and which everyone realized are presupposed. Sometimes,
however, the suppressed premises are not at all
obvious, and they may include unacknowledged prejudices and presuppositions which
would be rejected if they were brought to light.
For example, Judith Thomson's criticism of
many arguments about abortion which I mentioned in the introduction to this paper—that
they assume that the pregnant woman's moral

decision is on a par with the decision of any
other moral agent—is a criticism which reveals
an unacknowledged prejudice and presupposition. There are other suppressed premises, or
"gaps," in the argument from A to E to conclusion F which Judith Thomson reveals in the
course of her paper.

Using Hypothetical Cases

One tactic which Judith Thomson used, and
one which is a staple in her tradition, is that of
introducing hypothetical cases. Philosophers in
this tradition suppose moral agents understand
the arguments they are using, although that
understanding may need clarification; and
they suppose moral agents grasp the concepts
involved in the arguments. The philosopher
(so they say) merely clarifies the thinking and
the concepts which the moral agent already
grasps. The philosopher adds nothing new. In
fact, adding something new would not be doing
philosophy, they claim. It would be doing substantive morality, or moral persuasion. Sometimes philosophers talk of this in terms of
clarifying the *meaning of the moral terms*. In that
phrasing, it may seem even more obvious that
the philosopher is merely dealing with what the
moral agents already understand, and clarifying it.

Let me give the main hypothetical case
which Judith Thomson uses in her paper:

> . . . let me ask you to imagine this. You wake
> up in the morning and find yourself in bed
> with an unconscious violinist. A famous violin-
> ist. He has been found to have a fatal kidney
> ailment, and the Society of Music Lovers has
> canvassed all the available medical records and
> found that you alone have the right blood type
> to help. They have therefore kidnapped you,
> and last night the violinist's circulatory system
> was plugged into yours, so that your kidneys
> can be used to extract poisons from his blood
> as well as your own. The director of the hospi-
> tal now tells you, "Look, we're sorry the Society
> of Music Lovers did this to you—we would
> never have permitted it if we had known. But
> still, they did it, and the violinist now is
> plugged into you. To unplug you would be to
> kill him. But never mind, it's only for nine
> months. By then he will have recovered from
> his ailment, and can safely be unplugged from
> you." (Pp. 48–49)

Judith Thomson takes this hypothetical case to have obvious analogies to the abortion case, analogies she will use in examining the anti-abortion argument. I'll trace the outline of her discussion.

The conclusion of the antiabortion argument is

F. Abortion is impermissible.

Does this mean that the abortion is impermissible absolutely, under any and all circumstances? Or does it mean that it is impermissible under normal circumstances, but that there are extraordinary circumstances in which it might be permissible? To work that out, Judith Thomson begins clarifying premise E.

E. A person's right to life is stronger and more stringent than the mother's right to decide what happens in and to her own body and outweighs it.

But, she asks, what if the pregnant woman will die if the fetus is not aborted? In that case, we have the pregnant woman's right to life balanced against the fetal right to life. Judith Thomson insists that in order for the valid conclusion to be that abortion is absolutely impermissible, two important, suppressed premises have to be made explicit. They are

E(1) Performing an abortion would be *directly killing* the fetus and doing nothing will merely be *letting* the mother *die*.
E(2) Directly killing an innocent person is always and absolutely impermissible.

Judith Thomson now tests premise E(2) by bringing in the hypothetical violinist example. Suppose your kidneys will break down under the strain of purifying the violinist's blood and your own? If someone walks in and unplugs the violinist from you, he will be directly killing the violinist, which is impermissible, by E(2). But, she asks, what if you turn around and unplug *yourself* from the violinist. Is that impermissible? A low murmur rises from all the comfortable nooks in which people are reading Judith Thomson's paper. "Surely not," goes the murmur. "Surely unplugging *yourself* is not impermissible." The moral principle embodied in E(2), that directly killing an innocent person is absolutely impermissible, is overridden by a

principle of self-defense (or perhaps qualified by a principle of self-defense). We can see this clearly in the violinist example. But the abortion case also falls under E(2). So if it is not impermissible for you to unplug yourself from the violinist in the hypothetical case, then it is not impermissible for the pregnant woman to abort the fetus.

In the course of her discussion of the pregnant woman's decision to abort, Judith Thomson criticized other writings on abortion for having what amounts to a sexist bias (though she doesn't use that term):

> The main focus of attention in writings on abortion has been on what a third party may or may not do in answer to a request from a woman for an abortion. . . . So, the question asked is what a third party may do, and what the mother may do is decided, almost as an afterthought, from what it is concluded that the third party may do. But it seems to me that to treat the matter in this way is to refuse to grant to the mother that very status of person which is so firmly insisted on for the fetus. (P. 52)

This is a prime example of a woman working within the methods of a particular tradition in philosophy and correcting a bias which has its roots in sexism.

Clarifying Concepts

So far, we see that abortion is not *absolutely* impermissible. In some cases, the pregnant woman may abort herself—or at least her decision to do so may be morally justifiable. Now Judith Thomson goes on to argue that the pregnant woman's right to life and the fetus's right to life aren't on a par. She does this by using an analogy. The pregnant woman and the child, she says, aren't simply like "two tenants in a small house which has, by unfortunate mistake, been rented to both. The mother *owns* the house" (p. 53). She goes on to clarify this with another hypothetical example: "If Jones has found and fastened on a certain coat which he needs to keep him from freezing, but which Smith also needs to keep him from freezing, then is it not impartiality that says, 'I cannot choose between you' when Smith owns the coat. Women have said again and again,

'This body is *my* body!' " (p. 53). At this point, some readers may raise their eyebrows and ask what owning a house or coat has to do with the right to life. Many philosophers, including Judith Thomson, would say that property rights are the very model we work with in discussing rights, that our picture of what rights are, and our understanding of what they are, is gained by focusing on property rights.[7] The reader should pay heed also to the fact that Judith Thomson analyzes the pregnant woman's relation to her body by analogy with the legal relation of property ownership (as distinct from the legal relation of tenancy). She then uses this clarification in terms of property relations to help clarify the question of whether abortion is impermissible.

At this point, the murmur rising from the comfortable nooks may show ripples of shock. "Does this mean *I* have an obligation to seize the coat from Jones so that Smith won't freeze to death?" (Or, by analogy, to seize the woman's body back from the fetus by helping her with an abortion?) Judith Thomson saves us from such actions. We *decide* that it is right that Smith have the coat (or that the woman have her body), but we need not ourselves be the agent who does the confiscating. We must grant, she says, that a person has a right to refuse to confiscate that coat: "But then what should be said is . . . 'I will not *act*,' leaving it open that somebody else can or should and, in particular, that anyone in a position of authority with the job of securing people's rights, both can and should" (p. 54).

Judith Thomson's process of clarifying concepts here has been to show their links with other concepts in the broad conceptual scheme which we moral agents allegedly work within. This network includes the concept of *property* and also the concept of the *law*, which is presupposed in the concepts of property and tenancy (those being legalistic concepts). She also links the concept of rights to the concept of a *legitimate authority* who has the *responsibility* for seeing that rights are secured. We shall see later that these linkages are important. But at the moment, the concept of the right to life needs further clarification—a clarification which involves bringing in the additional moral concept of *justice*.

The Right to Life

Investigating the concept of a right to life is part of clarifying premises B and E of the anti-abortion argument:

B. Every person has a *right to life*.
E. A person's *right to life* is stronger and more stringent than the mother's *right to decide* what happens in and to her own body and so outweighs it.

Judith Thomson investigates the concept of the right to life in stages. First she asks, "Does having a right to life mean that you have the right to be given the bare minimum you need to continue life?" This is a specific application of the general question of whether having a right to something means that a person has the right to the means to that something, and is one of the very general clarifications of rights which she will make. Looking at the violinist example again, she concludes that although the violinist has a right to life, and he may need to use my kidneys as his means to keep on living, he has no right to their use. What is important here is that Judith Thomson has distinguished between having the right to something and having the right to the means to that something. She claims it is a feature of all rights and something any adequate account of rights must deal with (p. 56).

If the right to life doesn't necessarily involve the right to the means essential to life, what does it involve? Judith Thomson finally concludes that the right to life must simply be the right not to be killed *unjustly*. She then clarifies the concept of justice she is using by a hypothetical example, once again leaning on the concept of property rights (p. 60).

Suppose two brothers are given a single box of chocolates for Christmas, that is, it is their joint possession. Suppose further that the big brother grabs the box, won't let the little brother have any of the chocolates, and instead eats them all himself. We would all surely agree, she says, that the big brother is treating the little one unjustly, because the little brother has been given a right to half of them (p. 56). She goes on with the example. Suppose the older brother has been given the chocolates for his very own and he ate them all himself, refusing to give the little brother even a single one. He wouldn't be treating the little boy unjustly unless he had somehow given him a right to some of the chocolates. The big boy might be greedy, stingy, callous, and mean. But he would not be unjust.[8]

There are many different concepts of justice, and some of them certainly bear a resemblance to this one, which Judith Thomson claims is one we moral agents use. But according to her concept of justice, one may have a right to something by owning it, or by having been given a right to it (by its rightful owner or perhaps by God or by whatever gives natural rights). To act unjustly, then, seems to mean not letting someone have or use something that person has a right to. Having a right to life comes down to not being deprived of life unjustly.

The question of whether abortion is permissible in a given case, then, seems to turn on whether the woman has given the fetus a right to use her body. Once the area of explicit legal contract and long-standing custom is left behind, it becomes very difficult to decide under what conditions someone has given someone else a right to use something. In trying to clarify this in the abortion case, Judith Thomson brings in some of her most memorable hypothetical examples, about people seeds which float in through the living room windows and root themselves in the carpets. But the upshot is that there are cases of pregnancy in which the woman has not given the fetus a right to use her body and in which the fetus may be aborted without killing it unjustly. And so there are cases in which abortion is not impermissible.

Matters of Public Policy

I have discussed work in the Judith Thomson tradition so far as matters of private conscience go. But Joel Feinberg also said that the abortion issue raised questions for public policy and constitutional law, so it would seem that the tradition deals with moral aspects of those things too. I won't take up the question of constitutional law, but it is important to say some things about the way the tradition handles the moral aspects of matters of public policy.[9]

In Judith Thomson's discussion of rights, a person makes his or her decision of private conscience against a background environment that is fixed so far as the distinction of rights goes. Some rights everyone has, like the right to life. Other rights not everyone has, particularly rights to property or rights to some of the means which are necessary to exercise rights which everyone has. The result is that not everyone can exercise even the rights that everyone has. This background distribution may be changed by actions based on individual conscience; for example, the pregnant woman may decide that she ought to give the fetus a right to use her body. In the main, however, the distribution is changed by public policy; for example, the legislature or the courts may decide that public funds must be used to pay for the abortions of indigent women.

Interestingly enough, philosophers in this tradition clarify questions of public policy in the same way as they clarify questions of private conscience. The only difference they see is that in private conscience, individuals without special status are making decisions about their personal lives; and in public policy, individuals who are acting in certain offices (congressmen, circuit court justices, heads of public health divisions) are making policy decisions which will have effects on the public at large. These philosophers suppose that the process of moral reasoning is the same in both cases. In the public case, each individual supposedly clarifies his or her conscience and then votes. In cases of legislation or in board decisions this is exactly what happens. Executive decisions may be construed as decisions of one-member groups. In this view, public policy is made by aggregates of individuals each of whom reasons his or her way through the moral arguments and then votes.

This should serve as enough of a discussion of work in the Judith Thomson tradition to give the reader a feel for the style and to set out enough of the method, categories, and concepts so that I may later argue for bias in the tradition. I'll now turn to an altogether different sort of discussion of abortion.

Part III: Jane

In 1969, most state laws prohibited abortion unless the life of the pregnant woman was threatened.[10] A few states had reformed their abortion laws to allow abortion by doctors in hospitals in cases of threat to the health of the woman, threat of fetal deformity, or rape.[11] In the mid-1960s, the estimated death rate for abortions performed in hospitals was 3 deaths per 100,000 abortions; the rate for illegal abortions was guessed to be over eight times that— 30 deaths per 100,000 abortions was a rough estimate and almost certainly conservative.[12] For minority and poorer women, it was certainly very much higher.

The women's liberation movement was in its infancy in 1969. In that year, a group of Chicago women who had been active in radical politics formed an organization called Jane. Over the next year and a half, Jane evolved from an abortion counseling and referral service to a service in which abortions were actually performed by the Jane members themselves. By 1973 when they closed the service, over 12,000 abortions had been performed under Jane's auspices. The medical record equalled that of abortions done under legal, licensed conditions by physicians in hospitals. The service charged on a sliding scale; eventually all abortions were cheaper than the going rate, and some women paid nothing. Jane served many poor women, black women, and very young women who could not have had an abortion otherwise.

My discussion of Jane is based on one newspaper series and an interview with one member. Perhaps not all Jane members will agree with this member's interpretation, but that isn't the point here because I'm not doing a sociological study. I am investigating patterns of moral thinking and acting which the Judith Thomson tradition makes invisible. The fact that one person's thinking and action are concealed is enough to show bias. Pauline B. Bart has done a broader based study.[13]

What Jane Did

This is the way Jane operated, as reported in the June 1973 Hyde Park-Kenwood *Voices* article on the organization: "Jane was the pseudonym we chose to represent the service. A phone was opened in her name and an answering service secured, later replaced by a tape recorder. Jane kept all records and served as control-central." "Jane" was not a particular woman but the code name for whichever counselor was taking calls and coordinating activities on a given day.

> For four years, Jane kept the same phone number. . . . At first she received only eight to ten calls a week. A year later she was receiving well more than 100 calls a week.
>
> All phoned-in messages were returned the same day: "Hello, Marcia. This is Jane from women's liberation returning your call. We can't talk freely over the phone, but I want you to know that we can help you."
>
> Then Jane would refer the name to a counselor, who would meet personally with the woman and talk with her at length about available alternatives.
>
> The counselor would also help the woman arrange finances and, whenever possible, collect a $25 donation for the service loan fund. The counseling session was also a screening process for detecting conflicts and potential legal threats.[14]

Jane worked with several male abortionists. One of these was "Dr. C." Dr. C worked alone with his nurse in motel rooms until the day an abortion was interrupted by a pounding on the door and a man's voice shouting, "Come on out of there, baby killer!" After a wild chase between buildings and down alleys, Dr. C escaped the irate husband. When he caught his breath, he decided that it might be better to quit working in motels.

Jane members then began renting apartments for Dr. C and his nurse to work in. Jane describes the first day they used a rented apartment. "Seven women were done that day, in a setting where they could relax and talk with other women in a similar predicament. And when the first woman walked out of the bedroom, feeling fine and no longer pregnant, the other six were noticeably relieved. They asked her questions and got firsthand answers."[15] Another advantage of the new arrangement was that Jane counselors were with a woman during the abortion, giving her psychological and moral support and explaining what was going on to her. Still another was that the counselors gradually began assisting Dr. C in the abortion itself, and he began training them in the abortion procedures.

After a few months of operation, members of Jane had begun inducing miscarriages for women more than twelve weeks pregnant.[16] During this time, Dr. C was teaching the women of Jane more and more about the process of doing direct abortions. Finally, some counselors were doing the entire direct abortion themselves, under Dr. C's eye. In the midst of all this, they learned that Dr. C was no doctor at all, but just a man who had become an expert in the giving of abortions. Later, they broke off the relationship with Dr. C and began doing all of their own abortions. For good or ill, this meant that they had a sudden abundance of funds, since the abortion fee went to Jane instead of to Dr. C. In the eyes of the law, they became fullfledged abortionists: "We could no longer hide behind the label of 'counselor' or expect 'Dr. C' to act as a buffer, with his know-how and ready cash for dealing with a bust."[17] Jane members were arrested only once, although they were harassed by the police.[18]

The change in the abortion service meant that Jane members had to accept the full consequences of what they were doing—even if it resulted in illness, personal tragedy, or death—and they had to bear this without the protection that the doctor's professionalism gives him.[19] They worked under these conditions until 1 April 1973. Then, two months after the United States Supreme Court passed its opinion on the constitutionality of restrictive abortion laws, Jane officially closed.

What Jane Meant

In describing what Jane did, I selected data to a certain purpose. It was a selection different in many respects from the selection someone in Judith Thomson's traditon would have made. I didn't, however, use any special technical concepts or categories from some philosophical theory. In this section, I shall use Jane as a basis for discussing a moral theory which competes with theories of the Judith Thomson tradition, in order to reveal value implications of bias in that tradition.

Jane was an abortion clinic, and the women of Jane were working out moral and political beliefs and activities, not constructing a theory. I want to try to give a fragment of a theory which is able to capture their thinking and their work. The theory should be taken as *hypothesis* about what Jane meant, subject to correction through further investigation of Jane and groups like Jane, and through seeing what comes of acting on the theory. I believe the theory is based on anarchist, or anarchist-feminist principles, but I won't discuss that. Instead I'll call the tradition out of which the theory arises the Jane tradition, to contrast with the Judith Thomson tradition.

In March 1977, I interviewed one of the founders of Jane. She said that the women who founded the organization had been active in civil rights or anti-war work in the late 1960s. They wanted to begin work in the newly born women's liberation movement. But how should they begin? What should they do? Someone suggested abortion as an issue. It was a difficult decision, and they struggled over it for months. Deciding on an issue required an analysis of a network of larger issues, and of the place of the abortion issue in that network. According to the woman I interviewed, the question was one of a woman's opportunities for life choices: "It was a question of free choice about reproduction, free choice about life style, because the old roles for women weren't viable any more. In frontier times, childbearing was valuable and important. So was housework. But that role is gone. The old ways are gone. We felt nothing *could* come in to replace them unless women could make a choice about childbearing. That seemed necessary for any other choice." These alternatives had to be *created* within our social system. The members of Jane hoped that other groups within the women's movement would work on other alternatives—offering alternative living arrangements, working on ways that women could become economically independent, and so on—while Jane members tried to offer the alternative of choosing not to have the child by aborting. That is, they thought in terms of a division of labor among women working to change the society so that women would have real alternatives for meaningful lives.

As I mentioned in the introduction, the concept of a *meaningful life* (more often called "a good life") has traditionally been a central concept in moral philosophy. The pattern of thinking Jane members use requires a holistic analysis of the society in terms of the resources it actually offers for women to have meaningful lives, plus an analysis of how to change the society so that it can offer such resources. I'll take this up in more detail in Part IV.

In offering the alternative of abortion, Jane was offering a service that was badly needed. The alternative was open to all kinds of women—rich and poor, older and young, white and nonwhite, but it was a service most desperately needed by the poorer, younger, and minority women. One author says:

> In a comparison of blacks and whites, both for premarital and marital conceptions, we find that whites have higher percentages ending in induced abortions at the lower educational levels, while at the higher educational levels there is little or no difference between blacks and whites . . . the data point to the greater reliance upon abortion on the part of whites over blacks and on the part of the more affluent or more educated over the less affluent and less educated.[20]

When they did turn to illegal abortion methods, poorer and nonwhite women came out far worse. Nationally in 1968, the black death rate from abortion was six times that of the white death rate. In New York in the early 1960s, 42 percent of the pregnancy-related deaths resulted from illegal abortions; and of those women who died, half were black and 44 percent were Puerto Rican. Only 6 percent were white.[21]

More affluent women were also able to pay the high fees which all good, illegal abortionists charged.[22] Jane overcame this by calculating fees on a sliding scale according to income. Some women paid nothing.

Jane's purpose, however, was not simply to provide a service for women, however valuable that service might be. The Jane group could not provide abortions to all Chicago women who needed them. More than that, Jane members knew that when abortion was legalized, their service would have to disappear. Jane's purpose was to show women a much broader alternative than simply not having a baby, to show that by acting together, women can change society so that all women can have an opportunity to choose a meaningful life. They tried to show this in different ways. One way was through the sliding scale for fees. Counselors explained to a woman paying $300 that she was helping pay the cost for a woman who could pay only $5.00. She was, in a small way, helping to undercut the unfairness of a society which would allow her an abortion but not the poorer woman.

Jane itself was the most dramatic demonstration of an alternative for women acting together. Jane members were themselves future or past candidates for abortion, and in the present, they were doing something dangerous, exhausting, and illegal for the sake of changing society for all women. Jane showed that women could take change into their own hands. By coming to Jane for their abortions, other women were also acting for this change. They were trusting women to do things which traditionally were done by men in their society, and legally done only by doctors (overwhelmingly male) within the rigid, hierarchically ordered medical profession. This was a leap of trust.

In the structure of their service, Jane members were trying to build an alternative kind of medical structure as well.[23]

> We—the counselors—we learned the medical mystiques are just bullshit. That was a great up for us. Do you know, you're required to have a license as a nurse just to give a shot. Nurses can't even give an intravenous on their own. That takes a different kind of license. We would just explain to our workers how you had to fill the syringe, and how to be certain there was no air in it, and why that was important, and so on. We'd spend a lot of time explaining it. Then we would say to the patient, "Well this is the first time that Sue is giving anyone a shot. Maybe you can help her, and be patient with her." The patient was part of what was happening too. Part of the whole team.
>
> Sometimes in the middle of an abortion, we would switch positions to show that everyone in the service could do things, to show that the

woman who was counseling could give a shot, and the one who was giving a shot could counsel too. We did it to make people see that they could do it too. They have the power to learn to counsel and give a shot. They have the power to change things and build alternatives.

We here come to the central analysis within the Jane tradition, as it is expressed in Jane's practice. The analysis operates in a very general way to criticize our society and to offer direction to move toward change. Let me state it first in terms of the social structure of the institution of medicine in the United States today.

In the United States, medical people operate within a hierarchical system of dominance and subordination. Those higher in the hierarchy have power which those lower do not have— and the power to order those lower ones around is the least of it. One key aspect of that power is what Howard Becker calls "the right to define the nature of reality." He uses the notion of a "hierarchy of credibility": "In any system of ranked groups, participants take it as given that members of the highest group have the right to define the way things really are."[24] I would argue that this "right of definition" means not only that the word of the higher has heavier weight than that of the lower (teacher over student, doctor over intern or aide) but that the very categories and concepts that are used, the "official" descriptions of reality, are descriptions from the point of view of the dominant persons in the hierarchy. What counts as knowledge itself is defined in terms of that viewpoint, and the definition further legitimates the power of the dominant person.

The power of those in dominant positions in the hierarchy is *legitimate authority*. This contrasts with the *natural authority* of a person who, regardless of position, happens to have a great deal of knowledge, experience, or wisdom about a subject. A doctor's authority is legitimated by the criteria, standards, and institutions which control access to his place in the hierarchy. These criteria and requirements for training on the one hand are aimed at insuring that those with legitimate authority in the hierarchy also have the natural authority required to do the jobs they are doing. Although we all know there are incompetent doctors, these criteria do operate to screen out incompetence *as defined from the top of the hierarchy*. Do they insure that those at the top have natural authority? I think not, and that is because *legitimate authority* carries with it a definition of what counts as knowledge: the definition from the top of the hierarchy, the "official" point of view.

This outlook on knowledge is sometimes called "objective" or "the scientific outlook" of experts. In fact, it is absolutist, and when the definition of reality is given solely in terms of the tradition of the dominant in a dominant-subordinate structure, the outlook is, in fact, biased.

In part, Jane members were operating from the viewpoint of a subordinate group in our society: women. They were using this viewpoint to try to create new social structures which were not based on dominance and subordination and in which authority was natural authority—knowledge which suits the situation to the best degree that we know at the moment. When the woman I interviewed said that the members of Jane tried to show other women that they "have the power to learn to counsel and give a shot" and that they "have the power to change things and build alternatives," she is talking not only about the natural authority of knowledge but what we might call natural *moral* power, or *moral* authority.

In structuring the abortion service as they did, the members of Jane were developing an alternative to hierarchy, but they were also overcoming the vices of dependency and feelings of ignorance and impotence by showing women that they did have the power to learn and do things themselves. The Jane organization itself was built on nonauthoritarian, nonhierarchical principles, and Jane members tried to run it as a collective.

We tried to make it as nonauthoritarian as we could. We had rotating chairs. There wasn't a high value placed on one kind of work and a low value on another. Every position was so important to what we were doing, and it was treated as equally important, to the highest degree possible. This meant every one of us could do what she was best at. You didn't have people competing to do what was important, or feeling what they were doing wasn't valuable.

In April of 1973, the women of Jane asked themselves, "What next?" Whether abortion had been a good issue to move on or not, there was no place for an illegal abortion service now that abortions were legal. Some of the women went on to found a "well woman clinic," the Emma Goldman Clinic. They hoped to run the clinic on the nonauthoritarian, nonhierarchical model used by Jane.[25] The clinic was organized around the concept of self-help, in which the "patients" are trained too in the kind of medical knowledge they need to understand and care for their own bodies for a large range of normal functions and slight disorders.

Part IV: Bias in the World View

In my discussion here, both the Judith Thomson tradition and the Jane tradition were dealing with the problem of abortion. Neither would take it to be *the* problem. Abortion is a subsidiary problem chosen because of its connection with more central concerns. For Judith Thomson, it is a question of rights—we might even say a question of equal rights.[26] But it cannot be described that way for the Jane tradition without begging questions.

Within the Jane tradition, the problem was taken to be one of meaningful lives for women, or of free choice among genuine alternatives for meaningful lives. Some phrasing of the general problem in these terms seems appropriate to both traditions. Let me quote Betty Friedan, an activist who stands within traditions associated with Judith Thomson's:

> It is my thesis that the core of the problem for women today is not sexual but a problem of identity—a stunting or evasion of growth that is perpetuated by the feminine mystique. It is my thesis that as the Victorian culture did not permit women to accept or gratify their basic sexual needs, our culture does not permit women to accept or gratify their basic need to grow and fulfill their potentialities as human beings, a need which is not solely defined by their sexual roles.[27]

The statement of purpose of the liberal feminist National Organization for Women (NOW)

also concerns opportunities for a meaningful life and moral development as a human being: NOW pledges to "take action to bring women into full participation in the mainstream of American society now, exercising all the privileges and responsibilities thereof, in truly equal partnership with men."[28] This makes it appear that for both traditions, the problem may be stated as one of equality, particularly equality so far as it relates to the moral questions of being a full human being and of having a meaningful (or good) life. I believe that this is a central concern of those within the Judith Thomson tradition. But it may be that the problem cannot be resolved under that tradition or its associated world view.

Concealing Data

In Part III, I presented the moral activity of the organization Jane under one tradition. If we look at the Jane organization under the Judith Thomson tradition, we get a different selection of data. Here's a quotation from the newspaper article:

> From the beginning, we discussed the moral implications of abortion from all angles. We listened to right-to-lifers, Catholic clergy, population-control freaks and women's liberationists.
>
> We heard legislators and lobbyists and political commentators arguing fine points of "fetal viability." When does a fetus become a person? When it can survive outside the womb (after six months)? When it begins to move (after four months)? Or from the moment of conception?
>
> Many opponents of abortion called it "murder." We argued the logical counterarguments: If a fetus is a person, then why aren't abortionists and women who have abortions charged with murder?
>
> Or, if the fetus has the rights of a person, then does the woman who carries it become subject to its rights? What happens when the rights of the woman and those of the fetus come into conflict?
>
> All philosophical and legalistic positions lost relevance when we began doing and viewing abortions . . . we knew that we were grappling with matters of life and death and no philosophical arguments could alter that belief.[29]

Judith Thomson, or someone from her tradition, would have been a great help to the Jane women in these early discussions on abortion. On the other hand, these early discussions had no clear relevance to the central moral activity the women of Jane were engaging in—*by their own judgment.* The terms in which they saw the problem were different. Their perception and their moral activity constitute data which are important to solving the problem of equality, but the Judith Thomson tradition not only ignores those data: it makes them invisible. Let's look at some of the mechanisms by which the data are concealed.

One way a tradition conceals data is through the concepts and categories it uses. The Judith Thomson tradition would focus on the Jane discussions of rights. It would ignore the discussions of hierarchy, dominance, and subordination; and perhaps some within the tradition would not take these as morally relevant discussions at all. Any theory must use concepts. Through their very use, some data are selected and some ignored. Yet the question of whether the concepts properly capture the data, or of whether they are *appropriate,* is a central critical question about the adequacy of any tradition.

In a similar way, the categories a tradition uses to organize data reveal some and conceal others. For example, the Judith Thomson tradition uses the categories of moral agent and of groups of moral agents as aggregates. The tradition also uses a division of moral phenomena into questions of individual conscience and those of public policy, where the latter is a matter of *official* public policy, made by those with legitimate authority. I don't want to argue that the tradition *rules out* other sorts of moral phenomena. But using those categories, it cannot capture the sort of moral phenomena Jane members took to be central: people in a subordinate position acting to create a set of social relations which are not structured by dominance and subordination, through the subordinates' coming to know their own power (as opposed to legitimate authority) through acting in collectives (not aggregates).

But am I being fair to the Judith Thomson tradition? After all, people within it don't claim to cover *all* moral phenomena. Few theories claim to cover everything within their purview, and even within chemistry there are divisions into organic and inorganic. Mightn't there be divisions within the field of moral phenomena so that another part of the tradition might deal with Jane's moral activity and thus reveal it?

Perhaps any new moral tradition we develop will have to have something to do with the concept of rights (and associated concepts), and deal in some way with groups as aggregates and with public policy as officially handed down. But that new tradition could not be the Judith Thomson tradition, for a revolutionary change in the methodology of her tradition is necessary to uncover data like Jane's.

The Judith Thomson tradition supposes that there exists a set of moral concepts embedded in moral principles which "we" all know and understand. In her paper, Judith Thomson herself is clarifying concepts "we" grasp by the standard method of the tradition: the use of hypothetical cases. This method presupposes a very mentalistic view of concepts and word meanings—mentalistic in the way philosophical empiricists are mentalistic in their views on meanings as "ideas." The concepts exist in the speaker's understanding. If someone understands the concept, he or she knows whether it applies in any given case.[30] Considering hypothetical cases (in this view) points out cases the speaker might have overlooked; but once they are brought to his or her attention, the speaker allegedly knows whether the concepts apply or not, and so his or her explicit understanding of the concept is clarified. Similarly, one's explicit understanding of "our" moral principles is supposed to be clarified by considering hypothetical cases.

The most obvious thing to say about this method is that although bringing up hypothetical cases may clarify our understanding of concepts and principles, everyone knows that the selection of hypothetical cases also biases understanding. This bias may be (unintentionally) systematic. For example, Judith Thomson gives a case where Jones faces a frosty death because Smith owns the coat. Why not, instead, use a case where men, women, and children face poor diets, poor housing, and loss of dignity because the owner of a mill decides to move it out of one region into another having cheaper labor and lower tax rates? Philosophers may say the second example is too complicated, but the selection is not a trivial matter of simplicity. The coat example ignores an essential distinction in kinds of property ownership which the mill example reveals.

The method rules out empirical investigation to see what sorts of hypothetical cases might capture what is morally important to persons in a variety of circumstances in the United States. There seems to be no way whatsoever to insure that a fair consideration of hypothetical cases is made to reduce the bias. One can't develop a sampling procedure for hypothetical cases.

Worst of all, the method rules out empirical investigation to discover whether the moral concepts and principles the philosophers are dealing with are really the moral concepts which people use in the United States. It rules out empirical investigation to discover whether those concepts and those moral principles are relevant to the lives of people in different walks of life, investigation to discover whether they are relevant to solving those people's problems of human dignity and a meaningful life *as those people perceive* those problems.

The method itself has the mere appearance of being plausible only for ancient systems of concepts which are well worked out. It has not even the appearance of plausibility for a case like Jane's, in which people are in the process of creating new concepts through creating new social forms. The fundamental theory of meaning, of understanding, and of concept formation on which the method is based is not only inadequate: it is false.

All of this means that to encompass the Jane data, a revolutionary change is necessary in the methodology of the Judith Thomson tradition. Without it, the data remain concealed.

The data being concealed concern human moral activity and the possibilities of changing society. This constitutes a direct and very important value consequence. The Judith Thomson tradition dominates philosophy departments in the prestigious American universities, and even teachers in nonprestigious colleges are trained within it. This means that students are taught to see moral activity within that tradition. Activity requiring patterns of thinking and concepts and categories like Jane's is made invisible to them.

Official Points of View

From its beginnings, the tradition Judith Thomson works within has been centrally concerned with equality. People in this tradition have particularly been concerned that all human beings be equal under the moral law and under the positive law of the state. Equality before the moral or positive law means that the same laws and principles apply to all. Whether or not this is enlightened depends on which laws and principles one chooses and the society in which they apply.

The question of equality which those in the Jane tradition raise is one which takes dominant-subordinate structures in the society as *creators* of inequality. Their solution to the problem of equality is the use of the perception and power of the subordinate to eliminate dominant-subordinate structures through the creation of new social forms which do not have that structure. Those in the Judith Thomson tradition do not raise questions of dominance and subordination except in the moral, legal, and political spheres, where they are seen in terms of moral, legal, and political equality. Particularly, they do not raise the question of whether equality before the moral or positive law may not be rendered empty because of the dominant-subordinate structures in the economic or social (e.g., family) spheres.

It appears that there is a bias in our world view. It is a bias that allows moral problems to be defined from the top of various hierarchies of authority in such a way that the existence of the authority is concealed, and so the existence of alternative definitions that might challenge that authority and radically change our social organization is also concealed. But having acknowledged that, we must return to the question I asked at the beginning of the paper.

Part V: The Intellectual Pursuits

In this paper, I believe I uncovered a bias that requires a revolutionary change in ethics to remedy. But in the process of considering two approaches to the moral problem of abortion, it has become clear that there are serious questions to ask about the question with which I began the paper:

> Has a covert bias been introduced into our world view by the near exclusion of women from the domain of intellectual pursuits? If we ask about a bias in "our" world view, mustn't we ask who that "we" refers to? In fact, doesn't the question presuppose that "our" world view is constructed by people in the "intellectual pursuits"? That is, doesn't it presuppose a hierarchy of authority in which people in some occupations (academic humanists and scientists, professional writers, etc.) define a world view for everyone else? If so, then there is something further that the Jane case shows.

Judith Jarvis Thomson is a woman working in an established intellectual pursuit, and at the time she wrote her paper, she took a stand that amounted to criticizing certain ethical arguments for sex bias. She took her stand as an authority, she criticized other authorities, and her paper has been widely used by still other authorities who are certified to teach ethics classes. I have criticized her work in this paper, but I too write as an authority. This leads us to a certain conundrum—if I may call it that.

The women of Jane were certainly challenging the way men in important positions are certified to define the way we do things and, in fact, their authority to define "our" world view and say how things "really are." But some of the Jane members, at least, were not saying that we should remedy the problem by having women in important positions define the way we do things. They were saying that we should change the way we do things so that we do not have some important people giving the official world view for everyone else. That change cannot be accomplished merely by hiring more women to work in the intellectual pursuits. It requires changing the intellectual pursuits themselves. If Jane shows that we need a revolutionary change from the old moral theory, it is a change in the status of the authorities as well as a change in what has been taken to be moral theory. Unless we strive to find ways to do that, we violate the central moral and scientific injunction for respecting other human beings:

> . . . look upon human group life as chiefly a vast interpretive process in which people, singly and collectively *guide themselves* by *defining* the objects, events and situations they encounter.[31]

Notes

1. Judith Jarvis Thomson, "A Defense of Abortion," *Philosophy and Public Affairs* 1 (September 1971): 47–66. Reprinted in Chapter 8 of this volume.

2. Arlene Kaplan Daniels, "Feminist Perspectives in Sociological Research," in *Another Voice,* ed. Marcia Millman and Rosabeth Moss Kanter (Garden City, New York, 1975), p. 345.

3. Lyn Lofland, "The 'Thereness' of Women: A Selective Review of Urban Sociology," in Millman and Kanter, *Another Voice,* pp. 145–46, citing Herbert Blumer, *Symbolic Interactionism* (Englewood Cliffs, N.J., 1969), p. 132.

4. Lofland, "The 'Thereness' of Women," p. 162.

5. Thomas Kuhn, *The Structure of Scientific Revolutions,* 2nd ed. (Chicago, 1970).

6. Joel Feinberg, ed., *The Problem of Abortion* (Belmont, Calif., 1973), p. 1. All subsequent quotations from Judith Thomson's essay are from this edition.

7. John Locke's work forms an important foundation to this tradition, and the centrality of the concept of property to the concept of rights is explicit in his *Second Treatise of Government.*

8. Both the Marxists and the Freudians among us will raise their eyebrows at the use of this hypothetical case to explain the concept of justice. Plato, of course, would turn over in his grave.

9. Some repercussions for constitutional law are discussed in Betty Sarvis and Hyman Rodman, *The Abortion Controversy* (New York, 1974).

10. For their help in this part of the paper, I thank Howard Becker for his assistance with references on abortion and Shawn

Pyne for her zeal and imagination in searching the library.

11. For a discussion of abortion laws see Sarvis and Rodman, *The Abortion Controversy.* An excellent and more detailed discussion is given by Kristin Booth Glen in "Abortion in the Courts: A Laywoman's Historical Guide to the New Disaster Area," *Feminist Studies* (January 1978): 1–26. Glen traces the political implications of the fact that the decision turned on the right of physicians to make medical decisions, not on the rights of women. The Supreme Court declared state laws restricting abortion unconstitutional on 22 January 1973.

12. See Willard Cates and R. W. Rochat, "Illegal Abortion in the United States: 1972–74," *Family Planning Perspectives* 8 (March/April 1976): 86–92.

13. Pauline B. Bart, Abraham Lincoln School of Medicine, University of Illinois, Chicago, "Seizing the Means of Reproduction," in *Qualitative Sociology,* based on interviews with forty-two members of the Jane collective. I did not know of this study in time to incorporate it into my discussion in this section.

14. Jane, "The Most Remarkable Abortion Story Ever Told," Hyde Park-Kenwood *Voices,* June 1973, p. 2.

15. Ibid.

16. At this time, most abortionists refused to handle women more than twelve weeks pregnant. Nancy Howell Lee, *Search for an Abortionist* (Chicago, 1969), p. 6.

17. Op. Cit., Part VI, November 1973, p. 3.

18. The arrest was in the third year of the service. It appears to have been a renegade action by a few policemen, not a planned political arrest.

19. Jane members had to take on other duties too. Each week during its peak, the service used fifty ampules of ergotrate, ten bottles of xylocaine, a hundred disposable syringes, and six hundred tablets each of tetracycline and ergotrate. For a while, Dr. C's nurse had obtained the drugs. Eventually, Jane members had to devise ways of getting illegal supplies.

20. Lee, *Search for an Abortionist,* p. 161. In New York in the early 1960s, 93 percent of legal, therapeutic abortions were performed on white, private patients. During that period in the United States as a whole, the rate of legal abortions per 1,000 live births was 3.17 for private patients and 0.87 for clinic patients (those entering the hospital without a private physician). In Georgia in 1970, twenty-four times as many legal abortions were performed on unmarried white women as on unmarried black women. Sarvis and Rodman, *The Abortion Controversy,* p. 159.

21. Lee, *Search for an Abortionist,* pp. 169–70.

22. Information about illegal abortionists is spread through informal networks of acquaintances. More affluent women have more access to information about illegal abortionists of quality because they have acquaintances (some of them physicians) who have this information. Jane overcame this by publishing the telephone number of the service in underground newspapers and otherwise publicly spreading word about the service, through brochures, the Chicago Women's Liberation Union, and so on. See Lee, *Search for an Abortionist,* for extensive discussions on this.

23. I spoke with two women who worked with Jane, although only one interview is used in this paper. Both said that patients waited in the *living room.* They never called it the waiting room—although professionals using a house or apartment as an office, e.g., psychotherapists call the living room the waiting room. Both said that abortions were done in the *bedroom.* They never used the term *operating room* or anything similar. This was part of the attempt to demystify medicine. Some other abortionists made great efforts to cloak themselves in medical mystique—Dr. C is an example, since he called himself "Doctor" when he was not. For a description of one service which smothered the patient in medical mystique (and for a glaring contrast with Jane), see Donald W. Ball, "An Abortion Clinic Ethnography," *Social Problems* 14 (Winter 1967): 293–301.

24. Howard Becker, "Whose Side Are We On?" *Sociological Work* (New Brunswick, N.J., 1977), p. 126.

25. From what I had learned from other sources, it seemed to me that Emma Goldman had been less successful as a nonauthoritarian, nonhierarchical collective activity offering first-quality service. I asked Jane about this. She said that because the abortion service was illegal, it was free of many authoritarian and hierarchal pressures from the medical profession. Because Emma Goldman was a legal clinic, it had to accommodate itself to the medical profession—by maintaining relations with physicians, for example, who would let the clinic use their licenses. This introduced factors of authority because of the licensing procedure, and with it, hierarchy. For a discussion of self-help, see Boston Women's Health Book Collective, *Our Bodies, Ourselves,* 3rd ed. (New York, 1976), pp. 361–68.

26. For example, her interpreting women's remark, "This body is *my* body" by analogy with rights involved in property ownership parallels the great initial step toward equality made by John Locke when he interpreted a man's relation to his body and labor power by analogy with rights involved in property ownership.

27. Betty Friedan, *The Feminine Mystique* (New York, 1974), p. 69. The work, originally published in 1963, was a major force in initiating the "second wave" in feminism.

28. Ibid., p. 270. Betty Friedan was one of the founders of NOW. Liberal feminists share important parts of a world view with those in the Judith Thomson tradition. They are much more radical than the philosophers, however, in part because they are feminists, in part because they are activists.

29. Jane, "The Most Remarkable Abortion Story," Part VI, *Voices,* November 1973, p. 3.

30. Unless the concept is vague, in which case no one knows whether it applies in certain cases until some sort of definitional decision is made on whether it applies.

31. Blumer, *Symbolic Interactionism,* p. 132.

Study Questions

1. What is Addelson trying to show by using Judith Thomson's article on abortion?

2. What was "Jane"? What did it do, and what were the reasons for its activities?

3. What is the difference in the way the problem of abortion is viewed in the Thomson tradition and in the Jane tradition? How does the Thomson tradition "conceal data" about Jane's activities?

4. According to Addelson, what are the drawbacks of the method of considering hypothetical cases (a method she associates with the Judith Thomson tradition).

5. How does the Jane tradition view the problem of inequality? Why does Addelson think that Judith Thomson incorporates a dominant-subordinate structure?

In a Different Voice: Women's Conceptions of Self and of Morality

Carol Gilligan

The arc of developmental theory leads from infantile dependence to adult autonomy, tracing a path characterized by an increasing differentiation of self from other and a progressive freeing of thought from contextual constraints. The vision of Luther, journeying from the rejection of a self defined by others to the assertive boldness of "Here I stand" and the image of Plato's allegorical man in the cave, separating at last the shadows from the sun, have taken powerful hold on the psychological understanding of what constitutes development. Thus, the individual, meeting fully the developmental challenges of adolescence as set for him by Piaget, Erikson, and Kohlberg, thinks formally, proceeding from theory to fact, and defines both the self and the moral autonomously, that is, apart from the identification and conventions that had comprised the particulars of his childhood world. So equipped, he is presumed ready to live as an adult, to love and work in a way that is both intimate and generative, to develop an ethical sense of caring and a genital mode of relating in which giving and taking fuse in the ultimate reconciliation of the tension between self and other.

Yet the men whose theories have largely informed this understanding of development have all been plagued by the same problem, the problem of women, whose sexuality remains more diffuse, whose perception of self is so much more tenaciously embedded in relationships with others and whose moral dilemmas hold them in a mode of judgment that is insistently contextual. The solution has been to consider women as either deviant or deficient in their development.

That there is a discrepancy between concepts of womanhood and adulthood is nowhere more clearly evident than in the series of studies on sex-role stereotypes reported by Broverman, Vogel, Broverman, Clarkson, and Rosenkrantz (1972). The repeated finding of these studies is that the qualities deemed necessary for adulthood—the capacity for autonomous thinking, clear decision making, and responsible action—are those associated with masculinity but considered undesirable as attributes of the feminine self. The stereotypes suggest a splitting of love and work that relegates the expressive capacities requisite for the former to women while the instrumental abilities necessary for the latter reside in the masculine domain. Yet, looked at from a different perspective, these stereotypes reflect a conception of adulthood that is itself out of balance, favoring the separateness of the individual self over its connection to others and leaning more toward an autonomous life of work than toward the interdependence of love and care.

This difference in point of view is the subject of this essay, which seeks to identify in the feminine experience and construction of social reality a distinctive voice, recognizable in the different perspective it brings to bear on the construction and resolution of moral problems. The first section begins with the repeated observation of difference in women's concepts of self and of morality. This difference is identified in previous psychological descriptions of women's moral judgments and described as it again appears in current research data. Examples drawn from interviews with women in and around a university community are used to illustrate the characteristics of the feminine voice. The relational bias in women's thinking that has, in the past, been seen to compromise their moral judgment and impede their development now begins to emerge in a new developmental light. Instead of being seen as a developmental deficiency, this bias appears to reflect a different social and moral understanding.

This alternative conception is enlarged in the second section through consideration of research interviews with women facing the moral dilemma of whether to continue or abort a pregnancy. Since the research design allowed women to define as well as resolve the moral problem, developmental distinctions could be derived directly from the categories of women's thought. The responses of women to structured interview questions regarding the pregnancy decision formed the basis for describing a developmental sequence that traces progressive differentiations in their understanding and judgment of conflicts between self and other. While the sequence of women's moral development follows the three-level progression of all social developmental theory, from an egocentric through a societal to a universal perspective, this progression takes place within a distinct moral conception. This conception differs from that derived by Kohlberg from his all-male longitudinal research data.

This difference then becomes the basis in the third section for challenging the current assessment of women's moral judgment at the same time that it brings to bear a new perspective on developmental assessment in general. The inclusion in the overall conception of development of those categories derived from the study of women's moral judgment enlarges developmental understanding, enabling it to encompass better the thinking of both sexes. This is particularly true with respect to the construction and resolution of the dilemmas of adult life. Since the conception of adulthood retrospectively shapes the theoretical understanding of the development that precedes it, the changes in that conception that follow from the more central inclusion of women's judgments recast developmental understanding and lead to a reconsideration of the substance of social and moral development.

Characteristics of the Feminine Voice

The revolutionary contribution of Piaget's work is the experimental confirmation and refinement of Kant's assertion that knowledge is actively constructed rather than passively received. Time, space, self, and other, as well as the categories of developmental theory, all arise out of the active interchange between the individual and the physical and social world in which he lives and of which he strives to make sense. The development of cognition is the process of reappropriating reality at progressively more complex levels of apprehension, as the structures of thinking expand to encompass the increasing richness and intricacy of experience.

Moral development, in the work of Piaget and Kohlberg, refers specifically to the expanding conception of the social world as it is reflected in the understanding and resolution of the inevitable conflicts that arise in the relations between self and others. The moral judgment is a statement of priority, an attempt at rational resolution in a situation where, from a different point of view, the choice itself seems to do violence to justice.

Kohlberg (1969), in his extension of the early work of Piaget, discovered six stages of moral judgment, which he claimed formed an invariant sequence, each successive stage representing a more adequate construction of the moral problem, which in turn provides the basis for its more just resolution. The stages divide into three levels, each of which denotes a significant expansion of the moral point of view from an egocentric through a societal to a universal ethical conception. With this expansion in perspective comes the capacity to free moral judgment from the individual needs and social conventions with which it had earlier been confused and anchor it instead in principles of justice that are universal in application. These principles provide criteria upon which both individual and societal claims can be impartially assessed. In Kohlberg's view, at the highest stages of development morality is freed from both psychological and historical constraints, and the individual can judge independently of his own particular needs and of the values of those around him.

That the moral sensibility of women differs from that of men was noted by Freud (1925/1961) in the following by now well-quoted statement:

I cannot evade the notion (though I hesitate to give it expression) that for women the level of what is ethically normal is different from what it is in man. Their superego is never so inexorable, so impersonal, so independent of its emotional origins as we require it to be in men. Character-traits which critics of every epoch have brought up against women—that they show less sense of justice than men, that they are less ready to submit to the great exigencies of life, that they are more often influenced in their judgments by feelings of affection or hostility—all these would be amply accounted for by the modification in the formation of their super-ego which we have inferred above.

While Freud's explanation lies in the deviation of female from male development around the construction and resolution of the Oedipal problem, the same observations about the nature of morality in women emerge from the work of Piaget and Kohlberg. Piaget (1932/ 1965), in his study of the rules of children's games, observed that, in the games they played, girls were "less explicit about agreement [than boys] and less concerned with legal elaboration." In contrast to the boys' interest in the codification of rules, the girls adopted a more pragmatic attitude, regarding "a rule as good so long as the game repays it." As a result, in comparison to boys, girls were found to be "more tolerant and more easily reconciled to innovations."

Kohlberg (1971) also identifies a strong interpersonal bias in the moral judgments of women, which leads them to be considered as typically at the third of his six-stage developmental sequence. At that stage, the good is identified "with what pleases or helps others and is approved of by them." This mode of judgment is conventional in its conformity to generally held notions of the good but also psychological in its concern with intention and consequence as the basis for judging the morality of action.

That women fall largely into this level of moral judgment is hardly surprising when we read from the Broverman et al. (1972) list that prominent among the twelve attributes considered to be desirable for women are tact, gentleness, awareness of the feelings of others, strong need for security, and easy expression of tender feelings. And yet, herein lies the paradox, for the very traits that have traditionally defined the "goodness" of women, their care for and sensitivity to the needs of others, are those that mark them as deficient in moral development. The infusion of feeling into their judgments keeps them from developing a more independent and abstract ethical conception in which concern for others derives from principles of justice rather than from compassion and care. Kohlberg, however, is less pessimistic than Freud in his assessment, for he sees the development of women as extending beyond the interpersonal level, following the same path toward independent, principled judgment that he discovered in the research on men from which his stages were derived. In Kohlberg's view, women's development will proceed beyond Stage Three when they are challenged to solve moral problems that require them to see beyond the relationships that have in the past generally bound their moral experience.

What then do women say when asked to construct the moral domain; how do we identify the characteristically "feminine" voice? A Radcliffe undergraduate, responding to the question, "If you had to say what morality meant to you, how would you sum it up?" replies:

> When I think of the word morality, I think of obligations. I usually think of it as conflicts between personal desires and social things, social considerations, or personal desires of yourself versus personal desires of another person or people or whatever. Morality is that whole realm of how you decide these conflicts. A moral person is one who would decide, like by placing themselves more often than not as equals, a truly moral person would always consider another person as their equal . . . in a situation of social interaction, something is morally wrong where the individual ends up screwing a lot of people. And it is morally right when everyone comes out better off.*

Yet when asked if she can think of someone whom she would consider a genuinely moral person, she replies, "Well, immediately I think

---

*The Radcliffe women whose responses are cited were interviewed as part of a pilot study on undergraduate moral development conducted by the author in 1970.

of Albert Schweitzer because he has obviously given his life to help others." Obligation and sacrifice override the ideal of equality, setting up a basic contradiction in her thinking.

Another undergraduate responds to the question, "What does it mean to say something is morally right or wrong?," by also speaking first of responsibilities and obligations:

> Just that it has to do with responsibilities and obligations and values, mainly values. . . . In my life situation I relate morality with interpersonal relationships that have to do with respect for the other person and myself. [Why respect other people?] Because they have a consciousness or feelings that can be hurt, an awareness that can be hurt.

The concern about hurting others persists as a major theme in the responses of two other Radcliffe students:

> [Why be moral?] Millions of people have to live together peacefully. I personally don't want to hurt other people. That's a real criterion, a main criterion for me. It underlies my sense of justice. It isn't nice to inflict pain. I empathize with anyone in pain. Not hurting others is important in my own private morals. Years ago, I would have jumped out of a window not to hurt my boyfriend. That was pathological. Even today though, I want approval and love and I don't want enemies. Maybe that's why there is morality—so people can win approval, love and friendship.

> My main moral principle is not hurting other people as long as you aren't going against your own conscience and as long as you remain true to yourself. . . . There are many moral issues such as abortion, the draft, killing, stealing, monogamy, etc. If something is a controversial issue like these, then I always say it is up to the individual. The individual has to decide and then follow his own conscience. There are no moral absolutes. . . . Laws are pragmatic instruments, but they are not absolutes. A viable society can't make exceptions all the time, but I would personally. . . . I'm afraid I'm heading for some big crisis with my boyfriend someday, and someone will get hurt, and he'll get more hurt than I will. I feel an obligation not to hurt him, but also an obligation to not lie. I don't know if it is possible to not lie and not hurt.

The common thread that runs through these statements, the wish not to hurt others and the hope that in morality lies a way of solving conflicts so that no one will get hurt, is striking in that it is independently introduced by each of the four women as the most specific item in their response to a most general question. The moral person is one who helps others; goodness is service, meeting one's obligations and responsibilities to others, if possible, without sacrificing oneself. While the first of the four women ends by denying the conflict she initially introduced, the last woman anticipates a conflict between remaining true to herself and adhering to her principle of not hurting others. The dilemma that would test the limits of this judgment would be one where helping others is seen to be at the price of hurting the self.

The reticence about taking stands on "controversial issues," the willingness to "make exceptions all the time" expressed in the final example above, is echoed repeatedly by other Radcliffe students, as in the following two examples:

> I never feel that I can condemn anyone else. I have a very relativistic position. The basic idea that I cling to is the sanctity of human life. I am inhibited about impressing my beliefs on others.

> I could never argue that my belief on a moral question is anything that another person should accept. I don't believe in absolutes. . . . If there is an absolute for moral decisions, it is human life.

Or as a thirty-one-year-old Wellesley graduate says, in explaining why she would find it difficult to steal a drug to save her own life despite her belief that it would be right to steal for another: "It's just very hard to defend yourself against the rules. I mean, we live by consensus, and you take an action simply for yourself, by yourself, there's no consensus there, and that is relatively indefensible in this society now."

What begins to emerge is a sense of vulnerability that impedes these women from taking a stand, what George Eliot (1860/1965) regards as the girl's "susceptibility" to adverse judgments of others, which stems from her lack of power and consequent inability to do something in the world. While relativism in men, the unwillingness to make moral judgments that

Kohlberg and Kramer (1969) and Kohlberg and Gilligan (1971) have associated with the adolescent crisis of identity and belief, takes the form of calling into question the concept of morality itself, the women's reluctance to judge stems rather from their uncertainty about their right to make moral statements or, perhaps, the price for them that such judgment seems to entail. This contrast echoes that made by Matina Horner (1972), who differentiated the ideological fear of success expressed by men from the personal conflicts about succeeding that riddled the women's responses to stories of competitive achievement.

> Most of the men who responded with the expectation of negative consequences because of success were not concerned about their masculinity but were instead likely to have expressed existential concerns about finding a "non-materialistic happiness and satisfaction in life." These concerns, which reflect changing attitudes toward traditional kinds of success or achievement in our society, played little, if any, part in the female stories. Most of the women who were high in fear of success imagery continued to be concerned about the discrepancy between success in the situation described and feminine identity.

When women feel excluded from direct participation in society, they see themselves as subject to a consensus or judgment made and enforced by the men on whose protection and support they depend and by whose names they are known. A divorced middle-aged woman, mother of adolescent daughters, resident of a sophisticated university community, tells the story as follows:

> As a woman, I feel I never understood that I was a person, that I can make decisions and I have a right to make decisions. I always felt that that belonged to my father or my husband in some way or church which was always represented by a male clergyman. They were the three men in my life; father, husband, and clergyman, and they had much more to say about what I should or shouldn't do. They were really authority figures which I accepted. I didn't rebel against that. It only has lately occurred to me that I never even rebelled against it, and my girls are much more conscious of this, not in the militant sense, but just in the recognizing sense. . . . I still let things happen to me rather than make them happen, than to make choices, although I know all about choices. I know the procedures and the steps and all. [Do you have any clues about why this might be true?] Well, I think in one sense, there is less responsibility involved. Because if you make a dumb decision, you have to take the rap. If it happens to you, well, you can complain about it. I think that if you don't grow up feeling that you ever had any choices, you don't either have the sense that you have emotional responsibility. With this sense of choice comes this sense of responsibility.

The essence of the moral decision is the exercise of choice and the willingness to accept responsibility for that choice. To the extent that women perceive themselves as having no choice, they correspondingly excuse themselves from the responsibility that decision entails. Childlike in the vulnerability of their dependence and consequent fear of abandonment, they claim to wish only to please but in return for their goodness they expect to be loved and cared for. This, then, is an "altruism" always at risk, for it presupposes an innocence constantly in danger of being compromised by an awareness of the trade-off that has been made. Asked to describe herself, a Radcliffe senior responds:

> I have heard of the onion skin theory. I see myself as an onion, as a block of different layers, the external layers for people that I don't know that well, the agreeable, the social, and as you go inward there are more sides for people I know that I show. I am not sure about the innermost, whether there is a core, or whether I have just picked up everything as I was growing up, these different influences. I think I have a neutral attitude towards myself, but I do think in terms of good and bad. . . . Good— I try to be considerate and thoughtful of other people and I try to be fair in situations and be tolerant. I use the words but I try and work them out practically. . . . Bad things—I am not sure if they are bad, if they are altruistic or I am doing them basically for approval of other people. [Which things are these?] The values I have when I try to act them out. They deal mostly with interpersonal type relations. . . . If I were doing it for approval, it would be a very tenuous thing. If I didn't get the right feedback, there might go all my values.

Ibsen's play, *A Doll House* (1879/1965), depicts the explosion of just such a world through the eruption of a moral dilemma that calls into question the notion of goodness that lies at its center. Nora, the "squirrel wife," living with her husband as she had lived with her father, puts into action this conception of goodness as sacrifice and, with the best of intentions, takes the law into her own hands. The crisis that ensues, most painfully for her in the repudiation of that goodness by the very person who was its recipient and beneficiary, causes her to reject the suicide that she had intially seen as its ultimate expression and chose instead to seek new and firmer answers to the adolescent questions of identity and belief.

The availability of choice and with it the onus of responsibility has now invaded the most private sector of the woman's domain and threatens a similar explosion. For centuries, women's sexuality anchored them in passivity, in a receptive rather than active stance, where the events of conception and childbirth could be controlled only by a withholding in which their own sexual needs were either denied or sacrificed. That such a sacrifice entailed a cost to their intelligence as well was seen by Freud (1908/1959) when he tied the "undoubted intellectual inferiority of so many women" to "the inhibition of thought necessitated by sexual suppression." The strategies of withholding and denial that women have employed in the politics of sexual relations appear similar to their evasion or withholding of judgment in the moral realm. The hesitance expressed in the previous examples to impose even a belief in the value of human life on others, like the reluctance to claim one's sexuality, bespeaks a self uncertain of its strength, unwilling to deal with consequence, and thus avoiding confrontation.

Thus women have traditionally deferred to the judgment of men, although often while intimating a sensibility of their own which is at variance with that judgment. Maggie Tulliver, in *The Mill on the Floss* (Eliot, 1860/1965) responds to the accusations that ensue from the discovery of her secretly continued relationship with Philip Wakeham by acceding to her brother's moral judgment while at the same time asserting a different set of standards by which she attests her own superiority:

I don't want to defend myself. . . . I know I've been wrong—often continually. But yet, sometimes when I have done wrong, it has been because I have feelings that you would be the better for if you had them. If *you* were in fault ever, if you had done anything very wrong, I should be sorry for the pain it brought you; I should not want punishment to be heaped on you.

An eloquent defense, Kohlberg would argue, of a Stage Three moral position, an assertion of the age-old split between thinking and feeling, justice and mercy, that underlies many of the clichés and stereotypes concerning the difference between the sexes. But considered from another point of view, it is a moment of confrontation, replacing a former evasion, between two modes of judging, two differing constructions of the moral domain—one traditionally associated with masculinity and the public world of social power, the other with femininity and the privacy of domestic interchange. While the developmental ordering of these two points of view has been to consider the masculine as the more adequate and thus as replacing the feminine as the individual moves toward higher stages, their reconciliation remains unclear.

The Development of Women's Moral Judgment

Recent evidence for a divergence in moral development between men and women comes from the research of Haan (Note 1) and Holstein (1976) whose findings lead them to question the possibility of a "sex-related bias" in Kohlberg's scoring system. This system is based on Kohlberg's six-stage description of moral development. Kohlberg's stages divide into three levels, which he designates as preconventional, conventional, and postconventional, thus denoting the major shifts in moral perspective around a center of moral understanding that equates justice with the maintenance of existing social systems. While the preconventional conception of justice is based on the needs of the self, the conventional judgment derives from an understanding of society.

This understanding is in turn superseded by a postconventional or principled conception of justice where the good is formulated in universal terms. The quarrel with Kohlberg's stage scoring does not pertain to the structural differentiation of his levels but rather to questions of stage and sequence. Kohlberg's stages begin with an obedience and punishment orientation (Stage One), and go from there in invariant order to instrumental hedonism (Stage Two), interpersonal concordance (Stage Three), law and order (Stage Four), social contract (Stage Five), and universal ethical principles (Stage Six).

The bias that Haan and Holstein question in this scoring system has to do with the subordination of the interpersonal to the societal definition of the good in the transition from Stage Three to Stage Four. This is the transition that has repeatedly been found to be problematic for women. In 1969, Kohlberg and Kramer identified Stage Three as the characteristic mode of women's moral judgments, claiming that, since women's lives were interpersonally based, this stage was not only "functional" for them but also adequate for resolving the moral conflicts that they faced. Turiel (1973; Note 2) reported that while girls reached Stage Three sooner than did boys, their judgments tended to remain at that stage while the boys' development continued further along Kohlberg's scale. Gilligan, Kohlberg, Lerner, and Belenky (1971) found a similar association between sex and moral-judgment stage in a study of high-school students, with the girls' responses being scored predominantly at Stage Three while the boys' responses were more often scored at Stage Four.

This repeated finding of developmental inferiority in women may, however, have more to do with the standard by which development has been measured than with the quality of women's thinking per se. Haan's data (Note 1) on the Berkeley Free Speech Movement and Holstein's (1976) three-year longitudinal study of adolescents and their parents indicate that the moral judgments of women differ from those of men in the greater extent to which women's judgments are tied to feelings of empathy and compassion and are concerned more with the resolution of "real-life" as opposed to hypothetical dilemmas (Note 1, p. 34). However, as long as the categories by which development is assessed are derived within a male perspective from male research data, divergence from the masculine standard can be seen only as a failure of development. As a result, the thinking of women is often classified with that of children. The systematic exclusion from consideration of alternative criteria that might better encompass the development of women indicates not only the limitations of a theory framed by men and validated by research samples disproportionately male and adolescent but also the effects of the diffidence prevalent among women, their reluctance to speak publicly in their own voice, given the constraints imposed on them by the politics of differential power between the sexes.

In order to go beyond the question, "How much like men do women think, how capable are they of engaging in the abstract and hypothetical construction of reality?" it is necessary to identify and define in formal terms developmental criteria that encompass the categories of women's thinking. Such criteria would include the progressive differentiations, comprehensiveness, and adequacy that characterize higher-stage resolution of the "more frequently occurring, real-life moral dilemmas of interpersonal, empathic, fellow-feeling concerns" (Haan, Note 1, p. 34), which have long been the center of women's moral judgments and experience. To ascertain whether the feminine construction of the moral domain relies on a language different from that of men, but one which deserves equal credence in the definition of what constitutes development, it is necessary first to find the places where women have the power to choose and thus are willing to speak in their own voice.

When birth control and abortion provide women with effective means for controlling their fertility, the dilemma of choice enters the center of women's lives. Then the relationships that have traditionally defined women's identities and framed their moral judgments no longer flow inevitably from their reproductive capacity but become matters of decision over which they have control. Released from the passivity and reticence of a sexuality that binds them in dependence, it becomes possible for women to question with Freud what it is that they want and to assert their own answers to that question. However, while society may affirm publicly the woman's right to choose for herself, the exercise of such choice brings her privately into conflict with the conventions of femininity, particularly the moral equation of goodness with self-sacrifice. While independent assertion in judgment and action is considered the hallmark of adulthood and constitutes as well the standard of masculine development, it is rather in their care and concern for others that women have both judged themselves and been judged.

The conflict between self and other thus constitutes the central moral problem for women, posing a dilemma whose resolution requires a reconciliation between femininity and adulthood. In the absence of such a reconciliation, the moral problem cannot be resolved. The "good woman" masks assertion in evasion, denying responsibility by claiming only to meet the needs of others, while the "bad woman" forgoes or renounces the commitments that bind her in self-deception and betrayal. It is precisely this dilemma—the conflict between compassion and autonomy, between virtue and power—which the feminine voice struggles to resolve in its effort to reclaim the self and to solve the moral problem in such a way that no one is hurt.

When a woman considers whether to continue or abort a pregnancy, she contemplates a decision that affects both self and others and engages directly the critical moral issue of hurting. Since the choice is ultimately hers and therefore one for which she is responsible, it raises precisely those questions of judgment that have been most problematic for women. Now she is asked whether she wishes to interrrupt that stream of life which has for centuries immersed her in the passivity of dependence while at the same time imposing on her the responsibility for care. Thus the abortion decision brings to the core of feminine apprehension, to what Joan Didion (1972) calls "the irreconcilable difference of it—that sense of living one's deepest life underwater, that dark involvement with blood and birth and death," the adult questions of responsibility and choice.

How women deal with such choices has been the subject of my research, designed to clarify, through considering the ways in which women construct and resolve the abortion decision, the nature and development of women's moral judgment. Twenty-nine women, diverse in age, race, and social class, were referred by abortion and pregnancy counseling services and participated in the study for a variety of reasons. Some came to gain further clarification with respect to a decision about which they were in conflict, some in response to a counselor's concern about repeated abortions, and others out of an interest in and/or willingness to contribute to ongoing research. Although the pregnancies occurred under a variety of circumstances in the lives of these women, certain commonalities could be discerned. The adolescents often failed to use birth control because they denied or discredited their capacity to bear children. Some of the older women attributed the pregnancy to the omission of contraceptive measures in circumstances where intercourse had not been anticipated. Since the pregnancies often coincided with efforts on the part of the women to end a relationship, they may be seen as a manifestation of ambivalence or as a way of putting the relationship to the ultimate test of commitment. For these women, the pregnancy appeared to be a way of testing truth, making the baby an ally in the search for male support and protection or, that failing, a companion victim of his rejection. There were, finally, some women who became pregnant either as a result of a failure of birth control or intentionally as part of a joint decision that later was reconsidered. Of the twenty-nine women, four decided to have the baby, one miscarried, twenty-one chose abortion, and three remained in doubt about the decision.

In the initial part of the interview, the women were asked to discuss the decision that confronted them, how they were dealing with it, the alternatives they were considering, their reasons for and against each option, the people involved, the conflicts entailed, and the ways in which making this decision affected their self-concepts and their relationships with others. Then, in the second part of the interview, moral judgment was assessed in the hypothetical mode by presenting for resolution three of Kohlberg's standard research dilemmas.

While the structural progression from a pre-conventional through a conventional to a post-conventional moral perspective can readily be discerned in the women's responses to both actual and hypothetical dilemmas, the conventions that shape women's moral judgments differ from those that apply to men. The construction of the abortion dilemma, in particular, reveals the existence of a distinct moral language whose evolution informs the sequence of women's development. This is the language of selfishness and responsibility, which defines the moral problem as one of obligation to exercise care and avoid hurt. The infliction of hurt is considered selfish and immoral in its reflection of unconcern, while the expression of care is seen as the fulfillment of moral responsibility. The reiterative use of the language of selfishness and responsibility and the underlying moral orientation it reflects sets the women apart from the men whom Kohlberg studied and may be seen as the critical reason for their failure to develop within the constraints of his system.

In the developmental sequence that follows, women's moral judgments proceed from an initial focus on the self at the *first level* to the discovery, in the transition to the *second level*, of the concept of responsibility as the basis for a new equilibrium between self and others. The elaboration of this concept of responsibility and its fusion with a maternal concept of morality, which seeks to ensure protection for the dependent and unequal, characterizes the *second level* of judgment. At this level the good is equated with caring for others. However, when the conventions of feminine goodness legitimize only others as the recipients of moral care, the logical inequality between self and other and the psychological violence that it engenders create the disequilibrium that initiates the *second* transition. The relationship between self and others is then reconsidered in an effort to sort out the confusion between conformity and care inherent in the conventional definition of feminine goodness and to establish a new equilibrium, which dissipates the tension between selfishness and responsibility. At the *third level*, the self becomes the arbiter of an independent judgment that now subsumes both conventions and individual needs under the moral principle of nonviolence. Judgment remains psychological in its concern with the intention and consequences of action, but it now becomes universal in its condemnation of exploitation and hurt.

Level I: Orientation to Individual Survival

In its initial and simplest construction, the abortion decision centers on the self. The concern is pragmatic, and the issue is individual survival. At this level, "should" is undifferentiated from "would," and others influence the decision only through their power to affect its consequences. An eighteen-year-old, asked what she thought when she found herself pregnant, replies: "I really didn't think anything except that I didn't want it. [Why was that?] I didn't want it, I wasn't ready for it, and next year will be my last year and I want to go to school."

Asked if there was a right decision, she says, "There is no right decision. [Why?] I didn't want it." For her the question of right decision would emerge only if her own needs were in conflict; then she would have to decide which needs should take precedence. This was the dilemma of another eighteen-year-old, who saw having a baby as a way of increasing her freedom by providing "the perfect chance to get married and move away from home," but also as restricting her freedom "to do a lot of things."

At this first level, the self, which is the sole object of concern, is constrained by lack of power; the wish "to do a lot of things" is constantly belied by the limitations of what, in fact, is being done. Relationships are, for the most part, disappointing: "The only thing you are ever going to get out of going with a guy is to get hurt." As a result, women may in some instances deliberately choose isolation to protect themselves against hurt. When asked how she would describe herself to herself, a nineteen-year-old, who held herself responsible for the accidental death of a younger brother, answers as follows:

I really don't know. I never thought about it. I don't know. I know basically the outline of a character. I am very independent. I don't really want to have to ask anybody for anything and I am a loner in life. I prefer to be by myself than around anybody else. I manage to keep my friends at a limited number with the point that I have very few friends. I don't know what else there is. I am a loner and I enjoy it. Here today and gone tomorrow.

The primacy of the concern with survival is explicitly acknowledged by a sixteen-year-old delinquent in response to Kohlberg's Heinz dilemma, which asks if it is right for a desperate husband to steal an outrageously overpriced drug to save the life of his dying wife:

I think survival is one of the first things in life and that people fight for. I think it is the most important thing, more important than stealing. Stealing might be wrong, but if you have to steal to survive yourself or even kill, that is what you should do. . . . Preservation of oneself, I think, is the most important thing; it comes before anything in life.

The First Transition: From Selfishness to Responsibility

In the transition which follows and criticizes this level of judgment, the words selfishness and responsibility first appear. Their reference initially is to the self in a redefinition of the self-interest which has thus far served as the basis for judgment. The transitional issue is one of attachment or connection to others. The pregnancy catches up the issue not only by representing an immediate, literal connection, but also by affirming, in the most concrete and physical way, the capacity to assume adult feminine roles. However, while having a baby seems at first to offer respite from the loneliness of adolescence and to solve conflicts over dependence and independence, in reality the continuation of an adolescent pregnancy generally compounds these problems, increasing social isolation and precluding further steps toward independence.

To be a mother in the societal as well as the physical sense requires the assumption of parental responsibility for the care and protection of a child. However, in order to be able to care for another, one must first be able to care responsibly for oneself. The growth from childhood to adulthood, conceived as a move from selfishness to responsibility, is articulated explicitly in these terms by a seventeen-year-old who describes her response to her pregnancy as follows:

I started feeling really good about being pregnant instead of feeling really bad, because I wasn't looking at the situation realistically. I was looking at it from my own sort of selfish needs because I was lonely and felt lonely and stuff. . . . Things weren't really going good for me, so I was looking at it that I could have a baby that I could take care of or something that was part of me, and that made me feel good . . . but I wasn't looking at the realistic side . . . about the responsibility I would have to take on . . . I came to this decision that I was going to have an abortion [because] I realized how much responsibility goes with having a child. Like you have to be there, you can't be out of the house all the time which is one thing I like to do . . . and I decided that I have to take on responsibility for myself and I have to work out a lot of things.

Stating her former mode of judgment, the wish to have a baby as a way of combating loneliness and feeling connected, she now criticizes that judgment as both "selfish" and "unrealistic." The contradiction between wishes for a baby and for the freedom to be "out of the house all the time"—that is, for connection and also for independence—is resolved in terms of a new priority, as the criterion for judgment changes. The dilemma now assumes moral definition as the emergent conflict between wish and necessity is seen as a disparity between "would" and "should." In this construction the "selfishness" of willful decision is counterposed to the "responsibility" of moral choice:

What I want to do is to have the baby, but what I feel I should do which is what I need to do, is have an abortion right now, because sometimes what you want isn't right. Sometimes what is necessary comes before what you want, because it might not always lead to the right thing.

While the pregnancy itself confirms femininity—"I started feeling really good; it sort of made me feel, like being pregnant, I started feeling like a woman"—the abortion decision becomes an opportunity for the adult exercise of responsible choice.

> [How would you describe yourself to yourself?] I am looking at myself differently in the way that I have had a really heavy decision put upon me, and I have never really had too many hard decisions in my life, and I have made it. It has taken some responsibility to do this. I have changed in that way, that I have made a hard decision. And that has been good. Because before, I would not have looked at it realistically, in my opinion. I would have gone by what I wanted to do, and I wanted it, and even if it wasn't right. So I see myself as I'm becoming more mature in ways of making decisions and taking care of myself, doing something for myself. I think it is going to help me in other ways, if I have other decisions to make put upon me, which would take some responsibility. And I would know that I could make them.

In the epiphany of this cognitive reconstruction, the old becomes transformed in terms of the new. The wish to "do something for myself" remains, but the terms of its fulfillment change as the decision affirms both femininity and adulthood in its integration of responsibility and care. Morality, says another adolescent, "is the way you think about yourself . . . sooner or later you have to make up your mind to start taking care of yourself. Abortion, if you do it for the right reasons, is helping yourself to start over and do different things."

Since this transition signals an enhancement in self-worth, it requires a conception of self which includes the possibility for doing "the right thing," the ability to see in oneself the potential for social acceptance. When such confidence is seriously in doubt, the transitional questions may be raised but development is impeded. The failure to make this first transition, despite an understanding of the issues involved, is illustrated by a woman in her late twenties. Her struggle with the conflict between selfishness and responsibility pervades but fails to resolve her dilemma of whether or not to have a third abortion.

> I think you have to think about the people who are involved, including yourself. You have responsibilities to yourself . . . and to make a right, whatever that is, decision in this depends on your knowledge and awareness of the responsibilities that you have and whether you can survive with a child and what it will do to your relationship with the father or how it will affect him emotionally.

Rejecting the idea of selling the baby and making "a lot of money in a black market kind of thing . . . because mostly I operate on principles and it would just rub me the wrong way to think I would be selling my own child," she struggles with a concept of responsibility which repeatedly turns back on the question of her own survival. Transition seems blocked by a self-image which is insistently contradictory:

> [How would you describe yourself to yourself?] I see myself as impulsive, practical—that is a contradiction—and moral and amoral, a contradiction. Actually the only thing that is consistent and not contradictory is the fact that I am very lazy which everyone has always told me is really a symptom of something else which I have never been able to put my finger on exactly. It has taken me a long time to like myself. In fact there are times when I don't, which I think is healthy to a point and sometimes I think I like myself too much and I probably evade myself too much, which avoids responsibility to myself and to other people who like me. I am pretty unfaithful to myself . . . I have a hard time even thinking that I am a human being, simply because so much rotten stuff goes on and people are so crummy and insensitive.

Seeing herself as avoiding responsibility, she can find no basis upon which to resolve the pregnancy dilemma. Instead, her inability to arrive at any clear sense of decision only contributes further to her overall sense of failure. Criticizing her parents for having betrayed her during adolescence by coercing her to have an abortion she did not want, she now betrays herself and criticizes that as well. In this light, it is less surprising that she considered selling her child, since she felt herself to have, in effect, been sold by her parents for the sake of maintaining their social status.

The Second Level: Goodness as Self-Sacrifice

The transition from selfishness to responsibility is a move toward social participation. Whereas at the first level, morality is seen as a matter of sanctions imposed by a society of which one is more subject than citizen, at the second level, moral judgment comes to rely on shared norms and expectations. The woman at this level validates her claim to social membership through the adoption of societal values. Consensual judgment becomes paramount and goodness the overriding concern as survival is now seen to depend on acceptance by others.

Here the conventional feminine voice emerges with great clarity, defining the self and proclaiming its worth on the basis of the ability to care for and protect others. The woman now constructs the world perfused with the assumptions about feminine goodness reflected in the stereotypes of the Broverman et al. (1972) studies. There the attributes considered desirable for women all presume an other, a recipient of the "tact, gentleness and easy expression of feeling" which allow the woman to respond sensitively while evoking in return the care which meets her own "very strong need for security." The strength of this position lies in its capacity for caring; its limitation is the restriction it imposes on direct expression. Both qualities are elucidated by a nineteen-year-old who contrasts her reluctance to criticize with her boyfriend's straightforwardness:

> I never want to hurt anyone, and I tell them in a very nice way, and I have respect for their own opinions, and they can do the things the way that they want, and he usually tells people right off the bat. . . . He does a lot of things out in public which I do in private. . . . it is better, the other [his way], but I just could never do it.

While her judgment clearly exists, it is not expressed, at least not in public. Concern for the feelings of others imposes a deference which she nevertheless criticizes in an awareness that, under the name of consideration, a vulnerability and a duplicity are concealed.

At the second level of judgment, it is specifically over the issue of hurting that conflict arises with respect to the abortion decision. When no option exists that can be construed as being in the best interest of everyone, when responsibilities conflict and decision entails the sacrifice of somebody's needs, then the woman confronts the seemingly impossible task of choosing the victim. A nineteen-year-old, fearing the consequences for herself of a second abortion but facing the opposition of both her family and her lover to the continuation of the pregnancy, describes the dilemma as follows:

> I don't know what choices are open to me; it is either to have it or the abortion; these are the choices open to me. It is just that either way I don't . . . I think what confuses me is it is a choice of either hurting myself or hurting other people around me. What is more important? If there could be a happy medium, it would be fine, but there isn't. It is either hurting someone on this side or hurting myself.

While the feminine identification of goodness with self-sacrifice seems clearly to dictate the "right" resolution of this dilemma, the stakes may be high for the woman herself, and the sacrifice of the fetus, in any event, compromises the altruism of an abortion motivated by a concern for others. Since femininity itself is in conflict in an abortion intended as an expression of love and care, this is a resolution which readily explodes in its own contradiction.

"I don't think anyone should have to choose between two things that they love," says a twenty-five-year-old woman who assumed responsibility not only for her lover but also for his wife and children in having an abortion she did not want:

> I just wanted the child and I really don't believe in abortions. Who can say when life begins. I think that life begins at conception and . . . I felt like there were changes happening in my body and I felt very protective . . . [but] I felt a responsibility, my responsibility if anything ever happened to her [his wife]. He made me feel that I had to make a choice and there was only one choice to make and that was to have an abortion and I could always have children another time and he made me feel if I didn't have it that it would drive us apart.

The abortion decision was, in her mind, a choice not to choose with respect to the pregnancy—"That was my choice, I had to do it." Instead, it was a decision to subordinate the pregnancy to the continuation of a relationship that she saw as encompassing her life—"Since I met him, he has been my life. I do everything for him; my life sort of revolves around him." Since she wanted to have the baby and also to continue the relationship, either choice could be construed as selfish. Furthermore, since both alternatives entailed hurting someone, neither could be considered moral. Faced with a decision which, in her own terms, was untenable, she sought to avoid responsibility for the choice she made, construing the decision as a sacrifice of her own needs to those of her lover. However, this public sacrifice in the name of responsibility engendered a private resentment that erupted in anger, compromising the very relationship that it had been intended to sustain.

> Afterwards we went through a bad time because I hate to say it and I was wrong, but I blamed him. I gave in to him. But when it came down to it, I made the decision, I could have said, "I am going to have this child whether you want me to or not," and I just didn't do it.

Pregnant again by the same man, she recognizes in retrospect that the choice in fact had been hers, as she returns once again to what now appears to have been missed opportunity for growth. Seeking, this time, to make rather than abdicate the decision, she sees the issue as one of "strength" as she struggles to free herself from the powerlessness of her own dependence:

> I think that right now I think of myself as someone who can become a lot stronger. Because of the circumstances, I just go along like with the tide. I never really had anything of my own before . . . [this time] I hope to come on strong and make a big decision, whether it is right or wrong.

Because the morality of self-sacrifice had justified the previous abortion, she now must suspend that judgment if she is to claim her own voice and accept responsibility for choice.

She thereby calls into question the underlying assumption of Level Two, which leads the woman to consider herself responsible for the actions of others, while holding others responsible for the choices she makes. This notion of reciprocity, backwards in its assumptions about control, disguises assertion as response. By reversing responsibility, it generates a series of indirect actions, which leave everyone feeling manipulated and betrayed. The logic of this position is confused in that the morality of mutual care is embedded in the psychology of dependence. Assertion becomes personally dangerous in its risk of criticism and abandonment as well as potentially immoral in its power to hurt. This confusion is captured by Kohlberg's (1969) definition of Stage Three moral judgment, which joins the need for approval with the wish to care for and help others.

When thus caught between the passivity of dependence and the activity of care, the woman becomes suspended in an immobility of both judgment and action. "If I were drowning, I couldn't reach out a hand to save myself, so unwilling am I to set myself up against fate," begins the central character of Margaret Drabble's novel, *The Waterfall* (1971), in an effort to absolve herself of responsibility as she at the same time relinquishes control. Facing the same moral conflict which George Eliot depicted in *The Mill on the Floss*, Drabble's heroine proceeds to relive Maggie Tulliver's dilemma but turns inward in her search for the way in which to retell that story. What is initially suspended and then called into question is the judgment which "had in the past made it seem better to renounce myself than them."

The Second Transition: From Goodness to Truth

The second transition begins with the reconsideration of the relationship between self and other, as the woman starts to scrutinize the logic of self-sacrifice in the service of a morality of care. In the interview data, this transition is announced by the reappearance of the word selfish. Retrieving the judgmental initiative, the woman begins to ask whether it is selfish or responsible, moral or immoral, to include her own needs within the compass of her care and concern. This question leads her to reexamine the concept of responsibility, juxtaposing the outward concern with what other people think with a new inner judgment.

In separating the voice of the self from those of others, the woman asks if it is possible to be responsible to herself as well as to others and thus to reconcile the disparity between hurt and care. The exercise of such responsibility, however, requires a new kind of judgment whose first demand is for honesty. To be responsible, it is necessary first to acknowledge what it is that one is doing. The criterion for judgment thus shifts from "goodness" to "truth" as the morality of action comes to be assessed not on the basis of its appearance in the eyes of others, but in terms of the realities of its intention and consequence.

A twenty-four-year-old married Catholic woman, pregnant again two months following the birth of her first child, identifies her dilemma as one of choice: "You have to now decide; because it is now available, you have to make a decision. And if it wasn't available, there was no choice open; you just do what you have to do." In the absence of legal abortion, a morality of self-sacrifice was necessary in order to insure protection and care for the dependent child. However, when such sacrifice becomes optional, the entire problem is recast.

The abortion decision is framed by this woman first in terms of her responsibilities to others: having a second child at this time would be contrary to medical advice and would strain both the emotional and financial resources of the family. However, there is, she says, a third reason for having an abortion, "sort of an emotional reason. I don't know if it is selfish or not, but it would really be tying myself down and right now I am not ready to be tied down with two."

Against this combination of selfish and responsible reasons for abortion is her Catholic belief that

> . . . it is taking a life, and it is. Even though it is not formed, it is the potential, and to me it is still taking a life. But I have to think of mine, my son's and my husband's, to think about, and at first I think that I thought it was for selfish reasons, but it is not. I believe that too, some of it is selfish. I don't want another one right now; I am not ready for it.

The dilemma arises over the issue of justification for taking a life: "I can't cover it over, because I believe this and if I do try to cover it over, I know that I am going to be in a mess. It will be denying what I am really doing." Asking "Am I doing the right thing; is it moral?," she counterposes to her belief against abortion her concern with the consequences of continuing the pregnancy. While concluding that "I can't be so morally strict as to hurt three other people with a decision just because of my moral beliefs," the issue of goodness still remains critical to her resolution of the dilemma:

> The moral factor is there. To me it is taking a life, and I am going to take that upon myself, that decision upon myself and I have feelings about it, and talked to a priest . . . but he said it is there and it will be from now on, and it is up to the person if they can live with the idea and still believe they are good.

The criteria for goodness, however, move inward as the ability to have an abortion and still consider herself good comes to hinge on the issue of selfishness with which she struggles to come to terms. Asked if acting morally is acting according to what is best for the self or whether it is a matter of self-sacrifice, she replies:

> I don't know if I really understand the question. . . . Like in my situation where I want to have the abortion and if I didn't it would be self-sacrificing, I am really in the middle of both those ways . . . but I think that my morality is strong and if these reasons—financial, physical reality and also for the whole family involved—were not here, that I wouldn't have to do it, and then it would be a self-sacrifice.

The importance of clarifying her own participation in the decision is evident in her attempt to ascertain her feelings in order to determine whether or not she was "putting them under" in deciding to end the pregnancy. Whereas in the first transition, from selfishness to responsibility, women made lists in order to bring to their consideration needs other than their own, now, in the second transition, it is the needs of the self which have to be deliberately uncovered. Confronting the reality of her own wish for an abortion, she now must deal with the problem of selfishness and the qualification that she feels it imposes on the "goodness" of her decision. The primacy of this concern is apparent in her description of herself:

> I think in a way I am selfish for one thing, and very emotional, very . . . and I think that I am a very real person and an understanding person and I can handle life situations fairly well, so I am basing a lot of it on my ability to do the things that I feel are right and best for me and whoever I am involved with. I think I was very fair to myself about the decision, and I really think that I have been truthful, not hiding anything, bringing out all the feelings involved. I feel it is a good decision and an honest one, a real decision.

Thus she strives to encompass the needs of both self and others, to be responsible to others and thus to be "good" but also to be responsible to herself and thus to be "honest" and "real."

While from one point of view, attention to one's own needs is considered selfish, when looked at from a different perspective, it is a matter of honesty and fairness. This is the essence of the transitional shift toward a new conception of goodness which turns inward in an acknowledgement of the self and an acceptance of responsibility for decision. While outward justification, the concern with "good reasons," remains critical for this particular woman: "I still think abortion is wrong, and it will be unless the situation can justify what you are doing." But the search for justification has produced a change in her thinking, "not drastically, but a little bit." She realizes that in continuing the pregnancy she would punish not only herself but also her husband, toward whom she had begun to feel "turned off and irritated." This leads her to consider the consequences self-sacrifice can have both for the self and for others. "God," she says, "can punish, but He can also forgive." What remains in question is whether her claim to forgiveness is compromised by a decision that not only meets the needs of others but that also is "right and best for me."

The concern with selfishness and its equation with immorality recur in an interview with another Catholic woman whose arrival for an abortion was punctuated by the statement, "I have always thought abortion was a fancy word

for murder." Initially explaining this murder as one of lesser degree—"I am doing it because I have to do it. I am not doing it the least bit because I want to," she judges it "not quite as bad. You can rationalize that it is not quite the same." Since "keeping the child for lots and lots of reasons was just sort of impractical and out," she considers her options to be either abortion or adoption. However, having previously given up one child for adoption, she says: "I knew that psychologically there was no way that I could hack another adoption. It took me about four-and-a-half years to get my head on straight; there was just no way I was going to go through it again." The decision thus reduces in her eyes to a choice between murdering the fetus or damaging herself. The choice is further complicated by the fact that by continuing the pregnancy she would hurt not only herself but also her parents, with whom she lived. In the face of these manifold moral contradictions, the psychological demand for honesty that arises in counseling finally allows decision:

> On my own, I was doing it not so much for myself; I was doing it for my parents. I was doing it because the doctor told me to do it, but I had never resolved in my mind that I was doing it for me. Because it goes back to the fact that I never believed in abortions. . . . Actually, I had to sit down and admit, no, I really don't want to go the mother route now. I honestly don't feel that I want to be a mother, and that is not really such a bad thing to say after all. But that is not how I felt up until talking to Maureen [her counselor]. It was just a horrible way to feel, so I just wasn't going to feel it, and I just blocked it right out.

As long as her consideration remains "moral," abortion can be justified only as an act of sacrifice, a submission to necessity where the absence of choice precludes responsibility. In this way, she can avoid self-condemnation, since, "When you get into moral stuff then you are getting into self-respect and that stuff, and at least if I do something that I feel is morally wrong, then I tend to lose some of my self-respect as a person." Her evasion of responsibility, critical to maintaining the innocence necessary for self-respect, contradicts the reality of her own participation in the abortion decision. The dishonesty in her plea of victimization creates the conflict that generates the need for a more inclusive understanding. She must now resolve the emerging contradiction in her thinking between two uses of the term right: "I am saying that abortion is morally wrong, but the situation is right, and I am going to do it. But the thing is that eventually they are going to have to go together, and I am going to have to put them together somehow." Asked how this could be done, she replies:

> I would have to change morally wrong to morally right. [How?] I have no idea. I don't think you can take something that you feel is morally wrong because the situation makes it right and put the two together. They are not together, they are opposite. They don't go together. Something is wrong, but all of a sudden because you are doing it, it is right.

This discrepancy recalls a similar conflict she faced over the question of euthanasia, also considered by her to be morally wrong until she "took care of a couple of patients who had flat EEGs and saw the job that it was doing on their families." Recalling that experience, she says:

> You really don't know your black and whites until you really get into them and are being confronted with it. If you stop and think about my feelings on euthanasia until I got into it, and then my feelings about abortion until I got into it, I thought both of them were murder. Right and wrong and no middle but there is a gray.

In discovering the gray and questioning the moral judgments which formerly she considered to be absolute, she confronts the moral crisis of the second transition. Now the conventions which in the past had guided her moral judgment become subject to a new criticism, as she questions not only the justification for hurting others in the name of morality but also the "rightness" of hurting herself. However, to sustain such criticism in the face of conventions that equate goodness with self-sacrifice, the woman must verify her capacity for independent judgment and the legitimacy of her own point of view.

Once again transition hinges on self-concept. When uncertainty about her own worth prevents a woman from claiming equality, self-assertion falls prey to the old criticism of selfishness. Then the morality that condones self-destruction in the name of responsible care is not repudiated as inadequate but rather is abandoned in the face of its threat to survival. Moral obligation, rather than expanding to include the self, is rejected completely as the failure of conventional reciprocity leaves the woman unwilling any longer to protect others at what is now seen to be her own expense. In the absence of morality, survival, however "selfish" or "immoral," returns as the paramount concern.

A musician in her late twenties illustrates this transitional impasse. Having led an independent life which centered on her work, she considered herself "fairly strong-willed, fairly in control, fairly rational and objective" until she became involved in an intense love affair and discovered in her capacity to love "an entirely new dimension" in herself. Admitting in retrospect to "tremendous naiveté and idealism," she had entertained "some vague ideas that some day I would like a child to concretize our relationship . . . having always associated having a child with all the creative aspects of my life." Abjuring, with her lover, the use of contraceptives because, "as the relationship was sort of an ideal relationship in our minds, we liked the idea of not using foreign objects or anything artificial," she saw herself as having relinquished control, becoming instead "just simply vague and allowing events to just carry me along." Just as she began in her own thinking to confront "the realities of that situation"—the possibility of pregnancy and the fact that her lover was married—she found herself pregnant. "Caught" between her wish to end a relationship that "seemed more and more defeating" and her wish for a baby, which "would be a connection that would last a long time," she is paralyzed by her inability to resolve the dilemma which her ambivalence creates.

The pregnancy poses a conflict between her "moral" belief that "once a certain life has begun, it shouldn't be stopped artificially" and her "amazing" discovery that to have the baby she would "need much more [support] than I thought." Despite her moral conviction that she "should" have the child, she doubts that she could psychologically deal with "having the child alone and taking the responsibility for it." Thus a conflict erupts between what she considers to be her moral obligation to protect life and her inability to do so under the circumstances of this pregnancy. Seeing it as "my decision and my responsibility for making the decision whether to have or have not the child," she struggles to find a viable basis on which to resolve the dilemma.

Capable of arguing either for or against abortion "with a philosophical logic," she says, on the one hand, that in an overpopulated world one should have children only under ideal conditions for care but, on the other, that one should end a life only when it is impossible to sustain it. She describes her impasse in response to the question of whether there is a difference between what she wants to do and what she thinks she should do:

> Yes, and there always has. I have always been confronted with that precise situation in a lot of my choices, and I have been trying to figure out what are the things that make me believe that these are things I should do as opposed to what I feel I want to do. [In this situation?] It is not that clear cut. I both want the child and feel I should have it, and I also think I should have the abortion and want it, but I would say it is my stronger feeling, and that I don't have enough confidence in my work yet and that is really where it is all hinged, I think . . . [the abortion] would solve the problem and I know I can't handle the pregnancy.

Characterizing this solution as "emotional and pragmatic" and attributing it to her lack of confidence in her work, she constrasts it with the "better thought out and more logical and more correct" resolution of her lover who thinks that she should have the child and raise it without either his presence or financial support. Confronted with this reflected image of herself as ultimately giving and good, as self-sustaining in her own creativity and thus able to meet the needs of others while imposing no demands of her own in return, she questions not the image itself but her own adequacy in filling it. Concluding that she is not yet capable of doing so, she is reduced in her own eyes to what she sees as a selfish and highly compromised fight

for my survival. But in one way or another, I am going to suffer. Maybe I am going to suffer mentally and emotionally having the abortion, or I would suffer what I think is possibly something worse. So I suppose it is the lesser of two evils. I think it is a matter of choosing which one I know that I can survive through. It is really. I think it is selfish, I suppose, because it does have to do with that. I just realized that. I guess it does have to do with whether I would survive or not. [Why is this selfish?] Well, you know, it is. Because I am concerned with my survival first, as opposed to the survival of the relationship or the survival of the child, another human being . . . I guess I am setting priorities, and I guess I am setting my needs to survive first. . . . I guess I see it in negative terms a lot . . . but I do think of other positive things; that I am still going to have some life left, maybe. I don't know.

In the face of this failure of reciprocity of care, in the disappointment of abandonment where connection was sought, survival is seen to hinge on her work which is "where I derive the meaning of what I am. That's the known factor." While uncertainty about her work makes this survival precarious, the choice for abortion is also distressing in that she considers it to be "highly introverted—that in this one respect, having an abortion would be going a step backward; going outside to love someone else and having a child would be a step forward." The sense of retrenchment that the severing of connection signifies is apparent in her anticipation of the cost which abortion would entail:

> Probably what I will do is I will cut off my feelings, and when they will return or what would happen to them after that, I don't know. So that I don't feel anything at all, and I would probably just be very cold and go through it very coldly. . . . The more you do that to yourself, the more difficult it becomes to love again or to trust again or to feel again. . . . Each time I move away from that, it becomes easier, not more difficult, but easier to avoid committing myself to a relationship. And I am really concerned about cutting off that whole feeling aspect.

Caught between selfishness and responsibility, unable to find in the circumstances of this choice a way of caring which does not at the same time destroy, she confronts a dilemma which reduces to a conflict between morality and survival. Adulthood and femininity fly apart in the failure of this attempt at integration as the choice to work becomes a decision not only to renounce this particular relationship and child but also to obliterate the vulnerability that love and care engender.

The Third Level: The Morality of Nonviolence

In contrast, a twenty-five-year-old woman, facing a similar disappointment, finds a way to reconcile the initially disparate concepts of selfishness and responsibility through a transformed understanding of self and a corresponding redefinition of morality. Examining the assumptions underlying the conventions of feminine self-abnegation and moral self-sacrifice, she comes to reject these conventions as immoral in their power to hurt. By elevating nonviolence—the injunction against hurting—to a principle governing all moral judgment and action, she is able to assert a moral equality between self and other. Care then becomes a universal obligation, the self-chosen ethic of a postconventional judgment that reconstructs the dilemma in a way that allows the assumption of responsibility for choice.

In this woman's life, the current pregnancy brings to the surface the unfinished business of an earlier pregnancy and of the relationship in which both pregnancies occurred. The first pregnancy was discovered after her lover had left and was terminated by an abortion experienced as a purging expression of her anger at having been rejected. Remembering the abortion only as a relief, she nevertheless describes that time in her life as one in which she "hit rock bottom." Having hoped then to "take control of my life," she instead resumed the relationship when the man reappeared. Now, two years later, having once again "left my diaphragm in the drawer," she again becomes pregnant. Although initially "ecstatic" at the news, her elation dissipates when her lover tells her that he will leave if she chooses to have the child. Under these circumstances, she considers a second abortion but is unable to keep the repeated appointments she makes because of

her reluctance to accept the responsibility for that choice. While the first abortion seemed an "honest mistake," she says that a second would make her feel "like a walking slaughter-house." Since she would need financial support to raise the child, her initial strategy was to take the matter to "the welfare people" in the hope that they would refuse to provide the necessary funds and thus resolve her dilemma:

> In that way, you know, the responsibility would be off my shoulders, and I could say, it's not my fault, you know, the state denied me the money that I would need to do it. But it turned out that it was possible to do it, and so I was, you know, right back where I started. And I had an appointment for an abortion, and I kept calling and cancelling it and then remaking the appointment and cancelling it, and I just couldn't make up my mind.

Confronting the need to choose between the two evils of hurting herself or ending the incipient life of the child, she finds, in a reconstruction of the dilemma itself, a basis for a new priority that allows decision. In doing so, she comes to see the conflict as arising from a faulty construction of reality. Her thinking recapitulates the developmental sequence, as she considers but rejects as inadequate the components of earlier-stage resolutions. An expanded conception of responsibility now reshapes moral judgment and guides resolution of the dilemma, whose pros and cons she considers as follows:

> Well, the pros for having the baby are all the admiration that you would get from, you know, being a single woman, alone, martyr, struggling, having the adoring love of this beautiful Gerber baby . . . just more of a home life than I have had in a long time, and that basically was it, which is pretty fantasyland; it is not very realistic. . . . Cons against having the baby: it was going to hasten what is looking to be the inevitable end of the relationship with the man I am presently with. . . . I was going to have to go on welfare, my parents were going to hate me for the rest of my life, I was going to lose a really good job that I have, I would lose a lot of independence . . . solitude . . . and I would have to be put in a position of asking help from a lot of people a lot of the time. Cons against having the abortion is having to face up

to the guilt . . . and pros for having the abortion are I would be able to handle my deteriorating relation with S. with a lot more capability and a lot more responsibility for him and for myself . . . and I would not have to go through the realization that for the next twenty-five years of my life I would be punishing myself for being foolish enough to get pregnant again and forcing myself to bring up a kid just because I did this. Having to face the guilt of a second abortion seemed like, not exactly, well, exactly the lesser of the two evils but also the one that would pay off for me personally in the long run because by looking at why I am pregnant again and subsequently have decided to have a second abortion, I have to face up to some things about myself.

Although she doesn't "feel good about having a second abortion," she nevertheless concludes,

I would not be doing myself or the child or the world any kind of favor having this child. . . . I don't need to pay off my imaginary debts to the world through this child, and I don't think that it is right to bring a child into the world and use it for that purpose.

Asked to describe herself, she indicates how closely her transformed moral understanding is tied to a changing self-concept:

I have been thinking about that a lot lately, and it comes up different than what my usual subconscious perception of myself is. Usually paying off some sort of debt, going around serving people who are not really worthy of my attentions because somewhere in my life I think I got the impression that my needs are really secondary to other people's, and that if I feel, if I make any demands on other people to fulfill my needs, I'd feel guilty for it and submerge my own in favor of other people's, which later backfires on me, and I feel a great deal of resentment for other people that I am doing things for, which causes friction and the eventual deterioration of the relationship. And then I start all over again. How would I describe myself to myself? Pretty frustrated and a lot angrier than I admit, a lot more aggressive than I admit.

Reflecting on the virtues which comprise the conventional definition of the feminine self, a definition which she hears articulated in her mother's voice, she says, "I am beginning to think that all these virtues are really not getting me anywhere. I have begun to notice." Tied to this recognition is an acknowledgement of her power and worth, both previously excluded from the image she projected:

I am suddenly beginning to realize that the things that I like to do, the things I am interested in, and the things that I believe and the kind of person I am is not so bad that I have to constantly be sitting on the shelf and letting it gather dust. I am a lot more worthwhile than what my past actions have led other people to believe.

Her notion of a "good person," which previously was limited to her mother's example of hard work, patience and self-sacrifice, now changes to include the value that she herself places on directness and honesty. Although she believes that this new self-assertion will lead her "to feel a lot better about myself" she recognizes that it will also expose her to criticism:

Other people may say, 'Boy, she's aggressive, and I don't like that,' but at least, you know, they will know that they don't like that. They are not going to say, 'I like the way she manipulates herself to fit right around me.' . . . What I want to do is just be a more self-determined person and a more singular person.

While within her old framework abortion had seemed a way of "copping out" instead of being a "responsible person [who] pays for his mistakes and pays and pays and is always there when she says she will be there and even when she doesn't say she will be there is there," now, her "conception of what I think is right for myself and my conception of self-worth is changing." She can consider this emergent self "also a good person," as her concept of goodness expands to encompass "the feeling of self-worth; you are not going to sell yourself short and you are not going to make yourself do things that, you know, are really stupid and that you don't want to do." This reorientation centers on the awareness that:

I have a responsibility to myself, and you know, for once I am beginning to realize that that really matters to me . . . instead of doing what I want for myself and feeling guilty over how selfish I am, you realize that that is a very usual way for people to live . . . doing what you want to do because you feel that your wants and your needs are important, if to no one else, then to you, and that's reason enough to do something that you want to do.

Once obligation extends to include the self as well as others, the disparity between selfishness and responsibility is reconciled. Although the conflict between self and other remains, the moral problem is restructured in an awareness that the occurrence of the dilemma itself precludes non-violent resolution. The abortion decision is now seen to be a "serious" choice affecting both self and others: "This is a life that I have taken, a conscious decision to terminate, and that is just very heavy, a very heavy thing." While accepting the necessity of abortion as a highly compromised resolution, she turns her attention to the pregnancy itself, which she now considers to denote a failure of responsibility, a failure to care for and protect both self and other.

As in the first transition, although now in different terms, the conflict precipitated by the pregnancy catches up the issues critical to development. These issues now concern the worth of the self in relation to others, the claiming of the power to choose, and the acceptance of responsibility for choice. By provoking a confrontation with these issues, the crisis can become "a very auspicious time; you can use the pregnancy as sort of a learning, teeing-off point, which makes it useful in a way." This possibility for growth inherent in a crisis which allows confrontation with a construction of reality whose acceptance previously had impeded development was first identified by Coles (1964) in his study of the children of Little Rock. This same sense of possibility is expressed by the women who see, in their resolution of the abortion dilemma, a reconstructed understanding which creates the opportunity for "a new beginning," a chance "to take control of my life."

For this woman, the first step in taking control was to end the relationship in which she had considered herself "reduced to a nonentity," but to do so in a responsible way. Recognizing hurt as the inevitable concomitant of rejection, she strives to minimize that hurt "by dealing with [his] needs as best I can without com-promising my own . . . that's a big point for me, because the thing in my life to this point has been always compromising, and I am not willing to do that any more." Instead, she seeks to act in a "decent, human kind of way . . . one that leaves maybe a slightly shook but not totally destroyed person." Thus the "nonentity" confronts her power to destroy which formerly had impeded any assertion, as she considers the possibility for a new kind of action that leaves both self and other intact.

The moral concern remains a concern with hurting as she considers Kohlberg's Heinz dilemma in terms of the question, "who is going to be hurt more, the druggist who loses some money or the person who loses their life?" The right to property and right to life are weighed not in the abstract, in terms of their logical priority, but rather in the particular, in terms of the actual consequences that the violation of these rights would have in the lives of the people involved. Thinking remains contextual and admixed with feelings of care, as the moral imperative to avoid hurt begins to be informed by a psychological understanding of the meaning of non-violence.

Thus, release from the intimidation of inequality finally allows the expression of a judgment that previously had been withheld. What women then enunciate is not a new morality, but a moral conception disentangled from the constraints that formerly had confused its perception and impeded its articulation. The willingness to express and take responsibility for judgment stems from the recognition of the psychological and moral necessity for an equation of worth between self and other. Responsibility for care then includes both self and other, and the obligation not to hurt, freed from conventional constraints, is reconstructed as a universal guide to moral choice.

The reality of hurt centers the judgment of a twenty-nine-year-old woman, married and the mother of a preschool child, as she struggles with the dilemma posed by a second pregnancy whose timing conflicts with her completion of an advanced degree. Saying that "I cannot deliberately do something that is bad or would hurt another person because I can't live with having done that," she nevertheless confronts a situation in which hurt has become inevitable.

Seeking that solution which would best protect both herself and others, she indicates, in her definition of morality, the ineluctable sense of connection which infuses and colors all of her thinking:

> [Morality is] doing what is appropriate and what is just within your circumstances, but ideally it is not going to affect—I was going to say, ideally it wouldn't negatively affect another person, but that is ridiculous, because decisions are always going to affect another person. But you see, what I am trying to say is that it is the person that is the center of the decision making, of that decision making about what's right and what's wrong.

The person who is the center of this decision making begins by denying, but then goes on to acknowledge, the conflicting nature both of her own needs and of her various responsibilities. Seeing the pregnancy as a manifestation of the inner conflict between her wish, on the one hand, "to be a college president" and, on the other, "to be making pottery and flowers and having kids and staying at home," she struggles with contradiction between femininity and adulthood. Considering abortion as the "better" choice—because "in the end, meaning this time next year or this time two weeks from now, it will be less of a personal strain on us individually and on us as a family for me not to be pregnant at this time," she concludes that the decision has

> got to be, first of all, something that the woman can live with—a decision that the woman can live with, one way or another, or at least try to live with, and that it be based on where she is at and other people, significant people in her life, are at.

At the beginning of the interview she had presented the dilemma in its conventional feminine construction, as a conflict between her own wish to have a baby and the wish of others for her to complete her education. On the basis of this construction she deemed it "selfish" to continue the pregnancy because it was something "I wanted to do." However, as she begins to examine her thinking, she comes to abandon as false this conceptualization of the problem, acknowledging the truth of her own internal conflict and elaborating the tension which she feels between her femininity and the adulthood of her work life. She describes herself as "going in two directions" and values that part of herself which is "incredibly passionate and sensitive"—her capacity to recognize and meet, often with anticipation, the needs of others. Seeing her "compassion" as "something I don't want to lose" she regards it as endangered by her pursuit of professional advancement. Thus the self-deception of her initial presentation, its attempt to sustain the fiction of her own innocence, stems from her fear that to say that *she* does not want to have another baby at this time would be

> an acknowledgement to me that I am an ambitious person and that I want to have power and responsibility for others and that I want to live a life that extends from 9 to 5 every day and into the evenings and on weekends, because that is what the power and responsibility means. It means that my family would necessarily come second . . . there would be such an incredible conflict about which is tops, and I don't want that for myself.

Asked about her concept of "an ambitious person" she says that to be ambitious means to be

> power hungry [and] insensitive. [Why insensitive?] Because people are stomped on in the process. A person on the way up stomps on people, whether it is family or other colleagues or clientele, on the way up. [Inevitably?] Not always, but I have seen it so often in my limited years of working that it is scary to me. It is scary because I don't want to change like that.

Because the acquisition of adult power is seen to entail the loss of feminine sensitivity and compassion, the conflict between femininity and adulthood becomes construed as a moral problem. The discovery of the principle of nonviolence begins to direct attention to the moral dilemma itself and initiates the search for a resolution that can encompass both femininity and adulthood.

Developmental Theory Reconsidered

The developmental conception delineated at the outset, which has so consistently found the development of women to be either aberrant or incomplete, has been limited insofar as it has been predominantly a male conception, giving lip-service, a place on the chart, to the interdependence of intimacy and care but constantly stressing, at their expense, the importance and value of autonomous judgment and action. To admit to this conception the truth of the feminine perspective is to recognize for both sexes the central importance in adult life of the connection between self and other, the universality of the need for compassion and care. The concept of the separate self and of the moral principle uncompromised by the constraints of reality is an adolescent ideal, the elaborately wrought philosophy of a Stephen Daedalus, whose flight we know to be in jeopardy. Erikson (1964), in contrasting the ideological morality of the adolescent with the ethics of adult care, attempts to grapple with this problem of integration, but is impeded by the limitations of his own previous developmental conception. When his developmental stages chart a path where the sole precursor to the intimacy of adult relationships is the trust established in infancy and all intervening experience is marked only as steps toward greater independence, then separation itself becomes the model and the measure of growth. The observation that for women, identity has as much to do with connection as with separation led Erikson into trouble largely because of his failure to integrate this insight into the mainstream of his developmental theory (Erikson, 1968).

The morality of responsibility which women describe stands apart from the morality of rights which underlies Kohlberg's conceptions of the highest stages of moral judgment. Kohlberg (Note 3) sees the progression toward these stages as resulting from the generalization of the self-centered adolescent rejection of societal morality into a principled conception of individual natural rights. To illustrate this progression, he cites as an example of integrated Stage Five judgment, "possibly moving to Stage Six," the following response of a twenty-five-year-old subject from his male longitudinal sample:

[What does the word morality mean to you?] Nobody in the world knows the answer. I think

it is recognizing the right of the individual, the rights of other individuals, not interfering with those rights. Act as fairly as you would have them treat you. I think it is basically to preserve the human being's right to existence. I think that is the most important. Secondly, the human being's right to do as he pleases, again without interfering with somebody else's rights. (p. 29)

Another version of the same conception is evident in the following interview response of a male college senior whose moral judgment also was scored by Kohlberg (Note 4) as at Stage Five or Six:

[Morality] is a prescription, it is a thing to follow, and the idea of having a concept of morality is to try to figure out what it is that people can do in order to make life with each other livable, make for a kind of balance, a kind of equilibrium, a harmony in which everybody feels he has a place and an equal share in things, and it's doing that—doing that is kind of contributing to a state of affairs that go beyond the individual in the absence of which, the individual has no chance for self-fulfillment of any kind. Fairness; morality is kind of essential, it seems to me, for creating the kind of environment, interaction between people, that is prerequisite to this fulfillment of most individual goals and so on. If you want other people to not interfere with your pursuit of whatever you are into, you have to play the game.

In contrast, a woman in her late twenties responds to a similar question by defining a morality not of rights but of responsibility:

[What makes something a moral issue?] Some sense of trying to uncover a right path in which to live, and always in my mind is that the world is full of real and recognizable trouble, and is it heading for some sort of doom and is it right to bring children into this world when we currently have an overpopulation problem, and is it right to spend money on a pair of shoes when I have a pair of shoes and other people are shoeless. . . . It is part of a self-critical view, part of saying, how am I spending my time and in what sense am I working? I think I have a real drive to, I have a real maternal drive to take care of someone. To take care of my mother, to take care of children, to take care of other people's children, to take care of my own children, to take care of the world. I think that goes back to your other question, and when I am dealing with moral issues, I am sort of saying to myself constantly, are you taking care of all the things that you think are important and in what ways are you wasting yourself and wasting those issues?

While the postconventional nature of this woman's perspective seems clear, her judgments of Kohlberg's hypothetical moral dilemmas do not meet his criteria for scoring at the principled level. Kohlberg regards this as a disparity between normative and metaethical judgments which he sees as indicative of the transition between conventional and principled thinking. From another perspective, however, this judgment represents a different moral conception, disentangled from societal conventions and raised to the principled level. In this conception, moral judgment is oriented toward issues of responsibility. The way in which the responsibility orientation guides moral decision at the postconventional level is described by the following woman in her thirties:

[Is there a right way to make moral decisions?] The only way I know is to try to be as awake as possible, to try to know the range of what you feel, to try to consider all that's involved, to be as aware as you can be to what's going on, as conscious as you can of where you're walking. [Are there principles that guide you?] The principle would have something to do with responsibility, responsibility and caring about yourself and others. . . . But it's not that on the one hand you choose to be responsible and on the other hand you choose to be irresponsible—both ways you can be responsible. That's why there's not just a principle that once you take hold of you settle—the principle put into practice here is still going to leave you with conflict.

The moral imperative that emerges repeatedly in the women's interviews is an injunction to care, a responsibility to discern and alleviate the "real and recognizable trouble" of this world. For the men Kohlberg studied, the moral imperative appeared rather as an injunction to respect the rights of others and thus to protect from interference the right to life and self-fulfillment. Women's insistence on care is at first self-critical rather than self-protective,

while men initially conceive obligation to others negatively in terms of noninterference. Development for both sexes then would seem to entail an integration of rights and responsibilities through the discovery of the complementarity of these disparate views. For the women I have studied, this integration between rights and responsibilities appears to take place through a principled understanding of equity and reciprocity. This understanding tempers the self-destructive potential of a self-critical morality by asserting the equal right of all persons to care. For the men in Kohlberg's sample as well as for those in a longitudinal study of Harvard undergraduates (Gilligan & Murphy, Note 5) it appears to be the recognition through experience of the need for a more active responsibility in taking care that corrects the potential indifference of a morality of noninterference and turns attention from the logic to the consequences of choice. In the development of a postconventional ethic understanding, women come to see the violence generated by inequitable relationships, while men come to realize the limitations of a conception of justice blinded to the real inequities of human life.

Kohlberg's dilemmas, in the hypothetical abstraction of their presentation, divest the moral actors from the history and psychology of their individual lives and separate the moral problem from the social contingencies of its possible occurrence. In doing so, the dilemmas are useful for the distillation and refinement of the "objective principles of justice" toward which Kohlberg's stages strive. However, the reconstruction of the dilemma in its contextual particularity allows the understanding of cause and consequence which engages the compassion and tolerance considered by previous theorists to qualify the feminine sense of justice. Only when substance is given to the skeletal lives of hypothetical people is it possible to consider the social injustices which their moral problems may reflect and to imagine the individual suffering their occurrence may signify or their resolution engender.

The proclivity of women to reconstruct hypothetical dilemmas in terms of the real, to request or supply the information missing about the nature of the people and the places where they live, shifts their judgment away from the hierarchical ordering of principles and the formal procedures of decision making that are critical for scoring at Kohlberg's highest stages. This insistence on the particular signifies an orientation to the dilemma and to moral problems in general that differs from any of Kohlberg's stage descriptions. Given the constraints of Kohlberg's system and the biases in his research sample, this different orientation can only be construed as a failure in development. While several of the women in the research sample clearly articulated what Kohlberg regarded as a postconventional metaethical position, none of them were considered by Kohlberg to be principled in their normative moral judgments of his hypothetical moral dilemmas (Note 4). Instead, the women's judgments pointed toward an identification of the violence inherent in the dilemma itself which was seen to compromise the justice of any of its possible resolutions. This construction of the dilemma led the women to recast the moral judgment from a consideration of the good to a choice between evils.

The woman whose judgment of the abortion dilemma concluded the developmental sequence presented in the preceding section saw Kohlberg's Heinz dilemma in these terms and judged Heinz's action in terms of a choice between selfishness and sacrifice. For Heinz to steal the drug, given the circumstances of his life (which she inferred from his inability to pay two thousand dollars), he would have "to do something which is not in his best interest, in that he is going to get sent away, and that is a supreme sacrifice, a sacrifice which I would say a person truly in love might be willing to make." However, not to steal the drug "would be selfish on his part . . . he would just have to feel guilty about not allowing her a chance to live longer." Heinz's decision to steal is considered not in terms of the logical priority of life over property which justifies its rightness, but rather in terms of the actual consequences that stealing would have for a man of limited means and little social power.

Considered in the light of its probable outcomes—his wife dead, or Heinz in jail, brutalized by the violence of that experience and his life compromised by a record of felony—the

dilemma itself changes. Its resolution has less to do with the relative weights of life and property in an abstract moral conception than with the collision it has produced between two lives, formerly conjoined but now in opposition, where the continuation of one life can now occur only at the expense of the other. Given this construction, it becomes clear why consideration revolves around the issue of sacrifice and why guilt becomes the inevitable concomitant of either resolution.

Demonstrating the reticence noted in the first section about making moral judgments, this woman explains her reluctance to judge in terms of her belief

> that everybody's existence is so different that I kind of say to myself, that might be something I wouldn't do, but I can't say that it is right or wrong for that person. I can only deal with what is appropriate for me to do when I am faced with specific problems.

Asked if she would apply to others her own injunction against hurting, she says:

> See, I can't say that it is wrong. I can't say that it is right or that it's wrong because I don't know what the person did that the other person did something to hurt him . . . so it is not right that the person got hurt, but it is right that the person who just lost the job has got to get that anger up and out. It doesn't put any bread on his table, but it is released. I don't mean to be copping out. I really am trying to see how to answer these questions for you.

Her difficulty in answering Kohlberg's questions, her sense of strain with the construction which they impose on the dilemma, stems from their divergence from her own frame of reference:

> I don't even think I use the words right and wrong anymore, and I know I don't use the word moral, because I am not sure I know what it means. . . . We are talking about an unjust society, we are talking about a whole lot of things that are not right, that are truly wrong, to use the word that I don't use very often, and I have no control to change that. If I could change it, I certainly would, but I can only make my small contribution from day to day, and if I don't intentionally hurt somebody, that is my contribution to a better society. And so a

chunk of that contribution is also not to pass judgment on other people, particularly when I don't know the circumstances of why they are doing certain things.

The reluctance to judge remains a reluctance to hurt, but one that stems now not from a sense of personal vulnerability but rather from a recognition of the limitations of judgment itself. The deference of the conventional feminine perspective can thus be seen to continue at the postconventional level, not as moral relativism but rather as part of a reconstructed moral understanding. Moral judgment is renounced in an awareness of the psychological and social determinism of all human behavior at the same time as moral concern is reaffirmed in recognition of the reality of human pain and suffering.

I have a real thing about hurting people and always have, and that gets a little complicated at times, because, for example, you don't want to hurt your child. I don't want to hurt my child but if I don't hurt her sometimes, then that's hurting her more, you see, and so that was a terrible dilemma for me.

Moral dilemmas are terrible in that they entail hurt; she sees Heinz's decision as "the result of anguish, who am I hurting, why do I have to hurt them." While the morality of Heinz's theft is not in question, given the circumstances which necessitated it, what is at issue is his willingness to substitute himself for his wife and become, in her stead, the victim of exploitation by a society which breeds and legitimizes the druggist's irresponsibility and whose injustice is thus manifest in the very occurrence of the dilemma.

The same sense that the wrong questions are being asked is evident in the response of another woman who justified Heinz's action on a similar basis, saying "I don't think that exploitation should really be a right." When women begin to make direct moral statements, the issues they repeatedly address are those of exploitation and hurt. In doing so, they raise the issue of nonviolence in precisely the same psychological context that brought Erikson (1969) to pause in his consideration of the truth of Gandhi's life.

In the pivotal letter, around which the judgment of his book turns, Erikson confronts the contradiction between the philosophy of nonviolence that informed Gandhi's dealing with the British and the psychology of violence that marred his relationships with his family and with the children of the ashram. It was this contradiction, Erikson confesses,

which almost brought *me* to the point where I felt unable to continue writing *this* book because I seemed to sense the presence of a kind of untruth in the very protestation of truth; of something unclean when all the words spelled out an unreal purity; and, above all, of displaced violence where nonviolence was the professed issue.

In an effort to untangle the relationship between the spiritual truth of Satyagraha and the truth of his own psychoanalytic understanding, Erikson reminds Gandhi that "truth, you once said, 'excludes the use of violence because man is not capable of knowing the absolute truth and therefore is not competent to punish.'" The affinity between Satyagraha and psychoanalysis lies in their shared commitment to seeing life as an "experiment in truth," in their being

somehow joined in a universal "therapeutics," committed to the Hippocratic principle that one can test truth (or the healing power inherent in a sick situation) only by action which avoids harm—or better, by action which maximizes mutuality and minimizes the violence caused by unilateral coercion or threat.

Erikson takes Gandhi to task for his failure to acknowledge the relativity of truth. This failure is manifest in the coercion of Gandhi's claim to exclusive possession of the truth, his "unwillingness to learn from *anybody anything* except what was approved by the 'inner voice.'" This claim led Gandhi, in the guise of love, to impose his truth on others without awareness or regard for the extent to which he thereby did violence to their integrity.

The moral dilemma, arising inevitably out of a conflict of truths, is by definition a "sick situation" in that its either/or formulation leaves no room for an outcome that does not do violence. The resolution of such dilemmas, however, lies not in the self-deception of rationalized violence—"I was" said Gandhi, "a cruelly kind husband. I regarded myself as her teacher and so harassed her out of my blind love for her"—but rather in the replacement of the underlying antagonism with a mutuality of respect and care.

Gandhi, whom Kohlberg has mentioned as exemplifying Stage Six moral judgment and whom Erikson sought as a model of an adult ethical sensibility, instead is criticized by a judgment that refuses to look away from or condone the infliction of harm. In denying the validity of his wife's reluctance to open her home to strangers and in his blindness to the different reality of adolescent sexuality and temptation, Gandhi compromised in his everyday life the ethic of nonviolence to which in principle and in public he was so steadfastly committed.

The blind willingness to sacrifice people to truth, however, has always been the danger of an ethics abstracted from life. This willingness links Gandhi to the biblical Abraham, who prepared to sacrifice the life of his son in order to demonstrate the integrity and supremacy of his faith. Both men, in the limitations of their fatherhood, stand in implicit contrast to the woman who comes before Solomon and verifies her motherhood by relinquishing truth in order to save the life of her child. It is the ethics of an adulthood that has become principled at the expense of care that Erikson comes to criticize in his assessment of Gandhi's life.

This same criticism is dramatized explicitly as a contrast between the sexes in *The Merchant of Venice* (1598/1912), where Shakespeare goes through an extraordinary complication of sexual identity (dressing a male actor as a female character who in turn poses as a male judge) in order to bring into the masculine citadel of justice the feminine plea for mercy. The limitation of the contractual conception of justice is illustrated through the absurdity of its literal execution, while the "need to make exceptions all the time" is demonstrated contrapuntally in the matter of the rings. Portia, in calling for mercy, argues for that resolution in which no one is hurt, and as the men are forgiven for their failure to keep both their rings and their word, Antonio in turn foregoes his "right" to ruin Shylock.

The research findings that have been reported in this essay suggest that women impose a distinctive construction on moral problems, seeing moral dilemmas in terms of conflicting responsibilities. This construction was found to develop through a sequence of three levels and two transitions, each level representing a more complex understanding of the relationship between self and other and each transition involving a critical reinterpretation of the moral conflict between selfishness and responsibility. The development of women's moral judgment appears to proceed from an initial concern with survival, to focus on goodness, and finally to a principled understanding of nonviolence as the most adequate guide to the just resolution of moral conflicts.

In counterposing to Kohlberg's longitudinal research on the development of hypothetical moral judgment in men a cross-sectional study of women's responses to actual dilemmas of moral conflict and choice, this essay precludes the possibility of generalization in either direction and leaves to further research the tasks of sorting out the different variables of occasion and sex. Longitudinal studies of women's moral judgments are necessary in order to validate the claims of stage and sequence presented here. Similarly, the contrast drawn between the moral judgments of men and women awaits for its confirmation a more systematic comparison of the responses of both sexes. Kohlberg's research on moral development has confounded the variables of age, sex, type of decision, and type of dilemma by presenting a single configuration (the responses of adolescent males to hypothetical dilemmas of conflicting rights) as the basis for a universal stage sequence. This paper underscores the need for systematic treatment of these variables and points toward their study as a critical task for future moral development research.

For the present, my aim has been to demonstrate the centrality of the concepts of responsibility and care in women's constructions of the moral domain, to indicate the close tie in women's thinking between conceptions of the self and conceptions of morality, and, finally, to argue the need for an expanded developmental theory that would include, rather than rule out from developmental consideration, the difference in the feminine voice. Such an inclusion seems essential, not only for explaining the development of women but also for understanding in both sexes the characteristics and precursors of an adult moral conception.

Notes

1. Haan, N. *Activism as moral protest: Moral judgments of hypothetical dilemmas and an actual situation of civil disobedience.* Unpublished manuscript, University of California at Berkeley, 1971.

2. Turiel, E. *A comparative analysis of moral knowledge and moral judgment in males and females.* Unpublished manuscript, Harvard University, 1973.

3. Kohlberg, L. *Continuities and discontinuities in childhood and adult moral development revisited.* Unpublished paper, Harvard University, 1973.

4. Kohlberg, L. Personal communication, August, 1976.

5. Gilligan, C., & Murphy, M. *The philosopher and the "dilemma of the fact": Moral development in late adolescence and adulthood.* Unpublished manuscript, Harvard University, 1977.

Study Questions

1. What theme runs through the essays cited by Gilligan?

2. What does Gilligan think this recurring theme indicates about women's taking moral stands? Does the trait revealed indicate that women are like children?

3. What do women's constructions of the abortion dilemma reveal?

4. Kohlberg distinguishes three perspectives on moral conflict and choice. How does Gilligan view these three stages, or perspectives, in relation to women?

5. How does the first perspective show up in the abortion decisions? The second?

6. How does the third perspective differ from these in regard to abortion decisions?

Maternal Thinking

Sara Ruddick

We are familiar with Victorian renditions of Ideal Maternal Love. My own favorite, like so many of these poems, was written by a son.

> There was a young man loved a maid
> Who taunted him, "Are you afraid,"
> She asked, "to bring me today
> Your mother's head upon a tray?"
>
> He went and slew his mother dead,
> Tore from her breast her heart so red,

Condensed from *Feminist Studies*, Vol. 6, No. 2 (Summer 1980), pp. 342–67. Reprinted by permission of the publisher, Feminist Studies, Inc., c/o Women's Studies Program, University of Maryland, College Park, MD 20742. (Notes deleted.)

> Then towards his lady love he raced,
> But tripped and fell in all his haste.
>
> As the heart rolled on the ground
> It gave forth a plaintive sound.
> And it spoke, in accents mild:
> "Did you hurt yourself, my child?"[1]

Though many of the story's wishes and fantasies are familiar, there is an unfamiliar twist to the poem. The maid asked for the mother's head, the son brought her heart. The maid feared and respected thoughts; the son believed only feelings are powerful. Again we are not surprised. The passions of maternity are so sudden, intense, and confusing that we often remain ignorant of the perspective, the *thought* that has developed from mothering. Lacking pride, we have failed to deepen or articulate that thought. This is a paper about the head of the mother.

I speak about a mother's *thought*—the intellectual capacities she develops, the judgments she makes, the metaphysical attitudes she assumes, the values she affirms. A mother engages in a discipline. That is, she asks certain questions rather than others; she establishes criteria for the truth, adequacy, and relevance of proposed answers; and she cares about the findings she makes and can act on. Like any discipline, hers has *characteristic* errors, temptations, and goals. The discipline of maternal thought consists in establishing criteria for determining failure and success, in setting the priorities, and in identifying the virtues and liabilities the criteria presume. To describe the capacities, judgments, metaphysical attitudes, and values of maternal thought does not presume maternal achievement. It is to describe a *conception* of achievement, the end to which maternal efforts are directed, conceptions and ends that are different from dominant public ones.

In stating my claims about maternal thinking, I use a vocabulary developed in formulating theories about the general nature of thought. According to these theories, *all* thought arises out of social practice. In their practices, people respond to a reality that appears to them as given, as presenting certain *demands*. The response to demands is shaped by *interests* that are generally interests in preserving, reproducing, directing, and understanding individual and group life.

These four interests are general in the sense that they arise out of the conditions of humans-in-nature and characterize us as a species. In addition, particular practices are characterized by specific interests in meeting the demands that some reality imposes on its participants. Religious, scientific, historical, mathematical, or any other thinking constitutes a disciplined response to a reality that appears to be "given." Socially organized thinkers name, elaborate, and test the particular realities to which they respond.

Maternal practice responds to the historical reality of a biological child in a particular social world. The agents of maternal practice, acting in response to the demands of their children, acquire a conceptual scheme—a vocabulary and logic of connections—through which they order and express the facts and values of their practice. In judgments and self-reflection, they refine and concretize this scheme. Intellectual activities are distinguishable but not separable from disciplines of feeling. There is a unity of reflection, judgment, and emotion. This unity I call "maternal thinking." Although I will not digress to argue the point here, it is important that maternal thinking is no more interest-governed, no more emotional, and no more relative to a particular reality (the growing child) than the thinking that arises from scientific, religious, or any other practice.

The demands of children and the interests in meeting those demands are always and only expressed by people in particular cultures and classes of their culture, living in specific geographical, technological, and historical settings. Some features of the mothering experience are invariant and nearly unchangeable; others, though changeable, are nearly universal. It is therefore possible to identify interests that seem to govern maternal practice throughout the species. Yet it is impossible even to begin to specify these interests without importing features specific to the class, ethnic group, and particular sex-gender system in which the interests are realized. In this essay I draw upon my knowledge of the institutions of motherhood in middle-class, white, Protestant, capitalist, patriarchal America, for these have expressed themselves in the heterosexual nuclear family in which I mother and was mothered. Although I have tried to compensate for the limits of my particular social and sexual history, I principally depend on others to correct my interpretations and translate across cultures.

Interests Governing Maternal Practice

Children "demand" their lives be preserved and their growth fostered. Their social group "demands" that growth be shaped in a way acceptable to the next generation. Maternal practice is governed by (at least) three interests in satisfying these demands for preservation, growth, and acceptability. Preservation is the most invariant and primary of the three. Because a care-taking mother typically bears her own children, preservation begins when conception is recognized and accepted. Although the form of preservation depends on widely variant beliefs about the fragility and care of the fetus, women have always had a lore in which they recorded their concerns for the baby they "carried." Once born, a child is physically vulnerable for many years. Even when she lives with the father of her child or other female adults, even when she has money to purchase or finds available supportive health and welfare services, a mother typically considers herself, and is considered by others, to be responsible for the maintenance of the life of her child.

Interest in fostering the physical, emotional, and intellectual growth of her child soon supplements a mother's interest in its preservation. The human child is typically capable of complicated emotional and intellectual development; the human adult is radically different in kind from the child it once was. A woman who mothers may be aided or assaulted by the help and advice of fathers, teachers, doctors, moralists, therapists, and others who have an interest in fostering and shaping the growth of her child. Although rarely given primary credit, a mother typically holds herself, and is held by others, responsible for the *malfunction* of the growth process. From early on, certainly by the middle years of childhood, a mother is governed by a third interest: she must shape natural growth in such a way that her child becomes the sort of adult that she can appreciate and others can accept. Mothers will vary enormously, individually and socially, in the traits and lives they will appreciate in their children. Nevertheless, a mother typically takes as the criterion of her success the production of a young adult acceptable to her group.

The three interests in preservation, growth, and acceptability of the child govern maternal practices in general. Not all mothers are, as individuals, governed by these interests, however. Some mothers are incapable of in-

terested participation in the practices of mothering because of emotional, intellectual, or physical disability. Severe poverty may make interested maternal practice and therefore maternal thinking nearly impossible. Then, of course, mothers engage in practices other than, and often conflicting with, mothering. Some mothers, aware of the derogation and confinement of women in maternal practice, may be disaffected. In short, actual mothers have the same relation to maternal practice as actual scientists have to scientific practice, or actual believers have to religious practices. As mothers, they are governed by the interests of their respective practices. But the style, skill, commitment, and integrity with which they engage in these practices differ widely from individual to individual.

Interests in the preservation, growth, and acceptability of the child are frequently and unavoidably in conflict. A mother who watches a child eagerly push a friend aside as she or he climbs a tree is torn between preserving the child from danger, encouraging the child's physical skills and courage, and shaping a child according to moral restraints, which might, for example, inhibit the child's joy in competitive climbing. Although some mothers deny or are insensitive to the conflict, and others are clear about which interest should take precedence, mothers typically know that they cannot secure each interest, they know that goods conflict, and they know that unqualified success in realizing interests is an illusion. This unavoidable conflict of basic interests is one objective basis for the maternal humility I will shortly describe.

The Interest in Preserving the Life of the Child

A mother, acting in the interest of preserving and maintaining life, is in a peculiar relation to "nature." As childbearer, she often takes herself, and is taken by others, to be an especially "natural" member of her culture. As child tender, she must respect nature's limits and court its favor with foresightful actions that range from immunizations, to caps on household poisons, to magical imprecation, warnings, and prayers. "Nature" with its unpredictable varieties of dirt and disease is her enemy as much as her ally. Her children are natural creatures, often unable to understand or abet her efforts to protect them. Because they frequently find her necessary direction constraining, a mother can experience her children's own liveliness as another enemy of the life she is preserving.

No wonder, then, that as she engages in preservation, a mother is liable to the temptations of fearfulness and excessive control. If she is alone with and responsible for two or more young children, then control of herself, her children, and her physical environment is her only option, however rigid or excessive she appears to outsiders. Though necessarily controlling their acts, *reflecting* mothers themselves identify rigid or excessive control as the likely defects of the virtues they are required to practice. The identification of liability as such, with its implication of the will to overcome, characterizes this aspect of maternal thought. The epithet "controlling mother" is often unsympathetic, even matriphobic. On the other hand, it may, in line with the insights of maternal thought, remind us of what maternal thinking *counts as* failure.

To a mother, "life" may well seem "terrible, hostile, and quick to pounce on you if you give it a chance."[2] In response, she develops a metaphysical attitude toward "Being as such," an attitude I call "holding," an attitude governed by the priority of keeping over acquiring, of conserving the fragile, of maintaining whatever is at hand and necessary to the child's life. It is an attitude elicited by the work of "world-*protection*, world-*preservation*, world-*repair* . . . the invisible weaving of a frayed and threadbare family life."[3]

The priority of holding over acquiring distinguishes maternal thinking from scientific thinking and from the instrumentalism of technocracy. To be sure, under the pressures of consumerism, holding may become frantic accumulating and storing. More seriously, a parent may feel compelled to preserve her *own* children, whatever befalls other children. The more competitive and hierarchical the society, the more thwarted a mother's individual, autonomous pursuits, the more likely that preservation will become egocentric, frantic, and

cruel. Mothers recognize these dangers and fight them.

Holding, preserving mothers have distinctive ways of seeing and being in the world that are worth considering. For example, faced with the fragility of the lives it seeks to preserve, maternal thinking recognizes humility and resilient cheerfulness as virtues of its practice. In so doing it takes issue with popular moralities of assertiveness and much contemporary moral theory.

Humility is a metaphysical attitude one takes toward a world beyond one's control. One might conceive of the world as governed by necessity and change (as I do) or by supernatural forces that cannot be comprehended. In either case, humility implies a profound sense of the limits of one's actions and of the unpredictability of the consequences of one's work. As the philosopher Iris Murdoch puts it: "Every natural thing, including one's own mind, is subject to chance. . . . One might say that chance is a subdivision of death. . . . We cannot dominate the world."[4] Humility that emerges from maternal practices accepts not only the facts of damage and death, but also the facts of the independent and uncontrollable, developing and increasingly separate existences of the lives it seeks to preserve. "Humility is not a peculiar habit of self-effacement, rather like having an inaudible voice, it is selfless respect for reality and one of the most difficult and central of virtues."[5]

If, in the face of danger, disappointment, and unpredictability, mothers are liable to melancholy, they are also aware that a kind, resilient good humor is a virtue. This good humor must not be confused with the cheery denial that is both a liability and, unfortunately, a characteristic of maternal practice. Mothers are tempted to denial simply by the insupportable difficulty of passionately loving a fragile creature in a physically threatening, socially violent, pervasively uncaring and competitive world. Defensive denial is exacerbated as it is officially encouraged, when we must defend against perceptions of our own subordination. Our cheery denials are cruel to our children and demoralizing to ourselves.

Clear-sighted cheerfulness is the virtue of which denial is the degenerative form. It is clear-sighted cheerfulness that Spinoza must have had in mind when he said: "Cheerfulness is always a good thing and never excessive"; it "increases and assists the power of action."[6] Denying cheeriness drains intellectual energy and befuddles the will; the cheerfulness honored in maternal thought increases and assists the power of maternal action.

In a daily way, cheerfulness is a matter-of-fact willingness to continue, to give birth and to accept having given birth, to welcome life despite its conditions. Resilient good humor is a style of mothering "in the deepest sense of 'style' in which to discover the right style is to discover what you are really trying to do."[7]

Because in the dominant society "humility" and "cheerfulness" name virtues of subordinates, and because these virtues have in fact developed in conditions of subordination, it is difficult to credit them and easy to confuse them with the self-effacement and cheery denial that are their degenerative forms. Again and again, in attempting to articulate maternal thought, language is sicklied o'er by the pale cast of sentimentality and thought itself takes on a greeting-card quality. Yet literature shows us many mothers who in their "holding" actions value the humility and resilient good humor I have described. One can meet such mothers, recognize their thought, any day one learns to listen. One can appreciate the effects of their disciplined perseverance in the unnecessarily beautiful artifacts of the culture they created. "I made my quilt to keep my family warm. I made it beautiful so my heart would not break."[8]

The Interest in Fostering the Child's Growth

Mothers must not only preserve fragile life. They must also foster growth and welcome change. If the "being" preserved seems always to be endangered, undone, slipping away, the "being" that changes is always developing, building, purposively moving away. The "holding," preserving mother must, in response to change, be simultaneously a changing mother. Her conceptual scheme in terms of which she makes sense of herself, her child, and their common world will be more the Aristotelian

biologist's than the Platonic mathematician's. Innovation takes precedence over permanence, disclosure and responsiveness over clarity and certainty. The idea of "objective reality" itself "undergoes important modification when it is to be understood, not in relation to the world described by science, but in relation to the progressing life of a person."[9]

Women are said to value open over closed structure, to eschew the clear-cut and unambiguous, to refuse a sharp division between inner and outer or self and other. They also are said to depend on and prize the private inner lives of the mind. If these facets of the "female mind" are elicited by maternal practices, they may well be interwoven responses to the changeability of a growing child. A child is itself an "open structure" whose acts are irregular, unpredictable, often mysterious. A mother, in order to understand her child, must assume the existence of a conscious continuing person whose acts make sense in terms of perceptions and responses to a meaning-filled world. She knows that her child's fantasies and thoughts are connected not only to the child's power to act, but often are the only basis for her understanding of the child and for the child's self-understanding.

A mother, in short, is committed to two philosophical positions: she is a mentalist rather than a behaviorist, and she assumes the priority of personhood over action. Moreover, if her "mentalism" is to enable her to understand and love, she must be realistic about the psyche whose growth she fosters. *All* psyches are moved by fear, lust, anger, pride, and defenses against them; by what Simone Weil called "*natural* movements of the soul" and likened to laws of physical gravity.[10] This is not to deny that the soul is also blessed by "grace," "light," and erotic hungering for goodness.[11] Mothers cannot take grace for granted, however, nor can they force or deny the less flattering aggrandizing and consolatory operations of childhood psychic life.

Her realistic appreciation of a person's continuous mental life allows a mother to expect change, to change with change. As psychologist Jean Baker Miller puts it: "In a very immediate and day-to-day way women *live* for change."[12] Change requires a kind of learning in which what one learns cannot be applied exactly, often not even by analogy, to a new situation. If science agrees to take as real the reliable results of *repeatable* experiments, its learning will be different in kind from maternal learning. Miller is hopeful that if we attend to maternal practices, we can develop new ways of studying learning that are appropriate to the changing natures of all people and communities, for it is not only children who change, grow, and need help in growing; those who care for children must also change in response to changing reality. And we all might grow—as opposed to aging—if we could learn how. For everyone's benefit, "women must now face the task of putting their vast unrecognized experience with change into a new and broader level of operation."[13]

Miller writes of achievement, of women who have learned to change and respond to change. But she admits: "Tragically in our society, women are prevented from fully enjoying these pleasures [of growth] themselves by being made to feel that fostering them in others is the only valid role for all women and by the loneliness, drudgery and isolated non-cooperative household setting in which they work."[14]

In delineating maternal thought, I do not claim that mothers realize, in themselves, the capacities and virtues we learn to value as we care for others. Rather, mothers develop *conceptions* of abilities and virtues, according to which they measure themselves and interpret their actions. It is no great sorrow that some mothers never acquire humility, resilient good humor, realism, respect for persons, and responsiveness to growth—that all of us fail often in many ways. What is a great sorrow is to find the task itself misdescribed, sentimentalized, and devalued.

The Interest in Shaping an Acceptable Child

The third demand that governs maternal practice is the demand, at once social and personal, that the child's growth be shaped in a manner that makes life acceptable. "Acceptability" is defined in terms of the values of the mother's social group—whatever of its values she has internalized as her own plus values of group members whom she feels she must please or is fearful of displeasing. Society demands that a mother produce an adult acceptable to the next generation. Mothers, roughly half of society, have an interest in meeting that demand. They are also governed by a more stringent form of acceptability. They want the child they produce to be a person whom they themselves, and those closest to them, can appreciate. The demand of appreciability gives an urgency—sometimes exhilarating, sometimes anguishing—to maternal practice.

The task of producing an appreciable child gives a mother a unique opportunity to explore, create, and insist on her own values; to train her children for strength and virtue; and ultimately to develop openness and reciprocity in regard to her child's most threatening differences from her, namely, moral ones. As a mother thinks upon the appreciability of her child, her maternal work becomes a self-conscious, reflective expression of a disciplined conscience.

In response to the demand of acceptability, maternal thinking becomes contradictory—that is, it betrays its own interest in the growth of children. Almost everywhere, the practices of mothering take place in societies in which women of all classes are less powerful than men of their class to determine the conditions under which their children grow. Throughout history, most women have mothered in conditions of military and social violence and often of extreme poverty. They have been governed by men, and increasingly by managers and experts of both sexes, whose policies mothers neither shape nor control. Out of maternal powerlessness, in response to a society whose values it does not determine, maternal thinking has often and largely opted for inauthenticity and the "good" of others.

By "inauthenticity" I designate a double willingness—first, a willingness to *travailler pour l'armée*,[15] to accept the uses to which others put one's children; and second, a willingness to remain blind to the implications of those uses for the actual lives of women and children. Maternal thought embodies inauthenticity by taking on the values of the dominant culture. Like the "holding" of preservation, "inauthenticity" is a mostly nonconscious response to Being as Such. Only this attitude is not a caretaker's response to the natural exigencies of child tending, but a subordinate's reaction to a social reality essentially characterized by the domination and subordination of persons. Inauthenticity constructs and then assumes a world in which one's own values do not count. It is allied to fatalism and to some religious thought—some versions of Christianity, for example. As inauthenticity is lived out in maternal practice, it gives rise to the values of obedience and "being good"; that is, to fulfill the values of the dominant culture is taken as an achievement. Obedience is related to humility in the face of the limits of one's powers. But unlike humility, which respects indifferent nature, the incomprehensible supernatural, and human fallibility, obedience respects the actual control and preferences of dominant people.

Individual mothers, living out maternal thought, take on the values of the subcultures to which they belong and the men with whom they are allied. Because some groups and many men are vibrantly moral, these values are not necessarily inadequate. Nevertheless, even moral groups and men almost always accept the relative subordination of women, whatever other ideals of equality and autonomy they may hold. A "good" mother may well be praised for colluding in her own subordination, with destructive consequences to herself and her children. Moreover, most groups and men impose at least some values that are psychologically and physically damaging to children. Yet, to be "good," a mother may be expected to endorse these inimical values. She is the person principally responsible for training her children in the ways and desires of obedience. This may mean training her daughters for powerlessness, her sons for war, and both for crippling work in dehumanizing factories, businesses, and professions. It may mean training both daughters and sons for defensive or arrogant power over others in sexual, economic, or political life. A mother who trains either for powerlessness or abusive power over others betrays the life she has preserved, whose growth she has fostered. She denies her children even the possibility of being strong and good.

The strain of colluding in one's own powerlessness, coupled with the frequent and much greater strain of betraying the children one has tended, would be insupportable if conscious. A mother under strain may internalize as her own some values that are clearly inimical to her children. She has, after all, usually been rewarded for such protective albeit destructive internalization. In addition, she may blind herself to the implications of her obedience, a blindness excused and exacerbated by the cheeriness of denial. For precariously but deeply protected mothers, feminist accounts of power relations and their cost call into question the worthiness of maternal work and the genuineness of maternal love. It is understandable that such women fight insight as others fight bodily assault, revealing in their struggles a commitment to their own sufferings that may look "neurotic" but is in fact, given their options, realistic.

When I described maternal thought arising out of the interests in growth and preservation, I was not speaking of the actual achievement of mothers, but of a conception of achievement. Similarly, in describing the thought arising out of the interests in acceptability, I am not speaking of actual mothers' adherence to dominant values, but of a conception of their relations to those values in which obedience and "being good" is considered an achievement. Many individual mothers "fail," that is, they insist on their own values and will not remain blind to the implications of dominant values for the lives of their children. Moreover, given the damaging effects of prevailing sexual arrangements and social hierarchies on maternal lives, it is clearly outrageous to blame mothers for their (our) obedience.

Obedience is largely a function of social powerlessness. Maternal work is done according to the Law of the Symbolic Father and under His Watchful Eye, as well as, typically, according to the desires, even whims, of the father's house. "This is my Father's world/Oh let me ne'er forget/that though the wrong be oft so strong,/He is the ruler yet." In these conditions of work, inauthentic obedience to dominant patriarchal values is as plausible a maternal response as respect for the results of experiment is in scientific work.

As I have said, the work of mothering can

become a rewarding, disciplined expression of conscience. In order for this opportunity to be realized, either collectively or by individual mothers, maternal thought will have to be transformed by feminist consciousness.

> Coming to have a feminist consciousness is the experience of coming to know the truth about oneself and one's society. . . . The very *meaning* of what the feminist apprehends is illuminated by the light of what ought to be. . . . The feminist apprehends certain features of social reality *as* intolerable, as to be rejected in behalf of a transforming project for the future. . . . Social reality is revealed as deceptive. . . . What is really happening is quite different from what appears to be happening.[16]

Feminist consciousness will first transform in-authentic obedience into wariness, uncertain reflection, and at times, anguished confusion. The feminist becomes "marked by the experi-ence of moral ambiguity" as she learns new ways of living without betraying her women's past, without denying her obligations to others. "She no longer knows what sort of person she ought to be, and therefore, she does not know what she ought to do. One moral paradigm is called into question by the laborious and often obscure emergence of another."[17]

Out of confusion will arise new voices, rec-ognized not so much by the content of the truths they enunciate as by the honesty and courage of enunciation. They will be at once familiar and original, these voices arising out of maternal practice, affirming its own criteria of acceptability, insisting that the dominant values are unacceptable and need not be accepted.

The Capacity for
Attentive Love

Finally, I would like to discuss a capacity—attention—and a virtue—love—that are central to the conception of achievement that maternal thought as a whole articulates. This capacity and virtue, when realized, invigorate preserva-tion and enable growth. Attention and love again and again undermine a mother's in-authentic obedience as she perceives and en-dorses a child's experience though society finds it intolerable. The identification of the capacity

of attention and the virtue of love is at once the foundation and the corrective of maternal thought.

The notion of "attention" is central to the philosophy of Simone Weil and is developed, along with the related notion of "love," by Iris Murdoch, who was profoundly influenced by Weil. Attention and love are fundamental to the construction of "objective reality" un-derstood "in relation to the progressing life of a person," a "reality which is revealed to the patient eye of love."[18] Attention is an *intellectual* capacity connected even by definition with love, a special "knowledge of the individual."[19] "The name of this intense, pure, disinterested, gratuitous, generous attention is love."[20] Weil thinks that the capacity for attention is a "mira-cle." Murdoch ties it more closely to familiar achievement: "The task of attention goes on all the time and at apparently empty and everyday moments we are 'looking,' making those little peering efforts of imagination which have such important cumulative results."[21]

For Weil and Murdoch, the enemy of atten-tion is what they call "fantasy," defined not as rich imaginative play, which does have a central role in maternal thinking, but as the "prolifera-tion of blinding self-centered aims and im-ages."[22] Fantasy, according to their original conception, is intellectual and imaginative activity in the service of consolation, domina-tion, anxiety, and aggrandizement. It is reverie designed to protect the psyche from pain, self-induced blindness designed to protect it from insight. Fantasy, so defined, works in the ser-vice of inauthenticity. "The difficulty is to keep the attention fixed on the real situation"[23]—or, as I would say, on the real children. Attention to real children, children seen by the "patient eye of love, . . . teaches us how real things [real children] can be looked at and loved without being seized and used, without being appropri-ated into the greedy organism of the self."[24]

Much in maternal practices works against attentive love: intensity of identification, vicarious living through a child, daily wear of maternal work, harassment and indignities of an indifferent social order, and the clamor of children themselves. Although attention is eli-cited by the very reality it reveals—the reality of a growing person—it is a discipline that requires effort and self-training. The love of children is not only the most intense of attachments, but it is also a detachment, a giving up, a letting grow. To love a child without seizing or using it, to see the child's reality with the patient, loving eye of attention—such loving and attending might well describe the separation of mother and child from the mother's point of view. Of course, many mothers fail much of the time in attentive love and loving attention. Many mothers also train themselves in the looking, self-restraining, and empathy that is loving attention. They can be heard doing so in any playground or coffee klatch.

I am not saying that mothers, individually or collectively, are (or are not) especially wonderful people. My point is that out of maternal practices distinctive ways of conceptualizing, ordering, and valuing arise. We *think* differently about what it *means* and what it takes to be "wonderful," to be person, to be real.

Murdoch and Weil, neither mothers themselves nor especially concerned with mothers, are clear about the absolute value of attentive love and the reality it reveals. Weil writes:

> In the first legend of the Grail, it is said that the Grail . . . belongs to the first comer who asks the guardian of the vessel, a king three-quarters paralyzed by the most painful wound, "What are you going through?"
>
> The love of our neighbor in all its fullness simply means being able to say to him: "What are you going through?" . . . Only he who is capable of attention can do this.[25]

I do not claim absolute value, but only that attentive love, the training to ask "What are you going through?" is central to maternal practices. If I am right about its place in maternal thought, and if Weil and Murdoch are right about its absolute value, the self-conscious inclusion of maternal thought in the dominant culture will be of general intellectual and moral benefit.

Some Social and Political Implications

I have described a "thought" arising out of maternal practices organized by the interests of

preservation, growth, and acceptability. Although in some respects the thought is "contradictory" (i.e., it betrays its own values and must be transformed by feminist consciousness), the thought as a whole, with its fulcrum and correction in attentive love, is worthy of being expressed and respected. This thought has emerged out of maternal practices that are oppressive to women and children. I believe that it has emerged largely in response to the relatively invariable requirements of children and despite oppressive circumstances. As in all women's thought, some worthy aspects of maternal thought may arise out of identification with the powerless and excluded. Nevertheless, oppression is largely responsible for the defects rather than the strengths of maternal thought, as in the obedient goodness to which mothers find themselves "naturally" subscribing. When the oppressiveness of gender arrangements is combined with the oppression of race, poverty, or the multiple injuries of class, it is a miracle that maternal thought can arise at all. On the other hand, that it does indeed arise, miraculously, is clear both from literature (Alice Walker, Tillie Olsen, Maya Angelou, Agnes Smedley, Lucille Clifton, Louisa May Alcott, Audre Lorde, Marilyn French, Grace Paley, and countless others) and from daily experience. Maternal thought *identifies* priorities, attitudes, and virtues; it *conceives* of achievement. The more oppressive the institutions of motherhood, the greater the pain and struggle in living out the worthy and transforming the damaging aspects of thought.

Maternal thinking is only one aspect of "womanly" thinking. In articulating and respecting the maternal, I do not underwrite the still current, false, and pernicious identification of womanhood with biological or adoptive mothering of particular children in families. For me, "maternal" is a social category. Although maternal thinking arises out of actual childcaring practices, biological parenting is neither necessary nor sufficient. Many women and some men express maternal thinking in various kinds of working and caring with others. And some biological mothers, especially in misogynistic societies, take a fearful, defensive distance from their own mothering and the maternal lives of any women.

Maternal thought does, I believe, exist for all women in a radically different way than for men. It is because we are *daughters,* nurtured and trained by women, that we early receive maternal love with special attention to its implications for our bodies, our passions, and our ambitions. We are alert to the values and costs of maternal practices whether we are determined to engage in them or avoid them.

It is now argued that the most revolutionary change we can make in the institution of motherhood is to include men equally in every aspect of childcare. When men and women live together with children, it seems not only fair but deeply moral that they share in every aspect of childcare. To prevent or excuse men from maternal practice is to encourage them to separate public action from private affection, the privilege of parenthood from its cares. Moreover, even when men are absent from the nursery, their dominance in every other public and private room shapes a child's earliest conceptions of power. To familiarize children with "natural" domination at their earliest age in a context of primitive love, assertion, and sexual passion is to prepare them to find equally "natural" and exhaustive the division between exploiter and exploited that pervades the larger world. Although daughter and son alike may internalize "natural" domination, neither typically can live with it easily. Identifying with and imitating exploiters, we are overcome with self-hate; aligning ourselves with the exploited, we are fearful and manipulative. Again and again, family power dramas are repeated in psychic, interpersonal, and professional dramas, while they are institutionalized in economic, political, and international life. Radically recasting the power-gender roles in those dramas just might revolutionize social conscience.

Assimilating men into childcare both inside and outside the home would also be conducive to serious social reform. Responsible, equal childcaring would require men to relinquish power and their own favorable position in the division between intellectual/professional and service labor as that division expresses itself domestically. Loss of preferred status at home might make socially privileged men more suspicious of unnecessary divisions of labor and damaging hierarchies in the public world.

Moreover, if men were emotionally and practically committed to childcare, they would reform the work world in parents' interests. Once no one "else" was minding the child, good day-care centers with flexible hours would be established to which parents could trust their children from infancy on. These day-care centers, like the workweek itself, would be managed flexibly in response to human needs as well as to the demands of productivity, with an eye to growth rather than measurable profit. Such moral reforms of economic life would probably begin with professions and managers servicing themselves. Even in nonsocialist countries, however, their benefits could be unpredictably extensive.

I would not argue that the assimilation of men into childcare is the primary social goal for mothers. Rather, we must work to bring a *transformed* maternal thought in the public realm, to make the preservation and growth of *all* children a work of public conscience and legislation. This will not be easy. Mothers are no less corrupted than anyone else by concerns of status and class. Often our misguided efforts on behalf of the success and purity of our children frighten them and everyone else around them. As we increase and enjoy our public effectiveness, we will have less reason to live vicariously through our children. We may then begin to learn to sustain a creative tension between our inevitable and fierce desire to foster our own children and the less compulsive desire that all children grow and flourish.

Nonetheless, it would be foolish to believe that mothers, just because they are mothers, can transcend class interest and implement principles of justice. All feminists must join in articulating a theory of justice shaped by and incorporating maternal thinking. Moreover, the generalization of attentive love to *all* children requires politics. The most enlightened thought is not enough.

Closer to home again, we must refashion our domestic life in the hope that the personal will in fact betoken the political. We must begin by resisting the temptation to construe "home" simplemindedly, as a matter of justice between mothers and fathers. Single parents, lesbian mothers, and coparenting women remind us that many ways to provide children with examples of caring do not incorporate sexual inequalities of power and privilege. Those of us who live with the fathers of our children will eagerly welcome shared parenthood—for overwhelming practical as well as ideological reasons. But in our eagerness, we must not forget that as long as a mother is not effective publicly and self-respecting privately, male presence can be harmful as well as beneficial. It does a woman no good to have the power of the Symbolic Father brought right into the nursery, often despite the deep, affectionate egalitarianism of an individual man. It takes a strong mother and father to resist temptations to domination and subordination for which they have been trained and are socially rewarded. And whatever the hard-won equality and mutual respect an individual couple may achieve, as long as a mother—even if she is no more parent than father—is derogated and subordinate outside the home, children will feel angry, confused, and "wildly unmothered."[26]

Despite these reservations, I look forward to the day when men are willing and able to share equally and actively in transformed maternal practices. When that day comes, will we still identify some thought as maternal rather than merely parental? Might we echo the cry of some feminists—there shall be no more "women"—with our own—there shall be no more "mothers," only people engaging in childcare? To keep matters clear I would put the point differently. On that day there will be no more "fathers," no more people of either sex who have power over their children's lives and moral authority in their children's world, though they do not do the work of attentive love. There will be mothers of both sexes who live out a transformed maternal thought in communities that share parental care—practically, emotionally, economically, and socially. Such communities will have learned from their mothers how to value children's lives.

Notes

1. From J. Echegaray, "Severed Heart," quoted by Jessie Bernard in *The Future of Motherhood* (New York: Dial, 1974), p. 4.

2. The words are Mrs. Ramsay's in Virginia Woolf's *To the Lighthouse* (New York: Harcourt, Brace and World, 1927), p. 92.

3. Adrienne Rich, "Conditions for Work: The Common World of Women," in *Working It Out,* edited by Sara Ruddick and Pamela Daniels (New York: Pantheon, 1977), p. xvi (italics mine).

4. Iris Murdoch, *The Sovereignty of Good* (New York: Shocken Books, 1971), p. 99.

5. Ibid., p. 95.

6. Spinoza, *Ethics,* Book 3, Proposition 42, demonstration. See also Proposition 40, Note, and Proposition 45, both in Book 3.

7. Bernard Williams, *Morality* (New York: Harper Torchbooks, 1972), p. 11.

8. The words are those of a Texas farmwoman who quilted as she huddled with her family in a shelter as, above them, a tornado destroyed their home. The story was told to me by Miriam Schapiro.

9. Murdoch, *Sovereignty of Good,* p. 26.

10. Simone Weil, "Gravity and Grace," in *Gravity and Grace* (London: Routledge & Kegan Paul, 1952; first French ed., 1947), passim.

11. Ibid, and other essays in *Gravity and Grace.* Both the language and concepts are indebted to Plato.

12. Jean Baker Miller, *Toward a New Psychology for Women* (Boston: Beacon Press, 1973), p. 54.

13. Miller, *Toward a New Psychology,* p. 56.

14. Ibid., p. 40.

15. I am indebted to Adrienne Rich, *Of Woman Born* (New York: W. W. Norton, 1976), especially chapter 8, both for this phrase and for the working out of the idea of inauthenticity. My debt to this book as a whole is pervasive.

16. Sandra Lee Bartky, "Toward a Phenomenology of Feminist Consciousness," in *Feminism and Philosophy,* edited by Mary Vetterling-Braggin, Frederick A. Elliston, and Jane English (Totowa, N.J.: Littlefield, Adams, 1977), pp. 22–37. Quotes from pp. 33, 25, 28, 29.

17. Ibid., p. 31. On the riskiness of authenticity, the courage it requires of women, see also Miller, *Toward a New Psychology,* chapter 9.

18. Murdoch, *Sovereignty of Good,* p. 40.

19. Ibid., p. 28.

20. Simone Weil, "Human Personality," in *Collected Essays,* chosen and translated by Richard Rees (London: Oxford University Press, 1962). Also *Simone Weil Reader,* edited by George A. Panichas (New York: McKay, 1977), p. 333.

21. Murdoch, *Sovereignty of Good,* p. 43.

22. Ibid., p. 67.

23. Ibid., p. 91.

24. Ibid., p. 65.

25. Simone Weil, "Reflections of the Right Use of School Studies with a View to the Love of God," in *Waiting for God* (New York: G. Putnam's, 1951), p. 115.

26. Rich, *Of Woman Born,* p. 225.

Study Questions

1. What does Ruddick mean by "maternal thinking"? Do men have or can they acquire maternal thinking? Does such thinking grow out of biology?

2. Ruddick takes the view that thinking arises from practice. What is "maternal practice"? What three interests govern maternal practice?

3. Discuss how the maternal attitude Ruddick calls "holding" grows out of maternal practice. Why does this attitude manifest itself (among other ways) as humility?

4. A second aspect of maternal thinking that Ruddick discusses is the avoidance of the "clear-cut and unambiguous," that is, fluidity of conceptual outlook. How might such a form of thought grow out of maternal practice?

5. What are some of the "degenerate forms" of the maternal perspective?

6. In Ruddick's opinion, how should feminism transform maternal thought?

7. Ruddick says, "The identification of the capacity of attention and the virtue of love is at once the foundation and the corrective of maternal thought." Explain.

8. How does Ruddick feel about men becoming involved in childcare?

Ethics from the Standpoint of Women

Nel Noddings

Until quite recently, the idea of ethics from the standpoint of women—or "female ethics" as some prefer to call it[1]—would have been called a contradiction in terms. Women had long been considered morally inferior to men and were

From Deborah L. Rhode, ed., *Theoretical Perspectives on Sexual Difference* (New Haven, CT: Yale University Press, 1990). Reprinted by permission.

thought to be ethically dangerous to them.[2] This inferiority was considered irremovable; it was a permanent privation inherent in a creature made explicitly for reproduction.[3] Women were credited with a certain goodness if they met the standards men established for them, but this goodness was not the ethical goodness that genuine moral agents can achieve. Such goodness requires a level of objective thinking and detachment considered beyond the capabilities of females. Female goodness, in the standard male version, consisted in obedience, industry, silence, and service. Woman's goodness, like that of animals and instruments, was measured in relation to her usefulness to males.[4]

It is not surprising, then, that there should be controversy—even among feminists—over the value of an ethics built on women's traditional role as nurturers. (An ethics of caring is not the only possible version of "female ethics," and I mention alternatives later.) Objections to this approach to ethics come from a variety of sources. One objection to an ethics of caring comes from those who believe that caring and nurturing are somehow natural or instinctive. Women are to be appreciated for their dedication and self-sacrifice in family life, but there is no reason to regard their nurturing as a manifestation of ethical agency. A second objection, coming largely from feminists, expresses the fear that an ethics built on such experience (if it were possible to build one) might be used to maintain women's servitude and aggravate the unfortunate tendency of women to blame themselves for everything that goes wrong in their relationships.[5] A third objection is that the very idea of a female ethic contradicts the supposed universality of ethics as the philosophical study of morality. A female ethic, from this perspective, would have to be classified with "business ethics," "personal ethics," and other specialized ethics that apply philosophical ethics to particular problems and domains. A genderized ethic could not, by definition, attain the status of ethics in philosophy.

But the construction of ethics from the standpoint of women is an important enterprise that may contribute significantly to both ethical thinking and general human welfare. Such an ethic has much in common with Christian agape; for example, it emphasizes needs over rights and love over duty, but it does not depend on divine commandment or seek divine favor. It contrasts sharply with the Kantian and utilitarian ethics that have dominated philosophical thinking. The first step in establishing the credibility of a project aimed at the construction of a female ethic is to defend the idea of a genderized ethic.

Male Ethics

Under what circumstances can we properly say that a philosophy—in particular, an ethic—is male? In a careful analysis of this question, Jean Grimshaw separates unimportant from important senses in which one might describe philosophy as "male."[6] First, Grimshaw contends that just because almost all philosophers have been male, it cannot be said that their philosophical theories are necessarily male. This way of branding philosophy male is not, however, quite so easy to brush off as Grimshaw suggests. Our judgment depends on how we assess philosophy's traditional claim to universality. If philosophical thought is by definition universally applicable, then the claim that philosophy has been male because men have been doing it would clearly be false. If we can show, however, that philosophy—or any other body of theorizing—is necessarily constructed from a perspective, then the fact that philosophers have been men becomes a more salient bit of evidence for the maleness of philosophy. But Grimshaw is right in pointing out that argumentation is required to support the complaint, and the argument might have to proceed branch by branch. It may or may not be easier to show the maleness of ethics than the maleness of, say, logic.

Second, the well-documented misogyny found in the writings of important philosophers cannot be used to label their entire body of thought as male. This seems clearly right. As Grimshaw points out, misogynist statements in one essay do not necessarily contaminate work in which women are not even mentioned.

If we suspect, however, that ethical thought does indeed proceed from a perspective, we may begin a search for ways in which a male perspective affects ethics implicitly. This procedure will at best show that *some* philosophy is male and cast some doubt on its claim for universality.

Consider Kant as the first example.[7] In an essay entitled "Of the Distinction between the Beautiful and Sublime in the Interrelations of the Two Sexes," Kant attributes a form of inherent, aesthetically motivated goodness to women; women are identified with the beautiful. In contrast, men are at their best associated with the noble and sublime. Women do not need to think deeply, Kant declared, because they have "a strong inborn feeling for all that is beautiful." If they are so foolish as to undertake and actually succeed at "laborious learning" or "painful pondering," they lost the very charm and goodness that would have developed naturally. Kant says, "A woman with a head full of Greek . . . or . . . mechanics . . . might as well even have a beard; for perhaps that would express more obviously the mien of profundity for which she strives."[8] Not only are most women incapable of thinking at the level required for moral reasoning: they *should not,* since such thinking tends to destroy the merits "proper to the sex."

When Kant develops his ethical theory, it is not surprising that he elevates duty and principle to positions far above love and inclination. For Kant, acts done out of love do not qualify as moral acts. Only those committed out of a conscious sense of obedience to principle are moral acts. Feelings and emotions are not to be trusted. One must detach himself from personal loves and longings to be truly moral, and Kant (along with Aristotle and Aquinas) clearly believes women are incapable of this sort of detachment. Confined to the morally supportive arena of home and family, guided by good husbands or fathers, women can contribute through their inherent gentleness and love of beauty to the joy and comfort of private life. But they are clearly unsuited for academic and political life.

The obvious congruence between Kant's view of the difference between men and women and his separation of moral acts from loving ones may lead us to infer that his moral philosophy is thoroughly contaminated by his views of gender. But as Grimshaw points out, "Kant could, without inconsistency, have retained his view about "moral worth' but changed his view of women."[9] What we do not know, of course, is whether Kant would have changed his view of women or his view of ethics if he had been challenged with a thoughtful development of ethics based on some of the virtues he himself attributed to women. He

might have been led to modify both, for the creation of a female ethics would have forced him to acknowledge that women can think philosophically, and an emphasis on caring and response to needs in that ethic might press him to admit that genuinely moral acts (acts reflectively committed) can be motivated and jusified by fidelity to persons as well as fidelity to principles.

The important point is that Kant's moral philosophy, certainly one of the most influential in all of Western ethics, is apparently unconsciously genderized. Recognizing this, we might respond in one of several ways when we attempt to construct an ethical system. We might, for example, vow to avoid genderizing our own ethical thinking; we might adopt a deliberately genderized view that extols the virtues of our own sex; we might adopt a genderized view critically on the grounds that no other is honestly available.

To construct an ethic free of gendered views may be impossible in a thoroughly gendered society. It is not even clear that such a construction is desirable, but if it is one might argue that it cannot be accomplished until we have something like a balanced set of genderized ethics to analyze and then to transcend. Joan Tronto has argued that "although an ethic of care could be an important intellectual concern for feminists, the debate around this concern should be centered not in discussion of gender difference but in discourse about the ethic's adequacy as a moral theory."[10] Her reasons for making this recommendation are cogent. She fears, for example, that any assertion of gender difference in a society "that identifies the male as normal" will relegate the distinctly female view to inferiority. This is an important point, but there are a few others to keep in mind. First, it is not clear that discussion of care would ever have arisen if women had not initiated the discussion and responded to it with such recognition;[11] second, given that males have developed the criteria of adequacy for moral theories, female discourse concentrated on these may find itself oddly handicapped; and third, it may simply be necessary for women as moral and intellectual agents to develop moral theories (and other theories as well) through a careful articulation of their own female experience. Those who do such work can remain mindful of Tronto's warning, and I believe she is right that we should not get bogged down in disputes over empirical claims concerning moral orientation. Even if many women do not display signs of a caring orientation, and many men do, theories of care can clearly be developed from analysis of the activities of care that have dominated female experience for centuries. In this sense, the development of theories of care may be genderized for a long time before the "transvaluation" suggested by Tronto can even be approached.

The second possibility, building a frankly genderized ethic that favors certain virtues thought to belong to one's own sex, is illustrated in the work of Nietzsche. Here we encounter a consciously held and boldly articulated masculine ethic. Nietzsche's ethic is not just male in the sense that Kant's is; it does not simply reflect in its parallel structure a posited difference between men and women. Rather, it is built on a deliberately chosen model of masculinity that provides a foundation for the entire ethic. The morally best man, the one to be emulated and obeyed, is the courageous warrior. Slaves and women are to be despised. Any institution that embraces womanly "virtues" or exhibits female-like traits is also to be despised. The church, with its gentle (if sometimes hypocritical) message of love and forbearance, falls into this category. Nietzsche said of churchmen that they "smash the strong, contaminate great hopes, cast suspicion on joy in beauty, break down everything autocratic, manly, conquering, tyrannical, all the instincts proper to the highest and most successful of the type 'man.' "[12]

Nietzsche uses his description of the warrior to build a prescription for human (masculine) life at its best, a new morality that goes beyond traditional conceptions of good and evil. Simultaneously, he uses his own description of women as a foil to illustrate much of what he takes to be wrong with Western culture. Both men and women can find admirable insights in Nietzsche's work despite his depraved misogyny,[13] but it is hard to imagine any significant change in his view of women that would not have necessitated a correspondingly profound change in his moral philosophy. His philoso-

phy is overtly and proudly masculine, and much of it depends directly on the devaluation of women and all that is associated with the feminine.

Views very similar to Nietzsche's abounded into the twentieth century. Otto Weininger, whose work was apparently admired by Freud, published a book that was even more vitriolic than Nietzsche's in its condemnation of women. Like Kant, Weininger held that the truly feminine woman was incapable of genuine moral reasoning, but his assessment lacked a compensating admiration. Speaking of women he said, "In such a being as the absolute female there are no logical and ethical phenomena, and, therefore, the ground for the assumption of a soul is absent."[14] Weininger's "ethical" views were, like Nietzsche's, profoundly influenced by his misogyny. Unlike Nietzsche, however, who despised Kant's moral philosophy as unmanly in its emphasis on duty prescribed by universal principles, Weininger greatly admired Kant. As Bram Dijkstra points out, Weininger admired the individualism in Kant's position: "The birth of the Kantian ethics, the noblest event in the history of the world, was the moment when for the first time the dazzling conception came to him, 'I am responsible only to myself; I must follow none other; I must not forget myself even in my work; I am alone; I am free; I am lord of myself.' "[15] Where Nietzsche saw in Kant an emphasis on duty and therefore on weakness and subordination, Weininger detected the individualism that would characterize modern society and mark the admirable man.

All three men, Kant, Nietzsche, and Weininger, while differing dramatically on major points, carefully avoided anything in their ethical thinking that seemed to them to resemble the feminine. Traits that were admired had either to be denied of women (honesty and the capacity for rational thought are examples) or restricted to women (submissiveness and childlike innocence were often named in this category), and traits restricted to women had nothing to do with ethics. This way of approaching moral theory is both intellectually dishonest and morally wrong. When I speak of ethics from the standpoint of women, I do not mean that men should be excluded from either its descriptive or its prescriptive contents. Instead the ethic should frankly be developed from the experience of women. This leaves open the question whether it might also grow out of some forms of male experience.

The third possibility, that of adopting a genderized ethic for critical purposes, is hinted at in the work of William James, though he does not choose this strategy, letting the opportunity slip by. In his discussion of the warrior, James expresses the admiration traditionally directed toward this paradigm of masculinity, but he deplores the savagery and destruction of war. In an important sense he retains a masculine ethic while subjecting it to some criticism. Even though he wants to avoid the senseless violence of war, he wants also to avoid "effeminacy." "The fact remains," he says,

> that war is a school of strenuous life and heroism; and, being in the line of aboriginal instinct, is the only school that as yet is universally available. But when we ask ourselves whether this wholesale organization of irrationality and crime be our only bulwark against effeminacy, we stand aghast at the thought, and think more kindly of ascetic religion. . . . What we now need to discover in the social realm is the moral equivalent of war: something heroic that will speak to men as universally as war does, and yet will be compatible with their spiritual selves as war has proved itself to be imcompatible.[16]

James suggests poverty as a life equally strenuous and heroic, a suggestion in part motivated by a fear of softness, of being like a woman. "Does not . . . the worship of material luxury and wealth, which constitute so large a portion of the 'spirit' of our age, make somewhat for effeminacy and unmanliness?"[17] he asks. He sees the violence, greed, and "prevalent fear of poverty," which he regards as the "worst moral disease from which our civilization suffers,"[18] but he does not seem to see that the traditional view of masculinity—one that defines itself in opposition to femininity—may be a substantial cause of this moral disease. James was on the right track when he began to call into question the kinds of commitments men should make in exercising their virtues. If he had realized that his analysis was embedded in a genderized perspective, he might have

been able to explore the full range of human possibilities.

It is not necessary either to extol the virtues of one's sex blindly or to reject them wholesale in taking a genderized perspective, but if one is not aware that his or her perspective *is* genderized, one will miss a set of potential insights entirely. A female ethic built along Nietzschean lines might be instructive, but the notion is too outrageous for most of us even to consider, and at bottom it would be self-contradictory. What must be shown is that female experience, like male experience, can be reflected upon in a way that produces genuine moral insight and that failure to consider such experience and the virtues associated with it may condemn all of us to a state of moral dullness and incompleteness.

Female Ethics

The introduction of female ethics can hardly be construed as an attempt to genderize a field that has hitherto been gender-free; thus one objection to female ethics can be set aside. The other two objections remain. The first contends that the traditional activities and attitudes of women have nothing to do with ethics or even with a moral orientation from which ethics might be developed. The second expresses a concern that an ethics of caring might perpetuate the subordinate condition of women.

The first objection has two main parts: the common notion that traditional women's work does not require the kind of thought needed for moral agency and the more general claim that everyday experience is something to which ethics is applied, not something out of which ethics is developed.

Taking the first part of the objection, suppose that a phenomenology of work and interpersonal relations is necessary for the construction of ethics, is there reason to believe that a phenomenology of women's traditional work will uncover attitudes, ways of thinking, or modes of being that will contribute to ethical thought? This question has already been answered positively by a number of feminist thinkers and involves the analysis of such concepts and phenomena as caring,[19] virtues displayed in feminine life,[20] reproduction,[21] religious beliefs,[22] and maternal thinking.[23] The phenomena of caring are deeply embedded in ethical life, although theorists differ on the exact role of caring and its centrality to ethical theory.[24] Certain virtues have been attributed to women in their standard roles, but these virtues have not been considered important or even appropriate for men to develop, and both the philosophical account of birth and reproduction and the discussion of maternal thinking have induced lively debate on the relations between gender and ethical thought. A considerable revival of interest has taken place in restoring the role of ordinary life experience in ethics. Why, then, should there be resistance to the development of ethics from the traditional standpoint of women?

One reason for resistance is that, strictly speaking, there is no such thing as *the* standpoint of women.[25] Women's lives and voices differ. I, for example, speak not only as a woman but as middle-class, white, mother, and academic. Using such an expression as "the standpoint of women" risks an error similar to that in standard philosophy—a claim for universality that is patently false. This is an important objection, but it still may be important to articulate an ethical orientation that arises in the context of women's traditional work and gives attention to women's concerns. In doing this, we must choose topics that touch as many women's lives as possible, and we must also remember to invite a broad range of perspectives to join our own.

Another reason for resistance is the fear of being like a woman. Fear of being like a woman—of succumbing to effeminacy—has frequently influenced male philosophers, and now the same fear has infected many feminist thinkers. The feminist fear is not of being a woman but of being "like a woman"—of actualizing a hated stereotype. This fear is not entirely unfounded: as we have seen, the traditional view has not credited women with the capacity to think deeply about moral matters. It follows that the tasks traditionally charged to women cannot be either cognitively or morally demanding. Why, then, should we look at such activities as child-rearing, homemaking, and

cooking and the "admirable" attitudes that have long accompanied them when we are interested in moral thinking? Some feminists have insisted that women must free themselves from these oppressive tasks if they are to attain full personhood and, by implication, moral agency.

An alternative view interprets female ethics as a field that attends philosophically to matters of moral significance to women: abortion, divorce, equal employment opportunity, pornography, rape, child care, surrogate motherhood, and the like. These are important topics for ethics to address, and one sense in which ethics can be approached from the standpoint of women is to begin with problems that are especially relevant to them. No feminist can object to the careful study of such problems, but some might object to analyzing them in the standard mode. They have an understandable fear of being "like a man," of treating problems as though they can be coldly abstracted from the situations in which they arise and from the people who experience them. A strength of the program to develop an ethics of caring is that it does not invoke already established theoretical frameworks through which to study the problems of women but assumes that taking the standpoint of women requires starting with the life experiences of women. And this does not imply that the traditional experience of women must be exalted or fully accepted. Such a start acknowledges that our foremothers often worked at worthwhile tasks, thought clearly and effectively, and developed virtues as valuable as those James wanted to preserve for men from the warrior model, while criticizing the way of life that confined women to a specific set of tasks. The process of working from experience toward ethics offers the possibility of locating new ethical issues and gaining critical insights into existing frameworks.

As an example of this last possibility, let us see what can be uncovered through a consideration of one task, cooking, that has figured prominently in female experience. Cooking has been so important in women's lives that it has come under scathing attack by some feminists. Charlotte Perkins Gilman led the way in this rebellion by warning women that trying to find the way to men's hearts through their stomachs would produce "fat, greasy husbands" along with vice and indigestion.[26] She wanted women to be freed from the task of home food preparation, and she hoped that cooking would become a professional enterprise. Gilman's vehement attack on home cooking is similar to Shulamith Firestone's polemic against childbearing.[27] Both women felt that the activity under attack had to be abolished if women were to gain equality in public life, and both are subject to the same basic criticism: to attack activities that have been fundamental in women's lives is to elevate man's way of life above woman's prematurely and unreflectively. It risks losing the special contribution to thought that might be forthcoming from a careful analysis of women's experience in connection with these activities. One does not have to embrace the activities uncritically to take the standpoint of women, because female views arise from both participation in and resistance to these activities. But a woman's view cannot ignore them, as traditional views—those purporting to be man's (in the generic sense)—have done.

Gilman formulated her critique from a Marxist framework. Marx held that there are three components of labor: purposeful activity (the work itself), an object to be transformed, and an instrument to be used in accomplishing the work. When we read or listen to the stories women tell about food preparation, we see that something vital is missing in the Marxist view.[28] We need to ask not only what is being accomplished and how but *for whom*, in what setting, and with what attitude. To consider work as an economic concept seems right, but to consider it only an economic concept misses a large part of human experience. Much of women's work has been done, as Jane Roland Martin points out, with an emphasis on "caring, compassion, and connection,"[29] and one must ask how these attitudes can be maintained if the tasks under study lose their intimacy and become mere economic enterprises. As Marx worried over workers' alienation from their own labor under capitalism, women might be concerned with the loss of the tender personal interest that has often characterized "women's work." This concern need not culminate in a recommendation that all women rush back into the kitchen, but it

might encourage us to think deeply about the sharing, cultural knowledge, and intimate responsibility for others that may be learned and practiced in the ordinary tasks of everyday life. The result of such thinking might be a recommendation in direct opposition to Gilman's: instead of converting cooking to a completely professional occupation, all family members should be involved in the preparation of meals.

Insights may also spring from considering the struggles of largely female occupations toward professionalization. Teaching, nursing, and early childhood education (or child care) are semiprofessions wrestling with important dilemmas. On the one hand, professionalization usually means a separation from intimate contact with clients. Why, for example, should a highly educated nurse be involved in spooning food into those who cannot feed themselves; washing, powdering, and gently rubbing sore bodies; assisting in the evacuation of bladder and bowels; soothing, cooling, warming; wrapping, dressing, combing; comforting? On the other hand, many nurses and nurse-theoreticians recognize these tasks as central to nursing. Jean Watson, for example, counsels that these tasks present "caring occasions," occasions in which both nurse and patient must decide how to relate to each other.[30] A professional nurse, in contrast to a kindhearted volunteer, can learn a good deal about a patient's condition and treatment through performing these tasks, and the loving attention of an authorized professional seems to raise the spirit of a patient. Just as a child or a tired spouse appreciates a special dish made just for him or her, a patient feels *regarded* when a professional nurse cares for his or her personal needs. The dilemma pits the natural desire of well-educated women to be "true professionals" against the hard-earned wisdom that values direct contact even when it requires what is called "menial labor." Resolution of the dilemma demands a careful redefinition of what it means to be professional, and taking the standpoint of women is a first step in this direction.

But is it appropriate to work this way in ethics? This question is not so controversial now as it would have been a few years ago.

There is considerable philosophical interest today in ethical life as it appears in communities, occupations, and whole societies. The role of philosophy, in this view, is not to create ethics out of the heads of philosophers but to critique ethical life and bring some coherence to it. Some forms of foundational ethics, for example, clearly depend on background theories about the nature of experience, persons, and their relations to each other. A foundational ethics that does not posit self-evident basic premises, the intuition of basic moral knowledge, or an authoritatively established set of initial premises must build on a convincing description of human nature or experience.[31] Even if the ethical theory is neither foundational nor primarily concerned with moral knowledge and its justification, focusing instead on moral behavior and its correlate attitudes, such a grounding is necessary.

Recognition of the need to ground ethical theory in a psychology of human nature or experience is sometimes taken to mean that the moral orientation under development as an ethic requires empirical verification. This is only partly true. Studies showing that women are more concerned than men with human relationships,[32] that professional women may have greater sensitivity for moral issues than their male counterparts,[33] and that women are more likely than men to be politically concerned with issues of war and poverty[34] are interesting and important. They contribute to the convincing description of human experience that will ground an ethics of caring. But from a philosophical perspective it is not essential to show that all women think this way or that the "different voice" to which Gilligan refers belongs only to women. The ethic is concerned with the logic and phenomenology of caring, not with the number of people who actually invoke it or live by it. Although a program of this sort does develop out of a certain opposition to the ways of the opposite sex (fear of being like a stereotypical man does influence some feminist thinkers—certainly those concerned with the ethics of caring), it does not necessitate a claim for the moral superiority of women. Most feminists rightly reject such a claim on the dual grounds that it is undemonstrable and that arguments from nature

have not served women well in the past. The idea is to develop a phenomenology of women's experience that will provide an adequate grounding for the construction of ethics from the standpoint of women.

One must be cautious in assessing the present philosophical climate as receptive to the sort of program I have been discussing. The current revival of interest in practical ethics often centers on Aristotelian approaches.[35] Much of what I have said about studying ways of life and the tasks and attitudes characteristic of them is compatible with Aristotelian method, but an important difference must be noted and maintained. Aristotle's identification of virtues depended almost entirely on the establishment of exclusive classes and the activities appropriate to each. The virtues of women and of slaves were not those of educated citizens. He made no attempt to identify virtues in one class that might be cultivated in others by extending the range of privilege or sharing the array of common tasks. If he had made such an attempt, it would surely have moved in only one direction. One might try to inculcate the virtues of the highest class into lower classes, but one would never try to develop, say, feminine virtues in men.

Much of the same form of elitism can be found in current works that favor a return to Aristotle. Alasdair MacIntyre, for example, wants to begin the search for virtues in the sets of activities that he calls "practices," but he defines *practice* in an excruciatingly careful way to exclude all forms of therapy and management as well as many ordinary occupations from the class of practices.[36] Using such an approach we would surely end up with a hierarchy of jobs, persons, and virtues.

The feminist program outlined here has quite a different objective. It recognizes that, as Grimshaw says, "Theories . . . are not *only* ways of 'making sense' of the world. They may also be means by which one group of people may dominate or exercise control over another."[37] In our theorizing, we begin with ways of life in order to describe both strengths and weaknesses. The virtues we locate are not assigned permanently to a particular group or activity. Rather, we want to ask: If these virtues are worth maintaining, can they be developed if the ways of life in which they arose are abandoned? If not, can the ways of life be extended so that all human beings may develop them?

Caring and Self-Sacrifice

The final objection to an ethic of caring as an example of a genderized ethic is expressed well by Barbara Houston:

> When I reflect on the history of women, I realize how much our caring has nurtured and empowered others. I see how good it has been, for others. However, I also see how terribly costly it has been for women. And so the first question that arises for me is one that arises for many of Gilligan's subjects. Can an ethics of care avoid self-sacrifice?[38]

This is an important question motivated by a realistic fear. Women who maintain a moral orientation of caring are often exploited, find themselves dependent on men or on welfare in order to care for their children, and are sometimes physically abused. In most such cases, philosophical questions could be raised about the interpretation these women put on caring. We could probably show that their interpretation is "not really caring" as it has been defined theoretically. Although there is some justification for such a theoretical approach—all of us, both men and women, need to learn more about appropriate forms of caring—it would be an arrogant and self-defeating response. An ethical theory constructed from the standpoint of women is not designed to control and dominate women (or men) but to make the world better and to make better sense of it. The reality described by Houston must be faced.

The most powerful response to Houston is that the ethics of caring is not intended as an ethic only for women. An ethical orientation that arises in female experience need not be confined to women. The possibility of confinement to women was a cogent reason for rejecting an Aristotelian approach to moral life. If only women adopt an ethic of caring, the present conditions of women's oppression are indeed likely to be maintained. This is exactly why an ethic of caring puts great emphasis on

human interdependence and on moral education. An important task of moral education is teaching people how and why to care.

Kari Waerness has argued convincingly for "the rationality of caring."[39] She argues (as I did earlier) that any social theory resting its entire argument on an economic base is deficient. In her discussion of caring, she refers to "both labor and feelings":

> Caring is about relations between (at least two) people. One of them (the carer) shows concern, consideration, affection, devotion, towards the other (the cared for). The one needing care is invaluable to the one providing care, and when the former is suffering pain or discomfort, the latter identifies with her/him and attends to alleviating it. Adult, healthy people feel a need to be cared for by others. . . . Worn out, dejected, tired, depressed . . . we need or desire others "to care for us." In such situations we may feel that we have a *right* to our need for care being met. This means there must be others who feel that it is their duty or desire to honor this right.[40]

Waerness' concern to maintain or extend the attitude of love characteristic of private caring into public caring reflects the dilemma of the nursing profession. For present purposes, the important message in her argument is that caring is rational, that our universal desire to be cared for logically suggests the need for caring. Houston's worry is that the world can be too easily divided into two groups—the carers and the cared fors—and that women are all too likely to land in the first set. This problem is not one found only in ethics of caring. The so-called free-rider problem is a tough one whenever matters of charity (as contrasted with justice) are discussed.[41] People may acknowledge potential desires and needs, want remedies available for their own protection, yet not respond by making a personal contribution.

The solution probably has to involve both coercion and education. Corporations, professions, and educational institutions can be forced to provide better conditions for caring: child care, parental leaves, more time for interpersonal communication, cooperative evaluation. But coercion must not be pushed to the point where its users begin to model something that contradicts caring. Education must provide the attitudes that will make coercion acceptable. Sometimes adults, like children, welcome rules that give them legal reasons for doing what they really want to do or feel they should do. This is why educational programs of the sort suggested by Jane Roland Martin are so important: caring, compassion, and connection must become important values for all human beings, not just for many women.[42]

Although I have already said that I think it would be unproductive to respond to Houston solely in philosophical terms, a closer look at the philosophical underpinnings of caring is warranted. An ethics of caring is based on a relational ontology. It takes as a basic assumption that human beings are defined in relation. It is not just that "I" as a preformed, persistent individual enter into relations; the "I" of which we all speak so easily is itself a relational entity. I really am defined by the set of relations into which my physical self has been thrown. From this perspective, when I do something for someone else, I do it at least partly for me, too, since the other and I are members of a relation. A relational ontology is clearly at odds with the individualism that has dominated the last two centuries of Western thought and is still so powerful in the United States.[43]

Even though on an ontological level the self is already a relational entity, in practical, everyday life, people do enter relations, and Houston is concerned not only that women will too often occupy the position of carer (or "one-caring") in these relations but also that the moral worth of the carer seems to be conditional. She comments:

> Since an ethics of care takes as its ontology persons-in-relation and endows this fact of human relatedness with moral significance, the attribution of moral worth to persons appears to apply to them only as one-caring. . . . The unconditional worth of the *cared for* is unequivocally assumed. . . . But it is less obvious that unconditional value is assumed for the one-caring.[44]

Here I think Houston makes the error of supposing that a given person is either the one-caring or the cared for in some stable context. But this is not at all how the two are defined in my *Caring*.[45] Every human being capable of

response is potentially both, and roles shift. As a possible cared for, each human being is worthy of moral regard. It is true that those who are capable of acting as carers occupy a special position in this moral scheme. Without people able and willing to care, there could be no cared fors, regardless of the need. But this is not a moral orientation in which only duty bearers can belong to the moral community. Even in the language of justice and rights, many theorists recognize that people may be rights bearers although they cannot for some reason assume moral duties (infancy would be an example).[46] In the language of caring and response, all beings capable of human response (and that has to be defined, of course) can call forth the obligation to respond. The one-caring, then, is unquestionably awarded what Houston calls "moral worth," for by definition she or he is capable of the most significant form of human response—caring.

Notes

1. See Jean Grimshaw, *Philosophy and Feminist Thinking* (Minneapolis: University of Minnesota Press, 1986).

2. See Rosemary Radford Ruether, "Misogynism and Virginal Feminism in the Fathers of the Church," and Eleanor Commo McLaughlin, "Equality of Souls, Inequality of Sexes: Woman in Medieval Theology," both in Rosemary Radford Ruether, ed., *Religion and Sexism* (New York: Simon & Schuster, 1974).

3. This view may be traced to Thomas Aquinas, *Summa Theologica,* and before him to Aristotle, *Politics.*

4. See Judith Hauptman, "Images of Women in the Talmud," in Ruether, ed., *Religion and Sexism.*

5. See Larry Blum, Marcia Homiak, Judy Housman, and Naomi Scheman, "Altruism and Women's Oppression," *Philosophical Forum* 5 (1973–74): 222–47; also Barbara Houston, "Prolegomena to Future Caring" (paper presented at the an-

nual meeting of the Association for Moral Education, Toronto, September 1985).

6. Grimshaw, *Philosophy and Feminist Thinking*, 36.

7. Ibid.; also Mary Briody Mahowald, ed., *Philosophy of Women* (Indianapolis: Hackett, 1983).

8. Kant, "Of the Distinction between the Beautiful and Sublime in the Interrelations of the Two Sexes," in Mahowald, ed., *Philosophy of Women*, 194.

9. Grimshaw, *Philosophy and Feminist Thinking*, 49.

10. Joan Tronto, "Beyond Gender Difference to a Theory of Care," *Signs* 12 (1987): 646.

11. The response to Gilligan's work (Carol Gilligan, *In a Different Voice* [Cambridge: Harvard University Press, 1982]) has been tremendous. Several writers have argued that the response itself is a phenomenon of importance. See, for example, Betty Sichel, *Moral Education* (Philadelphia: Temple University Press, 1988), chap. 6.

12. Friedrich Nietzsche, *Beyond Good and Evil*, trans. R. J. Hollingdale (1886; Harmondsworth, Middlesex, England: Penguin, 1973), 70.

13. Some of these insights are noted, for example, in Mary Daly, *Beyond God the Father* (Boston: Beacon, 1973).

14. Otto Weininger, *Sex and Character* (Vienna: W. Braumueller, 1903), 186.

15. Ibid., 161. Quoted in Bram Dijkstra, *Idols of Perversity* (New York: Oxford University Press, 1986), 219.

16. William James, *The Varieties of Religious Experience* (New York: Mentor, 1958), 284.

17. Ibid., 282.

18. Ibid., 285.

19. Nel Noddings, *Caring: A Feminine Approach to Ethics and Moral Education* (Berkeley: University of California Press, 1984).

20. See, for example, Jane Roland Martin, *Reclaiming a Conversation* (New Haven: Yale University Press, 1985); also Barbara Hilkert Andolsen, Christine E. Gudorf, and Mary D. Pellauer, eds., *Women's Consciousness, Women's Conscience* (Minneapolis: Winston, 1985).

21. See Mary O'Brien, *The Politics of Reproduction* (London: Routledge & Kegan Paul, 1981).

22. See, for example, Paula M. Cooey, Sharon A. Farmer, and Mary Ellen Ross, eds., *Embodied Love* (San Francisco: Harper & Row, 1987); Daly, *Beyond God the Father;* Elisabeth Schussler Fiorenza, *In Memory of Her* (New York: Crossroads, 1983); Beverly Wildung Harrison, *Our Right to Choose* (Boston: Beacon, 1983); Catherine Keller, *From a Broken Web* (Boston: Beacon, 1986); and Sharon D. Welch, *Communities of Resistance and Solidarity* (Maryknoll, N.Y.: Orbis, 1985).

23. Sara Ruddick, "Maternal Thinking," *Feminist Studies* 6 (1980): 342–67. Reprinted in Chapter 8 of this volume.

24. See the discussion in Owen Flanagan and Kathryn Jackson, "Justice, Care, and Gender: The Kohlberg-Gilligan Debate Revisited," *Ethics* 97 (1987): 622–37.

25. This is one of Tronto's ("Beyond Gender Difference") points. It is also a point well made by Deborah L. Rhode, "The 'Woman's Point of View,'" *Journal of Legal Education* 38 (1988): 39–46.

26. Charlotte Perkins Gilman, *Woman and Economics,* ed. Carl N. Degler (New York: Harper & Row, 1966); see also the account in Page Smith, *Daughters of the Promised Land* (Boston: Little, Brown, 1970), 245–51.

27. Shulamith Firestone, *The Dialectic of Sex* (New York: William Morrow, 1970).

28. A wonderful source for these stories is cookbooks. See, for example, Jean Anderson, *The Grass Roots Cookbook* (New York: Times Books, 1977).

29. Martin, *Reclaiming a Conversation*, 197.

30. Jean Watson, *Nursing: Human Science and Human Care* (Norwalk, Conn.: Appleton-Century-Crofts, 1985).

31. See Mark Timmons, "Foundationalism and the Structure of Ethical Justification," *Ethics* 97 (1987): 595–609.

32. See Gilligan, *In a Different Voice.*

33. See Muriel J. Bebeau and Mary M. Brabeck, "Integrating Care and Justice Issues in Professional Moral Education: A Gender Perspective," *Journal of Moral Education* 16 (1987): 189–203.

34. See Susan Moller Okin, "Thinking Like a Woman," in *Theoretical Perspectives on Sexual Difference,* Deborah L. Rhode, ed. (New Haven, Conn: Yale University Press, 1990).

35. See, for example, G. E. M. Anscombe, "Modern Moral Philosophy," *Ethics, Religion and Politics,* vol. 3 of *Collected Philosophical Papers of G. E. M. Anscombe* (Minneapolis: Univerity of Minnesota Press, 1981), 26–42; also Alasdair MacIntyre, *After Virtue* (Notre Dame: University of Notre Dame Press, 1984).

36. MacIntyre, *After Virtue,* 187–203, 29–32.

37. Grimshaw, *Philosophy and Feminist Thinking,* 99.

38. Houston, "Prolegomena to Future Caring," 7.

39. Kari Waerness, "The Rationality of Caring," *Economic and Industrial Democracy* 5 (1984): 185–211.

40. Ibid., 188.

41. See Allen Buchanan, "Justice and Charity," *Ethics* 97 (1987): 558–75.

42. See Martin's *Reclaiming A Conversation,* also her "Bringing Women into Educational Thought," *Educational Theory* 34 (1984): 341–54, and "Transforming Moral Education," *Journal of Moral Education* 16 (1987): 204–13.

43. See Robert N. Bellah, Richard Madsen, William M. Sullivan, Ann Swidler, and Steven M. Tipton, *Habits of the Heart* (Berkeley: University of California Press, 1985).

44. Houston, "Prolegomena to Future Caring," 8.

45. Noddings, *Caring,* 69.

46. For a view that restricts rights bearing to duty bearers, see A. I. Melden, *Rights and Persons* (Oxford: Oxford University Press, 1977); for a more generous view, see L. Wayne Sumner, "Abortion: A Third Way," in Jan Narveson, ed., *Moral Issues* (Toronto: Oxford Universty Press, 1983), 194–214.

Study Questions

1. According to Noddings, what are two objections to female ethics? How does she respond to them?

2. What assumptions does she find in male ethics? Why does she think that ethics cannot be gender-neutral?

3. Noddings expects resistance to the expression, "*the* standpoint of women." Why? Would all feminists agree?

4. What is her response to Tronto's objection to an ethics of caring?

5. Why does Noddings feel that women's work might be the basis of an ethics? Discuss with an example.

6. In what ways might an ethics of caring be grounded? Explain.

7. How does Noddings address this question: Does an ethics of caring maintain the subordination of women?

Women and Honor:
Some Notes on Lying

Adrienne Rich

These notes were first read at the Hartwick Women Writers' Workshop, founded and directed by Beverly Tanenhaus, at Hartwick College, Oneonta, New York, in June 1975. They were published as a pamphlet by Motheroot Press in Pittsburgh, 1977; in Heresies: A Feminist Magazine of Art and Politics, *vol. 1, no. 1; and in a French translation by the Québecois feminist press,* Les Editions du Remue-Ménage, *1979.*

It is clear that among women we need a new ethics; as women, a new morality. The problem of speech, of language, continues to be primary. For if in our speaking we are breaking silences long established, "liberating ourselves from our secrets" in the words of Beverly Tanenhaus, this is in itself a first kind of action. I wrote Women and Honor *in an effort to make myself more honest, and to understand the terrible negative power of the lie in relationships between women. Since it was published, other women have spoken and written of things I did not include: Michelle Cliff's "Notes on Speechlessness" in* Sinister Wisdom *no. 5 led Catherine Nicolson (in the same issue) to write of the power of "deafness," the frustration of our speech by those who do not want to hear what we have to say. Nelle Morton has written of the act of "hearing each other into speech."* How do we listen? How do we make it possible for another to break her silence? These are some of the questions which follow on the ones I have raised here.*

(These notes are concerned with relationships between and among women. When "personal relationship" is referred to, I mean a relationship between two women. It will be clear in what follows when I am talking about women's relationships with men.)

1. The old, male idea of honor. A man's "word" sufficed—to other men—without guarantee.

2. "Our Land Free, Our Men Honest, Our Women Fruitful"—a popular colonial toast in America.

3. Male honor also having something to do with killing: *I could not love thee, Dear, so much/ Lov'd I not Honour more.* ("To Lucasta, On Going to the Wars"). Male honor as something needing to be avenged: hence, the duel.

4. Women's honor, something altogether else: virginity, chastity, fidelity to a husband.

From Adrienne Rich, *On Lies, Secrets, and Silence, Selected Prose, 1966–1978.* Copyright © 1979 by W. W. Norton & Company, Inc. Reprinted by permission of W. W. Norton & Company, Inc.

*Nelle Morton, "Beloved Image!", paper delivered at the National Conference of the American Academy of Religion, San Francisco, California, December 28, 1977.

Honesty in women has not been considered important. We have been depicted as generically whimsical, deceitful, subtle, vacillating. And we have been rewarded for lying.

5. Men have been expected to tell the truth about facts, not about feelings. They have not been expected to talk about feelings at all.

6. Yet even about facts they have continually lied.

7. We assume that politicians are without honor. We read their statements trying to crack the code. The scandals of their politics: not that men in high places lie, only that they do so with such indifference, so endlessly, still expecting to be believed. We are accustomed to the contempt inherent in the political lie.

8. To discover that one has been lied to in a personal relationship, however, leads one to feel a little crazy.

9. Lying is done with words, and also with silence.

10. The woman who tells lies in her personal relationships may or may not plan or invent her lying. She may not even think of what she is doing in a calculated way.

11. A subject is raised which the liar wishes buried. She has to go downstairs, her parking meter will have run out. Or, there is a telephone call she ought to have made an hour ago.

12. She is asked, point-blank, a question which may lead into painful talk: "How do you feel about what is happening between us?" Instead of trying to describe her feelings in their ambiguity and confusion, she asks, "How do *you* feel?" The other, because she is trying to establish a ground of openness and trust, begins describing her own feelings. Thus the liar learns more than she tells.

13. And she may also tell herself a lie: that she is concerned with the other's feelings, not with her own.

14. But the liar is concerned with her own feelings.

15. The liar lives in fear of losing control. She cannot even desire a relationship without manipulation, since to be vulnerable to another person means for her the loss of control.

16. The liar has many friends, and leads an existence of great loneliness.

17. The liar often suffers from amnesia. Amnesia is the silence of the unconscious.

18. To lie habitually, as a way of life, is to lose contact with the unconscious. It is like taking sleeping pills, which confer sleep but blot out dreaming. The unconscious wants truth. It ceases to speak to those who want something else more than truth.

19. In speaking of lies, we come inevitably to the subject of truth. There is nothing simple or easy about this idea. There is no "the truth," "a truth"—truth is not one thing, or even a system. It is an increasing complexity. The pattern of the carpet is a surface. When we look closely, or when we become weavers, we learn of the tiny multiple threads unseen in the overall pattern, the knots on the underside of the carpet.

20. This is why the effort to speak honestly is so important. Lies are usually attempts to make everything simpler—for the liar—than it really is, or ought to be.

21. In lying to others we end up lying to ourselves. We deny the importance of an event,

or a person, and thus deprive ourselves of a part of our lives. Or we use one piece of the past or present to screen out another. Thus we lose faith with our own lives.

22. The unconscious wants truth, as the body does. The complexity and fecundity of dreams come from the complexity and fecundity of the unconscious struggling to fulfill that desire. The complexity and fecundity of poetry come from the same struggle.

23. An honorable human relationship—that is, one in which two people have the right to use the word "love"—is a process, delicate, violent, often terrifying to both persons involved, a process of refining the truths they can tell each other.

24. It is important to do this because it breaks down human self-delusion and isolation.

25. It is important to do this because in so doing we do justice to our own complexity.

26. It is important to do this because we can count on so few people to go that hard way with us.

27. I come back to the questions of women's honor. Truthfulness has not been considered important for women, as long as we have remained physically faithful to a man, or chaste.

28. We have been expected to lie with our bodies: to bleach, redden, unkink or curl our hair, pluck eyebrows, shave armpits, wear padding in various places or lace ourselves, take little steps, glaze finger and toe nails, wear clothes that emphasized our helplessness.

29. We have been required to tell different lies at different times, depending on what the men of the time needed to hear. The Victorian wife or the white southern lady, who were expected to have no sensuality, to "lie still"; the twentieth-century "free" woman who is expected to fake orgasms.

30. We have had the truth of our bodies withheld from us or distorted; we have been kept in ignorance of our most intimate places. Our instincts have been punished; clitoridectomies for "lustful" nuns or for "difficult" wives. It has been difficult, too, to know the lies of our complicity from the lies we believed.

31. The lie of the "happy marriage," of domesticity—we have been complicit, have acted out the fiction of a well-lived life, until the

day we testify in court of rapes, beatings, psychic cruelties, public and private humiliations.

32. Patriarchal lying has manipulated women both through falsehood and through silence. Facts we needed have been withheld from us. False witness has been borne against us.

33. And so we must take seriously the question of truthfulness between women, truthfulness among women. As we cease to lie with our bodies, as we cease to take on faith what men have said about us, is a truly womanly idea of honor in the making?

34. Women have been forced to lie, for survival, to men. How to unlearn this among other women?

35. "Women have always lied to each other."

36. "Women have always whispered the truth to each other."

37. Both of these axioms are true.

38. "Women have always been divided against each other."

39. "Women have always been in secret collusion."

40. Both of these axioms are true.

41. In the struggle for survival we tell lies. To bosses, to prison guards, the police, men who have power over us, who legally own us and our children, lovers who need us as proof of their manhood.

42. There is a danger run by all powerless people: that we forget we are lying, or that lying becomes a weapon we carry over into relationships with people who do not have power over us.

43. I want to reiterate that when we talk about women and honor, or women and lying, we speak within the context of male lying, the lies of the powerful, the lie as false source of power.

44. Women have to think whether we want, in our relationships with each other, the kind of power that can be obtained through lying.

45. Women have been driven mad, "gaslighted," for centuries by the refutation of our experience and our instincts in a culture which validates only male experience. The truth of our bodies and our minds has been mystified to us. We therefore have a primary obligation to each other: not to undermine each other's

sense of reality for the sake of expediency; not to gaslight each other.

46. Women have often felt insane when cleaving to the truth of our experience. Our future depends on the sanity of each of us, and we have a profound stake, beyond the personal, in the project of describing our reality as candidly and fully as we can to each other.

47. There are phrases which help us not to admit we are lying: "my privacy," "nobody's business but my own." The choices that underlie these phrases may indeed be justified; but we ought to think about the full meaning and consequences of such language.

48. Women's love for women has been represented almost entirely through silence and lies. The institution of heterosexuality has forced the lesbian to dissemble, or be labeled a pervert, a criminal, a sick or dangerous woman, etc. etc. The lesbian, then, has often been forced to lie, like the prostitute or the married woman.

49. Does a life "in the closet"—lying, perhaps of necessity, about ourselves to bosses, landlords, clients, colleagues, family, because the law and public opinion are founded on a lie—does this, can it, spread into private life, so that lying (described as *discretion*) becomes an easy way to avoid conflict or complication? Can it become a strategy so ingrained that it is used even with close friends and lovers?

50. Heterosexuality as an institution has also drowned in silence the erotic feelings between women. I myself lived half a lifetime in the lie of that denial. That silence makes us all, to some degree, into liars.

51. When a woman tells the truth she is creating the possibility for more truth around her.

52. The liar leads an existence of unutterable loneliness.

53. The liar is afraid.

54. But we are all afraid: without fear we become manic, hubristic, self-destructive. What is this particular fear that possesses the liar?

55. She is afraid that her own truths are not good enough.

56. She is afraid, not so much of prison guards or bosses, but of something unnamed within her.

57. The liar fears the void.

58. The void is not something created by patriarchy, or racism, or capitalism. It will not fade way with any of them. It is part of every woman.

59. "The dark core," Virginia Woolf named it, writing of her mother. The dark core. It is beyond personality; beyond who loves us or hates us.

60. We begin out of the void, out of darkness and emptiness. It is part of the cycle understood by the old pagan religions, that materialism denies. Out of death, rebirth; out of nothing, something.

61. The void is the creatrix, the matrix. It is not mere hollowness and anarchy. But in women it has been identified with lovelessness, barrenness, sterility. We have been urged to fill our "emptiness" with children. We are not supposed to go down into the darkness of the core.

62. Yet, if we can risk it, the something born of that nothing is the beginning of our truth.

63. The liar in her terror wants to fill up the void, with anything. Her lies are a denial of her fear; a way of maintaining control.

64. Why do we feel slightly crazy when we realize we have been lied to in a relationship?

65. We take so much of the universe on trust. You tell me: "In 1950 I lived on the north side of Beacon Street in Somerville." You tell me: "She and I were lovers, but for months now we have only been good friends." You tell me: "It is seventy degrees outside and the sun is shining." Because I love you, because there is not even a question of lying between us, I take these accounts of the universe on trust: your address twenty-five years ago, your relationship with someone I know only by sight, this morning's weather. I fling unconscious tendrils of belief, like slender green threads, across statements such as these, statements made so unequivocally, which have no tone or shadow of tentativeness. I build them into the mosaic of my world. I allow my universe to change in minute, significant ways, on the basis of things you have said to me, of my trust in you.

66. I also have faith that you are telling me things it is important I should know; that you do not conceal facts from me in an effort to spare me, or yourself, pain.

67. Or, at the very least, that you will say, "There are things I am not telling you."

68. When we discover that someone we trusted can be trusted no longer, it forces us to reexamine the universe, to question the whole instinct and concept of trust. For awhile, we are thrust back onto some bleak, jutting ledge, in a dark pierced by sheets of fire, swept by sheets of rain, in a world before kinship, or naming, or tenderness exist; we are brought close to formlessness.

69. The liar may resist confrontation, denying that she lied. Or she may use other language: forgetfulness, privacy, the protection of someone else. Or, she may bravely declare herself a coward. This allows her to go on lying, since that is what cowards do. She does not say, *I was afraid,* since this would open the question of other ways of handling her fear. It would open the question of what is actually feared.

70. She may say, *I didn't want to cause pain.* What she really did not want is to have to deal with the other's pain. The lie is a short-cut through another's personality.

71. Truthfulness, honor, is not something which springs ablaze of itself; it has to be created between people.

72. This is true in political situations. The quality and depth of the politics evolving from a group depends in very large part on their understanding of honor.

73. Much of what is narrowly termed "politics" seems to rest on a longing for certainty even at the cost of honesty, for an analysis which, once given, need not be reexamined. Such is the deadendedness—for women—of Marxism in our time.

74. Truthfulness anywhere means a heightened complexity. But it is a movement into evolution. Women are only beginning to uncover our own truths; many of us would be grateful for some rest in that struggle, would be glad just to lie down with the shreds we have painfully unearthed, and be satisfied with those. Often I feel this like an exhaustion in my own body.

75. The politics worth having, the relationships worth having, demand that we delve still deeper.

76. The possibilities that exist between two people, or among a group of people, are a kind

of alchemy. They are the most interesting thing in life. The liar is someone who keeps losing sight of these possibilities.

77. When relationships are determined by manipulation, by the need for control, they may possess a dreary, bickering kind of drama, but they cease to be interesting. They are repetitious; the shock of human possibilities has ceased to reverberate through them.

78. When someone tells me a piece of the truth which has been withheld from me, and which I needed in order to see my life more clearly, it may bring acute pain, but it can also flood me with a cold, sea-sharp wash of relief. Often such truths come by accident, or from strangers.

79. It isn't that to have an honorable relationship with you, I have to understand everything, or tell you everything at once, or that I can know, beforehand, everything I need to tell you.

80. It means that most of the time I am eager, longing for the possibility of telling you. That these possibilities may seem frightening, but not destructive, to me. That I feel strong enough to hear your tentative and groping words. That we both know we are trying, all the time, to extend the possibilities of truth between us.

81. The possibility of life between us.

Study Questions

1. How does Rich view the relationship between lying and the unconscious?

2. In what ways have women been traditionally expected to lie? Have lesbians been less pressured to lie than nonlesbian women?

3. According to Rich, what is the liar afraid of?

4. What possibility does the liar lose sight of?

Conceiving Women: Notes on the Logic of Feminism

Joyce Trebilcot

Feminism is not just a matter of reordering what exists, of, say, moving women from one "place" to another; feminism involves, rather, changes in the very nature of things. In this paper I want first to explicate one reason why feminism requires ontological change and then to give some examples of ways in which these changes are taking place in our redefinings of women.

If we begin with the assumption that women should not be mutilated, violated, locked up, exploited, restricted—dominated, because we are women, we have the basis for feminism in a narrow sense, a feminism that would concern itself only with the mistreatments of women which arise out of perceptions of us as female.

From *Sinister Wisdom* 11 (Fall 1979). © 1978 by Joyce Trebilcot. Reprinted by permission of Joyce Trebilcot.

But to be a feminist is to care about women, and it is arbitrary to limit our concern to just those aspects of our sufferings and limitations which arise from a particular cause; so feminism, it seems to me, must be concerned with all of the harm done to women, regardless of its source. This means that because women are oppressed not only because we are women but also because we are Black or Hispanic or Jewish, because we are Lesbian, because we are poor or paraplegic or fat or young or old or (fill in the blanks), we must, as feminists, seek to identify, understand, , and eliminate all these oppressions.

They all have something in common. Their form is that a distinction is made, which is a division into two; and one part or half is held to be superior to the other; and it is claimed that the "superior" is justified in having power over the "inferior." This, of course, is dualism. It is a dualism that is essentially evaluative and that functions primarily as an excuse for power over.

The dualistic pair is the unit of hierarchy—that is, a hierarchy consists of overlapping dualistic pairs. A classical rendering is the pyramid with God at the apex, then angels, then man, then beasts, then the rest of the natural world. On this scheme, God is distinct from and better than man, and entitled to exercise control over him; man is distinct from and better than beasts, and entitled to exercise control over them; etc. The pyramid, of course, represents quantity: one on top, then a few, then more and more. While this particular version of the pyramid is perhaps antiquated, the form itself permeates dominant Western cultures.

It permeates received reality. At the epistemological level, it determines perception: we see—sight rather than, for example, touch, is primary—it is objects that are seen, and they are seen as having sharp boundaries. More obviously, dualism/hierarchy is the form of social organizations—governments, businesses, schools, families. It structures the person—self/other, mind/body, conscious and unconscious. There is even a dualism of right and left—the right hand, the right side, take precedence over the left. And so on.

In feminism, there is movement toward the elimination of all dualism, not just of those manifestations of it that oppress women as women or as members of other groups. One reason for this movement is the belief that only by getting rid of dualism in all of its manifestations can oppressions such as sexism, racism, and classism be permanently and thoroughly eradicated. Another reason is the sense that dualism as a form is discordant with women's values; even if no "inferior" category included women, dualism would block the flowering of women's modes.

The elimination of dualism—of either a specific manifestation of it or all of it—requires change in the nature of entities that are related to one another in dualistic/hierarchical orderings. This is because the nature of the entities is determined at least in part by their participation in the orderings. In academic terms, the relations among them are internal rather than external. An example of an external relation is the distance between two cups on a table; a change in the distance does not alter the nature of the cups. A change in an internal relation, however, does alter the nature of the things related. A nurse, for instance, cares for the sick by assisting and following the orders of doctors; if we eliminate her subordinate relationship to doctors, we change the meaning of the word "nurse." Similarly, what it is to be a worker, a deaf person, an Asian American, a wife—or, of course, a woman—is determined in part by relations between these and other concepts in hierarchical orderings. Because the relationships among items in dualistic/hierarchical orderings are internal, then, feminism, insofar as it is committed to the elimination of dualism/hierarchy, is committed to changing the nature of things.

Here I want to give examples of just some of the ways in which internal connections among items in hierarchies are broken by feminist reconceivings. I focus on reconceivings of women because they are starting points and centers of feminist theorizings. These reconceivings are, I take it, political strategies that weave bridges from patriarchy to women's spaces.

I use the distinction from academic philosophy between the descriptive and evaluative meanings of a term. The descriptive meaning is characterized as value neutral; it is supposed to imply only some facts about the thing in question. The evaluative meaning commends or condemns the facts described. To call someone forceful, for example, is to ascribe a certain style of behavior; this is the descriptive meaning of "forceful." But in addition, in most contexts, to say that someone is forceful commends if the subject is male and condemns if she is female; commending or condemning is the evaluative meaning of "forceful."

Because we engage in feminist theorizings in order to re-experience, to reconceive, that is, to bring forth new meanings, when we use a conventional word as central in our theorizings, the descriptive meaning of that word shifts. Sometimes the evaluative meaning shifts as well. Here I discuss three patterns of shift in evaluative and descriptive meaning. The words used to exemplify these shifts are "strong," "nurturant," and "lesbian." As these words, which are used by feminists to describe women, are given new meanings, the meaning of "woman" changes too—and the conceptual bonds which hold us in our traditional places in dualistic/hierarchical orderings are frayed.

1. *Descriptive meaning changes, evaluative meaning remains the same: Strength:* In patriarchy, a strong man is one who deals with difficulty calmly, quietly, unobtrusively. According to the cliché, he is the strong silent type—paradigmatically, the John Wayne character.

The patriarchal strong woman, like the strong man, handles or endures difficulties quietly, without disturbing others. But in other respects she differs from him. In particular, in accordance with the patriarchal practice of defining women in terms of our relationships to men and of our sexuality, the strong woman is typically one who both lacks a heterosexual partner and is thought to be sexually unattractive to men. She has no husband or mate (or, if she has, he is absent from the situation in which she is called strong) because if an appropriate male is present it is presumed that he takes care of and protects her, not that she does this for herself, and so the term "strong" is reserved for him. But even if she has no man, she can't be strong unless she is heterosexually unattractive—usually she is imaged as old—because if she is attractive she should or might have a man, and again the term "strong" is reserved, this time not for an actual but for a possible man. In patriarchy, then, we generally must be both unattached to a man and unattractive to men in order to qualify for strength.

The feminist concept of the strong woman preserves the notion of strength as dealing well with adversity—this is the common thread by virtue of which the same term, "strength," is used in both contexts. But of course the heterosexist limitations of women's strength drop out. A feminist strong woman may have a man—in many cases her strength is manifested primarily in her struggle against a husband or lover. And she need not be unattractive to men—we know that there are many young and conventionally beautiful women who are strong indeed.

Further, in feminism the idea of strength as quietly, privately, unobtrusively dealing with difficulty drops out. The feminist strong woman is likely to be noisy, even loud; she is inclined to protest, to complain, to call attention to her difficulty. This difference of course is based on the political difference between patriarchy's interest in preserving present systems and feminism's interest in changing them.

Thus, while the evaluative meaning of the expression "a strong woman" is the same in patriarchy and in feminism—it is positive in both contexts—the descriptive meaning shifts: *what* is valued changes. This change is the basis for a partial redefinition of the concept of women. Whereas in patriarchy, strength in women is an anomaly, in feminism there is a tendency to understand it as essential, as an element in the definition of woman: all women are potentially strong. But this move breaks one link in the internal connection between the concepts of woman and man. In patriarchy, women are weak as compared to men; therefore women are inferior; therefore women may justifiably be dominated by men. But if women are by nature strong, the syllogism fails.

2. *Descriptive meaning changes, evaluative meaning changes: Nurturance.* The term "nurturance," whose root idea, of course, is that of a mother nursing her child, is being given both new descriptive and new evaluative meaning by feminists. For example, Barbara Love and Elizabeth Shanklin, in their article, "The Answer is Matriarchy," provide an account of a feminist definition of nurturance which clearly differs from patriarchal ones.[1] To nurture a child, they say, is to support "the unique will of the child to grow into its full potential as a self-

regulating individual": again, to nurture is to strengthen "the unique will of each individual to form open, trusting, creative bonds with others" (184).

This concept of nurturing retains the connection with mother-child relationships, but otherwise contrasts sharply with patriarchal views of nurturance. In patriarchy, the aim of childrearing is not to strengthen the child's will, but to direct and control it, to dominate it. In patriarchy, the aim of the "training" of children is not to enable them to think for themselves, but rather to prepare them to take their places in existing institutions. Barbara and Elizabeth note that "in capitalism the child's will is directed toward serving the interests of corporations; in socialism it is directed toward serving the state" (184). Their concept of nurturing as supporting the unique will of each individual to develop as self-regulating and self-realizing constitutes, then, a clear shift in the descriptive meaning of "nurturance."

Evaluatively, nurturance is viewed positively in patriarchy, but as second-rate. Nurturing is a good thing for women to do, but not good enough for men. In matriarchal theory, however, the value of nurturing is expanded. The nurturant mother-child relationship is to serve as the model of all relationships, and all social institutions are to be designed so as to support nurturing. Here, nurturing, a women's value, becomes a primary value.

But from a feminist perspective it is probably a mistake to say that matriarchal theories make nurturing primary, for feminists tend not to be concerned to order values hierarchically. We may say, then, that what matriarchal theory does is to horizontally expand the range of nurturance. Traditionally, only women are supposed to be nurturant, and we are expected to nurture men and children but not one another or ourselves. But a matriarchal society is one in which nurturing is valued for everyone, in all contexts. Thus, matriarchal theory not only gives nurturing a new descriptive meaning, it also radically expands its sphere as a value. And if nurturing is not second-rate, then women are not in this respect

inferior to men, and one of the struts holding up the patriarchal hierarchy is toppled.

3. *Descriptive meaning changes, evaluative meaning is reversed: Lesbian.* Another way in which patriarchal evaluative meanings are altered in feminism is by simply reversing them. The patriarchal intention to keep us in line by calling us dykes or witches or hags is blocked when we describe ourselves in these terms with pride and pleasure. We break out of secondary status, out of hierarchy, by flipping their evaluations over, by gladly acknowledging that we are what they condemn.

This reversal of value is based on a reconceptualizing of the descriptive meaning of the term in question. While patriarchal concepts of lesbianism focus on women "having sex" with women—and on men (lesbians are women who can't get men, who need men, who hate men, etc.)—feminist conceivings retain only the emphasis on women, and transform it. Here are some samples. From the Radicalesbians: "A lesbian is the rage of all women condensed to the point of explosion."[2] From Ti-Grace Atkinson: Lesbianism is the "commitment, by choice, full-time, of one woman to others of her class."[3] From Sally Miller Gearhart: "A lesbian is a woman who seeks her own self-nurturance."[4] Such ways of understanding lesbianism depart from the patriarchal concept in description and reverse it in evaluation. And they not only move lesbians out of our patriarchal places as inferior to heterosexuals and to men, they also have implications for the concept of woman: if some women—lesbians—are not dependent on and inferior to men, then no women need be.

I have so far talked about ways feminists re-create ourselves by giving new meanings to words that are used in both patriarchy and feminism to describe women. But not everything we need to say about ourselves can be expressed in this way. So feminists also describe women in terms not conventionally used to describe women at all. I have chosen three examples here. One is "together," an adverb in standard English, an adjective in slang, and a feminist adjective in the work of Inez Smith Reid. A different sort of example is a new combination of ordinary words: "woman-identified." The third case is a materially new word, a word formed by combining parts of standard words—"gynergy." These are terms we have appropriated or invented for ourselves. One might say, that, unlike the words I discussed earlier, they are not old words given new meanings, but rather new words; they are, anyway, new descriptions of women. So to understand them as contributing to feminist conceivings of ourselves is not to trace shifts in their meanings from patriarchy to feminism—"gynergy," for example, has no meaning in patriarchy at all; it is, rather, just to understand why we need these new words, what they mean.

"Together" is used by Inez Smith Reid in her book *"Together" Black Women* to describe politically conscious Black women.[5] Many of these women do not define themselves as feminists, but in their struggle against racism as a hierarchy of power they are clearly sisters of feminists. Inez's account of how she came to use the word "together" in thinking about these women helps to illuminate one sort of politically-based conceptual shift.

Inez began her project with the intention of studying militant Black women and so she selected her subjects on the basis of their "reputation in the community for militancy." One of the questions the women were asked was to define militancy. Among the responses: "To be militant you have to be aware . . ."; "Militancy is when you can actually analyze . . ."; "a militant person is, for Black people, anybody who decides it's time for White folks to stop kicking my ass. It's just anybody who's tired of being messed over" (17, 18).

But most importantly, many of the responses carry a sense of dissatisfaction with the term "militant" itself. This sense is perhaps best expressed by the woman who says: "I really feel it's just a name that the White people gave to the Black people. They call them that name because they speak the right things for the race. . . . I don't think there's such a word as that" (20). *There is no such word as that.* This woman not merely refuses to accept a characterization imposed on her by the dominant group, she denies the very existence of the word.

As Inez listened to the women she was studying and began to appreciate their tendency to reject the standard concept of militancy, she herself moved away from this notion and came to think of these women not as militant, but as "together." She cites the definition of "together" from the *Dictionary of Afro-American Slang:* "to have one's mind free of confusion; to be positive; functional; to emerge as a whole person." Inez adds that in her work, "together" has "a more collective connotation," it is "characterized by a spiritual closeness in a common endeavor—that of a singular or peculiar commitment to erase oppression." Further, the term "denotes a refusal to take on, uncritically, the total value structure of the White community" (29). So here we have the discovery of the negative evaluative meaning of a term and its replacement with a new word, that is, with a word which in the standard language of the dominant culture is not used to describe persons at all.

The description of some women as "together" has, of course, implications for the concept of woman. Inez Smith Reid's work suggests that all women can be "together"—that is, free of confusion, whole, and sharing commitment; insofar as this conception of women is inconsistent with patriarchal ideas of women as scattered, incomplete, and at odds with one another, it tends toward transforming the concept of woman and so breaking the bonds which hold us in our traditional places in hierarchical orderings.

Another approach to reconceiving ourselves is to make up terms. The expression "woman-identified woman," introduced in the Radicalesbians' 1970 paper, names a woman who creates her identity in relation to women rather than in relation to men and who makes women her primary commitment: ". . . we must be available and supportive to one another, give our commitment and our love, give the emotional support necessary to sustain this movement. Our energies must flow toward our sisters, not backward toward our oppressors" (215). The paper provides a new, positive description of the lesbian feminist, along with a new name for her: woman-identified.

The meaning of the expression "woman-identified woman" has shifted somewhat within feminism. The expression has been used widely since its introduction, with the understanding that while not all lesbians are woman-identified, all women-identified women are perceived by patriarchy as lesbians. But then at the 1978 founding convention of the National Lesbian Feminist Organization, a resolution was adopted which specified that membership in the new organization is open to "all lesbians and/or woman-identified women who agree with the purpose of this organization." "Woman-identified woman" was included partly to make space for lesbians who cannot publicly say they are lesbians. But it was understood also that this provision would admit to membership women who in patriarchal terms are not lesbians.

So the concept of the woman-identified woman has taken on a life of its own. Arising out of the rejection of the male practice of defining women in narrowly sexual terms, and specifically out of the rejection of the narrowly sexual patriarchal definition of lesbianism, the new concept at first simply added to the sexual: a woman-identified woman was a lesbian who lived primarily with and for women. But then the term was used in such a way that the sexual criterion dropped out entirely. Thus our reconceivings of women change.

Another new word invented by feminists is "gynergy." Like "woman-identified woman," it has become a regular part of the vocabulary of many feminists. (The women I know pronounce it with a soft "g.") Janice Raymond describes gynergy as "the woman power/spirit/strength that is building up in 'woman-identified women' " and as both individual and social: ". . . it proceeds not only from an individual woman's realization of her own power of being but from a collective consciousness, i.e., a feminist collective consciousness."[6]

Unlike the other concepts discussed here, gynergy is not an attribute of individual women; we do not speak of a "gynergetic woman." Gynergy is something we as individuals feel ourselves participating in. I can think of no patriarchal concept which works in the same way—that is, which expresses something personal (not merely an atmosphere) which is at the same time not an attribute of persons. It may happen, of course, that we will

come to say things like "Sybil has great gynergy." Then the term "gynergy" would be rather like "spirit." But for now, it appears that gynergy is not only a new concept, but a new kind of concept. And it too is part of our redefinings of "woman."

These are just some of the ways in which we are reconceiving ourselves: taking on conventionally positive characteristics like strength, and changing them; redescribing and reevaluating aspects of ourselves like nurturance and lesbianism; and using words not conventionally used to describe women to express our becoming. These shifts all break internal definitional connections that exist in patriarchal systems between concepts of women and other concepts, particularly between concepts of women and of men. By breaking away from definitional connections that determine women's place in patriarchal conceptual systems and so in "the world," we move out of traditional dualistic/hierarchical orderings.

From a patriarchal perspective, all the concepts of women discussed here would be said to carry positive evaluative force, or to establish new ideals for women. But this account misrepresents the spirit in which these ideas are set forth. It is men who have invented the concepts of good and bad and for whom the making of value judgments is a major occupation. Feminists make vigorous value judgments about the patriarchy, but in our own worlds our concern tends to be more one of understanding and making space for processes than of evaluating persons and acts. Feminists are highly sensitive to the needs of women to create ourselves out of our own experiences, to our needs not to be told what we should do or be. The concepts of women I have discussed here then are not ideals or models, but gifts from some women to others, to be modified, transformed, abandoned, as each woman feels.

These conceivings of women are exercises of power: the power of naming ourselves, and the power in our new names. This is not different from "real" power. Although I have written here of words and concepts, the shifts I have sketched are also ontological; they are shifts from being women in patriarchy to becoming women in our own times and spaces. What patriarchy might see as logic, feminism understands as political strategy.

Notes

1. In *Our Right to Love: A Lesbian Resource Book*, edited by Ginny Vida (Englewood Cliffs, N.J.: Prentice-Hall, 1978).

2. "The Woman-Identified Woman" in *Radical Feminism*, edited by Ellen Levine and Anita Rapone (New York: Quadrangle/The New York Times Book Co., 1973), p. 240.

3. *Amazon Odyssey* (New York: Links Books, 1974), p. 132.

4. "The Spiritual Dimension: Death and Resurrection of a Hallelujah Dyke," in *Our Right to Love*, p. 187.

5. *"Together" Black Women* (New York: Emerson Hall Publishers, 1972).

6. "The Illusion of Androgyny" in *Quest: A Feminist Quarterly*, Vol. II, No. 1 (Summer 1975), pp. 64, 65.

Study Questions

1. What "dualism" does Trebilcot speak of, and how does it permeate our view of the world?

2. Why are feminists committed to eliminating dualism? What does this commit them to changing, and why?

3. What patterns of meaning change does Trebilcot discuss? Devise other examples besides the ones she gives.

4. What examples of term-formation (i.e., the creation—by feminists—of new words or phrases) does she discuss? Try to cite other examples.

Moral Wisdom in the Black Women's Literary Tradition

Katie Geneva Cannon

I first began pondering the relationship between faith and ethics as a schoolgirl while listening to my grandmother teach the central affirmations of Christianity within the context of a racially segregated society. My community of faith taught me the principles of God's universal parenthood that engendered a social, intellectual, and cultural ethos embracing the equal humanity of all people. Yet my city, state, and nation declared it a punishable offense against the laws and mores for Blacks and whites "to travel, eat, defecate, wait, be buried,

From *Weaving the Visions*, Judith Plaskow and Carol P. Christ, eds. (New York: Harper & Row, 1989). Copyright © Carol P. Christ and Judith Plaskow. Reprinted by permission of HarperCollins Publishers.

make love, play, relax and even speak together, except in the stereotyped context of master and servant interaction."[1]

My religious quest tried to relate the Christian doctrines preached in the Black Church to the suffering, oppression, and exploitation of Black people in the society. How could Christians who were white flatly and openly refuse to treat as fellow human beings Christians who had African ancestry? Was not the essence of the Gospel mandate a call to eradicate affliction, despair, and systems of injustice? Inasmuch as the Black Church expressed the inner ethical life of the people, was there any way to reconcile the inherent contradictions in Christianity as practiced by whites with the radical indictments of and challenges for social amelioration and economic development in the Black religious heritage? How long would the white church continue to be the ominous symbol of white dominance, sanctioning and assimilating the propagation of racism in the mundane interests of the ruling group?

In the 1960s my quest for the integration of faith and ethics was influenced by scholars in various fields who surfaced the historical contributions of Afro-Americans that had been distorted and denied. Avidly I read the analysis exposing the assumptions and dogmas that made Blacks a negligible factor in the thought of the world. For more than three and a half centuries, a "conspiracy of silence" rendered invisible the outstanding contributions of Blacks to the culture of humankind. From cradle to grave the people in the United States were taught the alleged inferiority of Blacks.

When I turned specifically to theological ethics, I discovered the dominant ethical systems implied that the doing of Christian ethics in the Black community was either immoral or amoral. The cherished ethical ideas predicated upon the existence of freedom and a wide range of choices proved null and void in situations of oppression. The real-lived texture of Black life requires moral agency that may run contrary to the ethical boundaries of mainline Protestantism. Blacks may use action guides that have never been considered within the scope of traditional codes of faithful living. Racism, gender discrimination, and economic exploitation, as inherited, age-long complexes, require the Black community to create and cultivate values and virtues in their own terms so that they prevail against the odds with moral integrity.

For example, dominant ethics makes a virtue of qualities that lead to economic success—self-reliance, frugality, and industry. These qualities are based on an assumption that success is possible for anyone who tries. Developing confidence in one's own abilities, resources, and judgments amidst a careful use of money and goods—in order to exhibit assiduity in the pursuit of upward mobility—have proven to be positive values for many whites. But the oligarchic economic powers, and the consequent political power they generate, own and control capital and distribute credit in a manner detrimental to Blacks. As part of a legitimating system to justify the supposed inherent inferiority of Blacks, the values so central to white economic mobility prove to be ineffectual. Racism does not allow all Black women and Black men to work and save in order to develop a standard of living that is congruent with the American ideal.

Theory and analysis demonstrate that to embrace work as a "moral essential" means that Black women are still the last hired to do the work that white men, white women, and men of color refuse to do, and at a wage that men and white women refuse to accept. Black women, placed in jobs proven to be detrimental to their health, are doing the most menial, tedious, and by far the most underpaid work, if they manage to get a job at all.

Dominant ethics also assumes that a moral agent is to a considerable degree free and self-directing. Each person possesses self-determining power. For instance, one is free to choose whether or not she or he wants to suffer and make sacrifices as a principle of action or as a voluntary vocational pledge of crossbearing. In dominant ethics a person is free to make suffering a desirable moral norm. This is not so for Blacks. For the masses of Black people, suffering is the normal state of affairs. Mental anguish, physical abuse, and emotional agony are all part of Black people's daily lives. Due to the white supremacy and male superiority that pervade this society, Blacks and whites, women and men are forced to live with very different ranges of freedom. As long as the white-male experience continues to be established as the ethical norm, Black women, Black men, and others will suffer unequivocal oppression. The range of freedom has been restricted by those who cannot hear and will not hear voices expressing pleasure and pain, joy and rage as others experience them.

In the Black community, qualities that determine desirable ethical values of upright character and sound moral conduct must always take into account the circumstances, paradoxes, and dilemmas that constrict Blacks to the lowest rungs of the social, political, and economic hierarchy. Black existence is deliberately and openly controlled.

. . . How we travel and where, what work we do, what income we receive, where we eat, where we sleep, with whom we talk, where we recreate, where we study, what we write, what we publish.[2]

The vast majority of Blacks suffer every conceivable form of denigration. Their lives are named, defined, and circumscribed by whites.

The moral wisdom of the Black community is extremely useful in defying oppressive rules or standards of "law and order" that degrade Blacks. It helps Blacks purge themselves of self-hate, thus asserting their own validity. But the ethical values of the Black community are not identical with the obligations and duties that Anglo-Protestant American society requires of its members. Nor can the ethical assumptions be the same, as long as powerful whites who control the wealth, the systems, and the institutions in this society continue to perpetuate brutality and criminality against Blacks.

Black Women's Literature as an Ethical Resource

The method used in this study departs from most work in Christian and secular ethics. Data is drawn from less conventional sources and probes more intimate and private aspects of Black life. The Black women's literary tradition has not previously been used to interpret and explain the community's socio-cultural patterns from which ethical values can be gleaned. I have found that this literary tradition is the nexus between the real-lived texture of Black life and the oral-aural cultural values implicitly passed on from one generation to the next.

Black women are the most vulnerable and exploited members of the American society. The structure of the capitalist political economy in which Black people are commodities, combined with patriarchal contempt for women, has caused the Black woman to experience oppression that knows no ethical or physical bounds.

As a black, she has had to endure all the horrors of slavery and living in a racist society; as a worker, she has been the object of continual exploitation, occupying the lowest place on the wage scale and restricted to the most demeaning and uncreative jobs; as a woman she has seen her physical image defamed and been the object of the white master's uncontrollable lust and subjected to all the ideals of white womanhood as a model to which she should aspire; as a mother, she has seen her children torn from her breast and sold into slavery, she has seen them left at home without attention while she attended to the needs of the offspring of the ruling class.[3]

This essay shows how Black women live out a moral wisdom in their real-lived context that does not appeal to the fixed rules or absolute principles of the white-oriented, male-structured society. Black women's analysis and appraisal of right and wrong, good and bad develop out of the various coping mechanisms required by their own circumstances. Black women have justly regarded survival against tyrannical systems of triple oppression as a true sphere of moral life.

Black women are taught what is to be endured and how to endure the harsh, cruel, inhumane exigencies of life. The moral wisdom does not rescue Black women from the bewildering pressures and perplexities of institutionalized social evils; rather, it exposes those ethical assumptions that are inimical to the ongoing survival of Black womanhood. The moral counsel of Black women captures the ethical qualities of what is real and what is of value to women in the Black world.

Black women writers function as symbolic conveyors and transformers of the values acknowledged by the female members of the Black community. In the quest for appreciating Black women's experience, nothing surpasses the Black women's literary tradition. It cryptically records the specificity of the Afro-American life.

For instance, Zora Neale Hurston in *Jonah's Gourd Vine* recorded a series of proverbial sayings between a dying mother and her nine-year-old daughter. The mother is providing the child with the moral wisdom of coping when life goes awry.

Stop cryin', Isie, you can't hear whut Ahm
sayin', 'member tuh git all de education you
kin. Dat's de onliest way you kin keep out from
under people's feet. You always strain tuh be
de bell cow, never be de tail uh nothin'. Do de
best you kin, honey, 'cause neither yo' paw or
dese older chillun is goin' tuh be bothered too
much wid you. But you goin' tuh git 'long.
Mark mah words. You got spunk, but mah po'
lil'l sandyhaired child goin' suffer uh lot 'fo'
she git tuh de place she can 'fend fuh herself.
And Isie, honey, stop cryin' and lissen tuh me.
Don't you love nobody bettern'n you do yo'self.
Do, you'll be killed 'thout being struck uh blow.
Some us dese things Ahm tellin' yuh, you won't
understand 'em fuh years tuh come, but de
time will come when you'll know.[4]

The mother's instruction was concerned not
so much with the ascertainment of fact or
elaboration of theories as with the means and
ends of practical life. The mother spelled out
those things that the daughter needed to do in
order to protect the quality and continuity of
her life. The Black female need not be a muzzled, mutilated individual but must continue to
grow as a woman-child with a vibrant, creative
spirit. This moral wisdom, handed down from
mother to daughter as the crystallized result of
experience, aimed to teach the next generation
not only how to survive but also how to consider
more deeply the worth and meaning of their
lives.

My goal is not to arrive at my prescriptive or
normative ethic. Rather what I am pursuing is
an investigation that will help Black women,
and others who care, to understand and to
appreciate the richness of their own moral
struggle through the life of the common people
and the oral tradition. I seek to further
understandings of some of the differences between ethics of life under oppression and established moral approaches that assume freedom and a wide range of choices. I am being
suggestive of one possible ethical approach, not
exhaustive.

I make no apologies for the fact that this
study is a partisan one. For too long the Black
community's theological and ethical understandings have been written from a de-
cidedly male bias. This study is not merely a
glorification of the Black female community,
but rather an attempt to add to the far too few
positive records concerning the Black woman
as moral agent. This method should enable us
to use the lives and literature of Black women to
recognize the contribution to the field of ethics
that Black women have made. One test will be
whether those who know this literary tradition
find that I have done justice to its depth and
richness. The second test is whether Black
women recognize the moral wisdom they utilize. The third test is whether Black feminists
who have given up on the community of faith
will gain new insights concerning the
reasonableness of theological ethics in deepening the Black woman's character, consciousness, and capacity in the ongoing struggle for
survival. If these criteria are met, I will have
reached my objective.

It is my thesis that the Black women's literary
tradition is the best available literary repository
for understanding the ethical values Black
women have created and cultivated in their
participation in this society. To prevail against
the odds with integrity, Black women must
assess their moral agency within the social conditions of the community. Locked out of the
real dynamics of human freedom in America,
they implicitly pass on moral formulas for survival that allow them to stand over against the
perversions of ethics and morality imposed on
them by whites and males who support racial
imperialism in a patriarchal social order.

The Evidence of Black Women's Stories

The story of the Afro-American has been told
quite coherently, but has repeatedly left out the
Black woman. Seldom in history has a group of
women been so directly responsible for insuring the well-being of both the Black family and
the white. At the same time, this story has not
been told. The work of Black women writers
can be trusted as seriously mirroring Black
reality. Their writings are important chronicles
of the Black woman's survival.

Despite their tragic omission by the literary
establishment, Black women have been ex-

pressing ideas, feelings, and interpretations about the Black experience since the early days of the eighteenth century. Throughout their history in the United States, Black women have used their creativity to carve out "living space." From the beginning, they contended with the ethical ambiguity of racism, sexism, and other sources of fragmentation in this acclaimed land of freedom, justice, and equality. The Black women's literary tradition delineates the many ways that ordinary Black women have fashioned value patterns and ethical procedures in their own terms, as well as transcending, radicalizing, and sometimes destroying pervasive, negative orientations imposed by the mores of the larger society.

Toni Morrison describes the moral agency of old Black women reared in the South in this way:

> Edging into life from the back door. Becoming. Everybody in the world was in a position to give them orders. White women said, "Do this." White children said, "Give me that." White men said, "Come here." Black men said, "Lay down." The only people they need not take orders from were black children and each other. But they took all of that and recreated it in their own image. They ran the houses of white people, and knew it. When white men beat their men, they cleaned up the blood and went home to receive abuse from the victim. They beat their children with one hand and stole for them with the other. The hands that felled trees also cut umbilical cords; the hands that wrung the necks of chickens and butchered hogs also nudged African violets into bloom; the arms that loaded sheaves, bales and sacks rocked babies to sleep. They patted biscuits into flaky ovals of innocence—and shrouded the dead. They plowed all day and came home to nestle like plums under the limbs of their men. The legs that straddled a mule's back were the same ones that straddled their men's hips. And the difference was all the difference there was.[5]

The bittersweet irony of Afro-American experience forces Black women to examine critically the conventional, often pretentious, morality of middle-class American ideals.

The Black women's literary tradition provides a rich resource and a cohesive commentary that brings into sharp focus the Black community's central values, which in turn frees Black folks from the often deadly grasp of parochial stereotypes. The observations, descriptions, and interpretations in Black literature are largely reflective of cultural experiences. They identify the frame of social contradiction in which Black people live, move, and have their being. The derogatory caricatures and stereotypes ascribed to Black people are explicitly rejected. Instead, writings by Blacks capture the magnitude of the Black personality. Spanning the antebellum period to today's complex technological society, Black women writers authenticate, in an economy of expressions, how Black people creatively strain against the external limits in their lives, how they affirm their humanity by inverting assumptions, and how they balance the continual struggle and interplay of paradoxes.[6]

Parallels with Black History

The Black women's literary tradition is a source in the study of ethics because it is tied historically to the origin of Black people in America. Most writing by Black women captures the values of the Black community within a specific location, time, and historical context. The literary tradition is not centered automatically upon the will and whims of what an individual writer thinks is right or obligatory, nor even upon whatever she personally believes to be true for her own localized consciousness. The majority of Black women who engage in literary compositions hold themselves accountable to the collective values that underlie Black history and culture. Dexter Fisher makes the point this way:

> . . . To be totally centered on the self would be to forget one's history, the kinship of a shared community of experience, the crucial continuity between past and present that must be maintained in order to insure the future.[6]

The patterns and themes in Black women's writings reflect historical facts, sociological realities, and religious convictions that lie behind the ethos and ethics of the Black community. As recorders of the Black experience, Black women writers convey the community's consciousness of values that enables them to find meaning in spite of social degradation, economic exploitation, and political oppression. They record what is valued or regarded as good in the Black community. Seldom, if ever, is their work art-for-art's-sake. "Whatever else may be said of it, Black American writing in the United States has been first and last, as Saunders Redding once observed, a 'literature of necessity.' "[7]

> The appeal of a basically utilitarian literature written to meet the exigencies of a specific historical occasion usually declines after the occasion has passed. That this is much less true of Black literature is due to constant factors in Afro-American history—the Black presence and white racism.[8]

Oral Narrative Devices

The irresistible power in the Black women's literary tradition is its ability to convey the assumed values of the Black community's oral tradition in its grasp for meaning. The suppression of book learning and the mental anguish of intellectual deprivation obliged Black literature to be expressed mainly in oral form. What is critical for my purpose is that these women reveal in their novels, short stories, love lyrics, folktales, fables, drama, and nonfiction, a psychic connection with the cultural tradition transmitted by the oral mode from one generation to the next. As serious writers who have mastered in varying degrees the technique of their craft, Black women find themselves causally dependent on the ethics of the Black masses. Black women writers draw heavily upon the Black oral culture.

The folk tales, song (especially the blues), sermons, the dozens, and the rap all provide Black writers with the figurative language and connotations of dim hallways and dank smells, caged birds and flowers that won't sprout, curdled milk and rusty razors, general stores and beauty parlors, nappy edges and sheened legs. The social and cultural forces within the Black oral tradition form the milieu out of which Black writers create.

Black women writers document the attitudes and morality of women, men, girls, and boys who chafe at and defy the restrictions imposed by the dominant white capitalist value system. They delineate in varying artistic terms the folk treasury of the Black community: how Black people deal with poverty and the ramifications of power, sex as an act of love and terror, the depersonalization that accompanies violence, the acquisition of property, the drudgery of a workday, the inconsistencies of chameleonlike racism, teenage mothers, charlatan sorcerers, swinging churches, stoic endurance, and stifled creativity. Out of this storehouse of Black experience comes a vitally rich, ancient continuum of Black wisdom.

This capacity to catch the oral tradition also means an ability to portray the sense of community. Barbara Christian in *Black Women Novelists: The Development of a Tradition, 1892–1976* recognizes this unique characteristic common to Black women's literature as the "literary counterpart of their communities' oral tradition."

> The history of these communities, seldom related in textbooks, are incorporated into the tales that emphasize the marvelous, sometimes the outrageous, as a means of teaching a lesson. In concert with their African ancestors, these storytellers, both oral and literary, transform gossip, happenings, into composites of factual events, images, fantasies and fables.[9]

This important characteristic of Black women's writing is increasingly recognized by literary interpreters. Jeanne Noble says, "We would be scripted in history with little true human understanding without the black writer telling it like it is."[10] Mary Helen Washington says that this deeper-than-surface knowledge of and fondness for the verbal tradition is a truth that is shared by the majority of Black women writers. "This remembrance of things past is not simply self-indulgent nostalgia. It is essential to her vision to establish connections with the values that nourish and strengthen her."[11]

Verta Mae Grosvenor captures the essence of the oral tradition at the very outset of her book, *Vibration Cooking:* "Dedicated to my mama and my grandmothers and my sisters in appreciation of the years that they have worked in miss ann's kitchen and then came home to TCB in spite of slavery and the moynihan report."[12] Marcia Gillespie, in the 1975 May editorial of *Essence* magazine, concludes that recording the oral tradition is a way of releasing the memories of mamas and grandmamas— "the race memory of our women who, though burdened, neither broke nor faltered in their faith in a better world for us all."[13]

Black women's combination of the Western literary form with oral narrative devices expresses with authority, power, and eloquence the insidious effects of racism, sexism, and class elitism on members of their communities. By not abandoning the deeply ingrained traditions of the Black community, these writers utilize common sources to illustrate common values that exist within the collective vision of Blacks in America.

The Insularity of the Black Community

Black women writers, as participant-observers, capsulize on a myriad of levels the insularity of their home communities. Due to systemic, institutionalized manifestations of racism in America, the Black community tends to be situated as marginated islands within the larger society. The perpetual powers of white supremacy continue to drop down on the inhabitants of the Black community like a bell jar—surrounding the whole, yet separating the Black community's customs, mores, opinions, and system of values from those in other communities. Black women authors emphasize life within the community, not the conflict with outside forces. In order to give faithful pictures of important and comprehensive segments of Black life, these writers tie their character's stories to the aesthetic, emotional, and intellectual values of the Black community.

For instance, Anne Petry's *The Street* (1946) depicts the inevitability of crime that Black mothers, who provide for their families against all odds in hostile urban environments, must face.

A lifetime of pent-up resentments went into the blows. Even after he lay motionless, she kept striking him, not thinking about him, not even seeing him. First she was venting her rage against the dirty, crowded street. She saw the rows of dilapidated old houses; the small dark rooms; the long steep flight of stairs; the nar-

row dingy hallways; the little lost girls in Mrs. Hedges' apartment, the smashed homes where the women did drudgery because their men had deserted them. She saw all of these things and struck them.

Then the limp figure on the sofa became in turn Jim and the slender girl she'd found him with; became the insult in the moist-eyed glances of white men on the subway; became the greasy, lecherous man at the Crosse School for Singers; became the gaunt Super pulling her down into the basement.

Finally, and the blows were heavier, faster, now, she was striking at the white world which thrust black people into a walled enclosure from which there was no escape; and at the turn of events which had forced her to leave Bub alone while she was working so that he now faced reform school, now had a police record.

She saw the face and the head of the man on the sofa through waves of anger in which he represented all these things and she was destroying them.[14]

Gwendolyn Brooks's novel *Maud Martha* (1953) focuses on the coming of age for the Black woman-child who has dark complexion and untameable hair and who must learn how to ward off assaults to her human dignity.

I am what he would call sweet. But I am certainly not what he would call pretty. Even with all this hair (which I have just assured him, in response to his question, is not "natural," is not good grade or anything like good grade) even with whatever I have that puts a dimple in his heart, even with these nice ears, I am still definitely not what he can call pretty if he remains true to what his idea of pretty has always been. Pretty would be a little cream-colored thing with curly hair. Or at the very lowest pretty would be a little curly-haired thing the color of cocoa with a lot of milk in it. Whereas, I am the color of cocoa straight, if you can be even that "kind" to me.[15]

Margaret Walker's *Jubilee* (1966) captures the richness of Black folk culture: the songs, sayings, customs, foods, medicinal remedies, and the language. This historical novel is the character Vyry's mosaic movement from slavery to freedom.

I wants you to bear witness and God knows I tells the truth, I couldn't tell you the name of the man what whipped me, and if I could it wouldn't make no difference. I honestly believes that if airy one of them peoples what treated me like dirt when I was a slave would come to my door in the morning hungry, I would feed 'em. God knows I ain't got no hate in my heart for nobody. If I is and doesn't know it, I prays to God to take it out. I ain't got no time to be hating. I believes in God and I believes in trying to love and help everybody, and I knows that humble is the way. I doesn't care what you calls me, that's my doctrine and I'm gwine preach it to my childrens, every living one I got or ever hopes to have.[16]

Black women writers find value consciousness in their home communities that serve as the framework for their circular literary structure. They transform the passions and sympathies, the desires and hurts, the joys and defeats, the praises and pressures, the richness and diversity of real-lived community into art through the medium of literature. As insiders, Black women writers venture into all strata of Black life.

Using the subject matter close to the heart of Black America, the Black women's literary tradition shows how slavery and its consequences forced the Black woman into a position of cultural custodian. Black female protagonists are women with hard-boiled honesty, a malaise of dual allegiance, down-to-earth thinking, the ones who are forced to see through the shallowness, hypocrisy, and phoniness as they struggle for survival. Alice Childress paints the picture in this manner:

The emancipated Negro woman of America did the only thing she could do. She earned a pittance by washing, ironing, cooking, cleaning, and picking cotton. She helped her man, and if she often stood in the front line, it was to shield him from the mob of men organized and dedicated to bring about his destruction.

The Negro mother has had the bitter job of teaching her children the difference between the White and the Colored signs before they are old enough to attend school. She had to train her sons and daughters to say "Sir" and "Ma'am" to those who were their sworn enemies.

She couldn't tell her husband "a white man whistled at me," not unless she wanted him to lay down his life before organized killers who strike only in anonymous numbers. Or worse, perhaps to see him helpless and ashamed before her.

Because he could offer no protection or security, the Negro woman has worked with and for her family. She built churches, schools, homes, temples and college educations out of soapsuds and muscles.[17]

Conclusion

The work of Black women writers can be trusted as seriously mirroring Black reality. Their writings are chronicles of Black survival. In their plots, actions, and depictions of characters, Black women writers flesh out the positive attributes of Black folks who are "hidden beneath the ordinariness of everyday life." They also plumb their own imaginations in order to crack the invidiousness of worn-out stereotypes. Their ideas, themes, and situations provide truthful interpretations of every possible shade and nuance of Black life.

Black women writers partially, and often deliberately, embrace the moral actions, religious values, and rules of conduct handed down orally in the folk culture. They then proceed in accord with their tradition to transform the cultural limitations and unnatural restrictions in the community's move toward self-authenticity.

The distinctiveness of most Black women writers is their knack for keeping their work intriguing and refreshing amidst its instructiveness. They know how to lift the imagination as they inform, how to touch emotions as they record, how to delineate specifics so that they are applicable to oppressed humanity everywhere. In essence, there is no better source for comprehending the "real-lived" texture of Black experience and the meaning of the moral life in the Black context than the Black women's literary tradition. Black women's literature offers the sharpest available view of the Black community's soul.

Notes

1. Pierre L. Van Der Berghe, *Race and Racism: A Comparative Perspective* (New York: Wiley, 1967), 77.

2. W. E. B. Du Bois, *Dusk at Dawn* (New York: Harcourt, Brace and Co., 1940).

3. Frances M. Beal, "Slave of a Slave No More: Black Women in Struggle," *The Black Scholar* 12 (November/December 1981): 16–17; reprinted from vol. 6 (March 1975).

4. Zora Neale Hurston, *Jonah's Gourd Vine* (Philadelphia: J. B. Lippincott Co., 1934; reprint, 1971), 206–7.

5. Toni Morrison, *The Bluest Eye* (New York: Holt, Rinehart and Winston, 1970), 109–10.

6. Dexter Fisher, ed., *The Third Woman: Minority Women Writers of the United States* (Boston: Houghton Mifflin Co., 1980), 148.

7. Quoted by Arna Bontemps in "The Black Contribution to American Letters: Part I," in *The Black American Reference Book*, ed. Mable M. Smythe (Englewood Cliffs, NJ: Prentice-Hall, Inc., 1976), 752.

8. Richard K. Barksdale and Kenneth Kinnamon, eds., *Black Writers in America: A Comprehensive Anthology* (New York: Macmillan Publishing Co., 1972), 59.

9. Barbara Christian, *Black Women Novelists: The Development of a Tradition, 1892–1976* (Westport, CT: Greenwood Press, 1980), 239.

10. Jeanne Noble, *Beautiful, Also, Are the Souls of My Sisters: A History of the Black Woman in America* (Englewood Cliffs, NJ: Prentice-Hall Inc., 1978), 63.

11. Mary Helen Washington, *Midnight Birds: Stories of Contemporary Black Women Writers* (Garden City, NY: Doubleday, 1979), 95–96.

12. Verta Mae Grosvenor, *Vibration Cooking* (New York: Doubleday, 1970).

13. Marcia Gillespie. Editorial, *Essence*, May 1975, 39.

14. Ann Petry, *The Street* (1946; reprint, New York: Pyramid Books, 1961), 266.

15. Gwendolyn Brooks, "Maud Martha," in *The World of Gwendolyn Brooks* (New York: Harper & Row, 1971), 178–79.

16. Margaret Walker, *Jubilee* (1966; reprint, New York: Bantam Books, 1981), 406.

17. Alice Childress, "The Negro Woman in American Literature," in *Keeping the Faith: Writings by Contemporary Black Women*, ed. Pat Crutuchfield Exum (Greenwich, CT: Fawcett Publications, 1974), 32.

Study Questions

1. What contradictions set Cannon upon her quest? Discuss with an example.

2. In what sense does Cannon think that an ethics of freedom has not applied to the Black community?

3. What does she mean by the moral wisdom of Black women? How does she see it as enabling for them?

4. What does Cannon see as the goals of an ethic? What three goals does she mention?

5. How have Black women writers delineated moral agency? Cite the example by Toni Morrison.

6. How does the literary tradition of Black women reflect values of the Black community?

7. What is the centrality of the oral tradition in Black women's writings? In particular, why is this important for Cannon?

Notes on the Contributors

Chapter 1

Jane Flax is at Howard University, Washington D.C., where she teaches in the Political Science Department. She is the author of *Thinking Fragments*.

Nancy Hartsock, a political scientist at the University of Washington, is the author of *Money, Sex, and Power*.

Maria C. Lugones is at Carleton College, Northfield, Minnesota, in the Department of Philosophy.

Elizabeth V. Spelman teaches at Smith College, Northampton, Massachusetts, in the Philosophy Department. She is the author of *Inessential Woman*.

Chapter 2

Caroline Whitbeck is at the Center for Policy Alternatives, Massachusetts Institute of Technology, and teaches at Massachusetts General Hospital Institute.

Nancy Holmstrom teaches in the Philosophy Department at Rutgers University, Newark, New Jersey.

Sherry B. Ortner is on the faculty of Stanford University in the Department of Anthropology.

Hélène Cixous is professor of English at University of Paris VIII. Her books include *The Newly Born Woman*.

Chapter 3

Sarah Lucia Hoagland, who teaches philosophy at Northeastern Illinois University, is the author of *Lesbian Ethics*.

Shulamith Firestone, a feminist activist and theorist, is the author of *The Dialectic of Sex*.

Jeffner Allen, a feminist philosopher, is on the faculty of the State University of New York, Binghamton. She is the author of *Lesbian Philosophy: Explorations*.

Anne Donchin teaches philosophy at Indiana University, Indianapolis.

Alison M. Jaggar, author of *Feminist Politics and Human Nature*, teaches philosophy at the University of Colorado, Boulder.

Chapter 4

Ti-Grace Atkinson, a feminist philosopher and teacher in New York City, is the author of *Amazon Odyssey*.

Charlotte Bunch is a feminist activist and theorist in New York City. Her works include *Passionate Politics*.

Marilyn Frye, author of *The Politics of Reality*, teaches philosophy at Michigan State University.

Sandra Bartky is a professor of philosophy at the University of Illinois, Chicago.

Bell Hooks is on the faculty of Oberlin College, where she is in the Department of English. Her books include *Feminist Theory: From Margin to Center*.

Chapter 5

Rosemarie Tong is in the Philosophy Department of Davidson College, North Carolina, and is the author of *Women, Sex and the Law*.

Helen E. Longino, a feminist theorist, teaches philosophy at Rice University, Houston, Texas.

Susan Griffin, a feminist poet and theorist who teaches in Berkeley, is the author of *Woman and Nature, Pornography and Silence,* and other works.

Catharine A. MacKinnon is a professor of law at the University of Michigan and is the author of *Sexual Harassment of Working Women*.

Chapter 6

Mary Daly, a feminist philosopher and teacher in Boston, is the author of *Beyond God the Father, GynEcology,* and *Pure Lust*.

Carol P. Christ has taught at Pomona College and Harvard Divinity School and is the author of *Laughter of Aphrodite*.

Gail Stenstad teaches philosophy at East Tennessee State University, Johnson City.

Chapter 7

E. Ann Kaplan, whose works include *Women and Film,* is Director of the Humanities Institute at the State University of New York, Stony Brook.

Mary Russo is a professor of literature and critical theory at Hampshire College, Amherst, Massachusetts.

Sue-Ellen Case, of the Drama Department at the University of California, Riverside, is the author of *Feminism and Theatre*.

Trinh T. Minh-ha is a professor of cinema at San Francisco State University. She is the author of *Woman, Native, Other*.

Chapter 8

Judith Jarvis Thomson is on the faculty of the Massachusetts Institute of Technology, where she is in the Department of Philosophy.

Mary Anne Warren teaches philosophy at San Francisco State University and is editor of *The Nature of Woman*.

Kathryn Pyne Addelson is on the faculty of Smith College, Northampton, Massachusetts, where she teaches in the Philosophy Department.

Carol Gilligan, author of *In a Different Voice*, teaches in the School of Education, Harvard University.

Sara Ruddick, who teaches philosophy at the Seminar College, New School for Social Research, is the author of *Maternal Thinking*.

Nel Noddings, the author of *Caring*, is a professor of education at Stanford University.

Adrienne Rich, feminist poet and theorist, is the author of many books of poems and the prose work *Of Woman Born*.

Joyce Trebilcot teaches philosophy and women's studies at Washington University and is the editor of *Mothering*.

Katie Geneva Cannon is a professor at Episcopal Divinity School, Cambridge. She is the author of *Black Womanist Ethics*.